SIMPLIFIED SIGNS

VOL. 1

Simplified Signs:
A Manual
Sign-Communication System
for Special Populations

Volume 1:
Principles, Background, and Application

John D. Bonvillian, Nicole Kissane Lee,
Tracy T. Dooley, and Filip T. Loncke

Illustrated by Val Nelson-Metlay

https://www.openbookpublishers.com

ISBN Paperback: 978-1-78374-923-2

ISBN Hardback: 978-1-78374-924-9

ISBN Digital (PDF): 978-1-78374-925-6

ISBN Digital ebook (epub): 978-1-78374-926-3

ISBN Digital ebook (mobi): 978-1-78374-927-0

ISBN XML: 978-1-78374-928-7

DOI: 10.11647/OBP.0205

Cover Image and design by Anna Gatti.

Contents

*This book is gratefully dedicated to our
parents and to the members of our families.*

Preface and Acknowledgments

The inspiration for the development of the Simplified Sign System occurred some years ago, in the late 1980s. A former student and I had recently completed a research project that examined various factors associated with non-speaking children's success in learning signs to communicate (Bonvillian & Blackburn, 1991). Most of the participants in that study were students diagnosed with autism at the Grafton School in Virginia. Because these students had failed to make significant progress in learning to speak, they had been taught to communicate through American Sign Language (ASL) signs. ASL is the principal language of the Deaf community in the United States.

After the research project ended, I met with Gail Mayfield, the director of the autism program at Grafton, to discuss the results. One of the findings was that scores on tests of the students' motor abilities predicted their acquisition of ASL signs. Many of the students had also obtained quite low scores on these tests of motor abilities. Furthermore, those children with more impaired motor skills tended to acquire relatively few signs and rarely combined them into more complex utterances.

These results surprised me because previous investigators had consistently stated that motor skills in children with autism were largely unimpaired. These findings, however, did not surprise Gail. As the director of a program that had used signs with children with autism for over a decade, Gail had seen firsthand the difficulties that many of her students experienced with motor tasks and sign formation. Gail made a point of underlining what she perceived as a serious problem in her students' communication training: many of them clearly had problems accurately forming the signs that they were being taught. In her opinion, the combination of the students' motor difficulties and the formational complexity of many ASL signs made her students' sign learning only a limited success.

  https://doi.org/10.11647/OBP.0205.10

Gail then made a fervent request: would it be possible to address the problems she witnessed daily by developing a simplified form of sign communication that would be easier for her students to learn? I told her that such an undertaking, properly conducted, would likely prove quite difficult and time-consuming. To accomplish such a task, I felt that more research needed to be conducted in several different areas. One such area was sign acquisition in developing children: how do young children without discernible motor or cognitive disabilities learn to form signs? At that time, very little was known about the early stages of sign acquisition in typically developing children. This was an important first step because it is difficult to distinguish atypical patterns of development without first knowing how development typically proceeds. A second research area that needed to be carefully examined was the type of sign production errors made by children with autism, in addition to the kinds of signs that they more easily acquired. A third area that needed to be systematically explored was the fine and gross motor problems that children with autism experienced. A sign-communication system developed for these children would need to avoid their areas of motor difficulty while emphasizing areas of relative strength. After the meeting with Gail, I agreed to make a determined effort to develop a simplified sign system, but not until much more had been learned about sign language acquisition, sign formation errors in children with autism, and the motor difficulties of children with autism.

The person most responsible for mapping out the course of young children's sign formation development was a then doctoral student, Theodore Siedlecki, Jr. Together, we investigated both the order of acquisition of sign phonemes (the individual formational parameters that make up a sign: handshape, location, and movement) as well as the types of sign formation errors made by the typically developing children of Deaf parents (Bonvillian & Siedlecki, 1996, 1998, 2000; Siedlecki & Bonvillian, 1993, 1997). These studies provided valuable background information on which formational parameters (or aspects) of signs were more easily learned and more accurately produced by young, typically developing children.

Another former University of Virginia doctoral student, Brenda C. Seal, investigated the sign formation errors made by children with autism (Seal & Bonvillian, 1997).[1] The present Simplified Sign System largely avoids those sign formational elements that children with autism had difficulty producing.

In her doctoral dissertation, Georgina R. Slavoff examined the gross and fine motor problems of children with autism, as well as their gestural imitation abilities (Slavoff, 1998). Her research documented the serious motor functioning problems of many of these children. In particular, her studies of gestural imitation helped shape how we might create or modify signs for inclusion in our sign system by revealing that we needed to limit the number of movements in each sign. Several years later, Ashley Fitzgerald Logan provided additional valuable information about the gestural imitation and memory abilities of children with autism in her distinguished (undergraduate) major thesis at the University of Virginia (Fitzgerald, 2001).

Another critical step in the development of the Simplified Sign System occurred while I was spending a year at Gallaudet University on a University of Virginia Sesquicentennial Associateship.[2] Because I was trying to write up the findings of a number of previously conducted research studies during the year, I requested the use of a desk in a remote corner of Gallaudet's library to minimize the number of interruptions that would occur while I was writing. Gallaudet's staff graciously complied with my request, and I was provided the use of a desk at the far end of the bottom floor of the library. What I soon realized, however, was that my ability to focus on my writing was limited mostly by my own ability to concentrate — I needed a break or change of pace about every 45–50 minutes. For my writing breaks, I would typically wander among the bookcases located near my desk and examine the many different volumes on the shelves.

Fortuitously, the section of the library near my desk at that time housed numerous volumes on sign languages from different countries around the world. (Most countries have their own distinct sign language.) I soon found myself taking several sign language dictionaries at a time to my desk and examining them before returning to my writing.

---

1   This research was supported by Social and Behavioral Sciences Research Grants from the March of Dimes Birth Defects Foundation.
2   Gallaudet University, located in Washington, DC, was the world's first institution of higher learning for deaf students.

I soon became interested in how the same concept might be expressed by a sign in different sign languages. What I quickly realized was that I could not accurately guess the meanings of the large majority of the signs I saw depicted through drawings or photographs in the different dictionaries. Nevertheless, periodically I would find a drawing of a sign for a particular concept in one sign language dictionary whose meaning was readily apparent to me, whereas, in other sign language dictionaries that I examined, I often could not discern a clear relationship between the signs for that very same concept and how the signs for that concept were formed. That is, in some sign languages, the meaning of a sign for a particular concept was quite apparent to me, but in most sign languages, the sign-to-meaning relationship for the same concept was not at all clear to me.

Over time, as I examined more and more dictionaries of sign languages and sign systems, it occurred to me that it might be possible to assemble a large collection of signs with readily apparent meanings (highly iconic signs) if one were to review enough sign language dictionaries from around the world. This seemed to me an important insight, since previous investigators (Konstantareas, Oxman, & Webster, 1978) had reported that sign-learning children with autism (and other children with intellectual disabilities) typically learned and remembered highly iconic signs better than they did signs with less transparent meanings. In other words, if one were to develop a sign-communication system that was more easily learned by non-speaking children with autism, then it would be a good strategy to try to include as many highly iconic signs as possible.

With this background information on sign learning and motor functioning established, I felt that the development of a simplified form of signing could begin in earnest. The actual onset of the Simplified Sign System project also occurred, in part, by chance. Nicole Kissane, a then first-year undergraduate pre-medical student at the University of Virginia, was taking my Introduction to Child Psychology class in the fall semester of 1997. The lectures on childhood deafness, sign language acquisition, and the use of signs and other (non-oral) augmentative and alternative communication systems with various non-speaking populations had intrigued her. At the end of the term, Nicole spoke with me about her interest in sign-communication training for hearing, but non-speaking, individuals. She explained that the topic was of particular interest to her because one of her grandfathers had suffered a series of strokes that had adversely affected his speech skills. Although much of his speech slowly returned during the remaining years of his life, he often struggled to communicate, occasionally using gestures to convey his needs. Nicole stated that if a research project involving the use of signs with non-speaking populations were to be undertaken, then she would very much like to assist. I told Nicole that such a project would probably take at least several years to complete, but that I would happily supervise her efforts. With the onset of the spring semester in January 1998, the development of the Simplified Sign System began. For the next three and a half years, Nicole would lead the way in this project.

We began the project by searching for signs that would be good candidates for inclusion in the Simplified Sign System lexicon. Because different countries usually have their own distinct sign languages, an initial step was to secure a collection of sign language dictionaries from around the world. This appeared to be a logical first step because it seemed easier to locate potentially useful signs for the Simplified Sign System from already existing sign languages than to try to create hundreds of new ones. (If, however, the dictionaries failed to yield a viable sign for a needed word or concept, then we would need to create that sign.) The acquisition of sign language dictionaries was ably assisted by the staffs of two libraries: the Gallaudet University Library and the University of Virginia Library. Gallaudet University generously allowed me to examine much of its extensive collection of sign language dictionaries. Aside from examining numerous dictionaries at Gallaudet, this accessibility enabled me to determine which dictionaries would most likely be helpful to the project. The University of Virginia library staff then helped us borrow copies of these dictionaries from libraries around the world through the interlibrary loan program. Over the years, Vicky L. Ingram, Sandra B. Dulaney, Dagmawi Abebe, Edward Abse, Heidi L. Dodson, Hang Dong, Ian T. Hickox, Jung W. Hong, Jing Lu, Rebecca Martin, Whitley Morton, and Rebecca A. Pappert proved especially helpful to the project in all aspects of library assistance. Vicky Ingram also provided many valuable suggestions for improvement on early drafts of this manuscript.

Nicole and several other University of Virginia undergraduate students, Erin McDaniel Catlett, Kathryn Thomas, and Kelly Tyree, carefully reviewed these dictionaries during the next few years looking for highly iconic signs. (Highly iconic signs are signs that bear a close resemblance to the actions, objects, or characteristics that they represent.) As they examined the dictionaries, Nicole and the other research assistants selected signs from the dictionaries whose meanings they were able to guess from looking only at the drawings. They then conducted much of the testing of these signs with University of Virginia undergraduate students to determine which individual signs were more easily remembered, recognized, and formed.

Filip Loncke joined the Simplified Sign project in the fall of 2000. At that time, he became one of the faculty advisors for Nicole's distinguished (undergraduate) major thesis. Filip also developed some of the signs that were incorporated into the Simplified Sign lexicon, supervised some field testing, and wrote an important section of this book's introduction (Chapter 1) and much of the chapter on how to use the signs with non-speaking individuals (Chapter 9). His involvement with sign language programs for non-speaking persons, however, has a much longer history than just the past decade and a half. He began using signs to foster communication in children with autism, cerebral palsy, and Down syndrome in his native Belgium over thirty years ago. By the early 1990s, he had become convinced that many signs used by most prelingually deaf persons in Belgium were too complicated for many non-speaking children to acquire. In light of this concern, he prepared a volume of signs for these children based on his efforts to modify Belgian Sign Language signs in order to make them easier to produce (Loncke & Bos, 1997).[3] Finally, it should be noted that during the period 2002–2004, Filip served as President of the International Society for Augmentative and Alternative Communication (ISAAC).

In May of 2001, Nicole submitted her distinguished major thesis, "Memory and Recall of Signs: The Development of a Simplified Sign System," to the University of Virginia. She also established a website that included the full text of her thesis, as well as copies of the

---

3   It should be noted that, in recent years, some researchers have asserted that there are two separate sign languages in Belgium: Flemish Sign Language (Vlaamse Gebarentaal or VGT) and French Belgian Sign Language (Langue des Signes Belge Francophone or LSFB).

approximately 500 signs that had been developed up to that point. Nicole's parents, William and Antoinette Kissane, should be recognized for their considerable support on this aspect of the project. Her mother helped primarily by drawing some of the initial illustrations of how the signs were formed. Her father was invaluable for his contribution to many of the technical aspects of the project. He devoted many hours to the development of the website, scanning and inputting the initial sign images, cleaning up those images, as well as copying and merging documents.

With the submission of Nicole's thesis and the establishment of a website, the project began to receive local, national, and even international media attention. Newspaper stories, magazine articles, and television shows covered the project. The website received many thousands of visitors and we were inundated with enthusiastic emails from parents, caregivers, and professionals who encouraged the completion of the Simplified Sign System. These individuals also requested that we expand the scope of our research to include other populations with communication disorders or difficulties.

In light of the outpouring of interest in the Simplified Sign System and the many requests to expand its scope, we elected to make a determined effort to add or develop new signs. At this time, undergraduate students Meaghan D. Hewitt and Sylvia A. Jasiurkowski joined the project. New signs were selected from additional dictionaries of sign languages and sign systems. However, because highly iconic signs often could not be found for needed concepts, we embarked on a program of creating signs for those perceived needs. This approach of creating or inventing new signs and then testing them to determine whether they were easily learned and remembered has continued until recently.

Shortly after her graduation from the University of Virginia, Nicole entered medical school at the Medical College of Virginia at Virginia Commonwealth University. This new educational and training focus necessitated that she somewhat curtail her involvement in the project, although she still managed to stay actively engaged, devoting many hours during vacations, weekends, and evenings to the project. After receiving her medical degree, Nicole did her residency in General Surgery at the University of Florida College of Medicine. In 2013, she earned a Master of Education degree from Harvard University in

Cambridge, Massachusetts. Nicole, now Nicole Kissane Lee, is currently Assistant Professor of Surgery in the Department of Surgery at Indiana University School of Medicine located in Indianapolis, IN. She is also the Director of the Surgical Skills Center there.

In the fall of 2002, Adrianne Walvoord and Heather Emmons joined the project. Adrianne was a fourth-year undergraduate student at the University of Virginia who had become deeply interested in the language and communication development of exceptional children. She also worked part-time for a family who lived nearby, helping to care for their two sons with autism. Heather was a graduate student at the University of Virginia in the Linguistics and Psychology programs with a principal research interest in children's sign language acquisition. In her senior year as an undergraduate at Grinnell College, she had taught the nine-year-old autistic son of an English professor to communicate for the first time by teaching him ASL signs. After first making progress in learning to communicate through signs, this boy subsequently acquired considerable proficiency in spoken English.

The primary intent of Adrianne's and Heather's research efforts was to assess systematically whether Simplified Signs were more easily learned and accurately formed than ASL signs by fully functioning young adults. If Simplified Signs were not more easily learned and accurately formed than ASL signs, then there would be little justification for recommending their use instead of ASL signs. To accomplish this task, Heather and Adrianne presented lists composed of ASL signs and Simplified Signs to undergraduate students. These students were then tested on their ability to recall signs immediately after a list was presented. The results of this research showed that Simplified Sign System signs were recalled significantly more often and accurately than ASL signs.

In the 2003–2006 academic years, we continued our program of systematic assessments of the relative ease of learning and remembering ASL signs and Simplified Sign System signs, as well as the creation of new signs. The focus of our new comparisons was the ability of undergraduate students to remember signs after a twenty-four-hour delay; again, the results showed greater recognition and recall of Simplified Signs. Assisting Heather Emmons in this project were undergraduate students Jessie Kora Wiley Hagger, Laura J. Moore, and Suellen Woodcock Robinson. Laura Moore, together with fellow undergraduates Alicia M. Dean, Ashley N. Paré, and Laura E. West, also helped during this period in the creation of new signs and in trying them out on other students.

In the summer of 2003, Tracy Dooley joined the project. To some extent, this was a reunion. During the early 1990s, Tracy had been a part of our laboratory group; she had studied the emergence of hand preference in young sign-learning children (Bonvillian, Richards, & Dooley, 1997). After graduating from the University of Virginia, Tracy went on to earn a Master of Divinity degree from Emory University's Candler School of Theology. While in Atlanta, Tracy also pursued training in sign language interpreting and worked with a deaf child with an intellectual disability.[4] Since returning to Virginia, Tracy completely recast the descriptions of the signs and thoroughly edited each of the book's chapters. Indeed, she helped to write or rewrite substantial portions of several key chapters. Tracy also assisted in the formation of new signs, the revision of existing signs, and was heavily involved in the review and approval of each of the sign illustrations. She also created a sign index with synonyms (see Volume 2), compiled the subject and name indices, and developed a glossary of terms for the benefit of readers. In more recent years, Tracy was very actively involved in the expansion of the lexicon of the Simplified Sign System.

In March 2005, the Simplified Sign System project took another turn in its development. Filip Loncke, Amanda M. England (a graduate student), and I made up the University of Virginia contingent at a conference on simplified signing for non-speaking persons held in Pforzheim, Germany. The conference convener, Klaus-Peter Böhringer, urged the participants to expand the scope of their sign systems so that the resulting system could be used worldwide. From his perspective, a sign-communication system that would transcend national borders and facilitate communication across spoken language barriers would be an important contribution as well. The German hosts were most gracious in their hospitality and generously shared with us many of the signs they were using.

During 2006 and 2007, the focus of the Simplified Sign System project shifted in response to requests for an expanded sign vocabulary. The

---

4   On the term *intellectual disability*, see Chapter 4, Footnote 1.

new emphasis was on the development of signs that would facilitate communication in medical settings and international travel, as well as prove of assistance to older individuals with impaired hearing. This effort was led by Ashleigh Holeman DeFries; her work was supported by a Harrison Award for Undergraduate Research. Two other undergraduate students, Alicia M. Dean and Rachel L. Yates, helped in the development and evaluation of these signs. Gregory M. Propp, the Director of the American Sign Language Program at the University of Virginia, provided valuable assistance in the development of signs for medical terms.

The illustrations depicting each of the handshapes (see Appendix B), the palm, finger, and knuckle orientations (see Appendix C), and the initial lexicon of 1000 Simplified Signs (see Volume 2) were adeptly drawn by Valerie Nelson-Metlay. Val showed incredible patience responding to the authors' requests for revisions to her drawings. To facilitate Val's drawings of the signs, the authors made videotapes of how the signs were formed. Assisting the authors in the videotaping of the 1000 signs from the initial lexicon and their subsequent editing were University of Virginia students Elizabeth A. Elder, Amanda R. Hulsey, Alexandria K. Moore, Heather J. Parrott, and Leigh E. Spoden.

In more recent years, we have continued to develop the Simplified Sign System in two principal areas. One on-going project has focused on creating new or revising existing Simplified Signs for use with persons who have paralysis of or serious difficulty using one of their arms and/or hands. This project was inspired in part by feedback we received about our signs by family members or professionals who worked with individuals who had the use of only a single arm or hand.

The other principal on-going project has been to increase the size of the Simplified Sign lexicon. The reason for this push to expand the size of the lexicon was the realization that the signs might be effectively used as vehicles of instruction in students' learning of foreign language vocabulary items. The initial impetus for this project came from an observation by Filip Loncke in response to a query from me as to why Europeans often were better foreign language learners than Americans. Filip observed that Europeans often tried to acquire a new language by living the language rather than trying to learn the language through classroom drills frequently stressing vocal repetition. As I reflected on

Filip's comment, it occurred to me that many of our Simplified Signs consisted of the sensorimotor actions one would produce if one were "living a language" while immersed in another language and culture. Perhaps there was something about producing a motor action related to or congruent with a word and its underlying concept that helped a person to learn and retain that word.

Not long after Filip's observation about "living a language," a then undergraduate psychology student, Talia S. Coney, came to see me in my university office in need of a research project for her upcoming alternative spring break trip. I soon learned that Talia was headed to Central America for spring break and would be working with a dozen orphan boys ranging in age from ten to twelve years. Because Talia was proficient in Spanish and had a background in ASL, we designed a project that would examine two different ways of teaching English vocabulary items to the boys. Half the boys would receive daily vocabulary lessons that included pictures of the to-be-learned words, and the other half would learn the same English words together with their sign language equivalents (typically iconic ASL signs). At the end of the week, Talia tested each boy individually on his ability to produce the appropriate English words after she uttered the Spanish translation equivalents for the words. The teaching approach that combined the use of manual signs with English words resulted in significantly greater English-word learning by the boys than the approach using pictures of the to-be-learned words.

With the results of this preliminary investigation in mind, we elected to increase the size of the Simplified Sign System lexicon. A number of University of Virginia undergraduate students provided invaluable assistance in this endeavor. Their efforts included reviewing dozens of different sign language dictionaries to help identify potential new signs for the system, making suggestions as to how some signs might be formed to make them easier to produce, testing many dozens of research participants to determine which potential new signs were more readily learned and recalled, and helping in the resulting data tabulation and analyses. The names of the current and former University of Virginia students who assisted in this phase of Simplified Sign vocabulary expansion are: Laila Y. Abbas, Jordan B. Adams, Katherine A. Becker, Kira R. Bolton, Katherine F. Bracaglia, Karsten Coates, Meghan M.

Cotton, Anna Cronin, Jessica A. Davis, Tayler E. Engelhardt, Hollis B. Erickson, Kelly E. Flynn, Chandler M. Hubbard, Amanda R. Hulsey, Ian M. Lamb, Henry T. Matthews, Alexandria K. Moore, Zenobia S. Morrill, Jacob S. Pittman, Benjamin Rost, Celeste R. Rovito, Ka Eun Song, Brigitte I. Sujik, Alexis A. Tew, Justin Bradley Torrence, and Nicole M. Waitzman.

Furthermore, I would like to extend special thanks to Kira R. Bolton, Jessica A. Davis, Alexandria K. Moore, and Zenobia S. Morrill who most adeptly managed my laboratory during this period. Without their dedication, interpersonal skills, and attention to detail the laboratory would not have functioned nearly as effectively as it did. With their invaluable assistance, we added approximately 850 new signs to the Simplified Sign System. In July of 2015, Karsten Coates ably assisted the authors in digitally recording the formations of these new signs that had reached criterion over the previous three to four years. (These signs will be included in a future expanded edition of the Simplified Sign System.)

The cost of the illustrations in the present volumes was covered in part by two generous contributions. The first was from the University of Virginia Research Support in the Arts, Humanities, and Social Sciences. The second was from my very dear friend Edward H. Rice. Not only did he most magnanimously help with the book's publication costs, but Ed and his family also generously hosted me on trips to Washington, DC and Gallaudet University during the preparation of this book.

During the preparation of this manuscript, I was supported by a pair of Sesquicentennial Associateships from the University of Virginia. These awards enabled me to devote the majority of my time during two academic years to the development of the Simplified Sign System and the writing of Volumes 1 and 2.

Finally, over the years, many students, colleagues, and friends gave their time, thoughts, and advice to assist in the development and refinement of the Simplified Sign System. Without their enthusiastic effort, this project would not have been successfully completed. I would like to acknowledge the many helpful comments and suggestions for the conduct of the project and for revision of these volumes made by David F. Armstrong, Elizabeth B. Bonvillian, Marjorie A. Boone, Virginia L. Casanova, Steven L. Converse, Eve Danziger, Alicia M. Dean, Chad S. Dodson, Alev Erisir, Neal P. Fox, Allison E. Jack, Vikram K. Jaswal, Linda A. Meyer, Eleni M. Papageorge, Brenda C. Seal, and Janis A. Sposato.

Virginia Casanova, Allison Jack, and Eleni Papageorge, in particular, made numerous suggestions that improved the text.

Unfortunately, there is one sad note to this research endeavor that should be mentioned. Gail Mayfield, the director of the Grafton School's autism program and the person who helped inspire this project, passed away from cancer before the project was completed. I like to think that she has continued to monitor our progress.

John D. Bonvillian
University of Virginia
2018

Postscript

In May of 2015, my brother, Dr. John D. Bonvillian, retired from his professorship in the Department of Psychology at the University of Virginia and was named emeritus. During his thirty-seven years at the University, John advised and taught thousands of students in classes on general psychology, child psychology, and developmental psycholinguistics. He also directed the linguistics program. The Simplified Sign project was the capstone project of his career. Although formal testing related to the Simplified Sign System ended with his retirement, John maintained an office at the University and continued to work on the Simplified Sign project.

Sadly, in early 2018, John was diagnosed with pancreatic cancer. He spent the next several weeks composing and editing a chapter on sign acquisition development in hearing children with autism, which was subsequently published in *Manual Sign Acquisition in Children with Developmental Disabilities* (a 2019 NOVA publication edited by Nicola Grove and Kaisa Launonen, who dedicated their book to John). After honoring his commitment to contribute to this wonderful new work, John started a course of chemotherapy while completing his work on these volumes. Although this treatment ultimately was not successful (John passed away on May 8, 2018), John was able to spend the last few months of his life communing with many friends, colleagues, students, family members, and loved ones, who visited him in the hospital and rehabilitation facility where he spent the last two months of his life. I think it is safe to say that we all greatly miss him.

In addition to the many people whom John thanked for their contributions to the Simplified Sign project, I want to single out for special recognition Tracy T. Dooley, one of the co-authors of this book. She worked for years with John preparing the signing lexicon, making major contributions. When John died, Tracy stepped into the breach and took responsibility for the manuscript preparation and editing that was essential to bringing the Simplified Sign project to publication. It was no small effort, and without Tracy's dedication, energy, and professionalism, we would not have been able to fulfill John's dying wish to have the Simplified Sign System published and available to the world.

I also would like to thank the two professional reviewers, Chloë Marshall and an anonymous reviewer, who offered many helpful and informative comments that allowed Tracy to update and polish the text as it neared completion. Finally, I would like to acknowledge all of the work done by the wonderful people at Open Book Publishers, including Dr. Alessandra Tosi, our editor Adèle Kreager, Luca Baffa for digital enhancement, Laura Rodriguez for marketing and online distribution, Javier Arias for data collection and management, and Anna Gatti for her beautiful cover design.

Much as John believed that Gail Mayfield continued to monitor our progress after her passing, I believe that John's spirit remains a strong and positive force that still infuses and gives energy to the Simplified Sign project. May the memory of John's infectious enthusiasm continue to guide our path forward, and may this publication have a positive impact on the lives of all those for whom John had so much love and respect.

William Boone Bonvillian
Great Falls, Virginia
2020

1. Introduction

Language and communication abilities are vital to human development. With them, one can interact effectively with others, obtain valuable information, and strive to accomplish important goals. Without them, one may struggle to form social bonds, acquire knowledge, and survive within a community. Simply stated, the development of useful language and communication skills is essential for many critically important aspects of human life. Unfortunately, large numbers of persons either fail to acquire adequate language and communication skills or lose their once existing abilities.

Most people become competent in using one or more of the world's thousands of spoken languages (see Eberhard, Simons, & Fennig, 2020 for listings). These languages rely on a person's ability to hear speech sounds and to produce them. In addition to this auditory-vocal channel of communication, spoken languages can be perceived through their printed or written forms. Systems of communication based on spoken languages, however, are not the only ways in which people can effectively communicate their thoughts or feelings.

People who grow up deaf typically communicate with other deaf persons through a sign language such as American Sign Language (ASL), the principal language of members of the Deaf[1] community in the United States. Deaf persons in most countries have their own sign languages, which have their own distinct sign vocabularies and grammars. In contrast to the auditory-vocal transmission of spoken language, signs in sign languages are produced manually by the hands

---

1   The spelling of *Deaf* with a capital *D* has emerged as a convention for indicating those deaf persons who communicate primarily through a sign language and who interact frequently with other signers. Such persons often self-identify with Deaf culture. The spelling of *deaf* with a lowercase *d* is used to refer to any person with a substantial hearing loss. It is also used to indicate the medical condition of deafness or when focusing on the physical aspects of hearing loss (Woodward, 1975, 1982).

    https://doi.org/10.11647/OBP.0205.01

and arms and perceived visually through the eyes. In some cases, such as with persons who are deaf and blind, signs are perceived through touch (Deuce & Rose, 2019; Mesch, 2013). This reliance on vision, movement, and touch to convey information is a testament to the human brain's remarkable ability to generate and process language regardless of the modality of production and transmission.

Both spoken languages and signed languages[2] are highly effective means of communication for their users. Nevertheless, many persons throughout the world have difficulty communicating proficiently with others either in a spoken language or in a full and genuine sign language such as ASL. Among these individuals are some persons with an intellectual disability,[3] cerebral palsy, or autism spectrum disorder (ASD), and persons who have suffered strokes or head injuries that have left them with a moderate to severe loss of language (aphasia).[4] Difficulties in communication often cause these individuals major problems in their education, social interaction, and general well-being. Other individuals who may experience difficulties in communication through spoken language are those persons who travel extensively in foreign lands and those who have relocated to another country. Although these individuals typically do not have cognitive or sensory impairments that limit their language learning or processing, they often face the arduous task of acquiring proficiency in another tongue.

Over the last twenty years, we, the authors, have developed a manual sign-communication system designed to address the communication needs of many of these individuals with complex communication needs. That system, known as the Simplified Sign System, consists of manual signs that are relatively easy to learn, remember, and form. It is important to note that the Simplified Sign System is not a full sign language and is not intended to replace one. Instead, it is a system of visual-motor communication that may or may not be used in conjunction with a spoken language. Although this system was originally developed

---

2   In this text, the terms *sign languages* and *signed languages* are used interchangeably to refer to the visual-motor (or visual-gestural) languages used as the principal means of communication among persons who have grown up Deaf. Hearing persons may also acquire fluency in signed languages.

3   On the term *intellectual disability*, see Chapter 4, Footnote 1.

4   Those individuals who are unable to effectively communicate their daily needs through spoken, written, or sign language, especially those individuals with multiple disabilities, are often described as having *complex communication needs*.

primarily to meet the communication needs of persons with disabilities, we hope that many other individuals may find the system worthwhile as well.[5] Among those who might benefit from this sign system are parents adopting internationally, infants and young children who are not yet fluent in a spoken language, healthcare professionals, immigrants, tourists abroad, military personnel and aid workers overseas, and persons of all ages who are learning a new spoken language.

The principal goal of these two initial volumes is to make available a collection of manual signs, the Simplified Sign System, together with information on how to form and use these signs. Most of the signs in the Simplified Sign vocabulary or lexicon were selected from existing sign languages or sign systems used by Deaf persons from around the world. Some of these signs were subsequently modified to make them easier to produce.[6] Other signs in the lexicon were developed solely for the Simplified Sign System; this typically occurred when we were unable to locate signs that were relatively easy to learn and remember in existing sign languages for concepts that we felt were needed. We believe that the resulting sign system has the potential to help many persons to communicate more effectively.

The primary goal of Volume 1 is to examine the research literature on the acquisition of sign-communication skills in various groups whose members have limited spoken language proficiency. From this examination, it should be evident that sign-communication training and teaching programs have significantly enhanced the communication skills and lives of numerous hearing children and adults who have difficulties using spoken language or need to improve their spoken language skills. This review should also make it clear that there are often

---

5   The fact that the principles of development for the Simplified Sign System not only meet the needs of a range of persons with disabilities but also serve to benefit many other people is consistent with the ethos of universal design. Universal design is defined as the "design and composition of an environment [or product or service] so that it can be accessed, understood, and used to the greatest extent possible by all people regardless of their age, size, ability, or disability" (Centre for Excellence in Universal Design, 2020).

6   The notion that one might modify how signs are formed to make them easier to produce is not a new one. Concerned about the difficulties that many persons with disabilities encountered when they tried to form ASL signs, Bornstein and Jordan (1984) made a number of observations about how the handshape, movement, and location parameters of signs might be changed while still being understandable by other sign users.

wide individual differences in the outcomes of these signing programs. While some individuals acquire a large vocabulary of signs and learn to combine signs into relatively complex sign utterances, others make only very limited progress (Grove, 2019a). Although much of this variability in program outcomes may depend on the characteristics of the learners, some of the variability in outcomes may be attributable to the nature of the signs themselves. That is, some signs in existing sign languages are more difficult to remember and produce than others. In general, the manual signs that resemble what they stand for and that are composed of more basic hand configurations and movements are more readily learned by hearing persons. Thus, if signs that have more transparent meanings and that are relatively easier to form were used instead of signs that are more difficult to understand and form, then the outcomes of sign-communication training and teaching programs likely would be more consistently positive for the participants.

The current chapter provides an introduction to sign communication in general and the Simplified Sign System in particular. First, however, we address common concerns and misconceptions about sign language training and teaching programs and provide some observations about those individuals most likely to benefit from such programs.

Addressing Concerns about Sign-Communication Training and Teaching

Concern 1: Learning to Sign Will Prevent Spoken Language Development

One reason that sign-communication training and teaching programs have not been more widely established is that many persons who teach or care for non-speaking, hearing individuals express a reluctance to embrace a communication system that relies on manual signs or gestures (Silverman, 1995; Sutherland, Gillon, & Yoder, 2005). This reluctance appears to result primarily from the mistaken belief that using such a system would prevent or hinder non-speaking persons' acquisition of spoken language skills. Concerned caregivers often fear that an individual who learns how to communicate through signs (or other augmentative and alternative communication systems) will have little or no motivation to learn to speak. This assumption, however, is unfounded; indeed, there is substantial evidence to the contrary (Branson & Demchak, 2009; DeThorne et al., 2009; Pattison & Robertson, 2016; Sheehy & Duffy, 2009; Silverman, 1995; Singh et al., 2017; Vandereet et al., 2011). In a number of instances, gains in signing skills have been accompanied by considerable progress in learning to speak (Grove & Walker, 1990; Launonen & Grove, 2003; Millar, Light, & Schlosser, 2006).

One possible reason why signing may help to promote spoken language development is that using signs may "exercise" areas of the brain critical for language. Brain regions involved in the fine motor control of the hands are closely related to those regions involved in the production of the coordinated movements responsible for speech (that is, the movements of the lips, tongue, larynx, and jaw). Evidently, progress in the acquisition of language skills in one modality often has a positive effect on language skills in another (Fouts, 1997; Millar, 2009). In particular, the combination of manual signs with speech (a process known as simultaneous communication) frequently results in improved spoken language skills.

Signing may also foster spoken language development indirectly by reducing an individual's need to communicate by speech. That is, if a non-speaking person learns to communicate through manual signs, then this accomplishment may result in a lessening of pressure on that individual to communicate through speech (DeThorne et al., 2009; Sheehy & Duffy, 2009). Because an effective avenue of communication has been established through manual signs, that non-speaking person's level of anxiety may be reduced and he or she may be more receptive to interventions designed to facilitate spoken language development.

Regardless of the particular reasons advanced to account for the apparently counterintuitive claim that learning to sign often facilitates spoken language development, one thing should be clear: teachers and caregivers should not worry that the acquisition of signs prevents spoken language development. Furthermore, the sooner that a sign-communication program is implemented (preferably with simultaneous spoken language input), the greater the chances of positive results with both signing and speech skills (Creedon, 1973; Goodwyn & Acredolo, 1998; Launonen, 1996, 1998, 2003, 2019a, 2019b; Launonen & Grove, 2003).

Concern 2: Non-Oral Forms of Communication, such as Manual Signs and Gestures, Are Unnatural and Stigmatizing

Those who care for a non-speaking individual may also hesitate to implement a signing program because communication that does not rely on spoken language may seem strange or foreign to them. Yet, even those people with little exposure to sign languages or sign systems typically make extensive use of gestures and other forms of nonverbal communication in their everyday conversations (Remland, 2004). Moreover, children who have been blind from birth use gestures along with their speech (Iverson & Goldin-Meadow, 1997). As we go about our daily lives, we are often unaware of the many ways in which we communicate through gestures or interpret the communicative gestures of others. Recognizing the extent of our own nonverbal or gestural communication may serve to reduce concerns about using a manual sign-based communication system with a non-speaking person.

In fact, for young children, the use of gestures to communicate is not only natural, it is the way that young children typically begin to communicate effectively (Bates et al., 1979; Goldin-Meadow, 1998; Iverson, Capirci, & Caselli, 1994; te Kaat-van den Os et al., 2015). Indeed, this strong reliance on gestures to communicate in infancy and early childhood often is a positive indicator of future language ability. That is, early gesture usage in children predicts their subsequent spoken language vocabulary production and comprehension (Goldin-Meadow et al., 2014; Iverson & Goldin-Meadow, 2005; Rowe & Goldin-Meadow, 2009a, 2009b; Rowe, Özçalişkan, & Goldin-Meadow, 2008). One way that this vocabulary learning may have taken place is that parents often responded to their young children's gestures by translating them into spoken words. The children then would often subsequently acquire these words. Moreover, this pattern of facilitated word learning through parental translation of their children's gestures held not only for typically developing children, but also for children with autism or Down syndrome (Dimitrova, Özçalişkan, & Adamson, 2016). The use of gestures in young children should not be viewed as unnatural, but rather, in most instances, as a positive indicator of future successful learning and development.

Concern 3: Learning Sign Language Will Require Too Great an Investment of Time on the Part of the Clinician, Teacher, or Caregiver

Becoming adept at a full, genuine sign language, such as ASL, involves extensive study and practice over a period of years, as well as experience interacting with persons who sign. While learning enough signs from a genuine sign language to interact effectively with a non-speaking person requires less of a time commitment from teachers and caregivers than acquiring sign language fluency, the effort involved is not insignificant. An easier to learn sign-communication system might be more readily embraced by already overburdened teachers and caregivers (Budiyanto et al., 2018; Cornforth, Johnston, & Walker, 1974; Glacken et al., 2019; Mistry & Barnes, 2013). Consideration for the needs of instructors and communication partners, as well as those of the primary learner, has helped guide the development of the Simplified Sign System.

Concern 4: Sign-Communication Programs Seem neither as Common nor as Firmly Established as Many Programs Promoting Spoken Language Development

Initially, the development of effective sign-communication training and teaching programs was slowed because of a relative lack of systematic scientific investigations of sign languages. Not until the 1970s did research into the structure of sign languages and the communicative use of manual signs really begin to flourish. This late emergence of sign language linguistics as a field of inquiry was largely the unfortunate consequence of a long-standing negative attitude toward sign languages and signers by many hearing professionals working with deaf students. Since then, numerous sign languages used by Deaf peoples throughout the world have been at least minimally studied and documented. The growing acceptance of sign languages and sign systems as worthwhile areas of scientific inquiry has helped spur investigations into how manual signs might be used to help persons with severe language impairments acquire better communication skills. In turn, these investigations provided the empirical foundations for successful sign-communication training and teaching programs. While not yet as common as certain forms of speech or spoken language therapy, this is probably attributable to the relatively recent introduction of sign-communication intervention approaches and not to their lack of efficacy. Indeed, as we shall see in the following section, there are a number of groups likely to benefit from a therapeutic approach that includes signing.

Special Populations

Some persons with an intellectual disability, cerebral palsy, autism, or aphasia experience considerable difficulty communicating effectively. Over the years, speech-language pathologists, researchers, and teachers who work with such persons have employed various approaches or strategies to enhance these individuals' communication abilities. Foremost among these approaches has been speech therapy or intervention. This therapy or training approach has resulted in many persons with severe spoken language impairments making great strides in their communication abilities, although gains in speech intelligibility often have varied widely.

One form of spoken language intervention or training — behavior modification speech training — often is quite successful with those individuals with autism who already have some useful spoken language or the ability to imitate speech (Lovaas, 1977). For those children with autism who are non-speaking or have very limited spoken language skills, however, a singular focus on speech training or therapy may not be the most effective approach to establishing effective communication skills. The same may be true for members of other groups of non-speaking persons.

Why does speech therapy or training sometimes result in only limited gains in communication skills? For some individuals with impaired language and communication skills, speech training may not be successful because of a significant hearing loss that adversely affects spoken language acquisition. A substantial proportion of children with Down syndrome (a frequently occurring form of intellectual disability), for instance, have some degree of hearing loss (Dahle & McCollister, 1986; Roizen, 1997, 2007). This deficit may make phonological processing slower and more difficult, as well as possibly delaying the development of speech skills. Hearing loss may be present in some persons with cerebral palsy as well (Pellegrino, 2007), with this loss affecting their spoken language acquisition and use.

Other individuals with a communication impairment may derive little benefit from speech training not because of hearing loss, but rather because the presence of neurological deficits may result in atypical processing of sounds. Many persons with aphasia, for example, may be able to *hear* speech sounds, but experience a serious disturbance in their *understanding* of spoken language. For these individuals, speech sounds enter their ears without obstruction, but their brains fail to recognize the sounds and sound patterns, or the sound signals are lost or distorted on the way to or in the areas of the brain responsible for comprehension of spoken language. While many children and adults with aphasia have auditory-processing problems in general (Corriveau, Pasquini, & Goswami, 2007), others may experience particular difficulty processing the rapid sequences of sounds present in speech (Alvarez et al., 2015; Tallal, 2003; Tallal & Stark, 1981). Auditory-processing disturbances also occur frequently in children with autism (Baranek, 2002; Condon, 1975; Greenspan & Weider, 1997). Some such children may have a hearing loss, but many more possess atypical neural circuitry, such that spoken language makes little or no sense to them. Furthermore, for some individuals with autism, certain speech sounds may actually be aversive and painful (Grandin, 1995; see also Grandin & Panek, 2013).

Other obstacles to speech training lie not in an individual's ability to comprehend spoken language, but rather in the ability to produce it. During spoken language production, cognitive and oral-motor processes must be finely coordinated in order to generate a rapid succession of speech sounds that are accurately timed and articulated to be recognizable. If any element of this process — whether planning, sequencing, or control of oral musculature — becomes disrupted, spoken language will be laborious, or may cease altogether. Children with autism, for example, often have problems controlling their oromotor skills, which results in poor coordination of tongue and lip movements (Page & Boucher, 1998). This, in turn, makes it difficult for them to produce clear, well-timed speech. For persons with cerebral palsy, early brain abnormalities may result in impaired voluntary muscular control and coordination, and may substantially affect spoken language production as well. Children with Down syndrome also frequently have serious articulation disorders. Difficulties with verbal memory and sound sequencing, together with recessed mandibles (lower jaw bones), may make their production of recognizable speech quite effortful (Barnes et al., 2006; Hamilton, 1993; Kumin, 2006). Finally, the spoken language of many individuals with aphasia often is quite slow and labored because the areas of the brain responsible for the production of speech have been damaged (Beukelman & Mirenda, 2013; Davis, 2007; Kertesz, 1979). In light of the substantial difficulties or disturbances in spoken language comprehension and production among members of these different populations, a nonspeech-based communication intervention approach might prove a very worthwhile addition to these individuals' language therapy programs.

Sign-Communication Training and Teaching

Fortunately, over the last few decades, various non-oral means of communication have been added to the array of strategies or approaches used by speech-language pathologists to facilitate their non-speaking clients' acquisition of communication skills. These approaches include employing signs from sign languages; and making use of a variety of other augmentative and alternative communication techniques, such as pictures, writing, physical objects, and speech-generating electronic devices. In many instances, the use of these different approaches with children or adults who are non-speaking or who have great difficulty using spoken language has resulted in noticeable gains in their communication skills (Beukelman & Mirenda, 2013; Romski et al., 2015; von Tetzchner & Martinsen, 2000).

Marked improvement in social or emotional behavior and well-being often has accompanied individuals' increased ability to communicate through manual signs or other non-oral approaches (Bryen & Joyce, 1985; Carr & Durand, 1985; Cooney & Knox, 1981; Grove & Walker, 1990; Horner & Budd, 1985; Mira Pastor & Grau, 2017; Prizant with Fields-Meyer, 2015; Schwartz et al., 2009; Wacker et al., 1990). Children with autism who have been taught to communicate through signs, for example, typically show a substantial reduction in such undesired behaviors as tantrums and soiling, and a corresponding increase in such desired behaviors as improved attention span and greater social interaction.

Even for an individual who has learned only a small number of signs, the ability to indicate that she or he needs to use the bathroom or desires something to eat can represent a real improvement in that person's daily life. In addition, an enhanced ability to communicate successfully with other individuals may greatly lessen the isolation that often surrounds a non-speaking person. Thus, the use of signs from sign languages or sign systems may serve not only as an effective communicative intervention strategy, but also as a path by which persons with spoken language impairments may attain a higher level of functioning and fulfillment through other aspects of their lives.

Sign-communication training and teaching programs, however, have not proven to be a panacea, as progress in learning to communicate through signs often has been quite uneven among participants. Although some non-speaking persons have shown remarkable improvements in communication skills when taught to sign, in other instances progress in communication skills has been quite limited or virtually non-existent (Bonvillian & Blackburn, 1991; Konstantareas, 1985; Layton, 1987). Some children in sign-communication programs make very limited progress, acquiring only a small sign vocabulary despite years of teaching. Other individuals acquire hundreds of signs, learn to combine signs to form more complex utterances, and make great strides in their communication skills overall.

The finding that some persons with language impairments make only limited progress in learning to sign may rest on underlying disabilities that also have adversely impacted their spoken language development. Many non-speaking individuals who experience difficulty learning to sign have various motor and cognitive impairments that may interfere with their acquisition and use of a full and genuine sign language (Beukelman & Mirenda, 2013; Bonvillian & Nelson, 1978; Kilincaslan & Mukaddes, 2009; Pellegrino, 2007; Seal & Bonvillian, 1997; Slavoff, 1998; Zhang, Oskoui, & Shevell, 2015). ASL and other Deaf sign languages contain many sign handshapes and movements that may be too complex for a person with motor difficulties to produce accurately. Many persons with disabilities also may have problems remembering how to form various signs, in recalling a number of signs, or understanding the grammatical rules of a particular sign language. In other words, the acquisition of a full and genuine sign language may prove inordinately difficult for some individuals with language, communication, and neuromotor impairments.

The Simplified Sign System

What, then, might one do to help foster communication skills in persons who are unable to fully understand or produce spoken language and who, because of cognitive, memory, or motor disabilities, may be unable to benefit substantially from instruction in a full and genuine sign language? One alternative that may increase the likelihood of such persons' successful communication is to use a system of signs or gestures specifically developed to be relatively easily learned, remembered, and formed. The Simplified Sign System is such a system.

The Simplified Sign System is more than just a collection of signs and gestures.[7] The signs that comprise the Simplified Sign System were selected, modified, and/or created according to a number of underlying principles or guidelines with the goal of increasing non-speaking individuals' accessibility to communicative symbols and symbol use through signs. These principles or guidelines include a considerable visual resemblance or connection between the signs and what they stand for; this resemblance should make the signs relatively easy to learn and remember. Because many of the intended users of this system experience some degree of motor disability in addition to cognitive dysfunctions (see Dennis et al., 1982), Simplified Signs also were developed to be easily formed. This was accomplished largely by creating or modifying signs so that they typically were formed with only a single movement and a basic handshape. Basic handshapes, also known as unmarked handshapes, tend to be produced relatively frequently and accurately by persons acquiring a sign language, including individuals with autism (Seal & Bonvillian, 1997), ASL-learning children of Deaf parents

---

7   The Simplified Signs included in Volume 2 have diverse origins. Most initially came from the sign languages used by Deaf persons in different countries around the world. In many instances, however, these signs needed to be modified to make them easier to form. Other important sign sources were the signs used by various Native American nations and signs used by members of monastic orders who embraced silence in their contemplative lives. All too often, however, we were unable to find existing signs that met both perceived communication needs and our criteria for inclusion. On those occasions, we created new signs (see Chapter 8 for a description of our procedures).

(Bonvillian & Siedlecki, 1996, 1998, 2000; Siedlecki & Bonvillian, 1993, 1997), and undergraduate students who had reported that they were unfamiliar with any sign language (Wright, Bonvillian, & Schulman, in press). These easier to articulate handshapes, including the pointing-hand, the fist, the flat-hand, and the spread- or 5-hand, are typically among the first handshapes that young children produce in many sign languages (Carmo et al., 2013; Clibbens, 1998; Juncos et al., 1997; Morgan, Barrett-Jones, & Stoneham, 2007). Other handshapes, such as the C-hand, the tapered- or O-hand, the L-hand, and the baby O-hand (also known as a pincer grip), also were produced frequently, albeit with higher error rates. When adjusting signs for ease of formation, we often replaced more complicated handshapes with these handshapes.

Another factor that guided our development of Simplified Signs was that many of the signs should represent relatively broad semantic concepts or categories, instead of denoting a one-to-one relationship between one sign and a specific word from the spoken language. This flexibility enables individual signs to represent an idea that may be expressed by different spoken words depending on the context in which they are used. Furthermore, we strove to pick one sign or gesture to represent each concept in the System, even though various acceptable possibilities existed. We standardized the lexicon to limit the confusion that may result from the use of multiple signs or sign variations to represent a single concept. Consistently using one specific sign helps to teach the underlying concept to the non-speaking individual and reinforces the use of that corresponding sign. Finally, the signs are limited to an initial vocabulary of 1000 signs; we have included those signs that the different target populations are likely to need in a wide range of situations.

Pointing, Iconicity, Transparency, and Translucency

One group of readily understood signs or gestures that we have included in the Simplified Sign System consists of signs that directly indicate a part of the body or draw attention to something. This is typically done by pointing with the index finger. These indicating signs are also known as deictic gestures or indexical signs (Cartmill, Beilock, & Goldin-Meadow, 2012). In these signs, the user simply points to (or touches) the intended location, person, object, or part of the body. Pointing is often a highly successful communication strategy; it is learned early in the development of most children. For most persons learning to sign, these indicating signs can be acquired and employed almost immediately.

Many of the signs we have selected or created for the system visually resemble the objects, actions, or properties they represent (their referents). The extent to which a sign resembles its referent is known as its iconicity. Iconicity may be expressed through a pantomimic expression of an action (e.g., moving one's hand to one's mouth as in EAT) or part of an object (e.g., the steering wheel of a CAR that one wishes to DRIVE); a depiction of an object's shape (e.g., tracing the shape of a TRIANGLE in the air); an evocation of an emotion (e.g., showing that one is ANGRY by shaking one's fist); a display of a prominent characteristic of a referent (e.g., raising one's hand high for TALL); or an indication of the meaning of a property (e.g., waving one's hand back and forth in front of one's face to show that one is HOT) or of an abstract concept (e.g., touching one's temple with one's index finger and then moving the hand away to show the emergence of an IDEA).[8] Iconic signs typically are easier for children with autism or intellectual disabilities to learn and remember than non-iconic signs (Konstantareas et al., 1978). In addition, many adults can often guess the meanings of highly iconic signs without having had any prior exposure to them. These signs are considered to have transparent meanings (Hoemann, 1975).

Even though many of the Simplified Signs we have selected or developed for our system have readily transparent meanings or are clearly iconic, it is important to understand that the degree of iconicity varies from sign to sign. Actions and objects generally are relatively easy to depict iconically (Cartmill et al., 2012; Fay et al., 2014; Perlman et al., 2018; Perniss et al., 2017) and these signs often have readily transparent meanings. For example, the sign for BALL is made by using one's hands to represent the round shape of a ball. Playing a GUITAR is portrayed by mimicking the strumming of a guitar's strings. In these instances, a prominent feature or characteristic of the concept is represented by the handshape, location, and/or movement of the sign. Signs that portray

---

8   It should be noted that throughout this volume, translations of signs, or sign glosses, are shown in upper case.

properties, thoughts, and emotions, however, frequently have to rely on a more metaphorical representation. For example, the sign for COLD is made by clenching one's fists in front of the chest as the arms shiver. LOVE is shown by holding someone or something close to the heart. The meanings of some of the signs in the Simplified Sign System, therefore, may not be as readily transparent as certain highly iconic signs or the pointing gestures in the system. Although the degree of resemblance between a sign and its referent may vary, we have tried to maximize each sign's iconicity or transparency.

Unfortunately, we were unable to identify or develop highly iconic signs for a number of the vocabulary items we wished to include in our sign system. Because of this difficulty, we opted to include translucent signs in our system as well. In sign language research, the extent to which the relationship between a sign and its meaning can be discerned after an explanation has been given is called the sign's translucency. Many more people report that they can perceive the relationship between a sign and the concept for which it stands after the sign's meaning has been provided to them (its translucency) than can correctly guess the meaning of an unfamiliar sign (its transparency) (Bellugi & Klima, 1976; Emmorey & Sevcikova Sehyr, 2018). Furthermore, a person's age, linguistic experience, and cultural background may influence his or her perceptions of iconicity (Ortega, 2017), as seen in studies of Italian Sign Language. Hearing non-signers who were Italian outperformed hearing non-signers from other cultures in their ability to correctly guess the meanings of iconic Italian signs (Grosso, 1993; Pizzuto & Volterra, 2000), a finding that reinforces the theory that cultural experience may be required to understand the mappings between a sign's formation and its meaning. It should also be noted that deaf signers consider the signs in their native sign language to be more iconic than signs from unfamiliar sign languages that are presented to them (Occhino et al., 2017). However, once the relationship between a sign and its referent is discerned, many people find it easier to remember that sign. The inclusion of numerous translucent signs in our lexicon is the principal reason why we have provided readers with both a brief sentence or phrase (a memory cue) that concisely ties each Simplified Sign to its referent and a more detailed explanation of the relationship between a sign and its referent (see Chapter 11, Volume 2). These explanations of the relationship between a sign and its meaning may help some persons better learn and remember that sign.

This strategy of providing information on how the formation of a sign is related to its meaning will probably be extremely helpful to non-speaking persons' teachers, caregivers, and family members because of their ability to understand the explanation of the relationship between a sign and its referent. Students using the signs to help them learn foreign language vocabulary items also will likely benefit from having an explanation provided about how the formation of each sign is related to its meaning. Elderly users with hearing impairments and those persons suffering from aphasia who are still able to read or understand spoken language may benefit from this information as well. It will likely be of less use to very young children or persons with a severe intellectual disability or autism spectrum disorder. Indeed, some users of the system, although they may learn iconic signs more easily than other signs, probably will not consciously understand the connection between an iconic sign and its meaning, even when an explanation is given. Instead, they may learn iconic signs more readily because the movements involved in forming them are familiar actions.

Ease of Production or Formation

Many signs in existing sign languages used by Deaf persons may be too complex formationally for some non-speaking persons to produce accurately. Each sign in a signed language requires that the signer form a particular hand configuration or handshape, make the sign in a certain area or location, and generate one or more movements of the hands and arms. These formational parameters or aspects of signs are referred to as a sign's handshape (HS), location (LOC), and movement (MOV), respectively. Non-speaking individuals often experience difficulty accurately making particular sign handshapes, controlling certain arm and hand movements, or remembering signs with multiple or complex movements. Because many potential users of the Simplified Sign System have motor impairments, the signs in our system have been selected, modified, and/or created with their ease of production in mind. Handshapes that were easier to form often were substituted for handshapes that were more difficult to make. Signs with multiple movements were simplified to a single movement whenever possible, and movements that were difficult to produce were excluded or changed to movements that were more accurately produced (e.g., contacting action with the body) (see Dennis et al., 1982).

In addition, many signs in the Simplified Sign lexicon can be made with just one arm. If a signer is able to move only one arm, then the signer uses whichever arm is available to perform the main action of the sign. Furthermore, some users of our system may prefer to produce signs that are typically formed with a single hand by moving both of their hands symmetrically; many of the signs in the lexicon can be made in this manner without confusion or a change in meaning. Overall, these various features should make Simplified Signs easier to produce both by individuals with psychomotor disabilities and by typically developing infants and young children.

Concept-Based Signs

Many signs in the Simplified Sign System often refer to relatively broad concepts or categories. In other words, many signs in the system are more flexible in their meanings than the words that we chose to pair them with in our lexicon. It is also important to know that a sign is not a direct translation of any specific word; rather, a sign is a visual representation of a concept — a concept that in turn may be represented by multiple words in a spoken language. For example, the sign CHAIR refers to something that can be used by an individual for sitting: a kitchen chair, a rocking chair, a portable car seat for a baby, or a seat in a vehicle. In the Simplified Sign System lexicon, all of these variations in meaning of the concept CHAIR are represented by one sign.[9] Although the lexicon (see

---

9   To be clear, the Simplified Sign lexicon includes signs for other furniture items on which a person may sit, for example, on a SOFA (bench, booth, couch, pew, etc.) or on a STOOL (although this sign is not a part of our initial lexicon). However, just because we have three separate signs for these similar concepts does not mean that every signer will learn or use all three formations. Although some people may benefit from finer conceptual distinctions, other signers may be better served by the broader conceptual category of CHAIR (and thus use that sign to refer to everything on which he or she can sit, including benches, sofas, and stools). An intermediate strategy could also be employed by using two options (e.g., lumping STOOL in with CHAIR but using SOFA for larger furniture pieces). Ultimately, the decision about which sign(s) to employ will rely on environmental context and the particular needs and characteristics of the individual (e.g., age, interests, level of linguistic development).

Chapter 11, Volume 2) lists each sign under the English word that we think most accurately reflects each sign's underlying concept, we also provide many synonyms or words closely related to that concept for ease of reference.[10]

As a result of combining the associated meanings of related words into one or two signs, the size and level of complexity of the Simplified Sign lexicon is limited. Much of the initial vocabulary is basic or general in nature, which should make it more mentally accessible to users under various conditions, according to the basic-level advantage phenomena observed in the categorization or retrieval of words or concepts within semantic hierarchies (see Rogers & Patterson, 2007). This approach of not having a sign for virtually every possible word or variation in meaning is one aspect that distinguishes the Simplified Sign System from full languages. We anticipate that this approach will not result in any confusion when the sign is used in a communicative context. Grouping related meanings under a single sign, however, may present challenges to children with autism spectrum disorder. Many of these individuals have difficulty applying one sign to multiple versions of a particular concept. For example, individuals with autism may think that the sign BALL only applies to the red dodge ball they play with; they may not understand that the sign can also apply to a basketball, a tennis ball, a ping-pong ball, or balls of varying sizes and colors that may be present in their environments. Many children with autism spectrum disorder and some persons with a severe or profound intellectual disability must be painstakingly and deliberately taught the skill of generalization. Whereas typically developing children perceive the underlying conceptual basis for BALL (spherical shape), some individuals may need to be taught this through tying each example of a ball to the sign for BALL. This challenge, however, is present when attempting to teach

---

10   Although both words in spoken languages and signs in sign languages stand for underlying concepts, one should not directly equate individual words with specific signs. As an example, the English word *ground* or *grounding* has a number of meanings, including soil, an object that makes an electrical connection with the earth, a basis for belief or argument, an area of knowledge, and a football offense. The different meanings of this word would require different signs to convey the range of meanings or concepts accurately. In our system, if a listed English word or gloss has two or more divergent meanings, we often provide a parenthetical word or phrase that clarifies which meaning is appropriate for that sign's formation (e.g., RIGHT (CORRECT) and RIGHT (DIRECTION) are two different signs).

any communication skill to children with autism spectrum disorder and to many other individuals with complex communication needs, and is not specific to Simplified Signs.[11]

Standardization

A number of the signs in the Simplified Sign lexicon may not seem to differ noticeably from gestures that people generate spontaneously. For example, many people tap their head when they need a gesture to indicate *head*. However, there also may be variability across individuals in their gestures: one person may point to the head with an index finger, another may use both hands to tap the head, and a third may make a circular movement around the head. All of these are acceptable and readily understood gestures; a non-speaking individual with severe cognitive and motor disabilities, however, may be confused by this variability. To lower the chance of confusion among communication partners, we have selected one particular gesture or sign for each concept, even though many suitable variations may exist. Moreover, this single, distinct form of a sign should then be used by all people in the signer's environment. This approach of using a single, consistent form for each sign may be especially important in interactions with persons with autism spectrum disorder. Individuals with ASD may experience real difficulty in discerning the underlying structural regularities in input (Hellendoorn, Wijnroks, & Leseman, 2015) if there is wide variability in how signs are formed. This strategy should help reinforce the acquisition of that sign and encourage its use by everyone.

Core Vocabulary

In contrast to the thousands of signs found in the full and genuine sign languages used by Deaf persons, the size of the Simplified Sign System lexicon has been restricted initially to 1000 distinct signs. The smaller size of the lexicon limits the complexity of the system and should make it easier for non-speaking individuals, as well as their teachers and caregivers, to learn. Not everyone will want to or need to learn all of

---

11   See Chapter 5 for more information on teaching generalization.

the signs in the lexicon, though; some individuals may learn and use only 30 to 50 signs. These numbers are generally comparable to studies of core vocabulary in preschool children, in which as few as 50 words comprised half or more of the total words used by those children (Banajee, Dicarlo, & Stricklin, 2003; Beukelman, Jones, & Rowan, 1989; Burroughs, 1957; Deckers et al., 2017; Fallon, Light, & Paige, 2001; Fried-Oken & More, 1992; Trembath, Balandin, & Togher, 2007). The number of signs a particular user learns to recognize and how many he or she produces will depend in large part on the extent of that person's cognitive and motor abilities, as well as on the dedication and persistence of that person's sign-using caretakers. Those individuals with less severe impairments will be able to learn and use many more signs than those with more profound impairments. The teachers and caregivers of each potential user will need to decide which concepts are the most important and helpful for that individual to learn and then concentrate on teaching the signs for those concepts. The main user's sign vocabulary can then be expanded as his or her communication needs grow (Dark, Brownlie, & Bloomberg, 2019; Grove & Walker, 1990; Walker, Mitha, & Riddington, 2019). Although the present lexicon is restricted in size, we believe that it is sufficiently large to meet many basic needs over a wide range of educational, institutional, and family settings. For those persons who wish to use Simplified Signs as an instructional vehicle to facilitate the acquisition of a substantial foreign language vocabulary, a noticeably larger lexicon of Simplified Signs will probably be needed. As a direct result of this potential use of the system, we tested and added 840 more signs to the lexicon. These additions considerably expand the lexicon's breadth and its resulting ability to address the communication needs of individuals in both general and more specialized settings. In the future, we hope to provide the expanded lexicon to the public and to develop teaching materials and a smartphone app for the lexicon as a whole.

By developing signs that are relatively easy to learn, remember, and form, we hope that we have removed an obstacle to more effective sign communication for many non-speaking individuals. We also hope that the signs that comprise the Simplified Sign System lexicon prove to be quite helpful to those who use them.

Goals, Clarifications, and Recommendations

We mentioned earlier that one of the principal goals that guided our development of the Simplified Sign System was that of increasing non-speaking individuals' accessibility to communicative symbols and symbol use. It would be a mistake, however, to assume that our motivation as authors and investigators was to create a symbol system that would be taught to and used solely by persons with autism spectrum disorder, intellectual disability, cerebral palsy, or aphasia. These individuals often struggle to communicate successfully with other people in their environment. To increase the likelihood of these individuals communicating successfully, other people in their environment also will need to learn and use the Simplified Sign System. The Simplified Sign System is more of a tool for enhancing the ability of its principal users to interact meaningfully with others in their environment. This ability thus serves a social function as well. Ultimately, the Simplified Sign System is an approach to communication by which an individual's quality of life can be comprehensively addressed and improved.

We think that the Simplified Sign System has a distinct advantage over many other augmentative and alternative communication systems (discussed in Chapter 5) because it has substantial potential to be integrated into a more expansive environment. Even though signing is not the norm within hearing and spoken language-based communities, it is becoming increasingly accepted and more prevalent. The Simplified Sign System provides the non-speaking individual an opportunity to engage more successfully with the public and to produce signs that should be recognizable to many people who have never been exposed to them. Our system, then, may help expand non-speaking persons' horizons that in the past may have been limited to their teachers, caregivers, staff members, and other non-speaking individuals involved in an educational or residential program. Therefore, this system may help non-speaking persons be integrated more fully as valuable and contributing members of their own communities and of the larger societies in which they live.

In addition, adoption of the Simplified Sign System is not an admission that one has given up on an individual acquiring speech skills or proficiency in their native sign language, or that the non-speaking person has no capacity to improve his or her spoken language or native sign language skills. In fact, just the opposite is true. Indeed, the use of Simplified Signs provides a foundation upon which subsequent communication and language development may occur — even the acquisition of useful speech skills. Whereas in the past, a non-speaking individual may have undergone extensive speech therapy with little or no progress, a change of strategy to that of accompanying speech with manual signs may somewhat paradoxically lead to an improvement in speech skills (Creedon, 1973; Fouts, 1997; Millar, 2009; Millar et al., 2006).

Even if spoken language skills fail to emerge with this change in strategy, the non-speaking individual likely will acquire enhanced communication skills through the effective use of signs. The Simplified Sign System has been tailored to the specific needs of various groups of non-speaking persons. However, it is not only for the main users; it is for everyone who encounters and interacts with them. This includes family members, caregivers, friends, teachers, medical and nursing staff, therapists, and the public. This sign system represents a response to the communication difficulties experienced by the *entire community* of people who interact with non-speaking persons. The Simplified Sign System helps to address this communicative need by meeting the vocabulary needs of diverse groups of individuals. The wide range of vocabulary items in the sign system may provide these individuals with their best chance of moving forward. From an initial focus on single vocabulary items, we hope that users of our sign system will progress to signing short sentences or utterances and then longer and more complex utterances — one step at a time, each one building on the steps that came before.

Before this process can occur, however, each non-speaking person's current level or status of communicative abilities should be accurately evaluated and assessed. This evaluation or communication assessment helps the speech-language pathologist or professional caregiver understand the *individual needs* of a target sign user before tailoring a specific plan or strategy to improve his communication skills and track his progress. Unfortunately, we cannot at this time accurately predict either which individuals will benefit most from using the Simplified Sign System, or how much they will benefit. What we do know is that those who try out the system will respond to it based on their individual abilities, characteristics, circumstances, and goals. These individuals will also be affected by whether or not the other members in their families and communities accept their responsibility to address the shortfall in communication being experienced by all. These family and community members should provide consistent encouragement to the main sign user and become actively involved in his or her life.[12]

Finally, it is important to recognize that the Simplified Sign System is not necessarily exclusive of other communication methods. For some individuals, it may be their sole means of effective communication. For others, it may be their primary means of communication that is then supplemented with other techniques (such as the use of objects, pictures, speech-generating devices, or software applications). For still others, it may be an augmentative communication system that supports another primary technique or approach. The Simplified Sign System is not only flexible in terms of how it is employed, but also in when it is employed. Although it is best (and highly preferable) to implement the system as soon as possible in a child's development or in an adult's rehabilitation, it can still have a positive impact if introduced later. Furthermore, the use of the Simplified Sign System may either grow over time as an individual responds positively to it, or its use may actually diminish as a person's spoken language or native sign language skills improve. This prediction is in line with the results of studies of other sign-communication systems used with persons with intellectual disability, cerebral palsy, autism, or aphasia.

Other Potential Users of the Simplified Sign System

Although the Simplified Sign System was originally developed primarily to facilitate the communication of non-speaking children and adults, other populations or groups of people may find that learning this manual sign system will benefit them as well. Among those who might benefit from learning and using Simplified Signs are persons (both hearing and deaf) who travel to foreign countries or work in the travel industry, parents who adopt children internationally, older persons who have lost their hearing, members of the military or foreign

---

12 We provide recommendations for enhancing this sign-learning environment in Chapter 4.

aid organizations, and healthcare professionals. Simplified Signs may also be useful to language instructors as an aid to teaching vocabulary from a person's primary spoken language, to learners of foreign or additional languages, and to children from economically disadvantaged backgrounds. The need to develop highly effective and efficient foreign language instruction materials, moreover, has been underlined by the plight of millions of migrants and refugees who are currently overwhelming existing aid resources.

International travelers frequently encounter situations where their spoken language skills are unable to overcome communication barriers. Although travelers may address this by using the services of an interpreter, finding such an individual might prove difficult, costly, and time-consuming. If time were of the essence, as when one has a plane to catch or requires assistance in an emergency, then the failure to communicate quickly and accurately might have serious negative consequences. In addition, it may be easier for people to learn and use an iconic sign-communication system when traveling within a foreign country for a limited period rather than attempting to learn and use that nation's spoken language(s). If Simplified Signs were acquired by many persons worldwide, especially by travelers who frequently go abroad and those individuals involved in the travel or hospitality industries, then many communication problems might be avoided or minimized.

Those persons who elect to adopt children from countries other than their own constitute another group that might find learning and using a simplified sign-communication system helpful and beneficial. The number of international adoptions increased greatly for several decades (Judge, 1999; Krakow, Tao, & Roberts, 2005; Tan & Yang, 2005; Tessler, Gamache, & Liu, 1999) before slowing in recent years. In the U.S., the decline in adoptions from abroad this past decade has been quite steep partly because of geopolitical reasons, as there apparently is no shortage of parents who wish to adopt (Jordan, 2016). In most instances, the children who have been adopted encounter not only new caregivers and unfamiliar surroundings, but new languages as well. While the parents may find that communicating effectively with their newly adopted children is rather frustrating at first, the children involved may find the change in their language environments truly bewildering. Whereas these children may have successfully understood and produced a spoken language prior to adoption, their change in circumstances typically places them in situations where their birth language is not spoken and their efforts at speech either poorly understood or not understood at all. Not surprisingly, these children's use of their birth language either declines or is arrested at its level of development at the time of adoption as the children encounter the language of their new environment (Glennen, 2002).

The process in which international adoptees learn the language of their adoptive parents often is referred to as second-first language acquisition. Fortunately, most internationally adopted children develop skills in their new language similar to their non-adopted peers within a few years of adoption (Glennen & Bright, 2005; Glennen & Masters, 2002; Rygvold & Theie, 2016; Scott, Pollock, Roberts, & Krakow, 2013). Although most internationally adopted children eventually perform in the typical range on tests of language abilities, their language skills often lag behind those of children from comparison groups closely matched for age, gender, and family socioeconomic status (Gauthier & Genesee, 2011); additionally, there is often wide variability in language outcomes among adopted children (Scott, Roberts, & Glennen, 2011). Particular attention and intervention services probably should be directed towards those children who were reared in especially impoverished environments prior to their adoption (Hwa-Froelich, 2009). Children between three- and four-years of age at adoption more frequently experience difficulty transitioning to their new language and social environments than children aged two and younger, but often make rapid strides toward attaining language proficiency (Glennen, 2009; see also Tan et al., 2012). For children who may be even older at the time of their adoption, the outcome often is not as positive as it is for infants or younger children (Beverly, McGuinness, & Blanton, 2008). Many of these older children have communication disorders, with their parents frequently reporting that they have language or articulation impairments. Some of these difficulties may be attributable to the children's pre-adoption experiences, often in orphanages, which were not adequately stimulating or supportive.

An approach that would likely facilitate internationally adopted children's transition from their birth language to their new adopted language would be to have the parents use manual signs together with spoken language when interacting with their children. In particular, if the parents were to use manual signs that had readily transparent meanings together with spoken language, then the meanings of their utterances would likely be much clearer to their children. An increased understanding of their parents' efforts at communicating with them might, in turn, lead the children to pay better attention and to respond appropriately more often. Once the children demonstrated knowledge of their parents' spoken utterances, then the parents would no longer need to pair signs with words. If this approach were to enhance the communication environment for these newly adopted children, then these youngsters' new homes would likely seem less confusing and frightening to them and lead to their better social adjustment.

As more people live longer, the number of persons who become hearing-impaired as part of the aging process is increasing substantially (Chen, 1994; Humes et al., 2012; Strawbridge et al., 2000; Trosman et al., 2012). The numbers involved are not small: in the U.S., 48 million people have hearing loss (Kelley, 2017), with nearly two out of every three persons older than seventy years experiencing a significant loss in hearing (Lin, 2017). For the large majority of these persons, speech will remain their principal form of communication. Although their own spoken language skills may be fully adequate, they may not understand the attempts of others to communicate with them through speech. This situation may be frustrating to all parties involved and socially isolating to those individuals with newly acquired hearing impairments. One way to cope with such a problem would be to request that others write down what they wished to convey. Such an approach, however, might prove cumbersome, time-consuming, and ultimately fatiguing. Although learning a full and genuine sign language certainly is an option, many older individuals and those who interact with them may not want to devote the time and effort needed to become proficient in a full sign language. Rather, a more effective strategy might be for individuals to learn a number of Simplified Signs and combine them with spoken language when communicating with persons who have impaired hearing. In group settings, those individuals who have at least some useful hearing would likely benefit primarily from the spoken words, while those who have become deaf or hard-of-hearing would likely find that the signs help them to understand the communication of others.

When serving overseas, members of the military and international aid organizations often encounter serious communication problems when they need to interact with the citizens of those countries. If they were to use iconic manual signs and gestures to supplement and clarify their efforts at spoken communication, then many potentially harmful confrontations might be avoided. The use of sign communication might also be of great benefit to the many injured veterans who have returned home over the years, especially those who have suffered brain injuries. These injuries, depending on their severity and the particular areas of the brain affected, may adversely affect or interfere with a veteran's ability to communicate successfully using speech. The addition of a sign-communication system to a veteran's rehabilitation program might help to overcome initial limitations in the use of spoken language.

Furthermore, as societies become more multicultural in nature, healthcare providers increasingly interact with patients (or their family members) who have recently immigrated to the country and who do not yet speak the principal language or languages of that country. In an emergency situation, securing the services of a knowledgeable interpreter might not be a viable or timely option. If emergency personnel were to use easily understood gestures or signs to interact with a severely injured person with limited speech communication skills in the local language, then this approach could truly prove to be a lifesaver.

Manual signs and iconic gestures also have been shown to be a useful aid to teaching English (or other languages) to students, including economically disadvantaged students, as a first or second language (Daniels, 2001; Mancini, 2005; Schunk, 1999). One reason for this success may rest on the finding that input or instruction in more than one modality often improves students' learning on a range of tasks in comparison with instruction in only a single medium (Gellevij et al., 2002; Loncke et al., 2006; Mayer & Sims, 1994). Learning language through more than one sense may result in that language being learned more effectively and remembered for a longer period of time. Because we feel that the topic of using iconic manual signs to facilitate the learning and processing of first and subsequent languages by members of the broader hearing population is of considerable importance, we discuss the literature on this topic in more detail in Chapter 7.

Research has shown that having students enact iconic signs or gestures as they say the to-be-learned words that correspond with these signs is a very powerful way for students to learn these new vocabulary items. We surmise that the production of iconic signs or gestures might enhance learning in a number of other domains as well. That is, if concepts in mathematics, science, and engineering were to be acted out gesturally, then the concepts so embodied might be learned more effectively and robustly (Cook, Yip, & Goldin-Meadow, 2010; Radford, 2009). We say this in part because there appear to be several partially separable human memory codes or representations: word or verbal codes, visual or pictorial codes, and motor or action codes (Cartmill et al., 2012; Engelkamp & Zimmer, 1984). Overall memory performance appears to be especially strong when the different memory codes are involved; people tend to remember those things that they say, see, and do. When describing a concept or an event in a signed language, this action is a form of enactment. It will be of interest to determine if seeing how concepts are described through signs by experienced teachers of deaf students would facilitate the learning of these concepts by hearing students.

From these brief overviews of some of the diverse populations who might benefit from the use of manual signs, it should be clear that the Simplified Sign System has the potential to successfully facilitate communication in a variety of locations and circumstances. To use the Simplified Sign System effectively, however, it will likely be helpful for the reader to examine background information on the nature of sign languages and the characteristics of sign-using populations, as well as learn how the Simplified Sign System was developed. To obtain this information, it is recommended that the reader first understand the structure and contents of these volumes.

Contents and Structure of the Two Volumes

Different people may want to read and use these two volumes in different ways. Individuals knowledgeable about signing with special populations or those who would like to use signs to facilitate foreign language vocabulary acquisition may wish to turn directly to Chapters 10 and 11 (Volume 2) for the listing of Simplified Signs, descriptions of how the signs are formed, explanations of the relationships between sign formation and sign meaning, and tips on using the lexicon and sign index. Those persons with little or no background in sign languages or teaching sign communication, however, would likely benefit from reading all or some of the chapters in Volume 1 before proceeding to the sign descriptions and drawings contained in Volume 2. For those persons interested in historical perspectives on the use of signs by hearing persons, Chapter 2 provides evidence that manual signs and gestures have long been used to overcome various spoken language barriers. In Chapter 3, the emphasis is on the nature and structure of the sign languages used by Deaf persons (particularly ASL). This background material should prove helpful in understanding the reasoning behind our selection, modification, and creation of signs for the Simplified Sign System.

Persons considering adopting a sign-communication intervention program with children or adults with spoken language difficulties should read the chapters that review the studies of signing with such individuals. We first focus on the sign acquisition of persons with an intellectual disability or with cerebral palsy (Chapter 4). In subsequent chapters, we explore the use of sign communication with individuals with autism spectrum disorder (Chapter 5) and with adults and children with aphasia or a developmental language disorder (DLD) (Chapter 6). In many instances, the participants in these studies had more than one condition or disability that may have adversely affected their use of spoken language, and as a result they had complex communication needs. To some extent, our discussion of the results of certain studies in a particular chapter may appear to be the product of a rather arbitrary placement decision, even though we strove to identify the participants' primary disabling condition.

Chapter 7 concentrates on how learning to sign, and how the use of Simplified Signs, might benefit typically developing children and school-age students. Included in this chapter are reviews of the emerging literature on the use of manual signs to foster vocabulary skills in students learning a foreign language, in children from economically disadvantaged backgrounds acquiring English, and in other groups of hearing individuals with different communication and learning needs. We also include information in this chapter on how learning to sign may enhance a person's cognitive processing, paying special attention to findings on spatial memory and mental rotation. From reading this chapter, it should be apparent that learning to sign likely has much to offer to a wide range of persons with normal hearing levels.

In Chapter 8, we recount the steps we followed in developing our system, in case others wish to add new signs to the Simplified Sign lexicon. Those individuals electing to initiate a program of sign-communication training and teaching with non-speaking persons are strongly urged to read Chapter 9. Included in this chapter are a number of recommendations about how to make such a program more effective and how to maximize one's chances for successful sign interactions.

We also wish to draw the reader's attention to the presence of various appendices and supporting materials. In Volume 1, a Glossary of terms is included to assist readers by offering definitions or explanations of more technical terms. This glossary may be especially relevant for family members, caregivers, and SLP students who are not already familiar with sign language linguistics, various disabilities or conditions, or research methods and procedures. Appendix A provides a listing of the diverse sign resources we consulted when developing the initial 1000 signs of the lexicon. Appendix B offers a drawing and a short description of each of the handshapes used in the Simplified Sign System. Likewise, Appendix C provides a drawing and an explanation of the formation of each of the palm, finger, and knuckle orientations found in our written descriptions. In Volume 2, there is a sign index with synonyms. The synonyms were provided to assist users of the Simplified Sign System by identifying those words, other than the principal lexicon entries, whose meanings could be conveyed by particular signs. We hope that this inclusion of synonyms in the sign index greatly expands the usefulness of our sign system. Regardless of how these two volumes are read and utilized, we hope that it will enhance the communicative interactions of many different people.

2. Use of Manual Signs and Gestures by Hearing Persons

Historical Perspectives

There are many situations in which spoken language communication is not feasible or successful, even if all persons involved have the physical ability to produce speech. In these cases, a viable option may be the use of signs or gestural communication; history provides multiple examples of the success of such a strategy. The early Europeans who landed on the shores of what to them was the New World encountered Native Americans[1] with whom they could not effectively communicate through spoken language. Faced with this difficult situation, they quickly resorted to the use of gestures and manual signs. Not only did these Europeans employ signs and gestures in their efforts to communicate, but the Indigenous peoples they met often made use of manual signs and gestures in these first contact situations as well (Bonvillian, Ingram, & McCleary, 2009).

---

[1] In this text, the term *Native American* is mainly used to refer to the Indigenous peoples that lived on the North American continent prior to the arrival of European colonizers. In particular, we focus most of our attention on interactions between Europeans and the Indigenous peoples of the present-day continental United States, northern Mexico, and southern Canada. Needless to say, there are other examples of such interactions in both North America and South America, as well as in many other parts of the world. As a full account of such cross-cultural contact situations is far beyond the scope of this chapter (and, indeed, this book), we have constrained ourselves to the denoted regions. As such, we have generally chosen to use the term *Native American* in a limited capacity as opposed to the more inclusive phrasing *Indigenous peoples of the Americas*, which is gaining popularity as the preferred way to refer to the multiple different cultural groups found throughout North, Central, and South America.

    https://doi.org/10.11647/OBP.0205.02

In fact, many of the Indigenous peoples that Europeans encountered had very effective sign-communication systems of their own. Because the various Native American tribes or nations spoke hundreds of different languages, they needed to find a way to overcome the spoken language barriers that they frequently experienced. The use of sign-communication systems enabled many Native Americans to communicate easily and efficiently across a wide geographical area (Davis, 2010, 2016). Manual signs also enabled Native Americans to communicate effectively while hunting without disturbing their prey. So widespread was signing among Native Americans at one time that when the sixteenth-century Spaniard Cabeza de Vaca learned one of their sign systems, he was able to use it to communicate effectively during his epic trek across much of continental North America (Bonvillian et al., 2009). Apparently, the sign-communication system that Cabeza de Vaca acquired and used was both easily learned and remembered.[2]

Communication through signs, however, was not a phenomenon limited solely to Native Americans and the occasional European. Manual signs have also been employed over the centuries by a wide range of persons in quite diverse settings. Although most people today probably think of sign communication as the language of those persons who have grown up Deaf (see Chapter 3), signing has a long history with hearing persons as well. Europeans often used manual signs to facilitate communication in everything from dramatic performances to business transactions. The utilization of manual signs was also a long-established part of monastic life. By signing instead of speaking, monks could successfully communicate in silence and avoid distracting the religious contemplation of others.

Using manual signs as an alternative to speech and as a potential universal language was also a recurring topic of philosophical inquiry across the centuries. Furthermore, there are biological and linguistic bases for believing that humankind's first language was a gestural one. Some support for this view has come from an experiment conducted centuries ago in which children were deliberately isolated so as to not

---

2   Cabeza de Vaca's success, indeed his survival, often depended on his ability to communicate through signs with people living across a wide geographical area who spoke many different languages. His experiences interacting with so many different cultural groups emphasize the potential usefulness of a sign-communication system for modern travelers as well. Such a possibility is discussed in Chapter 1.

be exposed to spoken language. These children were reported to have learned and used manual gestures to communicate instead of speech.

The Origins of Language

Various scholars over the centuries have speculated about humankind's first language. Where did this remarkable ability come from? Was it divinely inspired, part of our biological heritage, or the product of learning by a social creature? Which language was humankind's first? In discussions of the nature and origins of language, most people start from the perspective that languages are spoken and transmitted in an auditory-vocal manner. It is only in the past several decades that many linguists have expanded their views to include as genuine languages the sign languages used by members of Deaf communities. Some linguists and neuroscientists, moreover, have ventured past this point and theorized that human language emerged from manual sign or visual-gestural communication (e.g., Armstrong, 2008; Armstrong, Stokoe, & Wilcox, 1995; Armstrong & Wilcox, 2007; Corballis, 2002, 2009, 2013, 2017b; Fay et al., 2014; Gentilucci & Corballis, 2006; Hewes, 1976; Kimura, 1976, 1993; Levinson & Holler, 2014; Stokoe, 2001). According to this view, our human ancestors communicated primarily through manual signs or gestures, with their hands being used to represent a wide range of objects and actions (Armstrong, 2011; Wilson, 1998); spoken language did not appear until much later in human evolution. In this account, the relatively rapid emergence of spoken language as the predominant form of human communication occurred because it was based on an already established gestural means of communication that relied on sequentially produced manual signs.

How, then, would gestural communication itself have developed, and why would it have developed before spoken communication? One hypothesis advanced to explain an early emergence of manual communicative gestures is that such gestures stemmed from a neural mechanism already present in our prehominid ancestors (Arbib, 2005, 2013; Rizzolatti & Arbib, 1998). This neural mechanism, composed of a set of neurons called mirror neurons (as first observed in the brains of macaques), is active not only when an individual produces a specific action, but also when that same motor action or a similar one is viewed.

It appears that mirror neurons enable an individual to understand actions performed by others if the individual also has the ability to perform those actions (Corballis, 2010; Rizzolatti & Sinigaglia, 2008). Our current knowledge of human neurophysiology from brain imaging suggests that a mirror system for grasping, believed to be critical to our ability to imitate, is located in close proximity to neural systems devoted to manual control as well as the syntactic aspects of language production (Binkofski & Buccino, 2004). The co-representation of all these mechanisms in the same region of the brain has led a number of researchers to advance the view that the mirror neuron system helped lead humankind to first develop a gestural communication system or language, based on the ability to recognize, imitate, and build upon the hand movements used by others (Arbib, 2013; Ferrari, Gallese, Rizzolatti, & Fogassi, 2003; Rizzolatti & Arbib, 1998). In this approach, a mechanism for language presumably emerged from a mechanism not initially related to communication, such as the capacity to generate and recognize actions.

Many current researchers also think that control of the vocal mechanisms necessary for autonomous speech emerged only relatively recently in humans, long after humans had acquired proficiency in gestures and other voluntary motor actions (Corballis, 2002, 2009, 2017a; Lieberman, 1998; Stokoe, 2001). If this were indeed the case, then it implies that our human ancestors had more limited speech capabilities. Without being able to produce a sufficiently diverse array of sounds, these ancestral humans most likely would have found speech a less effective means of communication. In turn, they may have relied more heavily on their manual or gestural abilities to describe or represent aspects of their world. Sounds certainly would have played important roles in conveying alarms and indicating where one was located, but they may not have been as useful as manual gestures or signs in representing many objects, actions, or locations in the environment.[3]

Manual signs or gestures, on the other hand, clearly can be made to resemble or describe many objects, animals, actions, or properties; this

---

3   As stated in Fay et al. (2014), contemporary studies of gestural use by non-human primates also provide some support for the gestural theory of language origins (see Gardner & Gardner, 1969, 1971; Pollick & de Waal, 2007; Savage-Rumbaugh et al., 1986), but see Cartmill, Beilock, & Goldin-Meadow (2012) for information regarding the differences between human gestures and modern ape gestures in terms of their structure, meanings conveyed, and representational aspects.

characteristic is known as iconicity. Pantomime, for example, is highly iconic in nature. This representational capacity of gestures is largely equivalent to the meaning, or semantic, component of languages. Iconic signs or gestures, because they closely resemble the objects or actions for which they stand (their referents), probably would have been readily understood by others.

Another characteristic of gestures, movement, makes them an even more effective means of communication. When a person's gestural communications incorporate movement or motion, additional information beyond the identification of an object can be conveyed (Fay et al., 2014; Goldin-Meadow, 2003; Stokoe, 1991, 2001; Wilcox, 2009). Movement not only can indicate action, a property of verbs, but it can indicate the direction or location of the action (depending on where the gesture is produced). Movement can also indicate who or what is causing the action, as long as the location of the agent or the instrument used to perform the action is specified gesturally. Furthermore, movements can be systematically varied (e.g., slowed down, repeated) to show modification of the action. In light of these capacities, one can make an argument that gestural production can convey to the viewer considerable information that is syntactic in nature as well. The emergence of an ability to combine iconic gestures or mime sequences, moreover, may have facilitated early peoples' planning of forthcoming actions and the recounting of past events. For our early human ancestors, with their spoken language likely limited by biological constraints, gestures may well have been used quite extensively and effectively. In fact, the current focus on the gestural origins of language may help change scholars' views on the nature of speech itself. Once viewed exclusively as a system for sound production, speech is now considered by some researchers to be primarily a system for producing articulatory gestures (Gentilucci & Campione, 2013; Gentilucci & Corballis, 2006; Liberman, Cooper, Shankweiler, & Studdert-Kennedy, 1967).

Although many linguists and neuroscientists have only recently begun to seriously consider the idea that humankind first used gestures or manual signs to communicate, the idea itself is not an entirely new one. In 1746, a manuscript by prominent French scholar Etienne Bonnot de Condillac entitled *Essay on the Origin of Human Knowledge* (Trans. H. Aarsleff, 2001) was published describing the early communication of two imaginary children, a boy and a girl. In this essay, one child first used gestures to convey that he wanted something out of his reach. The second child understood the movement of the other's head, arm, and body and came to his assistance. Eventually a language emerged from these gestures as the children learned to connect ideas with gestural signs. Sounds often accompanied the children's gestural production, but speech did not replace the children's gestural language until later. This depiction of language as emerging solely out of human agency also challenged the view presented in the Book of Genesis of a divine origin of language (Rosenfeld, 2001).

Condillac's essay was largely speculative, without any basis in empirical evidence, yet it hints at how one might determine the answer to the question of what humankind's first language was. One approach to resolving this question that was discussed by different scholars over the centuries was to rear children from early infancy without exposure to any spoken language and then determine what language, if any, they spontaneously produced.[4] Such a language, generated without the benefit of spoken language input, was deemed by these scholars as likely to be the most fundamental of human languages: humankind's first and oldest language.

There is compelling evidence that at least one experiment was conducted that systematically examined the development of children reared without exposure to spoken language.[5] That experiment was conducted over 400 years ago by Akbar, emperor of Hindustan (Bonvillian, Garber, & Dell, 1997). If children, without benefit of spoken language input, were to utter a certain tongue, then Akbar felt that this language would be the oldest language. Akbar, according to his court historian, Abul Fazl, also was motivated to conduct his language experiment to resolve the question of whether speech arises spontaneously in children.

In Akbar's experiment, a number of children were taken from their parents (for a monetary consideration) while they were still in early

---

4　This approach might be seen as an effort to simulate the perceived conditions surrounding the initial emergence of human language. What these scholars evidently did not consider is that the language-learning skills of modern-day children would differ substantially from those of children eons ago when human language was first emerging (Botha, 2007; Goldin-Meadow, 2003).

5　This example from history of a highly unethical experiment conducted on children would not be acceptable today in reputable scientific communities.

infancy and then reared in a secluded house by nurses who refrained from speaking to them. Guards were posted at the house to ensure that speech did not intrude. The children remained in the house for periods of three to four years, receiving nourishment and interaction, but no spoken language input.

When the children were about four years old, Akbar had their language skills assessed. The children spoke no language at all; their only vocalizations were the noises associated with people born deaf. This was seen as a disappointing outcome because it failed to resolve the question of which spoken language was the oldest human language. The outcome did, however, provide evidence for the view that speech does not arise spontaneously in children. Children apparently need at least some minimal level of exposure to a particular tongue in order to acquire it.

Although the children in Akbar's language experiment failed to acquire even limited facility in speech, they did not fail to learn how to communicate. Rather than using spoken language, they "merely expressed their thoughts through gestures which answered the purpose of words" (Tylor, 1878, p. 81). Unfortunately, the accounts of Akbar's study do not provide sufficient detail about the children's gestures or manual signs to determine whether the children's gestural communication should be viewed as a genuine sign language. Nor do we know whether the nurses used gestures or signs in front of the children. Still, it is an interesting finding that the children acquired an ability to communicate through gestures or signs. In fact, Akbar and the scholars in his court may have been premature in dismissing the findings of the experiment. In light of contemporary views that our human ancestors probably communicated mostly through signs or gestures, the finding that the children communicated gesturally may have been an accurate resolution of the issue of language origins after all!

Signs as a Natural and Universal Form of Communication

In addition to the philosophical inquiries of various early scholars about the origins and emergence of human language, the potential utility of manual gestures has long been recognized. Through the ages, certain European scholars embraced the view that manual signs and gestures constituted a natural and effective means of communication that might take the place of speech. By "natural" it was meant that signs and gestures could be understood without needing to be learned or translated. This view about the nature of signs and gestures may have encouraged Europeans to use signs in North America, inspired investigators to study Native American signs, and influenced some of the early teachers of deaf students.

The view that someone unable to speak could communicate quite effectively through manual signs or gestures has a long history; it goes back at least to classical antiquity (Knowlson, 1965). In Plato's *Cratylus*, Socrates advanced the view that if one were without voice or tongue, then one could convey information effectively through the use of the hand, head, and rest of the body, much like the signing of deaf and mute persons. In making such a sign, "We should imitate the nature of the thing" (Plato, Trans. B. Jowett, 1961, p. 457). As an example, "if we were describing the running of a horse, or any other animal, we should make our bodies and their gestures as like as we could to them" (Plato, Trans. B. Jowett, 1961, p. 458). In this approach, the manual signs or gestures produced by deaf and mute persons were seen as resembling the basic nature of things or having a natural affinity to the concepts for which they stood. This natural resemblance meant that the meanings of manual signs were seen as sufficiently transparent that they could be understood without needing to be formally learned and that signs thus formed a natural language.[6] This belief about the nature of signs, it should be noted, was based on impressions, not systematic observations.

A small number of scholars over the centuries also advanced the view that a language of the hand or manual signs might serve as a universal language for humankind. Such signs would transcend spoken language barriers because they were based on actions known by everyone. John Bulwer, an ardent seventeenth-century advocate of this view, wrote about the capacity of the language of the hand:

---

6   The meaning of the term *natural language* has changed considerably over the years. In contemporary usage, a natural language would be understood to mean a language with its own grammar and lexicon that is acquired by native signers or speakers (Fischer, 2002). Examples of natural languages would be American Sign Language, French, Russian, Swahili, Spanish, Argentinian Sign Language, and Mandarin (Chinese).

> It speaks all languages, and as an universal character of reason, is generally understood and known by all nations among the formal differences of their tongue. And being the only speech that is natural to man, it may well be called the tongue and general language of human nature which, without teaching, men in all regions of the habitable world do at the first sight most easily understand. (Bulwer, 1644/1974, p. 16)

According to Bulwer, only spoken languages had been confounded at the Tower of Babel in the Genesis account. That is, when God punished men for their hubris in attempting to build a tower to the heavens, the resulting confusion caused by a proliferation of languages was limited to spoken language. The language of the hand, in contrast, "had the happiness to escape the confusion of Babel" (Bulwer, 1644/1974, p. 19). Although Bulwer may have been correct in the sense that gesture likely would prove a more effective form of communication than speech between individuals who spoke different languages, he failed to recognize that gestures varied widely by a person's cultural background (Knox, 1990).

An early indication that the manual signs used by persons who had grown up Deaf were much more than simple, readily understood pantomimic gestures came from the observations of a Dutch jurist, Cornelius Haga (Rée, 1999; Sibscota, 1670/1967). Haga served as an ambassador to the Court in Constantinople (present-day Istanbul) from 1611 to 1639. At his court, the Ottoman Sultan maintained a retinue of deaf and mute servants because he believed that they would not be able to betray court secrets to outsiders. Haga, intrigued by this situation, briefly studied these servants' signing. Haga observed that whereas he readily understood the meanings of some of the signs, the meanings of most were not apparent. With the assistance of sign language interpreters, Haga discovered that he could communicate in-depth on all topics with the deaf servants. He concluded that their system of signing was capable of expressing a wide range of ideas quite effectively.

Some of the first educators of deaf students also advanced the view that manual signs potentially constituted a universal natural language system for humankind (Knowlson, 1965). If that were the case, then manual signs might effectively overcome language barriers worldwide. Roch-Ambroise Bébian, an educator of deaf students in the early nineteenth century, nevertheless recognized that selecting a sign with a natural relationship to an idea was often not a straightforward undertaking. This was the case because the things signified frequently had a range of distinctive characteristics or features. Bébian observed that one "must choose between the possible signs for depicting an idea" (Bébian, 1817, Trans. F. Philip, 1984, p. 152) and "where there is a choice, error is possible" (Bébian, 1817, Trans. F. Philip, 1984, p. 150). If an error were made and an imprecise sign selected, Bébian hoped that educators would help rectify the situation and select a more precise sign. From such an approach, an effective natural language of signs or gestures might emerge.

The notion that there could be a natural gestural or sign language of humankind that was essentially universally understood rested, however, on a rather tenuous assumption. That assumption was that there were basic representative characteristics of actions, objects, or properties that could be rendered in gestures and be accurately perceived by most everyone. One problem with this approach, as Bébian observed long ago, is that there likely are a number of particular characteristics that might be selected as the basis of a "representative" gesture or sign. Furthermore, the selection of a "representative" gesture becomes noticeably more difficult when one moves from depicting concrete objects or overt actions to depicting abstract ideas. Another problem is that each individual confronting the task of creating a representative gesture would approach the task with a different viewpoint (Eco, 1995). What is a salient characteristic for one person might not be so for the next. Finally, the meaning or significance of objects, actions, or properties may vary considerably across cultures. This variation in meaning cross-culturally compounds the difficulty of selecting a representative gesture that would be universally understood.

Gestural and Sign Use Cross-Culturally

Indeed, there are imposing obstacles to developing a universal gestural or sign-communication system. Growing up in a particular culture, one often is not consciously aware of the large number of nonverbal behaviors and rules that one has acquired. However, travel to a foreign land with a different culture and one can very quickly recognize just how acutely different these cultures are nonverbally. Rules for body postures, greetings, eye gaze, hand use, and gesture production may vary dramatically. Furthermore, gestures seen as having transparent meanings in one culture may not be so viewed by someone in another culture.

One particular difficulty in developing a universal gestural or sign-communication system is that certain handshapes and gestures may have quite distinct meanings in different countries or cultures. A specific gesture that would be responded to in an approving manner in one country might be considered terribly rude, obscene, or provocative in another (Grosse & Reker, 2010). An example of such a potential gestural bombshell is the American "O.K." sign (the tips of the thumb and index finger touch to form a circle, with the remaining fingers extended and separated). In the U.S., this gesture has historically been used to indicate that things are fine or that one is doing well. The same gesture would be considered quite rude or vulgar in Brazil, Russia, and Germany (Axtell, 1991). Conversely, a handshape deemed offensive in the U.S., the extended middle finger, might be entirely acceptable in much of the rest of the world and be used in many signed languages (Holcomb, 2013). Moreover, gestures can have different meanings within the same country, take on new meanings as societies and cultures change, be appropriated by smaller groups or sub-cultures for their own purposes (whether benign or nefarious), or even pass out of usage altogether.

Fortunately, as people from disparate parts of the world learn more about each other, often from movies, television, videos, apps, and the internet, there is growing recognition that certain signs, gestures, and other nonverbal behaviors may have quite different meanings in other countries or cultures. As a result, those gestures or nonverbal behaviors that might be interpreted as offensive if made by a fellow citizen might be allowed to pass without alarm if made by a visitor. Correspondingly, with much more known today about cross-cultural differences in nonverbal behavior, it behooves the visitor to proactively learn what signs, gestures, and other nonverbal behaviors should be avoided when travelling to a particular area. Another useful option is to employ the services of an experienced travel guide or interpreter to help avoid or smooth over potential cross-cultural misunderstandings.

Because identical signs, gestures, and other nonverbal behaviors can have different meanings around the world, it is likely that efforts to generate a universal or nearly universal gestural communication system will include some gestures that are offensive to someone somewhere. One approach to resolving this issue would be to have users of any sign-communication system modify the offending gesture for use in that particular culture or to recommend that signs with related meanings be used in place of the offending one (see Mindess 2014 for a discussion of multicultural issues in the context of sign language interpreting). A second way to resolve this problem would be to note which signs might be offensive in which cultures so that the learner of a particular sign system might know beforehand which gestures or signs should be avoided while in that certain country. Despite these obstacles, if a gestural or sign-communication system could be developed that was both relatively easy to learn and useful in many different situations, then it would likely be helpful in overcoming many spoken language barriers.

Finally, it should be remembered that a widely used and easily learned sign-communication system was developed at least once before — by the Indigenous inhabitants of North America. Their success in this domain shows that it is possible for a sign-communication system to be embraced by a wide range of people who speak (or sign) many different languages. Furthermore, some of the same telecommunications technology that is bringing the world closer together might also be harnessed to disseminate information about such a sign-communication system.

Sign Communication in North America

With estimates of at least 400 different spoken languages (and probably hundreds more) in existence in North America at the time of Christopher Columbus' arrival (Farb, 1968; Goddard, 1996; Silver & Miller, 1997), communication through speech alone among members of separate Native American nations or tribes was a serious problem. Members of different nations needed a system of communication that could help them overcome numerous spoken language barriers. This problem was largely resolved by the use of a manual sign-communication system, Plains Indian Sign Language (PISL), also known as North American Indian Sign Language or American Indian Hand Talk (Davis, 2006, 2010). Members of a Native American nation typically would employ signs when they interacted with members of another nation who did not understand their spoken language. With members of many different nations able to sign, sign communication served as a common "language" or lingua franca (Campbell, 1997; Davis, 2005, 2010, 2016). In addition to this intertribal usage, Plains Indian Sign Language was commonly used as an alternative means of communication within a tribe, not only with deaf tribal members, but with hearing members as well (Davis, 2017). Moreover, signing was used concurrently with the spoken language of a tribe, or rather, as an augmentative means of communication. PISL also has been transmitted as a native language across multiple generations (Davis, 2017).

Because the culture of most Native Americans in North America historically was not a written one, obtaining information about their sign communication proved an arduous task for outsiders in early contact situations. The frequent hostilities between Native Americans and European immigrants made earning the confidence of tribal members, much less learning their language and culture, a difficult undertaking. Much of what we know about Native American sign communication was acquired during the nineteenth century through the efforts of a relatively small number of individuals, among them Garrick Mallery, William P. Clark, and Lewis Hadley.[7] Mallery had become quite knowledgeable about Native American signs and culture during his service in the west as a lieutenant colonel in the U.S. Army. His 1881 *Sign Language among North American Indians* contains information on the history and nature of signed languages together with written descriptions of Native American signs that he and other early investigators had recorded. Clark, a captain in the U.S. Army, provided detailed written descriptions of over 1000 signs in his 1885 volume *The Indian Sign Language*. His thoroughness proved quite helpful both to contemporary and subsequent investigators. Finally, Hadley's 1893 *Indian Sign Talk* included drawings, many for the first time, of how nearly 600 different signs were formed.

---

7   Lewis F. Hadley was a missionary of Quaker parentage allegedly born in Salem, Massachusetts and who lived for some time in what was then Anadarko (Oklahoma), Indian Territory. Hadley travelled widely among Native Americans for much of his life, initially compiling vocabularies of various Native American spoken languages before focusing on their Indigenous sign languages (Foreman, 1949). It is unclear which Native American nation or individual(s) bestowed upon Hadley the name of Ingonompashi, but there is some evidence that Hadley preferred this designation over his given birth name, especially in his published works on their sign language.

The use of manual signs to communicate was, at one time, quite widespread among Native Americans (Mallery, 1880, 1881/2001). Mallery reported that signs were used as far north and west as Alaska, in the north and east among the Cree and Iroquois, and south into Mexico.[8] Although Mallery marveled at the extent to which sign communication permeated North America, he was at pains to point out that there was not a single, universal sign system used throughout the continent by all Native Americans. In support of this latter claim, Mallery described the situation of the Utes and Paiutes (of western North America). Mallery observed that the Utes and Paiutes not only had their own signs, but that they recognized clear differences between their own signs and those of other Native American nations. These differences in sign systems, however, should not obscure the observation that there was considerable similarity in the signs used by many different nations, especially those signs used by members of the nations who inhabited the Great Plains of North America (e.g., Cheyenne, Comanche, Kiowa). The sign-communication system of the Plains Indians was used over a vast geographical area, extending from present-day Texas northward into Canada (McKay-Cody, 1998).

Since this sign system served to facilitate communication among members of many different Indigenous nations, it needed to be relatively easy to learn, as it typically would not be the principal means of communication for those who used it. It also needed to be easily understood and remembered by all. The Plains Indians used a sign vocabulary that met these important criteria by creating manual signs that often resembled the concepts for which they stood (that is, the signs were iconic or representative). In many ways, the development of this sign system was a remarkable human intellectual achievement and its widespread dissemination a testament to its practical value in overcoming communication barriers. Indeed, Mallery (1880, 1881/2001), who saw the elements of many of the signs he observed as reflections of

---

8 There is evidence that manual signing was used even farther north than Mallery envisioned. Sailors who accompanied the Englishman Martin Frobisher on his three voyages to the Arctic during the 1570s commented on the widespread use of signs by the Indigenous people they encountered there, the Inuit. The sailors and the Inuit of present-day Baffin Island, the largest island of the Arctic Archipelago, interacted with each other primarily through manual signs and gestures (Sherley-Appel & Bonvillian, 2014).

images from nature, advanced the view that such a manual sign system might help overcome many barriers to communication worldwide.

What were the origins of the sign-communication systems used by Native Americans? Some of the early investigators asked members of various tribes or nations about the origins of their signs (Dodge, 1882/1978; Scott, 1898/1978). Members of all these tribes and nations indicated that the sign language they used was of great antiquity and that it had been passed down from one generation to the next much like spoken language. Unfortunately, a definitive response as to a specific origin was not forthcoming. Members of many different nations, however, did observe that the Kiowa nation traditionally had been credited with inventing it. In one account, the Kiowas were depicted as often conducting raids among Native Mexicans, capturing numerous horses. The other tribes on the Northern Plains would then journey to the Kiowa and trade for horses. Because the Kiowa were already adept at sign communication, members of other Indigenous nations learned to sign from them.

Although this traditional account provided an explanation for the similarity of the signs used on the Great Plains, it did not explain how the Kiowa came to have such a system. This account also suggested that sign communication followed the re-introduction of horses to the Americas by Europeans. Mallery (1881/2001), however, observed that the conditions favorable for the emergence of a sign-communication system (many distinct spoken languages in one geographical area) predated the arrival of Europeans and their horses to North America. It is quite possible that the Indigenous peoples of present-day Mexico and Guatemala had sign-communication systems that long preceded the arrival of Europeans (Fox Tree, 2009), and that one of these sign-communication systems was learned by members of the Kiowa (or other groups) through intertribal contact (Brennan, 1998).

Alternatively, perhaps, the occurrence of hearing impairment or deafness among tribal members may have spurred the creation of manual signs.[9] Such signs might then have been adapted for communication

---

9   Native American children have a much higher incidence of otitis media, or middle ear inflammation, than American children with European ancestry (Bluestone, 1998; Bluestone & Klein, 2007). This much higher incidence of otitis media in Native Americans may result in overall increased rates of impaired hearing or

across spoken language barriers. Deaf members of Native American communities, moreover, apparently played important roles historically in the development and transmission of these sign-communication systems (Davis, 2016). Signs, either produced alone or accompanying speech, also played important roles in various other tribal activities such as storytelling (Farnell, 1995), rituals, prayers, conversation, and games (Davis, 2014). Furthermore, it should be noted that various Indigenous groups, including Native Americans, made considerable use of manual sign communication when hunting (Davis, 2017). To successfully bring down medium- or large-sized animals, Indigenous hunters often operated in groups (Divale & Zipin, 1977). A likely reason for this group action is that such animals typically needed to be wounded multiple times before the fatal blow was delivered. With the limited range of their weapons (e.g., bows and arrows, spears), the hunters also needed to get relatively close to their prey without being detected. The use of manual signs or gestures enabled members of a hunting party to effectively coordinate their actions in silence, greatly increasing the likelihood that they would not be detected. This ability to communicate silently in the presence of large predators may also have increased the likelihood that people would survive such encounters. These different uses and advantages provided by manual signs may help explain why signing became so widely used on the Great Plains in particular and more generally throughout North America.[10]

One explanation advanced for the origin of Native American signs that is not well supported is the hypothesis that European newcomers introduced the practice of communicating through signs to Native Americans (Samarin, 1987). Although many Europeans may have been exposed to the use of pantomime or gestural communication before embarking for America, the journals of a number of early Europeans

---

deafness in this population (Hammond & Meiners, 1993; McShane & Plas, 1982). Contemporary deaf children from Native American communities often attend schools for deaf students where they acquire facility in American Sign Language as opposed to their Indigenous sign language (Davis, 2016).

10 Over the past century, many of the spoken languages of the Indigenous peoples of North America have become endangered, as these languages often are not being transmitted to children (Hornberger, 1998; McCarty, 2008). In an effort to reverse this trend, gestures and manual signs currently are being used as effective vehicles of vocabulary learning in various programs of Native American language instruction (Borgia, 2014; Kipp, 2007).

underlined the presence of signing among the Native Americans at the time of the Europeans' arrival in North America. One such European was Cabeza de Vaca, whose trek took place only a few years after forces under the command of Hernán Cortés toppled the Aztec Empire (which eventually resulted in the conquest of Mexico for Spain). It is extremely unlikely that any system of manual communication introduced by Cortés or other colonizers could possibly have spread so widely throughout North America in such a brief period. To the contrary, there is considerable evidence that the Spaniards encountered sign communication in their interactions with Native Americans in their early travels into present-day Mexico and the area north of Mexico (Díaz del Castillo, Trans. A. P. Maudslay, 1908; Mallery, 1881/2001; Wurtzburg & Campbell, 1995).

Europeans in the New World and their Communicative Interactions through Signs

Álvar Núñez Cabeza de Vaca was not the first or only European to rely on manual communication in his interactions with Indigenous peoples in North America, but the story of his travels is a particularly compelling and illustrative one. Filled with twists and turns of fate and fortune, Cabeza de Vaca was able to parlay a rather inauspicious start to an expedition focused on exploiting and absconding with the natural resources of a foreign land into a more equitable and respectful relationship with various Native American nations he encountered (Bonvillian, Ingram, & McCleary, 2009).

The Adventures of Cabeza de Vaca

> We passed through a great number and diversity of languages. With all of them God our Lord favored us, because they always understood us and we understood them. And thus we asked and they responded by signs as if they spoke our language and we theirs... (Cabeza de Vaca in Adorno & Pautz, 1999, p. 233)

In the English translation of his report to his king quoted above, the Spaniard Álvar Núñez Cabeza de Vaca provided an account of his incredible trek across much of North America. It was a story of survival and perseverance in a foreign land, despite great hardships and innumerable obstacles. Essential to the survival of Cabeza de Vaca and his three companions from the Old World was the fact that they were able to communicate successfully with Native Americans by using manual signs. Without this ability, Cabeza de Vaca's odyssey might have had a very different, and perhaps fatal, ending.

Cabeza de Vaca was chosen to serve as the treasurer on an ill-fated Spanish expedition that reached present-day Florida in 1528. About 300 Spaniards disembarked there and began an overland campaign in search of riches in gold. Cabeza de Vaca observed that the native people he encountered in this expedition were quite active in their use of manual signs. Furthermore, both the Europeans and Native Americans relied heavily on manual signs and gestures in their communicative exchanges. Disease, a serious lack of food, and hostilities between the two groups, however, brought this part of the expedition to its end.

Unable to locate the ships that had brought them to Florida some months before, the Europeans constructed five rafts that they used for transportation along the Gulf Coast as they searched for Spanish-controlled territory. The rafts eventually washed ashore on the coast of present-day Texas; Cabeza de Vaca was one of only a small number of survivors. Taken captive by members of a tribe who lived on an island in the area of present-day Galveston Bay, Cabeza de Vaca suffered mightily as a result of forced labor before escaping to the mainland. On the mainland, he experienced better treatment and eventually established himself as a neutral merchant among many different Native American nations. His trading ventures brought him deep into the interior of North America and into contact with diverse groups of people. Because the members of many of these nations spoke different languages, Cabeza de Vaca likely acquired and used the manual sign-communication system employed by the Native Americans he encountered (Wurtzburg & Campbell, 1995).

In 1534, Cabeza de Vaca and three other survivors of the expedition began another attempt to locate Spanish-controlled territory. Initially, they moved slowly along the Gulf Coast, crossing the Rio Grande before turning to the northwest in the summer of 1535 (Adorno & Pautz, 1999). In the ensuing year, these four men wandered widely. Although their precise route remains a topic of scholarly debate, they most likely traveled through present-day northern Mexico, then southwest Texas, and probably into southern New Mexico. The men then changed direction again, this time heading to the southwest until they reached the Gulf of California in early 1536. From this point, they moved down the coast until they arrived at Spanish-controlled territory in present-day Mexico. In the course of their journey, Cabeza de Vaca and his three companions gained much respect among the Native Americans as great faith healers. Their reputation as healers preceded them in their travels, facilitating their movement among tribes or nations hostile to one another (Howard, 1997). Nevertheless, their trek is an incredible tale of human endurance in the face of extreme privation (Reséndez, 2007).

An important aspect of Cabeza de Vaca and his three companions' survival was their ability to communicate effectively in signs with the different tribes or nations that they encountered. Cabeza de Vaca claimed that although he passed among peoples who used many dissimilar tongues, he successfully asked questions and received answers by signs (Tomkins, 1931/1969). In his account, Cabeza de Vaca made clear that the sign-communication systems he encountered (particularly the one used by the Native American nations or tribes of the Great Plains) were both quite widespread and highly efficient (Wurtzburg & Campbell, 1995).

Other Early Contact Situations

Indeed, manual communication played an important role in many of the early explorations and settlements of the New World by Europeans. When Europeans first arrived in North America, they encountered a serious communication barrier with the Indigenous inhabitants. Not only was there no shared spoken language, but two vastly different cultures were colliding. This communication dilemma was resolved to some extent by both parties (the Europeans and the Native Americans) using manual signs and pantomime.

Christopher Columbus, in his log book entry on the first day of contact between his crew and Native Americans, 12 October 1492, described how he tried to make sense out of what he was seeing: "Many of the men I have seen have scars on their bodies, and when I made signs to them to find out how this happened, they indicated that people from other nearby islands come to San Salvador to capture them; they defend themselves the best they can" (Columbus, 1492, Trans. R. H. Fuson, 1987, pp. 76–77). Columbus apparently felt that this gestural communication was relatively effective. He observed: "I asked by signs," "I could find out by means of signs" (Ohler, 1986, Trans. C. Hillier, 1989, p. 75), and "I already understood something by means of signs" (Columbus, 1492, Trans. R. H. Fuson, 1987, p. 158). Columbus' assessment of how much he was learning through signs, however, likely was an overly optimistic interpretation (Axtell, 2000).

Although early Europeans in North America made frequent use of manual signs and gestures in their interactions with Native Americans (Greenblatt, 1991; Quinn, 1979), their assessments of the effectiveness of this approach varied considerably. Giovanni da Verrazzano, who explored the east coast of North America in 1524, observed on one occasion that the Native Americans "showed us by signs where we could more conveniently secure our boat" (Verrazzano, 1524, Trans. J. G. Cogswell, 1841/[1896], p. 2), whereas on another occasion he complained: "As to the religious faith of all these tribes, not understanding their language, we could not discover either by sign or gestures any thing certain" (Verrazzano, 1524, Trans. J. G. Cogswell, 1841/[1896], p. 11). Perhaps Verrazzano's effort to probe Native Americans' depth of religious understanding was too complicated an undertaking for an early encounter involving signs and gestures. The same, however, cannot be said for the Frenchman Jacques Cartier (1491-1557), the first European to travel the Gulf of St. Lawrence. Cartier became frustrated when his efforts at gestural communication did not have the effect he intended: "...we did not care to trust to their signs and waved to them to go back, which they would not do but paddled so hard that they soon surrounded our long-boat with their seven canoes. And seeing that no matter how much we signed to them, they would not go back, we shot off over their heads two small cannon" (Cartier, 1534, in Quinn, 1979, p. 299). That action resulted in the Native Americans paddling a safe distance away. Unfortunately, this was just one instance of how gestural and spoken communications between Europeans and Indigenous peoples did not produce the desired result.

Certainly, among the most effective manual sign communication that any of the early Europeans encountered was that of the Plains

Apache. Pedro de Castañeda was a member of the 1540–1542 expedition led by Francisco Vázquez de Coronado that travelled much of what was to become the southwestern United States and parts of the Great Plains. Castañeda observed of the Plains Apache: "That they were very intelligent is evident from the fact that although they conversed by signs they made themselves understood so well that there was no need of an interpreter" (Castañeda, Trans. G. P. Winship, 1933, p. 38). Evidently, when signing was done skillfully, information was clearly transmitted.

These early communicative interactions between Europeans and Native Americans underline several important points. One is that the Europeans recognized aspects of the communication barriers they would face and, starting from their very first encounters, tried to overcome these barriers by using manual signs, pantomime, and gestures. Correspondingly, the Native Americans, who often signed when interacting with members of other Indigenous nations, relied heavily on manual communication in their interactions with Europeans. Another point is that these early communicative interactions in some instances were not entirely successful. It became evident that certain manual signs or gestures whose meanings were viewed as readily apparent or transparent in one culture might prove unclear to members of another. A final observation is that the Europeans came to recognize that certain individuals and groups were more adept at manual communication than others and that people could acquire proficiency in sign communication. Indeed, in the famous eighteenth-century voyages conducted by James Cook, considerable reliance was made on sign communication, and Cook himself was seen as becoming "adept at sign language" in these encounters (Hough, 1994, p. 244).

Early European Gestural Communication

What background in gestural or manual communication did the early Europeans bring to their encounters with Native Americans? One view is that the use of signs and gestures by Europeans in the years before Columbus was already a well-established approach and deemed sufficiently commonplace not to merit particular attention. Hewes (1974, p. 5) wrote:

> Encounters between people ignorant of each other's language are
> frequently described in the narratives of travel and exploration prior
> to 1492, although explicit reference to sign-communication is rare, not
> because it did not occur, but because resort to it has been usually taken
> for granted.

Why might this be so?

Apparently, the use of signs and gestures in communication was quite
widespread in medieval Europe (Nitschke, 1997). In the Middle Ages,
mimes and jesters relied on members of the audience rapidly discerning
the relationships between the gestures they produced and their
meanings (Rée, 1999). Actors in medieval drama also made extensive
use of pantomime and gestures to convey important information to their
audiences (Enders, 2001). Indeed, the use of mimetic gestures in theatrical
productions has a very long history, extending back to the ancient
Greeks (Golder, 1996; Lawler, 1964). Orators and preachers during the
Middle Ages and Renaissance often utilized a variety of gestures to
supplement and to clarify their oral presentations. Many of the gestures
used by actors and orators in their presentations were common across
much of Europe (Barnett, 1990). This use of widely recognized and
easily understood gestures helped many people overcome considerable
spoken language barriers. The Europeans also may have benefited from
witnessing the behavior of merchants involved in international trade.
These merchants frequently encountered situations where their spoken
language skills did not suffice. To overcome this obstacle, the merchants
often relied on easily understood manual signs or gestures.

Use of Signs by Monastic Orders

Other sources of manual signs for Europeans were the sign lexicons
developed and used by members of various monastic orders. Over the
centuries, certain groups of devout hearing persons made a concerted
effort to communicate without using speech. For these groups, an
atmosphere of silence was an important aspect of their contemplative
lives. Silence was perceived as assisting the monks in their religious
reflection, with manual communication used when and where spoken
language was not permitted. For some in the monastic world, being
silent also was in accord with a heavenly ideal that was devoid of human
speech (Bruce, 2007). The Benedictines were an early Christian religious

order in which the monks frequently employed manual or signed forms of communication (Bragg, 1997). Cistercian monks were another such group (Barakat, 1975).

The precise date of introduction of signs to Christian monastic orders is uncertain. There is, however, every appearance that early monastic orders relied on the use of signs when speech was deemed undesirable (Barakat, 1975; Bruce, 2007). The use of signs as an alternative to spoken language in monasteries was set forth explicitly in the tenth century (Kendon, 1990). Benedictine monks needed to use signs to communicate in certain areas of the monastery during hours when speech was disallowed (Bragg, 1997).[11] By 1068, a list of the distinct signs being used by monks was drawn up; it totaled 296 in number. This document and subsequent sign compilations over the centuries provided valuable information on what signs were being used as well as descriptions of how they were formed. These lists served to standardize sign formation across a religious order and, to some extent, control the range of discourse. In spite of a relatively short list of signs, the monks were able to convey many other concepts by combining or compounding two, three, or more individual signs (Barakat, 1975; Kendon, 1990). Monks also created their own signs as communication needs arose in their particular monastery. As a result, each monastery evidently developed, in part, its own sign lexicon (Kendon, 1990).

For many of the manual signs created and used by monks, there was a clearly discernible tie between the sign and what it stood for (its referent). A sign for an object often visually resembled the object as a whole or a prominent feature of the object. Another frequent basis for a sign was the habitual action associated with the referent (Bruce, 2007). These discernible ties between the signs and their referents likely made the signs easier for the monks to learn and remember. Although the use of manual signs enabled the Benedictines, Cistercians, and other monastic groups to communicate extensively in silence, their sign systems should not be viewed as constituting distinct languages (Stokoe, 1978/1987). This is because the monks typically produced their sign utterances in the word order patterns of the spoken languages they knew, as their sign systems had no separate grammatical or syntactical structures of their own.

---

11   With the Second Vatican Council (founded 1962), however, this policy of silence and corresponding use of manual communication was largely set aside.

Monasteries, in addition to helping spread Christianity and serving as seats of learning, provided a safe place for medieval travelers to eat and to sleep. The monks' reliance on sign communication may also have helped many travelers overcome spoken language barriers (Ohler, 1986, Trans. C. Hillier, 1989). A traveler needed to know only a small number of the manual signs used by the monks to be able to communicate adequately with members of monastic orders located over a wide geographical area. This use of manual signs by European travelers, members of monastic orders, and performers in the Middle Ages may have helped inspire Europeans to use manual signs and gestures during their voyages to North America and in their encounters with Native Americans.

Concluding Remarks

Historical records have shown us that when people who did not speak the same language needed to communicate with each other, they often made use of gestures or manual signs. To facilitate communication in such settings, the meanings of many of the signs or gestures needed to be relatively transparent in order to be understood. In addition, because the signs used would not be the principal language of members of any party, the signs needed to be relatively easy to learn and to remember. This outcome provides a basis for believing that a sign-communication system such as the Simplified Sign System can be a successful alternative or supplement to spoken communication. This approach to overcoming spoken language barriers may also be an effective communication strategy for persons who are unable to speak because of cognitive, motor, or language impairments. Such persons include individuals with an intellectual disability, cerebral palsy, autism spectrum disorder, or aphasia (these groups are discussed in Chapters 4, 5, and 6). Before addressing these different populations, however, it is first important to understand the basic properties of the full and genuine sign languages used as the principal means of communication by persons who grow up Deaf. An analysis of the general characteristics of such sign languages will prove helpful in comprehending the choices we made when selecting or developing signs for the Simplified Sign System.

3. Deaf Persons
and Sign Languages

Before focusing more specifically on the Simplified Sign System that we have developed, it is important to first have a basic understanding of sign languages and the main group of persons who use them — Deaf people. To obtain this necessary background information, we strove to answer the following questions: what is the historical evidence for the use of sign languages among Deaf persons? How did educational programs for deaf students emerge, and what communication approaches did these programs use? How did sign languages gain linguistic recognition? How are individual signs and sign languages structured? How do deaf children typically acquire a sign language and does this acquisition process mirror or differ from hearing children's acquisition of a spoken language? We felt that without this background information, it would be difficult to understand how we selected, modified, and created signs for our system.

The goal of the Simplified Sign System is to provide signs that are easily learned, remembered, and formed by a wide range of individuals. Some of these individuals may have motor, memory, and/or cognitive disabilities that prevent them from effectively communicating through speech or a full and genuine sign language. Clues about which formational parameters of signs (their handshapes, locations, and movements)[1] are easier to form and to remember, as well as which types of signs typically are more readily recognized, come from a variety of studies of sign acquisition and learning in deaf and hearing children. These clues assisted us in developing signs for our system. Furthermore, the discussions in this chapter about the formational parameters of signs

---

1   See also the "Ease of Production or Formation" subsection in Chapter 1.

© Bonvillian, Kissane Lee, Dooley & Loncke, CC BY 4.0   https://doi.org/10.11647/OBP.0205.03

and the general characteristics of sign languages provide the foundation for understanding the Simplified Sign System.

Deaf Education and the Recognition of Sign Languages

Deaf persons have always been part of human society. Because they generally have used manual signs to communicate, their signed communication also has been present throughout human history. Although deaf persons were long known to interact through signs or gestures, very little was known about such signs until relatively recently as systematic investigations of sign languages were lacking. For many centuries, signs were perceived as mostly pantomimic, easily understood, and useful for communication at only a primitive level. An important reason behind this lack of understanding is that the large majority of deaf children are born to hearing parents (Mitchell & Karchmer, 2004). During the Middle Ages in Europe, families with a deaf member often would create signs or gestures to facilitate interaction with that individual. However, because there were no schools or institutions for deaf students during this period, the signs that had been created and learned at home were often lost at the time of that deaf person's death. As for the absence of schools for deaf students, persons born deaf historically were viewed as incapable of being educated by persons with European cultural backgrounds. This notion that deaf and mute persons were not capable of benefiting from formal instruction rested largely on the widely held belief that knowledge was acquired primarily through conventional language: spoken and written words (Knowlson, 1965).

The first systematic instruction of deaf students is credited to Pedro Ponce de León, who lived in sixteenth-century Spain. A Benedictine monk who spent most of his life at the Monastery of San Salvador de Oña (Abernathy, 1959; Chaves & Soler, 1974; Plann, 1997), Pedro Ponce de León would have learned to communicate in signs by using them in his monastic community.[2] Starting in the mid-1540s, the monastery's abbot entrusted a small number of deaf pupils, the children of Spanish noble families, to Ponce de León's care. He devoted himself to teaching these students to read, to write, and to speak. His pupils' accomplishments

---

2   See the "Use of Signs by Monastic Orders" subsection in Chapter 2 for more information on the centuries-long use of manual signs and gestures in monasteries.

in these domains were seen as remarkable; previously, deaf and mute youngsters had been viewed as not educable. Unfortunately, Ponce de León's manuscript account of his teaching methods is lost. Others' accounts indicate that he initially focused his instruction on teaching his students to write and that at least some of the children learned to form the letters of the alphabet on their hands (Chaves & Soler, 1974). There is, however, only "circumstantial evidence" (Stokoe, 1978/1987, p. 327) that Ponce de León relied on signs in his instruction.

Chaves and Soler saw the educational situation this way: "In the world of silence of the Benedictine monasteries the lack of speech of the deaf children was less noticeable. It is most likely that Fray Pedro Ponce made use of these [monastic] signs with the Velasco boys [Ponce de León's first deaf pupils]" (Chaves & Soler, 1974, p. 60). Ponce de León's students also likely brought with them the gestures or "home" signs they had used while growing up with mostly hearing relatives.[3] The children's homesigns and the monastery's manual signs may have been shared and together contributed to Ponce de León's educational efforts as well as the pupils' general communicative interactions.

Another early milestone in the education of deaf students occurred with the publication of the letters of the manual alphabet. Although Melchor de Yebra's depiction of the appropriate handshapes for each letter was, in the early 1590s, an important step, it was Juan Pablo Bonet's published version in 1620 that received most of the attention and was widely disseminated. Bonet's book resulted in the one-handed manual alphabet eventually spreading across continental Europe and to the Americas. This system enabled persons to spell words from a spoken (and written), alphabetical language on their hands (fingerspelling) by producing the individual letters of those words (Abernathy, 1959; Plann, 1997). Fingerspelling thus helped to tie the education of deaf students to the learning of words from the spoken and written languages of the larger hearing societies in which Deaf persons lived. Fingerspelling also

---

3   Homesigns, which typically are highly iconic, likely provided the roots for many of the signs that eventually became incorporated into conventional signed languages (Fusellier-Souza, 2006). Contemporary studies of deaf homesigners (see Goldin-Meadow, 2003; Goldin-Meadow et al., 1994) show that they use iconic gestures to communicate and that "gesture affords an easily accessible way to convey action, and suggests that our experimental paradigm is capturing an early stage of an important aspect of language creation" (Fay et al., 2014, p. 10).

enabled people to communicate manually about a person or topic for which no sign was yet available.

Up until the latter half of the eighteenth century, the education of deaf students was available only for the privileged few. This situation changed dramatically in 1760 when Abbé Charles-Michel de l'Épée founded the first school for the education of deaf students, irrespective of social condition, in Paris, France (Seigel, 1969). Abbé de l'Épée's educational approach relied heavily on manual signs, many of which were created and used by French Deaf persons. He also worked in association with his pupils to create signs for concepts that he felt were necessary for their education and development (Knowlson, 1965).

This school would subsequently greatly influence the education of deaf students worldwide, both through its training of teachers, and through the dissemination of signs from its sign language. One of the outstanding Deaf teachers at the school in Paris, Laurent Clerc, traveled to the United States with Thomas H. Gallaudet, an American who had come to Europe to learn about educational programs for deaf children. These two men were instrumental in establishing the first public school for deaf students in the U.S., now known as the American School for the Deaf, in 1817 (Lane, 1984).[4]

Clerc, during his many years of devoted teaching and program development at the American School for the Deaf, relied heavily on his knowledge of French signs. It is probably because of Clerc that many American Sign Language (ASL) signs are clearly related to corresponding signs in French Sign Language (LSF or Langue des Signes Française) and gestures from French culture (Shaw & Delaporte, 2010; Woodward, 1978). Some of the pupils who attended this school brought their own native sign-communication systems with them; signs from these systems were added to the emerging ASL lexicon. And, inasmuch as ASL is a living language, new sign vocabulary items were added (and continue to be added) as needs arose.

Although public education for deaf students in the U.S. and much of continental Europe initially embraced signing and fingerspelling as primary vehicles of instruction, this situation was not to last. Instead, various nineteenth-century educators argued that signing should be

---

4   The first institution for higher learning for deaf students in the world, Gallaudet University, is named in honor of Thomas H. Gallaudet.

prohibited in schools for deaf students and that all efforts should be placed on teaching the spoken language of the hearing society in which the deaf persons lived (Moores, 1996, 2010). This focus on oral-only education emerged as the dominant approach in deaf education in the latter half of the nineteenth century; it was to continue as the principal educational approach for nearly a century (Moores, 2010).

An important reason for the ascendancy of oral-only approaches in the nineteenth century was that many deaf students at that time had lost their hearing after making considerable progress learning to speak. These students' hearing loss was often the product of childhood diseases or accidents (Moores, 1996). Oral language educational programs often were successful in stimulating speech skills in these postlingually deafened and hard-of-hearing pupils.[5] In making their case, oral-only advocates also argued that signing was not a real language and that its use kept deaf people apart from the larger hearing society (Lang, 2003). However, as advances in medicine and sanitation were made in the twentieth century, the percentage of postlingually deafened pupils among the deaf student population steadily declined with each passing decade. By the latter half of the twentieth century, postlingually deafened students were a small minority. As the proportion of postlingually deaf pupils declined, an increasing proportion of congenitally or prelingually (children who become deaf before 18 months of age) deaf students filled their places. Moreover, it became evident to researchers that the sign-using deaf children of Deaf parents were clearly outperforming other groups of deaf students on a host of measures of academic achievement and social adjustment (Mindel & Vernon, 1971; Vernon & Koh, 1970, 1971). Additionally, a recent report showed that sign-using children of Deaf parents clearly outperformed non-sign-using deaf children of hearing parents in a study that examined intelligence test performance after both groups of children had received cochlear implants (to facilitate their hearing) relatively early in their childhood (Amraei, Amirsalari, & Ajalloueyan, 2017). In light of these changes in population characteristics and the findings of systematic research investigations, the case for prohibiting signing in educational programs for deaf students largely evaporated,

---

5   Postlingual deafness refers to hearing impairments that develop after the acquisition of speech and language, in contrast to prelingual deafness.

although the legacy of this oral-only approach may continue to impact deaf students in many ways.[6]

Even though the efforts of Abbé de l'Épée and others changed many persons' views about the educability of deaf students, the sign languages used by Deaf persons historically were not regarded as real or genuine languages. Instead, the signs from which these languages were composed often were characterized as consisting mostly of pantomimic gestures. Such gestures frequently were not deemed to be true symbols; spoken words, because they were seen as rarely resembling what they stood for, were considered true symbols. Sign languages also were viewed as having little evidence of grammatical structure. If some regularities in Deaf persons' sign production were discerned, they were interpreted as reflections of the grammars of the spoken languages of the larger hearing societies in which Deaf persons lived. These notions, that individual signs were disadvantaged compared with words because signs were not true symbols and that sign languages did not have their own grammatical systems, helped relegate sign languages to a level beneath that of spoken languages. For many language scholars, the study of sign languages was not seen as a topic worthy of linguistic analysis.

Although the view that sign languages were not real languages was quite long-standing, a dramatic change in perspective has occurred in the last several decades (Baker et al., 2016). Today, linguists accord full linguistic status to the sign languages used by Deaf persons. This recognition of sign languages as full and genuine languages resulted largely from the pioneering efforts of William C. Stokoe. Stokoe's investigations focused primarily on the structure of signs in American Sign Language (ASL), the principal language of members of the Deaf community in the U.S. Stokoe showed that signs in ASL had a distinct linguistic structure and that this formational structure was quite different from the structure of words in English and other spoken languages (Stokoe, 1960; Stokoe, Casterline, & Croneberg, 1965).

There is an important similarity, however, between how words in a spoken language and how signs in a signed language (such as ASL) can

---

6   *Deaf People Around the World: Educational and Social Perspectives* (Moores & Miller, 2009) provides accounts of the history of the education of deaf students, including changing perspectives on the use of sign languages, in thirty different countries.

be analyzed. Words in spoken languages are composed of phonemes, the smallest units of speech or sound that can signal a difference in meaning of an utterance (for example, the words *pat* and *hat* differ only in their initial sounds, or phonemes, but these differences signal two distinct meanings.) Although each individual word in a language has a definite meaning, the individual phonemes from which words are composed are essentially meaningless (the initial phonemes in the above example, /p/ and /h/, do not have meaning in and of themselves). The different spoken languages of the world vary greatly in their number of phonemes and the specific phonemes they employ. The words of English, for example, are composed from a collection of about forty-four different phonemes. This number, it turns out, is a little above the average for spoken languages. Stokoe applied the same approaches used for determining the phonological structure of spoken languages to determine the structure of ASL signs.

After systematically examining numerous ASL signs, Stokoe proposed that there were three formational aspects that differentiated any one ASL sign from another (Stokoe, 1960; Stokoe et al., 1965). These three aspects were the place or location where a sign was made, the shape or configuration of the hand(s) while making a sign, and the action or movement of the hand(s) in forming a sign. Although Stokoe identified these three aspects as a sign's tabula, designator, and signation, they are more commonly referred to as location, handshape, and movement.[7]

Stokoe's systematic analysis of ASL sign structure showed that each of the three formational parameters (or aspects) he had identified consisted of a limited set of elements. For ASL, he identified twelve different locations on or near the signer's body where signs were made, nineteen different handshapes used in forming signs, and twenty-four different types of sign movements. Altogether, according to Stokoe's model, there were fifty-five different formational parameters from which all the signs in ASL were composed. These fifty-five different formational elements (*cheremes* in Stokoe's terminology) functioned in a structural manner largely analogous to that of phonemes in spoken languages. In fact, many investigators use the term *sign phonemes* to designate these sublexical formational elements or cheremes. Although

---

7   In more recent years, the word *parameter* often has been used by sign language linguists in preference to Stokoe's term *aspect* (Valli, Lucas, & Mulrooney, 2005).

individual phonemes of spoken languages traditionally have been considered essentially meaningless, it should be noted that the same claim should not be made about individual sign phonemes, as where a sign is made, the handshape used, and the movement involved can be assigned meaning to a significant extent and can convey representational features in a way that vocal phonemes do not.

In the years since Stokoe proposed his model of sign structure, other parameters have been advanced to define signs more precisely (i.e., palm orientation[8] and non-manual or facial expression), but most researchers have continued to use the three parameters first described by Stokoe as the basic formational units of signs. Stokoe's approach of identifying the location, handshape, and movement parameters of ASL signs also has been used effectively to analyze the structure of signs from other sign languages. These investigations have shown that although there is substantial overlap in the sign phonemes used in many different sign languages, sign languages also differ in the particular handshapes, movements, and locations they employ. Stokoe's structural analytic approach also has been used to document the problems various individuals experience when they are learning how to form signs. Indeed, we used this same approach to sign structure during the development of signs for the Simplified Sign System (see Chapter 8) and in the descriptions of how these signs are formed (see Chapter 11, Volume 2).

---

8   A recent study (Koulidobrova, Luchkina, & Palmer, 2019) of deaf participants who were learning ASL as a second language and of non-signing hearing speakers of English involved a discrimination task between matched ASL sentence pairs that differed in only a single parameter (handshape, orientation, movement, or location). This study revealed that orientation and location were significant contrastive features for both groups, suggesting that orientation is a more important articulatory feature than previously suggested. Other researchers consider orientation to be a subordinate category of the handshape parameter (Sandler, 2012; Sandler & Lillo-Martin, 2006; van der Hulst, 1993; van der Kooij, 2002). It should be noted that in the written descriptions of each of the signs in the Simplified Sign System (see Chapter 11, Volume 2), we include both the orientation of the palm as well as the orientation of the fingers/knuckles of the hand(s). We found that providing this information helped to clearly specify the formation of each of our signs. In addition, this information sometimes disambiguates between related signs that have similar formations.

Sign Production

As a person starts forming a sign, there is essentially a simultaneous production of that sign's location, handshape, and movement phonemes. This simultaneity of production of sign phonemes differs somewhat from the sequential production of spoken language phonemes. That is, phonemes in spoken languages are uttered over time from the beginning of a word to its end. In signed languages (also known as visual-motor or visual-gestural languages), most of the information needed for a sign's recognition (its location, handshape, and movement) occurs at nearly the same time (Vermeerbergen, Leeson, & Crasborn, 2007).[9] Moreover, the information necessary for a viewer to recognize a sign typically becomes evident once the direction of the movement parameter is established at the beginning of the sign action (ten Holt et al., 2009).

Although Stokoe emphasized the simultaneous characteristics of ASL signs, he also described some of their sequential characteristics. In particular, he noted the sequential nature of the movement parameter. Movements include such actions as up-and-down movement of the hands and arms, nodding or bending of the wrists, and wiggling of the fingers. In the sign notational system developed by Stokoe, it is possible for a sign to have up to three movement phonemes. These sequential or consecutive movements may create a rhythm in a sign that is similar to syllables in spoken words. An outgrowth of this interest has been a series of explorations into the sequential segments and syllable-like structure in sign phonology (Coulter, 1990; Hildebrandt & Corina,

---

9   We should note that the location, handshape, and movement components of a sign's production correspond to some extent with the location, shape, and movement components of the speech apparatus (such as the tongue) during a word's production. However, most hearing people who use spoken languages do not typically concentrate on or even consciously perceive this oromotor information (an exception occurs for those hearing, hearing-impaired, or deaf persons who rely on speech-reading or lip-reading skills in certain situations). Perhaps it is the more clearly visible nature of signs that makes their various components or parameters appear more simultaneous than their less visible speech counterparts. After all, much of the speech apparatus is internal and concealed, whereas the sign apparatus (the hands, arms, face, head, and body) is external and easily seen. In the case of persons who are deaf and blind, this externally available information can still be perceived through laying their hands on top of the signer's hands. Signs can thus be distinguished through the sense of touch (Mesch, 2013). Some deaf and blind persons may also perceive speech through putting their hands on a speaker's mouth and jaw.

2002; Johnson & Liddell, 2010; Liddell & Johnson, 1989; Sandler & Lillo-Martin, 2006; Wilbur, 1993, 2011). This emphasis on the sequential nature of sign production suggests that there are additional important parallels between sign production and that of sequentially produced speech.[10]

In Stokoe's system of sign structure (1960; Stokoe et al., 1965), sign locations are designated primarily by the part of the body where the sign is made; for example, on the chin, chest, forehead, or arm. Not all signs, however, are made on or near a part of the signer's body. Some signs are made in the area directly in front of the signer; this area is known as the *neutral space* or *neutral place*. In addition, some signs are made on the signer's stationary hand, and some may require movement from one location to another (Battison, 1978).

Stokoe identified nineteen different handshapes from which ASL signs are composed. To designate these different handshapes, Stokoe used the letters from the manual alphabet and numbering system that most closely corresponded with the handshapes. For example, the C-hand, the 5-hand, and the L-hand are the terms he used to identify three different ASL handshapes. Many of the handshapes that are found in ASL may also be found in other sign languages; however, it is important to note that different sign languages make use of different handshapes and variations of those handshapes (Eccarius, 2008; Fischer & Gong, 2010, 2011; Sandler, 2012; Tang, 2007). Some signs require only a single handshape whereas others may involve a change in the handshape of one or both hands while making the sign (Battison, 1978; Sandler, 2012).

Some signs in the sign languages used by Deaf persons are made with a single hand, whereas other signs are made with both hands. In some two-handed signs, the handshape and movement parameters are identical, with one hand the mirror image of the other. These signs often are referred to as two-handed symmetrical signs. In other two-handed signs, the handshapes may differ or one hand may be primarily involved in the movement or action (the *active hand*) while the other hand serves mostly as a stationary base (the *stationary hand*) for the other hand's action. These signs often are referred to as two-handed asymmetrical

---

10 An important difference across language modalities is that most signs in a signed language are monosyllabic (Brentari, 1998), unlike words in spoken languages.

signs. Recent investigations have shown that, across a wide range of sign languages, two-handed signs often convey lexically plural concepts (Östling, Börstell, & Courtaux, 2018).

In forming one-handed signs or two-handed asymmetrical signs, a signer typically uses his or her dominant hand to perform the sign's movement. In most persons, this is the right hand. Sometimes, however, the right arm and hand may be temporarily occupied and not immediately available for signing. This may occur, for example, when a person is carrying a baby or a bag of groceries in his right arm. In such circumstances, a typically right-handed individual will likely switch and use his left hand to sign. There does not appear to be any appreciable loss in intelligibility caused by switching hands for native signers. An individual whose left hand is dominant typically will use his left hand as the active hand in one-handed signs and two-handed asymmetrical signs. Again, the use of the left hand does not appear to confuse the viewer.[11]

In some cases, serious bodily injury may result in the loss of use of a hand or arm that is relatively permanent. Such a serious injury may greatly limit the signer's ability to control her arm and hand movements. For one-handed signs, this limitation is not usually a problem: the signer simply uses the other hand and arm to produce the sign. For two-handed symmetrical signs (the handshapes, movements, and locations are mirror images of each other), the signer makes the sign with the available hand and the viewer imagines the other hand performing the same action with the same handshape in the mirror-image location. Two-handed asymmetrical signs, however, are more problematic. The signer uses her available hand to perform the critical action or movement parameter of the sign. In many instances, the injured or impaired hand and arm (or an available surface such as a counter, table, or desk) may be used as the stationary base for the sign's action. That is, the signer

---

11   The same, however, may not be true of naïve signers or persons unfamiliar with a sign language when trying to copy another person's signs. Meier (2019) reports that perceptual problems may come into play when a viewer is opposite a signer and must perform a spatial transformation in order to correctly copy a sign (as opposed to when he or she is standing or sitting to the side of a signer, where each person's body and hands are oriented in the same direction). Spatial transformations can be difficult for signing deaf children with autism spectrum disorder (Shield & Meier, 2012) and for adult learners of ASL (Chen Pichler & Koulidobrova, 2015; Rosen, 2004; Shield & Meier, 2018).

may make the sign directly on the injured limb (or available surface) and the viewer will need to imagine that the injured limb (or available surface) is in the correct location and has the correct handshape.

Sign Formation and Meaning

Contrary to popular impression, there is no universal sign language used by all Deaf persons. Rather, Deaf persons in most countries have their own distinct sign language, which has its own unique vocabulary and grammar.[12] In recent years, much has been learned from systematic studies of the world's different sign languages. These studies have shown that there are various general characteristics or tendencies present in the formational parameters of signs that are evident in many different sign languages from around the world. For example, the location of where a sign is made on or near the signer's body often is related to the meaning of the sign. Signs made on or near the forehead generally pertain to cognitive processes. Signs made near the heart often are connected to different emotions. Signs made near the abdomen or the body's midsection frequently have sexual or eliminative connotations.

In a relatively recent study, Cates et al. (2013) systematically probed the relationship between the location where a sign in ASL was formed and the meaning of the sign. Examination of hundreds of ASL signs showed that the location parameter of signs often was critical in conveying information about the signs' meaning. As examples, ASL signs made on or near the eyes typically encoded information related to vision (e.g., EYEGLASSES), signs made near the ear often were related to hearing (e.g., HEARING AID), and those signs made on the legs frequently were used for items of clothing for the lower body (e.g., SKIRT).[13] Although the location parameter alone would not be sufficient

---

12 Some examples of the various sign languages of the world include Kenyan Sign Language (KSL), Warlpiri Sign Language, Japanese Sign Language (JSL), Taiwanese Sign Language (TSS), Persian Sign Language (PSC), Czech Sign Language (CSE), Portuguese Sign Language (LGP or Língua Gestual Portuguesa), Quebec Sign Language (LSQ or Langue des Signes Québécoise), Argentine Sign Language (LSA or Lengua de Señas Argentina), Mexican Sign Language (LSM or Lenguaje de Señas Mexicanas), and Australian Sign Language (AUSLAN). A number of countries have now recognized their national sign language(s) through legislative action (De Meulder, 2015).

13 As noted in the Introduction, sign glosses, or their closest translations, are denoted in upper case throughout this volume.

for someone to guess the precise meaning of a particular sign, the location of where a sign was made evidently often provided important information about the meaning of a sign. These observations about the iconicity of the location parameter of manual signs hold for a variety of sign languages (Östling et al., 2018).

The handshape used in the formation of a particular sign is often related to the meaning of that sign (Pietrandrea, 2002). Signs made with a flat handshape (the hand is flat with the fingers together and extended) frequently refer to objects that have a flat surface. A fist handshape (the hand is clenched to form a fist) might be used in signs to convey roundness or a grasping action. From these instances and many others, it becomes clear that in sign languages there is often an association between the form of a handshape used in a particular sign and the meaning the sign conveys.

Various characteristics of the movement parameter of signs also are related to the meanings of signs in signed languages. In signs used to convey bigness, the distance between the signer's hands typically is quite large. In contrast, the hands are much closer together in signs used to convey smallness. Whether a sign is repeated or not may be important; repetition may indicate plurality. In ASL, the sign CHILD becomes CHILDREN if it is repeated. Repetition of a sign for an action may indicate the continuation of that action over an extended period of time rather than a single instance of the action. In ASL, if one repeats the movement in the sign TEACH, then the notion conveyed is TEACHING. Another characteristic tied to the movement parameter of a sign is the force or energy with which a sign is made. A sign that is made slowly might connote weariness, leisureliness, or boredom. A sign that is made forcefully commands the viewer's attention and underscores its importance. To a considerable extent, the speed and energy with which signs are produced correspond with the use of vocal inflections in spoken languages (Schein & Stewart, 1995). Signers, by making these variations in sign size, repetition, force, and speed, may noticeably expand the range of meanings that they are able to convey. This increased richness in meaning, however, also entails some additional complexity in sign formation.

Another characteristic of all or nearly all signed languages is their use of classifier constructions (Emmorey, 2003a; Engberg-Pedersen,

1993; Glück & Pfau, 1999; Marshall et al., 2015; Schembri, Jones, & Burnham, 2005; Sutton-Spence & Woll, 1999). A classifier construction is a sign that often is used in place of a noun or pronoun that has already been mentioned in a sign sentence or conversation. Classifiers typically consist of particular handshapes that symbolically represent classes of objects, such as vehicles or animals (or people), and convey the location and movement of these objects (or people) in space. For example, if a signer wanted to convey to another person that the route he took that day in his automobile was a very winding or meandering one, he might first establish that he had gone for a drive in his car and then subsequently use his classifier sign for vehicle to demonstrate his meandering route. It would probably be formationally easier for the signer (and more understandable for the viewer) if he moved his classifier handshape for vehicle in the desired motion than if he repeatedly made his sign for car along his path of movement. In many instances, classifier constructions are employed by signers when they wish to convey motion events or spatial relationships among objects (or people). In addition to the type of classifier that refers to objects or people (as described above), other types of classifiers exist that specify size, shape, handling, and other important characteristics of a referent.

In light of these observations, it appears that there are many underlying similarities across signed languages in how signs are formed and used that are related to the meanings of those signs. Furthermore, it is possible that these similarities may make communication in signs among signers from different nations more readily accomplished than is usually the case for people who communicate in different spoken languages.

Different Sign Languages and Obstacles to Sign Communication Worldwide

Over the last few decades, various sign languages used by Deaf peoples throughout the world have been at least minimally studied and documented. There is not, however, a fully comprehensive inventory of all the different sign languages in the world. One effort (Harrington, 2006; Harrington & Hamrick, 2010) at compiling a list of all known sign languages has resulted in the identification of 271 sign languages, sign dialects, and sign systems in the world.[14] Whether a particular sign system is a full and genuine sign language, a dialect of a sign language, or a signed version of the spoken language of the larger hearing society may still be a source of contention in some instances. Information on lesser-known sign languages is often scarce and difficult to find.

Despite a continuing need for research into the sign languages of the world, it is already apparent that there is great variety within the realm of sign languages worldwide. Likewise, a particular sign language may display additional complexity through regional variations that are akin to dialects in spoken languages. Deaf people may also adjust their sign vocabulary and register (i.e., level of sign formality) depending on the communicative setting, their communication partners, or other sociocultural factors such as age, gender, or race. Finally, sign languages, much like spoken languages, can be influenced by contact with other languages. In fact, sign languages can be affected by spoken languages. Some signs may have been created to represent concepts or specific words found in the hearing society's spoken language. Deaf people also create signs as new technologies and cultural expressions arise. Lastly, sign languages can be influenced not only by a related sign language (such as ASL was influenced by French Sign Language), but also by unrelated sign languages.

Throughout history, Deaf people of various countries have interacted; this exposure has offered Deaf people multiple opportunities to borrow or adopt signs from "foreign" sign languages. The expansion of technology (starting with video, then the internet, computer software applications, and now extending to smart phone apps) has also given Deaf people the opportunity to learn sign languages or communicate with Deaf people from other countries without actually physically traveling to those countries. This does not mean, however, that there is not a need for a sign language or a sign-communication system that transcends national boundaries. In the past, Deaf people have devoted a substantial amount of time to creating such a system. Deaf persons frequently meet in international settings; providing interpreters for

---

14 The *Gallaudet Encyclopedia of Deaf People and Deafness* (Van Cleve, 1987) also provides basic information on a number of sign languages. For videos of how specific concepts are signed in over two dozen sign languages from around the world, visit the *Spread the Sign* website (European Sign Language Centre, 2018) and/or download the *Spread Signs* app (available for iPhone/iPad and Android).

each country's participants at these events often is both costly and time-consuming. Deaf persons also travel as tourists to other countries where they may encounter Deaf persons whose sign languages are quite different from their own and which they do not understand.[15]

International Sign

Deaf people long ago recognized that the presence of many distinct national sign languages could prove an obstacle to effective communication in international settings (Moody, 2002). After years of committee work trying to resolve this problem, the efforts of a commission, whose members were British, Danish, Russian, American, and Italian, culminated in the publication in 1975 of *Gestuno: International Sign Language of the Deaf* (World Federation of the Deaf, Unification of Signs Commission, 1975). The reactions of many Deaf persons to Gestuno, however, were not positive. According to Moody (2002, p. 16), "Deaf people soon began complaining that the signs in the Gestuno lexicon were not iconic enough to be readily understood." Another concern was that the signs in Gestuno were predominantly from a small number of European sign languages and American Sign Language and relatively few were from African and Asian sign languages. Thus, the signs in the lexicon did not represent the diversity of the world's sign languages nor the diverse interests and perspectives of the Deaf persons who used them.

In the years that followed Gestuno's unpromising debut, various individuals have continued to work on codifying a limited number of signs for Deaf persons' use worldwide. This effort has resulted in a system known as International Sign (Rosenstock & Napier, 2016). Rather than having a committee or commission decide somewhat arbitrarily which signs to include in the system, the inclusion of a particular sign has been allowed to occur naturally. If a sign is useful, easily learned, and easily formed, then it is likely to be included in the system. This approach of waiting until there is consensus about the inclusion of a particular sign

---

15 Typically, Deaf persons are quite adept at negotiating understanding in these situations. However, using a lexicon of signs that are iconic and more easily understood than most of the signs from full and genuine sign languages may present another option for Deaf travelers when interacting with Deaf (and hearing people) from another country.

in International Sign has meant that the size of the lexicon of agreed upon signs has grown rather slowly over the years. The relatively small vocabulary size and lack of familiarity with the system may contribute to the noticeably longer time that it takes signers to convey information in International Sign than it does in their native sign languages (Allsop, Woll, & Brauti, 1995).

In recent years, investigators have conducted examinations of how International Sign is interpreted and have compared its linguistic content and structure with that of various natural sign languages also being interpreted. One major difference was that International Sign interpreters made much more frequent use of pointing signs in comparison with the natural sign language interpreters (Whynot, 2016). International Sign interpreters also made abundant use of depicting signs (illustrating the event or object encoded), indicating verbs (showing who was doing what to whom), and gestures in general (Stone & Russell, 2016; Whynot, 2016). In the future, more systematic comparisons between International Sign and other natural sign language interpreting will need to be conducted to help determine how best to achieve interpreter quality and audience comprehension.

Although International Sign remains a "work in progress," various concerns have been expressed about this emerging system (Rosenstock, 2004). One concern is the aforementioned problem that the lexicon of International Sign is rather limited in size. A second concern is that, like Gestuno before it, a substantial majority of the signs come from ASL and European sign languages. Also, although some signed languages may have arisen from the interactions of deaf persons in Indigenous communities around the world, in a number of instances western missionaries and educators may have exported their national sign languages to different countries (Green, 2014). This latter occurrence has meant that some sign languages from different parts of the world are closely related even though their spoken languages are not.

A third concern is that there is not clear agreement as to the grammatical and syntactic structure of International Sign. In fact, efforts at standardizing International Sign have focused almost entirely on its lexicon and not on its grammatical structure (Hiddinga & Crasborn, 2011). Moreover, it will probably be important to make extensive use of iconicity or iconic aspects in grammatical and syntactic components as well (Rosenstock, 2008). Although reliance on ASL and European signs and sign structures may not have been an especially large communication obstacle for many participants at international meetings in past decades, the communication hurdles may increase in magnitude in the future. In recent years, there has been increasing participation by representatives from Asian and African countries at international conferences and sporting events. The concern is that sign communication that is viewed as transparent in meaning to signers from many western countries may not be readily understood by signers from quite different cultural backgrounds. However, it is important to note that this is also true in the other direction — signs grounded in various Asian and African cultures may not be readily understood by persons from western countries. These observations reflect a general acknowledgement that some amount of exposure to a culture may be necessary in order to understand the significance of signs (or gestures) originating from that culture (see Ortega, 2017).

Unique Aspects of Sign Languages

The sign languages used by Deaf persons, despite many functional similarities with spoken languages, often convey information in quite different ways. For example, the visual-gestural modality of signed communication enables individuals simply to point to the referents that they are discussing rather than explicitly naming them (Meier, 2002). Another characteristic of sign languages that has no parallel in spoken languages is that certain signs may be produced simultaneously. For example, a signer might shake her head to indicate NO (or negation) while simultaneously making another sign with her hands. In contrast, words in spoken languages are produced sequentially. There is also a nonmanual component to signing that usually occurs simultaneously with the production of the manual component (Herrmann & Steinbach, 2013). Facial expression, together with head, eye, mouth, and upper body movements, combine with the manual component to constitute a multi-channel system. For sign language users, these different nonmanual components contribute at all levels of grammar and meaning (Dachkovsky & Sandler, 2009; Nespor & Sandler, 1999; Reilly, McIntire, & Bellugi, 1990; Sandler, 2012; Sandler & Lillo-Martin, 2006). In spoken languages, facial expression and body movements play important roles in conveying how an utterance should be interpreted, but do not appear to play a syntactic or grammatical role.[16]

Many of the differences between signed and spoken languages appear attributable to their different modes of production and reception (the language modality). Sign languages rely on the visual and manual (or gestural) modes to convey meaning effectively. Changes in speed, direction, location in space, and size of the signs produce variations in meaning (Fischer, 1973; Fischer & Gough, 1978; Liddell, 2003; Valli et al., 2005). Some signs (e.g., verbs like HIT, GIVE, and SHOW) vary their direction of movement to indicate who is performing the action, who is the recipient of the action, and where the action takes place (Hou & Meier, 2018; Lillo-Martin & Meier, 2011; Schembri, Cormier, & Fenlon, 2018; Schembri et al., 2005). In spoken languages, such information might be conveyed by word order or vocal inflections, but not by changing the direction of one's voice!

Signed languages take advantage of space and spatial relations to convey meanings (Campbell & Woll, 2003; Poizner, Klima, & Bellugi, 1987) in a way not possible with spoken languages. To do this, signers utilize the physical space in front of them (their signing spaces) to facilitate their communication. One way this might be done would be for a signer to develop a sort of topographic map in his signing space of the information that he wished to transmit. For example, if the signer wished to depict a particular farming scene to another person, the signer might establish where key items or elements in the scene were located. That is, a silo might be located near the barn, a tractor next to the barn, and so on, with the signer allocating each item a position in his signing space according to its location in the actual scene. A likely outcome of this effort would be that the viewer would obtain an accurate mental picture of the key elements of the scene that the signer was trying to convey. Another way that space might be effectively used would be for signers to locate agents and referents in their signing space without specifically tying them to their real-world locations. In this approach, a signer might

---

16 Visual short-term memory limitations appear to constrain the number of simultaneously articulated sign and non-manual components to a maximum of four independent propositions (Napoli & Sutton-Spence, 2010). Spoken languages, of course, can increase the number of simultaneous propositions they convey by accompanying their words with gestures.

establish the location of an agent and a recipient in his signing space and then denote the relationship between the two by directing the action from the agent to the recipient of the action on this imaginary stage. Or a signer might place absent objects in different locations in his signing space and, during a conversation, refer to those objects by pointing to their recently established locations in his signing space.

Many sign languages also use space to convey temporal relations. Often, an imaginary time line runs forward from the signer's cheek to indicate events in the future and behind the signer to indicate events in the past. As examples, the ASL sign WEEK arcs forward to indicate NEXT WEEK or a week from now and arcs backward toward the shoulder to indicate LAST WEEK or a week ago. In British Sign Language (BSL), the sign for TOMORROW moves forward whereas the sign for YESTERDAY moves backward (Marshall, Denmark, & Morgan, 2006). Events that are in the present or are just occurring are made relatively close to the signer's body. Furthermore, ASL verbs that refer to actions in the future tend to have forward movement whereas verbs with references to the past tend to have backward movement (Fischer & Gough, 1978).

These modality differences in how information is effectively transmitted probably resulted in the emergence of quite different grammatical systems for spoken and signed languages. By their very nature, spoken languages are linear in the sense that words are produced sequentially. Signed languages differ in that certain signs may be produced simultaneously and that signed languages make extensive use of space to convey grammatical relations. Also, signers often first establish the topic of their utterances and then comment on or elaborate on this topic (Holcomb, 2013). This phenomenon of first establishing the topic of a conversation at the beginning of a signed sentence is known as topicalization.[17] Even when the general word and sign order are similar, as in English and ASL (i.e., subject-verb-object), there are important differences in how syntactic relations are indicated. Slobin (2008) pointed out that whereas in English the pronouns convey who is the subject or object, this information is instead indicated by the verb in ASL. Furthermore, while word order is recognized as critical for the

---

17 It should be noted that English does have some flexibility and variation in word order that allows writers and speakers to make use of topicalization as well, particularly with regard to poetic forms and interrogatives. However, such constructions tend to be more prevalent in archaic texts than in daily modern usage (Wikipedia, 2020).

accurate transmission of meaning in English and is relatively fixed, there is considerable debate about the relative importance of sign order in signed languages. Another difference is that signed languages do not make use of the verbal form known as the copula *be* in English (Pfau & Bos, 2016).[18] This difference is hardly unique to signed languages, however, as various spoken languages (e.g., Mandarin Chinese) also do not have such a copula verb form.

The observations of our acquaintances who are fluent in both speech and a signed language suggest that it is either extremely difficult or impossible to simultaneously use the grammar of a spoken language and that of a signed language used by Deaf persons. For example, the two modalities of speech and sign enable one to produce a word and a sign essentially simultaneously. However, because the grammars of spoken and signed languages are quite different, it does not appear possible to simultaneously generate sentences in both. Rather, what often happens when one needs to communicate simultaneously in speech and sign, as when addressing an audience composed of both deaf and hearing individuals, is that one takes the signs from the particular sign language used by the Deaf persons and puts them in the word order of the spoken language as one speaks.

It should be noted that there have also been a number of special sign-communication systems designed to reflect the grammatical structure of a society's spoken language. These sign systems often were developed with the goal of teaching the spoken language's grammar to deaf students. Signed English, for example, puts ASL signs in English word order. In Signed English, the handshape parameter of the ASL signs is often modified to denote specific English words; in these cases, the handshapes frequently reflect the beginning letters of the English words. The signs may also be further modified to denote plurality or verb tense (e.g., -s, -ed, -ing) (Bornstein, 1974; Bornstein, Saulnier, & Miller, 1984). Signed English, although it borrows signs from ASL, should be considered a visual or manually coded form of English, rather than a natural sign language used by Deaf persons, because it reflects English grammatical structure.

---

18 A copular verb expresses either that the subject and its complement denote the same thing, or that the subject has the property denoted by its complement (e.g., "the grass is green").

Iconic Signs

Another important difference between signs and words is that a number of signs resemble the concepts they denote, whereas the relationship between spoken words or sounds and their meanings is often less apparent. That is, quite a few signs are at least somewhat visually iconic in nature, while relatively few words clearly resemble their underlying concepts from an aural perspective as in onomatopoeia (see Dingemanse, 2012 for a more expansive view of onomatopoeic words and ideophones in diverse spoken languages). A sign is considered iconic if it bears a close resemblance to the action, object, or characteristic it represents (Armstrong, 1983; Klima & Bellugi, 1979). Some iconic signs consist of actions that represent themselves; these signs are considered highly iconic and are often labeled *pantomimic* signs. For example, the ASL sign for KNOCK is made by producing the action involved when knocking on a door (Stokoe et al., 1965). Other highly iconic signs may emphasize certain salient features of objects or actions and use these specific features to represent the whole. For example, the ASL signs for CAR and DRIVE are made by having the signer's hands grip and move an imaginary steering wheel (the movements of the two signs are related, but different). Although only one prominent feature of a car or of the action of driving is used — gripping an imaginary steering wheel — this feature represents the entire car or the action of driving (Stokoe et al., 1965). Most individuals would probably easily tie the mimetic action of gripping and turning a steering wheel with the concept of driving a vehicle.[19]

While the resemblance of a sign to its referent is evident in many signs, it should be noted that highly iconic or pantomimic signs constitute only a small proportion of signs in sign languages. In the case of ASL, 10–15% of signs were rated as highly iconic (Lloyd, Loeding, & Doherty, 1985), with most signs viewed as having low iconicity values (Caselli et al., 2017). This low level of iconicity may not, however, have always been the case. A study of historical changes in ASL signs has shown that when

---

19 Because highly iconic signs typically are more easily recognized, learned, and remembered by hearing persons than less iconic signs, we have tried to make many of the signs in our Simplified Sign System highly iconic. This should benefit a wide range of sign-learning individuals, including persons with ASD, an intellectual disability, cerebral palsy, or aphasia, not to mention the teachers and caregivers who interact with them.

signs change over time, they typically move away from their imitative or pantomimic origins to more arbitrary or less transparent relationships with their referents (Frishberg, 1975). This change in a sign from iconic to arbitrary may be driven by such factors as ease of sign formation and a tendency by experienced signers to concentrate sign lexical information on the hands and away from the face and body.

Although only a minority of signs in Deaf sign languages are highly iconic in the sense that they closely resemble their referents and their meanings are readily apparent to the untrained observer, this does not mean that there is not an iconic component or base in many of the remaining signs. We have seen previously that where a sign is made, the handshape used, and the movements involved often are related to some extent to the meaning that a particular sign conveys (Cates et al., 2013; Östling et al., 2018; Pietrandrea, 2002; Schein & Stewart, 1995). Also, some signs may be based on relatively minor features or unexpected characteristics of their referents; Stokoe et al. (1965) categorized these signs as *metonymic*. Although the meanings of these signs may not be immediately apparent to most people, it cannot be said that these signs are not iconic to some degree. Indeed, those signs with no discernible ties whatsoever between the signs and their referents (*arbitrary signs*) probably constitute only a minority of the signs in the sign languages used by Deaf persons. In light of these observations, sign iconicity probably should be seen as extending across a wide range of form to meaning relationships, with "various types and degrees of iconicity" (Deuchar, 1990, p. 175). Other researchers have supported the theory that there is a continuum of iconicity in which some signs are more clearly iconic than others and that the forms and types of iconicity may vary based on the language involved (Emmorey, 2014; Klima & Bellugi, 1979; Meir et al., 2013; Ortega, 2017; Padden et al., 2013, 2015; Perlman et al., 2018).

Even those signs that are considered clearly iconic in sign languages often involve a degree of cognitive processing by the observer for the signs to be understood. In many semantic categories (e.g., trees, houses), the individual members of a category do not look alike — they vary substantially in appearance. For example, although pine trees and oak trees have certain features in common, they differ noticeably in their sizes and shapes. For such semantic categories, a useful iconic sign would need to depict the shape or structure of an especially good instance or exemplar of that category (Taub, 2001). In ASL, the sign HOUSE is made by having the signer's hands first touch at the imagined peak of a roof, then separate and move diagonally down to convey the slope of the roof, and finally move straight down to portray the sides or walls of the house.[20] The observer needs both to perceive the sign that has been produced as resembling the form of a particular instance or exemplar of a semantic category and to understand that the particular exemplar stands for the semantic category as a whole. Furthermore, the signer and the observer need to understand the correspondences between the sign they are producing or viewing and what it represents in the real world, a task involving conceptual integration skills (Napoli & Sutton-Spence, 2011). It should be noted that some very young or non-speaking sign learners may not have attained the level of cognitive functioning necessary to consciously understand these relationships (Griffith, Robinson, & Panagos, 1981; Ortega, 2017).

Although scholars often have used the term *pantomimic signs* to refer to signs that clearly resemble their referents, it would be incorrect to convey the impression that the performance of pantomime and the production of pantomimic signs are the same thing. Highly iconic or pantomimic signs differ from pantomime or mime in at least two important ways. One readily observable difference is that the mime artist may employ his whole body in imparting information through a series of image-evoking movements or actions. In reality, this means that the mime artist is free to move about a stage and often produces motor actions that involve the entire body in generating realistic movements. In contrast, a signer typically is much more stationary, usually sitting or standing upright. A less observable difference is that highly iconic or pantomimic signs in a particular sign language are composed from the same limited collection of sign phonemes (locations, handshapes, and movements) from which all other signs in that sign language are composed. That is, highly iconic signs in a particular sign language must be composed of phonetically acceptable forms from that sign language (Taub, 2001). In contrast, in pantomime, the artist is free to use any conceivable gesture or movement to transmit the desired image.

---

20   Many ASL users will form this sign without including the downward movement for the walls of the house.

When one looks at highly iconic or pantomimic signs from a sign language with which one is not familiar, one may be able to accurately guess some of their meanings. Such signs are considered to have transparent meanings (Hoemann, 1975), and the degree to which their meanings can be discerned is known as their *transparency*. It should be noted, though, that perception of sign transparency may vary depending upon one's particular background. The transparency of some signs seems to be essentially universal, with virtually everyone correctly discerning their meanings; however, some experience in a particular culture may be necessary to correctly guess the meanings of other signs (Grosso, 1993; Ortega, 2017; Pizzuto & Volterra, 2000).

Most hearing people with little or no formal sign language training find it difficult to accurately guess the meanings of many signs used in the sign languages of Deaf persons. When one has learned the meaning of a particular sign, though, it is often possible to discern how the sign and its meaning are related. The extent to which the relationship between a sign and its meaning can be discerned "after the fact" is called the sign's *translucency*. Many more people report that they can perceive the relationship between a sign and what it stands for after the sign's meaning has been explained to them (its *translucency*) than can accurately guess the meaning of an unfamiliar sign (its *transparency*) (Bellugi & Klima, 1976; Emmorey & Sevcikova Sehyr, 2018). Having the tie between a sign and its referent explained also can help many individuals in their initial learning and longer-term retention of signs (see "Step Six: Memory Aids" in Chapter 8). Although the transparency and translucency of some signs may make them easier to learn and remember, it is important to note that such an iconic aspect is not readily evident in a number of signs, especially those used to refer to abstract concepts (Meier, Cormier, & Quinto-Pozos, 2002).

Although it might be easier for signers in different sign languages to generate iconic signs for many objects or observable actions, this does not mean that iconic signs are restricted solely to the domains of concrete objects and observable actions. Rather, sign languages are capable of incorporating iconic signs for a number of more abstract concepts, including emotions and ideas. The key component present in iconic signs for abstract concepts is the tying of an abstract notion to a concrete representation or form (Taub, 2001). For example, a sign for the concept of being angry might involve the forceful shaking of one's fist or depicting fire or flames in one's belly. By using such an approach of tying abstract concepts to concrete forms, sign languages are able to express some abstract notions both iconically and effectively.

Because certain concepts (e.g., *house, throw*) are easier for people to depict iconically than others (e.g., *honor, imagine*), there may be highly iconic signs for many of the same concepts across a number of different sign languages. Even when the signs for a particular concept are clearly iconic in several different sign languages, however, this does not mean that the signs in each language will closely resemble each other. The reason for this is that different characteristics or features of the concept may be emphasized in different languages. As an example, let us take various signs for the concept *tree* (Klima & Bellugi, 1979). Signers in China curve their index fingers and thumbs into arcs to indicate the roundness of a tree's trunk and then move their hands up to show the tree's height. Signers in Italy, Argentina, India, and Japan use a similar formation according to videos on the *Spread the Sign* website (European Sign Language Centre, 2018). Signers in the U.S., Mexico, Spain, and Greece use their upright forearm to indicate the tree's trunk and their spread fingers to convey the notion of branches and/or leaves. Signers in other countries may vary this formation by curving their fingers to represent the top of the tree or by adding a chopping motion with a flat-hand to mimic cutting down a tree. The point of this example is to underscore that even when signs from different sign languages are iconic or physically resemble what they represent, these signs may still vary substantially in how they are formed from one sign language to the next.

Various contemporary investigators have examined more closely the different types of iconicity present in manual signs (Emmorey, 2014; Padden, Hwang, Lepic, & Seegers, 2015). Among the different strategies that signers have been found to exploit when producing an iconic sign for an object have been: performing the action associated with the object, tracing the outline of the object's shape, touching the location where the object often is found, and representing or depicting a perceptual feature of the object. These different types or forms of iconicity, moreover, may make the learning of iconic signs more readily accomplished by tying the signs' formations with the learners' past sensory-motor experiences and with the learners' mental representations of the signs' referents.

If the sign languages used by Deaf persons were comprised mostly of highly iconic or pantomimic signs, as many surmised before Stokoe's analysis of ASL, then one would expect that the sign languages used by Deaf people in different countries would be mutually intelligible; however, they are not. Rather, most signs, like words in spoken languages, have a particular meaning because users of the language employ them in a certain way. Or stated another way, signs and words have particular meanings by convention, or tacit agreement, among the users of a language. In fact, in some instances, formationally identical signs have quite different meanings in different sign languages.

In spoken languages, a phenomenon similar to that of iconic signs is evident in a small number of words: onomatopoeia. Onomatopoeic words are words made by imitating the sound associated with the thing designated (e.g., quack, cuckoo). The manual and visual nature of sign languages, however, appears to allow for a higher incidence of sign and concept resemblance than occurs for the majority of spoken words and their underlying concepts (see Fay et al., 2014; Fusellier-Souza, 2006). Thus, although only a minority of signs in a particular sign language are highly iconic or pantomimic, the proportion of such signs appears to be considerably greater than the incidence of onomatopoeic words in spoken languages.

Although this higher incidence of iconic signs in signed languages than of onomatopoeic words in spoken languages was once viewed as a limiting factor of signed languages (because iconic signs were not seen as true symbols), this view has been re-examined and contested in recent years (e.g., Meir, 2010). Rather than a limitation, the perceived resemblance between a manual sign and its referent might instead be viewed as a positive aspect, helping many hearing people learning to sign as a second language more easily learn and remember such signs (Baus, Carreiras, & Emmorey, 2013; Lieberth & Gamble, 1991). The relative absence of resemblance between spoken words and their referents might then be viewed as an impoverishing characteristic of spoken languages (Armstrong, 1983, 1988; Hockett, 1978). It also should be noted that the view that the relationship between a spoken word and its referent is in nearly all instances an arbitrary one has changed; there is growing recognition that the particular sounds from which words are composed often are related at least somewhat to the words' meanings (Taub, 2001; Ortega, 2017; Perlman et al., 2018; Perniss & Vigliocco, 2014). This view that the sounds of words often give clues to these words' meanings is known as sound symbolism. Spoken language researchers consider verbal iconicity or sound symbolism to exist on a continuum across many different linguistic forms in many different languages of the world (Akita, 2009, 2013; Assaneo, Nichols, & Trevisan, 2011; Dingemanse, 2012; Dingemanse et al., 2015; Perniss, Thompson, & Vigliocco, 2010), much like the views of sign language researchers on visual iconicity. Children, moreover, typically become more sensitive to sound symbolism with increasing age, and this ability may facilitate their learning of word-referent mappings (Tzeng, Nygaard, & Namy, 2017). Various scholars also have advanced the view that iconicity plays an important role in grammatical and syntactical forms in spoken languages as well (Haiman, 1980, 1985).

Finally, users of all natural languages appear to make abundant use of manual gestures to help them convey meanings effectively (Goldin-Meadow & Brentari, 2017; Kendon, 2014; McNeill, 1992; McNeill & Duncan, 2005); many of these accompanying manual gestures are iconic or pantomimic. The extensive use of gestures together with speech in most persons' utterances has led some scholars to view language as a multimodal communication system (Kendon, 2011, 2014; Vigliocco, Perniss, & Vinson, 2014). Whereas spoken language users often rely on producing image-evoking iconic gestures to help them convey the meaning of their utterances (McNeill, 1992), signed languages incorporate gestures (Goldin-Meadow & Brentari, 2017) and real-world visual and spatial information into signed utterances (Brennan, 2005). This incorporation of visual and spatial aspects of the world in signed utterances makes many such signed utterances relatively iconic or representative. Thus, an iconic or pantomimic component appears to be present to some extent across a wide range of human communication regardless of whether the principal language modality is speech or sign.

Sign Language Acquisition

How are sign languages learned? Throughout recorded history, Deaf persons have learned and used sign languages to communicate (Schein & Stewart, 1995). For most persons who are either born deaf or who lose their hearing in childhood, sign languages constitute their principal means of communication. These individuals often embrace signing and are responsible for the transmission of sign languages from one generation to the next. When Deaf parents have children, these children (whether they are deaf or hearing) typically learn to sign from their parents. These signing parents model the language to their children and engage them in developmentally appropriate conversation. For these children and their Deaf parents, the transmission of a sign language to the next generation is very similar to what occurs when hearing children learn a spoken language from their parents.

When investigators examined how Deaf mothers interacted with their infants, investigators found that the mothers made a number of modifications in their signing in comparison with how they signed to other Deaf adults or older children (Pizer, Meier, & Shaw Points, 2011; Spencer & Harris, 2006). The mothers typically would produce their infant-directed signs more slowly, make them larger, and locate them so that their infants could easily see them (Holzrichter & Meier, 2000). The mothers' infant-directed sign utterances also tended to be relatively short, often only several signs in length. Overall, the Deaf mothers' sign input to their infants appeared to be designed to promote the young children's understanding and to facilitate their language development (Masataka, 2000).

For deaf children as a whole, this pattern of parental transmission of sign language to the next generation has been the exception rather than the rule. This has been the case because the large majority — over 90% — of deaf children are born to hearing parents (Lu, Jones, & Morgan, 2016; Meadow, 1980; Meadow-Orlans, 1990; Schein & Delk, 1974). Indeed, one investigation put the percentage of deaf children born to one or two deaf parents at less than 5%, although it should be acknowledged that precise percentages are difficult to obtain (Mitchell & Karchmer, 2004). Historically, hearing parents often were advised to make every effort to develop their children's speech skills and to refrain from signing with their children. The reasoning behind this advice to not use signs when interacting with their deaf children was that many professionals believed that sign input would adversely affect the children's spoken language development. There was not, however, good evidence to support this recommendation. To the contrary, there is substantial evidence that early sign input, when used in a program that also includes speech input, does not negatively influence deaf children's oral-language development (Notoya, Suzuki, & Furukawa, 1994; Spencer & Tomblin, 2006). Moreover, there is some evidence that programs that use both manual and oral communication from early in development actually facilitate deaf children's acquisition of spoken language skills (Schlesinger & Meadow, 1972; Yoshinaga-Itano, 2006).

Most hearing parents of deaf children have been unfamiliar with manual sign communication until after their children's deafness was identified (Lu et al., 2016; Marschark, Lang, & Albertini, 2002; Schick, 2003). Not surprisingly, then, the ages at which deaf children of hearing parents have been introduced to sign communication have varied widely across families (Mason et al., 2010; Marshall et al., 2015; Morgan, Herman, & Woll, 2007).[21] In some instances, hearing parents have made an effort to acquire signing skills and begin signing with their deaf children during their infancy. Other deaf children with hearing parents have commenced their signing when placed in special preschool programs. More often, though, deaf children with hearing parents have learned to sign when attending a school for deaf students. In these schools, incoming students may acquire facility in signing from fellow students and from teachers and staff members who are relatively accomplished signers. Because the ages at which pupils have entered schools for deaf students have varied widely, the ages at which these pupils have been introduced to signing also varied widely. Finally, some deaf children of hearing parents, because they attended either local public schools that did not have a sign program or private schools that had an oral-only (no signing permitted) instructional policy, may not have started acquiring signing skills until adulthood.

The wide range in ages at which deaf children have begun learning to sign has enabled investigators to examine the relationship between age of acquisition and eventual signing proficiency. In general, the younger the individual at the age of sign acquisition, the greater the likelihood that the individual will become a skilled signer (Mayberry, 1994). Those individuals whose exposure to a natural language is either significantly

---

21   It should be noted that the recent introduction of neonatal screening for hearing loss has meant that many more parents are learning of their children's hearing loss when the children are very young.

delayed or absent may not develop the same language-processing abilities and brain-functioning areas as those youngsters who learn a natural language early in life (Malaia & Wilbur, 2010). Furthermore, the establishment of two-way sign communication between hearing parents and their young deaf children may have important social benefits for the children as well (Magnuson, 2000).

Children who acquire a sign language in the first few years of life are considered native users of that sign language, just as children who acquire a spoken language from their parents are native users of that spoken language. It is the acquisition of signing skills in native signers that has been the focus of many studies of sign language development. These very young sign-learning children, deaf or hearing, often have been the offspring of Deaf parents.

Studies of how young children learn the formational parameters of signs (that is, the acquisition of sign language phonemes by young children) typically have relied heavily on Stokoe's model of ASL structure. Of the three formational parameters in Stokoe's model, location is the one most often produced correctly by young children learning sign languages (Cheek et al., 2001; Conlin et al., 2000; Juncos et al., 1997; Karnopp, 2002; Marentette & Mayberry, 2000; Morgan, Barrett-Jones, & Stoneham, 2007; Siedlecki & Bonvillian, 1993). This tendency to accurately produce the location parameter of a sign emerges early in development. In fact, the location parameter usually is correct in the very first signs made by a child. One explanation advanced for this high formational accuracy rests on the observation that location phonemes (the areas on or near the body where signs are made) are often relatively broad categories. To form a sign in the correct location may require that the sign-learning infant make only gross motor movements. An alternative explanation for the high formational accuracy of the location parameter is that parents and investigators may recognize an infant's signs only when they are made in certain locations.

The movement parameter of signs is acquired by young ASL-learning children with intermediate accuracy (Conlin et al., 2000; Marentette & Mayberry, 2000; Siedlecki & Bonvillian, 1993). In general, there is little change in overall production accuracy of the movement parameter of signs during the first two years of life. Although young children show improved formational accuracy of the movement phonemes that they produced early in their development, these same children also add new movement phonemes to their signing repertoire with increasing age. That is, what changes is that the number of different movement phonemes and the complexity of those sign movements increase with age and vocabulary size. Errors made in the production of these more complex movement phonemes often cancel out the gains in production accuracy of the less complex movement phonemes. Other studies of movement errors in signing children have shown that they frequently repeat movements (Meier et al., 2008; Morgan et al., 2007), mirror movements with the other hand (Cheek et al., 2001; Marentette & Mayberry, 2000; Meier et al., 2008), or change the location of the movement from the correct joint to a joint closer to the body — a proximalization error (Lavoie & Villeneuve, 2000; Meier et al., 2008; Takkinen, 2003).[22] Of the different types of sign movements in Stokoe's model of sign formational structure, contacting action is by far the one most often produced by young children. Apparently, having a sign touch or make contact with one's own body is something young children master quite readily.

Of the three formational parameters, handshape initially is produced by young, typically developing children with the lowest accuracy (Cheek et al., 2001; Conlin et al., 2000; Karnopp, 2002; Marentette & Mayberry, 2000; Siedlecki & Bonvillian, 1993; Takkinen, 2003; von Tetzchner, 1984b). Unlike the location and movement parameters of signs, young children show clear improvement in the accuracy of their handshape formation with increasing age. In addition, most young children acquire the different handshapes in a definite sequence (Clibbens & Harris, 1993; Siedlecki & Bonvillian, 1997). For example, children learn to make the spread- or 5-hand (the hand is flat with fingers spread apart and extended) early in their development (Carmo et al., 2013; Juncos et al., 1997; Meier, 2019; Morgan et al., 2007). In contrast, the horns-hand (the little finger and thumb are extended from an otherwise closed hand) typically is acquired much later. Those handshapes that are easier to form or articulate, such as the spread- or 5-hand, often replace those handshapes that are more difficult to form motorically in young children's early sign productions. Both anatomical and physiological

---

22 It should be noted that adult learners of sign language also display proximalization errors (Mirus, Rathmann, & Meier, 2001).

factors appear to strongly influence children's handshape acquisition order (Boyes Braem, 1973/1990).

Once scholars began accepting Stokoe's position that American Sign Language was a genuine language, they started asking whether the course of language acquisition was the same regardless of language modality. That is, were signed languages and spoken languages acquired at about the same rate and in the same general acquisitional pattern as spoken languages? To answer this question, investigators often have compared the sign language development of children of Deaf parents with the spoken language development of children of hearing parents.

The answer to this question at a general level is that the course or path of language development is quite similar across modalities. Systematic comparisons between the sign-learning children of Deaf parents and their speech-learning counterparts have shown many parallels in language acquisition (Chamberlain, Morford, & Mayberry, 2000; Meier, 1991, 2019; Morgan & Woll, 2002; Newport & Meier, 1985; Schick, 2003; Schick, Marschark, & Spencer, 2005). Most typically developing children, regardless of language mode, first babble (vocally or manually). Manual babbling often is evident in the many sign-like gestures produced by children of deaf parents during the latter half of their first year (Meier & Willerman, 1995; Petitto & Marentette, 1991). In addition, many of the handshapes, hand arrangements, palm orientations, and hand-internal movements (such as the opening and closing of the hand) that occurred in the children's prelinguistic gestures subsequently were present in the same children's early signs (Cheek et al., 2001). Young children then produce their first recognizable words or signs, and soon after begin using these words or signs to name or label things and actions in their environments. Indeed, the content of the vocabularies of young children learning ASL and those learning spoken English is remarkably similar (Anderson, 2006; Anderson & Reilly, 2002; Bonvillian, Orlansky, & Novack, 1983; Folven & Bonvillian, 1991). These early language milestones are typically followed by a rapid growth in vocabulary size, the combination of lexical items, and the formation of short sentences, either signed or spoken (Bonvillian, 1999; Meier, 1991, 2019; Morgan, Barrière, & Woll, 2006; Woolfe et al., 2010).

Additional evidence of similarities in development across language modalities can be seen in studies of how negation is expressed (Anderson

& Reilly, 1997), the acquisition of verb agreement (Meier, 1981, 1987; Morgan et al., 2006; Quadros & Lillo-Martin, 2007), and the emergence of different types of semantic relations or functions (Morgan et al., 2008; Newport & Ashbrook, 1977). In their two-sign combinations, young deaf children typically produce the full range of semantic relations also found in hearing children's two-word spoken utterances [e.g., the genitive or possessive, such as MOTHER PENCIL (i.e., 'that's mom's pencil'), and the locative or the location of an object or action, such as SWEATER CHAIR (i.e., 'the sweater is on the chair')]. Furthermore, when the order of emergence of different types of semantic relations was examined within individual children, it was found that the order was virtually the same regardless of language modality (Newport & Ashbrook, 1977).

It might be anticipated that young children of Deaf parents learning to sign would find signs that are highly iconic or pantomimic much easier to learn than non-iconic signs, and that iconic signs would constitute a large portion of their early vocabularies. Certainly, there is some evidence that the Deaf parents of sign-learning children believe that iconic signs will be easier for their children to learn than non-iconic signs. These parents often commented that they consciously used highly iconic or pantomimic signs more often when they interacted with their young children.

Do the young, typically developing children of Deaf parents acquire iconic signs more easily? Although the evidence on this issue is not clear-cut, it appears to indicate that sign iconicity is not a critically important factor in the sign acquisition of very young children of Deaf parents. In two studies (Folven & Bonvillian, 1991; Orlansky & Bonvillian, 1984) that examined young children's initial ASL lexicons, highly iconic or pantomimic signs accounted for about one-third of the children's vocabularies. Although this proportion is apparently greater than the overall proportion of highly iconic signs in ASL (Boyes Braem, 1986; Lloyd et al., 1985), it shows that the large majority of signs in these very young children's vocabularies were not highly iconic. Furthermore, many of the signs these young children learned showed no discernible resemblance to their referents. In addition, if parents were deliberately exposing their children to a greater proportion of clearly iconic signs, the level of iconic signs in their children's vocabularies may, in part, simply reflect parental input. And when the sign productions of ASL-learning Deaf infants were examined, there was very little evidence that the infants tended to form signs that were more iconic than the adult model of the sign; in contrast, there were many more instances where the infant-produced sign was judged to be less iconic (Meier et al., 2008). Factors other than iconicity, such as ease of sign formation, phonological similarity to other signs, parental sign input frequency, and objects and activities of interest to the very young children, likely contribute to much of the sign-learning infants' early vocabulary (see Caselli & Pyers, 2017).

Although iconicity may play only a small positive role in sign comprehension and production in infancy, its importance in sign learning appears to grow as young children increase in age (Thompson et al., 2012). This claim is based primarily on the study of the acquisition of British Sign Language signs by thirty-one Deaf children ranging in age from eight months to thirty-six months. Iconicity also played a much greater role in hearing four- and five-year-old children's gestural learning than it did for hearing three-year-olds (Magid & Pyers, 2017). Deaf three-year-olds, in contrast, showed a facilitative effect of iconicity in their gestural learning; this latter finding suggests that the ability to access iconicity may depend in part on one's signing experience. There may also be a change in the preferred form of sign iconicity present in individuals' signing with their increasing age. Preschool- and school-aged (under ten years old) children in Turkey produced more iconic signs that incorporated actions associated with the signs' referents than iconic signs that were based on perceptual features of the signs' referents (Ortega, Sümer, & Özyürek, 2017). In contrast, the iconic signs produced by adult users of Turkish Sign Language, who were unrelated to the child participants in the study, showed a clear preference for iconic signs that were based on perceptual features of the referents in their signing. Thus, it appears that the importance of sign iconicity in vocabulary development not only increases with age in sign-learning children, but that these children also show a preference for producing iconic signs where the iconicity is directly related to the actions these children make with these signs' referents.

One of the few areas where there have been reports of differences in acquisition across language modalities is in the rate that initial vocabulary is acquired. Various investigators (Anderson & Reilly, 2002; Bonvillian et al., 1983; Folven & Bonvillian, 1991; Holmes & Holmes, 1980; McIntire, 1977; Orlansky & Bonvillian, 1988; Prinz & Prinz, 1979) have advanced the view that the young children of Deaf parents initially acquire signs more rapidly than the children of hearing parents acquire spoken words. These claims of accelerated early acquisition of signs, however, have not gone unchallenged (Petitto, 1988; Volterra & Caselli, 1985). The principal criticism is that those investigators who have argued for a "gestural advantage" (or that speech is "disadvantaged") may have attributed linguistic status to a sign based on its form rather than on how a sign was used. If, the critics argue, the investigators had focused on the context of the children's early sign use rather than whether recognizable signs were formed, then many early signs would have been seen as imitations of adults' signs or as part of familiar gestural interactional routines between parents and their children. Regardless of the outcome of this particular debate, the studies of sign language development in children have shown that acquiring facility in a sign language is a complex learning task that unfolds over a period of years in a manner similar to that of spoken language learning.

Overall, the course of sign language acquisition in young children of Deaf parents resembles in many ways that of spoken language development in children of hearing parents (Meier, 2019). There is some evidence, however, that certain early language milestones may be attained at younger ages by children learning to sign than by children learning to speak. The general finding of many parallels in development across language modalities, moreover, suggests that there is a human capacity for language that transcends its modality of expression.

Concluding Remarks

For centuries, very few scholars examined or wrote about the signed languages used by Deaf persons. This situation changed dramatically beginning about fifty years ago, once linguists recognized that signed languages were full and genuine languages worthy of systematic study. Indeed, the study of how sign languages are acquired and processed has emerged as one of the most exciting and vibrant areas of research in all the sciences. Some of this interest may stem from a desire to learn about and to assist in the education and development of children with deafness. Other scholars may have pursued their studies of signed languages in an effort to facilitate the development of communication skills in various groups of non-speaking, but hearing, individuals, such as children with autism. Still other scholars may have been motivated to learn about signed languages because they saw the study of sign language psycholinguistics as a way to learn about how the human brain functions. Although the particular interests and motivations of those individuals who studied and learned about signed languages may have varied widely, there is no denying that the fields of sign language research, teaching, and learning have witnessed explosive growth in the past several decades.

In addition to their widespread use among members of the Deaf community, sign languages and sign systems have been used to facilitate the communication of hearing individuals who either have failed to learn to speak or have lost such an ability. There were several accounts of the successful use of signs with non-speaking individuals during the nineteenth and first half of the twentieth centuries. Despite reports of their success, such sign intervention programs failed to catch on. The publication of Stokoe's findings (1960; Stokoe et al., 1965) about the linguistic structure of ASL signs, however, led to changes in many scholars' notions about the nature of language. The recognition that the signed languages used by Deaf persons were genuine languages helped many scholars to overcome their long-held view that language consisted of or was always based on speech. At this point, sign languages and systems based on sign languages began to be seen as potentially viable communication alternatives for non-speaking, albeit hearing, persons. Such persons include individuals with an intellectual disability, cerebral palsy, autism spectrum disorder (ASD), or aphasia. The successes and struggles of these people to communicate through spoken language and/or signs are explored next in Chapters 4, 5, and 6, and will shed further light on the choices we made when selecting, modifying, and creating signs for inclusion in the Simplified Sign System.

4. Sign Communication in Persons with an Intellectual Disability or with Cerebral Palsy

The 1970s brought a dramatic increase in the use of signs to foster language skills in non-speaking children and adults. When the decade began, there were only a few programs that utilized signs with hearing, but non-speaking, persons. By the time that Goodman, Wilson, and Bornstein (1978) conducted their national survey later that decade, however, there were over 10,000 students in North America alone who were participating in sign-communication training and teaching programs. Many of these individuals were children with an intellectual disability[1] who had extremely limited or no functional speech.

What led to this remarkable increase in the use of signs to facilitate language skills in non-speaking persons? One of the most significant factors was the recognition that the sign languages used by Deaf persons were genuine languages. This was an important conceptual breakthrough: language was no longer equated solely with speech. A second contributing factor was the large amount of attention given to the chimpanzee, Washoe. Washoe, taught by R. Allen and Beatrix T. Gardner (1969, 1971) to communicate through ASL signs, acquired a substantial sign vocabulary and learned to combine signs to express a

---

[1] The term *intellectual disability* now is being used in place of the term *mental retardation* (Schalock, Luckasson, & Shogren, 2007). This transition in usage is particularly evident in the renaming of the American Association on Mental Retardation to the American Association on Intellectual and Developmental Disabilities. Because, in the past, investigators who studied children with intellectual disabilities often employed the term *mental retardation*, it will sometimes be necessary to continue using this terminology when directly quoting their work.

wide range of concepts.[2] The press reports of Washoe's success helped inform a wide audience about the possibility of communicating through manual signs. Soon after, many non-speaking or minimally verbal persons with an intellectual disability entered sign-learning programs. Later, certain individuals with cerebral palsy, autism spectrum disorder (ASD), and/or aphasia also were exposed to these programs.

After sign-communication programs were introduced to a wide range of persons with serious communication disorders, there were a number of reports of substantial improvements in many individuals' language skills. In these reports, many non-speaking or minimally verbal children and adults were depicted as making great strides in their communication through programs that used either manual signs alone or signs combined with spoken language. With these accounts of positive outcomes, sign-communication programs rapidly became well established as a major form of intervention to increase individuals' abilities to communicate. Indeed, before 1990, programs using manual signs or signs combined with spoken language constituted the most frequently employed form of augmentative and alternative communication training for persons with cognitive impairments or childhood autism in the United States (Beukelman & Mirenda, 2005; Matas et al., 1985). The initial enthusiasm about manual signing interventions was soon tempered, however, by reports of more mixed outcomes among participants in those programs.[3] This variability in outcomes may have helped spark the development of other non-oral communication systems for intervention purposes (see Chapter 5). In some of these newer intervention approaches, signs may be combined with other non-oral communication systems in a more multimodal approach.

---

2   This project and similar manual sign-communication studies with primates (e.g., Miles, 1978; Patterson, 1978) were not without critique, however. See Lyn (2017) for an overview of methodological concerns regarding such animal language studies (as well as her rebuttals of many of them) and Pepperberg (2017) for a more personal view of the controversies surrounding the projects.

3   Many of these early manual sign intervention programs were performed in highly structured training sessions over a short period of time and did not focus on generalizing or incorporating sign use into more naturalistic settings or across multiple environments. Such limitations in program design probably had a negative impact on children's motivation to use signs outside of the specific training sessions. A more comprehensive approach to signing, such as immersion in a signing environment, would likely have generated better results or more consistently positive outcomes.

Reviews of the studies of sign-communication training and teaching with various non-speaking or minimally verbal populations, including those with more than one condition that affected their acquisition or use of spoken language, reveal important commonalities in their findings. There often has been a wide range in sign learning among participants, with certain types of signs more frequently acquired, and some environments more conducive to learning signs than others. As well as learning to communicate through signs, many participants in sign intervention programs show improvements in other areas, such as better understanding of spoken language, increased motivation, and improvement in academic skills (Kiernan, Reid, & Jones, 1982; Launonen, 1996, 1998, 2003, 2019b). In addition, as individuals with disabilities gain skills in controlling their environment and conveying their needs through signs, their level of frustration and incidence of tantrums often decrease. With an increased ability to communicate and reduction in behaviors associated with helplessness, these individuals also are more likely to comply with caretaker requests (Bryen & Joyce, 1985). Along with these benefits, the use of manual sign instruction has been consistently related to increases in most participants' spoken language production when signed input occurs together with speech (Dunst, Meter, & Hamby, 2011; Launonen, 2019b; Launonen & Grove, 2003; Millar et al., 2006; te Kaat-van den Os et al., 2015; Valentino & Shillingsburg, 2011). This is an important finding given concerns among parents and professionals that sign learning might adversely affect their children's or clients' spoken language development and use.

An Early Study

Although nearly all contemporary reviews of sign-communication training and teaching programs for non-speaking children with an intellectual disability focus only on studies conducted during the past several decades, it turns out that the use of signs with such children has a much longer history. In fact, many breakthroughs that we think of as recent achievements were known to certain professionals long ago. For example, the usefulness of sign instruction for children with significant cognitive impairments was spelled out in the middle of the nineteenth century by W. R. Scott, Ph.D. (Bonvillian & Miller, 1995).

Scott was the principal at a school for deaf students in the west of England. Although many schools for deaf students in England at that time stressed oral educational approaches, Scott embraced signing as well. He also was concerned about the development of children with serious intellectual disabilities. In 1847, he described a course of instruction for non-speaking individuals with an intellectual disability, observing in his report that those staff members with experience in the education of deaf students "...are not infrequently called upon to instruct children of very low intellectual capacity" (Scott, 1847, p. 7) as well. Scott noted that these children invariably improve as a result of the instruction they receive. With regard to their communication skills, Scott (1847) claimed that the children:

> ...generally obtain a sufficient knowledge of the sign language of the Deaf-mutes, to enable them to converse on the common subject, and furthermore generally learn the names of common objects and their more sensible qualities, and to perform the easier kinds of manual labor; but they seldom get to understand complicated forms of expression... (p. 8)

Along with these children's gains in communication, Scott observed noticeable improvements in their cleanliness, temper, and social behavior.

Scott offered a pair of explanations to account for the success of sign language training with these youngsters. One explanation was that gestural communication developmentally precedes spoken language. That is, virtually all infants use gestures to communicate before learning to speak, so gestural communication may be a more fundamental way to communicate.[4] His second explanation was that words and signs

---

4   Scott most likely was focused on how the production of meaningful and understandable gestures developmentally precedes the production of meaningful and understandable words. Contemporary studies show that children's gestures may be accompanied by either meaningless or meaningful vocalizations depending on the developmental stage of the child involved. In the early sessions of an observational study of gesture, speech, and word development in six typically developing children between the ages of twelve months and twenty-seven-and-a-half months, Goldin-Meadow (1998) reported that most of the children's communications were vocal in nature (between 60–80%). Of the 20–40% of the communications that did contain gestures, most of those gestures initially occurred without speech (in other words, speech and gestures were not yet part of an integrated system). The speech that the children did produce along with gestures in these early sessions was comprised of meaningless sounds not temporally matched with the peak of the gesture. This relationship, however, changed over time as the

differed in that there often was a discernible tie between a sign and what it stood for (its referent), whereas the relationship between a spoken word and its referent rarely was apparent. This discernible tie between a sign and its referent likely would make a sign more easily learned and remembered. As Scott observed, there frequently was "a natural relation to the notion taught" (1847, p. 34) for those signs the children learned (these signs would be considered iconic in nature). Scott evidently was a man ahead of his time: these explanations for the success of sign-communication programs for non-speaking children were to be advanced anew over a century later.

Although Scott's findings and observations about the merits of sign programs could have had a profound impact on the education of students with various intellectual disabilities, they did not. There probably were several reasons for this outcome, ranging from the publication of his report in an obscure academic pamphlet to the fact that many educators in the late nineteenth century adopted oral-only educational approaches for deaf students (that is, sign language and fingerspelling were prohibited). Regardless, if Scott's observations about the efficacy of sign-communication training and teaching had been more widely accepted, then the lives of many non-speaking persons with an intellectual disability might have been greatly improved.

Intellectual Disability

Intellectual disability is characterized by atypical (lower) cognitive functioning and impaired adaptive behavior. More precisely, intellectual disability is defined as "significant limitations both in intellectual functioning and in adaptive behavior as expressed in conceptual, social, and practical adaptive skills" (AAIDD Ad Hoc Committee on Terminology and Classification, 2010, p. 1). Furthermore, the onset needs to occur before the age of eighteen years. Many individuals with intellectual disabilities also have motor or neuromotor impairments that may adversely affect their communication skills (Beukelman &

---

children started to combine gestures with meaningful words and later started to temporally match their vocalizations (both meaningful and meaningless) with the gestures. At this point, the children's speech and gesture could be considered an integrated system.

Mirenda, 2013). Children with more severe cognitive impairments typically have very serious linguistic deficits as well (Bryen & Joyce, 1985). According to Romski and Sevcik, "the majority of children and youth with significant mental retardation fail to develop functional spoken words even with considerable speech and language instruction" (1996, p. 9). These communication deficits may lead them to experience frustration and indirectly result in a range of behavioral problems. Those persons who fail to acquire useful speech tend to have the lowest IQs (Sheehan, Martyn, & Kilburn, 1968) with many very low-scoring individuals having additional or multiple disabilities.

The particular etiology or cause of the intellectual disability also is an important factor that affects the level of language or communicative functioning that an individual may attain (Fowler, 1998). That is, persons with similar full-scale IQs may have quite different language profiles depending on whether they are identified as having Down syndrome, fragile X syndrome, Angelman syndrome, Williams syndrome, or other syndromes associated with an intellectual disability. Individuals with Williams syndrome, for example, tend to eventually acquire substantial productive spoken language skills, with their intellectual disability much more evident in the difficulties they experience with visuospatial skills (Brock, 2007; Vicari et al., 2004).[5] In contrast, the spoken language development of children with Down syndrome typically is not as advanced as their cognitive development (Barnes et al., 2009; Tager-Flusberg, 1999), with their visuospatial skills relatively well preserved (Dierssen, Herault, & Estivill, 2009; Vicari, 2006) although not immune to disruptions in spatial representation (Uecker et al., 1993; Vallar & Papagno, 1993; Woll & Grove, 1996, 2019).

Fragile X syndrome is a relatively common inherited form of intellectual disability, with males identified with the syndrome considerably outnumbering females.[6] Individuals with fragile X

---

5   Because signed languages rely heavily on visuospatial processing for effective communication, individuals with Williams syndrome might be expected to experience particular difficulty with this important aspect of sign communication. Findings from a case study of a deaf woman with Williams syndrome showed that she experienced significant difficulty using and understanding spatialized syntax and topographic relationships (Atkinson, Woll, & Gathercole, 2002; Woll & Morgan, 2012).

6   Estimates of the incidence of fragile X syndrome have varied widely, with the ethnic-group composition of the populations studied and the precise definition

syndrome typically are more impaired in their expressive language skills than in their receptive language skills (Martin et al., 2013), with impaired articulation a frequently occurring problem (Barnes et al., 2009; Finestack & Abbeduto, 2010). Some of the difficulties individuals with fragile X syndrome experience in their development of spoken language skills may be attributable to impaired phonological processing (Pierpont et al., 2011; see also Engineer et al., 2014). Although most individuals with fragile X syndrome eventually outperform individuals with Down syndrome on measures of grammatical ability (Finestack, Sterling, & Abbeduto, 2013) and expressive language (Finestack & Abbeduto, 2010), many youngsters with fragile X syndrome learn to communicate initially through augmentative and alternative communication strategies (Brady et al., 2006). The use of manual signs and PECS (Picture Exchange Communication System; see Chapter 5) are the two communication strategies most frequently mentioned by mothers of children with fragile X syndrome as being used by their children (Brady et al., 2006). Mothers of young children with fragile X syndrome, moreover, often facilitated their children's transition to spoken language by effective use of gestures during their interactions (Hahn et al., 2014).

Oral communication intervention programs often have proven unsuccessful in fostering spoken language skills in individuals with a severe or profound intellectual disability[7] even after intense therapy

---

of intellectual disability used affecting the results. Turner, Webb, Wake, and Robinson (1996) estimated a syndrome incidence of 1 per 4000 for males and 1 per 8000 for females from populations composed mostly of Caucasian families. Crawford, Acuña, and Sherman (2001) provided a range in syndrome prevalence for Caucasian males extending from 1 per 3717 to 1 per 8918. Males also typically are more adversely affected than females.

7   In many research studies, participants with a cognitive impairment have been grouped based on their scores on standardized tests designed to assess intelligence (IQ tests). Individuals who received an IQ score of 55–69 typically were identified as having a *mild* intellectual disability, those with IQ scores of 40–54 as having a *moderate* intellectual disability, those with IQ scores of 25–39 as having a *severe* intellectual disability, and those with IQ scores below 25 as having a *profound* intellectual disability. In more recent years, the distinction between these categories has gotten fuzzier and the boundaries have shifted, particularly in countries like the U.K. In such areas, the use of IQ tests as a basis for ID definition and for the provision of services to individuals with intellectual disabilities has been discouraged or deemphasized in favor of more social- or rights-based approaches that focus on giving families the support they need. In this volume, we acknowledge this ongoing cultural shift in terminology but will often continue to refer to the above

(Bonvillian & Nelson, 1978; Kopchick & Lloyd, 1976). Because the absence of communicative skills is such a serious problem, many researchers and educators who worked with these children eagerly embraced the use of signs several decades ago when it was first brought to their attention. The attention and recognition given to sign languages in the 1960s also helped spur the development of sign intervention programs. In many instances, the children who participated in these signing programs made considerable progress in learning to communicate more effectively (Kiernan et al., 1982).

Some studies that examined the learning of signs or gestures by individuals with cognitive impairments involved participants who had additional disabilities. Levett (1969, 1971) devised a system of mime for a group of non-speaking children with a severe intellectual disability and cerebral palsy. This system consisted of fifty gestures or movements that resembled activities or objects believed to be of interest or relevance to the children. Ten of the twelve youngsters who participated in the project learned to use the mime system effectively. This outcome indicated that a number of the participants had the ability to make important strides in communication skills when the modality was changed from a vocal one to a manual one. The fact that the signs and gestures had clearly visible ties to the concepts they represented probably also played a role in their successful learning. That is, signs and gestures that were pantomimic or highly iconic often were easier to learn and remember.[8]

In addition, sign vocabulary training was explored early on with individuals with an intellectual disability who were also deaf (Sutherland & Beckett, 1969). Prior to sign intervention programs, many of these persons had little or no exposure to a sign language. Deaf or hearing-impaired individuals with an intellectual disability traditionally were excluded from residential and community programs for Deaf persons because of their perceived low cognitive ability (Hall

---

categories largely because the research studies we reference used them as a basis for comparison. It is likewise helpful to point out that certain individuals have more complex communication needs than others, and as such, may require different intervention strategies, although which strategies to use with an individual should not be limited by his or her IQ scores.

8   The combination of cognitive age or intellectual, motor, and linguistic disabilities of an individual may prevent that person from consciously appreciating a sign's iconicity, especially if the tie between that sign and its referent is less clear. Regardless, highly iconic signs may still be remembered better than less iconic signs.

& Talkington, 1970). Because some of the factors that cause childhood deafness, such as maternal rubella or German measles, may also result in brain damage and cognitive impairment, deaf persons are over-represented in the population of individuals with a significant cognitive or intellectual disability (Bruce, DiNatale, & Ford, 2008; Guardino, 2008; van Dijk et al., 2010). The various studies of sign acquisition in individuals with intellectual disability showed that the large majority of the participants made some progress in acquiring sign-communication skills. Another important finding was that gains in communication skills among participants were not shared equally. Indeed, in one study involving sixteen participants with either a severe or profound intellectual disability (Hoffmeister & Farmer, 1972), the level of sign mastery extended from almost no learning to the acquisition of 200 or more signs by four participants; those four participants also learned to combine signs. Wide variation in sign mastery was again seen in a study by Cornforth, Johnston, and Walker (1974) in the U.K., where the number of expressive signs learned by fifty-one deaf adults with a severe intellectual disability ranged from 36 to 137. These findings underscore the wide differences in outcomes from relatively similar training and teaching experiences.

The success of deaf individuals with a cognitive impairment in learning to sign raises questions about the accuracy of their initial intellectual disability classification. That is, when an individual has low intellectual ability and deafness, the combination of disabilities may give the appearance of a much lower level of cognitive functioning than is actually present. The results of a systematic comparison back up this claim. Hall and Talkington (1970) compared the sign-learning abilities of thirty deaf students with an intellectual disability to those of thirty hearing students with an intellectual disability. The two groups were matched on IQ (on the performance, or non-language, IQ scale), sex, age, and length of institutional placement. After six months of training, the deaf students had learned to comprehend many more signs than the hearing students (deaf mean = 54.6 signs; hearing mean = 0.1 signs). This finding, together with those from additional studies, led to the conclusion that IQ measures of deaf students with an intellectual disability frequently were underestimating their ability to learn, especially their potential for acquiring signs.

Many children who are congenitally deaf and blind have been assessed as having a moderate to severe intellectual impairment (van Dijk, 2004). Once again, the presence of additional disabling conditions may give the appearance of a very low level of cognitive functioning in these individuals. Unlike deaf children who rely heavily on vision in their learning, deafblind children may need to rely more on touch and proprioception depending on their particular levels of vision and hearing (Deuce & Rose, 2019). Furthermore, it is important to understand that a child's visual and/or hearing skills may be relatively intact at birth but deteriorate further as he or she ages. Thus, family members and interventionists should take existing skill sets into consideration when developing communicative strategies and will then need to adapt these strategies as vision (and/or hearing) skills become more impaired (Deuce & Rose, 2019; Pease, 2000). Still, quite a few deafblind children manage to learn to produce and to understand manual signs and fingerspelling. In one study of 71 deafblind children in Denmark (Dammeyer & Ask Larsen, 2016), of those that had already developed language skills, 39% relied on a visually perceived sign language and 23% used the tactile modality to access sign language. Such use of signs from an existing sign language may in fact be built upon an earlier scaffold of natural gestures that have been developed or adapted by the deafblind person and his or her family members and caretakers for communicative purposes (Nafstad & Rødbroe, 2015; Souriau et al., 2008). A final factor that should be considered is that deafblind persons may also experience motor problems that necessitate changes to any manual signs that they produce. Signs should be altered in such a way as to emphasize that individual's relative strengths and avoid areas of particular difficulty (Deuce & Rose, 2019). These individuals' acquisition of manual communication skills often is associated with a reduction in negative behavioral patterns such as self-injurious behaviors (van Dijk, 2004).

Shortly after the publication of reports on the successful acquisition of signs by persons with both an intellectual disability and another disabling condition, a number of sign-communication programs were established for the broader population of individuals with intellectual disabilities or language impairments (Grove & Walker, 1990; von Tetzchner, 1984a). In these programs, many hundreds of persons, including participants without additional disabling conditions, showed marked improvement in their language skills through learning signs. The finding that many of these non-speaking children and adults could acquire a large lexicon or vocabulary of signs led to the establishment of numerous sign-based programs. Furthermore, once learned, signs often were retained for long periods even without additional training and teaching sessions (Hobson & Duncan, 1979).

One of the most widely used sign systems for non-speaking persons with severe language impairments is known as the Makaton Vocabulary. The Makaton Vocabulary was initially designed as a signing system to meet the needs of deaf adults with an intellectual disability. After it proved to be a viable communication approach for these individuals, it was successfully used with hearing adults and children with an intellectual disability, autism, a specific language disorder, or an acquired neurological disorder affecting communication (Grove & Walker, 1990; Sheehy & Duffy, 2009).

The signs for the original Makaton Vocabulary came from British Sign Language (BSL), the principal language used by members of the Deaf community in Great Britain. The BSL signs selected for inclusion in the Makaton Vocabulary were chosen based on the signs' perceived usefulness in meeting many of the basic needs and functions of the target populations. The signs were organized for teaching purposes into different stages reflecting the core concepts that needed to be expressed at different levels of development and use. Initially, there were 350 core concept signs; this was later expanded to 450 signs, and access to a much larger resource vocabulary was provided. After achieving a great deal of success in Great Britain, the Makaton Vocabulary was adapted for use in many other countries. In these adaptations, the signs for the Makaton Vocabulary were taken from the signed languages used by Deaf persons in those countries; for example, in Japan, the Makaton Vocabulary uses Japanese signs (Grove & Walker, 1990).

In the Makaton system, signs are used by teachers and caregivers in conjunction with speech. Rather than signing every word in a sentence, they sign only those words in a sentence that convey needed information. This focus on signing the principal content words in a sentence became known as *key word signing*.[9] Another aspect of the Makaton Vocabulary approach is the inclusion of graphic symbols. These symbols are largely

---

9   The signs from any signed language can be used in a key word signing approach.

pictorial representations of words or signs and operate in a manner similar to a rebus. Many teachers and caregivers who utilize the Makaton Vocabulary system reportedly teach by underlining the visual link between a sign and its equivalent graphic symbol (Grove & Walker, 1990). This inclusion of graphic symbols to help in sign learning and the establishment of a core concept vocabulary, as well as the development of various supplemental teaching aids, make the Makaton Vocabulary an innovative organizational approach to the fostering of communication skills in non-speaking persons (Sheehy & Duffy, 2009).

While many hearing persons with a severe or profound intellectual disability made progress in learning to sign, studies also revealed that there were wide individual differences in the level of sign mastery achieved. This observation of very uneven levels of mastery echoed the findings previously reported for deaf persons with an intellectual disability. Richardson (1975) reported that after one year of sign instruction, there was a range in mastery from one participant who learned only a small receptive vocabulary (understanding signs) to another participant who acquired a large expressive vocabulary, producing 400 different signs. This variability in language outcomes also is evident when considering the speech modality. When expressive communication skills, including both spoken words and manual signs, were examined in children with intellectual disabilities over the course of a two-year longitudinal study, there were very wide individual differences in the vocabulary sizes attained by the participants (Vandereet et al., 2010). Some of this variability in language learning across participants in a range of studies may be attributable to additional disabling conditions, other than cognitive impairment, that could have depressed certain individuals' IQ scores to a level lower than they should have been based on cognitive impairment alone. There also may be different skill patterns within different forms or types of intellectual disability (Dierssen et al., 2009; Jernigan & Bellugi, 1990; Prior, 1977; Vicari, 2006).

Examination of the findings from some of the early accounts of sign learning in individuals with an intellectual disability revealed that certain signs seemed easier to learn than others. This observation led investigators to probe more systematically those characteristics that were associated with more rapid sign acquisition. Signs that were rated as more highly iconic were found to be more readily learned (Griffith

& Robinson, 1980; Lloyd & Fuller, 1990; Snyder-McLean, 1978). Signs identified as high in translucency also were learned more readily by individuals with a moderate or severe intellectual disability (Doherty, 1985; Luftig, 1983).[10] Signs that are useful or relevant to the individual learner also tended to be learned and used more often (Dennis et al., 1982; Doherty, 1985; Meuris et al., 2014). Signs that involved touch or contact with the signer's body or the other hand frequently were learned more quickly (Dennis et al., 1982; Kohl, 1981; Stremel-Campbell, Cantrell, & Halle, 1977), as were those signs that involved symmetrical movements with each arm and hand. An important outgrowth of these results was that teachers and investigators began to focus more intensely on the formational characteristics and iconic nature of the signs they selected for vocabulary training.[11]

Not only may certain individual signs be acquired more easily than others, but signs from different sign systems or languages may be more readily learned as well. Amer-Ind is a sign-communication system based on Plains Indian Sign Language, a system of signs developed by members of different Native American tribes or nations who did not speak the same language.[12] In comparison with ASL signs, a larger proportion of Amer-Ind signs are described as highly iconic (Skelly et al., 1975; see also Kirschner, Algozzine, & Abbott, 1979) and less complex motorically (Daniloff & Vergara, 1984). These characteristics may make Amer-Ind signs easier to learn than ASL signs. This question

---

10   When a sign is identified as highly *iconic*, it often resembles the concept for which it stands and the sign's meaning is quite "guessable" or transparent. Although related to iconicity, a sign's *translucency* refers to the ease with which people discern the relationship between a sign and what it stands for once the sign's meaning has been provided. For more information on iconicity and translucency, see "The Simplified Sign System" section in Chapter 1.

11   It is important to note that many such studies of sign acquisition in special populations involved laboratory conditions, and thus their results may not fully translate into more naturalistic settings and/or in highly supportive signing environments, where the properties of the signs themselves may turn out to be of less significance than in laboratory settings. The criteria for judging successful acquisition of the signs also varied from study to study, so it is difficult to make direct comparisons among them. Still, it is likely that signs that are taught in laboratory conditions with stricter criteria for acceptance would also be just as likely, if not more likely, to be learned in a highly supportive signing environment that also accepts approximations of signs. Iconic signs also have a distinct advantage in that they have a much greater chance of being understood by persons in the larger environment than signs that have less transparent meanings.

12   Amer-Ind is discussed in further detail in Chapter 6.

of relative ease of acquisition of the two sign systems has been examined
in adolescents and adults with intellectual disabilities. In general,
participants tended to acquire and to retain more Amer-Ind signs than
ASL signs (Gates & Edwards, 1989). This difference in learning rates
was attributed to the more concrete and less formationally complex
nature of Amer-Ind signs. Although many non-speaking persons with
intellectual disabilities learned Amer-Ind signs more easily than ASL
signs, it should be noted that the characteristics of the sign learner are
quite important as well. In fact, one study (Marquardt, Sanchez, &
Munoz, 1999) reported that the best predictor of sign learning among
adults with Down syndrome was the cognitive, language, and motor
abilities of the participants themselves.

Down Syndrome

Down syndrome is a congenital condition typically characterized by a
mild or moderate intellectual disability and distinctive facial features.
With an occurrence rate of one in every 700–1000 births, Down syndrome
is the most common chromosomal cause of intellectual disability
(Dykens, Hodapp, & Finucane, 2000). Fifty years ago, expectations
about the educability and eventual level of development of children
with Down syndrome were quite low. In more recent years, largely
because of the results demonstrated by individuals who participated
in early intervention programs, expectations have become considerably
higher (Corby, Taggart, & Cousins, 2018; Launonen, 2019a; Spiker, 2011;
Turner, Alborz, & Gayle, 2008). Guralnick (2017, p. 214) notes that

> early intervention for all children remains a problem-solving process
> involving the family, the intervention team and other supports within
> the community. The information provided by etiology-specific
> developmental studies is of considerable value as all involved can better
> anticipate issues and construct intervention strategies more likely to have
> a positive impact.

Spoken language production often is an area of particular difficulty
for individuals with Down syndrome (Martin et al., 2009). Many
children with Down syndrome show delayed onset of spoken language
(Berglund, Eriksson, & Johansson, 2001), acquire new spoken words
at a rate well below what would be expected based on their level of

cognitive development (Zampini & D'Odorico, 2013), and fail to attain levels of expressive language that are expected for typically developing three-year-olds (Fowler, 1990). These delays are particularly evident in the domains of phonological and syntactical development (Barnes et al., 2009; Tager-Flusberg, 1999). Overall, verbal skills typically are areas of relative weakness for individuals with Down syndrome, whereas nonverbal skills often are areas of strength (Grieco et al., 2015). Indeed, gesture production is viewed as an area of strength for children with Down syndrome in comparison with their vocal language skills (Galeote et al., 2011). Perhaps because of the difficulties and delays that children with Down syndrome experience in spoken language development, representative gestures constitute a larger proportion of their utterances than they do for typically developing children (Stefanini, Recchia, & Caselli, 2008). Furthermore, delays in expressive language development continue to be evident with increasing age; many children and adolescents with Down syndrome show deficits in their production of syntax and vocabulary, as well as in the intelligibility or comprehensibility of their spoken language (Barnes et al., 2009; Chapman & Hesketh, 2000; Finestack & Abbeduto, 2010; see also Yoder, Woynaroski, & Camarata, 2016). Available evidence suggests that the marked delays in spoken language development often seen in individuals with Down syndrome may be greatly lessened if a program of language stimulation or intervention is initiated very early in these individuals' lives (Launonen, 2019a, 2019b; Roberts, Price, & Malkin, 2007; Sanz Aparicio & Balaña, 2002). In addition, the use of communicative gestures by young children with Down syndrome may serve as a helpful "bridge" to word production later in childhood (Zampini & D'Odorico, 2009; see also the review study by te Kaat-van den Os et al., 2015).

Are there factors other than cognitive impairment that may account for this particular difficulty with spoken language skills? There appear to be at least several factors that may delay the onset of spoken language in some individuals with Down syndrome and make their speech relatively unintelligible to people unfamiliar with them. One factor may be hearing impairment, as 40–80% of children with Down syndrome experience some hearing loss. A substantial proportion has a mild to moderate hearing impairment (Dahle & McCollister, 1986; Roizen, 1997,

2007), with severe impairment evident in many fewer cases (Marcell, 1995; Marcell & Cohen, 1992). Some of this relatively high incidence of hearing impairment may be attributable to recurrent otitis media or inflammation of the middle ear (Nightengale et al., 2017; Roberts & Medley, 1995; Shott, Joseph, & Heithaus, 2001; Strome & Strome, 1992). Individuals with Down syndrome appear to be especially vulnerable to otitis media because of physical anomalies of their ears and upper respiratory tract. Damage to the inner ear also contributes to their relatively high incidence of hearing impairment. Whereas inflammation of the middle ear is treatable, damage to the inner ear usually is not. Moreover, a hearing loss that occurs when children with Down syndrome are between the ages of two and four years old is likely to have a significant negative impact on the children's development of spoken language skills (Laws & Hall, 2014; Nightengale et al., 2017).

Another factor adversely affecting the spoken language acquisition of many children with Down syndrome is their severe problem with articulation. The production of the correct sounds and sound combinations needed for clear speech often is very difficult for these children (Kumin, 1996). In particular, they experience problems in the oral-motor planning, sequencing, and coordination that result in the production of the rapid movements of the tongue, lips, and other oral structures involved in speech (Barnes et al., 2006; Hamilton, 1993). This difficulty that many persons with Down syndrome experience in oral-motor planning, evident in their problems combining and sequencing sounds into words and sentences, means that they should be viewed as having a verbal (or oral-motor) apraxia (Kumin, 2006). Some of these individuals' articulation problems also may result from their recessed mandibles (lower jaw bones) and, as a consequence, protruding tongues.

A third factor that may influence the spoken language abilities of some children with Down syndrome is the occurrence of poor auditory or phonological memory (Kay-Raining Bird & Chapman, 1994; Laws & Gunn, 2004; Næss et al., 2015). Individuals with Down syndrome have a rather limited capacity for verbal material in their immediate memory system (Purser & Jarrold, 2005). This deficit in phonological memory or storage capacity, it should be noted, also is evident in children with intellectual disabilities more generally (Schuchardt, Maehler, & Hasselhorn, 2011; van der Schuit et al., 2011b). The limited capacity or poor memory for speech sounds may make spoken language more difficult to process than manual signs or gestures.

Although delayed or atypical development of the auditory system could account for some of the struggles many children with Down syndrome experience learning spoken language, more fundamental neuropathology or neurological abnormalities probably underlie some of their language difficulties. The hippocampus, a brain structure that plays a critical role in memory (Corkin, 2013), is impaired and disproportionately reduced in volume in persons with Down syndrome (Nadel, 2003). Individuals with Down syndrome also show diminished cerebellar size (Dierssen et al., 2009; Guidi et al., 2011; Uecker et al., 1993). This is important because the cerebellum is a brain structure that has long been recognized for its involvement in movement sequencing and motor abilities. More recent evidence indicates that it is also involved in higher order functions such as cognition and language (Kellett, Stevenson, & Gernsbacher, 2012). In contrast, individuals with Williams syndrome, who do not show the same difficulties with expressive spoken language that persons with Down syndrome do, have more normal-sized cerebellums (Chiang et al., 2007; Jernigan & Bellugi, 1990). Finally, persons with Down syndrome may have additional disabling conditions that adversely impact their communication skills, such as the 10–15% of children in one study who displayed early signs of autistic disorder or autism spectrum disorder at age two and then again at ages four or five (Hepburn et al., 2008). Early screening of children with Down syndrome before the age of three years for symptoms of autism and diagnostic evaluation by clinicians may provide critically important information to parents and caretakers. Such a diagnosis would aid in their search for appropriate social and communicative interventions to mitigate the additional disturbances not seen in the general population of persons with Down syndrome (Hepburn et al., 2008).

Parents of children with Down syndrome who have not developed spoken language skills frequently express concern that their children will never learn to speak if they learn how to communicate through signs. Therefore, one important research question has focused on whether signing interferes with spoken language acquisition among children with Down syndrome. When spoken language is combined with manual signs, such individuals evidently benefit from this bimodal input. For example, children with Down syndrome were shown to imitate novel spoken words more frequently when the words were paired with signs than when the words were presented in speech or sign alone (Kay-Raining Bird et al., 2000). Moreover, the production of manual signs by children with Down syndrome at two-and-a-half years of age positively predicted the size of their spoken language vocabularies one year later (Özçalişkan et al., 2016). That is, these children's success in producing signs in early childhood was highly related to their subsequent ability to produce spoken words. In many instances, the items in the expressive vocabularies of children with Down syndrome who have received multimodal input are in both spoken and signed modalities (Deckers et al., 2017). Overall, the available evidence suggests that signed input together with speech facilitates the development of spoken language and communication skills in children with Down syndrome rather than slowing them down, and that input early in development is particularly helpful (Clibbens, 2001; Dunst et al., 2011; Launonen, 2019b; Millar et al., 2006; Miller, 1992). In light of such findings, Deckers et al. (2016) recommended that parents of children with Down syndrome be told of the apparently beneficial effects of sign instruction on their children's early language development.

The outcomes of several case studies of sign-communication training and teaching in youngsters with Down syndrome illustrate how combining signs with speech may foster subsequent spoken language development. In a case study of a young girl with Down syndrome, Kouri (1989) observed that the girl, who received simultaneous spoken language and sign input, typically made the signs for words or concepts first and then relatively shortly afterward produced the spoken words for those concepts. In another case, the transition to spontaneous spoken language occurred only after a substantial sign vocabulary had been acquired. The boy with Down syndrome in this study (Layton & Savino, 1990) initially participated in an oral (speech-oriented) program, but when he failed to progress, was introduced to a simultaneous speech-and-sign program. He rapidly acquired sign-communication skills. He did not make impressive strides in spoken language, however, until after he had attained an expressive sign vocabulary of approximately 400 signs. At that time, his spoken language vocabulary increased rapidly in size and his use of signs declined dramatically.

In a third case-study report (Launonen & Grove, 2003; see also Launonen, 2019a), the transition from signs to spoken language occurred much later in development. In this study, a boy with Down syndrome was introduced to manual signs when he was three-and-a-half years old and had not yet started to speak. His parents and family learned and made extensive use of signing in natural everyday settings with him, a fact that supported and encouraged his own use of signs. This boy acquired a substantial sign vocabulary and relied on signs for communication throughout his childhood. He started to speak more often from ages twelve to thirteen, and his speech skills improved during his teenage years. Five years later, spoken language had become the resilient young man's dominant mode of communication; he generally signed only when others found his speech unintelligible.

Although the three youngsters described above made a successful transition from signs to spoken language, it might be argued that an intervention program using manual signs could result in more slowly developing or poorer speech skills than a program that did not include signs. This, however, does not appear to be what typically happens. In one longitudinal study (Launonen, 1996; see also Launonen, 2019a), twelve young children with Down syndrome received a communication intervention program that emphasized key word signing whereas twelve other children with Down syndrome had previously received a similar intervention program but without manual signing. It should be noted that the parents in the sign-communication intervention program were urged to sign the *key words* in their spoken utterances. When the children were assessed between three and five years of age, the dozen children who had received the key word signing input were well ahead of the children in the non-signing comparison group on measures of language ability. A follow-up assessment conducted when the children were eight years old (five years after the intervention program had ended) revealed that the children who had participated in the signing program remained ahead on a range of skills, including language comprehension, interaction, reading, and writing. With regard to expressive language, eight children in the key word signing group and five in the comparison group used spoken language as their principal means of communication. Two children in the key word signing group relied mostly on signs, and one child in each group combined manual signs and spoken words.

Of the remaining children, five in the comparison group and only one in the key word signing group were reported as having no functional expressive language (Launonen, 1998, 2003, 2019a).[13] Evidently, there were both short- and long-term benefits from using manual signs early in the development of youngsters with Down syndrome. The use of signs with non-speaking children with Down syndrome may not only provide them with an initial communication system and facilitate their eventual transition to spoken language, but may also help to reduce their frustration and challenging behaviors (Remington & Clarke, 1996).

In conclusion, there are at least several advantages to teaching signs to children with Down syndrome. Not only does sign-communication training and teaching in early childhood not impede spoken language development, it actually appears to facilitate it. Furthermore, as these children's speech becomes more intelligible, they typically reduce their signing. A second advantage is that by teaching children with Down syndrome to sign, they learn how to communicate effectively with other people who may then respond to the children and be interested in their communications (Launonen, 2019b). Finally, a third advantage is that once these children learn to sign with family members and people at school, their level of frustration is noticeably reduced (Miller, Leddy, & Leavitt, 1999). In light of these advantages, it should not be surprising to learn that manual signing is a popular form of augmentative and alternative communication for children with Down syndrome (Brady, 2008; Kumin, 2003).

At the same time, it should be noted that children with Down syndrome who are taught to sign also may show impairments in their use of signs, especially with regard to morphosyntactic skills. In a case study of hearing, identical twin girls with Down syndrome who were born to Deaf parents in the U.K. (Woll & Grove, 1996), the researchers reported that the bilingual girls had difficulties with both their spoken English and their use of British Sign Language (BSL). Consistent with expectations, assessments showed that the twins' nonverbal IQ and visual and motor skills were areas of relative strength in comparison with their verbal skills. However, when tested on their receptive and productive BSL signing skills, both girls showed difficulties with representing

---

13 One family in the comparison group elected not to participate in the follow-up assessment.

spatial relationships between objects in a way that is typical of adult BSL signers (who depict these relationships based on the location of their signs). Both twins had significant trouble modifying BSL signs to reflect plurality as well. On a third task, one girl correctly modified signs based on size and shape, whereas the other twin was less successful doing so. The girls, however, were adept at distinguishing between related noun-verb pairs. Taken together, these results show that certain sign forms, in particular those that require syntactic markings of spatial location, were an area of particular difficulty for the girls. Other studies have also suggested that children with Down syndrome may experience deficits in spatial representation (Carretti, Lanfranchi, & Mammarella, 2013; Uecker et al., 1993; Vallar & Papagno, 1993; Yang, Conners, & Merrill, 2014) and that these deficits may persist (Woll & Grove, 2019).

In a follow-up study of the bilingual twins when they were sixteen, their problems with BSL spatial grammar with regard to verbs remained. Also, both girls' noun/verb distinctions had declined quite a bit as well (Woll & Grove, 2019). Their skills with size and shape modifiers differed with one girl scoring perfectly but the other girl scoring poorly. However, both girls did relatively well on size, shape, and plurality modifications, and one girl understood some classifier constructions. These findings show that specific sign language skills in persons with Down syndrome may not be static over time — they can either improve or decline. Whether such changes are due to a change in language environment and input (e.g., having less consistent exposure to BSL, leading to a decrease in signing skills), a personal preference for the speech modality, or syndrome-related declines in memory as individuals age remains to be seen.

Angelman Syndrome

Some individuals identified with Angelman syndrome might also benefit from sign-communication programs. Persons with Angelman syndrome are often described as having a severe intellectual disability, a happy disposition, lacking movement coordination, and rarely producing recognizable spoken words (Micheletti et al., 2016; Pearson et al., 2019; Quinn & Rowland, 2017; Smith et al., 1997; Trillingsgaard & Ostergaard, 2004). The difficulties that persons with Angelman syndrome experience in controlling voluntary muscle movements may account in part for their frequent absence of spoken language (Penner et al., 1993). Another likely reason for the absence of spoken language in most children with Angelman syndrome is their lack of development of the arcuate fasciculus, the white matter tract that connects the language comprehension region with the speech-generating region of the brain (Wilson et al., 2011). Finally, a large percentage of persons with Angelman syndrome (80-90%) have some form of epilepsy (Conant, Thibert, & Thiele, 2009; Micheletti et al., 2016) and all of the ten participants in one Italian study had neurovisual impairments that could have impacted upon their daily activities and functioning (Micheletti et al., 2016).

The difficulties in coordinating muscular movements (ataxia) that may inhibit spoken language use by persons with Angelman syndrome would be expected to similarly affect their acquisition of manual signs. Nevertheless, there have been occasional reports of successful sign learning and usage in some individuals with Angelman syndrome (Didden et al., 2009; Pearson et al., 2019; Quinn & Rowland, 2017). For example, the four non-speaking children with Angelman syndrome studied by Smith et al. (1997) acquired between eight and thirty-five different signs, although it should be noted that three of these children had only relatively mild motor impairments. In another study, Clayton-Smith (1993) examined eighty-two patients with Angelman syndrome. Although the ability to use some sign language was reported for 90% of them, this signing consisted mostly of "personal" signs or gestures. These "personal" signs were based on gestures that a specific individual with Angelman syndrome would produce; these existing gestures were then adapted for communicative purposes with that person. A much lower proportion of the patients, 20%, was able to use Makaton Vocabulary signs. Apparently, not all of the individuals could master the greater complexity of the Makaton signs despite substantial input from both parents and professionals.

In recent years, there has been increased interest in the use of the gestures that individual children with Angelman syndrome already produce as the basis for an effective communication system. Two of the obstacles to the more widespread implementation of such a system were to get children with Angelman syndrome to use the gestures in spontaneous communication and to expand the use of the gestures to more communication partners in a wider array of settings. Calculator and Diaz-Caneja Sela (2015), using an approach similar to "personal" signs that they termed "natural gestures," succeeded in establishing some spontaneous communicative behaviors in several children with Angelman syndrome. According to the investigators, "The idea is to take actions individuals already associate with objects and events, based on their existing behaviours, and then shape them into purposeful communicative behaviours" (Calculator & Diaz-Caneja Sela, 2015, p. 148). Progress also has been made in getting parents of individuals with Angelman syndrome to establish programs using natural gestures in their homes, thus expanding the range of settings where such gestures are used (Calculator, 2016). A remaining obstacle to more widespread use of this natural gesture or personal sign approach is that because of the idiosyncratic nature of many of these children's gestures or signs, a number of potential communication partners will likely not recognize the meanings of the gestures and react appropriately. Regardless, in light of the difficulties many children with Angelman syndrome experience in acquiring signs from existing signed languages or sign systems, this approach of adapting gestures that the children already make for communication purposes would appear to have considerable promise.

It should be recognized that the communicative behaviors of children with Angelman syndrome vary quite widely. For example, some individuals with Angelman syndrome, while unable or unwilling to produce manual signs or gestures themselves, are able to communicate by manipulating their therapists' or caregivers' hands into recognizable signs (Pearson et al., 2019; Summers & Szatmari, 2009). Moreover, when a questionnaire was administered to twenty families of children with Angelman syndrome, it indicated that half of the children used signs; seven of them communicated spontaneously by producing signs (Alvares & Downing, 1998). The investigators concluded that manual communication, either signs or gestures, appeared "to be the preferred expressive modality for most individuals" (p. 21) with Angelman syndrome. In a review of the expressive communication skills of 300 persons with Angelman syndrome in the United States who were in the early developmental stages of communication (Quinn & Rowland, 2017), 40% of the participants used pointing gestures and 26% used manual signs. Most of these participants communicated to get or obtain something, to refuse something, or for social interaction purposes; many fewer communicated to exchange information (Quinn & Rowland, 2017). The authors, however, noted that their study did not include data from higher-functioning individuals with Angelman syndrome and thus they could not provide any insight into the use and purposes of gestures or manual signs by persons who were more developmentally advanced. Finally, it should be noted that the utilization of speech-generating devices to facilitate the communication of children with Angelman syndrome also has been reported to be a frequently used approach (Calculator, 2013b).

Some of the wide variability in communication development outcomes seen across participants in different studies may be attributable to the specific genetic mechanisms responsible for the various forms of Angelman syndrome. Those children who did not have the maternal chromosomal deletion form of Angelman syndrome were found to have better communication skills, including the use and understanding of spoken language, manual signs, and gestures (Calculator, 2013a; Jolleff et al., 2006; Pearson et al., 2019; Quinn & Rowland, 2017). Moreover, in general, those children with a severe level of intellectual disability as opposed to those with a profound level, who lived at home rather than at a residential facility, and who had no epilepsy, were the children who engaged more often in successful communication (Didden et al., 2009).

Complicating Factors

Although many intervention programs for young children and students with Down syndrome and other forms of intellectual disability reported considerable success in sign learning (Abrahamsen et al., 1991; Blischak, Loncke, & Waller, 1997; Kiernan et al., 1982; Romski & Sevcik, 1997; Toth, 2009), youngsters in a number of other programs failed to make substantial progress. The results of two longitudinal studies of sign language learning in students with a severe or profound intellectual disability underscored the limited progress some participants made. In one study, the students' signing skills were assessed after a mean training duration of nearly three years (Bryen, Goldman, & Quinlisk-Gill, 1988). These youngsters imitated an average of 9.2 signs and spontaneously used an average of only 4.2 signs. In the second study (Kahn, 1996), manual signs were taught to thirty-four children over a four-year period. Twenty of them failed to use a single sign spontaneously or independently. Although the remaining children were more successful (six formed sign combinations), the finding that the majority made very little progress learning to sign should make one cautious about expecting significantly positive outcomes in some children with a severe or profound intellectual disability.

One explanation advanced for the limited progress in spontaneous signing manifested by some persons with an intellectual disability was the "dismally limited" sign usage of staff members (Bryen & McGinley, 1991). Staff members at a community residence for individuals with intellectual disabilities were found to have sign vocabularies only slightly larger than the residents and to rarely interact with them through signs. These sign interactions also tended to occur in limited settings, rather than being incorporated in a naturalistic way throughout the entire day. Furthermore, the sign vocabulary used was not especially meaningful or tailored to the particular interests of the children, thereby limiting their motivation to use the signs (Bryen & McGinley, 1991). A more supportive signing environment, together with a simplified form of signing, might have enhanced the residents' sign-communication skills. Positive links have been established between the use of signs by teachers and staff members and higher signing levels by individuals with disabilities in school, day care, and group home settings (Grove & McDougall, 1991; Rombouts, Maes, & Zink, 2017a, 2017b, 2017c, 2018a, 2018b; Rombouts et al., 2019).

Even with an environment that is more supportive of signing and that employs manual signs that are easier to form, some individuals with an intellectual disability may never make substantial progress in signing. These persons might benefit from other augmentative and alternative communication systems (some of which are discussed in Chapter 5). Deciding which system to use will likely require considerable care. For example, one might intuitively believe that learning to point to pictures on a communication board or computer screen to indicate items would be an easier task than learning to produce signs to identify those same items. Yet, when a pair of studies (Sundberg & Sundberg, 1990; Wraikat, Sundberg, & Michael, 1991) systematically probed the use of manual signs and pointing with minimally verbal adults who had an intellectual disability, the clear majority of the adults were more successful in acquiring and using signs. It should be noted that the participants in these studies did not have discernible motor impairments that might have made their production of signs more difficult. Moreover, dynamic or moving stimuli may convey more information than static stimuli, such as photographs, thus facilitating the performance of persons with intellectual disabilities (see Moore, 2001).

Even among those persons who are quite successful in acquiring large expressive sign vocabularies, their sign usage typically remains relatively basic (Grove, 2019a; Grove & Dockrell, 2000). In particular, signing youngsters appear to experience a good deal of difficulty in making the transition from one- or two-sign utterances to mastering syntactic rules. Although a lack of fluent sign language input by their teachers, caregivers, and fellow students may account for some of this limited sign complexity, the youngsters' cognitive, language, and motor impairments probably play important roles as well. Despite these obstacles, however, the majority of the ten children in the Grove and Dockrell (2000) study made spontaneous, meaning-based modifications to their signs; most such changes were made on iconic verbs. Thus, it appears that persons with intellectual disabilities are capable of making creative changes to their signs even without prior prompting or modeling by others. It is therefore important for teachers and caregivers to watch out for, identify, and capitalize upon the use of such sign modifications as a way to build the children's nascent syntactic skills.

In recent years, investigators have deliberately made an effort to increase the complexity of the meanings that children with intellectual disabilities are capable of expressing through manual signs. These efforts have focused on getting children with moderate and severe intellectual disabilities and poor speech intelligibility to modify their signs to express more complex meanings. As examples, a sign's direction of movement might be changed to indicate who is the recipient of an action, a sign's width might be increased or decreased to indicate an object's relative size, or a sign might be repeated to indicate plurality. By learning these and other changes or modifications in how signs may be formed, a number of children with intellectual disabilities have been shown to be able to convey more complex meanings through signs (Molteni et al., 2010; Rudd, Grove, & Pring, 2007). Furthermore, these interventions can take advantage of modifications that the children are already making (Grove, 2019a; Rudd et al., 2007).

Finally, because many individuals with cognitive impairments have multiple disabilities, analysis of the usefulness of or progress in manual sign intervention of such persons can be quite complicated (Bonvillian & Nelson, 1978). Various medical factors and additional disabilities, although not directly related to a particular individual's level of cognitive functioning, may make the task of signing much more difficult. Teachers and caregivers may need to evaluate how much to emphasize signing as a communication skill and how much to focus on other methods with a particular individual. At the same time, caregivers should give serious consideration to using (or at least trying out or experimenting with) a sign-communication system that is based on signs that are more iconic and that have been modified to make their handshapes easier to form and their movements easier to remember. Systems such as Amer-Ind and the Simplified Sign System may produce better results with regard to sign comprehension, retention, and production than full and genuine sign languages or other sign systems.

Cerebral Palsy

Cerebral palsy occurs when children experience damage to the nervous system before, during, or just after birth. Long believed to be the consequence of an inadequate supply of oxygen during the birth process, in recent years there has been a major change in our understanding of the causes of cerebral palsy. Today, in preterm (premature) infants, cerebral palsy is seen as primarily the product of a cerebral hemorrhage (extensive bleeding from the rupture of a blood vessel in the brain) or of an injury to the white matter of the brain. With advances in medical care in recent decades, there has been an increase in survival rates after preterm births; this increase in survival rates has also resulted in an increase in the incidence of cerebral palsy (Krägeloh-Mann & Cans, 2009). The majority of cases of cerebral palsy, however, are the result of full-term pregnancies. In full-term infants, cerebral palsy is believed to be the product of a brain malformation during intrauterine development (Pellegrino, 2007). A disruption of the supply of oxygen to the brain during the birth process accounts for only a minority of the cases of cerebral palsy (Pellegrino, 2007). Although a number of children with cerebral palsy have some degree of intellectual impairment, many others have unimpaired intellects and a proportion fall into the gifted range (Stadskleiv et al., 2018).

As a result of abnormalities in their developing brains, children with cerebral palsy have disorders of posture and movement. These disorders of posture and movement, moreover, are both non-progressive (i.e., not increasing in severity or extent) and permanent. In addition to difficulties in their execution of motor movements, individuals with cerebral palsy also show deficits in their planning of such movements (Steenbergen & Gordon, 2006). The motor speech problems often evident in children with cerebral palsy (Pirila et al., 2007) are probably the outcome of disturbances or difficulties in their neuromuscular control of the speech mechanism. These neuromotor impairments may prevent typical spoken language development. This atypical spoken language development often is evident early, as infants with cerebral palsy may show delayed babbling and restricted phonetic repertoires (Levin, 1999). In general, those children with more severe gross motor impairments also had poorer communication skills (Coleman et al., 2013).

There are four main types of cerebral palsy: spastic, dyskinetic, ataxic, and mixed (National Center on Birth Defects and Developmental Disabilities, 2019). Spastic cerebral palsy, the most common form of cerebral palsy, is characterized by increased muscle tone and stiff muscles. It is subdivided into unilateral (also known as spastic hemiplegia or hemiparesis) and bilateral forms that include diplegia and quadriplegia (Anderson et al., 2008). Those persons with the most severe form of spastic cerebral palsy, quadriplegia, often have intellectual disabilities, seizures, vision problems, hearing difficulties, and/or issues with the production of speech. Dyskinetic cerebral palsy (also known as athetoid, dystonic, or choreoathetoid cerebral palsy) involves uncontrollable movements of parts of the body; muscle tone in persons with this subtype can alternate between too tight and too loose. In the Anderson (2008) study, most persons with dyskinetic cerebral palsy had severely impaired speech or no speech and 42% had epilepsy. Ataxic cerebral palsy causes problems in balance and coordination, having an effect on the rate of an individual's movement as well as his or her control of fine motor skills. Persons with mixed cerebral palsy experience symptoms of a combination of types (NCBDDD, 2019).

Many children with cerebral palsy have intact or relatively intact cognitive and receptive language abilities, but, as a result of their neuromuscular deficits, are unable to effectively communicate orally. Programs for these children frequently are able to take advantage of their ability to understand spoken language. Other children with cerebral palsy may have substantial hearing loss, vision problems, seizures, or cognitive impairments (Andersen et al., 2008; Bottos et al., 1999; Chan et al., 2005; Himmelmann et al., 2006; Pellegrino, 2007; Reid et al., 2011; Stadskleiv et al., 2018; Zhang, Oskoui, & Shevell, 2015). Among these additional impairments are a number of children who are also diagnosed as having autism spectrum disorder (Kilincaslan & Mukaddes, 2009). These additional disabilities may inhibit the use of communication programs based on the children's understanding of spoken language alone.

In the Andersen study (2008), Norwegian children born with cerebral palsy during a three-year period were examined extensively. This investigation represented an effort to provide an account of the varying abilities and different impairments associated with cerebral palsy in a national cohort. Of the children studied in-depth, 28% had severely impaired or no spoken language. Correspondingly, it should be pointed out that 72% of the participating children were assessed as having either normal speech or impaired speech that was still understandable. These findings indicate that while most children with cerebral palsy apparently will be able to rely primarily on spoken language to communicate, a sizeable minority will likely need a form of alternative or augmentative communication to interact effectively.

The Norwegian study (Andersen et al., 2008) provided information on a number of other impairments associated with cerebral palsy as well. Of those children whose cognitive development was assessed, 31% evidenced intellectual disability as determined by scores below 70 on IQ tests. In addition, 5% of the children examined had severely impaired vision and 4% had severely impaired hearing.[14] Finally, 35% of

---

14   A group of researchers (Reid et al., 2011) performed an international literature review of fourteen studies that included data on hearing loss in persons with cerebral palsy in Australia, Finland, Iceland, Ireland, Norway, Quebec, the U.K., and the United States. They found that the mean percentage of persons having cerebral palsy and

the children showed severely impaired fine motor functioning of their hands. When examined for typology, 33% of the Norwegian children in the study had spastic unilateral CP, 49% had spastic bilateral CP, 6% had dyskinetic CP, 5% had ataxic CP, and 7% of the children were not classified (Andersen et al., 2008). The authors reported that the distribution of the various subtypes of cerebral palsy in Norway was generally consistent with that found in Sweden (Himmelmann et al., 2006), Australia (Howard et al., 2005), Hong Kong (Chan et al., 2005), and Italy (Bottos et al., 1999).

In Norway, greater impairments in gross and fine motor functions were observed in spastic bilateral and dyskinetic populations (Andersen et al., 2008; see also Stadskleiv et al., 2018). The majority of the dyskinetic population and 35% of the spastic bilateral population had severely impaired or no speech. Intellectual disability was seen in significant numbers in spastic bilateral, dyskinetic, and ataxic subtypes but less so in the spastic unilateral subtype (Andersen et al., 2008; see also Stadskleiv et al., 2018). However, recent researchers note that it is important to adapt the response mode on tests of cognitive ability for persons with severe speech and motor disorders to include eye gaze (Stadskleiv et al., 2018). Previous determinations that did not allow for this alternative response mode (i.e., those dependent on verbal responses or pointing with one hand) may have underestimated the actual level of intelligence in such individuals.

Taken together, these findings draw attention to the wide range of disabilities often present in a population of children with cerebral palsy. This wide range in impairments also would appear to make it unlikely that a single form of augmentative and alternative communication would meet the needs or abilities of all children with cerebral palsy with spoken language impairments. Indeed, in one study of fourteen

---

severe hearing loss in these studies was 3%. The same researchers also recorded a similar level of severe-profound hearing loss in their own study of 685 children with cerebral palsy born between 1999 and 2004 in Australia (Reid et al., 2011). Of the forty-eight children with hearing loss in that population, most had sensorineural or mixed sensorineural/conductive hearing loss, although the vast majority of them were not due to genetic causes (unlike the wider population of persons with sensorineural hearing loss). In fact, no cause was identified for half (twenty-four) of the children. In addition, many of the Australian children with hearing impairment were also identified as having quadriplegia, serious motor problems, intellectual disability, visual impairment, and/or epilepsy (Reid et al., 2011).

children with cerebral palsy who used augmentative and alternative communication systems, eight relied primarily on Blissymbols (a form of pictographic line drawings), five primarily on manual signs, and one primarily on spoken language, with all the children using more than one system to communicate depending on the situation (Sundqvist & Rönnberg, 2010; see also Sandberg & Dahlgren, 2012). In another recent report (Watson & Pennington, 2015), the Picture Exchange Communication System or PECS (Bondy & Frost, 2002; see Chapter 5) also was identified by speech-language pathologists as a communication intervention approach that they used frequently in their interactions with children with cerebral palsy.

As noted earlier in this chapter, some children with cerebral palsy and an intellectual disability who failed to make progress learning to speak were able to learn to communicate through mimetic gestures (Levett, 1969, 1971). Those individuals with more severe motor impairments, however, may be unable to learn to communicate primarily through a sign or gestural system. These youngsters may be better served by learning to use a communication board or a system that relies on hand pointing or eye placement. These systems require only limited motor abilities to be effective. It should be noted that in a survey of 181 children with cerebral palsy in Hong Kong (Chan et al., 2005), 36 were rated as nonverbal. Of this nonverbal subgroup, six used communication books or boards and five used manual signs; the others communicated through simple gestures, vocalizations, and crying. It is possible that the provision of better and more consistent intervention support to parents could help the latter group of children to use one or more augmentative and alternative communication methods.

There are few systematic, large-scale studies of the relative success of using different non-oral programs with persons with cerebral palsy. This situation may seem somewhat surprising in light of the relatively high incidence of cerebral palsy — estimated in the U.S. (and in other developed countries) at about 1 in 500 children (Bottos et al., 1999; Himmelmann et al., 2006; Howard et al., 2005; Pakula, Van Naarden Braun, & Yeargin-Allsopp, 2009; Winter et al., 2002) — and the substantial frequency of speech problems in these children (Yorkston et al., 1999; Zhang et al., 2015). An important reason behind this dearth of large-scale studies is that most children with cerebral palsy have associated conditions or impairments that make systematic comparisons difficult to conduct — various types of cerebral palsy present with different levels of cognitive ability and distributions of motor skills. Regardless, a certain pattern of placement in communication intervention programs seems to have emerged for children who have not acquired adequate spoken language skills. Those children with more severe motor impairments and milder cognitive impairments typically were placed in programs that required only limited motor skills (e.g., programs utilizing communication boards that included printed words, letters, or pictographic line drawings such as Blissymbols). Those children with more severe cognitive impairments, but more intact motor abilities, often were placed in programs that utilized signs (Kiernan et al., 1982; Udwin & Yule, 1990). Hearing-impaired children with cerebral palsy also may be placed in a program that employs manual signs and graphic symbols (Hooper, Connell, & Flett, 1987).

One of the few systematic studies of sign acquisition in children with cerebral palsy (Udwin & Yule, 1990) followed twenty children in Great Britain as they were taught signs from the Makaton Vocabulary. This study also underscored some of the limitations of many sign-communication training and teaching programs. After 10.5 months of sign instruction, the children learned to produce an average of 28.2 different signs and to understand an average of 34.4 signs. These relatively substantial average scores, however, masked the finding that there were wide individual differences in the number of signs learned; the least able signer, for example, acquired only a single sign. Fourteen of the children continued in the sign-training program for eighteen more months and their sign vocabularies showed additional growth. These children produced an average of 65.1 different signs and understood an average of 72.1 signs. Thus, for most of the participants, increased duration in sign instruction was positively related to vocabulary size.

Although the children's acquisition of a core sign vocabulary represented an improvement in their language and communication skills, it should be recognized that these numbers contrast markedly with the thousands of words that children without disabling conditions acquire in their childhoods. Furthermore, most of the sign productions of the children with cerebral palsy were composed of only a single sign; only about 12% of their sign productions were multi-sign combinations.

In their effort to understand the sign-learning environments of children with cerebral palsy, Udwin and Yule (1991) examined the extent to which the children were exposed to signs. They observed that the children received between one hour and one-and-a-half hours of formal sign instruction per week. Exposure to signs outside of formal instruction, however, was quite limited. Relatively few of the children's teachers took advantage of opportunities to use signs outside of the sign-training sessions. Exposure to signs similarly was quite inconsistent in most of the children's homes. This occurred even when the parents had received training and instruction in the use of the Makaton vocabulary. This lack of sign exposure outside of the formal teaching setting may not only have restricted the children's sign learning but also adversely affected their spontaneous use of signs.

Although most individuals with impaired spoken language skills eventually make greater progress with signs when signs are introduced in early childhood, there may still be benefits to introducing signs at a later age. Tavares and Peixoto (2003) reported that adolescents with cerebral palsy often were able to make progress in learning to sign despite not being shown how to communicate with manual signs until late childhood or adolescence. The acquisition of signs, moreover, enabled these youngsters to become more independent through their more effective communicative interactions.

Another study into the use of signs to promote language development with similarly-aged individuals with cerebral palsy was conducted in the U.K. in the 1970s (Fenn & Rowe, 1975). Seven male students at the Meldreth Manor School in Royston, Hertfordshire who were between the ages of ten and thirteen years old were taught signs from the Paget-Gorman Sign System. Six of the boys had athetoid (dyskinetic) cerebral palsy (four were classified as severe, one moderate, and one mild) and the other boy had ataxic cerebral palsy. In addition, five of the boys were severely deaf and the remaining two had some degree of hearing impairment. Since earlier attempts to teach other students syntax through use of fully signed sentences were ineffectual (most students only used single signs), the authors decided to adopt a more limited or "telegraphic [approach] in which only the essential information in a sentence is signed in the early stages" (Fenn & Rowe, 1975, p. 4). This early key word signing approach initially focused on nouns and then expanded to include adjectives and verbs in a phrasal structure. The signs were taught to the seven students in naturalistic settings or situations (a milieu or incidental teaching approach) and were relevant to the boys' experiences. Furthermore, the researchers made sure that all of the staff members at the school were taught and regularly trained on the use of the signs, although they conceded that they could not guarantee the level of general sign exposure that the boys received. When the boys were assessed on their comprehension of simple sentences six months later, most demonstrated knowledge of a variety of lexical relations, although their word order was inconsistent (Fenn & Rowe, 1975). In addition, they were able to spontaneously combine signs and had even started to sign to one another. Thus, it appears that the researchers were quite successful in increasing sign usage and lexical knowledge in this group of students.

Finally, individuals with cerebral palsy or speech disorders who have at least some useful spoken language skills might wish to consider combining iconic gestures with their speech when they communicate. We say this for two reasons. One is that iconic gestures themselves often are an effective way to communicate and may be easily understood by communication partners and also by persons in the environment who are not familiar with the individual or with signing (Powell & Clibbens, 1994). The other reason is that when iconic gestures accompany spoken language, the speech of persons with cerebral palsy often is more intelligible (Hustad & Garcia, 2005), as is the speech of persons with Down syndrome (Powell & Clibbens, 1994). Greatly enhanced intelligibility of communication also is evident when signs are combined with speech in individuals with Cri du chat syndrome (Erlenkamp & Kristoffersen, 2010). Individuals with Cri du chat syndrome, a rare genetic disorder, have substantial intellectual disability and show either markedly delayed expressive language or fail to develop any recognizable spoken language. This increase in intelligibility when spoken language is accompanied by iconic gestures may be a result of the speakers slowing down their rate of articulation and their overall rate of speaking.

Recommendations for Enhancing
the Sign-Learning Environment[15]

When planning for the adoption of communication intervention programs with children with disabilities, it is important to first be aware of and, if possible, proactively address any overarching concerns or negative attitudes that may impact the children's general educational environment. As the education of persons with disabilities does not occur in a vacuum, but instead exists within an evolving matrix of wider legal, political, social, and other environmental variables, it is important to be aware that these factors can impact the decision-making processes of teachers, staff, and caregivers. Furthermore, those educators and advocates who view the inclusion of persons with disabilities through more of a human rights model or social diversity lens understand the importance of addressing structural and systemic barriers (Degener, 2016; Guralnick, 2017; Light & McNaughton, 2015). Teachers' and caregivers' attitudes are influenced by the political atmosphere with regard to official educational policy (e.g., whether there are laws requiring integration of special students into mainstream settings), the stance taken by school administrators and leaders toward inclusion, and the level of ongoing support provided to them in the form of resource materials, equipment, training, and personnel (Avramidis & Norwich, 2002; Budiyanto et al., 2018; Goldbart & Marshall, 2004; Light & McNaughton, 2015; Singh et al., 2017). In general, studies have shown that the more experience a teacher has with children with disabilities, the better and more positive his or her attitude toward their inclusion in mainstream settings (Avramidis & Norwich, 2002). Likewise, the more experience that teachers and staff members have with a particular communication intervention program, the greater their positivity toward it and the greater the chance of its successful implementation (Cologon & Mevawalla, 2018).

---

15 In Chapter 9, we discuss various teaching or training approaches that we believe will foster the individual sign learner's acquisition and use of Simplified Signs. Here, we comment on findings about the use of signs by teachers and staff members in educational and residential settings and by family members at home. These findings make it clear that if one wishes to provide a highly effective sign-learning environment, then an effort also needs to be made to facilitate sign acquisition and usage by those persons who care for and interact with the principal sign learner.

If the decision is made to implement a sign intervention program for non-speaking individuals with an intellectual disability, cerebral palsy, autism spectrum disorder, or aphasia, then an effort also should be made to facilitate the sign learning and usage of those persons caring for and interacting with them (Budiyanto et al., 2018; Cologon & Mevawalla, 2018; Dolly & Noble, 2018; Glacken et al., 2019; Grove & McDougall, 1991; Kent-Walsh et al., 2015; Launonen, 2019b; Light & McNaughton, 2015; Mackenzie, Cologon, & Fenech, 2016; Rombouts et al., 2019; Sheehy & Duffy, 2009; Woll & Barnett, 1998). All too often, programs have focused almost entirely on the sign learning of the non-speaking participants and their language teachers, while neglecting the signing abilities of all of the other persons with whom the participants come into contact (Bryen et al., 1988). When a signing program is implemented on a wider scale within a class or school, signing is often viewed with much less stigmatization than if signing is only used by a few people in limited contexts (Brereton, 2008; Budiyanto et al., 2018; Cologon & Mevawalla, 2018; Mistry & Barnes, 2013; Woll & Barnett, 1998).

This type of inclusive educational model, in which the needs of persons with disabilities are considered and then enacted on a broad scale to the benefit of everyone (not just those persons with disabilities), is consistent with the concept of universal design for learning (Meyer & Rose, 2000; Spratt & Florian, 2015). In this model, teachers view each and every student as an individual and take his/her needs into account when designing lesson plans. Indeed, it is a recognition that teachers already make adaptations for their students, regardless of whether labels are applied to them or not (Mackenzie et al., 2016; Spratt & Florian, 2015). Changes are also incorporated into the curriculum materials to support students who learn better through media such as illustrations, movies, games, audio, and software (Meyer & Rose, 2000). Such an approach may also include more collaborative efforts among children in a classroom, rather than focusing solely on individual work or projects (Spratt & Florian, 2015). A further consideration is that sign-communication programs often have utilized only a small portion of a participant's day for sign instruction and usage rather than embedding signing throughout the entire day. Although this approach is quite typical, it is not the optimal way to enhance signing skills or to maximize progress.

A range of programs for non-speaking children have been examined for their effectiveness in increasing the children's manual signing (Schepis et al., 1982). Those programs that encouraged caregivers to increase the amount of their sign communication throughout the day and in different situations tended to have children who signed more and who engaged in more spontaneous sign interactions (Dodd & Gorey, 2014; Launonen, 2019b; Rombouts et al., 2017a, 2017b). For sign intervention programs to be optimally successful, individuals should be immersed in an environment where most persons consistently rely on signs to communicate (Rombouts et al., 2019; Woll & Barnett, 1998). Because of the importance of family members in caring for and interacting with individuals with disabilities, it would be a good idea to include these family members in the decision-making process about which communication intervention systems to employ and how to implement them (Goldbart & Marshall, 2004; Granlund et al., 2008; Mandak et al., 2017). Regardless of which augmentative and alternative communication approach is selected for a child's instruction, increasing adult input at home is related to greater vocabulary growth by the child (Brady et al., 2013; Launonen, 2019b).

There seem to be several ways for families and institutions to enhance non-speaking individuals' sign language skills. For those who live at home, it would be extremely helpful if their parents, siblings, and other family members learned to sign and then used signs when interacting with them (Glacken et al., 2019; Launonen, 2019b; Smith, Romski, & Sevcik, 2013). The use of signs by family members would give these non-speaking individuals much more practice signing, as well as the opportunity to use signs outside of the school setting. This extension of sign usage beyond the educational setting is important because it will reinforce a child's spontaneous efforts at sign communication across a variety of environments. Involvement of family members in signing likely would also foster closer ties between the non-speaking children and their families and might help alleviate the frustration these children encounter when they are not able to communicate effectively with others (Glacken et al., 2019; Goldbart & Marshall, 2004; Grinnell, Detamore, & Lipke, 1976; Marshall & Goldbart, 2008). Furthermore, by embedding communication interventions throughout the day in natural settings, not only will the children make progress in their communication skills, but the level of parental stress typically will decline as well (Glacken et al., 2019; Guralnick, 2017; Koegel, Bimbela, & Schreibman, 1996; Launonen, 2019b; Singh et al., 2017).

The signing skills of many staff members at institutions or programs for non-speaking children should be improved as well. In many instances, it is only those teachers and language therapists who have direct and frequent contact with the children who learn signs. Other staff members continue to interact among themselves and with these youngsters exclusively in spoken language. Such a situation not only fails to take advantage of opportunities to enhance a sign learner's communication skills, but also may unintentionally convey the impression that signing is quite limited in its usefulness. In one of the early studies that examined the impact of a full-time signing environment, non-speaking participants with an intellectual disability showed rapid mastery of signing skills (Kopchick, Rombach, & Smilovitz, 1975).

Likewise, when support staff in a facility for adults with intellectual disabilities used key word signing in their communicative interactions in an immersion approach, there was a significant increase in sign usage (Grove & Walker, 1990; Meuris, Maes, & Zink, 2015; Schlosser & Sigafoos, 2006). Key word signing confers an additional benefit: it provides information to the learner in more than one modality and thus increases the chance that the individual will be able to understand the communication (Loncke et al., 2006). Furthermore, speaking and signing at the same time typically slows down the rate of speech, thus providing more time for persons with communication disabilities to comprehend the message (Loncke et al., 2012). These characteristics of speaking and signing the key words at the same time may be especially helpful to persons with multiple disabilities such as intellectual disability, visual impairment, hearing impairment, or autism. If such an individual misses some of the information contained in one modality (e.g., the auditory input), he or she may be able to pick up the same information from the other modality (e.g., the signed input).

Moreover, staff members in residential settings appear to be able to acquire a small number of useful signs each week without an undue expenditure of time or funds (Spragale & Micucci, 1990). In fact, if deliberately trained to combine signs, both teachers and staff members can successfully learn and model multi-sign utterances for students, thereby increasing the likelihood that the students themselves will combine signs (Dolly & Noble, 2018; Grove, 2019a). Once such communication partners learn how to accurately form a core vocabulary of useful signs, providing these individuals with some form of portable prompt system (e.g., reference card) as a memory aid is likely to prove helpful to them (Chadwick & Jolliffe, 2008). Such a portable prompt system or reference card probably should include a picture or drawing of each sign in the core vocabulary, each sign's translation or language equivalent, and a brief description of how each sign is made.

Even with some minimal training in signing, however, many staff members may be reluctant to use those signs because of a lack of confidence, the increased cognitive effort required to remember and produce the signs in the early stages of their training, or the perception that signing is only useful when spoken language communication fails (Rombouts et al., 2017a). Such attitudes and perceptions should be addressed during staff training sessions by stressing the importance of having staff model sign use throughout the child's environment not only so that the child can learn the signs, but also so that he or she can maintain sign use over longer periods of time. Furthermore, staff sign training, much like the sign training of persons with disabilities, should not be limited to discrete teaching sessions but instead should be incorporated in natural settings throughout the day with appropriate feedback from more experienced and trained signers and with open access to teaching materials (Dolly & Noble, 2018; Kent-Walsh et al., 2015; Rombouts et al., 2017a). Consistently reinforcing the use of signs at various points in the day, including during often-neglected times such as meals and non-communicative (i.e., crafts, play) activities (Grove & McDougall, 1991; Rombouts et al., 2018a, 2018b) helps to establish signing as a natural habit for everyone involved. Overall, when staff members at institutions commit to providing a more complete sign-communication environment, and when they receive consistent training and positive reinforcement to do so, they appear to positively influence non-speaking individuals' sign mastery (Grove & McDougall, 1991; Guralnick, 2017; Kent-Walsh et al., 2015; Mellon, 2001; Rombouts et al., 2019; Wooderson, Cuskelly, & Meyer, 2014).

Although there have been a number of attempts to create sign intervention programs for non-speaking children with an intellectual disability, the findings of a systematic review showed that only a minority of the programs significantly increased the children's competence in communicating with others (Bryen & Joyce, 1985). Communicative competence was defined as the ability to use signs to effectively convey one's needs, rather than the ability to produce signs out of context. The investigators tried to determine which sign intervention programs led youngsters to use signs to enhance their interactions with others across a range of settings, not just in the classroom. Two differences in the context of sign training and teaching were shown to be related to whether programs were successful or not in fostering communicative competence: (1) successful programs most often were those that used signs throughout much of the children's environment as opposed to those programs that relied on isolated sign-training sessions, and (2) successful programs also emphasized spontaneous sign usage as one of their goals. In fact, the importance placed on spontaneous signing was highly related to the participants' retention and use of signs (Bryen & Joyce, 1985).

In addition, teachers, staff, and caregivers should help promote the use of signs between peers in classrooms and in other settings. Grove and McDougall (1991) found that much of the sign activity they observed in their study of signing by children with various disabilities was directed toward adults; many fewer signs were directed at other children in the classroom. The researchers suggested that direct intervention techniques, including teaching non-disabled peers to sign, may help to promote and support more communicative activity both in the classroom and during other school activities and playtime (Grove & McDougall, 1991). Schools that promote the learning of signs by all teachers, staff, and children have a significant positive effect on the children's sign use (Bryen & Joyce, 1985). This type of environment also promotes signing by persons with autism who are educated in inclusive, mainstream settings (Mackenzie et al., 2016).

One of the approaches related to increased signing and communicative competence is called an incidental or milieu[16] teaching program. This approach utilizes natural interactions between caregivers and non-speaking participants throughout the day for instructional purposes (Launonen 1996, 1998, 2003, 2019b; Light & McNaughton, 2015; Mancil,

---

16　The word *milieu* refers to the participant's natural environment.

2009; Schepis et al., 1982). Communication training focuses on what the participant is paying attention to and likely is interested in, as well as modeling correct communication at the appropriate level (Wright et al., 2013). With this approach, many participants engage in markedly more spontaneous signing and rely less on prompting from their teachers or caregivers. Also, when staff are more responsive to participants' sign communications (e.g., by imitating or repeating the signs that the participants produce), persons with disabilities have a greater likelihood of producing novel or spontaneous signs (Broberg, Ferm, & Thunberg, 2012; Dodd & Gorey, 2014; Rombouts et al., 2017b, 2017c, 2018b). It should be noted that the sustained interactions in sign on the part of caregivers and teachers or therapists often are critical in maintaining the participants' use of signs. Moreover, teaching parents to use naturalistic language intervention strategies (enhanced milieu teaching or EMT) with their preschool children with intellectual disabilities typically results in greater increases in language and communication skills than if only the therapists are trained (Kaiser & Roberts, 2013; Launonen, 2019b). Also, the effectiveness of parents' teaching of words and signs through EMT evidently can be improved if the parents are provided coaching and feedback from trained therapists (Glacken et al., 2019; Wright & Kaiser, 2017).

Although probably not all non-speaking persons can acquire manual signs without direct teaching, at least some individuals evidently can learn signs primarily through exposure to others' signing (Valentino & Shillingsburg, 2011). In future research, investigators might wisely incorporate an incidental or milieu teaching approach into their methods and try to maximize the opportunities for non-speaking individuals to learn that way. In addition, many young children with intellectual disabilities, including Down syndrome, benefit more in terms of vocabulary growth when milieu communication teaching occurs at a higher rather than lower frequency each week (Yoder et al., 2014; see also Guralnick, 2017).

Another approach likely to foster increased signing in language-limited individuals is to work with parents and other caregivers to enhance their responsiveness to the non-speaking or minimally verbal person's efforts at communication. In such an approach, parents would try to follow their children's leads and react to the children's acts of communication rather than direct the communication process themselves (Broberg et al., 2012; Fey et al., 2006; Girolametto, Sussman, & Weitzman, 2007; Guralnick, 2017; Mahoney et al., 2006; Ruble et al., 2008; Trivette, 2007; Van keer et al., 2017). The parents' behavior would thus be largely contingent on and responsive to their children's communicative acts rather than the other way around. One tool for measuring the communication of parents when interacting with their children who use signs or other augmentative and alternative communication techniques is the Responsive Augmentative and Alternative Communication Style (RAACS) scale (Broberg et al., 2012). Communicative strategies measured by this instrument include attending to and confirming the child's communication, adjusting physically to the child, giving the child space and time to communicate, clarifying one's own communication, focusing on the child's topic of interest, expanding upon the child's communicative efforts, using AAC, adapting to and engaging in the situation, and adjusting to the child's level of communication (Broberg et al., 2012, p. 249). Important outcomes of this responsive approach would be an increase in the children's initiation of engagements or social interactions, as well as improvements by young children with Down syndrome in their level of developmental functioning (Karaaslan & Mahoney, 2013).

Further examination of the efficacy of different sign intervention programs found that successful learning of a sign-communication system was related to several additional factors in the environment (Avramidis & Norwich, 2002; Bryen & Joyce, 1986; Budiyanto et al., 2018; Cologon & Mevawalla, 2018; Glacken et al., 2019; Goldbart & Marshall, 2004; Grove & McDougall, 1991; Kent-Walsh et al., 2015; Loeding, Zangari, & Lloyd, 1990; Marshall & Goldbart, 2008; Rombouts et al., 2017a, 2017b, 2017c, 2018a, 2018b; Sheehy & Duffy, 2009; Singh et al., 2017; Woll & Barnett, 1998). Those factors included the attitudes of teachers, caregivers, and parents toward the use of manual sign communication, in-service training in the use of a particular sign system, and the level of caregiver competence in a sign system. One interview study that elicited the thoughts of eighteen parents about using key word signing (Lámh) with their children occurred in Ireland (Glacken et al., 2019). Many of the parents commented on the process they went through to understand and accept the potential of using Lámh with their children, noting the importance that healthcare professionals played in allaying their concerns. Parents appreciated the tailored nature of their initial training in the system, but also stressed the need to have continued access to ongoing training, including supporting materials online, in order to keep up with their developing children's vocabulary needs (Glacken et al., 2019). Frustrations were also expressed by parents of children who used various augmentative and alternative communication (AAC) techniques, including signs, in the U.K. and in Malaysia (Goldbart & Marshall, 2004; Marshall & Goldbart, 2008; Singh et al., 2017). In these interview studies, the parents expressed concerns about their children's social inclusion, societal attitudes toward AAC, financing of the devices they used, the various roles the parents had to play, and the many demands placed on them. They also noted the lack of support from other members of the family, insufficient assistance from some teachers, and not receiving enough information or resource materials about AAC from professionals (Goldbart & Marshall, 2004; Marshall & Goldbart, 2008; Singh et al., 2017).

Taken together, these findings about the importance of the involvement of instructional staff and family members and the effectiveness of certain sign-training approaches make clear that to be maximally beneficial, a sign-communication program needs to focus on enhancing aspects of the settings in which sign teaching and use will take place. Parents, teachers, staff, and other caregivers should also be supportive of signing (or other means of augmentative and alternative communication) in the wider environment (i.e., at stores, parks, sporting events, medical offices, etc.) or with persons with whom the child comes into contact on a less regular basis (Collier, McGhie-Richmond, & Self, 2010; Light & McNaughton, 2015). Beginning the program of sign intervention early in children's development also is associated with considerably greater long-term progress in communication skills (Branson & Demchak, 2009; Clibbens, 2001; Launonen, 2019b; Millar et al., 2006). Furthermore, even when multimodal language intervention programs are effective in enhancing the communication skills of young children with intellectual disabilities, these programs may need to be maintained for a period of years to ensure these children's continued progress (van der Schuit et al., 2011a).

An additional factor that has not yet received much attention is the impact of the attitudes of a signer's peers toward the use of signs.

Whereas multiple studies have addressed the attitudes and concerns of teachers, support staff, professionals, and other adults, a recent study (Bowles & Frizelle, 2016) focused on young children's attitudes toward signing in a mainstream school setting. In this study, investigators interviewed eight children (four from one school, four from another school) who had a classmate with Down syndrome and who had all been taught Lámh. Each of the children was asked various questions about their knowledge of Lámh, including where the signs were used, who used them, and how they felt about the signs. The researchers found that all of the peers had positive attitudes toward signing and also recognized the importance of signing for the person who had Down syndrome (see also Glacken et al., 2019). Thus, it seems that the use of key word signing was not stigmatized in the eyes of the children. The children did, however, express concerns about remembering all of the signs, having a hard time making some of the signs, and being able to use the signs in unstructured settings. In response to these concerns, the authors suggested that teachers focus on a smaller group of high-frequency signs and take a more consistent approach to teaching them (Bowles & Frizelle, 2016). It is also possible that teaching signs that are more iconic and easily formed would have had an impact on these typically developing children's recall abilities.

Although a limited signing environment may constrain the children's development of signing skills, it was not the problem mentioned most frequently by the teachers and language therapists of students with neuromotor disabilities. Rather, these staff members underlined their difficulties in interpreting their students' signing (Grove, 1990). One resolution to this problem might be for the teachers and therapists to accept consistent approximations of the signs. Indeed, one student's rudimentary sign approximations were more easily understood than his indistinct vocalizations (Grove, 1990). Another possible strategy would be to use a sign system that was formationally easier to produce by individuals with motor impairments, such as Amer-Ind or the Simplified Sign System.

Finally, it should be noted that the effectiveness of particular language intervention programs may vary depending on the etiology of the children's intellectual disability and on their levels of communicative abilities (Yoder & Warren, 2002). That is, particular intervention approaches may be more successful with children at different levels of communicative functioning or with children in certain diagnostic categories (e.g., Down syndrome). In the future, it may be possible for clinicians to confidently recommend a particular intervention program based on an individual's background characteristics and current level of communicative functioning. Alternatively, one may adopt a more holistic approach that maximizes an individual's exposure to multiple forms of input (e.g., speech, sign, symbols, speech-generating devices, etc.) that can all serve as models for his or her communicative development. In such an approach, all strategies would be considered viable and useful options unless specific evidence to the contrary arises for that individual; an ineffective strategy could then be discontinued or de-emphasized in favor of strategies that are more beneficial to that individual. It is also vitally important to consider the preferences of the individuals with developmental disabilities when trying to determine which augmentative and alternative communication options to pursue with them (van der Meer et al., 2011). A user's choice gives that person power in making decisions that affect his or her life and provides him or her with an opportunity to exercise autonomy and control over aspects of the surrounding environment (Light & McNaughton, 2015).

Selecting Signs

If a decision is made to implement a sign intervention program for a non-speaking individual with an intellectual disability or cerebral palsy, then care should be exercised in selecting those signs to be taught. Because some such individuals have pronounced motor difficulties, the signs selected should be relatively easy to form (Dennis et al., 1982). This means that they should consist of a single distinct movement and a basic or formationally simple handshape. Repetition of a particular sign movement typically has little or no impact on that sign's learning. If possible, the signs selected also should touch or make contact with the signer's body or other hand. If, in contrast, the selected signs are more difficult to form, then much more time and effort likely may need to be devoted to teaching the individual to produce recognizable signs. Such an outcome probably would prove frustrating for both teacher and learner, and slow the learner's development of communication skills.

Regardless, it should be acknowledged that systematic studies that probe the interrelationships between sign formational parameters and sign learning in persons with disabilities have rarely been conducted.

Signs taught also should be highly iconic, if possible. Highly iconic signs typically are learned and remembered more easily than signs that do not resemble their concepts (arbitrary signs). Signs high in translucency also are more readily acquired than arbitrary signs. Therefore, signs to be taught should be clearly iconic or high in sign translucency. If it is not possible to find or create a highly iconic or translucent sign for a certain concept, then use the best sign available and facilitate its acquisition by providing an explanation of the relationship between that sign and the concept for which it stands.

Although all sign languages used by Deaf persons have some highly iconic signs, these signs constitute a minority (generally one-third) of the lexicons of those languages (Boyes Braem, 1986; Lloyd et al., 1985). The sign-communication system developed by the Indigenous peoples of North America, Plains Indian Sign Language, evidently contains a larger proportion of highly iconic signs than Deaf sign languages. Unfortunately, many of the signs developed and used by Native Americans for intertribal communication and trade do not appear to be useful in a contemporary classroom setting. Furthermore, some of the signs in Deaf sign languages and Plains Indian Sign Language are relatively complex formationally. Since neither Deaf persons nor Native Americans typically have had difficulty motorically producing signs, this formational complexity was not a problem. Sign formational complexity, however, does factor into the sign-learning success of some individuals with an intellectual disability and/or with cerebral palsy.

Another factor that teachers or caregivers should keep in mind when selecting which signs will be taught is whether a particular sign might be potentially useful to the learner. If a sign does not serve a purpose or is not functionally relevant in some way to the learner, then it is unlikely to be used except in sign-learning sessions.

We believe that the signs that we have developed for the Simplified Sign System help overcome many of the memory and formational difficulties involved in learning to communicate through signs. Simplified Signs are relatively easy to form, typically are high in iconicity or translucency, and frequently will be useful in modern-day situations.

For these reasons, we feel that signs from the Simplified Sign System will be helpful additions to the educational and training programs of many persons with an intellectual disability or with cerebral palsy. These same characteristics also make them easier to learn and remember by young typically developing children (discussed in Chapters 3 and 7), individuals with autism (discussed next in Chapter 5), and individuals with aphasia (discussed in Chapter 6).

5. Childhood Autism and Sign Communication

When we began the Simplified Sign System project, our primary focus was on improving the communicative success of children with autism. Many of these individuals had serious difficulties understanding and producing speech. For these children, training in an augmentative and alternative communication strategy, such as manual signs, was a possible intervention approach. Unfortunately, the motor problems experienced by many persons with autism, coupled with the formational complexities of many of the signs of full and genuine sign languages, such as American Sign Language (ASL), have limited the success of sign intervention programs to some extent. To address these difficulties, we explicitly set out to develop a system composed of signs that were easier to form.

Because persons with autism may also have problems acquiring and remembering signs from genuine sign languages, we included signs that we felt would be more readily learned. In particular, we strove to ensure that the signs in the Simplified Sign System visually resembled the concepts they represented as much as possible. This iconic aspect of many of the signs should make them easier for individuals with autism to learn and remember by providing a visual "clue" to the meanings of the signs. The more transparent nature of the signs should also make them easier for family members, caregivers, teachers, peers, and other persons in the wider community to understand.

It is important to note that participation in an intervention program that utilizes an augmentative and/or alternative communication system, such as the Simplified Sign System, does not weaken or prevent the development of spoken language skills. Rather, sign-communication training and teaching may actually facilitate the development of

© Bonvillian, Kissane Lee, Dooley & Loncke, CC BY 4.0   https://doi.org/10.11647/OBP.0205.05

these skills, with some sign-learning children making considerable progress learning to speak. Finally, it is also important to point out that children with autism are a diverse group, and the Simplified Sign System is not to be thought of as the best or only approach for every child with communication difficulties. There are a variety of non-oral communication approaches or methods that may be utilized as either alternatives to speech or as supplementary or augmentative communication techniques.

Childhood Autism

It has been over seventy years since Leo Kanner (1894–1981) first described the syndrome of childhood autism in 1943.[1] He portrayed children with autism as self-absorbed with severe social, communication, and behavioral problems. More specifically, he described them as failing to interact socially, frequently displaying stereotyped gestures or mannerisms, often preoccupied with maintaining sameness or uniformity in their environment, and as having marked impairments in their use of language to communicate. In the years that followed, children who met Kanner's initial clinical description of the principal characteristics of autism have frequently been seen as having classic autism.

At about the same time that Kanner, located in Baltimore, MD, was developing his views about the nature of autism, Hans Asperger (1906–1980), a Viennese clinician, was working with and describing a number of youngsters who shared many of the characteristics of the children seen by Kanner. For many years, it was believed that the two investigators had worked in parallel and been unaware of each other's efforts. That view has changed recently, as it has become apparent that there were important ties between the personnel present in the two clinics (Silberman, 2015). In his work, Asperger described children with autism who varied across a wide range of abilities but who manifested difficulties in social interaction and who frequently engaged in repetitive

---

1   Although Kanner was the first investigator to specify the characteristics of childhood autism, there is considerable evidence that certain persons, who today would likely be identified as on the autism spectrum, have been present in society over a long period of time (Donvan & Zucker, 2016).

actions and pursued narrow interests. Because Asperger highlighted the performance of some of the more intellectually gifted children he worked with in his accounts, many children with autism with higher IQs and relatively good formal language skills were described in the scientific literature as having Asperger syndrome.[2]

Over time, the more inclusive view of autism advanced by Asperger, with its wide range of ability levels, has come to be the generally accepted version of the syndrome (Frith, 2008; Silberman, 2015). This diversity of abilities is captured by the term autism spectrum disorder (or ASD). Individuals with ASD are identified by several core features or diagnostic criteria (American Psychiatric Association, 2013; Frith, 2008): difficulties in engaging in reciprocal social interactions and social communication (including atypicalities in nonverbal communication, the production of few communicative gestures, and problems understanding facial expressions); repetitive actions, behaviors, or narrow interests (such as stereotyped movements, resistance to change, and object fixations); the presence of these symptoms in early childhood; and these symptoms are not attributable to an intellectual disability or a global developmental delay. There frequently is also a delay in spoken language development that is evident in both receptive (understanding) and expressive (productive) language in infants who are subsequently diagnosed with ASD (Lazenby et al., 2016). The wide range of abilities among persons on the autism spectrum can be seen in that some individuals are highly gifted intellectually while others have an intellectual disability.

Although much has been written about childhood autism over the last seven decades, the origin and neurophysiological basis of the disorder remain unclear. Kanner originally believed that parents, through their curtailed and frigid patterns of interaction with their children, likely caused the disorder; he was subsequently to abandon this view. Most contemporary investigators view the underlying issue in autism as some form of organic or neurochemical brain dysfunction that has not yet been specifically determined.[3] Although there have been numerous

2   It should be noted that in the recent edition of the *Diagnostic and Statistical Manual of Mental Disorders*, or DSM-5, that Asperger syndrome is no longer identified as a separate diagnosis (American Psychiatric Association, 2013).

3   Some evidence of brain dysfunctions related to atypicalities associated with autism is beginning to emerge. Post mortem examination of portions of the cortex from children with ASD has shown patches of disturbances in the cortical architecture

reports in recent decades of anatomical abnormalities located in the brains of individuals with ASD, it should be noted that many of these findings subsequently failed to be replicated in a larger sample (Haar et al., 2016). Moreover, multiple genetic and environmental risk factors likely contribute to the atypicalities associated with autism (Wozniak et al., 2017).

There is now considerable evidence of a substantial genetic component in childhood autism (Acosta & Pearl, 2006; Autism Genome Project Consortium, 2007; Bailey et al., 1995; Gamsiz et al., 2015; Muhle, Trentacoste, & Rapin, 2004; Rosenberg et al., 2009; Rutter & Thapar, 2014; Sutcliffe, 2008; Yuen et al., 2017). The evidence of a genetic component in childhood autism is particularly striking in studies involving monozygotic (identical) and dizygotic (fraternal) twins. If one monozygotic twin is diagnosed with autism, then the co-twin also is quite likely to be diagnosed. The concordance rates for autism among dizygotic twin pairs, in contrast, are much lower. There is also growing evidence, albeit indirect, that exposure to toxic chemicals early in development may contribute to childhood autism (Landrigan, 2010). In addition, the findings from a recent twin study suggest that shared environmental factors, including those present in the womb, likely play an important role in autism (Hallmayer et al., 2011). Two such factors reported as being associated with increased risk of ASD were maternal antidepressant use during pregnancy (Boukhris et al., 2016) and maternal exposure to fever during the second trimester of a pregnancy (Hornig et al., 2017).

The initial investigations that established a genetic role in the etiology of autism focused on families in which more than one member had been identified with ASD and emphasized classic Mendelian inheritance patterns. Over the past decade, however, a very different viewpoint has emerged as to the genetic origins of a large number of cases of autism. This new viewpoint is that ASD often arises from spontaneous (or *de novo*) mutations (Gamsiz et al., 2015; Iossifov et al., 2014; Sebat

---

of most of these individuals (Stoner et al., 2014). These patches of disorganized cortex, furthermore, were found in regions that mediated functions often impaired in persons with ASD. A reduced volume of the arcuate fasciculus also has been reported for persons with autism. The arcuate fasciculus is the major white matter tract that connects important language-processing regions in the brain. The reduction in arcuate fasciculus volume, moreover, also was significantly related to autism symptom severity (Moseley et al., 2016).

et al., 2007; Yuen et al., 2017). Such de novo mutations reportedly occurred more frequently in families where there was only a single child identified with autism as opposed to families where two or more children were affected. These mutations, moreover, frequently turned out to be complex genetically and to have taken place as the parents' eggs or sperm cells were developing. Additional research showed that whereas these spontaneous mutations individually were quite rare, collectively they appeared to account for a substantial number of cases of childhood autism (Hall, 2015; Iossifov et al., 2014; Yuen et al., 2017). In coming years, it will be important to continue to pinpoint more precisely the many genes associated with autism; if this is accomplished, then it will enable clinicians to prioritize those infants most in need of early diagnostic assessments and interventions (Yuen et al., 2017). The wide variety of individual de novo mutations involved might also help explain the great heterogeneity seen in the behavior of persons with autism. Finally, the finding that many such mutations occurred during egg and sperm cell development, rather than earlier in the development process, might help account for the reported increased rates of ASD in children with older parents.

Even though the precise cause of autism has remained elusive, the number of children diagnosed with it has increased steadily over the years (Hertz-Picciotto & Delwiche, 2009). Originally believed to be quite rare and to occur in only one or two children per 10,000, by the mid-1990s the incidence of autism spectrum disorder (ASD, that is, childhood autism and other closely related syndromes) was estimated at 1 in about every 500 children (Bristol et al., 1996). Recently, the incidence of children with ASD in the U.S. has been reported as being much higher: 1 in every 91 children in one study (Kogan et al., 2009) and 1 in about every 59 children in another (Centers for Disease Control and Prevention, 2018). Furthermore, the prevalence of autism spectrum disorder among elementary-school-aged children in a South Korean community has been found to be even higher, 2.64%, or 1 in about every 38 children (Kim et al., 2011). Finally, an estimate of the number of individuals with ASD worldwide was made recently at 67 million, with approximately 600,000 of these persons living in France (Bonnet-Brilhault, 2017). These large numbers helped lead France to recognize autism as a national public health priority.

One explanation advanced for the rapid increase in the prevalence of autism was that of diagnostic substitution; that is, many children who previously had been classified as having an intellectual disability were subsequently being classified with autism (Croen et al., 2002). Whether the apparent increase is the product of greater awareness of the characteristics of childhood autism (and thus more accurate diagnoses), the inclusion of milder forms of autism because of expanded diagnostic criteria (Gernsbacher, Dawson, & Goldsmith, 2005), greater availability of services spurring more families to come forward for assistance, diagnostic substitution, or the result of an actual increase in the number of individuals born with or developing autism has been a topic of considerable debate in recent years.

Childhood autism affects individuals of all races, ethnicities, and social backgrounds. Autism is much more common in boys, who are about four to five times more likely to be affected than girls (Centers for Disease Control and Prevention, 2018; Fombonne, 2005; Lajonchere & the AGRE Consortium, 2010).[4] Why autism occurs much more frequently in boys than girls remains unexplained. Childhood autism begins at birth or in early childhood and is highly likely to persist throughout adulthood. Some of these individuals require lifelong care from their parents, siblings, other caregivers, or state agencies.

While some individuals with ASD may demonstrate average or above-average intelligence, many do not. Earlier accounts of children with autism indicated that about three-quarters of this population earned scores in the intellectually disabled range on most intelligence tests (American Psychiatric Association, 1994; Fombonne, 2005). This proportion, it should be noted, may be too high as some of the characteristics of children with ASD may have interfered with the assessment of their intelligence (Edelson, 2006). Moreover, as the syndrome of childhood autism has become better known and more widely applied, the proportion of children with ASD being identified as intellectually disabled has decreased substantially (Baird et al., 2000; Kielinen, Linna, & Moilanen, 2000; Volkmar et al., 2014). More specifically, 31% of children with ASD have been identified as having intellectual disability (IQ of 70 or lower) and another 25% as scoring in

---

4   In the Centers for Disease Control study, the prevalence rate for boys was 1 in 37 and for girls was 1 in 151.

the borderline range on tests of intellectual ability (IQ scores of 71–85) (Centers for Disease Control and Prevention, 2018).

The view that a large proportion of children with ASD are cognitively impaired also has been challenged. In one study, thirty-eight children with autism were assessed using the Raven Progressive Matrices (Raven, Raven, & Court, 1998), a test of high-level analytical reasoning and problem solving. The children's scores were at the 56th percentile, indicating an average level of performance (Dawson et al., 2007). In contrast, these same children scored on average 30 percentile points lower on the Wechsler scales of intelligence (Wechsler, 1974, 1991), which rely heavily on verbal comprehension. Evidently, many individuals with ASD have average or above-average reasoning skills when they are tested in a particular nonverbal domain.

A recurring complicating factor both in the diagnosis and treatment of childhood autism is that of *comorbidity*. In other words, a substantial number of children with ASD have one or more additional medical conditions at the same time (Autism Speaks, 2017; Fombonne, 1999; Volkmar et al., 2014). Included among the many associated medical conditions are fragile X syndrome, epilepsy, disrupted sleep, depression, cerebral palsy, Down syndrome, and hearing and visual impairments. Like children with Down syndrome, children with ASD have a significantly increased rate of middle ear infections and otitis media-related complications in comparison with typically developing children (Adams et al., 2016), as well as a higher incidence of hearing impairment (Demopoulos & Lewine, 2016).[5] These difficulties in hearing may, in turn, adversely affect their spoken language development. In addition, it has been observed that many children with ASD also meet the diagnostic criteria for attention-deficit hyperactivity disorder (ADHD) (Autism Speaks, 2017). Indeed, the observation that individuals with ASD and ADHD share a large number of behavioral and neurophysiological features has led some investigators to suggest that the two disorders may exist along a continuum and have a common etiology (Kern et al., 2015). Aside from making the determination of an optimal intervention program for children with autism a more challenging endeavor, the

---

5   The prevalence of autism in deaf individuals is estimated at 1 in 59 (Szymanski et al., 2012), a number that matches the overall prevalence of autism in the general population (Centers for Disease Control and Prevention, 2018).

presence of these associated medical conditions likely has also resulted in an overdiagnosis of autism more generally.

A problem frequently encountered by teachers and caregivers of children with autism is their production of maladaptive or challenging behaviors. Such behaviors might include self-injury, the destruction of property, tantrums, stereotypies (frequently repeated behaviors, such as finger flicking), or aggression (Goldstein, 2002). For example, some infants diagnosed with autism may begin to rock or bang their heads against their cribs. One early approach to these behaviors was to try to eliminate them, sometimes through the use of painful physical punishment (Lovaas, Schaeffer, & Simmons, 1965). A different perspective on the nature of these challenging behaviors emerged when it was hypothesized that some of these behaviors were serving a communicative function (Carr & Durand, 1985; Wetherby, 1986). If this were in fact the case, then the administration of punishment (or aversives) would be curtailing the children's efforts to communicate. This change in perspective led investigators to focus more on determining the underlying purposes or functions of the challenging behaviors and then on teaching useful communication skills; this approach has led to a reduction in many maladaptive or challenging behaviors (Carr & Durand, 1985; Horner & Budd, 1985; Mira Pastor & Grau, 2017; Schwartz et al., 2009; Wacker et al., 1990). Some of the children's challenging behaviors may also be indicative of problems in emotional regulation. Again, rather than trying to eliminate these behaviors, a more productive approach may be to strive to understand the reasons for or causes of those behaviors and then address these causes (Prizant with Fields-Meyer, 2015).

Communication Interventions and Outcomes

Since the early 1960s, there have been two major innovations in language or communication therapy programs for children with autism. The first innovation, the use of behavior modification speech training, often proved successful in fostering spoken language skills in children already exhibiting some speech or oral language ability. The second innovation, the use of augmentative and alternative communication systems, such as sign communication, often provided non-speaking children with the ability to communicate for the first time.

Studies by Ivar Lovaas and his associates have been a major source of information about the use and effectiveness of behavior modification (or operant) speech training for children with autism. Operant conditioning of behavior may be defined as changes in a person's or "animal's 'voluntary' responses after they have been followed, on prior occasions, by the presentation or withdrawal of reward or punishment" (Cohen, 1969, p. 5). Operant conditioning thus seeks to change behavior by either administering or removing a rewarding (or punishing) consequence for the behavior. Through the careful application of rewards for behaviors that the investigators wished the children would produce more frequently and, in some instances, the use of punishment for behaviors the investigators wished to decrease in frequency, many children with autism made noticeable progress in their spoken language and social skills (Lovaas, 1977, 1987; Lovaas et al., 1973; but see Ospina et al., 2008, for qualifications of these claims).

In the approach pioneered by Lovaas, complex behaviors were broken down into smaller, discrete actions that were learned through repetition and the application of rewards. Individual participants needed to be very carefully and systematically taught almost every skill they acquired. This applied behavioral analysis approach typically consisted of intensive one-on-one daily training and teaching sessions in a highly structured environment.[6] In the years since the Lovaas approach was first reported, there have been a number of other behavioral-based programs developed, with some designed for use in school and in home settings. Many children in these programs made dramatic improvements in their spoken language skills and social behavior; others made only

---

6   It is important to acknowledge that applied behavioral analysis (ABA) has been heavily criticized for the use of negative reinforcement (punishment) and its emphasis on control (Gruson-Wood, 2016). In recent years, a number of therapists who embraced the ABA approach have opted to use more child-directed behavioral methods in a more natural setting rather than the highly structured approach developed by Lovaas. This newer approach, known as pivotal response treatment, has been associated with more rapid improvements in communication in children with ASD (Mohammadzaheri et al., 2014). It should also be noted that there are varying degrees of implementation within the ABA approach, with some adaptations stressing positive reinforcement over punishment of undesired behaviors (Kates-McElrath & Axelrod, 2006).

minimal gains. It should be noted, however, that even minimal gains through behavioral or operant programs often contrasted with findings of virtually no improvement whatsoever in more traditional therapy programs (e.g., play therapy, psychodynamic therapy). Moreover, recent assessments of the efficacy of the behavioral approaches have underlined the effectiveness of intensive early behavioral intervention with children with ASD (Eldevik et al., 2009; Reed, 2016).

In this operant or behavioral approach, the ability to imitate verbally plays a major role in speech training. By analyzing the records of the children who participated in his studies, Lovaas was able to determine that those who were mute (that is, not producing recognizable speech) at the time that they began to participate were those who were least likely to benefit from operant speech-training programs. Those children who were already echoing or repeating elements of others' speech, though generally in a nonmeaningful way (that is, they were echolalic), typically made progress in the operant speech-training or verbal imitation program. This echoing or repeating of others' speech by some children with autism may indicate that they are able to retain utterances in short-term memory, an early step in the course of language development (Roberts, 2014). Lovaas (1977, p. 118) noted this difference in his program's effectiveness between the two groups of children:

> It was striking to observe how clearly, richly, and "effortlessly" the echolalic child imitated the adults' speech. They "spoke" a lot and "played" with speech. The imitative behavior of the previously mute children, on the other hand, stayed closely dependent on the experimental reinforcers, frequently deteriorated and "drifted" away from criterion, and sounded stilted. In general, our language program was not as successful for the mutes as for the echolalics. If the child was already echolalic, even though he did not know the meaning of his vocal expressions or how to arrange them in sentences, then it seemed easy for us to rearrange behavior (syntax) and bring it under appropriate stimulus control (semantics).

Although Lovaas' operant speech-training program has proven to be a highly beneficial intervention approach for many children with autism, it evidently was not nearly as successful with non-speaking children.

The second important innovation in language interventions for children with ASD has been the use of augmentative and alternative communication systems, primarily with non-speaking or minimally verbal individuals. Such children also tended to score very low on IQ tests, even on those tests designed for nonverbal children. Those children who had very little or no useful speech historically constituted the largest single subgroup of autism, comprising between one-third and one-half of the children diagnosed with autism (Frankel, Leary, & Kilman, 1987; Lord & Paul, 1997; Mesibov, Adams, & Klinger, 1997; Peeters & Gillberg, 1999).

The proportion of children without any functional expressive speech, however, has decreased considerably in recent years. This has occurred in part because of the inclusion of more children with higher cognitive skills and less severe behavioral problems within the diagnostic category autism spectrum disorder, and because of the benefits in language processing achieved by those children who participate in very early intervention programs (Lord, Risi, & Pickles, 2004; Wetherby, 2006). Recent estimates are that about 20–30% of those children diagnosed with ASD do not acquire useful spoken language (Kim & Lord, 2014; Tager-Flusberg & Kasari, 2013; Wodka, Mathy, & Kalb, 2013). In the past, the prognosis for children who do not acquire useful spoken language has been very bleak (Eisenberg, 1956). For many such children, the outcome has been lifelong institutionalization (Lotter, 1974). In contrast, those individuals with ASD who acquire useful speech by age five or six typically have better long-term outcomes (Howlin et al., 2004; Lord & Bailey, 2002; Szatmari et al., 2003). Still, despite the many advances in language intervention programs in recent decades, the long-term outcome for nearly half of all individuals with autism is considered to be poor or very poor (Steinhausen, Mohr Jensen, & Lauritsen, 2016).

For decades, investigators in the field of autism typically have accepted the view that autism was a lifelong condition. In general, the stability of a diagnosis of ASD in toddlers has been shown to be quite high when the same children were reassessed about two or more years later (Brian et al., 2016; Chawarska et al., 2009). Considerable improvements might be made in certain behaviors, but some aspects of autism seemed to continue throughout the affected individual's life. Occasionally, there were claims of children with autism spectrum disorder showing full "recovery," but those reports often were greeted with skepticism. Perhaps those children had been initially misdiagnosed as "autistic."

In recent years, the view that autism was a lifelong condition has changed somewhat. One of the first scholars to articulate the view that autism might be effectively treated in some cases was Lovaas (1987). He reported that some of the children he studied who received intensive intervention (40+ hours per week) made enough progress that they were able to attend and pass first grade in a mainstream classroom. In fact, some children with ASD can show sufficient improvements in their language, face recognition, communication, socialization, and social-interaction skills that they are able to function within normal limits and no longer meet the diagnosis of autism (Fein et al., 2013). These individuals, however, typically had milder symptoms of autism at initial assessment early in their development (Moulton et al., 2016).

The results of a second study (Dawson et al., 2012) also underlined the importance of intensive early intervention in improving a wide range of behaviors in children with autism. In addition, this study showed for the first time that brain activity (i.e., EEG) within normal limits was a possible outcome for children with ASD after such intervention. The results of these two studies raise considerable hope for the future development and education of children with autism. At the same time, caution needs to be exercised before considering children "recovered." Although some children initially diagnosed with ASD evidently can improve sufficiently after early intervention that they no longer meet the criteria for ASD, it should be recognized that most such youngsters will continue to need support. Furthermore, in a longitudinal follow-up of a group of children who purportedly had "recovered" from autism, a number of these children once again met the criteria for ASD at the time of their later assessment (Olsson et al., 2015). Finally, it remains to be seen just which forms of intervention are the most effective for which children with autism.

Sign-Communication Training and Teaching

Teaching non-speaking children with autism to communicate through signs has been one of the principal non-oral communication intervention approaches. Since the early 1970s there has been considerable growth both in interest about signing and in research on children's sign learning (Kiernan & Reid, 1984). As a result of their manual sign training, many children who had failed to make progress acquiring spoken language skills learned to convey their basic needs for the first time through signs. Altogether, the results of more than thirty studies involving non-speaking children with ASD have underscored the potential effectiveness of teaching signs to this population (Bonvillian, Nelson, & Rhyne, 1981; Goldstein, 2002; Lal, 2010; Layton, 1987; Valentino & Shillingsburg, 2011; Wendt, 2009). In these studies, the children's teachers or caregivers typically took individual signs from existing sign languages or sign-communication systems and paired them with spoken words in their interactions with their children. The gains that the children made in sign-communication skills often were retained for long periods (e.g., Webster et al., 2016); in contrast, rather poor word retention generally was evident in vocal language interventions (Gaines et al., 1988). In addition, after first learning to communicate through signs, some of the children in the different studies went on to acquire spoken language skills.

One of the first attempts to teach manual sign communication to non-speaking children with autism took place at Benhaven, starting in 1971 (Lettick, 1972, 1979). At that time, Benhaven, located in New Haven, Connecticut, was a school for autistic and brain-damaged children ranging in age from six to twenty-one years. Many of the Benhaven students had failed to make progress in programs at other schools or agencies. With the arrival of a deaf student with autism, the school embarked on sign language lessons for the entire staff and a program of sign and speech input for all the students who did not appear capable of acquiring useful speech. The outcomes of this simultaneous sign and spoken language training were positive for all the students, although progress varied widely. At one end were those children whose sign learning consisted solely of understanding the meaning of a few signs. At the other end were children who learned to respond to questions in signed sentences and who engaged in signed conversations. Furthermore, it was observed that the use of signs did not appear to stifle the emergence of communication skills in other modes (e.g., speech).

Another early effort to teach manual signs to a hearing but non-speaking individual with autism took place in Palo Alto, California in 1972 (Bonvillian & Nelson, 1976). Researchers began to work with a nine-year-old non-speaking boy with autism and an IQ score below 40 who experienced great difficulty in his ability to communicate with others. Because this boy was mute, he learned signs as an alternative form of communication in lieu of spoken language. In teaching him signs, investigators would first demonstrate the sign, and then mold his hands into the shape of the sign. After working with the child for only six months, the investigators had taught him fifty-six different signs. After several years, he had acquired a lexicon of over four hundred signs and was able to combine five or six signs into short sentences. By learning to sign, this boy was able to overcome the barrier that was holding him back from interacting with others and understanding the world around him (Bonvillian & Nelson, 1976).

Investigations of manual sign acquisition by non-speaking or minimally verbal youngsters with autism continued in the decades following these pioneering studies. Many of these studies used a key word signing approach in which the teachers or therapists spoke in sentences or phrases while signing the principal or key words in their utterances. In one such key word intervention (Tan et al., 2014), the three young participants acquired a core vocabulary of signs and generalized their sign usage across activities. These children's sign learning, moreover, was associated with increased production of both spoken words and natural (non-sign) gestures.

Many of the studies of sign-communication training and teaching in non-speaking, albeit hearing, children with ASD also reported improvement in their adaptive behaviors (Lal, 2010). In many cases, these improvements were not the outcome of direct training, but were associated with the children's enhanced communication skills through signing. Frequently observed improvements included increased attention span, declines in the incidence of tantrums and stereotypic behaviors, improved bladder control and fewer soiling incidents, increased willingness to participate in group activities, and better self-help skills. As can be easily imagined, these improvements often had a positive effect on the children's caregivers as well.

A number of possible explanations have been advanced to account for the success some individuals with autism have shown in learning to sign after experiencing repeated failure in acquiring speech skills. One explanation is that spoken language may be difficult for some persons with autism because they process sound atypically. Most preschool children with ASD prefer non-speech signals to speech input, whereas the opposite pattern is present in typically developing youngsters (Kuhl et al., 2005). In infants subsequently identified with ASD, the presence of speech has been shown to disturb their visual scanning of facial features (Shic, Macari, & Chawarska, 2014). Abnormal processing of vocal stimuli, but not for non-vocal sounds, also has been reported for adults and children with autism (Gervais et al., 2004; Sperdin & Schaer, 2016). In general, auditory-processing problems are quite common in individuals with ASD (Baranek, 2002; Condon, 1975; Greenspan & Weider, 1997). Temple Grandin, an accomplished scholar and highly articulate individual with ASD, has observed that some persons with autism are hypersensitive to certain sounds, often finding them painful. She also has reported that many individuals with autism, herself included, find the processing of complex sounds, such as those in spoken language, particularly difficult or problematic (Grandin, 1995; Grandin & Panek, 2013). For many individuals with ASD, their visual and kinesthetic processing abilities may be more advanced and intact than their speech-processing abilities (Mirenda, 2014; Mitchell & Ropar, 2004).

A second explanation for the successful use of signs is that the manual mode may be more conducive to direct instruction than speech. That is, teachers and caregivers not only can hold their hands in the same position for a long time in order to facilitate the child's copying of a sign, but they also can directly mold the child's hand(s) into the correct sign formation.[7] A similar degree of control is not possible for spoken language. A third reason for this success in signing over vocal skills training may be that a number of signs clearly resemble the objects, actions, or properties for which they stand. This iconic or pantomimic aspect of signs may make them easier for many children to learn and to

---

7   This latter option should be used with caution and respect for the bodily autonomy of persons with disabilities; permission should first be obtained before physical contact is made. This contact should also be as gentle as possible and should last no longer than is necessary. Such molding of the hands and movement of another person's hand(s) and/or arm(s) should be faded as sign production skills improve. Furthermore, some persons with ASD have extreme sensitivities to touch that may prevent the successful use of a molding approach to sign formation (Herman, Shield, & Morgan, 2019).

remember (Doherty, 1985; Konstantareas et al., 1978). In contrast, most spoken words do not clearly resemble the objects, actions, or properties they represent.

Fourth, it has been suggested that by teaching children with autism to sign, caregivers may have indirectly been teaching them to control their stereotypic gestures and mannerisms (Bram, Meier, & Sutherland, 1977).[8] Because the production of these repetitive gestures may interfere with cognitive processing, lowering their frequency might enhance the children's ability to learn. Another explanation for the reduced incidence of motor stereotypies in autistic children learning to sign is that acquiring sign-communication skills may reduce these children's anxiety levels. Finally, because learning to speak may be associated with frustration and failure in many children, a switch from a focus on speech to an emphasis on signs may avoid these negative feelings.

Although signing programs overall have a quite positive record as a form of communication intervention for non-speaking children with ASD, there are limitations that should be acknowledged. Even though the finding that sign interventions often are effective is based on the outcomes of many studies, only a small proportion of these studies involved ten or more participants. Indeed, a number of these studies involved only a single participant. Furthermore, detailed assessments of the background characteristics of many of these participants frequently were lacking, as were baseline and intervention outcome data (Schwartz & Nye, 2006). This is a serious problem because the range of outcomes in sign learning varied quite widely across individual participants. Without this background information, it is difficult to determine who would be a prime candidate for sign-communication intervention and who might benefit more from other approaches.

---

8   This idea that the learning and use of manual signs is associated with reduced levels of motor stereotypies or repetitive behaviors (e.g., twirling, finger flicking) in children with autism has received support from a study of deaf children. In this study, deaf parents of deaf children with autism reported that their children did not produce the motor stereotypies typically seen in children with autism (Szymanski & Brice, 2008; see also Szymanski et al., 2012). Although the deaf children's signing may have enabled them to effectively control their motor movements, other explanations cannot be excluded; for example, the children's deafness may have prevented them from hearing aversive sounds that might have prompted their stereotypies.

Another important limitation of the studies of sign teaching in children with ASD is that relatively few involved very young children (Anderson, 2001). There appear to be two principal reasons for this. First, parents and teachers frequently wished to focus language training solely on spoken language; signing was an alternative to be explored if progress was not seen with speech. Only in recent years has there been recognition that language development in one mode fosters communication skills in another (Dunst et al., 2011; Millar, 2009; Millar et al., 2006; Rowe & Goldin-Meadow, 2009b).

A second reason that few young children with ASD participated in sign interventions is that the diagnosis of the disorder often was made at a later age. Today, children with ASD often are diagnosed at two to four years of age, and the average age of diagnosis is steadily decreasing. Although clear progress is being made at identifying children with ASD at younger and younger ages, diagnostic evaluations before the age of two years remain challenging (Zwaigenbaum et al., 2009). There is now evidence of high stability in diagnoses of ASD in children as early as eighteen months of age, but this appears to be the case for those children with more severe impairments; those children with more advanced language and adaptive skills often were not identified until three years of age (Zwaigenbaum et al., 2016).

Studies of very young children subsequently diagnosed with ASD have shown that certain behaviors (e.g., little response to name, lack of joint attention, poor eye control, lack of communicative gestures, and social touch aversion) may successfully distinguish these children from typically developing infants (Baranek, 1999; Chawarska et al., 2014; Osterling & Dawson, 1994; Veness et al., 2014; Watson et al., 2013; Werner et al., 2000). In the future, it may be possible to make accurate diagnoses relatively early in development in light of the above findings and of findings of movement atypicalities (Baranek, 1999; Bodison & Mostofsky, 2014; Teitelbaum et al., 1998) and of brain overgrowth (or accelerated head growth) during the first year of life in children subsequently identified with autism (Courchesne, Carper, & Akshoomoff, 2003; Dawson et al., 2007). Eventually, it may be possible to make accurate diagnoses relatively early in infancy. In fact, a recent examination (Hazlett et al., 2017) of cortical surface area expansion in infants from six to twelve months predicted subsequent diagnosis of autism in young children with familial high risk of ASD.

An accurate and early diagnosis of ASD is likely to be an important factor for intervention programs as there typically is greater neural plasticity or flexibility early in development (Knudsen, 2004; Knudsen et al., 2006; Nelson, 2000). That is, younger children often are more receptive to environmental interventions (such as signing) and thus have more potential for greater long-term progress than older children or adolescents. Moreover, there is evidence that even infants and toddlers with serious developmental disabilities, including ASD, can make progress in learning to communicate effectively through the use of manual signs, gestures, and other non-oral approaches (Branson & Demchak, 2009). Studies of deaf children with ASD who first learn a sign language also provide unique insights into the early application of sign intervention techniques (Herman et al., 2019; Shield, 2014; Shield, Cooley, & Meier, 2017; Shield & Meier, 2012, 2018; Shield, Meier, & Tager-Flusberg, 2015; Shield et al., 2016, 2017; Sparaci, Lasorsa, & Capirci, 2019). If very young children evidently can benefit from early intervention programs, then the question arises as to why so few young children participate in such programs. At the same time, it should be recognized that although the human brain is particularly adept at acquiring information early in life, there is considerable evidence to support the view that the brain is also a flexible structure that "can adapt and modify with age and with the acquisition of new motor and cognitive skills" (Denes, 2016, p. xiv). In fact, participants with ASD who demonstrated impressive skill gains after intensive early intervention showed recruitment of numerous additional regions of the brain to compensate for their atypical neural processing mechanisms (Eigsti et al., 2016).

Dispelling Myths

A concern frequently voiced by parents when therapists have suggested that their child with autism be introduced to sign language (or other forms of augmentative and alternative communication) is that he or she will never acquire spoken language (Cress & Marvin, 2003). For these parents, the prospect of using signs to communicate is tantamount to an admission that their child will not acquire speech and that the best outcome they can hope for is that he or she will learn a small vocabulary of signs or gestures. Their dream that their son or daughter will become a fully functioning and integrated member of a society that relies on spoken language is threatened.

In many instances, sign-communication training and teaching is initiated only after a child has failed to acquire functional language in a speech-training program. As Alpert (1980, p. 401) observed, "This is unfortunate, for not only does the child remain without a means of communicating during the entire training period, but as the child gets older, the probability that he will acquire functional communication skills may be reduced." Although there are many reported instances of children with ASD acquiring spoken language skills after a severe language delay (Wodka et al., 2013), the frequency at which such late onset of speech occurs declines sharply with increasing age after the age of six (Pickett et al., 2009). This approach of not introducing signs to a young, non-speaking child would make sense if there were compelling research findings that showed that implementing a sign system impaired the acquisition of speech skills. To the contrary, there is considerable evidence that using signs with speech may facilitate comprehension and production of spoken language in both mute and echolalic children with autism (Barrera et al., 1980; Barrera & Sulzer-Azaroff, 1983; Carr, Pridal, & Dores, 1984; Dunst et al., 2011; Millar, 2009; Remington & Clarke, 1983; Valentino & Shillingsburg, 2011; see also Carbone et al., 2010).

Although training involving the use of signs together with speech has been associated with many children's acquisition of language skills in both modalities, there has been wide variation in the degree of success achieved. Often, children with ASD first acquired a sign vocabulary and began combining signs before making a transition to spoken words (Layton & Watson, 1995). In many instances, those children who acquired both speech and sign skills had at least a minimal level of verbal imitative ability prior to training. A number of non-speaking children with ASD, however, made little or no progress in their verbal production ability despite substantial simultaneous speech and sign training. Such children who remain minimally verbal despite acquiring a sign lexicon in a simultaneous training program may make progress in vocal language production only when they are specifically rewarded for vocal production (Scarbro-McLaury, 2004).

It is not clear how the notion spread that learning to sign inhibits the acquisition of spoken language. Certainly, hearing children of Deaf parents typically master both the spoken language of the hearing population and the sign language used by their Deaf parents. Furthermore, hearing babies exposed to signs and speech often are more advanced in their spoken language acquisition than babies exposed only to speech (Goodwyn & Acredolo, 1998). The notion that signing inhibits speech probably came from educators of deaf students who wished to emphasize an oral-only (sign language prohibited) educational approach. These educators felt that deaf students who were allowed to communicate using signs and the manual alphabet would not be motivated to learn to speak. However, there is no evidence supporting this position, and indeed, if anything, the opposite appears closer to the truth: successful communication in one language modality is related to successful communication in another. According to multiple studies, "gestures and words constitute a single communication system with shared roots in development, underlying the multimodal nature of human communication" (Sparaci et al., 2019, p. 41; see also Goldin-Meadow, 1998; Kendon, 2014; Levinson & Holler, 2014; Vigliocco, Perniss, & Vinson, 2014). Moreover, one of the best predictors of the acquisition of expressive and receptive spoken language skills in young children with ASD is their use of communicative gestures (Luyster et al., 2008; Manwaring et al., 2017; Rowe & Goldin-Meadow, 2009a).

Although many parents of non-speaking children with ASD are reluctant to have them begin programs of sign-communication training and teaching because they feel they will have abandoned any chance of their children learning to speak, the results of a range of studies suggest that such concerns are not well-grounded. Of the thirty children with autism who were taught to sign in Creedon's pioneering study (1973; see Offir, 1976), seven also acquired considerable facility in spoken English and another 40% attained some speech skills. Success in learning both signs and speech also was reported by Fouts (Fouts, 1997; Fulwiler & Fouts, 1976). Fouts surmised that certain children with autism experience difficulty connecting information from the auditory channel to information from the visual channel. He felt that the result of this problem in cross-modal transfer was that "sound was confusing at best and terrifying at worst" (1997, p. 187). The two boys with whom he worked first learned to communicate in signs, then produced short sign phrases, next they uttered single words, and finally generated spoken phrases.

In reflecting on these children's dramatic progress in their ability to communicate, Fouts (1997) advanced the view that the key to their success was that both signs and speech involve precise and sequential motor movements. With signs, it is the fine motor movements of the hands; with speech, it is the fine motor movements of the tongue. That is, both speaking and signing involve planning, coordinating, and producing a sequence of fine motor movements. In the brain, the areas that control the movements of the tongue (and other areas involved in articulation) and the hands are closely interconnected. There is also a functional connection between the hand area of the motor cortex and the language-related areas of the motor cortex (Meister et al., 2003). Improved functioning in the motor areas related to sign production appeared to have had a side effect of benefiting the motor areas related to speech production. Another factor that may underlie the difficulties that persons with ASD experience in connecting information from the auditory channel to the visual channel is that they may process information from each channel at different rates. This difference in temporal processing rates across channels may make the perceptual integration of auditory and visual information much more problematic (Stevenson et al., 2016; see also So et al., 2015).

Additional support for the view that signing or the production of hand gestures may facilitate or bootstrap spoken language production in some individuals has come from studies of a phenomenon known as synesthesia, or blending of the senses. In instances of sensory blending, there may be cross activation of neighboring brain regions. Ramachandran and Hubbard (2003, p. 59) wrote that "a kind of spillover of signals occurs between two nearby motor areas: those that control the sequence of muscle movements required for hand gestures and those for the mouth... As Charles Darwin pointed out, when we cut paper with scissors, our jaws may clench and unclench unconsciously as if to echo the hand movements." If cross activation or spillover is occurring in the brain regions responsible for sign production and spoken language production, then this may account for the increased vocalization and speech of some sign-learning children with ASD.

Another approach to fostering communication in non-speaking children with autism combined a speech-imitation program with signing (Schaeffer et al., 1977; Schaeffer, Musil, & Kollinzas, 1980). In separate daily language sessions, three boys learned to imitate speech through a behavior modification program in one session and learned to sign spontaneously in the other. All three boys initially learned to sign spontaneously. After their sign-communication skills were firmly established, the investigators elected to have them combine their sign production with their spoken word production. That is, the boys were taught to utter the English word equivalents of the signs they were making. After four to five months of the boys communicating simultaneously in both signs and speech, the investigators gradually faded the boys' production of signs. The outcome was that all three boys eventually produced spontaneous speech (see also Valentino et al., 2011).

The results of the above studies should make it clear that teaching sign language to a child with ASD should not be equated with abandoning hope for the development of spoken language skills. In fact, the development of sign-communication skills may facilitate the subsequent development of spoken language skills. Although the results of the above studies and those of other investigations provide encouragement to many parents who dream of one day hearing their children's voices, it should be recognized that many non-speaking children with autism who are taught to sign do not acquire facility in speech. Rather, in most instances, gains in speech communication are relatively modest (Millar et al., 2006).

Teaching Generalization and Spontaneous Communication Skills

Many early attempts to foster language development in children with autism reported the successful teaching of a substantial vocabulary of words or signs. These communication intervention programs typically emphasized the children's production of the correct words or signs in response to discrete stimuli such as real objects, pictures, or teachers' prompts. A serious limitation to this approach is that children with ASD frequently experience difficulty in generalizing newly acquired words or signs to new instances of a concept or to new settings. As a result, they often would use their words or signs only in the structured learning environment in which they were taught and only for the items specifically trained. This outcome is problematic because the goal of most communication programs is for the learner to use words or signs to express needs and wants and to make requests in a variety of settings to a number of different persons. These children also were frequently passive, with their language or communication characterized by a lack of spontaneity (Carr, 1982; Carr & Kologinsky, 1983; Duffy & Healy, 2011; Schaeffer, 1978).

Examination of the children's language-learning environments showed that they often had been taught words or signs by a single instructor in a single setting using a single training format. In light of this narrow training environment and the children's difficulties in generalizing and in initiating communication, it should not come as a surprise to learn that their language production was quite limited or restricted. The children frequently failed to initiate communication, to generalize newly acquired vocabulary to new instances of items, or to use their vocabulary in different settings (Openden et al., 2009). Fortunately, procedures have been developed to increase communicative spontaneity and language generalization (Hundert, 1981; Reichle & Sigafoos, 1991; Schreibman, Stahmer, & Suhrheinrich, 2009).

One of the ways to facilitate children's spontaneous use of signs has been to have teachers identify natural opportunities to teach signs throughout the day. For example, signs for foods might be taught to children at mealtimes. Teachers also have been urged to capitalize on the children's desires and interests within the context of ongoing activities (McGee, Krantz, Mason, & McClannahan, 1983; Rogers, 2006). In particular, teachers should be alert to attempts by children to communicate and to use these incidental opportunities to teach new signs and to establish the usefulness of signs already learned. Indeed, this more naturalistic teaching strategy (or milieu therapy) typically results in greater progress in language development and more generalization of newly learned skills by children with autism (Delprato, 2001; Mancil, 2009). These incidental teaching practices, often essential in fostering the communication skills of children with ASD, typically prove quite helpful with children with other communication disabilities as well.[9]

How might one facilitate generalization of the different signs taught? That is, how might one promote the use of signs to different instances or examples of a particular concept, with different people, and in different settings? One important step would be to incorporate procedures or strategies designed to promote generalization in the plans for the language training and teaching prior to the actual commencement of language lessons (Openden et al., 2009). A number of strategies that might be helpful in promoting generalization include: teaching in a variety of settings, varying communication partners (e.g., language therapist, parents and siblings, babysitter) and locations, teaching during the day's naturally occurring routines, and varying the conditions of instruction and the materials used (Dodd & Gorey, 2014; Rombouts et al., 2019; Schreibman et al., 2009; Stokes & Baer, 1977). Because some children with autism become upset if their environments change, one may wish to implement the above recommendations gradually, rather than all at once. If a teacher varies the exemplars used and embeds instruction across the day and in a variety of settings, then generalization is much more likely to result.

Motor and Imitation Abilities

Before participating in a sign-communication program, a number of children with autism had spent long periods in speech-oriented language therapy programs without making noticeable progress. Although nearly all of the children who participated in sign programs made some progress, the range of individual outcomes was quite wide (Bonvillian & Blackburn, 1991; Konstantareas, 1985; Layton, 1987). Some children acquired hundreds of signs and learned to combine them into phrases to express a wide range of meanings. At the other end of the spectrum were those youngsters who made only very limited gains despite years

---

9   For more information on these practices, see the "Recommendations for Enhancing the Sign-Learning Environment" section in Chapter 4, as well as the following subsections in Chapter 9: "Use Environmental Cues or Contextual Information" and "Ensure a Positive Signing Environment" (under the "Guidelines for Using the Simplified Sign System" section).

of training and acquired only a receptive sign vocabulary or learned to produce just a few signs.

These wide individual differences in sign-learning success led investigators to try to determine what factors were associated with successful sign acquisition by children with autism. In general, those children who earned higher scores on intelligence tests and who had better social skills, receptive language abilities, and fine motor skills tended to make the greatest progress (Bonvillian & Blackburn, 1991; Gaines et al., 1988). In addition, the size of the children's vocabularies was positively related to how long they had participated. It should be noted, however, that most participants showed only a gradual increase in vocabulary size over time.

Of those factors found to be positively associated with sign learning, it was the children's scores on tests of fine motor skills that initially puzzled investigators. One reason for this confusion was that children with autism historically were depicted as having intact fine motor abilities (Kanner, 1943). This view that children with ASD had typical or near-normal motor abilities continued for some time. In 1988, Mirenda and Schuler referred to "The combination of severe social-cognitive limitations and relatively well-developed motor skills that is so typical of the autistic syndrome" (p. 25). This assumption that children with autism have near-normal motor abilities now appears to be fundamentally incorrect (Bo et al., 2016; Bodison & Mostofsky, 2014; Paquet et al., 2016).

Not only do children with autism frequently have deficits in fine motor skills, but they often have serious gross motor skill deficits as well (Chukoskie, Townsend, & Westerfield, 2013; Slavoff, 1998; see also LeBarton & Iverson, 2016a). Evidently underlying the many motor impairments or deficits reported for children with ASD are related patterns of atypical hemispheric lateralization of their motor circuits (Floris et al., 2016). These motor development difficulties may include such basic motor control processes as gait, balance and coordination, and posture (Gidley Larson & Mostofsky, 2006). The motor deficits of children with autism, furthermore, are developmentally stable; that is, motor performance typically continues to be substantially impaired with children's increasing age (Biscaldi et al., 2014). These deficits in motor skills that emerge early in the development of young children with ASD also apparently contribute to their problems in subsequent acquisition of executive functioning abilities (e.g., working memory, planning) (St. John et al., 2016). In light of these findings, motor impairments are now seen as occurring quite often among individuals with autism (Mirenda, 2008), and apparently constitute an integral part of the syndrome. Moreover, the motor atypicalities or impairments present early in the development of most children subsequently diagnosed with ASD may serve as behavioral markers of the syndrome and thus facilitate early diagnosis (May et al., 2016; Trevarthen & Delafield-Butt, 2013).

A likely reason why motor functioning difficulties in children with autism were not systematically probed until relatively recently is that motor disturbances may not be as striking or seem as important as other areas of developmental difficulty. When a child fails to acquire useful speech, does not respond emotionally to others in a typical way, and lags far behind his or her peers cognitively, then these difficulties or disturbances are both quite conspicuous and major sources of concern. Furthermore, when a child lags behind motorically after attaining the basic motor milestones of sitting, standing, and walking, such a deficiency may not be especially evident or seem of great importance. Today, however, motor disturbances and deficits in motor planning and sequencing are seen as vital aspects in the functioning of both younger and older children with ASD (Adams, 1998; Bodison & Mostofsky, 2014; Focaroli et al., 2016; Gidley Larson & Mostofsky, 2006; Herman et al., 2019; Hughes, 1996; Ming, Brimacombe, & Wagner, 2007; Mostofsky et al., 2006; Paquet et al., 2016; Vanvuchelen, Roeyers, & De Weerdt, 2007) and in deaf children with ASD (Bhat et al., 2016; Shield et al., 2017). The difficulties many children with autism experience combining actions into motor or action sequences may rest, in part, on their tendency to subdivide such sequences into smaller pieces. If children with ASD do not process motor or gestural sequences as whole units, they may have difficulty understanding the intentions of others' actions (Cattaneo et al., 2007; see also Angeleri et al., 2016).

In retrospect, it seems quite logical that children's scores on tests of fine motor skills would be positively related to their success in learning a visual-motor or sign-communication system. In fact, discussions with teachers of sign-learning children underscored the teachers' concerns about their students' motor problems in general and how these problems might impair their sign production (Bonvillian & Blackburn, 1991).

These teachers' concerns led directly to an investigation of the relationship between the sign production of children with autism and their motor functioning (Seal & Bonvillian, 1997). In this study, fourteen non-speaking students with autism were videotaped while they were signing with their teachers. These tapes subsequently were transcribed into the sign notation system developed by William C. Stokoe (1960; Stokoe et al., 1965). All of the students made errors in their sign formation, with the error rates varying widely among the participants. Those who acquired the most signs typically had low error rates, whereas those who learned relatively few signs had much higher error rates in sign formation.

The movement parameter of signs proved to be an area of particular difficulty in the sign production of these students (Seal & Bonvillian, 1997). Not only did the students have difficulty with various sign movements, but they often deleted movements from multi-movement signs and added extraneous movements to others. Eleven of these children subsequently were given an apraxia test battery to assess their purposeful motor actions or movements. The high incidence of errors by the students on the apraxia battery was consistent with a diagnosis of apraxia or dyspraxia.[10] Furthermore, the rate at which these students made errors in producing the movement parameter of signs was highly related to their scores on the apraxia battery. There was not, however, a strong relationship between the students' apraxia scores and their percentages of location or handshape errors.

These findings were interpreted as indicating that movement functioning played an important role in the signing of children with autism. Additional support for this interpretation of a frequently occurring apraxia component in children with ASD comes from the finding of a significant relationship between the apraxia scores of

---

10   Apraxia is a neuromotor disorder that precludes or limits an individual's planned, voluntary, and purposeful motor movements in the absence of muscle weakness or paralysis (Wertz, LaPointe, & Rosenbek, 1984). A loss of the ability to execute movements is usually referred to as *apraxia*, whereas a less profound impairment often is referred to as *dyspraxia*. While the term *apraxia* typically is used in the literature for adult-onset impairments, *developmental dyspraxia* frequently is used for impairments present from infancy or early childhood onward.

children with autism and their sign language production (Soorya, 2003). Because a large proportion of children identified with autism also have apraxia, it might be prudent to evaluate all children with autism and speech difficulties for apraxia (Bhat et al., 2016; Shield et al., 2017; Tierney et al., 2015). An elevated incidence of dyspraxia also has been reported to occur in adults with ASD (Cassidy et al., 2016).

Motor impairments in children with autism also were the focus of a study by Page and Boucher (1998). These investigators found that nearly 80% of the thirty-three children they examined exhibited marked impairments in various areas of motor functioning. The children's motor problems included oromotor skills (tongue and lip movements, chewing), manual skills (object manipulation, forming correct handshapes, sequencing handshapes), and gross motor skills (running, hopping). Although deficits were evident in all three skill areas, the most prevalent areas of difficulty were oromotor and manual skills. In light of their findings, the investigators suggested that oral and manual dyspraxia probably played an important role in the impaired speech and signing of many children with ASD. These concerns about the relationship of oral- and manual-motor difficulties to language proficiency appear to be well-founded. A more recent study demonstrated that the oral- and manual-motor skills of very young children with autism significantly predicted their level of speech fluency in middle childhood and adolescence (Gernsbacher et al., 2008).

One possible explanation for findings of dyspraxia in children with ASD is that their gestural and oromotor impairments might just reflect more general or basic motor impairments. Research results, however, suggest that findings of dyspraxia in these children cannot be fully accounted for by their basic motor skill deficits (Dziuk et al., 2007; see also Dowell, Mahone, & Mostofsky, 2009). Other factors, such as understanding others' intentions and the ability to sequence actions and keep them in memory, may be quite important as well (see also Angeleri et al., 2016 and Cassidy et al., 2016).

Not only do children with autism often show impairments in their gestural production, but they typically display nonverbal communication that is quite different from that of other children as well. Children with autism are much less likely than other young children to point, show objects, to use conventional gestures such as shaking or nodding one's head, or to gaze at another person to communicate, which may result in problems interpreting other people's facial expressions (Denmark et al., 2014; LeBarton & Iverson, 2016b; Mastrogiuseppe et al., 2015; Shield et al., 2015; So et al., 2015; Sparaci et al., 2019; Stone et al., 1997). When young children with ASD do use deictic gestures, they tend to extend an open palm toward an object (a "give" gesture) rather than using the extended index finger in a pointing gesture (Özçalişkan et al., 2017). Children with ASD also are less likely to integrate their gesture production with their spoken language than typically developing children (So et al., 2015). Some of these children's atypicalities in nonverbal or gestural communication, it should be noted, may rest on their impaired motor skills.

Another motor production factor involved in the speech and signing of children with autism is their sequencing of movements. In spoken language, the brain and oral musculature are involved in the rapid production of speech sounds over time. Sequential motor production is also an important dimension in the formation of signs from genuine sign languages such as American Sign Language (ASL). In ASL, many signs have more than one movement. Slavoff (1998) examined the gestural imitation and gestural sequencing of thirteen children with autism. Seven of the children communicated primarily through speech, six through signs. The vocabulary sizes of these children, regardless of language modality, were highly related to their scores on tests of gestural imitation and sequencing. That is, the better a child performed on the tests of gestural imitation and sequencing, the larger the size of his or her vocabulary. This finding of a substantial relationship between gestural imitation and sequencing scores and vocabulary size might be used as a predictor of which children with ASD would be good candidates for participation in a sign-communication program. Furthermore, the children's ability to imitate a gestural sequence declined sharply from one-movement gestures to three-movement gestures. These findings underscore an important movement component in the children's signing and speech, and probably an important imitation or memory component as well.[11] Moreover, not only do children with ASD imitate

---

11   Although it is not clear how best to account for this decline in performance, it is possible that those children who experienced considerable difficulty imitating multi-movement gestures may have had particular difficulty forming representations of more than a single action at a time. It is also possible that representations in their working memories may have decayed more quickly than normal.

actions less than typically developing children, they often successfully imitate only the final action of a sequence (Gonsiorowski, Williamson, & Robins, 2016). Another implication of these findings is that signs that involve more than a single movement are likely to prove difficult for some children with autism to remember and to produce.[12]

The finding that the gestural or motor imitation abilities of children with ASD were related to measures of vocabulary, language development, and language use (Slavoff, 1998; see also Ingersoll & Lalonde, 2010; Ingersoll & Meyer, 2011; Özçalişkan et al., 2017; Stone & Yoder, 2001; and Toth et al., 2006) in turn raises questions about how best to teach manual signs to youngsters with autism. That is, if a child with ASD has particular difficulty imitating another person's actions or gestures, then a sign-teaching approach that began by relying heavily on the modeling of a sign by the teacher likely would not be very effective. One approach would be to focus on enhancing the child's imitation skills prior to teaching signs. A promising procedure in this domain would be to have a communication therapist initially follow the child's lead by nearly simultaneously imitating all of the child's gestures, vocalizations, and actions on objects. If this approach is successful in gaining the child's attention, then the therapist would start interspersing bids for the child to copy or imitate the therapist's actions (Ingersoll & Schreibman, 2006).

Or, for a child who fails to imitate, it may be necessary to rely primarily on molding his hands into the correct sign handshape and then physically guiding his hands through the correct sign movement. This approach of molding and guiding the signer's hands may need to be employed often as deficits in imitation are quite widespread among children with ASD (Hepburn & Stone, 2006; Jiménez et al., 2015; Rogers & Bennetto, 2000; Rogers, Bennetto, McEvoy, & Pennington, 1996; Rogers & Williams, 2006; Smith & Bryson, 1998; Vanvuchelen et al., 2007, 2011; Williams, Whiten, & Singh, 2004). Moreover, deficits in gestural imitation are especially pronounced in non-speaking or minimally verbal children with autism (Heimann et al., 2016; Shield et al., 2017). Indeed, children

---

12 Studies concerning the motor difficulties of persons with ASD influenced the selection and development of signs in our Simplified Sign System. That is, we deliberately modified signs so that most had only a single movement and we excluded more complex handshapes. The fact that our signs resemble the concepts they stand for also should make them easier to learn and to remember.

with autism appear to rely more on proprioceptive feedback (sense of relative position of one's limbs) than on visual feedback to guide their motor learning (Bodison & Mostofsky, 2014).

The deficits in visual imitation seen in children with autism may be the product of a dysfunctional observation matching system (Bernier et al., 2007), motor-planning difficulties (Hughes, 1996; Lloyd, MacDonald, & Lord, 2011; Smith & Bryson, 1994), or problems in forming internal models or representations of actions (Haswell et al., 2009). In contrast to the motor deficits of children with ASD, which typically remain stable with increasing age, these children's difficulties in imitation skills tend to improve with age (Biscaldi et al., 2014). As a consequence, it may be possible for teachers to rely more on modeling and imitation in their students' learning of signs as the students get older.

A recent series of studies focusing on the signing of deaf children with ASD (Shield, 2010, 2014; Shield & Meier, 2012) has revealed that hand or palm orientation is another sign formational parameter that can be problematic. Some of the individuals in these studies occasionally reversed the palm orientation of the signs they made. This sign formational error, however, was interpreted as probably being a reflection of the children's difficulties in visual perspective-taking (Shield, 2010; Shield & Meier, 2012), rather than being the product of underlying motor impairments. Later, however, the authors surmised that persons with autism may approach imitation of gestures and signs in a manner different from typically developing individuals (Herman et al., 2019; Shield & Meier, 2018). Some deaf children with ASD also demonstrated sign echolalia or repetition of others' signs (Shield, 2014; Shield, Cooley, & Meier, 2017). This finding would indicate that echolalia in ASD is not modality dependent, as it evidently occurs both in sign and speech modes (see also Jure, Rapin, & Tuchman, 1991).

Although numerous studies in recent decades have underlined the many problems that children with ASD experience in their imitation of gestures (Vivanti & Hamilton, 2014), it is likely that these children will experience fewer difficulties imitating Simplified Signs than they do imitating gestures more generally. We say this because most of the signs in the Simplified Sign System are meaningful gestures. That is, the signs typically represent meaningful actions or the shapes of objects and thus are meaningful behaviors for most persons. In the past, investigators have reported that children with autism imitate meaningful gestures more accurately than gestures without clear meanings (Rogers et al., 1996; Smith & Bryson, 2007; Vanvuchelen et al., 2007).

Finally, the difficulties that children with ASD experience in the formation of words and signs and in their sequencing may be related to damage to or abnormalities of the cerebellum. The cerebellum is the hindbrain structure especially involved in muscular or motor control, the maintenance of equilibrium, learning, coordination, and the precise timing and sequencing of complex motor movements (Cheron, Márquez-Ruiz, & Dan, 2016). Because the cerebellum's developmental phase is a lengthy one, it is especially vulnerable to impairments associated with a number of different disorders (Becker & Stoodley, 2013). Cerebellar abnormalities often are evident in individuals with autism (Allen, 2005, 2006; Bauman & Kemper, 2005; Becker & Stoodley, 2013; Kemper & Bauman, 1998; Palmen et al., 2004). These abnormalities may negatively affect the musculature and sequencing involved in the production of spoken words and phrases and the motor movements and sequencing involved in the production of signs, fingerspelling, and multi-sign utterances. If, as some believe (Grush, 2004), the cerebellum plays a central role in the mimicking and the prediction of the outcome of motor actions, then it is easy to see why abnormalities in the cerebellum would adversely affect the learning and production of spoken words and manual signs. Furthermore, investigators have advanced the view that the cerebellum is involved in a variety of cognitive and linguistic functions (Becker & Stoodley, 2013; Leiner, Leiner, & Dow, 1989, 1993), including certain high-level linguistic processes (De Smet et al., 2007). It has also been hypothesized that the cerebellum may play an important role in the development of social cognition and emotion through its extensive connections in different areas of the cortex (Crippa et al., 2016).

Other Non-Oral Approaches

The serious motor and memory difficulties observed in some children with ASD may inhibit their acquisition of signs from the Simplified Sign System we have developed. Fortunately, there are a number of different augmentative and alternative communication systems that can be used in intervention programs for those individuals who fail to acquire speech and who experience great difficulty in learning to sign (Beukelman & Mirenda, 2005, 2013; Romski et al., 2015; von Tetzchner & Martinsen, 2000). These various systems are primarily visually-based communication systems and rest on the observation that many children with autism have better visual-processing skills than auditory-vocal processing skills. These approaches often make use of gestures, pictures, real objects, electronic devices, and computerized voice synthesizers or speech-generating devices.

The approaches that rely on pictures, real objects, and speech-generating devices to facilitate communication are known as aided communication. Approaches that do not include equipment, such as manual signs, speech, or gestures, are known as unaided communication. Among the advantages of the aided communication approaches are that they typically make only limited demands on the user's memory skills (especially if the symbols involved are iconic or representative), require only rather basic motor abilities, and often are understood by other persons in the user's environment (Wendt, 2009). Among the disadvantages of the aided systems are that they require that the equipment involved be carried by the user or communication partner to any change in location and that communicative exchanges often take longer than they do with unaided approaches.

Although it is beyond the scope of the present book to describe these systems in detail, we will provide brief overviews of a handful of these approaches for interested teachers and caregivers. At the same time, we should note that an important limitation of some of these systems is that the research evidence on which they are based often consists largely of descriptive accounts involving relatively few children.

One approach to facilitating communication is to have a non-speaking and non-signing child use real objects (or tangible symbols) to make requests or to convey information (Bondy & Frost, 2002; Rowland & Schweigert, 1990, 2000; Stillman & Battle, 1984; van Dijk, 1966). For example, a child might learn to bring his mother a paper cup if he is thirsty. Alternatively, another child might give his teacher a small ball if he wanted to play. In comparison with signs and speech, this approach involves little memory, imitation, or symbolic skills by the child and virtually no new learning by the caregiver. The motor demands on the child are also relatively minimal. Yet, it should be recognized that this approach has limited portability and that the desired objects may not be available when they are needed. It may also prove difficult to portray more abstract notions using real objects (Vanderheiden & Lloyd, 1986). The limitation in portability caused by having the child carry a collection of real objects with him wherever he goes may be overcome in part by switching to smaller versions of the objects. At the same time, it should not be assumed that young children will recognize that the much smaller version of the object will represent the full-sized object (DeLoache, Miller, & Rosengren, 1997). Communication, moreover, would still be restricted to the number of items one could easily carry in a bag and by the time involved in finding the desired item. The time needed to find the desired item from among a collection of objects also may make demands on the child's memory.

In comparison with real objects, photographs are more easily carried to different locations; thus, they do not have the same portability constraints. They also can be used to represent specific people, places, and activities (Bondy & Frost, 2002). Photographs, however, appear to require somewhat more symbolic sophistication by the child than the use of real objects because photographs transform a three-dimensional object into a two-dimensional representation. The ability to understand and interpret photographs usually unfolds over the first several years of life in typically developing children (DeLoache, Pierroutsakos, & Uttal, 2003). Teachers and caregivers working with a non-speaking child thus will need to ensure that the child understands that the photographs represent real objects and actions. Furthermore, these teachers and caregivers often will need to take photographs or clip pictures from magazines in order to establish the needed inventory of objects and activities. In the past, it might have taken considerable time to assemble a suitable and rich inventory of photos and pictures, but with the spread of computer technology (e.g., laptops, tablets), software, online resources, and the subsequent proliferation of smartphones with cameras and associated apps, this task is much less daunting today. Often, physical pictures are attached to a board or put into a communication book for a particular child, but it is also possible to put digital photos that serve the same function into a digital album on a child's portable computer and/or smartphone for use in public. Regardless of the specific form of the collection of photographs or pictures, such collections will need to be expanded periodically as the child's interests and desires change over time. If the collection of photographs or pictures gets large, then this communication approach likely will make demands on the child's memory and visual-tracking skills. Nonetheless, the use of picture boards or books has met with some success in fostering communication in children with autism (Mirenda & Santogrossi, 1985; Reichle, York, & Sigafoos, 1991).

One of the most popular picture systems is the Picture Exchange Communication System (PECS). PECS differs from other picture communication systems in that the developers, Andy Bondy and Lori Frost, devised a specific intervention protocol and that the system requires that a participating child interact with a communication partner (Bondy & Frost, 2009b). PECS was introduced as a communication system for children with autism who neither imitated vocally nor motorically, nor were they successful in pointing to pictures to communicate their needs or desires (Bondy & Frost, 1994, 2002). In this system, the first step is to determine what item or activity a particular child desires. A picture of this item (or activity) is then placed on a card. An adult, typically the teacher or caregiver, then holds the desired item in one hand while simultaneously extending the other hand to the child with the card representing the item. A second person, the physical prompter, typically sits near the child and guides the child's hand in first picking up the card and then releasing it back into the hand of the first adult. The item is then given to the child. Over time, the action of the physical prompter is faded or eliminated as the child learns to pick up and deliver the desired card to the first adult in exchange for receiving the desired item. The number of pictures is then expanded to include a wider array of items, activities, or persons.

An important aspect of the PECS approach is that it involves interaction with another person: the card recipient. Thus, the child not only is learning to use pictures to represent items or activities, but also is learning to initiate communication with a partner. Over time, children taught PECS typically show increases both in their frequency of communication and in the size of their PECS vocabulary (Flippin, Reszka, & Watson, 2010; Ganz et al., 2012; Ganz & Simpson, 2004; Gordon et al., 2011; Magiati & Howlin, 2003; Preston & Carter, 2009; Schwartz, Garfinkle, & Bauer, 1998), as well as in their spoken language skills (Bondy & Frost, 2009b). For some children with autism, the transition from PECS to spoken language skills will remain elusive; for these youngsters, the fostering of communication skills in another visual modality may be helpful (Bondy & Frost, 2009a).

There are a number of advantages to using PECS in comparison with other communication intervention approaches for non-speaking or minimally verbal children with autism. One advantage is ease of implementation. Time and effort do not need to be spent developing prerequisite skills, such as eye contact, verbal imitation, or gestural production in the participating children (Flippin et al., 2010; Preston & Carter, 2009). Also, teachers and therapists can acquire the skills needed to use PECS with children after only a relatively brief training period. In contrast, teachers and therapists who choose to use manual signs often need considerable training before they are sufficiently proficient signers to work effectively with children with ASD. Another advantage to using PECS is that progress in attaining functional communication skills by participating children often is quite quick. Finally, individuals not directly involved in PECS training frequently can recognize what participating children are requesting from looking at the pictures the children are holding, whereas outsiders may not understand the signs or vocal utterances that children produce. In light of these advantages, PECS has become a widely used intervention approach for many non-speaking children with ASD.

Although the results of a number of studies show that PECS can be readily learned by many young children with ASD who have little or no spoken language skills, some concerns remain about its effectiveness in certain domains. Anecdotal reports suggest that PECS may foster spoken language skills in some children. More systematic reviews, however, lead to the conclusion that it is unclear as to whether experience using PECS is associated with improvements in spoken language skills (Preston & Carter, 2009), and if there are benefits in speech, they appear to be small in magnitude (Flippin et al., 2010). Other concerns that investigators might wish to address include the efficacy of PECS in reducing challenging behaviors, whether PECS skills are maintained over time and generalized to new situations, and if PECS can fulfill more diverse communicative functions other than merely requesting items such as engaging in social interactions, commenting on current events, telling jokes or stories, or conveying other types of information (Bonvillian, 2019).

Line drawings are another option that may be effectively employed (Bloomberg, Karlan, & Lloyd, 1990; Hamilton & Snell, 1993). Line drawings have been used not only to depict persons, places, objects, and activities, but also to communicate properties or descriptors, feelings, and social etiquette messages such as please or thank-you (Bondy & Frost, 2002). In addition to creating one's own line drawings, there are a number of commercially available packages containing thousands of such symbols.

One of the earliest non-speech approaches to teaching children with autism to communicate involved the use of wooden or plastic symbols (McLean & McLean, 1974; Premack & Premack, 1974). In this approach, the symbols do not resemble their referents; they are equivalent to words or concepts in a spoken language. Using many of the same procedures first utilized by Premack (1971) to establish various language skills in a chimpanzee, McLean and McLean reported improved communication skills in children with autism. Two of their three non-speaking participants learned to use the symbols to describe a limited number of events or social interactions. It should be noted that these two children acquired a lexicon of manual signs as well.

Printed words or letters also may be responded to as visual symbols by children with ASD. Some success in developing communication skills has been reported in several studies that focused on learning printed or written words (LaVigna, 1977; Marshall & Hegrenes, 1972; Miller, 1969). These investigators began by training participants to recognize individual words and then teaching them to arrange the words in phrases. Training outcomes, though, varied widely across participants. A slightly different approach was used by Ratusnik and Ratusnik (1974) with a non-speaking ten-year-old with autism. This child initially was taught to spell individual words with plastic letters; he then learned to combine these words into phrases. At the study's conclusion, he occasionally combined words spontaneously into sentences. The use of words and letters to communicate may help some persons with autism to acquire literacy skills. However, in view of the fact that the meanings of written or printed words are not transparent, this might make them more difficult for children with autism to learn than the items used in most other approaches (Mirenda & Locke, 1989).

Improvements in technology also have benefited children with limited spoken language abilities. A number of these individuals have learned to use speech-generating devices or voice output communication aids (VOCAs) (Bornman & Alant, 1999; Schlosser, Sigafoos, & Koul, 2009; Sigafoos & Drasgow, 2001). These are portable electronic devices that produce digitized or synthetic speech output (Mirenda, 2003); these devices may help a child to interact effectively with people unfamiliar with the child's sign, symbol, or picture communication system. Unfortunately, a significant drawback to a number of these devices is that their output is limited to prestored messages (Schlosser et al., 2009), with the consequence that their use in new situations is considerably constrained. New messages may take considerable time to compose; children and adults who used speech-generating devices and their parents noted that some potential communication partners did not have the patience to wait long enough for a new message to be conveyed (Batorowicz et al., 2014). Furthermore, the batteries on many commercial speech-generating devices often become drained and need recharging, such devices frequently break down and may require weeks to repair, they may be more difficult to use in outdoor settings, particularly in bad weather or where electrical outlets for recharging are unavailable, or it may be hard to hear the voice output in public or noisy settings (Batorowicz et al., 2014; Iacono et al., 2013).

A more recently introduced software application for electronic devices, known as Proloquo2Go™ (Sennott & Bowker, 2009), shows much promise as an effective system of communication for many minimally verbal children with ASD. This application runs on a range of touchscreen devices. The screens on these devices display different pictures from which a user may choose. The user scrolls through and selects the item desired. The large storage capacities of these devices mean that users do not need to carry around large communication books or collections of pictures to ensure effective communication in diverse settings. Moreover, the public use of electronic devices (such as smartphones and tablets) by people of all ages is so common that children with autism using Proloquo2Go™ probably will not stand out as much, but rather fit in better with their peers and be more widely accepted (see Dada et al., 2016). The widespread availability and use of these portable electronic devices may also result in the children with ASD receiving more input and interaction throughout the day from their communication partners (Sennott, Light, & McNaughton, 2016).

Another important aspect of Proloquo2Go™ is that it offers a voice output system. That is, a user manually enters a desired phrase into the system, and the device then reads it aloud. This option should enable individuals unfamiliar with this communication application to respond appropriately to the user's requests. Because of the relative newness of this system, detailed evaluations of its effectiveness are limited in number. Among the early findings are reports that children with autism spectrum disorder are able to learn to make multistep requests (Alzrayer, Banda, & Koul, 2017) and to label aspects of their environments (Lorah & Parnell, 2017). These outcomes and others suggest that the speech-generating applications on smartphones and tablet-like devices are effective communicative approaches for many children with ASD, and that the results compare favorably with the use of manual signs or PECS (Kagohara et al., 2013). Overall, the Proloquo2Go™ application looks like it will be a very worthwhile addition to the array of communication approaches used by non-speaking individuals.

Comparison Studies

Although the past several decades have witnessed the emergence of a wide range of non-oral approaches designed to facilitate communication in children with ASD, there have been few systematic, large scale, long-term comparisons of the relative efficacy of these various sign, symbol, speech-generating, and picture communication systems with such children (Mirenda, 2003). This relative dearth of research comparing the effectiveness of different approaches has made it difficult for teachers, caregivers, and clinicians to make informed decisions or recommendations as to the optimal intervention strategy for particular children. This situation appears to be changing, however, as various investigators have conducted systematic comparisons in recent years (Couper et al., 2014; Gevarter et al., 2013; Mirenda, 2014; van der Meer et al., 2011; Wendt, 2009). One important difficulty with conducting such assessments is that children with autism constitute a very diverse group (Schaaf & Zoghbi, 2011) with widely differing abilities; this diversity makes it unlikely that a single intervention approach will be the optimal method for all children (Gevarter et al., 2013; Landa, 2007). A second difficulty is that the abilities and communication needs of individuals with ASD change from childhood to adulthood (Howlin et al., 2004). These changes, in turn, may need to be addressed by modifying or switching the intervention approach used.

In four carefully conducted comparison studies that examined the use of manual signs and PECS, the results did not clearly favor one approach over the other. In the first study (Anderson, 2001), six children, ranging in age from two to four years, were taught sign language or PECS in alternating sessions. As a group, the children showed a faster rate of acquisition and greater item generalization with PECS than sign language. In contrast, these same children demonstrated greater eye contact, higher levels of initiation of interaction and communication, and more frequent vocalization at post-treatment in sign training. Examining the performance of the participants individually, Anderson observed that three children behaviorally preferred PECS and that the other three behaviorally preferred sign language. Additional examination suggested that the children who preferred signs tended to be chronologically older, showed more advanced play behavior, and had higher fine- and gross-motor age equivalents than the children who preferred PECS. In interpreting her findings, Anderson observed that a certain level of cognitive and motor ability might need to be attained before sign language training is worthwhile. She speculated that very young children with autism might be effectively taught to communicate first with PECS and then later transitioned to signs.

In the second comparison study (Tincani, 2004), two elementary-school-aged children were trained on both manual signs and PECS. One child was more successful using signs; the other was more successful using PECS. Both participants vocalized more frequently during sign training. The finding that the children in both the Anderson (2001) and Tincani (2004) studies vocalized more frequently during sign training may be seen as additional evidence that acquiring manual signs not only does not inhibit vocal language development, but probably facilitates it. Furthermore, the finding that certain manual actions are positively related to the occurrence of vocal actions would be consistent with the emerging view that "systems of movement for mouth and for hand cannot be separated from one another, and that they are intimately linked in the production of language" (Iverson & Thelen, 1999, p. 35).

In the third study (Nollet, 2008), the three participants also were trained to communicate using manual signs and PECS. The two older children in this study acquired the two communicative methods at about the same rate, but when given the opportunity, they signed more frequently than they picture exchanged. The youngest participant, in contrast, learned picture-exchange skills more rapidly, and used this method more often. In addition, the incidence of problem behaviors (e. g., whining, tantrums) declined for all three participants over the course of the study, while vocal production increased for two.

In the fourth comparison study (Moodie-Ramdeen, 2008), three children were randomly assigned to PECS training whereas three others were taught American Sign Language signs. Although all six participants showed improvements in communication over the course of the study, progress was at a faster rate for those participants who received PECS training than those given sign instruction. More specifically, one child in PECS and one in manual sign training made quite substantial improvements whereas the other four children showed only minor improvements. The researcher, Moodie-Ramdeen, observed that young children with autism might well benefit from multiple forms of communication training. Moreover, the highly variable outcomes across these four studies suggest that the characteristics of the individual children often are critical in determining training program efficacy, not the particular system.

In more recent comparison studies, investigators have examined the acquisition and use of manual signs, PECS, and speech-generating devices (with Proloquo2Go™ application) to communicate in children with ASD (Achmadi et al., 2014; Couper et al., 2014; McLay et al., 2015). Across the studies, the children typically learned all three communication systems to the acquisition criterion. In general, though, the children tended to reach criterion more rapidly and to maintain performance better with the speech-generating devices and PECS. An explanation advanced for this pattern was that these two systems relied more on the children's recognition memory processes, whereas signs depended more on the children's recall skills. Furthermore, when assessments were conducted on the children's preferences, most of the children selected the speech-generating devices. The findings of these studies bode well for the continued and increased use of such speech-generating devices with minimally verbal children with ASD in the future.

Overall, more research needs to be conducted before one can make truly definitive statements about which individuals with ASD are more likely to benefit from which non-oral approaches. In particular, comparison studies need to examine which communicative system works best with which children over the long run. A determined effort also needs to be made to determine which training and teaching approaches are likely to optimize participants' progress in acquiring useful communication skills. Another factor that should be considered in selecting an intervention approach is the preference of the individual user for a particular system. Individual children with ASD (or other developmental disabilities) often show preferences for different communicative intervention approaches (van der Meer et al., 2011) and these preferences may change with increasing age. In addition, the teaching of signs that more closely resemble the concepts that they represent (that is, signs that are highly iconic or pantomimic, such as Simplified Signs) may positively influence the sign-learning abilities of a wide range of individuals with ASD. This potential enhancement of sign-learning abilities may, in turn, necessitate another round of comparison studies across the different intervention options.

Finally, it should be noted that when augmentative and alternative communication systems are used in an intervention program for children with autism, there is no evidence that the use of such systems will impede or hinder these children's speech production. Rather, systematic examination of the outcomes of numerous studies in which these systems were used indicate that children often showed gains in their speech production (Romski et al., 2015; Schlosser & Wendt, 2008). These gains, however, frequently were relatively modest ones.

Evaluative Comments

A large number of studies have reported that sign language training is an effective intervention strategy for teaching receptive and expressive language skills to non-speaking children with ASD. Indeed, in his review of communication intervention programs for children with autism, Goldstein (2002, p. 373) observed, "In particular, interventions incorporating sign language... have been used successfully to expand the communication repertoire of children with autism." At the same time, it should be acknowledged that relatively little is known about the interrelationships among participants' characteristics, types of instruction, the utilization of multiple intervention strategies, and sign-communication program outcomes.

Overall, there are both distinct disadvantages and advantages associated with using manual signs as opposed to other non-oral communication systems or approaches with children with autism (Wendt, 2009). Some individuals may have severe motor problems or impairments that may impede their sign learning (Bonvillian, 2002; Maurer & Damasio, 1982). In addition, although signs may be produced more slowly than speech, they are not as permanent or long lasting in the duration of their presentation as pictures or real objects. Some children may need a longer presentation time than is comfortable when signing. A third limitation of signing is that a learner needs sufficient memory skills to be able to recall and produce the signs that have been taught. Pictures and real objects require that the learner only recognize the needed concept or item from a display or collection.

Fourth, teachers and caregivers need to invest the time necessary to learn to communicate effectively through signs. Although the time commitment involved in keeping pace with the signing of most children with ASD is relatively small, it is not negligible; teachers and caregivers must make the commitment to use signs with the child throughout the day to maximize its effectiveness. Fifth, as the practice of adapting or modifying signs to make them easier to produce continues to grow, teachers and caregivers will need to learn the specific exceptions used with individual children. Finally, despite the increased popularity of signing in the general public over the past few decades, most members of society do not sign. This means that the usefulness of children's signing with persons outside of their homes, schools, and care centers will be considerably limited.

Although there are some disadvantages to using signs with non-speaking children with ASD, there are several distinct advantages as well. With signing, one does not need to carry around supplies or invest in expensive equipment. Additionally, conversations in sign, as opposed to other augmentative and alternative communication approaches, can be relatively fast-paced and spontaneous. The learner does not need to turn pages, find a picture or an object, or turn on equipment in order to communicate. A third advantage is that successful signing involves interaction with another person and, in particular, appears to foster increased eye contact. Finally, there is some evidence that the planning, coordinating, and sequencing of motor movements used in forming a sign are closely related neurobiologically to the specific oral-motor movements involved in uttering a spoken word. This close neurological association may help explain why some children learning to sign spontaneously start to vocalize.

If a decision is made to implement a signing program (or other augmentative and alternative communication interventions) for a child with ASD, the available evidence indicates that the earlier in the child's life that the program is begun, then the greater his or her acquisition of communication skills likely will be in the long run. With the diagnosis of childhood autism often being made in a child's second year, we see no compelling reason not to introduce signs as soon after the diagnosis as conveniently possible. This early introduction of signs contrasts markedly with the all too frequent approach of waiting to see whether a child with ASD will acquire useful speech and then teaching signs only after it appears that he or she will not speak. Implementing a sign-communication program early in development is likely to have lasting benefits.

If a sign-communication program is introduced, then progress in spoken language development is more likely to occur if speech accompanies the signed input. In most cases, the sign and speech input may be simultaneous. For those children with ASD who find spoken language input aversive, however, then a different strategy may need to be employed. One possibility would be to teach signing skills in a separate session from that of speech training. Once these children have learned to communicate spontaneously through signs, it may be possible to pair signs with speech to facilitate spontaneous spoken language usage and development.

Because of the motor and cognitive impairments present in many children with ASD, different signs may be learned and remembered more easily than others. In general, those signs that are easy to form, high in iconicity, and of interest or use to the children are acquired more readily. We selected or developed Simplified Signs to meet these criteria; therefore, they should constitute a good lexicon for individuals with autism. The Simplified Sign System also is a solid choice for others who experience cognitive, memory, and/or motor disturbances, such as persons with cerebral palsy, an intellectual disability, or aphasia. The language disorders of this last group of individuals often result from a severe head injury, brain tumor, brain infection, or stroke. In other words, after such an event, a person may have difficulty understanding speech (receptive aphasia) or producing recognizable speech (expressive aphasia). Our next chapter focuses on sign-communication training and teaching in persons who have aphasia.

6. Sign-Communication Intervention in Adults and Children with Aphasia

In the previous two chapters, the research focus has primarily been on the sign acquisition of non-speaking or minimally verbal children. A number of these individuals learn to communicate effectively, often for the first time, through the use of manual signs. Furthermore, while gaining proficiency in sign communication, a substantial proportion of these children are also able to acquire some spoken language skills. In the present chapter, our principal focus changes to the acquisition and use of manual signs by individuals who were once fluent spoken language users. These persons, typically as a result of a stroke or brain injury, experience severe losses of language functions, motor abilities, or both. Like non-speaking children, some of these individuals are able to learn to communicate effectively through the use of manual signs or gestures.

Manual signs have also been used by therapists to foster their clients' spoken language skills through the pairing of their clients' manual sign production with their efforts to produce recognizable words. In some instances, real improvements in speech intelligibility and articulation have been reported. Although manual sign-training and teaching programs have been shown to increase the communication abilities of many adults who have suffered extensive language losses, much remains to be learned about these individuals' sign acquisition. Many more research studies need to be conducted before we can determine how the location and severity of brain damage affect sign acquisition, how signs may best facilitate speech recovery, and which signs are more readily learned and why. Studies of deaf persons who have suffered strokes

 https://doi.org/10.11647/OBP.0205.06

that resulted in aphasia also provide a fascinating look at the distinction between these individuals' signing abilities and their gestural abilities.

It is important to note that children are not immune to strokes, head injuries, or brain trauma that result in loss of expressive and/or receptive language abilities. Furthermore, a number of children who have not suffered brain trauma may still be noticeably impaired in their spoken language development despite hearing levels and nonverbal cognitive abilities in the normal range. Many of these children have substantial and long-lasting vocabulary deficits (Rice & Hoffman, 2015), with such deficits raising concerns about the children's resulting success in learning to read and eventual educational attainment. Teaching signs to hearing children with Landau-Kleffner syndrome (acquired epileptic aphasia), a developmental language disorder (DLD), or childhood apraxia of speech may prove to be a useful strategy in improving their overall communication skills while also encouraging their development of speech skills. Finally, deaf children may be impaired in their sign language development despite normal cognitive abilities, consistent input from fluent sign language models, and the absence of other factors such as autism, head trauma, or stroke. The identification of deaf children with delayed or atypical sign language development is a relatively new expansion of the literature on developmental language disorder and presents unique challenges for families and educators.

Introduction to Aphasia and Apraxia

Individuals with aphasia, or loss of language ability, constitute another population with serious communication difficulties (Beukelman & Mirenda, 2013; Davis, 2007; Kertesz, 1979). Aphasia (or dysphasia)[1]

---

1   Technically, *aphasia* refers to a comprehensive loss of language and *dysphasia* refers to partial disruptions of language abilities. However, in many fields, the terms *aphasia* and *dysphasia* are used interchangeably to refer to losses of language ability of any degree. Furthermore, usage of these terms varies by geographical location. In the United States, the preferred term often is *aphasia*, whereas in other countries, the term *dysphasia* is more prevalent. In this text, we consider *aphasia* and *dysphasia* to generally be synonymous. For practical purposes, however, we use *aphasia* to refer to acquired language losses that are the result of strokes, head injuries, tumors, infections, and the like. In contrast, we use *developmental dysphasia* or *developmental language disorder* to refer to language problems that are present in children from an early age and which are not attributable to a specific trauma.

is primarily a language disorder that results from damage to areas of the brain responsible for various language functions. This damage can affect both the production of language (that is, *expressive language skills*) and its understanding (*receptive language skills*), as well as impairing the ability to read (*dyslexia*) or write (*dysgraphia*). Aphasia is often the product of a cerebrovascular accident or stroke, serious brain injury, brain infection, or brain tumor. Although aphasias are more common in older than younger individuals, children and adolescents may also lose all or portions of their language abilities.

Strokes are the leading cause of long-term disability among adults worldwide (Ward & Cohen, 2004). Strokes involve the relatively sudden loss of blood circulation to an area of the brain; this loss of blood circulation in turn results in impairment or loss of function performed by the brain area affected (Caplan, 1995; Kljajevic, 2012). In most instances, the cause of a stroke is a clot that blocks a blood vessel in the brain; this is known as an ischemic stroke. A less common form of stroke occurs when a blood vessel breaks and there is a discharge of blood into the brain; this is known as a hemorrhagic stroke. In the United States, there are over three quarters of a million new cases of cerebrovascular accident or stroke each year. Of those individuals who experience an acute stroke, a significant proportion (21-38%) suffer extensive language loss or aphasia (Geschwind, 1979; Laska et al., 2001; Pedersen et al., 1995). In addition to their language loss, persons with aphasia may suffer impairments in other areas of cognitive functioning, such as attention and executive function (Sandberg, 2017). Because advancements in medical care are both prolonging the average life span and improving the survival rates after strokes, there are increasing numbers of individuals with aphasia who become candidates for language therapy (Howard & Hatfield, 1987). A recent estimate is that aphasia affects about one million persons living in the U.S. (National Institute of Neurological Disorders and Stroke, 2019).

Another leading cause of disability among adults is traumatic brain injury (TBI). These serious injuries frequently are the product of an automobile accident, fall, or assault. Those individuals who suffer traumatic brain injuries are likely to experience impairments in their motor, cognitive, perceptual, communicative, and social abilities (Rispoli, Machalicek, & Lang, 2010). Individuals with acquired language impairment or aphasia after TBIs frequently make more extensive use of gestures, typically pointing and iconic gestures, when compared with healthy adults (Kim et al., 2015). Although the use of gestures may help such aphasic individuals convey information and enhance their communication, their loss of spoken language abilities may result in social isolation.

For some years, treatment programs for persons with aphasia, especially those with chronic aphasia, frequently were viewed as relatively ineffective. More recently, however, there has been a change in perspective about treatment outcomes and the optimal course of therapeutic intervention for persons with aphasia. This change was based on findings from investigations that showed that intense aphasia treatment over a short duration often resulted in substantial treatment gains and proved more effective than the same number of hours of treatment spread over a longer period (Bhogal, Teasell, & Speechley, 2003; Hillis, 2007). Greater treatment progress also was evident in those persons whose language therapy hours and frequency of language therapy were maximized (Pulvermüller & Berthier, 2008). These findings about the benefits of intensive language therapy held both for those persons whose language loss was of recent origin and for persons with chronic aphasia.

Many patients evidence substantial recovery from stroke-caused aphasia in the first three months after onset, with some persons continuing to show improvements in verbal communication over the next three months (Bakheit et al., 2007; El Hachioui et al., 2013). However, recovery often reaches a plateau about six months after stroke. In their course of language recovery, patients typically recover their semantic and syntactic skills before they recover their phonological skills (El Hachioui et al., 2013). This pattern of a longer recovery period for phonology, as opposed to semantics and syntax, apparently indicates that various components of language are often differentially affected in aphasia.

Additional patients, especially those with a severe aphasia, fail to reacquire most of their speech skills, even after intensive and prolonged speech therapy. Some of these latter individuals may be able to acquire needed communication skills through the use of manual signs or other augmentative and alternative communication intervention strategies

(Hux, Weissling, & Wallace, 2008). Yet, many such individuals, including those with severe, chronic aphasia, evidently are reluctant to embrace any augmentative and alternative communicative strategy out of fear that it might interfere with the return of their natural speech skills (Beukelman et al., 2007).

Persons who become aphasic may have serious motor or visual-processing difficulties, along with their language-processing disturbances. In general, however, visual and gestural skills are not as impaired as spoken language skills in persons with aphasia (Porch, 1970, cited in Kenin & Swisher, 1972; see also Cocks et al., 2009). This pattern may help explain why many individuals with aphasia make more frequent use of gestures, especially iconic gestures, in their communication than do neurologically healthy comparison group members (Kong et al., 2015; Pritchard et al., 2015). Many persons with aphasia experience muscular weakness (or hemiparesis) on one side of their bodies. If the impairment is quite severe and the side of the body is paralyzed, then the term hemiplegia is used (Patterson & Chapey, 2008). In the large majority of cases it is the right side of the body that is affected. In addition, some individuals may experience temporary or lasting paralysis on both sides of their bodies. Clearly, persons with lasting, bilateral paralysis would not be good candidates for a sign-communication system where movement of at least one arm is essential. Before starting a sign-communication intervention with such persons, control of movement of at least one arm would need to be re-established.[2] Furthermore, the visual problems experienced by certain individuals with aphasia often involve a cut in their visual fields (Davis, 2007), frequently on the right side. As a result, manual signs made in these persons' right visual fields would be largely inaccessible

---

2　Certain investigators have been examining the use of motor imagery as a way to improve the motor abilities of individuals who have suffered motor impairments after strokes (Hwang et al., 2010; Sharma, Pomeroy, & Baron, 2006). In this approach, patients form visual images of themselves successfully performing motor functions or movements without overtly performing these actions. It is possible that motor imagery may be a useful initial strategy in rehabilitating motor control in persons with bilateral paralysis or impairment. If use of this approach is successful in re-establishing control of movement in at least one arm, then these persons may become candidates for learning and using manual sign communication. Because manual signs are, to a considerable extent, motor actions, it might be possible to incorporate the learning of signs into the initial application of this motor imagery rehabilitation strategy (rather than after).

to them. If an individual has such a difficulty, then signs should be positioned to avoid these problems or another form of communication should be considered.

Over the last few decades, two contrasting representations of the relationships between gesture and speech have emerged from the research literature. In one, gesture and speech were viewed as products of a single bimodal process. If this approach were to be empirically verified in all or most individuals, then it would suggest that the use of manual gestures to compensate for spoken language losses from aphasia probably would be limited at best. That is, communication in both the speech and gestural channels would be impaired. The other major depiction of speech-gesture relationships has viewed spoken language and manual gestures as two highly coordinated but largely independent processes. In their test of these two approaches, Hogrefe et al. (2013) examined the use of gestures in adults with varying degrees of aphasia. More specifically, the participants were instructed to retell video clips they had seen: first, without narrative instruction (the patients typically used speech and gestures) and, subsequently, to do so silently through manual gestures (without speech). Because the comprehensibility of the gestures produced by a number of the aphasic participants was significantly enhanced in the silent condition, the investigators interpreted this finding as supporting the position that speech and manual gesture are largely separate communication channels. They also advanced the view that persons with aphasia could compensate, in part, for their spoken language impairments through the use of gestural communication (Hogrefe et al., 2013; see also Ahlsén, 1991; Béland & Ska, 1992; de Beer et al., 2017; de Ruiter, 2006; de Ruiter & de Beer, 2013; Goodwin, 2000, 2006; and Herrmann et al., 1988).

Although the comprehensibility of the gestures produced by many of the aphasic participants was found by Hogrefe et al. (2013) to be significantly enhanced in their silent condition, this should not be interpreted to mean that aphasic patients should communicate in the gestural mode alone. More specifically, listener comprehension has been shown to be greater when the speech of persons with aphasia is combined with pantomimic gestures than when efforts to communicate are made in speech or gesture alone (de Beer et al., 2017; Rose, Mok, & Sekine, 2017). It is also important to note that a person with aphasia may convey additional information through the gestural modality than is present in his or her speech (de Beer et al., 2017). In other words, gestures that people produce with their speech do not always provide redundant information — sometimes, the gestures augment or add new informational content to a spoken utterance (Bangerter, 2004; Beattie & Shovelton, 2011; Melinger & Levelt, 2004).

For most hearing patients with severe aphasia, the principal emphasis of their language therapy will be on restoring their spoken language skills. But if patients fail to show real improvements in their speech skills over time, then therapists should strongly consider embarking on a program of teaching communicative gestures to these patients. For instance, in one study, although the clear majority of the participants with severe aphasia acquired more vocabulary items through therapy using spoken and written words, a distinct minority learned many more vocabulary items through gesture communication therapy (Marshall et al., 2012).

Not only may some patients with aphasia benefit from learning gestures, but their therapists and caregivers may also wish to acquire a vocabulary of representative or iconic gestures to accompany their speech to their patients. We say this in light of findings from a recent study of co-speech gestural input (Eggenberger et al., 2016). In this study, if gestures were combined with spoken language input to patients with aphasia, then it was important that these co-speech gestures be congruent with (i.e., closely related to or highly similar in meaning) or match the principal content of the vocal utterances. More specifically, when gestures congruent with speech were used, the patients' comprehension of the input increased. In contrast, when gestures were not congruent with the speech input, then the aphasic patients' comprehension decreased significantly. This approach of using co-speech gestures congruent with the meaning of the spoken language input will likely make communicative interactions with aphasic patients more successful.

Finally, it should be noted that the study of aphasia, in addition to being central to a major and growing area of language and communication therapy, has contributed much to our understanding of the neurological bases of language. By pinpointing the location in the brain of a stroke or other lesion, investigators have been able to determine areas of the brain related to specific language functions. Depending on the precise location of the lesion and the severity of the damage, different language and motor processes may be affected. Not only do the lesions of hearing persons with aphasia provide useful information, but the lesions of deaf persons with aphasia who use signed languages also provide insight into the brain's neurological organization with regard to language.

In some cases, Deaf signers may experience brain injuries that severely and adversely affect their signing. This loss of language ability, or sign language aphasia, may occur when a signer suffers a stroke or cerebrovascular accident, typically in the left hemisphere of the brain. In such an instance, a signer often also loses the use of his or her right (or contralateral) arm. Although the use of the left arm may not be physically impaired, the damage to the brain's left hemisphere may constrain that Deaf person from producing useful sign utterances (Marshall et al., 2005). Systematic examinations of Deaf signers who have suffered aphasias have shown that the brain structures that control sign production and comprehension are highly similar to those involved in spoken language production and comprehension in hearing persons (Corina et al., 1992; Emmorey, 2002, 2003b; Hickok, Love-Geffen, & Klima, 2002; MacSweeney et al., 2009; Marshall et al., 2004; Poizner, Klima, & Bellugi, 1987; Sarno, Swisher, & Sarno, 1969). Furthermore, this seems to be true even when a deaf signer shows atypical brain lateralization (i.e., right hemisphere dominance for language). In a study of a left-handed deaf signer who had suffered a right hemisphere stroke and had sign language aphasia, the researchers found that the pattern of strengths and deficits in this deaf man's production and understanding of sign language very closely mirrored the pattern of strengths and deficits observed in hearing persons' production and understanding of spoken language (Pickell et al., 2005). Such a result implies that right hemisphere damage in persons with atypical brain lateralization for language may produce deficits similar to those exhibited by neurotypical persons who experience a left hemisphere stroke.

Improvement in the signing skills of Deaf persons with aphasia often depends on recovery or improvement of damaged brain functions. Many studies, however, have found that deaf persons who suffer brain damage and have impairments in the production of linguistically constrained signs may not have deficits in the production of gestures (Corina et al., 1992; Hickok et al., 2002; Marshall et al., 2004). That is, some deaf people with aphasia have difficulty producing signs from their native sign language within the phonological constraints imposed by those signs' particular handshapes, locations, movements, and orientations. In contrast, they may not have as much difficulty producing wider-ranging gestures or pantomimic enactments. Deaf persons may thus be able to access gestural abilities that are at least somewhat disassociated from their signing abilities despite the fact that both gestures and signs use the same visual-manual modality. Comparisons of the similarities and distinctions in linguistic processing in different modalities (e.g., speech, sign, and gestures) by normal and aphasic hearing persons and by normal and aphasic deaf persons may well illuminate further aspects of neural functioning that would otherwise remain hidden (Marshall et al., 2004, 2005).

Apraxia

A number of individuals who are severely aphasic also are identified as apraxic or dyspraxic[3] (Albert et al., 1981; Kertesz, 1979; Papagno, Della Sala, & Basso, 1993; Weiss et al., 2016). That is, many persons with severe aphasia experience significant difficulty in accurately and purposefully controlling their manual or oral-respiratory movements, even in the absence of motor paralysis. More specifically, in the Weiss et al. (2016) study, approximately two-thirds of their aphasic patients also had apraxia. Although apraxia commonly co-occurs with aphasia, it may also occur when no language deficit is present. This pattern, however, is relatively rare; Weiss et al. (2016) reported that only 4% of their patients were identified as apraxic without co-occurring symptoms of aphasia.

The lack of a strong correlation between severity of apraxia and severity of aphasia often is viewed as indicating that there is no causative relationship between the two (Albert et al., 1981). At the same time, it should be recognized that both language and purposeful motor movements (that is, *praxis*) are evidently vulnerable to injury in nearly the same areas of the brain, typically in the left hemisphere (Stamenova, Roy, & Black, 2010; Tartter, 1998). Most likely, the neural networks that

---

3   See Chapter 5, Footnote 10 for a discussion of the terms *apraxia* and *dyspraxia*.

support language and praxis are partly overlapping (Papagno et al., 1993). There is also evidence of a cerebellar role in verbal and manual apraxia, as the cerebellum is involved in the coordination and sequencing of complex motor movements (Paquier & Mariën, 2005).

It should be noted that not only may language and purposeful motor movement abilities be independently impaired by brain injury, but the movements that underlie speech and the use of the hands and limbs may be independently affected as well (Albert et al., 1981; Falchook et al., 2014). While language and purposeful motor movements may be independently impaired by brain injury, the loss of language skills may influence a patient's capacity to select purposeful actions (Falchook et al., 2014). Moreover, in one recent study, language impairment was strongly associated with the aphasic participants' deficits in the generation of pantomimes of tool use whereas other measures of apraxia were not similarly adversely affected (Goldenberg & Randerath, 2015). The investigators advanced the view that underlying this impairment in both pantomime of tool use and linguistic abilities was probably the participants' loss of access to their semantic memories or knowledge.

The various forms of apraxia also may differentially affect the usefulness of certain language and communication intervention programs. Those individuals with a severe oral-motor apraxia may find acquiring spoken language skills very difficult.[4] Correspondingly, because losses in motor planning and production skills involving the hands may negatively affect an individual's ability to acquire and use signs, learning a manual communication system may prove an inordinately difficult task for some persons, such as those with a limb apraxia.[5] In addition, when persons with more severe apraxia produce manual gestures, the meanings of these gestures may not be understood by others; that is, these gestures may be quite low in comprehensibility (Hogrefe et al., 2012). For aphasic individuals with severe apraxia, a less motorically demanding communication system, such as a communication board,

---

4   An oral apraxia is when an individual experiences difficulty performing, on request, such tasks as sticking out one's tongue or biting one's lip. Apraxia of speech is evident in impaired speaking skills such as imprecise articulation, slow overall rate of production, and errors of stress assignment. Apraxia of speech is believed to be the product of a disturbance in the planning or programming of movements for speech.

5   Limb apraxia is when an individual experiences difficulty performing, on request, such motor or gestural tasks as making a fist, waving good-bye, or throwing a ball.

picture cards, or speech-generating device may be a more beneficial approach.[6] Nevertheless, some aphasic individuals with moderate to severe limb apraxia are able to acquire a vocabulary of manual signs and to combine signs into short sign utterances (Coelho & Duffy, 1990). Furthermore, the signs of an individual with aphasia and apraxia may be more recognizable to their communication partners (and thus more functionally successful) than their spoken language utterances (de Beer et al., 2017; Goodwin 2000, 2006; Herrmann et al., 1988).

Sign-Communication Training Outcomes

Although the literature on sign-communication training and teaching in non-speaking populations has grown markedly over the last few decades, only a relatively small proportion of these studies have examined the sign-learning abilities of adults with aphasia. These studies show that some individuals who have lost their ability to speak may still be able to acquire a number of communicative signs (Christopoulou & Bonvillian, 1985; Peterson & Kirshner, 1981; Rose, 2006). Many of these studies, however, were primarily exploratory in nature, involved only a few participants, and failed to include detailed descriptions of participants' language and motor impairments. As a result, it remains difficult to draw firm conclusions about the efficacy of sign-communication training and teaching with adults with aphasia. This situation is somewhat perplexing in that there have been repeated observations, some dating back to the late nineteenth and early twentieth centuries (e.g., Seton, 1918), that adults with severe spoken language impairments might be taught to communicate effectively through the use of manual signs.

Unlike children with a severe or profound intellectual disability who were taught to sign, hearing adults with aphasia typically were fluent users of a spoken language for many years before their loss. Depending on the type and severity of their aphasia, these individuals may retain substantial receptive language skills (the ability to understand language). If a particular person has at least some receptive spoken language skills, it may be possible to explain the meanings of signs and how they are formed, which in turn may facilitate the learning

---

6   For more information on such systems, see the "Other Non-Oral Approaches" section in Chapter 5.

of those signs. We say this because some manual signs may be more easily learned and remembered if the relationships between those signs and what they stand for (their referents) can be readily discerned once the meanings of the signs have been provided.[7] In the paragraphs that follow, we review a small number of investigations that have examined manual sign acquisition in hearing individuals with aphasia.

As part of their investigation into the usefulness of sign-communication interventions, Eagleson, Vaughn, and Knudson (1970) developed a manual system that was designed to help persons with expressive aphasias communicate their self-care needs. In constructing this system, the investigators borrowed a relatively small number of signs from the sign languages used by Deaf persons and from the sign system used by Native Americans. These signs were then taught to a fifty-five-year-old man with a predominantly expressive aphasia; that is, he could understand considerable speech, but produced very little. His success in communicating manually appeared to encourage him to communicate verbally as well. Although Eagleson et al.'s efforts represent an early attempt to design a manual communication system for a hearing (albeit non-speaking) individual, the very limited size of the lexicon seriously constrained its usefulness with other persons.

In 1975, Holmes reported success in teaching a manual sign vocabulary to a sixty-year-old man diagnosed with Wernicke's aphasia. People with Wernicke's aphasia often produce speech that is markedly lacking in specific content or references because they experience difficulty in using meaningful content words such as nouns, verbs, adjectives, and adverbs. Over a relatively brief training period, this man acquired a lexicon of 120 signs from the Paget-Gorman sign system (a communication system devised in Great Britain to render English manually). Most of the signs this man learned were nouns, and he used many of those signs to refer to objects that he was unable to name orally. This outcome demonstrates that some individuals who are unable to produce specific words orally may retain the capacity to produce those same words manually.

Another early account of an adult with aphasoid characteristics acquiring signs was provided by Bonvillian and Friedman (1978). The forty-nine-year-old man in this case report suffered severe

---

7   This feature of signs is known as translucency; see Chapter 1 for a discussion of translucency, iconicity, and related concepts.

brain and bodily injuries as a result of an accident. He experienced nearly complete loss of his spoken language skills and was partially paralyzed. Several years of speech therapy followed the accident, but when no improvement occurred, it was discontinued. Some years later, over the course of nine months of one-hour-per-week teaching sessions using American Sign Language (ASL) signs, this man made substantial progress in his ability to use signs. He learned to produce 117 different signs and used 79 of those signs spontaneously (without immediate prior prompting or usage by others). Rarely, however, did he spontaneously combine signs; his multi-sign combinations seemed quite effortful. With his increase in communication skills through signs, this person appeared much less frustrated with his daily living situation and was reported by members of the nursing staff to be much easier to care for and interact with.

Some persons suffer extensive damage to their brains resulting in a severe language deficit known as global aphasia. These persons show deficits in both their comprehension and production of language, and typically experience severe movement restriction on the right side of their bodies (right hemiplegia) (Damasio, 2008). The prognosis for recovery of spoken language in these individuals is quite low. However, the results of two studies involving persons with global aphasia indicate that such persons may be able to make significant progress in learning to communicate again through manual signs and gestures. In one study (Moody, 1982), the participant acquired an active vocabulary of over 200 signs from Australasian Sign Language. Two-handed signs were modified into one-handed versions. Although the participant reportedly was able to understand longer utterances, this individual communicated mostly through single-sign utterances. In the second study (Baratz, 1985), the participant made gradual progress in learning to communicate over a twenty-month training period. He first learned to produce pantomimic gestures through therapeutic drills and then began to generate his own pantomimic gestures. In the ensuing months, the participant increased his communicative repertoire by learning signs from Amer-Ind and then from ASL. He also frequently combined gestures and signs, but he showed no evidence of acquiring syntactical rules. Taken together, these two studies show that at least some individuals with global aphasia may be able to make considerable progress in learning to communicate again when they participate in a program of manual sign and gestural communication.

Amer-Ind

Over the past several decades, Amer-Ind (derived from a Native American sign language variously known as Plains Indian Sign Language, North American Indian Sign Language, or American Indian Hand Talk) has become a widely used sign-communication system both for individuals with aphasia and for those with an intellectual disability. Amer-Ind was initially devised by Madge Skelly (Skelly, 1979; Skelly et al., 1974) and her colleagues to help meet the communication needs of patients who had undergone such surgical procedures as a glossectomy (removal of the tongue) or laryngectomy (removal of the larynx, which holds the vocal cords) as part of their cancer treatment. After Amer-Ind proved successful with these individuals, it was adapted for use with other groups of non-speaking persons.

The most extensive literature on the use of signs by individuals with aphasia or other severe communication disorders was compiled by Madge Skelly (1979). In this report, Skelly summarized the results of seven Amer-Ind training programs; altogether, 181 individuals participated. The report indicated that most of the participants were able to learn at least a limited number of signs and gestures, and that this enabled them to communicate their basic needs. Although one-half of them also acquired some speech skills, progress in this domain typically was much poorer. Unfortunately, wide differences across the various Amer-Ind training studies in treatment methods, duration of training, and characteristics of the participants make it difficult to reach more specific conclusions based on the report of the training studies' outcomes. For example, because no attempt was made to differentiate the various types of aphasia involved, it is not possible to predict the likely efficacy of sign-communication training for individuals presenting with different types of aphasia.

Two additional case studies of the acquisition of Amer-Ind signs and ASL signs (Heilman et al., 1979; Kirshner & Webb, 1981) have shown that at least some individuals with aphasia are able to combine signs. In both these cases, the participants acquired over one hundred different signs and learned to produce short sign sequences. This ability to sequence or combine signs enabled the participants to transmit more complex messages than would have been possible using only single signs. This seems to indicate that at least some of the participants' syntactic skills were still present, even with the loss of speech.

Skelly and her colleagues used several criteria in selecting signs from the Plains Indian Sign Language lexicon to constitute the Amer-Ind vocabulary (Skelly, 1979). Each sign was chosen because it was deemed to be readily understood by the inexperienced viewer, of some practical present-day value, and relatively easy to produce. These are some of the same criteria used in selecting and developing signs for the Simplified Sign System. Some Amer-Ind signs subsequently were modified to make them easier to produce. In particular, a single-hand version was developed for use with the left hand by right hemiplegic (paralyzed) patients (Skelly et al., 1975). In addition, a small number of signs were created to help meet the needs of persons using modern technology. Altogether, 236 distinct signs make up the Amer-Ind core vocabulary.

Since publication of Skelly's book in 1979, investigators working with individuals with aphasia increasingly have opted to use Amer-Ind signs instead of those from a sign language used by Deaf persons. One reason frequently given for selecting Amer-Ind is that many of its signs are highly iconic or pantomimic. Persons unfamiliar with the Amer-Ind system typically are able to accurately guess the meanings of about half of the Amer-Ind signs they see (Campbell & Jackson, 1995; Daniloff, Lloyd, & Fristoe, 1983; Vanderheiden & Lloyd, 1986). This is a much higher rate of accuracy than what occurs when they are tested on the signs of ASL or other Deaf sign languages (in 1985, Lloyd, Loeding, and Doherty estimated that only about 10–15% of ASL signs were highly iconic or pantomimic). The highly iconic nature of many Amer-Ind signs may help explain the finding that these signs typically are more easily learned than ASL signs for the same word or concept (Fritelli & Daniloff, 1982). This iconic or pantomimic aspect of many Amer-Ind signs may also facilitate their acquisition by those who care for persons with aphasia.

In a related study, investigators examined whether ASL or Amer-Ind signs were more often recognized and more accurately imitated by individuals with aphasia (Daniloff et al., 1986). Amer-Ind signs were found to be significantly easier both to recognize and to imitate. The investigators suggested that this outcome was largely the product of the greater motor coordination involved in the production of ASL signs than in the formation of Amer-Ind signs. Recall that in ASL, individual signs may have more than one movement (Stokoe et al., 1965). When examining which signs individuals with severe aphasia learned (Coelho & Duffy, 1986), motor complexity was found to have an impact on sign learning. The motor complexity of a sign is based on the number of movements contained in the sign, the particular location, handshape, and movement parameters used in the sign, and the spatial orientation of the sign. Those signs with a low or intermediate level of motor complexity were more frequently acquired than those signs with greater motor complexity.

Finally, it should be noted that there is a significant limitation to the Amer-Ind system. At 236 distinct signs, the overall size of the Amer-Ind lexicon is quite small in comparison with the many thousands of signs present in ASL and other sign languages used by Deaf persons and less than one-fourth the size of the initial Simplified Sign System lexicon. It is important to remember, though, that Amer-Ind is a communication strategy for individuals with moderate to severe language impairments and is not intended to be a full language. Nevertheless, Amer-Ind's limited vocabulary size is a serious constraining factor with regard to its more widespread adoption and use. Clinicians who adopt Amer-Ind for their clients may, if needed, create additional concepts through the process of combining or agglutinating two or more existing signs. For example, the concept *library* is conveyed by adding the sign for SHELTER or HOUSE to the sign for BOOK (Skelly et al., 1974). Although such combinations of signs noticeably increase the potential vocabulary size of Amer-Ind (and could also be used to increase the size of the Simplified Sign System lexicon), this process involves considerably more cognitive and motor skills on the part of the user and may be problematic for individuals with certain language or motor impairments.

Pantomime

Various investigators have suggested that one reason for the success of sign-communication interventions with some persons with aphasia has been the pantomimic aspect of many manual signs. Certain investigators (Methé, Huber, & Paradis, 1993; Sarno, 1998), moreover, have advanced the view that the areas in the brain that are involved in the processing of pantomime may have remained relatively intact in individuals with aphasia while their language-processing centers were severely damaged. Other investigators (e.g., Daniloff et al., 1986; Skelly, 1979) have claimed that it was the pantomimic or iconic nature of many manual signs that made them quite readily learned and particularly memorable for aphasic individuals. In light of this strong emphasis on pantomime processing in individuals with aphasia and the pantomimic aspect of many manual signs, we elected to explore this topic in more detail.

Examination of the pantomime abilities of adults with aphasia also has been seen as a way to test the hypothesis that aphasia is primarily a deficit in symbol processing. More specifically, proponents of this central symbolic deficit hypothesis of aphasia (Duffy & Duffy, 1981; Duffy, Duffy, & Pearson, 1975) have seen the language loss experienced by adults with aphasia as reflecting a more general deficit in symbolic representational skills rather than one limited to the domain of language.[8] According to this approach, if such a central symbolic deficit did exist, then persons with aphasia likely would show noticeably poorer pantomime recognition skills when compared with brain-damaged individuals without aphasia and when compared with same-age individuals with intact abilities. In a study testing this hypothesis, aphasic participants as a group performed more poorly on pantomime recognition tasks than did participants from the other groups, lending some support to the central symbolic deficit hypothesis (Duffy et al., 1975). Additional support for this view came from a study of pantomimic gesture comprehension conducted by Gainotti and Lemmo (1976). These investigators had their research participants first view a simple pantomime and then identify the object to which it was related from among a set of three pictures. Additional pantomimes and sets of pictures were then presented. Nearly two-thirds of the participants with aphasia were depicted as failing to comprehend simple pantomimic gestures. These findings of deficits in pantomime

---

8   A person with a central symbolic deficit would have difficulty understanding and using various symbol forms such as words, musical notes, and insignia. Pantomimes, because they generally resemble and stand for objects, actions, and properties, could be viewed as symbolic forms as well.

processing often were seen as valid predictors of aphasic individuals' likely success (or lack of it) in intervention programs that relied on manual signs or gestures.

Because the Simplified Sign System we have developed and Amer-Ind both rely heavily on signs that are highly iconic or pantomimic, a substantial deficit in comprehending pantomimic gestures would appear to be a very negative indicator for the use of Simplified Signs or Amer-Ind signs with persons with aphasia. Perusal of Gainotti and Lemmo's results, however, suggests that the picture is not so bleak. Of the fifty-three aphasic individuals they tested, twenty made no errors on the test of gestural comprehension and another ten made only a single error. Although the remaining participants performed relatively poorly, one could argue that the majority were successful in comprehending pantomimic gestures (Christopoulou & Bonvillian, 1985). Indeed, Gainotti (1988) has recognized that deficits in pantomime comprehension skills affect only a percentage, although often a sizeable one, of individuals with aphasia. Gainotti wrote: "that pantomime comprehension disorders are observed only in a subgroup of aphasic patients can be explained by assuming that aphasia is a complex, multicomponent syndrome and that only one (or some) of these components are intimately linked to pantomime recognition impairment" (p. 138).

Another complicating factor that may have affected Gainotti and Lemmo's results was the fact that participants chose from a list of pictures instead of from a collection of real objects. In other words, some individuals may have trouble interpreting two-dimensional pictures and/or relating them to the pantomimic gestures demonstrated by investigators, whereas those same individuals may not have trouble interpreting and relating real objects to pantomimic gestures (Rothi, Mack, & Heilman, 1986). This observation makes analysis of pantomime comprehension results difficult, as one cannot be sure whether a participant had poor pantomime recognition skills, difficulty perceiving two-dimensional pictures, problems relating the two-dimensional, static pictures to moving gestures, or some combination of factors. Perhaps the conclusion one should draw from this study is that some persons with aphasia are relatively good at understanding pantomimic gestures and recognizing their relationships to two-dimensional pictures, whereas others find some aspect of this task difficult.

In addition to difficulties with pantomime recognition, individuals with aphasia often have been reported to show marked deficits in pantomime expression. In general, those aphasic individuals with more severe verbal deficits typically scored lower on pantomime expression, with scores in this domain significantly correlated with their scores on pantomime recognition (Duffy & Duffy, 1981). These findings initially were interpreted as providing strong support for the view that the verbal deficits and pantomimic deficits present in individuals with aphasia were caused by a central symbolic deficit. Subsequent investigations, however, have revealed that the situation is a more complicated one. In addition to a central symbolic deficit, performance on pantomime recognition tasks evidently is affected by impairments in visual processing areas of the brain, and pantomime expression may be affected by the occurrence of limb apraxia (Duffy & Duffy, 1990). Difficulties in pantomime expression or production, moreover, may rest on aphasic participants' problems in selecting purposeful actions (Falchook et al., 2014) or in semantic processing more generally (Weiss et al., 2016). Aphasic individuals with predominantly phonological-processing impairments might not experience such pantomime production problems. Furthermore, individuals with apraxia show a particular deficit in the processing of sequential pantomimic actions (Weiss et al., 2008). This last finding may indicate that aphasic individuals with apraxia may be more successful in acquiring single-movement pantomimic gestures or iconic signs than they would be for more complex, multi-movement gestures or signs.

Thus far, the studies we have reviewed with regard to assessment of pantomime recognition ability, pantomime expression, and limb apraxia in individuals with aphasia have come from investigations that relied on formal testing of these abilities. Rose and Douglas (2003), however, questioned whether such results from standard tests of these abilities were actually indicative of aphasic individuals' spontaneous gestural performance in natural conversational settings. Rose and Douglas found that the presence of pantomimic deficits and limb apraxia in their participants (as determined from standard assessment tests) was not related to these individuals' production of pantomimic gestures in spontaneous communicative interactions. Apparently, the demand characteristics of the formal testing situations did not accurately predict performance in more natural settings. Following up on those initial findings, additional studies (Sekine & Rose, 2013; Sekine et al., 2013) examined gesture use in conversational discourse in a large number of individuals with aphasia. The investigators found that their aphasic participants produced a higher proportion of gestures than did members of their comparison group, which consisted of healthy individuals. Moreover, many of the gestures produced by those participants with a Broca's aphasia were clearly iconic and meaning-laden, including pantomimes and number gestures. These findings show that some individuals with aphasia may make frequent use of iconic gestures and pantomime when in more natural communication settings (de Beer et al., 2017).

In a comparative study of a sixty-eight-year-old man with Wernicke's aphasia versus a healthy control group (van Nispen et al., 2014), the investigators noted that the man almost always gestured along with his production of speech (his speech was incomprehensible). This study involved both an object naming task and a story retelling task within two conditions: the use of co-speech gesture (called the verbal condition that enabled gesticulation) and the use of gestures without speech (called the pantomime condition). Naïve viewers were asked to watch silent videos of the aphasic man while he performed each task. After each stimulus, the viewer had to interpret the meaning of the aphasic man's gestures and select from one of two possible options. Results indicated that the man's comprehensibility on the object naming task was greater in the pantomime condition (i.e., no speech, only gestures), and his comprehensibility on the story retelling task was greater in the verbal condition (i.e., using co-speech gestures). In the pantomime condition for object naming, the researchers noted that he used shape gestures for most of the items whereas the control group generally used handling gestures (van Nispen et al., 2014). However, in the verbal condition (co-speech gesture) for object naming, the aphasic man tended to use deictic and handling gestures. These interesting results show that some persons with aphasia may prefer certain types of pantomimic gestures to others and the form or type of gestures they prefer may vary based on whether or not they accompany speech. Indeed, persons with aphasia often use shape or outline gestures to convey meaning when communicating with others (Cocks et al., 2011, 2013; Mol, Krahmer, & van de Sandt-Koenderman, 2013). Finally, the ability of other people to understand such gestures may be somewhat dependent on the context in which they are used.

Overall, numerous investigations of the nonverbal cognitive abilities of persons with aphasia have shown wide ranges in performance across both the participants tested and the particular abilities examined (Gainotti, 1988). Often, persons with aphasia have significant deficits on tests of pantomime recognition and expression, but many other persons with aphasia perform satisfactorily on these tests. Furthermore, scores indicative of pantomimic deficits obtained from formal tests may not be related to aphasic individuals' production of pantomimic gestures in natural communication settings. In the future, it will be of interest to examine the interrelationships among scores on tests of pantomime recognition and expression, measures of severity of limb apraxia, the incidence of pantomimic gesturing in natural settings, and aphasic individuals' learning of Simplified Signs. How well an individual with aphasia learns signs from the Simplified Sign System might be predicted by his or her scores on one or more of these measures. Such an approach might be used to identify which individuals with aphasia are likely to benefit from sign training and teaching.

Predicting Sign Intervention Outcomes

Overall, the findings reviewed in this chapter indicate that a program that includes communicative gestures or manual sign-communication training and teaching may be a more successful intervention strategy with certain persons with aphasia than more traditional speech-based therapies. This outcome raises the question as to why this may occur. One interpretation is that manual signs may access abilities, such as pantomime and gesture, which may have remained relatively intact in contrast to more severely damaged linguistic centers (Methé et al., 1993; Sarno, 1998; see also van Nispen et al., 2014). A therapist, through switching the communication mode to a visual and manual one, might effectively bypass an area of particular difficulty for a client, such as apraxia of speech. Moreover, if a person's spoken language difficulties stemmed primarily from problems in the processing of auditory-vocal input, then the shift to manual signs would likely involve processing in different networks at a perceptual level, thus potentially avoiding an area of difficulty. Because many Amer-Ind (and Simplified Sign System) signs resemble the objects and actions for which they stand, such iconic signs may make only limited demands on an individual's memory and symbol-processing skills (Skelly, 1979). A second possibility that might account for the present findings of manual sign acquisition in some individuals with aphasia is that certain forms of learning or processing may recover more quickly than others. In these individuals, visual- and motor-processing skills may re-emerge faster and more completely than spoken language abilities. Another possible explanation for the success of sign intervention is that a therapist who teaches signs is able to mold and guide a person's hands and arms in the production of signs in a way that would not be possible in teaching speech. Finally, when some persons with aphasia observe the production of manual gestures or signs and then attempt to imitate these gestures, this process may aid the reassembly of damaged or incomplete neural networks, thus facilitating limb rehabilitation (Buccino, Solodkin, & Small, 2006).

Although the studies we have reviewed indicate that some individuals with severe aphasic impairments can make noticeable progress in learning to sign, it is important not to overstate the studies' outcomes. In many instances, the rate of sign acquisition by the participants was slow and the vocabularies attained relatively small in size (Kraat, 1990). The same lesion or injury that caused their initial communicative and language impairments may have adversely affected the persons' learning of manual signs as well. Some investigators have tried to identify which individuals with aphasia would be more likely to benefit from sign-communication training and teaching. The severity of an individual's aphasic impairment has been shown to be an important factor in predicting the outcome of this type of therapy (Coelho, 1990; Coelho & Duffy, 1987). More specifically, the number of signs that a participant acquired and whether that person learned to combine signs were strongly related to the severity of aphasic impairment. Persons with less severe aphasic impairments typically made much more progress learning to sign. In light of these findings, Coelho and Duffy (1987) advanced the view that there may be a threshold level of aphasic severity beyond which sign acquisition is either very limited or negligible (but see de Ruiter, 2006 and de Ruiter & de Beer, 2013).

Neuro-imaging techniques, which have enabled clinicians to determine the location and extent of the brain damage that caused an individual's language loss, also have the potential to be used to determine which individuals with aphasia would be more likely to benefit from sign interventions. One study that used this approach (Anderson et al., 1992) found that two severely aphasic patients with damage or lesions in the left posterior temporal and parietal regions of the brain were much more successful in learning to communicate with ASL signs and fingerspelling than a severely aphasic patient with damage to most of her left temporal cortex.[9] This study clearly shows that the location(s) of an individual's brain damage can have profound effects on that person's acquisition and use of manual signs. In light of the great strides that have been made in neuro-imaging techniques in recent decades, it is perplexing that more investigators have not probed the interrelationships between the locations of patients' brain injuries and their success in learning manual signs. If, in the future, systematic records were kept of the location and extent of different individuals' lesions and the outcome of sign-communication programs, then it should be possible to predict which persons would be more likely to benefit from such training.

An additional issue involved in evaluating the usefulness of different communication intervention approaches for persons with aphasia has come to light in another study (Pattee, Von Berg, & Ghezzi, 2006). That issue is participant preference. This study involved a middle-aged woman who had primary progressive aphasia as well as apraxia of speech.[10] This woman was taught both to produce ASL signs and to use a text-to-speech alternative communication (or speech-generating) device. She made progress in both communication approaches. At the end of the study, she was asked to indicate her preferred mode of

---

9   The parietal lobe is a region of the brain involved with the sense of touch and the experience of one's body in space and movement. The temporal lobe is primarily involved in audition and language. The cortex refers to the outer layers of the cerebrum, the part of the brain responsible for most mental processes.

10   Primary progressive aphasia is a gradual deterioration of language functioning over a period of at least two years while other cognitive abilities remain largely intact. Apraxia of speech is a motor speech disorder that results in impaired speaking or an inability to speak.

communication. Her clear preference across all situations was signing; the alternative communication device just did not feel "normal" to her. As the meanings of most ASL signs are not apparent to most hearing persons this woman may come into contact with, it is possible that the more highly iconic Amer-Ind signs and Simplified Signs would have proved even more effective and been preferred as a communication approach.

A final concern that has been expressed about the outcomes of sign-communication programs for persons with aphasia is that these programs focused primarily on the acquisition of sign vocabulary within a discrete training setting. Although the participants in these programs typically acquired a number of signs, the results were not shown to generalize to functional use outside of the training settings (Jacobs et al., 2004). To overcome this limitation, sign-communication programs in the future should be designed to extend the training and teaching to a variety of settings, to include a number of communication partners, and to incorporate signing into the day's naturally occurring routines.[11] If these procedures are followed, it is likely that the sign usage of persons with aphasia will be both more spontaneous and functionally useful.

Sign Facilitation of Spoken Language

For some individuals with aphasia, manual signs may constitute an effective alternative to speech as a primary means of communication (Rose, 2006). Manual signs, however, apparently can play another important role in aphasia therapy as a facilitator of spoken language (Rao, 2001). In some of the studies that examined the use of sign communication with persons with aphasia, oral language skills were reported to have improved along with sign-communication skills. This pattern occurred primarily when a therapist combined signed input with spoken words (Hoodin & Thompson, 1983; Kearns, Simmons, & Sisterhen, 1982). Some individuals with aphasia evidently benefit from

---

11 For more information on these approaches to facilitating sign use, see the "Recommendations for Enhancing the Sign-Learning Environment" section in Chapter 4 and the "Teaching Generalization and Spontaneous Communication Skills" section in Chapter 5, as well as the subsections "Use Environmental Cues or Contextual Information" and "Ensure a Positive Signing Environment" in Chapter 9 (under the "Guidelines for Using the Simplified Sign System" section).

the multimodal nature of this input (Rao & Horner, 1978; Rose, 2013; Skelly et al., 1974). Therefore, if one therapeutic goal is improved oral language skills, then therapists should strongly consider combining signs and communicative gestures with speech rather than using signs or speech alone.

Facilitation of verbal naming also may occur when nonfluent aphasic patients (that is, patients with hesitant, effortful, abbreviated speech; Broca's aphasia is one type of nonfluent aphasia) are instructed to produce communicative gestures with their more affected or impaired limb as they try to name or label pictures (Hanlon, Brown, & Gerstman, 1990). The more affected limb, usually the right arm and hand, is used because it is controlled by the same general area of the brain that controls speech. By focusing therapeutic intervention on the more affected arm, this limb may show greater improvement in its functioning. Enhanced action or motor functioning with the more affected limb often is associated with improvements in language abilities (Gauthier et al., 2008; Szaflarski et al., 2008). Improved word retrieval may also occur when aphasic participants simply observe others performing actions corresponding to the words to be retrieved (Marangolo et al., 2010) or by preactivation of the motor cortex through standing (Meinzer et al., 2011). This improvement across modalities may rest on the many interconnections between language and action systems in the brain (Pulvermüller & Berthier, 2008). Furthermore, in recent years, manual gestures and speech have come to be viewed by a number of investigators as an integrated system operating both in language production and language comprehension (Goldin-Meadow, 1998; Kelly, Özyürek, & Maris, 2010).

The improved spoken language skills present in some sign-trained individuals may be evidence of successful deblocking or cueing. In the aphasia treatment technique known as deblocking, a disturbed language function is paired with an intact or less impaired communication or language function (Benson & Ardila, 1996). The hope is that this systematic pairing, typically involving both receptive and expressive language tasks, will result in the more intact function having a positive effect on the more impaired function. In sign-communication deblocking therapy, a manual sign is paired with the spoken word for the same concept. For example, after learning an Amer-Ind sign for a particular concept, a client would be trained to synchronize the appropriate movements of the mouth for the associated word while producing the Amer-Ind sign. A frequent outcome of this pairing of language modalities has been improved verbal expression or speech intelligibility (Code & Gaunt, 1986; Rosenbek, LaPointe, & Wertz, 1989; Skelly et al., 1974). This outcome may rest, in part, on the fact that the areas of the brain involved in speech production are near or adjacent to the areas of the brain involved in manual sign production. In some instances, the activation and use of one brain area apparently has a positive crossover effect on the other. (For additional discussion of how signing skills may help a person regain or improve spoken language skills, see the "Addressing Concerns about Sign-Communication Training and Teaching" section in Chapter 1 and the "Dispelling Myths" section of Chapter 5.)

In the aphasia treatment technique known as cueing, emphasis is placed primarily on the use of prompts or prestimulation to facilitate a person's word retrieval or comprehension. Among the many possible cues that might be employed are pictures, letter tracing, manual signs, printed or written words, pantomime, object visualization, and pointing. Not all cues, however, are equally effective. In one study (Rose & Douglas, 2001), the production of iconic gestures resulted in significantly enhanced word naming abilities in half of the participants, whereas the use of other types of cues, such as pointing and visualization, did not have significant positive effects. In a second study (Pashek, 1997), cued naming was most effective when the participant's verbal training also included the production of iconic gestures (mostly Amer-Ind signs). In light of these findings and others, Marshall (2006) advanced the view that for gestures to cue words effectively, the gestures need to have "language-like" properties. The transparency of meaning and relatively close correspondence with words often present in Amer-Ind and Simplified Sign System signs may make them good gestural cues for individuals with aphasia.

A recurring observation among investigators who have examined the effects of signs or iconic gestures on the spoken language production of individuals with aphasia is that this treatment approach often is quite effective with some participants while not benefiting others (Rose, 2010). In a pair of studies, Rose and her associates (Lanyon & Rose, 2009; Rose & Douglas, 2001) examined the participant characteristics that were associated with successful use of iconic gesture production to resolve word retrieval difficulties. In both studies, it was the aphasic participants with predominantly phonological-level impairments who benefitted from using iconic gestures; facilitation effects of iconic gestures were not observed for the other participants. In the future, it will be important both to replicate this finding in additional participants and to try to determine if there are individuals with other forms of aphasic impairments who also would benefit from iconic gesture or sign-communication training and teaching.

What factor or factors might explain the improved spoken language skills of persons with aphasia when words are cued or paired with closely related iconic gestures or manual signs? One possibility is that because words and their corresponding signs (or iconic gestures) share lexical features, the activation provided by the manual or gestural modality may facilitate lexical retrieval of the spoken words (Krauss, Chen, & Gottesman, 2000). Another possibility is that the pairing of words and signs (or iconic gestures) activates related processes at the motor programming level. That is, in some individuals with aphasia, there might be cross-modal activation of the motor programming processes that underlie the subsequent production of spoken words. Of course, neither of these hypothesized processes may prove to be accurate explanations of a person's improved speech skills or both processes may be involved. Regardless, it is clear that improved spoken language skills often result when words and signs (or iconic gestures) are combined.

Finally, a recent investigation has shown that a person's motor system may play an important role in that individual's comprehension of spoken language (Willems et al., 2011). Although studies of the use of signs with persons with aphasia typically have focused on their language production, signed input may also play a role in facilitating their receptive language skills or language comprehension. Many individuals with aphasia have serious deficits in their comprehension or understanding of the spoken language produced by other people. If the communication partners of such individuals were to accompany their speech with signs that have clearly transparent meanings, then this approach might enhance their communicative effectiveness and be easier for persons with aphasia to understand (see Eggenberger et al., 2016). Furthermore, the combining of speech with signs (a process known as simultaneous communication)[12] may sufficiently slow the communication partners' rate of speaking to make their speech input more intelligible to persons with receptive language difficulties (Hyde & Power, 1991; Wilbur & Petersen, 1998), thus providing the opportunity for the information to be more fully and accurately processed by them.

Acquired Childhood Aphasia and Landau-Kleffner Syndrome

Although we have focused most of our discussion in this chapter on the language loss of adults, children certainly are not immune to brain injuries that result in a language loss or deficit. In most cases, children who experience aphasia as a result of external brain trauma are relatively good candidates to recover or reacquire their spoken language skills (Loonen & Van Dongen, 1990; Martins, 2004; Van Dongen & Loonen, 1977). Not all children, however, are so fortunate. Consider the case report of Johnny (Brookner & Murphy, 1975). According to hospital records, Johnny was a typically developing four-year-old until he fell on a concrete step, striking his head. He failed to reacquire speech, was very aggressive, and repeatedly suffered from seizures. After an eighteen-month stay in the hospital, Johnny was transferred to a state institution for persons with an intellectual disability; he had a diagnosis of global aphasia (substantial damage to all aspects of language) and severe intellectual disability. There, his foster parents observed that many of Johnny's aggressive outbursts were associated with his unsuccessful attempts to communicate. As a result, the foster parents helped craft a very basic gestural communication system for Johnny. The use of this system appeared to alleviate some of his frustration.

At the age of fifteen, Johnny was introduced to sign language signs together with speech input. He made rapid progress manually, acquiring a vocabulary of 160 signs after only nine months. The complexity of his signing increased as well: he began to combine signs after an initial

---

12   We recommend that teachers and caregivers use a specific form of simultaneous communication known as key word signing when interacting with non-speaking individuals. In this technique, the teacher or caregiver signs the principal, information-bearing words of a sentence at the same time that the corresponding words are uttered. All words in the sentence are spoken, but only the most important ones are signed. Key word signing is discussed in more detail in Chapter 9.

period of using only single signs. Johnny's significantly increased ability to sign also appeared to assist his social development. Soon after joining the sign language program, his social behavior improved and his in-school temper tantrums ceased. While Johnny's sign acquisition is quite impressive, the relatively late onset of the sign-communication training makes one wonder what he might have been able to achieve if this training had started much earlier.

When the cause of a child's loss of language is an internal event such as an infectious disease (e.g., herpes encephalitis, tuberculous meningitis), a tumor, or a progressive disorder, the prospects for rapid reacquisition of speech often are not as good as they are for losses caused by strokes or by external traumas (Loonen & Van Dongen, 1990; Martins, 2004).[13] Seizure activity also is associated with language loss or impairment in children. In some children who experience seizures, there is a nearly total loss of the ability to comprehend or produce spoken language. These seizures are believed to be localized primarily in cortical areas (outer layers) of the brain involved in speech-sound processing (Castillo et al., 2008). While their spoken language skills are seriously impaired, the nonverbal cognitive skills of most such children remain relatively intact. These children have the ability to learn and a desire to communicate despite serious auditory-processing difficulties.

Landau-Kleffner Syndrome

In acquired epileptic aphasia, also known as verbal auditory agnosia or Landau-Kleffner syndrome, children experience a severe and often prolonged loss of their receptive language skills (Landau & Kleffner, 1957; Pearl, Carrazana, & Holmes, 2001; Rapin et al., 1977; Stefanatos, 2011). Indeed, the children's difficulty in understanding spoken language and their deficits in the auditory processing of other sounds (e.g., environmental noises, music) may convey the impression that they are deaf. Typically, children with Landau-Kleffner syndrome first

---

13 In her study of acquired childhood aphasia, Martins (2004) reported that all nineteen of her patients who had become aphasic after suffering a stroke recovered their spoken language skills. This rate of recovery is much higher than that for adults. Kertesz (1979, 2000) reported that only around 25% of the sixty-seven adults he studied who became aphasic after suffering strokes regained enough language skills to be considered fully recovered. Another approximate 25% of this group made what Kertesz deemed a "good" outcome or recovery.

show a decline in their language comprehension;[14] this is often followed by difficulties in oral expression, with mutism a frequent outcome (Campos & Guevara, 2007; Chapman, Stormont, & McCathren, 1998; Kaga, 1999; Kuriakose et al., 2012; Pearl et al., 2001; Soprano et al., 1994; Tharpe & Olson, 1994). These children may also show declines or impairments in their reading skills (Sieratzki et al., 2001). As their speech comprehension and production skills deteriorate, some individuals begin to rely more heavily on pointing and gesturing (Paquier, Van Dongen, & Loonen, 1992; Sharma, Sharma, & Yeolekar, 2011). Deficits in the auditory processing of speech sounds tend to persist longer or be more severe than impairments in the processing of environmental sounds, which improve at least somewhat with age (Doherty et al., 1999; Kaga, 1999; Korkman et al., 1998; Sieratzki et al., 2001). Along with their language-processing difficulties, children with Landau-Kleffner syndrome frequently are hyperactive, aggressive, have difficulty following lengthy verbal directions, and experience mood swings and attentional problems (Chapman et al., 1998; Cockerell, Bølling, & Nakken, 2011; Korkman et al., 1998; Kuriakose et al., 2012; Sharma et al., 2011).

The age of onset of Landau-Kleffner syndrome occurs between eighteen months and fourteen years of age (Stefanatos, 2011). About 75% of these cases start when the children are between the ages of three and seven years. In general, the younger the child at syndrome onset, the poorer the prognosis for eventual spoken language development (Bishop, 1985; Chapman et al., 1998; Pearl et al., 2001). As with many forms of language disturbance, the syndrome occurs more frequently in boys than girls (Pearl et al., 2001; Woll & Sieratzki, 2019).[15] The long-term outcomes for individuals with Landau-Kleffner syndrome are quite variable. In one large-scale study (Caraballo et al., 2014), eight of the twenty-nine participants eventually showed complete recovery from their language disturbances, while the remaining twenty-one continued to evidence language and/or cognitive disturbances. These results are in line with other studies that show variable long-term outcomes

---

14 Some aspects of speech processing (e.g., understanding and production of prosodic features like intonation and syllables) may remain relatively intact in some individuals with Landau-Kleffner syndrome (Doherty et al., 1999; Korkman et al., 1998).

15 For exceptions to these general trends, see Robinson et al., 2001.

(Cockerell et al., 2011; Doherty et al., 1999; Duran et al., 2009; Kaga, 1999; Korkman et al., 1998; Woll & Sieratzki, 2019). Older children affected by Landau-Kleffner syndrome, children experiencing fluctuations in their speech skills, and children undergoing a shorter period of aphasia tend to recover more language functioning (Cockerell et al., 2011; Sharma et al., 2011).

Although most youngsters (about 70–85%) with Landau-Kleffner syndrome experience seizures at some point, these usually stop by the age of fifteen (but see Duran et al., 2009 for exceptions). Furthermore, some individuals do not have seizures but all show EEG abnormalities, some of which may persist (Campos & Guevara, 2007; Kuriakose et al., 2012; Pearl et al., 2001; Sharma et al., 2011; Tharpe & Olson, 1994). In some instances, seizures appear after disturbances in language development are already occurring. In the Caraballo et al. (2014) study, two of the participants experienced language disturbances prior to their first seizures, and in seven other cases, their initial seizures occurred at the same time as the onset of their language disturbances. This pattern of language disturbances sometimes preceding, following, or co-occurring with initial seizure activity may indicate that there is a common etiological factor (e.g., autoimmune reaction, encephalitis, meningitis) behind both the language disturbance and the seizures (Campos & Guevara, 2007; Soprano et al., 1994). Another view is that the children's language difficulties may be the product of a special form of epilepsy (Deonna, 2000). Regardless, in the future, investigators may wish to carefully chart each participant's course and pattern of syndrome onset together with the drug regimen (typically anticonvulsants or corticosteroids), surgical interventions or medical therapies (Castillo et al., 2008), and the language therapy programs subsequently employed (Van Slyke, 2002). Although the cessation of seizure activity and/or the resumption of normal EEG patterns may have a positive effect on the reacquisition of both receptive and productive language functions, this effect may be gradual and linguistic deficits often remain (Korkman et al., 1998; Van Slyke, 2002). This outcome is probably the result of lasting damage in the primary auditory cortex (Castillo et al., 2008). If, however, the language functions affected by this damage are able to be assumed by other areas of the brain (perhaps in the unaffected hemisphere) through a natural reorganization of neural pathways, better outcomes may result (Castillo et al., 2008).

In an important case study (Roulet Perez et al., 2001), a boy with acquired epileptic aphasia was taught to communicate quite effectively through a sign language. This boy began losing his speech comprehension and production skills when he was between the ages of three and four years. At the age of six, he was introduced to the vocabulary of Swiss-French Sign Language and at age seven began attending a school for deaf and for dysphasic students in Switzerland. In the ensuing years, he made rapid progress learning to sign, acquiring a substantial vocabulary and mature grammatical skills. Indeed, when this boy's sign proficiency was compared with that of a same-age congenitally deaf student, there was no clearly discernible difference in signing proficiency between them. This study showed that a youngster with acquired epileptic aphasia was capable of acquiring fluency in a sign language when placed in an environment that emphasized signing.

Although signing was this boy's preferred communication mode during his schooling, he made a great deal of progress in reacquiring speech skills. Progress in oral language development was quite slow at first, but increased with the help of speech therapy and auditory training. The investigators noted that signing did not compete with his spoken language development and may well have hastened his recovery of oral language. Meanwhile, this youngster was able to complete years of schooling while he was regaining his speech skills. While signing can result in significant gains in spoken communication skills, it should be noted that the specific technique of key word signing may not work as well with some persons with Landau-Kleffner syndrome because of auditory interference from the speech input (Woll & Sieratski, 2019). Such individuals may initially benefit more from signed input only and then be transitioned to both speech and signed input. In addition, the educational environment for a child with Landau-Kleffner syndrome should be adapted to that child's particular needs, a variety of language interventions may need to be employed, and adjustments should be made as the child's linguistic situation evolves (Chapman et al., 1998; Kuriakose et al., 2012; Vance, 1991; Van Slyke, 2002).

Other individuals with acquired epileptic aphasia or Landau-Kleffner syndrome in childhood also have learned to communicate manually, and some have become quite adept in using a sign language or in fingerspelling (Cockerell et al., 2011; Deonna, Peter, & Ziegler, 1989; Deonna et al., 2009; Doherty et al., 1999; Ege & Mouridsen, 1998; Pullens et al., 2015; Rapin et al., 1977; Sieratzki et al., 2001; Tharpe & Olson, 1994; Vance, 1991; Woll & Morgan, 2012; Woll & Sieratski, 1996, 2019). These youngsters' acquisition of sign language skills indicates that the higher language areas in the brain involved in sign language processing were essentially spared, in contrast with those involved in speech processing (Gordon, 2004). In addition, the acquisition of signing skills evidently did not interfere with spoken language recovery in individuals with Landau-Kleffner syndrome, and may have facilitated it (Deonna et al., 2009). Despite the evidence of successful use of manual signs to facilitate the communication of children with Landau-Kleffner syndrome, the implementation of such sign-based programs may still be met with resistance by some family members who worry that learning to sign might impede their children's re-acquisition of speech (Deonna, 2000). Such concerns should be addressed at the time of a child's diagnosis so that parents can understand both the short-term and long-term benefits of sign intervention.

Children's successful use of signs to communicate also can prevent or decrease the behavioral difficulties often associated with the syndrome (Chapman et al., 1998; Deonna, 1991; Tharpe & Olson, 1994). Furthermore, by becoming adept or proficient at using a sign language, these youngsters may be able to make educational progress and to interact socially with members of a signing community. Because students with Landau-Kleffner syndrome can still hear, both family attitudes and legal restrictions may need to be overcome if they are to attend a school for deaf students. If placement in a school for deaf students is not an option, another alternative that should be explored would be to teach these youngsters to communicate through manual signs by utilizing the services of language therapists in local school systems or mainstream settings.

Developmental Language Disorder
and Childhood Apraxia of Speech

Some hearing children experience a disorder in language and communication seemingly from birth onward without any clearly discernible cause (e.g., intellectual disability, brain trauma, autism spectrum disorder). These children often initially appear to be developing in a typical manner; it is only when the understanding and production of spoken language becomes important that a deficit becomes evident. Such children historically were diagnosed with developmental dysphasia. In later years, the more frequently used term became specific language impairment (SLI) (Hoff, 2009), although that term itself is in the process of being superseded by the umbrella term developmental language disorder (DLD) (Bishop, 2017).[16] In comparison with typically developing children, children with DLD in most instances acquire early spoken language milestones at later ages (Botting, 2014; Rudolph & Leonard, 2016), and their rate of language acquisition is noticeably slowed.

A small number of children with developmental language disorder respond to environmental sounds and short verbal commands but fail to acquire even the rudiments of expressive spoken language. In light of their ability to process visual information and their relatively intact nonspeech-based cognitive skills, it should not be surprising to learn that some of these children spontaneously create their own gestural or manual sign-communication systems. These systems often begin with pointing and other basic communicative gestures and then progress to a more elaborate system of mime or to manual signs. A similar phenomenon of spontaneous development of a complex gestural communication system has not been reported for non-speaking children with autism spectrum disorder. Although it is not clear why some children with DLD create their own gesture or sign-communication

---

16 Bishop (2017) provides an analysis of the debate process on the CATALISE (Criteria and Terminology Applied to Language Impairments: Synthesizing the Evidence) project as its participants were trying to reach consensus on the diagnostic terminology to apply to unexplained language problems, and the criteria for distinguishing such problems from other conditions. Also of note in this paper are panelist concerns about the resulting impact of any such determination on the provision or exclusion of intervention services and the allocation of resources to children and families who could benefit from them.

systems and children with autism do not, it is likely that the relatively more intact cognitive, motor, and social interaction abilities of children with developmental dysphasia are important contributing factors.

Caparulo and Cohen (1977) provided a case study account of a young child with developmental dysphasia named Todd who acquired gestural and sign-communication skills. When they first observed him, four-year-old Todd communicated with his mother through a vocabulary of twenty signs, most of which referred to concrete objects. During the eight months he was observed, Todd acquired additional signs and spontaneously began to combine them. This enabled him to convey a range of semantic relations, thus expanding the scope of his communicative abilities. Although Todd's sign-communication skills were far behind those expected of children of Deaf parents of his age, the system he created with his mother clearly expanded his range of communication and facilitated his growth and development.

In a case study of a young boy whose speech was unrecognizable and who also experienced delays in his receptive language skills, the introduction of Signed Norwegian proved extremely helpful (von Tetzchner, 1984a). Signs were taught to him in a formal training session on a daily basis, other signs were taught during play, and he learned some signs through general exposure. The boy often vocalized sounds along with his production of signs; initially, these sounds were difficult to interpret. However, as he learned a sign, the sounds he produced started to resemble the spoken word equivalent. Signing thus provided a means for his parents and teachers to better interpret his vocalizations and provide him with appropriate linguistic feedback (von Tetzchner, 1984a). Shortly after learning to pronounce a spoken word, he typically stopped using the sign for that word. After six months of sign training, the child had improved dramatically on both his receptive and productive speech skills, was able to learn most words without the help of signs, and had noticeable improvements to his temper.

Some success in acquiring a lexicon of manual signs in children with congenital aphasia or developmental dysphasia also has been reported by Phillips (1973). Over a six-week period, she taught seventeen children, ranging in age from six to thirteen years, a vocabulary of signs used in the U.S. In addition to teaching manual signs, Phillips also assessed the children's degree of aphasic impairment. While she reported that the children were able to acquire some facility in signing, their performance in the manual modality evidently was affected by their general language deficits (their degree of aphasic disturbance). That is, the children's proficiency in sign language was significantly related to their degree of aphasic impairment, with those children with lower levels of aphasic impairment showing greater proficiency in sign communication. This finding indicates that performance in the two language modalities of speech and sign are closely interrelated. A similar pattern of considerable impairment across modalities also was found in a recent study of gestural comprehension and production in children with developmental language disorder (Wray, Norbury, & Alcock, 2016). This finding of a breakdown in both spoken language and gestural communication provides additional support to the view that performance in both communication modalities is highly interrelated.

Although we have largely focused so far in this chapter on cases where language loss has been quite extensive or when little spoken language development has occurred, there are many more instances in which the disturbance in language is less severe. Many children identified with developmental language disorder communicate relatively effectively through speech, but begin to talk at a later age, have smaller vocabularies, exhibit deficits in grammatical and morphosyntactic skills, experience difficulties understanding complex utterances, and continue to show impairments in language relative to other abilities some years later (Bernstein Ratner, 2017; Bishop, 2006; Fey, Long, & Finestack, 2003; Haskill & Tyler, 2007; Tomblin et al., 1997; Tomblin et al., 2003). Most of these children are neither cognitively impaired nor hearing-impaired, have no clear evidence of brain dysfunction, and do not meet the criteria of autism spectrum disorder. Furthermore, the number of children who meet the diagnostic criteria for DLD is quite high, with estimates ranging from 5–7% of the population (Botting, 2014). As with most other language-related syndromes, the incidence is markedly higher among boys than girls (about 3:1).

There are also a large number of children who are identified between two and three years of age as "late talkers." This term is largely a descriptive one as many investigators feel that a diagnosis of developmental language disorder cannot be accurately made at this age. When these late-talking children have been followed longitudinally, over 75% of them moved into the normal range for vocabulary, grammar, and discourse skills by the time they were in kindergarten (Paul & Roth, 2011). Although these late-talking toddlers clearly improved their language skills with increasing age in comparison with language norms, it should be noted that their language abilities continued to be well below their nonverbal abilities throughout adolescence (Rescorla, 2009).

Some of the children who are quite delayed or late in their development of spoken or expressive language skills also are delayed in their development of receptive language abilities. Those children who experience delays in both expressive and receptive language domains also use gestures less frequently and score lower on measures of symbolic comprehension than do children who have a delay in expressive language skills only (O'Neill & Chiat, 2015). Those children who have delays in the development of both receptive and expressive language abilities have largely been excluded from studies of late talkers. As a consequence, relatively little is known about the course of their language development and what approaches to communication might be more effective in fostering their progress.

Late-talking children and youngsters with developmental language disorder often appear to have patterns of learning different from those of typically developing youngsters. That is, many late-talking children and youngsters with DLD have better visual and spatial learning abilities than learning abilities based on spoken language (Camarata, 2014). These children apparently learn more by watching and doing than by listening. Some of these learning preferences may be rooted in differences in hemispheric processing. When young adults with DLD were tested, the clear majority (about 55%) showed right-hemispheric dominance for language and a sizeable minority (about 27%) showed their language function to be dispersed bilaterally (Whitehouse & Bishop, 2008). In contrast, the overwhelming majority of typically developing young adults show strong left-hemisphere dominance for language. These differing patterns of learning abilities and hemispheric processing among late-talking children and individuals with DLD may, in turn, underlie their selection of different educational and career paths that embrace more analytical activities (e.g., engineering, accounting).

For the large majority of hearing children with developmental language disorder who eventually acquire substantial spoken language skills, manual gestures may help them compensate to some extent for their early expressive spoken language difficulties. This may be seen in the higher proportion of gesture use in the communications of language-impaired children than in typically developing children (Evans, Alibali, & McNeil, 2001; Iverson & Braddock, 2011; see also von Tetzchner, 1984a). In particular, children with DLD tend to produce more iconic or representative gestures to replace words in their communications than do children in comparison groups (Blake et al., 2008). In a study of mother-child shared book reading (Lavelli, Barachetti, & Florit, 2015), children with DLD used more co-speech gestures, especially representative gestures, than did their typically developing age-mates. In addition, the children with DLD were more sensitive to their mothers' use of gestures or gestural cues in these book-reading experiences. Manual gestures also apparently serve to "boot strap language development" in hearing children with developmental language disorder in much the same fashion as gestures aid younger, typically developing children to communicate (Botting et al., 2010, p. 65). In addition, children with DLD appear to access information more effectively when it is conveyed through gesture than when it is conveyed through speech alone (Kirk, Pine, & Ryder, 2011).

Because developmental language disorder apparently transcends language modality and is evident in the signing of some deaf children, an intervention approach that simply focused on switching language input to a child with DLD from speech to sign language might not be effective in establishing full language abilities. In such a child, sign language may be paired with speech not only to increase his or her productive speech skills, but also as a way to increase his or her receptive speech skills. For a hearing child to be able to understand speech, that child must be able to receive the auditory signal, keep it in memory, and be able to discern patterns within the auditory sequence. For a typically developing child, this process occurs very quickly. Many children with developmental language disorder, however, have auditory-processing difficulties (Corriveau et al., 2007) or deficits in auditory-temporal processing (Alvarez et al., 2015; Tallal, 2003; Tallal, Miller, & Fitch, 1993; Tallal & Stark, 1981) and may need much more time to accurately process the rapid sequences of sounds often present in speech.

In light of these concerns about some children's difficulties in rapid auditory-temporal processing, computer-based intervention programs were developed to improve these skills. Examinations of the outcomes of interventions using these computer-based programs (e.g., Fast ForWord®), however, have not provided evidence that these programs are effective language intervention approaches (Fey et al., 2010; Strong et al., 2011). Because combining manual signs with speech often slows a communication partner's rate of speaking (Hyde & Power, 1991; Wilbur & Petersen, 1998), some children with DLD may find speech input more intelligible when it is combined with manual signs. The use of iconic or representative signs together with speech may also facilitate such children's vocabulary development by making the meaning of many spoken words more transparent. Indeed, in some special classroom units for children with DLD, manual signing systems have been employed to support the children's learning (Conti-Ramsden & Botting, 2000).

Although hearing children with developmental language disorder experience difficulties across a wide range of expressive and receptive language skills, these children often have particular difficulty learning new words. This word-learning deficit results in a smaller vocabulary size and more limited word knowledge at a given age. Moreover, this vocabulary deficit emerges early in a child's life and continues at least into adulthood (Rice & Hoffman, 2015). Some children with DLD may need to hear a new word twice as often as their typically developing peers before gaining an understanding of that word's meaning. Similarly, many children with DLD also will need to practice saying a new word additional times before they are able to use it without assistance (Gray, 2003). In light of the importance of vocabulary knowledge for effective interpersonal communication and for reading comprehension, such deficits in word-learning abilities are a very serious concern for parents and educators.

What might account for these children's problems in learning new words? One view that has been advanced by a number of investigators is that many children with DLD have deficits in the phonological short-term memory component of their working memories (Archibald & Griebeling, 2016; Jackson, Leitao, & Claessen, 2016; Montgomery,

Simplified Signs — Vol. 1

Magimairaj, & Finney, 2010). That is, the working memories of many children with DLD often hold significantly less verbal information than those of their typically developing same-age peers. This smaller size combined with less effective processing of verbal material might help explain why children with DLD have difficulty forming stable phonological representations of newly encountered words as well as their smaller vocabulary sizes overall. One possibility that might be explored in the future would be to pair to-be-learned spoken vocabulary items with corresponding iconic or representative manual signs. Because children with DLD have nonverbal skills in the normal range, such an approach of harnessing visual and motor skills with phonological-processing deficits might assist these children in building their vocabularies.

Finally, although the primary deficit of children with developmental language disorder is, by definition, language, they may have deficits in other domains as well. These deficits include attention control (Noterdaeme et al., 2001), motor control (with deficits in fine and gross motor skills) (Hill, 2001), and the ability to imitate body postures and hand movements (Marton, 2009). Moreover, a subgroup of children with DLD also shows deficits in visual-motor integration (Nicola & Watter, 2016). In contrast, children with DLD typically show age-appropriate visuospatial immediate memory skills (Archibald & Gathercole, 2006). It is possible that teaching these children to sign may facilitate their development of motor control and motor imitation skills, as well as increase their ability to pay attention by having them look at others when they sign.

Developmental Delays in Deaf Children's Signing

Despite hearing loss officially excluding children from a diagnosis of developmental language disorder, hearing children are not the only individuals who may experience a disruption in their developing linguistic skills. It should be noted that DLD appears to affect the language acquisition and processing of deaf children learning to sign in many of the same ways it affects hearing children learning to speak (Herman et al., 2014; Herman, Shield, & Morgan, 2019; Marshall, Denmark, & Morgan, 2006; Marshall & Morgan, 2016; Marshall et al.,

2013, 2015; Mason et al., 2010; Morgan, Herman, & Woll, 2007; Quinto-Pozos, Forber-Pratt, & Singleton, 2011; Woll & Morgan, 2012; see also Metz-Lutz et al., 1999). Analysis of the linguistic development of deaf children is particularly difficult because of a number of factors. First, since most deaf children are born to hearing parents who do not know sign language (Lu, Jones, & Morgan, 2016; Mitchell & Karchmer, 2004), deaf children are rarely exposed to sign language until they are older, unlike hearing children that are exposed to spoken language from birth (Marschark, 1997). This simple demographic fact means that unless hearing parents are immediately aware of their newborn's deafness, choose to learn a sign language, and teach it to their infant, he or she will not receive complete linguistic input in any modality, especially if his or her deafness is severe or profound. This situation of linguistic deprivation means that deaf children are often delayed in their sign language development in comparison to typically developing hearing children (Herman et al., 2019).

Furthermore, with the relatively recent emergence of sign language linguistics as a field, particularly in countries where sign languages lack official linguistic status, studies of the typical course of sign language acquisition in a specific sign language may not be available. When the typical course of language acquisition is not known, it is difficult to impossible to figure out how or if a child is diverging from age-related linguistic norms. Even if such information is known, there may not be any official, evidence-based sign language assessment instruments for that particular sign language or for more specific skill sets within that language (Herman et al., 2019; Quinto-Pozos et al., 2011; Woolfe et al., 2010; see also Haug, 2005 and Haug & Mann, 2008). These concerns, as well as other multiple compounding factors, make it difficult to determine whether deaf children learning a sign language are delayed in their development.

Non-word repetition tasks in hearing children often are a good indicator of developmental language disorder in spoken languages (Bishop, North, & Donlan, 1996; Chiat & Roy, 2008; Conti-Ramsden, 2003; Conti-Ramsden & Hesketh, 2003; Dollaghan & Campbell, 1998; Ebbels, Dockrell, & van der Lely, 2012; Herman et al., 2019; Reuterskiöld-Wagner, Sahlén, & Nyman, 2005), so some sign language researchers worked to develop a non-sign repetition task and tested it on fifteen typically developing deaf children learning BSL (Marshall et al., 2006). The task involved variations in the complexity of the handshape and/or movement parameters of meaningless signs; the signs were phonologically possible but did not actually exist in BSL. Errors included producing the wrong handshape; using only one hand instead of two; changing, deleting, or adding a movement; performing internal and path movements consecutively rather than simultaneously; reversing the direction of the movement; and adding or deleting contact. In general, the greater the complexity of the sign, the more errors that were produced, and task performance tended to improve with age (Marshall et al., 2006). This task was later revised and tested on another ninety-one deaf children with no known language impairments (Mann et al., 2010). Results showed that the task was quite difficult and that deaf participants correctly repeated the non-signs with much less accuracy than hearing children repeated non-words (Marshall, Mann, & Morgan, 2011). Whereas non-word repetition tasks are indicative of DLD in hearing children, it appears that non-sign repetition tasks are hard for many typically developing deaf children and thus are not a clear diagnostic indicator of DLD in deaf populations.

One case study of a deaf five-year-old boy of deaf parents was conducted that found impairments in both the comprehension and production of certain aspects of British Sign Language (BSL) grammar (Morgan et al., 2007).[17] Since both of the boy's parents were deaf, the child had been exposed to BSL from birth; therefore, his signing deficits could not be attributed to linguistic deprivation. He also did not have any cognitive impairments or intellectual disability that could have explained his signing difficulties. The researchers noted that he had particular problems with regard to negation, noun-verb distinctions, spatial verbs, and classifiers. His expressive language was delayed by about two years, thus supporting a diagnosis of developmental language

---

17   The early course of language acquisition in British Sign Language is relatively well known; norms for age of acquisition, familiarity, and iconicity for 300 BSL signs were developed (Vinson et al., 2008). In addition, an adapted version of the MacArthur-Bates Communicative Development Inventories (which is for hearing children, see Fenson et al., 1993, 1994) was tested for the assessment of vocabulary development in deaf children learning BSL (Woolfe et al., 2010) and one is also available for deaf children learning ASL (Anderson & Reilly, 2002). Finally, there are assessment instruments for both receptive BSL skills (Herman, Holmes, & Woll, 1999) and for productive BSL skills (Herman et al., 2004).

disorder (Morgan et al., 2007). In contrast to hearing individuals with DLD, this young boy did not have impairments in phonology or receptive vocabulary.

A later study by these and additional researchers focused on identifying and assessing a wider population of deaf children (including those with hearing parents and deaf parents) who were suspected of having delays in their BSL acquisition (Mason et al., 2010). All of the deaf children had been exposed to at least three years of sign language input. Out of a larger group of children that were referred to the study for assessment, thirteen were fully assessed and showed evidence of language impairment. Over half of the children had deficits in receptive BSL skills and all failed at least one aspect of productive BSL skills on a narrative task (content, structure, grammar). The distribution and severity of the impairments varied, a finding in line with results of developmental language disorder in hearing children learning a spoken language (Mason et al., 2010).

In a comparison study of eleven deaf children with developmental language disorder and eleven typically developing deaf children on a sentence repetition task in British Sign Language (Marshall et al., 2015), researchers found that the children with DLD were much less accurate overall than the control group. The DLD group also performed more poorly on specific measures of repetition of lexical items, sign order, sentence meaning, facial expression, and verb agreement. The fact that the deaf children with DLD in this study had trouble with signed sentence repetition is in line with findings of poor verbal sentence repetition in hearing children with DLD (Chiat et al., 2013; Contemori & Garraffa, 2010; Conti-Ramsden, Botting, & Faragher, 2001; Riches et al., 2010; Stokes et al., 2006). Another comparison study examined the narrative abilities of seventeen deaf children with DLD to seventeen typically developing deaf children in British Sign Language who watched a language-free video (Herman et al., 2014). When later describing the content of this video, the DLD group produced shorter, less structured, and grammatically simpler signed narratives than the group of typically developing deaf children. Once again, verb agreement or morphology was an area of particular difficulty for the children with DLD, as were classifiers, role shifting, and their ability to infer meanings from the video (Herman et al., 2014). Similar findings of impairment in verbal narrative skills have resulted in this being seen as a marker of developmental language disorder in hearing children (Botting, 2002; Pearce, James, & McCormack, 2010; Reed et al., 2007; Wetherell, Botting, & Conti-Ramsden, 2007).

Finer distinctions between typically developing deaf children and deaf children with developmental language disorder have been observed in a study of semantic fluency (Marshall et al., 2013). In this study, twenty-two typically developing deaf signers and thirteen deaf signers with DLD (ten of the same participants from Mason et al., 2010's study) were tested on their ability to produce lists of different types of animals and food within a sixty-second time frame. Results from both the typically developing deaf signers and the deaf children with DLD were similar to results from semantic fluency tasks performed by typically developing hearing children (Marshall et al., 2013).[18] These results imply that semantic fluency is not a key marker of DLD in deaf signing children. However, the deaf children with DLD were slower to respond initially and also displayed word-finding errors that the typically developing deaf group did not.

Finally, in an interview study of educators and language professionals who worked with deaf students learning American Sign Language (ASL), the participants discussed atypicalities in the signing of deaf children with whom they were familiar (Quinto-Pozos et al., 2011). Examples of such atypicalities included sign stuttering/repetition, lack of facial expressions, errors in the formational parameters of signs, failing to properly use space to set up referents, poor role-shifting, and leaving out necessary referential information such as the time, place, and people involved in a story (Quinto-Pozos et al., 2011). These professionals also noted the difficulty of distinguishing between normal errors that children made while learning to sign and errors that are more attributable to atypical development or a potential communication disorder. Standards for the identification of such errors and for comparison with typically developing populations were not widely available. Many times, the educators and speech-language therapists within a school had to develop their own tools for analysis and intervention with a child they

---

18　This similarity in findings supports the idea that the development and structure of deaf children's semantic sign networks is largely comparable to the development and structure of hearing children's semantic word networks.

suspected of having a developmental language disorder. Such concerns reveal that much work remains to be done in defining, assessing, and creating therapeutic interventions for developmental language disorder in deaf children. Moreover, it is possible that the incidence of DLD in deaf children is equal to or greater than the 5–7% incidence of DLD in hearing children (Mason et al., 2010; Morgan et al., 2007). In order to receive proper consideration of and support for linguistic interventions in deaf children, it will be important for the definition of DLD to evolve to include the experiences of deaf populations.

Childhood Apraxia of Speech

Some children experience substantial difficulty in their production and sequencing of speech sounds. These children evidently have deficits in the planning and programming of the movements underlying their speech but do not show neuromuscular deficits in general (Aziz et al., 2010). The term frequently used to identify this condition is childhood apraxia of speech, although the terms developmental apraxia of speech, childhood verbal apraxia (or dyspraxia), childhood dyspraxia (of speech), and developmental articulatory apraxia have been employed as well.[19] The spoken language of children with apraxia of speech often is not intelligible, with inconsistency and variability of speech sound production underlying this problematic condition (Proctor, 2014). Childhood apraxia of speech frequently is viewed as being highly heritable; individuals with this disability often come from families where other members also manifest speech or language disorders (Lewis et al., 2004). Systematic efforts to determine a specific genetic cause of childhood apraxia of speech have not yet proved successful; indeed, the view is emerging that the syndrome has a complex heterogeneous genetic etiology (Peter et al., 2016). In addition to their speech difficulties, many youngsters with childhood apraxia of speech frequently have other impairments, such as an intellectual disability or autism spectrum disorder (Tierney et al., 2015). As a consequence, children with apraxia

---

19   When children get older and their apraxia of speech persists, their speech disorder is still considered childhood apraxia. This helps differentiate it from adult-acquired apraxia of speech. Adult-acquired apraxia of speech typically is the product of cerebrovascular accidents (strokes) or other brain trauma (Proctor, 2014).

of speech should be evaluated for these conditions as well. Academically, children with apraxia of speech also often experience difficulties in reading and other language arts areas (Beukelman & Mirenda, 2005; Davis, 2007).

Because the spoken language of many individuals with childhood apraxia of speech is largely unintelligible, they frequently participate in various augmentative and alternative communication programs. Selecting an effective communication program for these children, however, may prove difficult as they often are also identified as having a limb apraxia. This limb apraxia is evident in their difficulties with sequencing the motor movements of their hands and arms. Despite these impairments, some children respond well to interventions based on sign language or the manual alphabet. Other children may do better with communication boards or speech-generating devices. These various augmentative and alternative communication intervention approaches do not impede the children's progress in spoken language development and may even promote it (DeThorne et al., 2009). Additionally, with the children frequently more successful in their communicative interactions with others after intervention, they often show improvements in their behavior as well (Beukelman & Mirenda, 2005; Culp, 1989; Cumley & Swanson, 1999; Shelton & Garves, 1985).

Finally, Helfrich-Miller (1984, 1994) has reported promising results in reducing the frequency of articulation and phonemic sequencing errors in youngsters with childhood apraxia of speech by combining two different treatment approaches. More specifically, she combined Melodic Intonation Therapy, an approach often used with adults with aphasia, together with Signed English signs. In this combined approach, the verbal input to a child and the child's output would be slowed down and the rhythm and stress exaggerated. The signs were paired with spoken words because this procedure slowed both the rate of language presentation to each child and each child's rate of speaking, as well as helping to convey to each child the meanings of the words and phrases. In light of the promising results from this study and others using various augmentative and alternative communication approaches, it is hoped that larger and more systematic studies of the effectiveness of these approaches will be conducted in the future.

Concluding Remarks

After concentrating almost entirely on enhancing the often limited spoken language skills of individuals with aphasia, investigators in recent decades have expanded their focus to include the use of different non-oral approaches in fostering communication skills. Among the non-oral approaches that have shown some success are those that have used signs from various sign languages or sign systems. If persons with aphasia or developmental language disorder are able to acquire some signing skills, then that ability to communicate, regardless of language modality, should make their lives more fulfilling and considerably less frustrating. Additionally, the pairing of iconic manual signs with speech shows promise of facilitating spoken language development in some individuals.

Studies of manual sign learning in adults with aphasia have shown widely varying training outcomes among the studies' participants. Some participants have acquired substantial sign lexicons and learned to combine signs. Other participants have made only very modest gains in communication skills despite considerable investment of time and effort. Examination of these different studies and their participants reveal that there are at least several factors involved in successful sign learning by persons with aphasia. The type and severity of the aphasia affect sign learning, with the most severely impaired individuals typically making the most limited progress. The characteristics of a particular sign also affect its learning. A sign that is highly iconic and easy to form is likely to be learned more readily than a sign without such characteristics. The iconic nature and formational ease of many Simplified Sign System signs will likely make them relatively easier to learn than most signs from genuine sign languages. These characteristics should also make the signs easier to learn by children with aphasia, Landau-Kleffner syndrome, developmental language disorder, or apraxia of speech, not to mention the family members, friends, teachers, and medical staff with whom such individuals come into contact.

In fact, in recent years there has been growing recognition that hearing children and adults with full mental capacities might also benefit from learning and using manual signs. Some of the interest in this domain appeared to emerge after scholars began to discuss their findings about signing in babies. Rather suddenly, many thousands of hearing babies of hearing parents were being taught to communicate through manual signs and gestures. Moreover, this interest has continued to expand; manual signs and gestures have come to be recognized as potential vehicles of instruction in fostering language and cognitive development more generally. We discuss this growing interest in and excitement about the use of manual signs and gestures to facilitate learning in the larger population in Chapter 7.

7. Use of Manual Signs and Gestures by Hearing Persons

Contemporary Perspectives

So far in this volume, we have discussed the history of the sign languages of Deaf persons and their recognition as true and genuine languages, as well as the unique richness of meaning that can be conveyed through a visual-gestural mode of communication. Signs also have proven to be beneficial to the larger hearing societies in which Deaf people live, as shown by our exploration of the use of signs by hearing persons in various historical contexts. These contexts included the initial interactions of peoples who came from different cultures and/or who spoke different languages, the frequent use of pantomime or iconic gestures during artistic performances, and the use of signs as a means of communication during times of contemplative silence in monasteries. We also have discussed the more recent use of signs with hearing persons with autism spectrum disorder, intellectual disability, cerebral palsy, and aphasia.

In the introduction to this volume, we mentioned the potential use of a sign-communication system in contemporary contexts by other hearing persons. A sign-communication system that is easily remembered and that consists of gestures that visually resemble the concepts for which they stand could potentially be used by modern-day travelers, members of the military, or international aid workers while interacting with people in a foreign country whose language they do not understand. Highly iconic signs and gestures could also be used by healthcare professionals and staff members in nursing homes (whose residents often have experienced a decline in their hearing), emergency rooms

 https://doi.org/10.11647/OBP.0205.07

and hospitals (whose patients or staff may speak various languages), and medical emergency situations in areas that may include a wide range of first- or second-generation immigrants. Iconic or representative signs and gestures could also be used effectively with young children who have just been adopted from various countries overseas and who are faced with the daunting task of having to learn a new language with their new family.

Despite the wide range of existing and potential uses of sign languages and sign-communication systems that we have already discussed, there are many other applications that we have not yet covered. Among these is the use of signs by hearing parents with their young hearing infants as a means of fostering early successful communication. In addition, teaching signs to youngsters from economically disadvantaged families may increase their linguistic abilities and provide a sound basis for further academic achievement. In fact, utilizing iconic signs and gestures may be helpful to many young children in primary school and pre-kindergarten educational programs.

Iconic or representative signs may even facilitate the learning processes of persons with attention-deficit hyperactivity disorder (ADHD) and children who struggle with reading comprehension impairment. Highly iconic signs or gestures may also serve as a powerful bridge to learning the vocabulary of a second (or additional) language. Students of all ages may find that pairing to-be-learned foreign language vocabulary items with iconic or representative gestures aids the students in recalling the foreign language's vocabulary. Finally, learning to sign may result in enhanced cognitive abilities for all individuals, deaf or hearing, especially in the domains of spatial memory and mental rotation. Thus, iconic signs and gestures can provide a meaningful and positive impact on the cognitive and linguistic development of hearing persons in a wide range of contexts throughout their lifetimes. Indeed, in light of the many apparent advantages that may be attained by either learning a genuine sign language of Deaf persons or a large lexicon of iconic signs, we encourage everyone to take advantage of opportunities to learn to sign. Let us first focus on the use of signs by hearing parents with their hearing infants.

Teaching Signs to Hearing Infants of Hearing Parents

After investigators (e.g., Bonvillian et al., 1983; Folven & Bonvillian, 1991; McIntire, 1977) reported that very young children of Deaf parents often attained early language milestones in sign at younger ages than children learning to speak did so for spoken language, other investigators began to study the learning of signs or symbolic gestures by the young hearing children of hearing parents (Acredolo & Goodwyn, 1996; Goodwyn & Acredolo, 1993, 1998). In this research, those infants who were taught a collection of "baby signs" typically acquired the signs faster than speech-trained infants acquired a collection of target words, although there were wide individual differences in acquisition rates. The investigators attributed the children's slower acquisition of words to the difficulties and complexities involved in spoken language production early in a child's development. In other words, a child's physical ability to produce speech or control the muscles needed for recognizable speech seems to lag behind the child's physical ability to control the arm and hand movements needed for recognizable signs. This implies that most children have the mental capacity to communicate before they are able to effectively do so through spoken language (Loncke, 2019).

Sign-trained youngsters were then followed longitudinally by Goodwyn and Acredolo (1993, 1998) to determine whether there were any lasting effects of early signing or symbolic gesturing on subsequent development. In comparison with those children who had not had the sign intervention, the children in the sign-trained group showed an advantage on a number of verbal language acquisition measures throughout early childhood, as well as higher school-age IQ scores (Acredolo, Goodwyn, & Abrams, 2002; Goodwyn, Acredolo, & Brown, 2000). These findings clearly indicate that early signing or symbolic gesturing does not hamper verbal development and may, in fact, enhance it.

In an attempt to account for the positive outcomes associated with baby-signing in their research, Goodwyn and Acredolo have advanced the view that the children's symbolic gestures or signs may have elicited more spoken language input from the children's parents as well as indicated to the parents the specific topics in which the children were interested. There are, however, other possible interpretations. One is that combining sign and spoken language input may facilitate the vocal production of typically developing babies much as it apparently does for many children with Down syndrome (Özçalişkan et al., 2016; see Chapter 4) or autism (Özçalişkan et al., 2017; see Chapter 5). A second possibility is that because "baby-signing" typically involves caregivers producing signs for only the key words in their utterances, this combining of signs and spoken language may help infants segment the speech stream by making the signed words more prominent, thus facilitating their acquisition (Mueller & Acosta, 2015). Another possibility is that the combination of visual, auditory, and gestural processing that occurs when babies learn signs together with words may make information acquired that way more memorable. Although the use of multiple symbolic coding systems has been advanced as an explanation for findings of enhanced learning and retention in adults (Paivio, 1990), it is not clear whether the use of multiple representational or symbolic coding systems operates similarly in infants (cf. Lukowski et al., 2005).

Along with the claim of potentially fostering more rapid spoken language development, the early use of signs also has been associated with fewer and less severe temper tantrums in infancy and early childhood (Acredolo et al., 2002). Additional support for this claim of improved social behavior is seen in a study of hearing infants who were taught manual signs early in their lives. Once these infants acquired minimal functional sign skills, their incidence of crying and whining decreased substantially (Thompson et al., 2007).

The claims about the positive effects of signing apparently have resulted in signs making major inroads among hearing families with young children. This group consists of parents who have embraced baby-signing as a way to enhance their communicative exchanges with their babies before their babies can effectively communicate with them in spoken language. More specifically, hearing parents who have adopted baby-signing often express their hope that signing with their young children will result in earlier and clearer communication between them, as well as encourage more socially appropriate behaviors by their young children (Pizer, Walters, & Meier, 2007).

Two additional studies have examined the impact of mothers using manual signs together with spoken language on their infants' language development. In one study (Seal & DePaolis, 2014), the development of eight infants exposed to baby signs was compared with that of eight infants who were not exposed to baby signs. The data for this study came from videotapes of the sixteen infants obtained when they were between nine and eighteen months of age. Analyses of the tapes showed that the infants exposed to baby signs achieved the four-, ten-, and twenty-five-word points in development earlier than the non-signing infants, but that the differences in vocabulary acquisition rates between the groups were not statistically significant. The investigators also reported that the level of manual activity that accompanied vocal productions did not differ between the two groups. For both the infants exposed to signs and those not exposed to signs, there was a very high rate of manual activity accompanying vocal production. This finding underlines the view that manual activity and vocal activity are often closely interlinked.

In another investigation (Kirk et al., 2013) of the impact of "baby signs" or symbolic gestures on infant language development, forty infants were followed from the age of eight months to twenty months. Half of the mothers modeled signs or gestures for a limited number of target set signs, whereas the remaining half of the mothers focused on spoken language input. During the course of the study, many of the infants in the sign-input condition learned some or most of the signs or gestures modeled by their mothers. But these infants' sign learning evidently did not affect their language development more generally, as there were no differences on measures of spoken language comprehension or production between these infants and those who received only spoken language input. There was, however, one clear difference between the sign-input and the no-sign-input groups: the mothers in the sign- or gesture-input conditions became more sensitive to their infants' nonverbal cues than the mothers in the speech-only condition. This increased sensitivity to their infants' nonverbal cues may be an important benefit of sign input as such sensitivity may contribute to close mother-infant bonding.

We should also point out that the learning of signs by hearing children growing up in hearing families may not precisely mirror those patterns seen in children growing up in Deaf families. Although we noted earlier (see Chapter 3) that sign iconicity did not play an important role in the initial acquisition of signs by the very young children of Deaf parents, whether or not a sign is highly iconic may be important in the sign learning of slightly older hearing children of hearing parents. In several studies involving hearing children ranging in age from two to five years, the children associated iconic signs or gestures with their referents much more successfully than they associated arbitrary signs or gestures with their referents (Brown, 1979; Magid & Pyers, 2017; Namy & Waxman, 1998; Tomasello, Striano, & Rochat, 1999). In addition, children's ability to recognize the meaning of iconic signs evidently improves greatly during the preschool years (Tolar et al., 2008). Thus, sign iconicity may become a factor in the rate of sign learning and ease of retention as children mature. Young children also produce a wide range of representational gestures on their own, although the incidence of this spontaneous production may vary across cultures (Marentette et al., 2016). Finally, four-year-old children are able to use iconic gestures produced by a human adult to obtain a reward much more often than they could use an arbitrary gesture to secure a reward (Bohn, Call, & Tomasello, 2016). Chimpanzees, in contrast, were not nearly as adept in their understanding of iconic gestures as the children. This latter finding may suggest that humans are noticeably better at comprehending iconic gestures than their closest living relatives.

Evaluative Comments

In recent years, a controversy has arisen about some of the claims made by investigators about the positive effects of baby-signing. The issue that appears to be the principal source of controversy in the "baby sign" literature is whether signing with hearing babies facilitates these babies' acquisition of spoken language skills. There does not seem to be the same level of disagreement over whether most hearing babies are able to acquire a target vocabulary more rapidly in the visual-gestural modality as opposed to the auditory-vocal modality. As Kirk et al. observed (2013, p. 580): "...infants did acquire the gestures and used them to communicate about the target set of referents long before the onset of speech." So, if the question under examination were whether signing increased early communication and naming, regardless of communication modality, then a case could be advanced for the beneficial effects of signing.

Goodwyn and Acredolo's finding that signing with hearing infants does not interfere with these youngsters' acquisition of spoken words appears to be well supported. Parents and investigators, however, should exercise caution before accepting some of their other claims about the positive effects of baby-signing. There are several reasons for recommending such restraint. One is that their findings about the positive effects of signing on spoken language development were small in magnitude and not consistently statistically significant throughout the course of the study. A second reason is that the findings are not based on a very large number of study participants. Another methodological concern is the possibility that the participants in the parent-child sign-training group may have differed from the participants in the parent-child comparison group in important ways from the beginning of the study. That is, those parents who embraced the idea of signing with their babies back when the study started may have differed from the comparison-group parents in ways other than the use of signs.

It should also be noted that as the Goodwin and Acredolo study progressed, there was a fairly high participant attrition rate (Johnston, Durieux-Smith, & Bloom, 2005). This loss of participants over time means that the claims from the latter stages of the study were based on considerably fewer participants than those from the initial stages. Furthermore, those participants who did not continue in the study may have differed from those who did continue in ways undetected by the investigators, making the interpretation of any findings difficult at best. In light of these concerns, more scientific studies clearly need to be conducted and findings replicated before the various claims about the positive effects of baby-signing can be given substantial credence (Barnes, 2010).

Overall, a review of the various studies of baby-signing does not provide clear support for the view that signing with your baby during infancy will lead to significantly enhanced spoken language abilities in early childhood (Fitzpatrick et al., 2014); the evidence remains inconclusive. When differences have been reported, while tending to support the facilitative effect of baby-signing use, they have been relatively small and not long-lasting. These general trends, however, may mask some important differences that will need to be probed more thoroughly in the future. For example, in the Kirk et al. (2013)

study, three low-performing boys evidently benefited from the gesture-communication training they received. This finding led the investigators to "suggest that gesture is beneficial for infants who have weaker language abilities than others" (p. 581).

Another aspect that should be examined in the future is whether gesture- or sign-communication interventions affect young children from different socioeconomic classes in the same way. In the above studies of baby-signing, it appears that the large majority of participants came from middle-class families with strong educational backgrounds. For example, in the Kirk et al. (2013) study, only one of the participating mothers did not have an undergraduate university education. Children reared in such families often are bathed in language beginning in infancy. If studies of baby-signing were to include a much more diverse population, then it is possible that trends favoring the use of baby-signing to facilitate spoken language development might emerge among late-talking children and children from more economically disadvantaged households. Moreover, other aspects of child development besides spoken language development (e.g., cognitive growth, social development) probably should be examined as well in studies of baby-sign training. We say this in light of the array of positive findings of the effects of baby-signing on the development of young children from predominantly lower-income families in a Latino community (Mueller, Sepulveda, & Rodriguez, 2014).

Finally, it should be noted that in the studies of "baby-signing" discussed above, the participating parents typically were hearing persons who were neither fluent nor even proficient in a genuine sign language used by Deaf persons. Furthermore, the signs that the participating mothers used in their interactions with their hearing infants came primarily from baby-signing books and lists or lexicons of signs taken from dictionaries of genuine sign languages. The participating mothers thus were dependent on outside source materials as opposed to relying on a communication system that they had fully internalized. In addition, it appears that the mothers' use of baby signs accounted for only a small portion of their communicative exchanges with their babies. If the mothers who participated in these studies had been more fluent signers, it is likely that they would have begun to sign with their babies much earlier in their infancy than occurred in the studies examined, and that the infants would have been fully enveloped in a signing world. Instead, it appears that the "baby sign" infants existed primarily in a speaking world punctuated by periodic symbolic gesture or manual sign input from their mothers.[1] If the potential efficacy of baby-signing on young children's development were to be truly tested, then it would appear that it would be necessary to ensure that the participating mothers were adept and dedicated signers (see Snoddon, 2014).

Socioeconomic Intervention Programs and Language

During the 1960s, a view emerged among many educators and social scientists in the United States that intervention programs needed to be introduced to help combat the adverse effects of children being reared in poverty. The best known and largest of these programs was Project Head Start, although there was a wide range of other smaller-scale intervention programs as well. Project Head Start focused primarily on improving the lives of three- and four-year-old children from families with incomes below the poverty line. Participating children typically would receive nutritious meals in a safe educational environment along with regular medical and dental care.

Because Head Start has been in operation for decades, it is possible to assess its effectiveness over time. In many ways, those individuals who participated in Head Start showed significant long-term benefits. Head Start participants were more likely to graduate from high school and enroll in college and less likely to repeat grades or engage in adolescent drug use and acts of delinquency (Garces, Thomas, & Currie, 2002; Love, Chazan-Cohen, & Raikes, 2007). At-risk children who participated in Head Start preschool programs also were much less likely to be placed in foster care than those children who attended non-Head Start preschools or day care programs (Klein, Fries, & Emmons, 2017). This outcome may be a product of the additional support provided by Head

---

1   Although children under the age of twenty-four months do not effectively acquire new spoken words through video presentations (DeLoache et al., 2010), the same pattern does not occur for manual sign learning. When fifteen-month-olds were shown ASL signs at home through instructional videos, the infants demonstrated considerable sign learning (Dayanim & Namy, 2015). This study indicates that baby signs may be acquired through educational videos, even when a caregiver is not present.

Start programs to the children's entire families. The evidence in support of academic benefits, however, is more limited. In general, gains in IQ and academic achievement scores by Head Start participants were no longer evident by the end of first grade in comparison with those of non-participants (U.S. Department of Health and Human Services, 2010). More targeted analyses of the effectiveness of Head Start have shown that benefits varied widely among participants. Those children from the lowest risk subgroup of participants were largely unaffected by their participation in the program. In contrast, children from higher risk subgroups (e.g., children with lower initial academic skills, children with mothers with lower education levels) often benefited significantly from Head Start participation (Cooper & Lanza, 2014).

What might be behind the lack of progress in academic skills seen in many children from families with lower socioeconomic backgrounds? Children reared in economically disadvantaged (or less advantaged) families often are talked to less frequently and exposed to fewer different words by their parents (Hart & Risley, 1995, 2003; Hoff, 2003, 2013). Not only are children from lower socioeconomic backgrounds talked with much less frequently by their parents at home, but the complexity and diversity of the language that these children receive from their teachers in kindergarten is significantly more limited (Neuman, Kaefer, & Pinkham, 2018). This lower level of input is important as studies have shown that the quantity of words and the number of different words spoken by adults to infants and young children are strong predictors of their language development (Pan et al., 2005; Shneidman et al., 2013; Topping, Dekhinet, & Zeedyk, 2013; Zauche et al., 2016). Furthermore, smaller vocabulary sizes and lower language-processing abilities already are evident in children from lower socioeconomic backgrounds by eighteen months of age (Fernald, Marchman, & Weisleder, 2013).

Children from economically disadvantaged families typically do not have the experiences that foster reading acquisition skills, specifically the development of phonemic awareness, a substantial vocabulary, and oral language knowledge (Buckingham, Beaman, & Wheldall, 2014). Children reared in low income households also typically are read to at home much less frequently in the years before they enter first grade than children reared in higher-income homes (Adams, 1990; Whitehurst, 1997). These book reading experiences are important because children who are read to more frequently tend to have larger vocabularies, evidence greater language complexity, and demonstrate better cognitive outcomes than children who are read to less frequently or not at all (Needlman & Silverstein, 2004; Raikes et al., 2006; Rodriguez et al., 2009; Schmitt, Simpson, & Friend, 2011; Zauche et al., 2016).

There is also a social class difference with regard to maternal gestural input and infant gesture production. Mothers from higher socioeconomic backgrounds typically use more gesture types in their interactions with their infants than do mothers from lower socioeconomic backgrounds (Rowe & Goldin-Meadow, 2009a). That is, mothers from higher socioeconomic backgrounds use gestures to convey a wider range of meanings to their infants than do mothers from lower socioeconomic backgrounds. The participating children's subsequent spoken language vocabulary comprehension at four-and-a-half years was predicted by the number of gestures they produced as infants. Evidently, there are distinct differences by family socioeconomic background in both maternal gestural and spoken language input during infancy, and these two forms of communicative input are related to each other and with children's eventual language development. Children from economically disadvantaged families likely enter pre-school programs with less developed language skills than their peers from middle-class backgrounds. In general, the lower a family's socioeconomic status (SES), the greater the likelihood that the children have impaired language acquisition (Donkin et al., 2014).

Another possible reason for the lack of clear long-term benefits in language development and literacy for most Head Start participants may reside in the way Head Start classrooms are composed. Children in Head Start classrooms are grouped together with preschool-aged peers from families with very low incomes. Typically, children from such low SES backgrounds have low language skill levels. When preschool children with low language skills are placed in a classroom with peers with similarly low language skills, the children show noticeably less language growth than preschool children who are placed in a classroom with children with higher language skills (Justice et al., 2011). If it were possible to group preschoolers with lower language skills together with preschoolers with higher language skills, then the children with lower language skills likely would show greater gains in their language development. It should also be acknowledged that Head Start preschool programs often include children with disabilities. In one recent survey, the participating Head Start teachers reported that nearly one-fourth of the children in their classes had some form of disability, with speech or communication problems being the most prevalent disability (McDonnell et al., 2014). Such a high incidence of children with disabilities in Head Start classrooms might account for some of the reported difficulties observed in achieving desired literacy-related skills.

Concerns about the longer-term development of English language and literacy skills by children who participated in Head Start programs have prompted considerable re-thinking by policymakers of the program's structure. Because many three-year-olds spend a second year in their same Head Start classroom, a question has arisen as to whether this approach is an optimal one pedagogically. It is now possible to largely resolve this issue in that another option to combat the detrimental effects of poverty has emerged in the form of publicly funded pre-kindergarten programs for many four-year-olds. These pre-kindergarten programs often offer more intensive educational curricula than those of Head Start; there is typically a stronger focus on literacy, language, and mathematical skills. The research question that has been pursued is whether it is better educationally to keep children in Head Start programs for a second year or to transition them to a pre-kindergarten program. Although this question has not been answered definitively, it appears that children who attended Head Start at age three in most instances develop stronger prereading skills if they transition to a quality pre-kindergarten program at age four (Jenkins et al., 2016). Thus, a change in educational sequencing of academic programs may pay dividends developmentally.

Another approach that should be considered to enhance the spoken language vocabulary skills of young children from families with very low incomes would be to introduce manual sign-communication programs into their preschool and elementary school classrooms. In her book *Dancing with Words: Signing for Hearing Children's Literacy*, Marilyn Daniels (2001) makes the case for adding sign language training and teaching to the educational programs of typically developing, hearing preschool and school-age children from economically disadvantaged families to increase the children's spoken language vocabulary size. In a series of studies, Daniels convinced teachers to introduce sign instruction to their daily programs. In most of her investigations, hearing pre-kindergarten and kindergarten children were taught American Sign Language (ASL) signs by their teachers. The efficacy of the instruction typically was assessed by administering one version of a receptive English vocabulary test, Peabody Picture Vocabulary Test-Revised or PPVT-R (Dunn & Dunn, 1981), at the beginning of the school year and another at the end. In most instances, those children who participated in the sign language programs showed substantial gains in their English vocabulary size, whereas children in comparison groups did not. When English-language vocabulary scores were converted into standard scores (with a mean of 100 and standard deviation of 15), the children in the sign-learning condition typically showed increases of about 13–16 points over the school year, a highly significant improvement. (Although the PPVT-R is not an IQ test, it should be noted that scores on the PPVT-R correlate highly with full scale scores on the Stanford-Binet IQ test.) Furthermore, Daniels found that these gains continued over time. When children in a kindergarten program who had been taught signs the previous year were tested the next year, they continued to show evidence of increased English vocabulary size. These findings may be of particular importance to parents and educators of young children because vocabulary size in the preschool years has been shown to be predictive of language and literacy skills years later (Lee, 2011; Storch & Whitehurst, 2002).

There are several other aspects of Daniels' studies that merit discussion. One is that some of the teachers in her studies had only the most rudimentary knowledge of signing and fingerspelling. According to Daniels, teachers should not be discouraged by their lack of signing expertise; the teachers need only to be slightly ahead of their pupils in their knowledge of signs. A second aspect is that the findings of substantial gains in vocabulary scores came from students in schools in more disadvantaged neighborhoods. When students in more middle-class neighborhoods were taught ASL signs, there was not a similar gain in receptive vocabulary scores. It is likely that these children already were in quite stimulating language environments. A third aspect is that while the sign input was associated with English vocabulary gains by many children from more disadvantaged neighborhoods, it is not clear why these gains occurred. One possibility is that when vocabulary items are both taught and learned as signs and spoken words, this approach may more fully engage the children's sensory and motor abilities. The use by children of their visual and motor skills, in addition to their auditory-vocal skills, may result in vocabulary items being processed more deeply as well as in different ways. Although just which memory and recall processes are involved in children's vocabulary learning remains unclear, it is evident that language input in more than one modality often results in enhanced vocabulary learning. Another possibility is that sign instruction may help children learn to visually attend to their teacher and to better regulate their motor movements. These skills — paying attention and behavioral regulation — may then help children to learn more effectively in a classroom setting. Finally, it should be noted that most of Daniels' studies were relatively small in magnitude and short in duration. In the future, it will be important to gain a better understanding of just which children benefit, how long these benefits last, and why those benefits occurred.

The claims of a facilitative effect of manual signs and fingerspelling on the spoken language development of young hearing children are in accord with observations made long ago by Thomas H. Gallaudet, a pioneering educator of deaf students in the United States. Gallaudet had observed beneficial effects of having children who could hear and speak interact in an educational setting with children who were deaf and non-speaking. Bartlett, in 1853, summarized the principle upon which Gallaudet's view of a beneficial effect evidently was based: "The more varied the form under which language is presented to the mind through the different senses, the more perfect will be the knowledge of it acquired, and the more permanently will it be retained" (p. 33). Although Gallaudet's observations and theorizing were not based on the outcomes of systematic investigations, they appear to fit remarkably with much current thinking in education.

Another factor that may affect the efficacy of early intervention programs is the behavior of mothers from different backgrounds or ethnicities with their infants. Within low-income families, there is a wide range in the quality of mother-child communicative exchanges. Those mothers who engaged in higher quality verbal and nonverbal interactions (e.g., joint engagement, connected communication) with their two-year-olds typically had children with greater expressive language skills a year later (Hirsh-Pasek et al., 2015). Furthermore, when the behavior of mother-infant pairs from different ethnic backgrounds was compared, it was the African-American mothers who engaged in less gestural communication and language input to their infants than the mother-infant pairs from the other ethnicities examined (Tamis-LeMonda et al., 2012). Additionally, there were some suggestions that the African-American mothers felt that language is largely learned by their children on their own and not the product, to a considerable extent, of maternal language input.

Marilyn Daniels' studies provide evidence of what might be accomplished by introducing sign communication to preschoolers from low socioeconomic status backgrounds. At present, however, relatively little is known about any potential benefits that might be derived from having mothers from economically disadvantaged backgrounds sign with their preverbal infants. One study (Kirk, 2009) tried to examine this issue by comparing the language development of infants from low-income families placed in two different groups. A "general communication" group was composed of mother-infant pairs in which the mothers were urged to foster their infants' communication by including turn-taking, joint attention, etc. in their interactions. The mothers in a "gesture communication" group were urged to also include various signs or gestures (specifically, Makaton signs; see Chapter 4) in their interactions with their infants. Unfortunately, high participant attrition rates in this study substantially limited the strength of the conclusions that can be drawn from the study. Still, it should be noted that there was a trend for the mothers in the gesture group to have infants show greater improvements in their receptive and productive spoken language vocabularies than did the infants in the general communication group.

Some of the mothers in the gestural communication group were interviewed as the study came to its end. These participating mothers observed that they thought that the use of gestures had resulted in improved communication with and better understanding of their infants. The mothers also commented that for gestures to be useful for them as parents, the gestures needed to feel natural and to be produced virtually automatically. Apparently, in the demands of communicating with and taking care of their infants, there was little time for the mothers to reflect or to look up signs. Thus, it was important for signs or gestures to feel natural to the mothers and be readily formed, and for the gestures to be very easily recalled or remembered.

Finally, another issue in the educational development of children from economically disadvantaged families is that the academic progress demonstrated by many such children during the school year often does not continue during the summer months when schools are closed (Alexander, Entwisle, & Olson, 2014; Heyns, 1978). Many of the children do not advance in their academic skills during their summer break and may show declines. It is possible that some young students' academic skills might be more robust or longer lasting if they were acquired in a learning environment that incorporated more visual and gestural components and was less dependent on the children's listening skills (Daniels, 2001).

Attention-Deficit Hyperactivity Disorder (ADHD) in Academic Settings

Many children experience problems in attention control and impulsivity. For some children, these problems are much more severe than they are for most other children. Those children with more severe problems in attentional control and impulsivity often are identified as having attention-deficit hyperactivity disorder (ADHD). With increasing awareness of the characteristics of this disorder, more and more students are being diagnosed as having ADHD. Current estimates of the percentage of school-aged children who meet the diagnostic criteria for ADHD range from 3–11% of all school-aged children (Biederman & Faraone, 2005; Leung & Hon, 2016), with most estimates between 5–7%. With such a high incidence, ADHD is an issue of major concern in many contemporary classrooms and families worldwide. And, as with many syndromes involving children, boys are diagnosed with ADHD much more often than girls; the ratio is about 4 to 1.

Children with ADHD frequently are very impulsive, constantly fidgeting, inattentive, and quite disruptive of many classroom activities (Barkley, 2003; Brown, 2005; Goldstein, 2011). Individuals with ADHD often show difficulties or deficits in a range of executive functioning skills, as they have problems with organizing, focusing, and staying alert, as well as managing frustration. These difficulties, furthermore, often are long-lasting; about 40–50% of children with ADHD will continue to show impairments into adulthood (Biederman & Faraone, 2005; Leung & Hon, 2016). Persons with ADHD also typically experience various motor dysfunctions or deficits, although their imitation abilities appear to be intact (Biscaldi et al., 2015). The inability to stay focused on cognitive tasks and to inhibit motor actions in favor of thought processes often results in the children having both academic and social problems. In light of these issues, both parents and teachers frequently embark on treatment or intervention programs for the children involved to lessen the adverse effects of ADHD.

A frequently pursued treatment approach for students with attention-deficit hyperactivity disorder has been to administer a stimulant medication, such as Ritalin, to the students. This approach typically results in improved academic performance, attentiveness, and social interaction with peers. Although stimulant medications are effective with most individuals diagnosed with ADHD, they are not an effective treatment for all; about 20–30% do not show significant improvements in response to medications (Brown, 2005). Some parents, physicians, and students, however, have expressed a reluctance to embark on a long-term course of medication. Moreover, a number of professionals in the field of child mental health have become quite concerned about the use of stimulant medications with relatively young children (Fontanella et al., 2014; Olfson et al., 2010). Many preschoolers evidently are neither receiving mental health assessments prior to embarking on courses of psychoactive medication use nor are they receiving non-pharmacological treatment interventions. If alternative behavioral or educational intervention approaches were to be shown to be effective, then these non-drug approaches would be welcome additions to the ADHD treatment arsenal. And consideration should be given to combining these behavioral or educational interventions with pharmacological treatments in an effort to obtain optimal results.

One non-drug approach that might have substantial potential is to have teachers and parents communicate with their children with ADHD more extensively with representative gestures or signs. When teachers communicated with students with ADHD through gestures, these students' performance was much better than when the teachers' input to these same students was through spoken language alone (Wang, Bernas, & Eberhard, 2004). In the study conducted by Wang et al., the behavior of forty-five boys, between the ages of seven and eight, diagnosed with ADHD was videotaped while they worked to solve puzzles and while they interacted with one of twelve participating teachers. When the teachers communicated with the boys in gestures alone or in speech combined with gestures, the boys' task performance and attention to the teachers was many times better than when the teachers' input to the boys was solely through spoken language. The boys' task performance and attention to the teachers was especially impressive when the teachers combined their use of gestures with spoken language. In addition, when the investigators (Wang et al., 2004) examined their videotapes, they found that those gestures that were especially helpful to the boys with ADHD were those gestures that were classified as representational (gestures that resembled the shape or motion of an object) or deictic (pointing). In light of these promising results, it would appear that more systematic examination of the use of iconic or representational signs or gestures in communication with students with ADHD is merited.

Some other, more anecdotal, accounts provide support to the view that at least some students with ADHD respond better to visual-gestural (sign) input than auditory-vocal (speech) input. In an informal case study, one of my (John D. Bonvillian) then undergraduate research assistants devoted several hours each week during an academic term to teaching signs to three elementary-school aged students diagnosed with ADHD. One of the students was especially disruptive in class, and his teacher was interested in trying almost any reasonable approach that might result in improved behavior on his part. This lad, and another boy in the class with ADHD, responded very positively to their sign-learning sessions. The boys would often ask my research assistant for the sign-names for different objects and activities, as well as what signs to use in various social interactions. Aside from acquiring a substantial sign vocabulary, these boys' interactions at school also changed for the better. According to their teacher and my undergraduate research assistant, these boys frequently would go around their classroom and school yard during recess showing the other students and teachers the sign names for various objects and activities. At the end of the semester, the boys' teacher told my assistant that the sign training had been "extremely helpful" for one boy (the more disruptive one) and "very helpful" for the other boy. The teacher assessed the sign training as "helpful" for the girl who had participated, but that her behavioral improvement had been less dramatic than that of the boys. And when my research assistant visited the classroom to say "good-bye" to her students (she was about to graduate), the lad whose disruptive behavior had largely sparked the study thanked her and observed "...for the first time in my life, I was good at something."

Personal communication with some of my other undergraduate students provides additional support for the view that manual signing might be an effective educational approach for some students with ADHD. One University of Virginia student told me (John D. Bonvillian) that he had learned to translate or paraphrase his teachers' and professors' lectures into signs and fingerspelling during class. Prior to adopting this procedure, he observed that his ability to concentrate in classes largely disappeared after ten to fifteen minutes, that he often felt restless, and that he typically wanted to get up and move around the classrooms. He claimed that this approach of translating or paraphrasing much of his teachers' and professors' oral presentations into signs and fingerspelling enabled him to concentrate more effectively and to perform at a relatively high level academically. In order to not be overly disruptive to his classmates near him, he told me that he would typically make his signs in a much-reduced signing space; he called this approach "micro-signing."

Another of my undergraduate students related a similar account of how one of her best friends from high school learned to cope effectively with her ADHD without using physician-recommended stimulants. This person, struggling with ADHD, started to learn ASL during high school. She, too, learned that coding her instructors' spoken English into ASL signs greatly helped her to concentrate and noticeably enhanced her understanding of what her teachers were saying. It is, of course, not clear what is happening in the brains of these two students. One possibility is that spoken language is at some level either an aversive situation or too complex a form of input for some persons with ADHD.

Another possibility is that learning to sign and fingerspell helped the students to inhibit disruptive behaviors and to focus on their academic tasks more effectively. Regardless, by changing the modality to one that the students could control and by paraphrasing their teachers' spoken words, the students had discovered an effective way to learn while reducing their restlessness.

Finally, the use of manual signs with a particularly "disruptive" four-year-old girl in preschool resulted in her greatly improved behavior (Brereton, 2009). This finding adds to the emerging view that manual signs or gestures might be effectively used by teachers or parents with some very inattentive or disruptive students. In this study, the two teachers in the classroom combined spoken English with Signing Exact English[2] in their interactions with their preschool students. One of the children in the class, Alana, was observed often to be physically aggressive with her peers, to find social interactions very difficult, and not to be able to sit still for more than a couple of minutes. Fortunately, Alana rapidly became an excellent signer, acquiring proficiency in signing more quickly than most of her peers. As Alana acquired more signs, the incidence of her aggressive outbursts decreased substantially. Moreover, in light of her signing skill, Alana often found herself directly helping other students learn to correctly form a number of signs. And, when Alana was supposed to sit still, as in classroom "circle" time, she would usually produce signs along with her teacher. This sign production by Alana apparently provided an acceptable outlet for her need for movement.

The reported changes in Alana's behavior as she acquired more proficiency in signing were quite similar to those seen in the elementary-school aged students diagnosed with ADHD described above. In the future, investigators might wish to examine more systematically which students with ADHD would benefit from programs of manual sign or gestural input and under what circumstances. Investigators might also wish to determine which forms of sign or gestural input, with and without accompanying speech, are more effective in enhancing the behavior and learning of youngsters with ADHD.

---

2   Signing Exact English uses ASL signs in English syntactical order together with various hand gestures to indicate certain aspects of English morphology.

Using Manual Signs to Improve
Reading Comprehension

In recent decades, it has become apparent that many students in the U.S. and throughout the rest of the world have noticeable difficulty understanding the text passages that they have just adequately read aloud. This phenomenon has become known as reading comprehension impairment. According to Hulme and Snowling (2011, p. 139), "children with reading-comprehension impairment (often referred to as poor comprehenders) can read aloud accurately and fluently at a level appropriate for their age but fail to understand much of what they read." That is, these poor reading comprehenders evidently are adept at decoding the texts they are reading aloud, as they show fully adequate phonological or speech-sound skills.

Most of the students with reading comprehension difficulties have weak vocabulary knowledge, problems with listening comprehension, limited abilities in understanding figurative language, and problems in processing grammatical information (Clarke et al., 2010; Hulme & Snowling, 2011). Without adequate development of these language skills, such students probably are destined to remain poor reading comprehenders and to perform poorly in many school-learning domains. A number of poor reading comprehenders also experienced difficulties on verbal working memory tasks, but not on spatial working memory tasks (Pimperton & Nation, 2014).

Although problems in reading comprehension may not become clearly evident until students reach fourth grade, these problems appear to have their roots much earlier in development. In one study (Elwér et al., 2015), fourth grade students (aged nine to ten years) with poor reading comprehension initially were shown to have deficits in vocabulary, grammar, and verbal memory and that these skill deficits were highly related to their poor reading comprehension. These students' performance was then traced back to their results on different assessments or tests conducted earlier in their schooling. It turned out that the fourth grade students' deficits in oral language skills were already evident when the children were in preschool. A similar finding of oral language skills at three-and-a-half years of age predicting reading comprehension at eight-and-a-half years of age also was reported by

Hulme et al. (2015). Among the participants in this study were children at familial risk for dyslexia. Taken together, the results of these two studies indicate that not only are oral language skills important for the attainment of adequate reading comprehension, but that these skills emerge early in development. In light of these findings that difficulties in oral language skills emerge early in development, it might be a good strategy to focus on enhancing these skills while the children are young.

Of the various intervention approaches used with students with reading comprehension impairment, oral-language vocabulary training has achieved the best outcomes. The oral-language training approach in one important study (Clarke et al., 2010) included getting the children to use new vocabulary items in different and relevant contexts, to listen to reading passages, to learn about figurative language (e.g., idioms, metaphors), and to produce spoken narratives. Over time, the children's enhanced vocabulary and oral-language skills were associated with improved reading comprehension skills.

In a study of reading comprehension that involved first- and second-language learners in Norway, Lervåg and Aukrust (2010) found that it was vocabulary knowledge that predicted reading comprehension growth, and that this relationship was especially strong for second-language learners. More specifically, these investigators reached the conclusions that it was the semantic language component that caused much of the differences in comprehension performance between the two language-learning groups, and that oral-language vocabulary training should receive a heavy emphasis among second-language learners. Vocabulary knowledge also was found to be the principal factor that differentiated poor and average comprehenders in a study of English reading ability in Chinese adolescents learning English as a second language (Li & Kirby, 2014). These students, who apparently were all adequate readers in their first language, were participating in an English-immersion program in their eighth grade (aged thirteen to fourteen years) classrooms in China. In light of their findings, the investigators recommended that more attention be devoted to systematic vocabulary instruction.

In as much as vocabulary knowledge evidently is an important factor in reading comprehension and because students with reading comprehension deficits showed real improvements after vocabulary training, teachers and language therapists might seriously consider expanding their vocabulary training in the early school grades. We (the authors) also suggest that teachers consider combining spoken language vocabulary items with manual signs in their training programs for these students. We make this recommendation for several reasons. The first is that Marilyn Daniels (2001) reported strong and lasting gains in vocabulary knowledge for young children from economically disadvantaged families when their teachers combined signs with speech in their language input. Daniels (2004) also found that hearing kindergarten students from a rural background who received ASL instruction showed impressive gains in their receptive English vocabulary knowledge, as they averaged two years of vocabulary growth over the course of the nine-month school year.

The findings from two other studies provide additional support for including manual signs in the educational programs for young students. In a fourteen-month-long project in the United Kingdom, hearing children, ages five to six, were joined by deaf students one afternoon a week, and together they were taught in part in British Sign Language (BSL) (Robinson, 1997). At the end of the project, the use of signs was reported to have helped the hearing children with their English vocabulary development and assisted in their learning of concepts in mathematics and geography. An explanation advanced to account for this improved performance was that the use of signs had resulted in the young students looking at, listening to, and attending to their teachers more often. In a two-year pilot project conducted in the U.S. state of Louisiana, young deaf and hearing children were taught by teachers who used both spoken English and ASL signs simultaneously (Heller et al., 1998). At the end of the study, the children in this inclusive preschool classroom who had been taught to sign earned significantly higher receptive English vocabulary scores than those children in the other classrooms who had not been taught to sign.

A second reason behind our recommendation is that a number of studies have shown that students effectively learn and retain foreign language vocabulary items when the to-be-learned words are paired with iconic or representative manual signs. Because second-language learners are over-represented in the population of students identified as having reading comprehension impairments, the findings about iconic signs and foreign language vocabulary learning may be particularly relevant here. Third, when students with reading comprehension impairment produce representative or iconic signs when uttering the to-be-learned vocabulary items, the act of producing the highly iconic signs may serve as an instructional vehicle for learning the meanings of the vocabulary items themselves. To a substantial extent, each highly iconic or representative sign produced is an act of depiction of the meaning or referent of the to-be-learned word. With substantial benefits in terms of increased vocabulary knowledge potentially derived from combining iconic or representative manual signs with English (or other spoken language) input, and no perceived negative effects, we see no reason for teachers and parents not to embark on such a program. And, finally, because manual signs rely on visual and motor processing rather than the auditory-vocal modality, this change in modality might make signs a more effective vehicle of instruction than spoken words for students with verbal working memory weaknesses.

Facilitating Foreign Language Vocabulary Acquisition

A major challenge in acquiring a foreign or second language is learning the words of that language. For children in the U.S. growing up in non-English-speaking homes, English vocabulary knowledge is an area of particular difficulty (Snow, 2014). Foreign language and English-as-a-second-language instructors often devote substantial time trying to impart the meaning of new vocabulary items to their students. The students, in turn, frequently confront long lists of words that they need to store effectively in their memories if they are to make progress in learning that new language. The outcome of these efforts, at least in the U.S., often is not a very positive one. After studying a foreign language in school, the typical American student frequently has made little progress toward acquiring fluency in that language and may have acquired a negative or fearful attitude toward foreign language learning (Asher, 1969). The educational system in the U.S., moreover, is not producing enough students with sufficient foreign-language proficiency needed to compete effectively in a global market place (Wiley, Moore, & Fee, 2012). And with the world's economy becoming an ever more global one with each passing year, the need for students worldwide to acquire facility in a second or third language is increasing.

In recent years, another large group of individuals who need to acquire skills in a foreign language has emerged on the world's stage. These persons are among the millions of migrants and refugees currently fleeing areas in Africa, the Middle East, and other parts of the world (Clay, 2017). Many of these individuals are both seriously traumatized and in dire straits. If these refugees and migrants were to learn a core vocabulary of words from their potential host countries' languages, then their situation would likely prove less stressful.

Difficulties in acquiring a new or second language are not limited to the present; they extend into the distant past. Correspondingly, teachers have for a long time considered different ways that foreign languages might be taught and learned more effectively. One teacher and scholar, Claude-François Lyzarde de Radonvilliers, penned a book in 1768 on how a language could be effectively acquired. De Radonvilliers apparently was quite frustrated by his pupils' inability to remember their Latin vocabulary items after classroom instruction, which relied heavily on lecturing. Furthermore, he realized that it was not possible for his students to adequately acquire a language if they did not understand what the words meant.

Upon reflection, it is apparent that in contrast to the traditional classroom-learning situation, young children acquiring the vocabulary of their native language often learn these words in a context where they view either pictures or encounter instances of the words they are acquiring. Caregivers also frequently point out instances of a word or concept to young children. In addition, young children may acquire new words together with identifying or accompanying gestures. Certain eighteenth-century scholars, including Condillac (1746/2001; see Chapter 2), long ago recognized that a new or second language would be more readily learned and remembered by students if they followed some of the same processes that they had used to acquire their first language, namely through incorporating gestures and conversations in the learning process. Thus, it should be noted that concerns about traditional approaches to second-language learning and the potential benefits of using gesture to foster foreign language vocabulary acquisition were expressed hundreds of years ago (Rosenfeld, 2001).

Although scholars long ago may have recognized the potential usefulness of pairing foreign language vocabulary learning with related movements and gestures, this approach does not appear to have ever been firmly established as a teaching method until much more recently. About two centuries after Lyzarde de Radonvilliers' book was published, James Asher (1969) advanced the idea that foreign language instruction should begin with students acting out the meanings of the words and sentences that they had just heard. This approach, which Asher called Total Physical Response, emphasized students' initial comprehension of foreign language words and phrases and used the students' bodies as tools of learning along with their minds. Despite some empirical support for his claims of more effective language learning and instruction than traditional auditory-vocal instruction, Asher's approach did not succeed in becoming well established in American classrooms.

An emerging and promising approach to foreign language instruction is that being developed by AIM (Accelerative Integrated Methodology) Language Learning. This gesture- and movement-based approach was pioneered by Wendy Maxwell of British Columbia. Before developing this educational method, she was a foreign language teacher in Canada who had become quite concerned by her students' difficulties in learning and retaining foreign language materials. The approach she has developed uses pantomimic and emblematic gestures to help convey the meaning of foreign language words or phrases in video-based lessons and stories. The production and understanding of spoken language also are introduced with program onset.

As AIM Language Learning is of relatively recent origin, long-term systematic examinations of its efficacy in foreign language learning are largely lacking. One difficulty in conducting such systematic examinations of AIM's effectiveness in fostering foreign language learning has been that individual teachers apparently vary considerably in how closely they follow AIM routines and teaching strategies (Arnott, 2011). Two studies conducted in Canada that did compare the effectiveness of AIM with more established approaches to teaching French yielded inconclusive results; the AIM-instructed students in most instances were not significantly more proficient in French than their more traditionally educated peers (Bourdages & Vignola, 2009; Mady, Arnott, & Lapkin, 2009). Clearly, additional research investigations of the efficacy of AIM Language Learning will be needed before firm conclusions as to its effectiveness can be reached. Nevertheless, anecdotal accounts from teachers using the system often have been quite positive.

Meanwhile, noticeable progress has been made in the last few decades in understanding human memory through laboratory research. The findings from this laboratory research provide an empirical foundation for incorporating the use of gestures and actions in foreign language teaching and learning. In investigations that began about forty years ago, Johannes Engelkamp and Ronald Cohen independently found that if one encoded information through the production of actions, then the performance of these actions positively influenced one's ability to remember the information (Zimmer et al., 2001). Experimental studies showed that research participants recalled action phrases better if the participants simulated the actions in the phrases as opposed to forming visual images of the actions or through just listening to the phrases. This effect of gestures or actions on memory was called the *enactment effect* (Engelkamp & Krumnacker, 1980). Research also revealed that to obtain the maximum facilitative effect of gestural actions on memory, it was important for each participant to perform the action himself or herself (*subject performed task effect*) (Cohen, 1981), as viewing someone else perform the action was not quite as effective (Engelkamp & Zimmer, 1994). From the findings of these studies and others of the efficacy of self-performed actions on memory, it became evident that incorporating gestures into the learning and recall of verbal material often was a more effective approach than relying primarily on auditory-vocal rehearsal or repetition to facilitate recall.[3] Although the evidence for the efficacy of self-performed actions (or enactment effect) on adult participants' memory is quite compelling, the evidence for such an effect in children has been inconsistent (Foley & Ratner, 2001). At least some six-year-old children, however, are able to take advantage of the enactment effect to facilitate their verbal recall (Chatley, 2013).

With the use of gestures established as an effective way to learn and retain verbal material overall, a number of studies were conducted that

---

3   Although the primary focus of this section of the present chapter is on students' learning of foreign language vocabulary and phrases, we do not mean to suggest that the use of self-performed actions or gestures is limited to students' learning of foreign languages. To the contrary, self-performed task effects have been reported for different types of materials and for a wide range of participants (e.g., persons with intellectual disabilities, Alzheimer's disease patients) (Zimmer & Cohen, 2001).

demonstrated the effectiveness of gestures on the learning and retention of foreign language words and phrases. In a U.K. study (Mistry & Barnes, 2013), Makaton signs were taught in both a weekly discrete training session and also in child-led play settings in a classroom in which four of the pupils were learning English as an additional language. Makaton was found to noticeably increase those four students' production of English; the authors also noted that Makaton seemed to serve as a common language among all of the persons in the class. Allen (1995) showed that accompanying French expressions with emblematic gestures (e.g., "thumbs up") resulted in the students recalling more of the French expressions they were learning than the students in the no-gesture comparison groups. Lindstromberg and Boers (2005) found that when students pantomimed or demonstrated the meaning of foreign words or expressions, then they were more likely to retain and understand those foreign words and expressions than the students who relied on a more traditional verbal identification and translation approach. Finally, in a study that involved students' learning of pseudo-words (word-like constructions), the use of iconic gestures (Simplified Signs) was shown to facilitate the student participants' learning in comparison with various approaches that did not include iconic gestures (Loncke et al., 2009). Although the results of these studies and others established that the use of gestures was a potentially important way to increase foreign language vocabulary learning, a number of important questions about this approach still remained to be answered.

An important question about the use of gestures to accompany foreign language vocabulary learning that needed to be answered was whether the type of gesture used had an effect on the number of vocabulary items students learned. If it were simply the case that it is the production or enactment of any gesture that helped students learn new vocabulary, then it would not matter whether the learner produced either a meaningless gesture or an incongruent gesture (a gesture that did not match the meaning of the word being learned) as opposed to a congruent gesture or representative (iconic) gesture. The answer to this question is that the nature of the gesture is a very important factor in the learning and retention of foreign language vocabulary. Congruent or representative (iconic) gestures that accompany spoken word production greatly enhance foreign language vocabulary acquisition in comparison with the use of incongruent gestures or meaningless gestures (Kelly, McDevitt, & Esch, 2009; Macedonia, Müller, & Friederici, 2011). The use of an incongruent or unmatched gesture with a foreign language word typically has a negative or adverse effect on learning (Kelly et al., 2009). Thus, the production of gestures to successfully facilitate foreign language vocabulary learning appears to rely not on the attention-getting or dynamic movement that gesture production involves, but rather on how successfully the produced gesture is integrated with the word to be learned.

A second issue or question that needed to be examined was whether the use of gestures to accompany foreign language learning was effective with a wide range of word classes or whether it was limited to only certain types of words, such as concrete nouns or action verbs. It turns out that producing an iconic or representative gesture with a foreign language vocabulary item contributes to that item's learning regardless of whether that word is a concrete noun, verb, abstract noun, or adverb (Macedonia & Knösche, 2011). Although the learning of all four classes of words was significantly enhanced by the production of accompanying iconic or representative gestures, concrete nouns tended to be recalled the most frequently and adverbs the least. The investigators, Macedonia and Knösche, then examined their student participants' production of new sentences using the words that the participants had just learned. Again, the words that had been learned with accompanying iconic gestures were used significantly more frequently in the production of the new sentences. This latter finding would appear to indicate that foreign language vocabulary items learned with accompanying iconic gestures are more easily accessible in the learners' memories.

A third question that needed to be examined in determining the potential efficacy of using iconic or representative gestures in the acquisition of foreign language vocabulary items was whether the words acquired in that manner differed in how long they stayed in students' memories in comparison with words learned in the more traditional auditory-vocal approach. The findings from three studies answered this question. In Kelly et al. (2009), undergraduate students were tested on their recall and recognition of Japanese verbs after delays of five minutes, two days, and one week from their initial training. At all three of the time periods since training, the words learned through saying them while also producing congruent gestures were recalled and recognized at higher levels than words learned through the other approaches (i.e., speech, repeated speech, and speech with incongruent gestures).

In the Macedonia and Klimesch (2014) study on this issue of retention, German-speaking college students were assessed through cued recall of artificially constructed vocabulary items at five different points in time: day 1 (after a learning phase), day 8 (after a learning phase), day 15 (test only), day 73 (test only), and day 444 (test only). At all five time points, the artificially constructed "words" that were learned through hearing, reading, and saying the words while producing semantically related gestures were recalled much more frequently than the words learned the same way but without the production of synchronous, semantically related gestures. In a third study that examined retention over time, Mayer, Yildiz, Macedonia, and von Kriegstein (2015) found that adult participants remembered significantly more foreign language words two- and six-months post-learning when the words were learned with self-performed representative gestures than when learning was accompanied with pictures or with verbal presentation alone. The results of these three studies show that the inclusion of congruent or semantically related gestures to the process of learning foreign language vocabulary items has a strong positive effect on the likelihood that those items will be remembered over time. Also, it should be noted that the Macedonia and Klimesch study involved the teaching and testing of students in an on-going classroom situation, so the results obtained from this study are likely to generalize to other classrooms.

Another important question in the use of additional modalities in foreign language instruction is whether learning is better when the to-be-learned items are accompanied by pictures or when they are accompanied by related gestures. In one examination of this question, Tellier (2010) assessed whether five-year-old French-speaking children acquired more English words when each word was paired with a picture of the item (or of the activity involved) or when each word was paired with a representative gesture. In one group, the children repeated the English words they heard while looking at the associated pictures. In the other group, the children repeated the English words they heard and also produced the representative gestures they saw demonstrated.

By the end of the 4-week study, the children who had learned the words with accompanying gestures had produced significantly more English words than the children in the picture condition. In a second study (Porter, 2016), children's learning of short foreign language sentences was examined when the sentences were accompanied by pictures alone and when the sentences were accompanied by both pictures and related gestures. The children, ages four to seven years, remembered many more words from the sentences when gestures accompanied their presentation. And in a third examination of this question, Mayer et al. (2015) found that adult participants' learning of foreign language vocabulary items by performing representative gestures was a significantly more effective strategy than learning those items with accompanying pictures. Both these strategies were more effective learning strategies than traditional verbal learning approaches. While these results provide additional support for the view that the enactment of gestures related to foreign language vocabulary items facilitates their learning, it should be noted that the children and adults in these studies (and other studies) also were getting visual input from seeing the gestures demonstrated.

One final question that has been examined concerns the rate of foreign language vocabulary learning. It turns out that adults (age eighteen to sixty-five years) learned foreign language words to criterion noticeably faster when the words were paired with iconic gestures (Simplified Signs) than when the words were not paired with the gestures (Adams, 2016). With all the adult participants in this study learning foreign language vocabulary items faster when they were accompanied by iconic signs, this outcome would suggest that vocabulary acquisition might be effectively sped up by adopting such an iconic sign-based approach.

What might be behind the evidently successful use of iconic gestures or signs to facilitate students' acquisition of new or foreign language vocabulary? Unfortunately, a clear-cut or definitive answer to this question cannot be provided at present. Several possible explanations, however, may be advanced to help account for this finding. One explanation is that students may find that their teachers' (or experimenters') pairing of spoken words with iconic gestures or signs may make the words' meanings clearer and more understandable, as well as keeping the students alert and interested (Allen, 2000; Gullberg, 2006; Lazaraton, 2004). Another possible explanation is that when students see an iconic sign or gesture produced first by their teachers and then by themselves, those events may increase the likelihood that students will form a picture or visual image in their minds of that gesture or its referent (Kelly et al., 2009; Riseborough, 1981). The evocation of a visual image has long been known to improve memory performance (Paivio, 1971). Also, when individuals form visual images of concepts, such actions may facilitate the learning of those concepts by focusing the individuals' minds on core features or characteristics of those concepts (e.g., shape, movement, color). Moreover, when individuals produce gestures, that activity in itself may bring action into the individuals' mental representations, which in turn may affect both the individuals' behavior and thinking (Goldin-Meadow & Beilock, 2010).

A third possible explanation for the students' improved learning and retention rates rests on the students' production of the iconic signs or gestures that they had observed being produced. If the students were to actually form the signs or gestures, then the enactment of these gestures might help the students store and retrieve the words (Macedonia & Knösche, 2011) and gestures. Such embodied actions might also serve to anchor foreign language vocabulary items more firmly in the students' minds (Rivers, 1991; see also Asher, 1969).[4] If, subsequently, the students were to generate the iconic signs or gestures, then these actions might aid the students in lexical retrieval (Cartmill, Beilock, & Goldin-Meadow, 2012; Frick-Horbury & Guttentag, 1998). Furthermore, it has become apparent that language is not solely the province of a delimited area in the left frontal area of the cortex. Rather, language learning and processing now appear often to involve other areas of the cortex (Pulvermüller, 2005), as well as subcortical areas of the brain (Lieberman, 2000). In an exploratory study of the neural representation of novel (artificially created) words, Macedonia and Mueller (2016) found evidence of activation of areas in the brain outside the principal language regions for the words learned with self-performed iconic gestures. These areas included the learners' sensory and motor cortices (see also Kelly et al., 2009), as well as the basal ganglia, and the cerebellum. Apparently, the production of iconic signs

---

4   When language is embodied, it is said to be grounded in a person's bodily experiences, with bodily experience involved in conceptual representations (see Barsalou, 2008).

or representational gestures along with foreign language vocabulary items may help students to activate more areas of the brain, such as visual and motor areas (Mayer et al., 2015), than is typically the case for just the auditory-vocal repetition or rehearsal of those words.

Another explanation for the facilitative effect of iconic gesture or sign production on vocabulary learning is that these gestures may engage an additional memory system. Vocabulary knowledge is often thought to be part of a person's declarative memory, which consists of knowledge that can be expressed in words. But because the use of iconic signs or gestures in vocabulary learning involves the production of motor actions to a considerable extent, it is quite possible that the engagement of a participant's motor system may result in the use of one's procedural memory system in addition to that of the declarative memory system (Macedonia & Mueller, 2016; see also Corkin, 2013).[5] Because knowledge of how to do something often is especially long-lasting, then engagement of the procedural memory system in the vocabulary learning process might help explain why vocabulary items acquired through the use of iconic signs or gestures are retained for long time periods.

Each of the various processes described above probably contributes to some extent to enhanced foreign language vocabulary learning. The involvement of auditory-vocal, visual, pre-motor, and motor areas of the brain may result in the foreign language word or concept being widely interconnected in different areas of the brain (Klimesch, 1987). The use of gestural enactment, the formation of a visual image, and the hearing and saying of a word from a foreign language may also result in greater depth of processing (Craik & Lockhart, 1972) of that word. If a foreign language word undergoes greater depth of processing, and its meaning is fully understood, then its acquisition will likely be facilitated (Allen, 1995).

The findings reviewed above clearly indicate that language learners are much more likely to remember a new word from a foreign language if the learners produce an iconic or representative gesture as they say that word (Macedonia, 2014). What has yet to be determined is whether

---

5   The procedural memory system involves knowledge of how to do something and this knowledge is often expressed in actions or behaviors as opposed to words, as in declarative memory.

there is an optimal word-learning approach involving the enactment of iconic gestures, the viewing of pictures of the words or concepts, the reading of the words, and the repetition of the to-be-learned words. It will also be important to determine whether these various word-learning approaches are effective with all learners, or if certain groups of learners benefit more from particular approaches.

Learning to Sign May Positively Affect One's Cognitive Abilities

In addition to the potential benefits of learning to sign documented in previous sections and chapters, there is substantial evidence that acquiring signing skills may improve one's spatial cognitive abilities as well. This claim is based on studies of the performance of both deaf signers and hearing signers on standardized tests of intelligence, as well as on tests of spatial memory, mental rotation, and facial discrimination. While the enhanced performance of signing individuals in all these domains is noteworthy, it is the performance of signers on tests of spatial memory and mental rotation that may be of special significance. These skills evidently are very important in engineering and other scientific and mathematical domains (Sorby, 2009; Wai, Lubinski, & Benbow, 2009). One way to develop these skills may be to increase students' opportunities to learn to sign.

Intelligence Tests

One set of studies that examined the effects of learning to sign on cognitive development and processing consisted of studies that used standardized tests to measure intelligence. In one meta-analytic investigation (Braden, 1994) that involved using IQ test scores of large numbers of deaf students collected over a number of decades, the IQ scores of deaf students with deaf parents were compared with the scores of deaf students with hearing parents and with the scores of students with hearing in the normal range. Presumably, the children of deaf parents would in most instances have grown up in a signing environment, whereas hearing parents of deaf children historically were advised not to sign with their children but to emphasize spoken language acquisition instead. The most frequently used instrument to assess the intelligence of deaf students was the Performance IQ Scale (e.g., block design, puzzle completion) of the Wechsler Intelligence Scale for Children — Revised (WISC-R) (Wechsler, 1974). For the deaf students with hearing parents, their mean performance IQ score of 99 did not differ significantly from the mean of 100 for students with normal hearing. But the mean performance IQ score of the deaf students with deaf parents, 108, was significantly higher, clearly outperforming on average the students with normal hearing. Please note that deaf students as a group typically earn below average verbal IQ scores; in the U.S., the verbal IQ section of the Wechsler tests involves considerable mastery of English. A likely reason for the superior performance of the students with deaf parents on the performance scale is that their signing skills facilitated their processing on tasks entailing spatial knowledge and memory.

Other studies of the effects of learning to sign on intelligence test scores involved hearing children who were taught to sign. In a follow-up of the participants in their study of baby-signing, Acredolo and Goodwyn (2000) administered the WISC-III (Wechsler, 1991) IQ test to the children when they were eight years old. Those children who had learned signs in infancy scored significantly higher than the children in the (non-sign) comparison group, both on the Verbal IQ scale (116 vs. 103) and the Performance IQ scale (109 vs. 101). In a second investigation involving hearing children, Italian children were introduced to Italian Sign Language early in elementary school in two studies (Capirci et al., 1998). Those children who opted to learn to sign in each study received about two hours each week of sign instruction during the school year over a two-year period. Other children in the investigation chose to participate in one of several additional enrichment programs (e.g., music, English-language learning) for two hours each week. Although the children in each of the different enrichment and control programs scored very similarly (about the fiftieth percentile on the average) near the beginning of the school year as they began their participation, those children who were learning to sign, in comparison with their classmates who were not, improved much more rapidly over time in their test performance. The sign-learning children subsequently scored substantially higher than the other children on measures of visuospatial cognition and nonverbal reasoning, the Raven Progressive Matrices (Raven, 1949).[6] By the end of the second school year in which they participated, the mean score of the children in the non-signing enrichment groups remained at about the fiftieth percentile, whereas the scores of the children who learned to sign approached the ninetieth percentile on the Raven's test. In conclusion, the findings from these various investigations suggest that children, deaf and hearing, who learn to sign relatively early in their development often show real cognitive benefits as assessed by their performance on various tests of intelligence.

Spatial Memory

In addition to higher average scores on broad measures of intelligence, learning to sign also has been found to be associated with enhanced performance in a number of more specific domains (Hauser & Kartheiser, 2014). Among the domains investigated have been spatial memory, mental rotation, and face-processing. The Corsi block-tapping task (Milner, 1971; Orsini et al., 1987) is a frequently used instrument for assessing individuals' short-term visuospatial memory. In this task, an examiner taps a certain number of blocks arranged irregularly on a board; immediately afterward, the participant is asked to tap out the same pattern. The hearing children who had learned Italian Sign Language in the Capirci et al. (1998) study discussed above had significantly larger spatial memory spans than the children in the other (non-sign instruction) enrichment groups. Similarly, deaf children who sign have been found to outperform hearing, non-signing children on this task (Wilson et al., 1997).

This pattern of signers showing an advantage over non-signers also has been shown for adult participants on the Corsi block-tapping task. In one study (Romero Lauro et al., 2014), deaf signers significantly outperformed hearing non-signers on both versions (forward and backward) of the Corsi blocks. The deaf participants in this study reported that they had been exposed to Italian Sign Language before

---

6   The Raven Progressive Matrices measure an individual's ability to analyze figures and detect patterns. In this test, each participant needs to select the missing piece to complete the matrix.

the age of six years and had used it as their principal means of communication since early childhood. In a second study (Geraci et al., 2008), deaf signers also outscored hearing non-signers on the Corsi block-tapping task; the hearing participants, however, outperformed the deaf participants on a test of word/sign span. Even when signing skills are acquired in early adulthood, the experience appears to heighten spatial memory. Adult hearing participants with one to five years of signing experience also showed a greater spatial memory span (on the Corsi blocks) when compared with adult hearing non-signers of the same age (Keehner & Gathercole, 2007). However, in contrast to this superior performance on the Corsi block-tapping test, the deaf signers in the Romero Lauro et al. (2014) study did significantly worse than the non-signers on the Visual Patterns Test (Della Sala et al., 1999).[7] The investigators advanced the interpretation of their findings that the Corsi block-tapping tasks involved a spatial and movement component that appeared to be advantaged by signing skills, whereas the Visual Patterns Test involved a stable or static presentation. Furthermore, this presentation of stable shapes on the checkerboard might have facilitated their naming in a verbal code.

In a different approach to assessing spatial memory skills, the performance of deaf and hearing British Sign Language (BSL) users was compared with that of hearing non-signers on the game of *Concentration* (Arnold & Murray, 1998).[8] When the cards consisted of pictures of objects, there was no difference in the level of performance among the three groups. But when the cards consisted of human faces, both the deaf and hearing signers outperformed the hearing non-signers. The deaf signers, moreover, also showed better memory for the location of faces than the hearing signers, who had not acquired facility in BSL until adulthood. When Arnold and Murray examined the relationship between years of sign experience and memory for faces performance, they found that the two were highly related: the number of years signing highly predicted memory for faces performance. An interpretation advanced for these findings is that signing experience was tied to facial

---

7   This test, designed to assess visual short-term memory, requires participants to reproduce checkerboard patterns.

8   In this game, cards are placed face down and a player turns over two cards in an effort to find a matched pair. If the two cards match, then they are removed from the table; if they do not match, then the cards are returned to their original locations.

discrimination skills and to remembering the location of these faces, whereas the objects in the first task were easily nameable in both signs and speech and so did not differentiate among participants based on their language skills.

Finally, the performance of deaf and hearing signers was compared with that of hearing controls on a haptic (by touch) spatial configuration learning task (van Dijk, Kappers, & Postma, 2013). The deaf signers were prelingually deaf adults whose first language was the Sign Language of the Netherlands; the hearing signers were adult Dutch sign language interpreters; and the hearing controls were Dutch adults who reported no sign language experience. In the experimental task, the participants were instructed to match ten shapes by touch to cut-outs in a board as fast as possible while blindfolded. Both the deaf and hearing signers outperformed the hearing controls, as the signers were significantly faster than the non-signers across the three test trials. This pattern of results, furthermore, also occurred when the cut-out board subsequently was rotated 90°. These findings suggest that sign language experience may be related to improved spatial memory skills, especially that of relative location in space.

Mental Rotation

Signing experience also has been associated with enhanced performance on tests of mental rotation. In mental rotation tasks, a participant needs to be able to rotate an observed scene or stimulus in his or her mind. The adult participants in the Keehner and Gathercole (2007) study discussed above were assessed on their mental rotation abilities as well. The hearing participants who signed outperformed the hearing non-signers when the visual stimuli were rotated 90° and 180°, but not when the scene was tested at a 0° rotation (i.e., without rotation). In a related study (Emmorey, Kosslyn, & Bellugi, 1993), in which participants were asked whether the rotated shapes were the same as the target shape, both the hearing and deaf signers outperformed hearing non-signers when the stimulus shapes were rotated. Similarly, deaf signers were more accurate than hearing non-signers when they were examined on a task that involved both rotation of a scene and the orientation of an object (Emmorey, Klima, & Hickok, 1998). Although both groups of participants were less accurate when rotation was involved, the deaf signers were significantly better than the non-signers in mental rotation as well as in remembering object orientation.

Finally, in a fourth study (Talbot & Haude, 1993), fifty-one adult women (two reported that they were hearing impaired while forty-nine reported normal hearing) were tested on their mental rotation ability. The participants varied widely in their experience using American Sign Language. Those participants with more ASL experience scored significantly (and much) higher than those women with less experience signing. The findings from these four studies indicate that it is signing experience that apparently is the critical factor in enhanced mental rotation skills, not a person's hearing capacity. Another possible, although we think unlikely, interpretation is that persons, deaf or hearing, with a strong aptitude for mental rotation and spatial cognition tasks, tend to become more proficient signers.

Facial Discrimination

Signers have been shown to outperform non-signers on certain tests of face-processing as well. In the test of Facial Recognition by Benton et al. (1983), a participant views a person at the top of the page and then must identify that person from among pictures of other people at the bottom of the page. It should be noted that this test is seemingly more one of facial discrimination than facial recognition. What makes this task somewhat challenging is that the lighting conditions and angle of presentation are different for the person being identified at the bottom of the page than at the top. Signing deaf children performed better than hearing non-signers on this test (Bellugi et al., 1990).

This finding of better performance by signing deaf children in comparison with hearing non-signers raised the question as to whether this heightened performance was the product of sign language skills or the outcome of deaf persons compensating for a relative lack of auditory-vocal input. Additional studies showed that it was the former, the acquisition of signing skills, which contributed to this advantage. Deaf non-signers did not perform as well on the test of Facial Recognition as either the hearing signers or the deaf signers (Parasnis et al., 1996). And in a series of experiments, Bettger et al. (1997) showed that both deaf and hearing signers outperformed non-signers on facial discrimination tasks. From these results, it appears that it is the ability to sign that is the important factor in elevated results, not whether a person is deaf or hearing. If one learns to converse in a signed language, then one needs to attend to and interpret the facial expressions of others while they are signing. As a consequence, signers may become more adept at discriminating facial expressions (Emmorey, 2002).

Discussion

What factors or experiences might be contributing to sign-learning individuals' enhanced performance on measures of nonverbal intelligence and spatial cognition? If a person learns to sign, then that individual gains substantial experience in learning how to transmit information effectively in a visuospatial environment. For example, an individual acquiring a signed language will learn that the location of a sign and the direction of a sign's movement are important in transmitting information about who (or what) is performing the action and who (or what) is the recipient of the action. And as a sign learner becomes increasingly proficient in his or her signing, that individual likely will increasingly rely on establishing an imaginary stage and locating different persons or objects on that "stage" for subsequent reference. This "stage" typically is located in the space in front of the signer's body and reflects a direct representation of objects, persons, or actions on that stage. This approach probably results in increased efficiency in the sign learner's transmission of information, but also makes greater demands on the signer's and viewers' spatial and gestural memories.

If other persons sign to a sign-learning individual, then that individual needs to learn to process those sign utterances and grasp their meanings from different spatial or visual perspectives. Because most signers convey information to others from their own perspectives, a sign learner looking at a signer directly in front of him or her needs to mentally rotate or transform the signer's sign production 180° to fully comprehend what was just signed. If the sign learner is located to the signer's right or left, then he or she needs to mentally rotate the sign utterance about 90° to fully understand it. With time, the sign learner may become increasingly adept at understanding sign communications viewed from a wide range of visual angles. Indeed, as a person gains experience in comprehending others' signing, the process of rotating or transforming these utterances may become fully automatic! In addition, as the sign learner becomes proficient in understanding others' signed communications, the sign learner receives extensive practice in mental rotation skills with regard to manual signs. The mental skills needed to successfully understand another person's signed communication may provide a strong foundation for success in the mental rotation tasks assessed by various standardized tests.

Another way for an addressee of a signed utterance to understand the spatial relationships in such an utterance would be to adopt the viewpoint of the person generating the signed utterance. An initial step in developing this skill would be to recognize that visual perspectives differ depending on one's location. Then one would need to be able to create the scene as viewed from another's perspective. It appears that signers learn to imagine themselves in other persons' bodies (motor embodiment) in order to view the scene as depicted from those persons' vantage points (Pyers, Perniss, & Emmorey, 2015). This placement of oneself in other persons' vantage points may become easier with increasing age and signing experience, as well as prove cognitively less demanding than constantly mentally rotating the scene that is being depicted.

While signers often score higher than non-signers on tests involving visuospatial skills, it should be noted that there are exceptions to this pattern. In a number of instances, hearing individuals without signing skills have scored as high as or higher than deaf persons on measures of visuospatial abilities (Marschark et al., 2015). Moreover, one may not need to have learned to sign to show enhanced performance on spatial problem-solving tasks through the gestural modality. When hearing, non-signing college students simply were encouraged to gesture when solving such spatial visualization tasks as mental rotation and paper folding, they performed significantly better than those students who did not receive these instructions (Chu & Kita, 2011). Regardless, it should also be recognized that the finding that individuals, deaf or hearing, who learn to sign often score significantly higher on tests of spatial memory and mental rotation than non-signing individuals indicates that the visuospatial skills involved in these tests are, to at least some extent, learnable. That is, as one becomes more proficient in signing, one typically appears to become more adept at spatial memory and mental rotation tasks. These claims should not be considered as surprising ones in that the comprehension and production of a signed language involves the use of such visuospatial skills as memory for spatial locations, discrimination of handshapes and facial expressions, and mental rotation or transformation of visual scenes. Whereas users of a signed language would frequently be exercising those portions of their brains involved in spatial memory and cognition, users of spoken languages would not receive the equivalent practice effects (Hauser & Kartheiser, 2014).

This finding that learning to sign is associated with enhanced performance on measures of spatial skills is also consistent with other current reports that spatial thinking is malleable (Sorby, 2009; Uttal, Miller, & Newcombe, 2013; see also Casey, 2013); that is, with appropriate experience, spatial thinking can improve. And because women historically have been found to score lower on measures of visuospatial processing than men (Halpern et al., 2007), it would be of interest to see whether experience in signing would reduce or eliminate this reported sex difference in cognitive ability. Moreover, young girls might likely reap the most benefit from early spatial intervention programs (cf. Casey et al., 2008).

Finally, it is quite possible that the use of manual signs and gestures will prove beneficial in the learning of mathematics more generally (Macedonia & Repetto, 2017; Roth, 2001). When representational gestures were used to explain mathematical equivalence to school-age children, the children receiving this gestural input demonstrated significantly better performance than those children who did not receive the gestural input (Cook et al., 2017). Moreover, it has become apparent that both teachers and learners often make abundant use of pointing and representational gestures in their teaching and learning of mathematical concepts (Alibali & Nathan, 2012). What is not yet well understood, though, is just how such gestural production and processing improves students' learning.

Concluding Remarks

Although the original goal of the Simplified Sign System was to provide a manual sign-communication system that might facilitate the communication of minimally verbal individuals with autism, Down syndrome, cerebral palsy, or aphasia, the contents of the present chapter show that there are many other individuals who might benefit from learning to sign or using Simplified Signs. In fact, it seems likely to us that many more typically developing hearing individuals will make use of our Simplified Sign System than those individuals for whom we originally designed the system. A simple reason behind this assessment is that there are many millions of individuals who need to acquire a foreign language vocabulary for their economic livelihoods, much less the millions of children who need assistance in attaining literacy skills as the pathway to escaping poverty.

Worldwide, many children become fluent in their family's spoken language but encounter serious language issues when they enter school. The difficulty these young students encounter is that their native language, in which these students are fully fluent, may not have a written or printed form. For these students to have a chance at literacy and educational success, they will need to acquire substantial proficiency in a language that has a written form. Furthermore, this proficiency probably needs to be attained relatively quickly so that the students do not fall behind in their educational achievement. And, because many countries where such educational hurdles occur frequently have only limited resources to overcome such hurdles, then any intervention program ideally should be relatively inexpensive to operate.

In light of the findings about the facilitative effects on learning of having students produce iconic gestures as they utter foreign language words, we see no reason why this approach should not be widely used in the teaching of vocabulary items. If this approach were to be transferred to a classroom setting, teachers adopting such an iconic gesture approach to word learning could first produce an iconic gesture while simultaneously uttering the to-be-learned word. The students could then perform the gesture they just saw as they said the word they are trying to learn. A limiting factor with the widespread adoption of this pedagogical approach, however, is that many teachers would likely find it difficult and stressful to generate an effective iconic gesture for a particular word or concept on the spot while standing in front of a classroom of students. Fortunately, this task could be more easily accomplished and the problem largely overcome if these teachers were to avail themselves of the signs from the Simplified Sign System or another system of iconic signs or pantomimic gestures. And, if the students were to learn their foreign language vocabulary items on their own by pairing the to-be-learned words with their Simplified Sign equivalents, then the learning process would likely be much more successful and noticeably less tedious than traditional auditory-vocal rehearsal of the words on a foreign language vocabulary list. At the same time, it should be recognized that there is much more to learning a foreign language than mastering a core vocabulary. But if students could understand and produce a large number of words from a foreign language after having learned them by pairing them with iconic signs, then an important language acquisition hurdle would have been overcome.

We also can easily see many preschool teachers devoting at least a portion of their class days to showing their young students a small number of Simplified Signs. Teachers may wish to pair each sign with its spoken language equivalent and to show how each sign is formed. Although some young children may perceive the relationship between a sign and its meaning, many teachers may wish to point out how a sign's formation relates to its meaning. One benefit of including Simplified Signs (or iconic signs from a similar system) in the classroom routine by pairing signs with spoken words is that the children's vocabulary knowledge is likely to increase. This building of vocabulary knowledge through manual signs may prove of special importance to young children from lower socioeconomic backgrounds and to children whose parents are immigrants. The reasoning behind this claim is that these young children often do not receive the level of spoken language input at home that is necessary for attainment of full literacy in the language used in the school system.

A second potential benefit of preschool and kindergarten teachers including signs in their classes is that young children may acquire better motor control, manual dexterity, and improved eye-hand coordination through sign learning. Although Simplified Signs were designed to be relatively easy to form, they still entail some degree of motor skill to form accurately. Young children may need repeated demonstrations of how signs are formed by their teachers, as well as assistance from their teachers in molding their hands and fingers into the correct sign formation. This involvement of teachers in the demonstration of signs may also result in the children learning to look at their teachers more often. Another possible benefit of incorporating manual signs into the school experience is that some of the young children's restlessness and need to move around may be absorbed into their production of signs.

Furthermore, the findings of a number of studies on the impact of learning to sign on cognitive processing should be encouraging news to persons considering such a course of study for themselves or their children. In addition to learning to communicate in another modality, many hearing children who learn to sign show elevated scores on subsequent vocabulary and IQ tests. And if teachers or school officials are worried about the time commitment needed to obtain substantial effects, then they should review the study conducted by Capirci and her associates (1998). In the Capirci et al. study, Italian elementary school students received only two hours a week of training in Italian Sign Language for two school years, yet they demonstrated major gains in their nonverbal reasoning abilities over this period. It would be difficult to find another pedagogical intervention that would return benefits of this magnitude for such a limited investment of time and effort.

Finally, the results of studies on the impact of learning to sign on cognitive processing are of interest for another reason: they show that a language can affect one's thinking or cognitive processes. This notion that one's language could affect one's reasoning and mental activities was advanced in the nineteenth century by the German philosopher and linguist Wilhelm von Humboldt (von Humboldt, 1836, Trans. P. Heath & Intro. H. Aarsleff, 1988), but it is better known today as the Sapir-Whorf hypothesis. Support for this hypothesis, though, has been modest at best (McWhorter, 2014). This assessment, however, was based solely on examination of the outcomes of studies of spoken languages and their impact on cognitive processes. If one were to include signed languages in these analyses, one could reach a very different conclusion. That conclusion is that learning to sign may significantly affect one's cognitive abilities. In particular, persons who learn and use a sign language often show enhanced spatial memory, mental rotation, and nonverbal reasoning abilities. While key word signing with Simplified Signs may not bring the same boost in cognitive abilities as using a full and genuine sign language, it may have its own unique or similar benefits. At the same time, while learning to sign likely will improve various cognitive abilities, this does not mean that signers are viewing the world in fundamentally different ways or are endowed with new conceptual abilities.

In conclusion, acquiring signing skills and using Simplified Signs appear to bestow a number of educational benefits on the sign learners. Just how extensive such potential benefits will be and for whom will need to await the outcomes of future investigations. Regardless of who benefits and the magnitude of such benefits, it should be an exciting experience determining how best to use manual signs to elevate the lives of sign learners. We spent an extensive amount of time selecting, modifying, and creating signs to be as iconic, easily remembered, and easily formed as possible for all of these various sign-learning populations. In the next chapter, we discuss the steps we followed in developing the Simplified Sign System, including the testing of the signs with different individuals and groups.

8. Development of the Simplified Sign System

Background Information

The original goal of the Simplified Sign project was to develop a system of manual signs that would enhance the communication skills of a number of hearing, but non-speaking, persons. Initially, the focus of the project was to create a sign vocabulary that would meet many of the needs of children with autism or with other disabilities such as cerebral palsy or Down syndrome. We felt that these children would benefit from a new sign-communication system that was easy to learn since their motor and/or memory impairments often made learning and producing signs from existing sign languages very difficult. We also hoped that the system would prove beneficial to older individuals who had experienced a serious loss or impairment of their speech skills because of a stroke.

The focus of the project, however, was expanded while the system was still being developed. This occurred largely as a consequence of the media attention that the project started to receive in 2001. When information about the Simplified Sign System was first disseminated by the various media, we learned that certain individuals were using Simplified Signs with members of population groups that we had never considered. For example, we discovered that the signs were being used in nursing home settings with older individuals who had experienced some degree of hearing loss, but minimal disruption in their speaking abilities. Some of the healthcare professionals who used our signs with members of this population requested that we expand our lexicon to meet the communication needs they witnessed. In light of this feedback, we made a serious effort to do so.

    https://doi.org/10.11647/OBP.0205.08

Along with the requests for specific vocabulary additions that we received from individuals who were trying out the system, several published sources helped guide our selection of entries for the Simplified Sign System lexicon. One source was a proposed vocabulary list for non-speaking preschool children based on input from parents and clinicians, language samples from typically developing young children, and word lists prepared by these speaking children's parents (Fried-Oken & More, 1992). If our Simplified Sign System were to prove helpful to many non-speaking or minimally verbal preschool children, then we would need to have vocabulary items for those topics about which the children and their parents wanted to talk. As a result, we made a determined effort to find or to create signs for the large majority of terms on this list. A second published paper also alerted us to certain vocabulary items that we elected to include in the Simplified Sign System. This source was a listing of words used most frequently in conversations by adults between the ages of sixty-five and eighty-five (Stuart, Beukelman, & King, 1997). Because individuals in this age group are more likely to experience hearing loss or strokes that may adversely affect their understanding or production of speech, we felt that we should provide signs for their principal topics of conversation. A third source that helped guide our selection and development of signs for the Simplified Sign System was a manual that contained lists of vocabulary items that would be needed by many adults who used an augmentative and alternative communication system (Collier, 2000). This volume included recommendations for vocabulary items that would facilitate communication across a wide range of settings. If our sign system were to be of assistance to many different persons in diverse settings, then it would need to include signs for many of these recommended words and concepts.

We then elected to include signs in our initial lexicon that might be of assistance in medical settings and for international travel. We felt that the growing numbers of older, hearing-impaired individuals and of non-English-speaking persons in the United States might benefit from iconic manual signs for various medical terms. We also received requests to include signs for medical terms and for human physiology from individuals involved in medical intervention or rescue operations overseas. Such signs might prove especially helpful in instances of medical emergency where speed and accuracy of communication often are critically important. An important source for many of our signs for medical conditions or terms was the *Random House Webster's American Sign Language Medical Dictionary* (Costello, 2000). Finally, for international travel, we relied on various travel guidebooks and on our own intuitions as to what vocabulary items would likely be of assistance to travelers.

As the lexicon continued to be expanded to address the potential use of the system by persons learning a new or additional spoken language, we also strove to include more signs for concepts within various subject areas such as sports and games, personal care, animals, science, technology, numbers, math, food, law and criminal justice, music, months, countries, holidays, and religion. Moreover, we made a concerted effort to add related vocabulary or synonyms to as many of our existing signs as possible. This resulted in the addition of thousands of terms to the lexicon; many sign entries are supplemented with synonyms so that users can quickly see the range of meanings represented by that sign. Whereas the main entries or sign glosses in the lexicon represent relatively basic vocabulary, the synonyms provide access to a larger and more advanced vocabulary that can be conveyed by the signs. This more advanced vocabulary is less relevant to children, but may prove useful to teenagers, college students, and adults learning a new spoken language, as well as to elderly populations who wish to communicate on a range of topics.

Clarifications

Before describing how we went about developing the Simplified Sign System, we first wish to emphasize several points. The most important is that the system we have developed is not a genuine sign language and is not intended to replace one; it is a system of visual-motor communication that may or may not be used in conjunction with a spoken language. Genuine languages, whether signed or spoken, have much more extensive vocabularies than the Simplified Sign System, as well as underlying phonological systems and rule-based grammars. We have purposefully limited the formational complexity of the signs in our system to accommodate the memory, motor, and cognitive difficulties of many of its intended users. However, a person with a full complement of memory, motor, and cognitive skills, but who is unable to speak, might wisely consider acquiring a full and genuine sign language.

A second important point is that the Simplified Sign System is not the first serious effort to create or modify signs to make them easier to learn or use. In the last few decades, several different sign systems have been developed to foster communication in non-speaking individuals with autism, an intellectual disability, cerebral palsy, or aphasia (Loncke & Bos, 1997; Skelly, 1979; Windsor & Fristoe, 1991). Other systems that have been developed for persons with disabilities borrow signs from the sign language of a particular country's Deaf community without making any modifications to the signs (Grove 1994; Grove & Walker, 1990). Altogether, these sign-communication systems have proven beneficial to a large number of individuals with serious language and communication problems.

We believe that the success or efficacy of a sign-communication system will be enhanced if it is firmly based on empirical findings of how individuals learn and remember signs, the types of errors they make when forming signs, and their intended users' particular communication needs. Fortunately, much has been learned about how signs are acquired and the problems various individuals with language impairments experience when forming signs (Dennis et al., 1982; Doherty, 1985; Dunn, 1982; Grove, 1990). For many of these persons (and for most typically developing persons overall), signs with clearly transparent meanings (i.e., highly iconic or representative signs) are learned more quickly and recalled more readily than signs that do not resemble their referents. Therefore, our Simplified Sign System contains a large number of signs with clearly transparent meanings. Because many persons with language impairments experience difficulty forming various handshapes and remembering signs with more than one distinct movement, the signs in our system largely avoid these problem areas. The availability of this background information on both sign acquisition and sign formational difficulties was an important factor in our decision to undertake the development of a new sign system. The publication in recent decades of more sign language dictionaries from around the world also helped us. With a larger pool of potential signs from which to choose, our task of finding a sufficient number of useful signs was considerably eased. In more recent years, online resources such as the *Spread the Sign* website (European Sign Language Centre, 2018) have proven especially helpful when trying to find potential sign formations for specific concepts that we wished to include in an expanded version of our lexicon.[1]

If we have been successful in developing a sign system consisting mostly of signs that are easy to form and that have transparent meanings, then there likely will be additional benefits beyond that of enhancing the sign production and comprehension of the original target populations. One potential benefit is that teachers and staff members might experience less difficulty in interpreting their students' and clients' signs, thus facilitating communicative interaction. Another is that outsiders who do not have a background in sign communication might be able to accurately guess the meanings of some signs and to respond appropriately. If this were indeed the case, then the potential usefulness of such a sign system would be expanded greatly.

Increasing the number of people with whom sign-using children and adults could interact would likely provide further benefits. This interaction should help these individuals to become more socially integrated and to have better opportunities for progress than may currently be available to them. Because many persons with language disorders can feel quite isolated, one should not underestimate the impact of providing them an additional or alternative means of communication, especially if it gives them confidence to interact with other people in public. Even small gains in receptive or expressive vocabulary can have a profoundly positive effect on a person's life, emotional health, and physical well-being. Thus, the Simplified Sign System is not meant to be just a communicative strategy or method, but also a path by which persons with language impairments may attain a higher level of functioning and fulfillment throughout all aspects of their lives.

The final point we wish to mention is that although individuals who are minimally verbal or who have severe spoken language impairments may be the principal beneficiaries of the Simplified Sign System, many persons without any language production difficulties should also

---

1   In addition to the sources that we reference here, some sign languages have free online dictionaries (both official and unofficial), computer software for purchase, smartphone apps that can be downloaded, specialized books and supporting materials for teaching, and other resources available to the public. In the future, we hope to procure funding so that we can develop similar materials to support the use of the Simplified Sign System.

consider learning it. Indeed, we would be surprised if many children
in preschool programs and students in foreign language classes did
not find themselves using Simplified Signs to assist in their spoken
language vocabulary acquisition. In the past, it has often been the
case that only the teachers and caregivers directly responsible for non-
speaking individuals attempted to acquire and use a sign language.
Because of the time and effort involved, many individuals shied away
from learning to sign. (Kemp, 1998, reported that learning a true sign
language is much like learning any other foreign language.) As a result,
many relatives of non-speaking individuals and the staff members at
educational and medical institutions who cared for them did not learn to
sign. The outcome all too often was a signing, non-speaking individual
in an environment where most others did not sign — not an optimal
situation for sign mastery. This situation also did nothing to overcome
the isolation that many non-speaking individuals experienced. One
should realize that communication is a process that depends on mutual
give and take; in other words, the participation of more than one person.
Although our system was developed primarily to address the learning
and communicative needs of special populations, it is meant for use
by everyone in the non-speaking individual's life. A sign system that
is easily learned and remembered by family and staff members (such
as the Simplified Sign System) hopefully will result in an environment
where signs are used much more extensively; this should in turn
enhance the sign-communication skills and social interactions of non-
speaking individuals.

Overview

How, then, did we develop the Simplified Sign System? To accomplish
this task, we needed to develop a sign lexicon or vocabulary that would
be easy to learn, easy to remember, and easy to form. There were several
steps to this undertaking. In previous chapters, we reported that signs
that were highly iconic or pantomimic were more easily learned and
remembered by many non-speaking children and adults than signs that
were not as iconic.[2] As a first step, then, we needed to select or create

---

2   Iconicity refers to the physical resemblance between a sign and what it stands for, its
     referent. For more information, see Chapter 1 and Chapter 3.

signs that were highly iconic or representative. If we were unable to find or create highly iconic signs for needed concepts, then we selected or created signs that had clearly discernible ties to their referents once their meanings were explained. The ease with which a person can discern the relationship between a sign and its referent once the sign's meaning has been given is known as the sign's translucency. These highly translucent signs also are more easily acquired and retained than arbitrary signs. The second step in the development of the Simplified Sign System was to modify those signs that were relatively difficult to produce so that they became easier to form. The background information needed for this step came from previous studies of sign production by persons with autism, sign language acquisition in young children, and accuracy of sign recall by college students. The third step in the system's development involved the testing of these potential Simplified Signs with undergraduate students unfamiliar with a sign language. The signs that these students both remembered and formed accurately were kept in the system. Those signs that the students had difficulty remembering and forming were either discarded or modified structurally and then retested.

Once we had tested and approved most of the signs in the initial lexicon, we proceeded to a related step: testing undergraduate students to determine whether our Simplified Sign System (SSS) signs were easier to learn and to remember than American Sign Language (ASL) signs. In this fourth step, student participants were tested on their ability to remember SSS signs and ASL signs immediately after list presentation and after a twenty-four-hour delay. This testing showed that signs in our system were often easier to recall and to form than ASL signs. We have also completed some testing of student participants to see how well they recall Simplified Signs as opposed to Amer-Ind signs. The fifth step involved allowing various investigators to try out the system with different populations. From these investigators, we received valuable feedback with regard to specific signs that we needed to add to our lexicon and information they felt would be helpful in the teaching of our sign system. The final steps in the development of the Simplified Sign System were to provide an explanation of how each sign's formation was related to its underlying meaning and to furnish a short sentence or phrase that illustrated the tie between each Simplified Sign and its referent as a memory aid. The inclusion of this material was done to make the signs even more memorable. A brief definition of each item in the system also was included to assist non-native speakers of English in their learning of new vocabulary. We will now explore each of these steps in more detail.[3]

Step One: Iconic Sign Selection

A number of studies have reported that iconic signs are more rapidly learned and remembered than signs that are not as iconic or representative (e.g., Baus, Carreiras, & Emmorey, 2013; Coelho & Duffy, 1986; Emmorey & Sevcikova Sehyr, 2018; Griffith & Robinson, 1980; Konstantareas et al., 1978; Lieberth & Gamble, 1991; Ortega, 2017; Perniss et al., 2017; Thompson et al., 2013; Vinson et al., 2008; see also Chapter 3). The usefulness of this finding, however, has been constrained by the relatively low incidence of highly iconic or pantomimic signs in individual sign languages. Selecting signs for the Simplified Sign System from a single sign language therefore would not yield a very large lexicon or vocabulary of highly iconic signs. For this reason, we expanded our search for appropriate signs to the dictionaries of other sign languages and various sign systems. Examination of these dictionaries revealed instances where highly iconic signs for certain concepts existed in some sign languages but not in the others.

For more than eight years, various members of our research group pored over dictionaries of different sign languages and sign systems in search of highly iconic signs. Altogether, we examined a total of forty dictionaries for our initial lexicon of 1000 signs (see Appendix A).[4]

---

3   In the pages that follow, we provide a general overview of our methods and procedures for the benefit of family members, caregivers, and service providers. However, it is beyond the scope of this chapter to provide detailed research information on each of the six sign sets that formed the basis of the initial lexicon or the additional seventeen sign sets that formed the basis for the expanded lexicon. Information such as the list of signs tested in each set (and the groupings of signs within those lists), the formational parameters of those signs, the origins of each of the signs, the exact number of signs that passed or failed criterion in each set, errors made by the study participants during testing, specific modifications made to failed signs before retesting them, or detailed statistical analyses related to the testing are not given here. In the future, we hope to publish articles with this data and/or make the data available online for the benefit of sign language researchers.

4   In the years since we completed our initial lexicon of 1000 signs, we continued to examine additional sign language dictionaries (over 60) and to develop new Simplified Signs for our system.

Individual signs often were selected from these dictionaries when we were able to correctly discern the meaning of a sign solely from the picture or drawing of how the sign was formed. From this archival effort, we were able to identify hundreds of signs that we felt were either highly iconic or had readily transparent meanings and that we also felt might be of some use to various non-speaking individuals. When we were unable to find highly iconic or transparent signs for needed concepts from among our host of sign language dictionaries, we often selected translucent signs.[5] Persons with an intellectual disability typically acquire signs with high levels of translucency more easily than signs with more arbitrary ties to their referents (Doherty, 1985; Luftig, 1983).

This selection of signs from various sign languages or systems should make for a degree of international appeal for the Simplified Sign System. Individuals familiar with a sign language from a particular country may well recognize signs from that language in our lexicon. Selecting signs from many different sign language dictionaries also may make our system more usable worldwide because the signs are not based on one specific language or culture, but many. In addition, since we typically perceived the iconic or pantomimic nature of the signs without knowing the particular culture or language involved, it is likely that other individuals from around the world will do so as well.

Unfortunately, although the examination of the different sign languages resulted in a long list of potentially useful signs, there were still many important concepts or words for which we were unable to locate either highly iconic or translucent signs. For such concepts, we needed to create signs that were either highly iconic or translucent and easily formed. In creating these signs, we relied on our own intuitions and those of numerous friends and colleagues (both hearing and deaf). Some of these signs were based on common gestures, others on iconic visual symbols, and a few were related to or derivations of signs that had already passed criterion and were included in the system (for example, using the opposite formation of an action sign to represent that sign's antonym). Regardless of the conceptual origin of a particular sign or our intuitions about whether that sign would be easy to remember

---

5   Translucent signs are signs that have clearly discernible ties to their referents once the meanings of the signs have been provided. For more information, see Chapter 1.

and form, we always empirically tested each sign for recall and correct production before including it in the Simplified Sign System. Signs that did not meet the selection criterion were discarded. Thus, every sign in the Simplified Sign System lexicon underwent testing, regardless of whether or not it came directly from a full and genuine sign language or an existing sign system, whether or not its formation needed to be adjusted to make it easier to use by persons with memory and motor disabilities, or whether or not it was created specifically for the lexicon.

Although our efforts to find or to create highly iconic or translucent signs that were relatively easy to form was aimed primarily at facilitating the sign learning of non-speaking individuals, these same characteristics should make the signs relatively easy for other persons to learn as well. The highly iconic nature of many of the Simplified Signs should also enhance teacher and caregiver sign recognition and recall. Similarly, the effort to make Simplified Signs relatively easy to produce for non-speaking individuals with motor impairments should likewise make them easy for teachers and caregivers to form.

Step Two: Sign Formation Modification

After selecting signs for potential inclusion in the Simplified Sign System, the next step was the modification of those signs that we felt would be difficult for children with autism (or for individuals with other motor problems) to form. In addition, when we created new signs for needed concepts, we wished to avoid those formational characteristics of signs that likely would prove difficult for persons with motor and memory deficits. We obtained the background information needed for this task by examining videotape records of the sign production of several different groups.[6] One group consisted of students diagnosed with

---

6   The onset of the Simplified Sign System project occurred at the beginning of 1998; therefore, the studies that supported our initial work and that we mention here in this section occurred prior to 1998. In the two decades since we first started developing the system and testing signs for inclusion, many more studies have been published about the signing of children with autism (e.g., see Shield's work in Chapter 5), the acquisition of signs by the children of deaf parents (see Chapter 3), and signing by hearing persons in various situations (see Chapter 7). Much of this research reflects positively on the decisions we made related to the principles of the Simplified Sign System, particularly with regard to iconicity and revision of sign formational parameters.

autism; these students were videotaped while they signed with their teachers (Seal & Bonvillian, 1997). The videotapes were then analyzed to determine which sign formational characteristics (sign phonemes) were produced more frequently and accurately, and which were rarely produced or incorrectly formed.

The second group studied consisted of the ASL-learning children of Deaf parents (Bonvillian & Siedlecki, 1996, 1998, 2000; Siedlecki & Bonvillian, 1993, 1997). The videotapes of these children were analyzed not only to determine which sign phonemes tended to be produced more frequently and accurately, but also to document the order in which children typically acquired them. The third group consisted of undergraduate students who had reported that they were unfamiliar with any sign language (Wright, Bonvillian, & Schulman, in press). These students were videotaped as they tried to recall lists of ASL signs that had been presented to them, and the videotapes were then analyzed to determine which sign phonemes were produced more accurately. In all three sets of videotapes examined, the analysis focused on the sign formational parameters first identified by William C. Stokoe: location, handshape, and movement.[7] The information we gathered on sign phoneme production proved helpful when we needed to create new signs or modify existing signs to make them easier to form.

In all three of the groups studied, the location parameter of the signs was produced with relatively few errors, and considerably more accurately than the handshape and movement parameters. As a result, the location parameter of existing signs was less frequently the focus of revision than were the handshape and movement parameters. Regardless, it should be acknowledged that certain sign locations were acquired earlier in sign language development and produced more frequently and accurately than other locations. More specifically, the signer's trunk (the area of a signer's body from approximately the shoulders to the waist), neutral space (the area in front of the signer's body), chin, cheek, midface (the region near the eyes and nose), forehead, and the stationary hand when it was configured as a spread- or 5-hand (the hand is flat with fingers spread apart and extended) were all areas where signers produced signs frequently, accurately, and early

---

7   See Chapter 3 for more information on Stokoe's research into the structure of ASL.

in development. If we needed to modify the location parameter of a sign to make it easier to form correctly, then we typically revised the sign by using one of these locations. Furthermore, because one-handed signs were recalled correctly more often when they involved body contact, we endeavored to include such contact when we either created a new sign or modified a sign's formation.

The configuration of the hand(s) when making signs, the handshape parameter, was the source of numerous errors in the sign formation of all three videotaped groups. Even with this high overall incidence of errors, certain handshapes were produced relatively frequently and accurately. These handshapes were the pointing-hand (the index finger is extended from an otherwise closed hand), the fist (the hand forms a fist), the flat-hand (the hand is flat with fingers together and extended), and the spread- or 5-hand (the hand is flat with fingers spread apart and extended). Two other handshapes, the C-hand (the fingers are together and curved, with the thumb opposite the fingers) and the tapered- or O-hand (the fingers are together and curved, with the finger tips touching the thumb tip), also were produced frequently, but had higher error rates than the first group of handshapes listed. The L-hand (the index finger and thumb are extended from an otherwise closed hand and form a right angle) and baby O-hand (the index finger and thumb are curved and touch at their tips from an otherwise closed hand; also known as a pincer grip) were produced with intermediate accuracy. These easier to articulate handshapes often are known as unmarked or basic handshapes. When modifying existing signs, we typically substituted the above handshapes in place of handshapes that were produced less frequently and accurately.

The movement parameter of signs also was a focus of concern in our selection of signs from sign language dictionaries, in our modification of existing signs, and in our creation of new signs. In the sign languages used by Deaf persons, a substantial proportion of the individual signs require more than one sign movement for correct sign formation. Although such multi-movement signs are not a problem for typical signers, such signs are a source of difficulty for many persons with autism. When videotapes of sign production by students with autism were analyzed, one of the most frequently observed errors was a reduction in length of signs that consisted of more than a single movement to a single movement (Seal & Bonvillian, 1997; see also Slavoff, 1998). In light of this finding, we tried to create signs for our system that had only a single distinct movement or to modify existing multi-movement signs to a single movement.

An important exception to this procedure was contacting action. Because signs often were formed or recalled correctly when they involved contact with the body, we did not count contacting action as a distinct movement when reducing the number of movements in a sign. Examination of these videotapes also showed that the students typically produced certain types of sign movement (e.g., wrist nodding) less accurately than others. Again, we opted to avoid or modify signs with these more problematic movements.

Step Three: Testing of Simplified Signs with Undergraduate Students

In developing the Simplified Sign System, we felt that we needed to systematically evaluate our impressions as to which signs would be both easily remembered and accurately formed. We elected to assess the learning and recall of our potential Simplified Signs by first testing individuals without any discernible motor, memory, and cognitive impairments and who were unfamiliar with any sign language. In making this determination, we relied primarily on the participation of University of Virginia undergraduate students. We reasoned that if undergraduate students encountered any problems in remembering or forming a particular sign, then that sign would also prove difficult to learn for someone with a cognitive or motor disability. In addition, we felt that the undergraduates' success in learning particular signs would approximate the sign-learning abilities of the teachers, caregivers, and family members who will also need to learn the sign system. Altogether, over one hundred undergraduates participated in the assessment of sign learning and recall for the initial lexicon (and over two hundred fifty students did so for the expanded lexicon). In addition, several dozen other members of the university community provided helpful feedback on possible Simplified Signs.

The procedure adopted to test the undergraduate students' ability to remember and form potential Simplified Signs was a cued-recall memory task.[8] Each student was told that he or she was participating in a study of memory and recall of manual signs. Participants were tested individually in a laboratory office setting. They sat at a table and faced two experimenters. One experimenter demonstrated the signs and provided their English translations or word equivalents, then later cued each student participant for sign recall by uttering the English word equivalents. The second experimenter focused on scoring the accuracy of the participant's sign production. Each participant was presented six lists of twenty signs, together with their English translations (120 stimuli). Each sign and its translation equivalent were presented at four-second intervals. After each list was presented, the experimenter read aloud each word from that list and asked the student to produce its corresponding sign from memory. The participants were encouraged to provide their best guess for any signs about which they were unsure. This procedure was used in the development of the initial 650 signs in the Simplified Sign System lexicon. In ensuing years, as fewer signs were being tested at one time, the number of lists included in each testing set often was reduced to four lists of twenty signs (80 stimuli).

Each participant's sign recalls were scored for accuracy. A "perfect" recall was defined as a recall identical to the sign demonstrated by the experimenter. In deciding whether a sign was accurately recalled, however, certain sign characteristics typically were not counted. These included such characteristics as the speed at which a sign was produced, unless it was vital to the meaning of the sign (e.g., the sign SLOW must be produced slowly), the hand used to form the sign, or whether the

---

8   The fact that potential signs for the lexicon were tested in an artificial setting (rather than in a natural setting or within a larger communicative or semantic context) means that the signs that passed our criterion for inclusion did so without the assistance of additional support (with the exception of the use of facial expressions with emotion signs). In other words, the signs were able to be immediately remembered and properly formed by persons with no experience signing, who had received no explicit training (let alone sustained or repeated training), and who had not been provided environmental cues that may have assisted their recall. This bodes quite well for the signs that passed criterion, as signs that can be remembered in isolation would most surely also be remembered when explicitly taught in both specific sign-training sessions as well as in natural settings, throughout the day's normally occurring activities, and with the aid of environmental contextual information (e.g., teaching food signs at mealtime), of feedback from communication partners, and of the provision of pictures, photos, symbols, and/or real objects that could be used to directly link the sign's formation to its referent. The authors welcome future testing of the signs in these and various other contexts.

sign was made in a clockwise or counterclockwise direction. A sign recall was deemed "essentially correct" if it contained only a small error in its handshape, location, or movement. A sign recall was scored as "identifiable" if, despite being imperfectly formed, it sufficiently resembled the demonstrated sign as to be readily recognized as an attempt to produce that sign. A small number of the recalled signs had such substantial flaws that they could not be identified, and thus were considered unrecognizable. Recalls were marked as "wrong" if they consisted of the production of the incorrect sign for the word cue. A score of "no response" was given if the participant did not attempt to make a sign within ten seconds of the English word cue being presented.

Before testing the undergraduate students on their ability to remember and to form signs, we decided to establish a minimal level of recall accuracy that would need to be attained for a particular sign to be included in our Simplified Sign lexicon. The criterion that we selected was that an individual sign would need to be both recalled and formed perfectly by at least 70% of the undergraduate students tested on that sign before it would be included in the system. That is, for those student research participants tested on a particular sign, slightly more than two-thirds would need both to remember the sign and form it accurately in order for that sign to be added to our lexicon. We selected 70% as our criterion because we wished to include only those signs that most people successfully remembered and formed while at the same time not making the recall task so challenging or the selection criterion so stringent as to drastically limit the number of proposed signs that could be included in the lexicon.

Overall, our impressions as to which signs would be relatively easy to remember and to form were borne out by the undergraduate students' responses on the cued-recall task. These participants, as a group, recalled about 90% of the signs presented to them clearly enough that they could be identified as the signs on the list that they had just seen. The remaining 10% consisted of instances where participants either failed to give a sign response to the English word cue (no response), produced a sign from a previous list (list intrusion), or generated a sign that had such substantial structural flaws that it was unrecognizable. Probably because of the cued-recall format, the location of a sign on a list did not have any effect on whether or not a sign was recalled. Although the large majority of the participants' signs clearly were attempts at producing the demonstrated sign, a significant proportion of these signs were not formed perfectly. Many of the signs that were not perfectly recalled in their initial list presentation were subsequently modified and then retested with other students in a different list presentation.

Those signs that were not recalled perfectly by at least 70% of the undergraduate students on which they were tested were then examined for the types of formational errors that the participants had made. In a number of instances, the students were relatively consistent in the errors that they made when forming those particular signs. For example, most of the students recalled the initial version of the sign ELEVATOR with the palm of their active signing hand facing down rather than with the palm facing up as had been demonstrated. In instances such as this, the systematic nature of the errors in sign formation provided us with clues as to how to modify the signs to make them easier to form. In the case of the sign ELEVATOR, we changed the orientation of the active signing hand so that its palm faced down, and then retested this new, more easily formed version with another group of students. This revised sign was then recalled perfectly by nearly everyone.

For other signs that were recalled by the undergraduate students with small formational errors, we often revised the signs by changing their problematic handshapes or movements to ones that were more basic. After modifying the signs that initially had failed to meet our selection criterion, we then retested the revised versions with a new group of participants. These revised versions frequently met the selection criterion.

Unfortunately, many of the signs that were not recalled perfectly by 70% or more of the student participants on which they were tested either had major errors in their formation or were not sufficiently memorable to be recalled at all. These signs proved difficult to modify satisfactorily. In these instances, we looked at other sign language dictionaries for alternative signs for a particular concept, or we created our own versions. We then tested these new signs with another group of students.

Altogether, about two-thirds of the signs presented to the students were recalled sufficiently accurately that we included them in our initial lexicon. This proportion, however, somewhat masks what in fact happened. About 300 of the signs presented were recalled perfectly by all or nearly all of the individuals tested on those signs. The remaining signs tested often had appreciably lower levels of recall accuracy, although they still met or exceeded our selection criterion. What this means in terms of our Simplified Sign lexicon is that some of the signs were recalled perfectly by all of the people tested on them, whereas others were not as easily remembered and formed. Altogether, we tried out about fifteen hundred signs or sign formations before achieving our initial lexicon of 1000 Simplified Signs.

There appear to be several reasons for this variation in recall accuracy. First, many of the signs remembered by all participants were signs for discrete objects or easily demonstrated actions. For such concepts, it was not at all difficult to locate highly iconic signs that were relatively easy to form. The meanings of these signs would likely have been readily apparent to the participants and easily coded in memory.

A second factor that may have influenced sign recall is that the presentation of some signs was intentionally accompanied by an emphatic facial expression when produced by the experimenter. A number of signs recalled perfectly by the participants involved emphatic emotional expression and associated sentiment (e.g., a large grin for HAPPY, a frown for CRY, and a lowered brow for ANGRY). Facial expression was not scored as part of a sign's formational accuracy, but may have been helpful for the participants in recalling the sign. Ties to a sign's referent may have been underscored by accompanying such signs with strong and, sometimes, passionate emotional expressions. The fact that many signs incorporating emotional facial expressions were produced with high rates of accuracy seems to indicate that such emotional content added another dimension by which to place signs in context and associate them with their meanings. These facial expressions also may have enabled signs to be related more effectively to common gestures based on emotion.[9]

A third reason for the variation in recall accuracy is that as time progressed and more people became aware of the project, we received

---

9   Although the presence of emotional facial expressions may have facilitated sign recall in the undergraduate students tested, these facial expressions may not affect individuals with autism spectrum disorder (ASD) in the same way. Individuals with autism spectrum disorder often show delayed and atypical processing of emotional facial expressions (Dapretto et al., 2006; Denmark et al., 2014; Herman et al., 2019; Winkielman, McIntosh, & Oberman, 2009).

feedback from teachers, caregivers, and medical professionals with regard to concepts they felt should be added to the lexicon. For these requested additions, it frequently proved difficult to locate highly iconic signs with a single sign movement from our collection of dictionaries. As a result, we often had to create the signs ourselves. Fourth, as more and more signs were added to the Simplified Sign lexicon, it became increasingly difficult to find or create signs that did not substantially overlap or resemble signs already in the lexicon. Finally, in the latter stages of testing, we often had to try out multiple variants of a sign before we found one that met (or exceeded) the 70% perfect recall selection criterion. This occurred for words or concepts that we felt were essential to include in the initial Simplified Sign System lexicon. Indeed, we tried out a half dozen signs for SISTER before we found one that was sufficiently memorable to meet the selection criterion. All of these factors appeared to influence the relative ease (or difficulty) with which a particular sign was recalled and accurately formed.

Step Four: Comparison Testing of Simplified Signs

An important issue that we needed to examine was whether signs from the Simplified Sign System were easier to learn and to remember than signs from another sign language. If Simplified Signs were found to be more difficult to learn, then there would be little justification for the dissemination of yet another collection of signs to already over-burdened parents, teachers, and language professionals. One exception to this statement should be noted. If the Simplified Sign System contained a number of signs for concepts needed by particular populations that were not included in another sign language or system, then it would be worthwhile to disseminate it to members of those groups. With these concerns about evaluating our sign system in mind, we embarked on a program of systematic comparison.

Simplified Sign System Signs and ASL Signs

The focus of our study was a comparison of Simplified Sign System (SSS) signs and American Sign Language (ASL) signs. As the principal language of members of the Deaf community in the U.S., ASL has a number of important advantages over the Simplified Sign System. As a full and genuine sign language, ASL has a vocabulary of thousands of signs, many more than the SSS. ASL dictionaries and teaching materials are already available, and there are established ASL classes in much of the U.S. With these advantages, it would be important for us to show that Simplified Sign System (SSS) signs were more easily learned and recalled than ASL signs.[10]

In assessing the ease of learning ASL signs and SSS signs, we elected to examine the ability of individuals to recall signs immediately after lists of signs were presented to them and to recognize those signs after a twenty-four-hour delay (Emmons, 2004). In both these immediate- and delayed-recall studies, the participants were undergraduate students at the University of Virginia who were unfamiliar with any sign language. Although in the future we would like to compare the ease with which various non-speaking populations learn signs from different sign languages and sign systems, the abilities of the undergraduate students probably resemble those of the caregivers, teachers, and speech-language professionals who will also need to learn Simplified Signs.

In both the immediate- and delayed-recall studies, our first step was to develop lists of SSS signs and ASL signs that could be systematically compared. We randomly selected a number of SSS signs and then obtained the ASL signs for the same words or concepts. If the signs were identical or nearly identical in both ASL and the SSS, we excluded those signs from testing. One concern we had was that lists composed solely of ASL signs would contain a higher proportion of signs with more than

---

10   Although the ASL-SSS comparison study was the only one we were able to complete before John Bonvillian's retirement in 2015 and passing in 2018, this does not mean that it would not be fruitful to carry out further comparison studies with other deaf sign languages. Since our system takes inspiration from as many sign language dictionaries and sign systems as we were able to consult, it is important to note that such comparison studies would probably have to be performed on a one-by-one basis. As some of our sign language dictionary searches were more fruitful than others, certain sign languages have more representation in our system than others. In order to properly conduct comparisons in the future, it is necessary to follow the same steps that we did when designing the lists of SSS signs to be compared with ASL signs, including the elimination of signs that formationally resemble each other and taking into consideration the number of movements involved. With these factors taken into account, it is unlikely that a future study would use the exact same Simplified Signs found in the ASL-SSS comparison study; instead, each study would need to tailor its vocabulary lists to the particular sign language chosen for comparison.

one movement. Such lists would probably take longer to present and thus add another factor (time of presentation) to the study. In addition, because most ASL signs are not pantomimic or highly iconic, a list composed solely of ASL signs might be perceived by the participants as noticeably more difficult. Our solution to these concerns was to compose lists that had equal numbers of ASL signs and SSS signs. With this in mind, we prepared eight lists of thirty signs each (fifteen ASL signs and fifteen SSS signs). Each thirty-sign list was assigned to one of two groups. Half the participants in the immediate-recall study were shown one set of four thirty-sign lists (120 stimuli), and the other half were shown the second set (120 stimuli).

During each list presentation, an experimenter demonstrated how each sign was formed and provided its English word or translation equivalent twice. Participants were instructed not to physically imitate the signs as the experimenter presented them. After presenting each list, the experimenter cued the participant for recall of each sign by uttering its corresponding English word or translation equivalent. The participants were encouraged to provide their best guess for any signs about which they were unsure. Each participant's sign recalls were scored for accuracy in sign formation, as well as for whether the correct sign was recalled for the English word provided. Sign recall accuracy was analyzed with criteria similar to those used with the original testing of Simplified Signs. Those signs that were recalled and formed correctly were deemed "perfect" recalls, whereas those signs that were remembered but included a small formational error were deemed "essentially correct" recalls.

The sixty University of Virginia student participants in the immediate-recall study remembered significantly more SSS signs than ASL signs (Emmons, 2004). The participants' mean (average) percentage of perfect ASL sign recalls was 42.8%; the participants' mean percentage of perfect SSS sign recalls was much higher at 66.9%. Thus, the clear majority of the SSS signs were recalled perfectly, whereas fewer than half of the ASL signs were. We also analyzed the combination of the participants' perfect recalls and essentially correct recalls, a classification we called "recognizable" sign recalls. The undergraduate students' mean percentage of recognizable ASL sign recalls was 64.1% whereas their mean percentage of recognizable SSS sign recalls was 82.5%. Thus, even when analyzing formational accuracy of sign recall less strictly, many more SSS signs were recalled than ASL signs. Our analysis of the participants' sign recall productions showed that the handshape parameter of ASL signs proved to be an area of particular formational difficulty.

In our examination of the students' recall of ASL signs and SSS signs, we observed quite wide individual differences in recall scores. Some of the participants remembered the large majority of the signs presented to them, whereas other participants accurately recalled many fewer. This wide range in recall scores surprised us because all of the participants were undergraduate students at a highly selective university, not one of them had a clearly discernible motor disability, and none had reported ever having taken a sign language course (if a participant had taken or was taking a sign language course, then such a background likely would have assisted that particular individual on the sign recall task). Such variability in sign recall led us to ask whether there were any distinct patterns of responses among the participants. Two different patterns emerged. One consisted of students who accurately recalled many of the signs and who recalled only slightly more SSS signs than ASL signs. The other consisted of students who recalled relatively few ASL signs while remembering many more SSS signs. That is, those student participants who had the greatest difficulty remembering ASL signs remembered many more Simplified Signs. Although generalizing from undergraduate student research participants to clinical populations is fraught with difficulties, we thought that it was a good indicator for subsequent intervention programs that those individuals who encountered the most difficulty remembering ASL signs showed much better performance recalling Simplified Signs.

In the delayed-recall study, we showed a different group of students three lists of thirty signs each (90 stimuli) on one day and then tested them on their ability to recognize those signs the next day. As in the immediate-recall study, each list of thirty signs consisted of fifteen ASL signs and fifteen SSS signs. The experimenter demonstrated how each sign was formed and uttered its English word equivalent twice during the initial presentation of each list. Unlike the immediate-recall study, however, the experimenter cued the participants on the second day by producing each sign and then asking the participants to write down the sign's English translation. Even after a twenty-four-hour delay, the participants recognized significantly more SSS signs than ASL signs (Emmons, 2004). This pattern occurred for both scoring criteria: when only the precise English word equivalent was scored as correct (49.0% for SSS signs, 35.2% for ASL signs) and when synonyms of the English word equivalent also were scored as correct (52.9% for SSS signs, 36.2% for ASL signs). Therefore, both the immediate- and delayed-recall studies' findings consistently indicated that Simplified Sign System signs were noticeably easier to remember than ASL signs by typically functioning individuals.

Simplified Sign System Signs and Amer-Ind Signs

In addition to the ASL comparison study, we also conducted a preliminary comparison of undergraduate students' immediate- and delayed-recall of Amer-Ind signs (Skelly, 1979) and Simplified Sign System signs. Selecting the stimuli for this comparison study, however, proved more difficult than it did for the ASL-SSS comparison discussed above. There were several reasons for this. At 236 distinct signs, Amer-Ind's lexicon is rather limited in size and therefore does not offer as many choices for cross-system comparison. Furthermore, there are signs in Amer-Ind for various concepts (such as *bribe* or *buffalo*) that we felt were not sufficiently useful to include in our initial lexicon of 1000 signs, thus further reducing the number of concepts available for testing. Finally, because both systems relied on some of the same historical source materials about the signs of Native Americans, a number of the signs in Amer-Ind and the SSS are highly similar or identical. For these reasons, the number of contrasting sign pairs present in both systems was smaller than those available for the ASL-SSS study.

As in the comparison study involving ASL signs and SSS signs, undergraduate research participants were shown lists of signs and then cued for recall either immediately after list presentation or after a delay. Although this testing is far from completed, an initial examination of the participants' scores failed to show significant differences in recall scores as a function of sign system. The student participants remembered almost as many Amer-Ind signs as Simplified Sign System signs.

In reflecting on this absence of statistically significant differences in the immediate- and delayed-recall scores between SSS signs and Amer-Ind signs, it is important to consider the two systems' similarities. Both the Simplified Sign System and Amer-Ind primarily selected signs from existing dictionaries of sign languages or sign systems (in some cases, the same ones). The signs in both sets, moreover, were chosen because they were perceived as highly iconic or pantomimic and relatively easy to form. Another factor that may have contributed to the similar recall score levels is that in a few instances the same formational gesture or sign appeared in both sign systems, although with different glosses or English translations. For example, a flexed upper arm is identified as the sign for MAN in the Amer-Ind system whereas the same gesture is identified as the sign for STRONG (powerful, strength) in the Simplified Sign System. It should be noted that these signs were tested in different sign sets, and the same participant did not see both similarly formed signs. In light of these various similarities across the two systems, it should not be surprising that the student participants' recall scores did not differ noticeably. Indeed, the principal difference between the two systems appears to be the much larger size and probably greater usefulness and applicability of the Simplified Sign System.

Step Five: Feedback from Users

When we began working on the Simplified Sign System in 1998, our goal was to develop a communication system that would benefit non-speaking individuals and their teachers and caregivers. Although that goal has remained our primary one, we decided to expand our focus after receiving an email from a language therapist who was trying out our system with various groups of older individuals. In this email, she informed us that our Simplified Sign System was a very helpful addition to programs in nursing homes. Because we had not contemplated patients or clients in nursing homes as potential beneficiaries of the Simplified Sign System, we were intrigued by this information.

A substantial proportion of residents or clients in nursing homes or assisted living facilities has difficulty hearing, is in the process of losing their hearing, or has already become deaf. Because of their impaired hearing, these individuals may not be able to understand either the speech of the staff members at their nursing home or the speech of their fellow residents. Furthermore, staff members often find it rather cumbersome and time-consuming to write down information that needs to be conveyed.

To overcome some of the communication difficulties that she observed, the language therapist elected to teach Simplified Signs to interested staff members at the nursing homes where she was a consultant. She found that the staff members learned the SSS signs very quickly. These staff members then used the signs to augment their spoken language interactions with their clients. A limitation to the version of the Simplified Sign System that she used, however, was that it had not been designed for older individuals in a healthcare setting. In light of her feedback about the potential usefulness of our sign system with a population we had not previously considered, we began to create or find signs that likely would be needed in a nursing home or assisted living environment.

Additional impetus to generate new signs for a healthcare setting came from a nursing supervisor who commented that patients' impaired hearing was not the only communication problem that she or her staff members encountered. She explained that many of the patients in the facilities she supervised spoke languages other than English. She remarked that having an easily learned sign-communication system for everyday interactions would be quite helpful, and potentially life-saving in certain circumstances.

Worthwhile feedback about our system also came from an enthusiastic group of students, parents, and teachers from northeastern North Carolina who volunteered to carry out a pilot study of how well our Simplified Signs could be learned by youngsters with severe communication difficulties. The student volunteers first learned some Simplified Signs and then taught those signs to ten participants, ranging in age from nine to fifteen years, from the special education program of the Elizabeth City, N.C. public school system. These ten youngsters previously had been identified as having either a severe communication limitation or an intellectual disability.

During the first weekly individual thirty-minute session, the student volunteers put most of their effort into the teaching of three or four new signs to the participants with whom they were working. In subsequent weeks, not only were new signs introduced, but the participants were also tested on their sign retention and on the accuracy of their sign production. Although the number of signs acquired varied widely across individual participants (from eight to forty), as a whole these youngsters were able to learn most of the signs to which they had been introduced. One week after being shown several new signs for the first time, the participants were able to remember over 80% of those signs. Of the signs that these participants remembered, more than 95% were formed relatively accurately. These numbers compare quite favorably to the lower levels of mastery reported in many previous studies of non-speaking populations who were taught signs from existing sign languages.

In addition to providing useful information as to the potential efficacy of the Simplified Sign System, the volunteers in this pilot study unintentionally helped change our thinking about the format of our system. Soon after these student and teacher volunteers began using our sign system, many of them decided that having pictures of the referents (e.g., the objects, actions, or properties for which the signs stood) would probably enhance the learning of the signs. These volunteers sifted through magazines to locate appropriate pictures to go with the signs they wished to teach. They then cut out the pictures they needed and mounted them on cards to be used during their teaching sessions. The student volunteers would often pair the sign with the appropriate picture or drawing when first teaching it and later use the picture alone when prompting for sign production. In light of these volunteers' desire to have a picture accompany their sign-teaching efforts, we decided that we would eventually need to provide a picture of the concept underlying each sign in our Simplified Sign System as an instructional aid. In the future, we hope to develop flashcards, workbooks, software apps, and other materials that make effective use of pictures and the drawings of how Simplified Signs are formed.

Step Six: Memory Aids

The last step that we included in our effort to facilitate the learning and retention of signs was to provide the learner with information that might more effectively tie each Simplified Sign to its referent. We discovered from teaching our Simplified Signs to a small group of students from overseas that some potential learners for whom English was not their first language would not know the meanings of some of the English words in the lexicon. On those instances when the students failed to grasp the meaning of the English words, they also experienced difficulty understanding how our Simplified Signs related to these words. For this reason, we included a brief definition of each of the words in our lexicon.

We also provided information on how each sign in our system was tied to its meaning in two ways. One was a short sentence or phrase that concisely tied each sign to its referent. The other approach was to provide a more detailed explanation of the relationship between each sign's formation (its location, handshape, movement, and/or facial expression) and its conceptual basis or meaning. In crafting these two memory aids, we felt that the more detailed or explicit explanations of sign-referent relationships would prove especially helpful to individuals as they were first learning our Simplified Signs, and that this would be the case particularly for those persons largely unfamiliar with American culture. Then, once the learner had come to understand the link between a sign's formation and its meaning, we hoped that the shorter memory aids would be sufficient to jog the learner's memory in the future. Moreover, we felt that this additional information would be particularly important for those signs that were not as clearly iconic or pantomimic as others. An explanation of the tie between a sign and its referent often is provided in stories about a sign's origin in Deaf sign languages. For example, the sign for BOY in ASL is made with the hand at the top of the signer's forehead. The sign's action is indicative of a boy tipping his cap. Although our memory aids do not necessarily reflect the origin of a sign's formation in any particular Deaf sign language, they do provide useful information that concretely links the sign's formation to its underlying conceptual basis. One reason we wished to include these explanations is that we, the authors, often relied on such information when trying to remember signs. Secondly, there is a sound empirical basis for doing so.

The effect of providing information about the tie between a sign and its referent or an explanation of the sign has been examined in two studies. In one study (Maynard, Slavoff, & Bonvillian, 1994), undergraduate students unfamiliar with any sign language or sign system were presented lists of signs together with their English word or translation equivalents (word-sign pairs). The students were randomly assigned to one of three experimental conditions or groups. The students in the first experimental condition were given a brief explanation (a short sentence or phrase that helped tie that sign to its English word equivalent) for each sign they were to learn. These explanations consisted of either brief accounts of the origins of the signs or of how these signs were related to their referents. The students in the other two experimental conditions were urged to use alternative recall strategies (e.g., overt rehearsal of the signs). All of the students were tested for their ability to remember the signs after being cued by their English translation equivalents both immediately after each list was presented and again after a one-week delay. When tested for immediate recall, there were only slight differences among the three groups of participants in the number of signs that they recalled. After a delay of one week, however, those students who had received information about the origins of the signs or explanations of the ties between the signs and their referents remembered many more signs than did the students in the other two groups or conditions. Thus, it appears that giving a brief description of the tie between a sign and its referent serves as an important memory aid for longer-term sign recall.[11]

The results of a second study (Stedt, 1984) also showed that providing explanations of signs often enhanced individuals' recall of those signs. In this study, students in the second, fifth, and eleventh grades were shown ASL signs in sentences and subsequently asked to verbally identify the signed sentences in a recall task. Those signs that had received mnemonic (memory assisting) explanations were recalled much more often by the students than those signs without such explanations.

---

11   The results of this immediate- and delayed-recall study mirror the results of a different recall study involving the recognition of arbitrary signs versus iconic signs (Lieberth & Gamble, 1991). In that study, investigators found that participants remembered about the same number of arbitrary signs as iconic signs shortly after the signs were presented. In contrast, many more iconic signs were recognized after a longer delay (see also Ortega, 2017). Thus, iconic signs are easier to remember over longer periods of time (as in Lieberth & Gamble, 1991) and having an explanation of the tie between a sign and its referent also increases recall over the long term (as in Maynard et al., 1994). A combination of strategies from these two studies (i.e., using iconic signs plus giving memory aids) should result in even better long-term recall.

The findings from these two studies that showed that providing student learners with explanations of the ties between observed signs and their underlying meanings aided them in remembering the signs also are consistent with views about how the human mind or brain operates. Experimental psychologists showed some years ago that having research participants focus on the meaning of words (semantic encoding) was a particularly effective way for them to remember the words (Craik & Tulving, 1975). More recently, a view has emerged that the brain strives to find meaning in or to make sense of our environmental experience (Carey, 2015; Proulx & Inzlicht, 2012). By providing the student learners in the two studies discussed above with brief accounts of the signs' origins or how the signs were related to their referents, the signs likely became considerably more meaningful and memorable for the learners.

Although receiving explanations about the sign-referent connections aided undergraduate and school-age students in their ability to remember signs, such information probably would affect various sign-learning groups quite differently. The staff at facilities where non-speaking persons are taught to sign, the parents or caregivers of such youngsters, elderly persons with hearing impairments, certain individuals with expressive speech aphasias (i.e., those who have suffered a loss of productive language ability but who can still understand spoken language), students using signs to facilitate their acquisition of foreign language vocabulary, and children in preschool programs might benefit from having the tie between a sign and its referent provided to them. In contrast, non-speaking children with autism spectrum disorder or children with a severe or profound intellectual disability may not reap similar benefits from such explanations.

Concluding Remarks

We believe that the Simplified Sign System we have developed will prove beneficial to many individuals who encounter or experience serious communication difficulties. We say this because the signs included in our system were the product of research efforts to determine which signs should be included and what formational parameters of signs should be avoided. We are not aware of other sign languages or sign systems developed in a similar systematic manner. The finding that undergraduate students found Simplified Signs easier to remember and form than signs from a genuine sign language also bodes well for future use of the Simplified Sign System. Perhaps caregivers and staff members at programs for non-speaking individuals will be more inclined to learn and use signs if they perceive them as more readily acquired.

Careful examination of the next chapter, which focuses on how to teach and use signs from the Simplified Sign System, reveals many helpful methods for enhancing the communicative efforts and successful social interaction of minimally verbal or non-speaking individuals. In addition, we answer many questions that teachers, staff members, caregivers, and family members may have, including a response to those who have reservations about using signs in general or Simplified Signs in particular. We hope that the teaching guidelines we provide, as well as our overview of how to develop a communication plan for an individual, will result in a comprehensive strategy in which to encourage and accurately measure a person's progress with Simplified Signs.

Although the present sign system represents years of effort, we are under no illusion that it cannot be improved. We welcome recommendations for new signs to include in our vocabulary as well as suggestions for modifying existing signs to make them easier to form and to remember. We should note that we expanded the size of the Simplified Sign System lexicon (to about 1840 signs) and began work on the development of a one-handed version of our system. We anticipate that a larger vocabulary of Simplified Signs will make the system a more useful vehicle for the teaching and learning of foreign language vocabulary items. We also hope that a one-handed version of our system will help meet the communication needs of those individuals with severe motor impairments to one of their hands or arms. Finally, we would readily accept advice on any helpful teaching strategies, research, exercises, or other information that should be included in future editions of this book or in supporting materials such as workbooks or multimedia resources. Only when we obtain input from many different minds will the Simplified Sign System reach its full potential as a communication system.

9. Application and Use of the Simplified Sign System with Persons with Disabilities

In the last several decades, both clinical and research evidence have shown that individuals who cannot effectively use or understand speech (including persons with autism spectrum disorder, an intellectual disability, cerebral palsy, or aphasia) may be able to produce or understand visual-motor symbols such as manual signs. However, to obtain the best results for these persons, it is not sufficient to merely start using signs with them. One must adopt good practices concerning which signs to teach first and which ones later, what teaching methods to use, which supporting activities to introduce, and how to incorporate sign learning as part of a larger intervention program for an individual (Dark, Brownlie, & Bloomberg, 2019; Grove & McDougall, 1991; Sundberg & Partington, 1998). The attitudes and responses to the use of signs by people in the surrounding environment also can have either a positive or a negative impact on an individual's progress (Bowles & Frizelle, 2016; Brereton, 2008; Budiyanto et al., 2018; Glacken et al., 2019; Rombouts, Maes, & Zink, 2017a, 2017b, 2017c, 2018a, 2018b; Sheehy & Duffy, 2009; Singh et al., 2017; Spratt & Florian, 2015).

In this chapter, considerable attention is devoted to providing teachers and caregivers with information on how to be supportive communication partners and how to coach an individual who has language difficulties into successful communicative behavior. Although the focus of this chapter is on teaching and using Simplified Signs, many of the approaches that are recommended are applicable to other intervention strategies as well. Also addressed are many common questions that may arise from the teachers, caregivers, and family members who are

  https://doi.org/10.11647/OBP.0205.09

primarily involved in deciding what type of communication methods to employ with a non-speaking individual.

Approaches to Teaching the Simplified Sign System

It is important to realize that signs are not a personalized communication prosthesis that, once they are adapted to the main or target user, will automatically result in improvement. Communication is a process of interaction between more than one person: the main user, the main user's communication partners, and the wider environment in which the main user lives and interacts. Each of these components will need to be a part of the learning process. Slightly different teaching and learning goals can be defined for each of them.

Component	Motivations	Goals
Main user	Experience that learning and using signs can be helpful.	Produce and recognize signs in daily situations. Produce and recognize signs in a teaching situation.
Communication partners	Understand that signs can be a help and support for the main user. Understand that the efficacy of signs will increase if they are used receptively and expressively by all communication partners.	Produce and recognize signs in daily situations. Produce and recognize signs in a teaching situation. Encourage the use of signs.
People in the wider environment	Understand that non-speaking or minimally verbal people need augmentative and alternative means such as signs to communicate effectively.	Respect the use of signs.

In essence, there are several steps that must be mastered for the successful implementation of a sign intervention strategy. The main user and his or her communication partners will need to learn how to form individual signs and learn the meanings associated with those signs. Each of these people will also need to learn how to combine signs and how the combining of signs affects their meanings. In addition, the main user and his or her communication partners will need to learn how to produce their signs effectively in a range of communicative contexts (Beukelman & Mirenda, 2013; Dark et al., 2019; Launonen, 2019b).

Main User

The most significant person in the learning process, of course, is the non-speaking or minimally verbal individual who will make use of the Simplified Sign System as a principal form of communication or as an augmentative technique to existing communicative methods. It would be a misperception, however, to assume that he or she is the sole reason why we need Simplified Signs. Communication is not a one-way process, and a limitation in communication is always a shared condition: this includes every person in the user's environment who wants to or needs to communicate with him or her.

There are four general ways to teach signs to the main user of the system: through general exposure, an incidental or milieu approach, games and group sessions, and explicit instruction or specific training sessions (often discrete trial training). We recommend using all of these strategies to attain maximum results. The first method of teaching signs is through general exposure. If everyone in the individual's environment utilizes Simplified Signs while interacting, the main user may acquire signs spontaneously (Valentino & Shillingsburg, 2011). In fact, if a communication partner makes a sign at a moment that the user is especially attentive because the item of discussion is of particular interest to him or her, he or she may learn and remember that sign. This phenomenon is similar to the way typically developing hearing children acquire most spoken words and how typically developing deaf and hearing children of deaf parents acquire signs. It is extremely important that the user's communication partners sign whenever he or she is around. In this way, the partners model signing and help turn

Simplified Signs into the standard mode of communication throughout the environment. This, in turn, provides many more opportunities for social interaction and the learning of signs.

Many persons with severe developmental disabilities learn signs best within the course of their daily living situations. This incidental or milieu teaching technique may be used when a non-speaking individual's interest is raised by food, a toy, or another item (Carr & Felce, 2007; Launonen, 1996, 1998, 2003, 2019b; Light & McNaughton, 2015; Mancil, 2009; Schepis et al., 1982; Wright et al., 2013). In such a situation, the learner may be especially motivated to learn and use a sign. For example, a caregiver signs EAT before a meal and asks the individual to repeat that sign. If he or she succeeds in making this sign or at least attempts to make the sign, then he or she is rewarded with the food item. If the learner fails to sign, the caregiver may repeat the sign once or twice. If the learner still does not produce the sign, the communication partner may take the hands of the individual and carefully and respectfully "mold" them into the sign (Clibbens, Powell, & Atkinson, 2002). The caregiver then repeats the sign and the meal starts. In this context, the sign serves as a reference to an upcoming or current event. The sign learner is more likely to store the sign as an internal symbol that represents the concept *eat* than if the sign is presented out of context. This very useful strategy should be implemented often.

Another method of teaching signs to persons with disabilities is by turning the task into a game or by using signs in conjunction with music, dance, storytelling, poetry, puppets, and other creative expressions (Parkhouse & Smith, 2019; Sutton-Spence & Kaneko, 2016). The more fun that a potential user has in learning signs, the more likely that he or she will learn and use those signs (Dark et al., 2019; Grove, 2019a). This approach does not have to be limited to the main user — including other children in the classroom will make learning signs an enjoyable experience for everyone (Grove & Colville, 1990; Grove et al., 2019; Mistry & Barnes, 2013). Furthermore, teaching signs to a main user's peers in group sessions promotes and encourages the use of signs not just in the classroom setting, but also outside of the classroom (Bowles & Frizelle, 2016; Glacken et al., 2019; Mackenzie, Cologon, & Fenech, 2016; Woll & Barnett, 1998). Since many persons with disabilities tend to communicate mostly with the adults in their lives (e.g., teachers, caregivers, therapists, and parents), including children of the same age in signing sessions gives the main user more motivation and opportunities to engage with same-age peers, thereby offering more chances to develop healthy social relationships (Grove & McDougall, 1991; Mackenzie et al., 2016; Parkhouse & Smith, 2019).

The last approach is to organize regular teaching sessions in which the person is taught the association between a sign and its meaning. These sessions typically are highly structured and focus on the learning of targeted behaviors or signs. The way these sessions are organized will depend on the cognitive level of the user, as well as his or her interest level. In many instances, he or she will first need to learn to look at the person teaching the signs. Once this visual contact has been established, the teacher shows how a particular sign is formed. If the user fails to produce the sign after it has been demonstrated several times, the teacher may wish to mold the user's hand(s) into the correct handshape(s) and guide his or her hand(s) through the appropriate sign movement (for precautions about using the molding technique, see Dunn, 1982; Grove et al., 2019; and Herman, Shield, & Morgan, 2019). Once the user has learned to produce the correct sign formation, the teacher's motor control can be faded. To maintain the child's attention and involvement through these sign-learning sessions, the teacher may wish to reward the user's attempts at producing signs. For many such sign learners, these sessions can be held in a classroom or speech-language therapist's office. The therapist, parent, teacher, or caregiver may also work with real objects, pictures, or posters to teach desired concepts, depending on what works best for the sign learner (Dark et al., 2019). This is the most structured type of teaching session. For some sign-learning individuals, the specific sign-training sessions may need to take place outside of their usual environment. This move to a special environment may be done to increase the learners' attention and to avoid distractions. If teaching takes place outside of a main user's customary surroundings, then an effort will need to be made to ensure that any signs learned in the special setting transfer back and are incorporated into an individual's regular environment.

Finally, the earlier in a child's development that a system of signed communication is enacted, the greater the possibility of long-term progress and of positive results (Branson & Demchak, 2009; Broberg et al., 2012; Clibbens, 2001; Creedon, 1973; Goodwyn & Acredolo, 1998; Guralnick, 2017; Launonen, 1996, 1998, 2003, 2019a, 2019b; Launonen & Grove, 2003; Mahoney et al., 2006; Millar et al., 2006). In fact, delaying a sign intervention program (or other AAC techniques) may leave a child without the ability to communicate his or her needs in an effective manner. Such a deficit in communication skills may lead the child to develop behavioral control issues and may also result in social withdrawal or isolation from same-age peers. The introduction of signs and/or other communicative techniques provides a young child with a means of becoming involved in the world and experiencing a degree of control over his or her environment. Typically, this also results in declines in emotional outbursts, frustration levels, and other negative behaviors associated with minimally verbal or non-speaking individuals. Even when introduced at a later age, however, signs can provide these and other benefits. Parents, teachers, and other caregivers should therefore be open to using signs with non-speaking persons of any age.

Communication Partners

Teachers, caregivers, family members, friends, and other persons who regularly interact with the main user should become adept at signing and should employ Simplified Signs whenever that individual is present, especially when speaking with him or her. We recommend that a user's communication partners organize their own learning and practice sessions. These sessions can be fun; learning signs is an engaging way to broaden one's language skills (Dolly & Noble, 2018; Spragale & Micucci, 1990). Furthermore, being able to witness a person with serious communication difficulties make progress in learning signs and in improving the quality of his or her life can be especially rewarding. Providing direct and consistent training and guidance to communication partners on how they might best facilitate their non-speaking loved one's use of nonverbal communication methods should also be seriously considered (Broberg et al., 2012; Cologon & Mevawalla, 2018; Glacken et al., 2019; Grove & McDougall, 1991; Guralnick, 2017; Kent-Walsh et al., 2015; Mahoney et al., 2006; Mellon, 2001; Rautakoski, 2011; Rombouts et al., 2017a, 2017b, 2017c, 2018a, 2018b, 2019; Singh et al., 2017; Wooderson, Cuskelly, & Meyer, 2014).

Many non-speaking children and adults reside at home and need to interact frequently with family members. If parents, siblings, and other family members learn to sign, then the main user will have many more opportunities to learn signs and these signs likely will generalize to new situations (Dodd & Gorey, 2014; Launonen, 2019b; Smith, Romski, & Sevcik, 2013). For these reasons, enlisting the active participation of family members is an important step in establishing a successful sign-communication program. There are, however, hurdles that need to be overcome before a supportive family sign-learning environment can be fully implemented. One hurdle is that few hearing parents know much about the use of signs with speech when interacting with a hearing person (Kaufman, 2003). These family members should be given ample information on the nature of signing and why signing may benefit their non-speaking family member. These benefits often include a reduction in temper tantrums or challenging behaviors, improved classroom performance, and increased self-confidence and independence (Berry, 1987; Glacken et al., 2019; Goldbart & Marshall, 2004; Grinnell, Detamore, & Lipke, 1976; Marshall & Goldbart, 2008). A second hurdle is that many parents are apprehensive about whether signed input, together with speech, might adversely affect the main user's likelihood of acquiring speech (Berry, 1987; Iacono & Cameron, 2009; Kaufman, 2003). These family members should be informed that research findings indicate that combined sign and speech input does not negatively affect spoken language development, and often facilitates it (Blischak, Lombardino, & Dyson, 2003; Dunst et al., 2011; Millar et al., 2006). This particular issue is discussed later in this chapter under "Frequently Asked Questions."

Family members may also be reluctant to sign because they are self-conscious about doing so (Kaufman, 2003). Although sign interpreting and sign language classes are more widespread than in years past, it should be recognized that signing is still an unusual activity for most hearing persons. Moreover, family members may be hesitant to become involved in implementing a sign-communication (or other augmentative and alternative communication) intervention program because of concerns about the amount of time they will need to commit (Goldbart & Marshall, 2004; Iacono & Cameron, 2009). Although the amount of time needed by parents and other family members to acquire an initial lexicon of Simplified Signs will not be large, it will not be negligible.

This issue also is discussed later in this chapter under "Frequently Asked Questions." Considerable support and encouragement probably will need to be provided to overcome many hearing persons' reluctance to learn and use signs.

People in the Wider Environment

Individuals who have less frequent contact with the main user should at least be informed that he or she is being taught Simplified Signs (and/or other communication techniques), why the system is being tried, and how it can help him or her to communicate more effectively. Sometimes people in the wider environment may learn a few signs to enable them to interact more successfully with the main user (Collier, McGhie-Richmond, & Self, 2010; Light & McNaughton, 2015). Such interaction through signs likely would be beneficial to the main sign learner as it may help him or her become more fully integrated into society at large.

Guidelines for Using the Simplified Sign System

In the Introduction (Chapter 1), we put forth the basic principles of the Simplified Sign System. These principles include: choosing or creating signs that are high in iconicity (maximizing the transparency or translucency of the signs); making the signs as easy to form and to remember as possible; including signs that can describe many items within a broad concept category; standardizing the formation of those signs; and focusing the lexicon on a core vocabulary that will likely prove most helpful to the main users of the system. These are important characteristics of a communication system that will be taught to target populations who have a wide range of cognitive and motor abilities, as well as difficulties in recognizing, understanding, remembering, and producing symbols. The same principles used in selecting and developing Simplified Signs should also make them easier to learn by the teachers, caregivers, friends, and family members of the target groups.

Learning to communicate, however, is more than just recognizing or producing single signs or signs in combination. Many factors play a role in whether communication is successful. For example, the speed of communication can be an issue; too fast and the person may not understand, too slow and the person may not realize that someone is trying to communicate. A sign may also need to be repeated before it is understood. Eye contact, facial expression, and proper timing are all factors that influence whether or not a message will be successfully transmitted. The following guidelines will help caregivers and teachers establish good and consistent communication practices that likely will maximize a potential user's success with the Simplified Sign System.

Ensure a Positive Signing Environment

Signing is, at least initially, an unusual way for most hearing persons to communicate. Some people, including teachers, staff, caregivers, and the intended users, may have negative attitudes toward signing. This can have a profound impact on the willingness of individuals to learn and use signs. When introducing a program that relies on signs, try to estimate how well signs are accepted by the different persons in the main user's environment, including the non-speaking individual. It may be necessary to take steps to improve caregiver, teacher, and user perceptions and attitudes about signing (Avramidis & Norwich, 2002; Budiyanto et al., 2018; Goldbart & Marshall, 2004; Light & McNaughton, 2015; Marshall & Goldbart, 2008; Rombouts et al., 2017a; Sheehy & Duffy, 2009; Singh et al., 2017).[1]

It is also important that all or nearly all of the main user's regular communication partners employ signs while interacting with him or her. The consistent and regular use of signs will help the user to learn and retain signs and encourage spontaneous sign production (Glacken et al., 2019; Grove & McDougall, 1991; Kent-Walsh et al., 2015; Launonen, 2019b; Light & McNaughton, 2015; Mackenzie et al., 2016; Rombouts et al., 2019). If only a small number of people sign, or if they sign inconsistently or only at specific times, the main learner will be less likely to use signs. This is because communication is very much influenced by what is perceived to be the norm in any given environment. Individuals with communication impairments are still affected by the languages and communication approaches utilized

---

1   For a much more detailed account, we strongly urge readers to review the "Recommendations for Enhancing the Sign-Learning Environment" section in Chapter 4.

by the people around them, and they may not use signs, even if they have the ability to do so, if nobody or very few other people in their environment sign. If everyone uses signs, however, the learner will be much more likely to sign spontaneously (Bowles & Frizelle, 2016; Bryen et al., 1988; Grove & Walker, 1990; Meuris, Maes, & Zink, 2015; Mistry & Barnes, 2013; Rombouts et al., 2017b, 2017c, 2018a, 2018b; Schlosser & Sigafoos, 2006; Woll & Barnett, 1998). For sign intervention programs to be optimally successful, then, non-speaking individuals should be immersed in an environment where most people consistently rely on signs to communicate and where signing is the norm (Brereton, 2008; Budiyanto et al., 2018; Cologon & Mevawalla, 2018; Dolly & Noble, 2018). This does not mean that speech is excluded; we highly recommend the use of key word signing.

Establish Visual or Tactile Contact

Unlike the case for speech, non-speaking persons need to look at the signs to be able to learn them. Non-speaking persons who also are blind or severely visually impaired will need to feel a teacher's hands during sign production in order to learn those signs. How one secures the needed attention of a sign-learning individual, though, will depend to a large extent on the age and abilities of the learners themselves. For very young children, caregivers and teachers likely will need to adopt quite different sign-teaching strategies than they would for older learners. When deaf mothers of very young sign-learning children were observed interacting with them, the mothers often formed their signs within their children's existing areas of visual attention rather than in the mothers' signing space (Baker & van den Bogaerde, 1996; Clibbens et al., 2002; Dark et al., 2019; Holzrichter & Meier, 2000; Spencer & Harris, 2006). A variation of this approach was for the mothers to move the objects of their children's attention closer to the mothers' signing space. In both these approaches, the children were able to see their mothers' signs and the contextual referents at the same time. Deaf mothers of very young children also elected to make some of their signs directly on their children's bodies and to mold their children's hands into the correct sign formations (Clibbens et al., 2002; Harris et al., 1989; Pizer, Meier, & Shaw Points, 2011; Waxman & Spencer, 1997). These approaches were effective in getting the children to attend to the signed input as well (Dark et al., 2019; Masataka, 2000; von Tetzchner & Martinsen, 2000; Wright et al., 2013).

Many other non-speaking children or older individuals will need to look at their caregivers or family members to understand any signs made by them. These sign users must therefore be encouraged to look at and preferably to make eye contact with the persons with whom they wish to communicate. Another reason to make eye contact is that a signer's facial expression is important in conveying the emotional content of a signed utterance. Some of the candidates for learning the Simplified Sign System may have fluctuating attention spans or rarely make eye contact with other people. Persons with autism spectrum disorder often fail to establish eye contact with others; these individuals, however, may be attending covertly by using their peripheral vision (Gernsbacher et al., 2008). And even though deaf children with ASD do not recognize emotions conveyed on a signer's face as well as typically developing deaf children, they still extract information conveyed on a signer's face to some extent (Denmark et al., 2014). In those cases involving persons with autism, teachers or caregivers may choose to implement a program of systematic training to increase the amount of time the user spends looking at or toward them. For example, during a teaching session, each time that the main user looks in the teacher's direction, he or she is rewarded. Regular use of rewards should increase both the number and length of attentive gazes.

Once consistent attention is established, the teacher can progress to incorporating Simplified Signs into interactions with the intended user. It should be noted, however, that establishing eye contact is not essential to the learning of signs. To see another person's signs, one must look in the general direction of that signer, but not necessarily at that signer's eyes. Indeed, for many sign learners, it may prove difficult to gaze into another person's eyes while simultaneously looking at that individual's manual sign productions and one's own sign productions (von Tetzchner & Martinsen, 2000). Finally, for non-speaking individuals with severe visual impairments, teachers and caregivers will need to rely much more on the sense of touch when teaching signs. The hands and arms of these non-speaking individuals will need to be molded into the correct sign formations, and they will need to learn to understand their teachers' and caregivers' signs and fingerspelling by feeling them made in their hands.

Use Key Word Signing

We encourage teachers and caregivers to use Simplified Signs in conjunction with speech, a process known as simultaneous communication. Using both signs and spoken words helps to enhance and reinforce communication. Speaking and signing *every* word in a sentence, however, is both difficult and time-consuming. In a study involving fluent users of American Sign Language and English, it was found that, on average, about twice as many words were produced per second than signs (Klima & Bellugi, 1979). Conveying the content of full sentences, however, took about the same amount of time in both language modalities. This is largely because individual signs often convey more information than individual words. Yet if one were to produce a sign to accompany each spoken word in a sentence, the greater time required for individual sign production might noticeably increase the time needed for effective communication (and might increase it to a point where comprehension is negatively affected).

The technique of key word signing seeks to overcome the difficulties in simultaneous communication by limiting the number of signs to those that contain the most essential information — these are the *key words* (Windsor & Fristoe, 1991). In this approach, the teacher or caregiver in a country produces a sentence in the standard word order of that country's spoken language while simultaneously signing the principal information-carrying words of the sentence. The fact that only the more important words are signed makes combining speech with signs less difficult. For a sentence of six to ten words, probably only three or four signs will be used. For example, the caregiver or teacher says, "The plate is on the table" and makes the signs for PLATE, ON, and TABLE as the corresponding words are uttered (Grove, 1980). As another example, the question "Do you feel well?" would require only the signs YOU and GOOD. Facial expression, in this case raising one's eyebrows, will convey that a question is being asked, and eye contact will help make it clear that the question is directed at the user. Speech intonation and the speech itself also will help support the meaning of the sign. If necessary, one can add the sign QUESTION for clarification.

When deciding which words to sign, be sure to think about the underlying meaning of what is said; this will help determine which words to sign and also which signs to use. Remember that signs in our Simplified Sign System have relatively flexible meanings and are usable across a range of contexts. Whereas the teacher or caregiver is expected to integrate speech with signs, the non-speaking user is not; rather, he or she is first expected to imitate signs and then encouraged to initiate communication through those signs (Grove & Walker, 1990).

There are a number of reasons for teachers and caregivers to use a key word signing approach. Many words in a spoken utterance primarily play a structural role by making the utterance grammatical; providing signs for such words probably would not enhance signed communication. Additionally, because many signs take longer to form than their spoken word equivalents, speaking and signing the key words at the same time helps to slow down communication (Loncke et al., 2012). Speech often is more understandable if its rate of production is slowed down slightly. This may be a benefit for individuals who have difficulty processing rapid speech input; slowing down sign communication may also benefit persons who need a longer visual presentation time to understand the signed input. Third, a teacher or caregiver using key word signing often is interacting in an environment where there are individuals with widely varying abilities. Although hearing a full sentence may not directly benefit some non-speaking individuals, it may be of assistance to others. A fourth reason for the key word approach is that the exposure to a spoken language may facilitate the non-speaking individual's development of spoken language processing skills (Loncke et al., 2006). Furthermore, if a sign learner misses some of the information contained in one modality (e.g., speech), he or she may be able to understand the information provided by the other modality (e.g., signs). Signs can have a positive effect on speech recognition similar to what a yellow marker does on written text: it highlights what is essential to understanding the message. Finally, the teacher or caregiver may feel more comfortable using spoken language and supplementing speech with signs rather than relying solely on signs for communication.

Sign Correctly but Accept a User's Imperfect Signs

It is important for teachers or caregivers to produce signs accurately and consistently so that the main user has a better chance of learning them. Caregivers and teachers need to monitor themselves to make sure that the signs are made as they are described in the lexicon (see Chapter 11, Volume 2). This way, a main or target user is not confused by wide variations in how a sign is produced. This need for consistency in caregivers' and teachers' sign formation has been underlined recently through the concerns expressed about the difficulties individuals with ASD have in processing input that is not relatively stable in form (Hellendoorn et al., 2015). One should strive to make all communications as clear as possible, and limiting the variation within a particular sign is part of this strategy. Related to this strategy of standardization of sign formation is the commitment to teaching and using the particular Simplified Sign listed in the lexicon under a certain concept, even if other common gestures or signs may be just as clear and understandable. This ensures that everyone who interacts with the main user learns and uses the same sign, thereby increasing the chances that the sign will be incorporated into that individual's sign vocabulary. Again, the goal is for the main user to not be confused by exposure to different signs that represent the same concept. An exception to this principle is if the non-speaking individual has already learned a sign or gesture from another source and uses it successfully to represent that concept. In this case, make sure everyone uses the previously learned sign or gesture instead of the Simplified Sign. If, however, this "known" sign is produced inconsistently or with great difficulty, one may wish to introduce the Simplified Sign version and determine whether it is produced with greater ease and is retained better than the other sign.

Although teachers or caregivers may learn signs relatively quickly, it is important to understand that it may take much longer for the main or target users to learn them (Grove et al., 2019). The target users may not be accustomed to processing visual linguistic information or they may never have learned how to successfully communicate symbolically until they are taught Simplified Signs. Using signs means a dramatic change in the strategies non-speaking or minimally verbal persons employ to interact with their environments. This learning process may take a substantial amount of time because it requires users to learn how to associate symbols (signs) with objects, activities, or concepts, then store and later retrieve those same symbols (signs).

Some individuals may need to learn to replace their current form of communication with the use of signs. Sometimes, this current form of "communication" may be a problem or challenging behavior (Wetherby, 1986). For example, a child with ASD may have learned to get what he wants by looking at something and throwing a tantrum. From the viewpoint of the child, this behavior is extremely effective: the attention of a teacher or a caregiver is obtained and subsequently the desired object is provided. The use of signs will be a much less disruptive form of communication; however, the child will need to learn that using signs is as effective as or more effective than the problem behavior that had worked up until that point (Hetzroni & Roth, 2003). Often this will require a systematic approach by the teachers or caregivers to promote the use of signs and to discourage tantrums. Once a sign is taught for a certain concept, the child should be rewarded for using that sign so that the likelihood of it being used again will increase.

For those individuals with aphasia who communicated effectively before their loss of speech, one should still expect gradual progress in learning signs. Even with existing linguistic ability or lengthy experience with spoken language, it will take time for an individual to become accustomed to processing or "reading" another person's signs (their handshapes, locations, and movements) as well as producing them (Doherty, 1985). This point is applicable to anyone learning the system who has not already been exposed to a sign language or sign system. In addition to the time needed to become accustomed to using signs, time is required for a person to learn how to accurately produce a *specific* sign. Many persons who will benefit from the Simplified Sign System have motor difficulties that will directly affect their ability to form particular signs. Caregivers should expect that signs produced by individuals in the early stages of intervention may only approximate how the signs are actually made. Much like an infant who is learning to utter words for the first time, but who leaves out syllables or substitutes easier-to-make sounds for more difficult ones, signs typically are not produced perfectly on the first try. Users may initially leave out part of a sign, produce it in the wrong location, form it with a different handshape, or make incorrect movements.

Caregivers or teachers may wish to adopt a strategy of shaping or molding the user's imperfect signs into the correct forms. As the individual becomes more familiar and comfortable with signing, his or her signs should become more accurate. Depending on the specific cognitive and psychomotor abilities of the learner, however, certain signs may never be correctly produced. Even if a person can only make approximations of certain signs, caregivers and teachers should be supportive. It is important that the user feel that his or her communication is recognized and rewarded, and most of all, appreciated and encouraged (Grove et al., 2019). Keep in mind that signing may still be much easier for a person than speaking, and his or her signs may be more understandable than his or her speech (Grove, 1990). Lastly, some individuals may prefer to produce many Simplified Signs with both of their hands. That is, in addition to a signer using his or her dominant hand to perform the handshape and movement of a one-handed sign, he or she may mirror that handshape and movement with the non-dominant hand (Doherty, 1985; Grove et al., 2019; McEwen & Lloyd, 1990; Meier et al., 2008). Transforming a one-handed sign into a two-handed symmetrical sign usually should not be considered an error. Many of the signs in our system can be made in this manner without any confusion or change in meaning. Caregivers and teachers should, of course, continue to use the standard form of each sign. It is also possible that as a particular signer gains or develops more control over his or her motor abilities, he or she will learn to inhibit the extraneous movement of the non-dominant hand.

Reward the User for Progress

Eventually, successful communication will be enough of a reward in and of itself to use the Simplified Sign System. A user's experience of being understood by his or her communication partners is one of the strongest incentives to keep using signs. In the beginning, however, he may not be able to see the relationship between producing a sign and getting a specific response. Some form of age-appropriate encouragement will typically increase the chances that the user will intentionally sign to express what he or she wants. Rewards can take several forms: a desired food, overt cheering, a hug, verbal reinforcement or encouragement, or some kind of gift or token. The right amount of an item or an activity serving as a reward is enough to increase the likelihood that the sign being taught will be produced again, but not so much that the sign learner no longer desires the reward. Caregivers and teachers should rely on their understanding of the particular characteristics of a potential sign user when choosing what type and amount of a reward to employ, because different rewards will be effective with different individuals. These rewards may be faded out as the need for them decreases.

Use Facial Expression

Facial expression is a powerful tool in helping to clarify or support the meaning of a signed communication. In fact, our testing of Simplified Signs revealed that signs accompanied by an emphatic facial expression often were more easily recalled than those that did not incorporate facial expression (see Chapter 8). Facial expression serves to underscore a signed or spoken communication and helps to make the message more understandable and more memorable. A sign may not be understood at all if not accompanied by the proper facial expression, or worse, if it is accompanied by the wrong one. For example, a frown while making the sign for HAPPY would be confusing; on the other hand, a smile would be appropriate and would help to clarify the meaning of that sign. We suggest appropriate facial expressions in the written descriptions of some of the signs in our Simplified Sign lexicon. Use of facial expression also may help keep the sign learner's attention. However, this emphasis on appropriate facial expression is more of a concern in the signing of teachers and caregivers. Indeed, a small number of non-speaking individuals have difficulty generating different facial expressions and should not be expected to produce them.

Use Environmental Cues or Contextual Information

Make communication multimodal: maximize the use of environmental cues to make the message as transparent and as clear as possible and to reduce any ambiguity in meaning. Teachers are encouraged to produce signs in conjunction with a desired activity or object. For instance, pick up or point to a book when using the sign BOOK. However, one should be careful not to mismatch cues; it would be confusing to introduce the sign for SLEEP while an individual is taking a walk or eating. Instead, one should introduce the sign when the context is right: at bedtime or naptime. Pictures, posters, drawings, toys, and other objects in the environment can serve as contextual cues to both the caregiver's communication efforts and the child's communication efforts as well. Using environmental cues to decode linguistic input is a skill learned in early childhood (Bezuidenhout & Sroda, 1998; Loukusa et al., 2017). This receptive language skill can also be used proactively by children to support their expressive language skills (i.e., their linguistic output) in multimodal ways through the use of pointing at people or objects, gesturing, signing, pantomiming actions, vocalizing, and facial expressions (Borghi et al., 2014; Grove, 2019b; Hill, Reichart, & Korhonen, 2014; Kusters et al., 2017; Launonen & Grove, 2019; Morgan, 2014; Parkhouse & Smith, 2019). When at all possible, point to or pick up the object being discussed. Continue to make use of objects or activities occurring in the environment until an individual user has learned and employed a sign multiple times in a variety of contexts. A caregiver may then consider gradually fading out the use of the objects.

Use the Sign for the Underlying Concept

Try to be sensitive to the underlying meaning or concept behind a spoken word and use the sign for that concept instead of trying to find a sign for a specific word. For example, the sentence "Stay where you are" would be conveyed by the sign HALT. HALT signals to the user to interrupt his or her movement, which is the underlying meaning of the spoken sentence. Notice that there is no separate sign for the word *stay* in the lexicon. Instead, we tried to find or create signs that are usable in various contexts. The spoken sentence "I will ask the receptionist" can be signed with QUESTION and MAN or WOMAN. In this instance, the sign for MAN or WOMAN is a suitable substitute for the word *receptionist*. Alternatively, one can point directly to the person if he or she is visible. If a specific concept is used often, however, one may wish to find or create a sign for it (we offer suggestions on how to do this later in the chapter).

Adapt the Size, Rate, and Frequency of Signing

For very young children, persons with visual impairments, individuals with autism, or older persons with memory impairments, it may be important to provide a longer presentation time for signs to be imitated correctly and learned. Indeed, deaf mothers teaching their children sign language often make modifications to their signing, including making the sign larger, slowing down the rate of signing or increasing the duration of the sign to clarify its movement, using fewer signs in an utterance, and repeating the sign multiple times (Pizer et al., 2011). This last strategy of repetition may be specifically designed to increase the likelihood that a child will attempt to produce the sign (Woll, Kyle, & Ackerman, 1988). These strategies may also be useful when teaching signs to siblings, caregivers, family members, and adult communication partners who have not already been exposed to a sign language.

Viewing someone else producing a sign and then successfully imitating that sign often requires a person to perform a spatial transformation that reverses the sign's movement (Shield, 2010; Shield & Meier, 2018; see also Grove et al., 2019). Persons with autism have particular difficulty with visual perspective-taking and may produce errors with lateral movements, inward-outward movements, and palm orientations (Edwards, 2014; Hamilton, Brindley, & Frith, 2009; Shield, Cooley, & Meier, 2017; Shield & Meier, 2012, 2018). One way to avoid many of these errors is for the sign teacher to physically reorient his or her body so that he or she is positioned next to the signer and facing in the same direction (Dunn, 1982; Shield, 2010). This allows individuals who have trouble with spatial transformations to perform the signs using an easier and more direct matching strategy. Typically, as a sign learner gains experience in both viewing and producing signs, his or her visuospatial skills will improve to the point where this teaching strategy is no longer necessary. Children with autism, however, may continue to make visuospatial errors even after years of signing experience (Shield & Meier, 2018).

Frequently Asked Questions

Which Signs Should Be Taught First?

Once one chooses to implement the Simplified Sign System, one needs to decide which signs a potential user should try to learn first. Many educators are inspired by the first words (e.g., *ball, doggie, up, mommy, daddy*) of typically developing young children. These first words are often those that refer to the most important objects, actions, and persons in the young child's environment. In studies of vocabulary use in preschool children, as few as fifty words comprised half or more of their total number of words (Banajee, Dicarlo, & Stricklin, 2003; Beukelman, Jones, & Rowan, 1989; Burroughs, 1957; Deckers et al., 2017; Fallon, Light, & Paige, 2001; Fried-Oken & More, 1992; Trembath, Balandin, & Togher, 2007). While beginning with signs that have a strong interest value is a good principle, we must consider that the world of individuals who need Simplified Signs frequently is quite different from the world of typically developing young children. Therefore, the content of the first lexicon of a Simplified Sign System user may be substantially different (von Tetzchner & Martinsen, 2000).

The first step in developing a teaching plan is to start with an assessment of the principal learner's interests, needs, desires, and current successes and challenges in communication (Beukelman & Mirenda, 2013; Light et al., 1998; Reichle, York, & Sigafoos, 1991; Vandereet et al., 2010, 2011). During this assessment, the caregiver or teacher should include a list of situations in which communication is or is not successful. The selection of the first signs to be taught should emphasize situations in which teachers and caregivers report a real need for a sign and in which there is sufficient indication that the principal learner or user will experience an improvement in communication by using signs. Indeed, because the rate of sign or manual gesture learning often is quite slow for many individuals, therapeutic interventions should concentrate on teaching those signs or gestures that promise to have a direct benefit or practical relevance to the principal learner (Daumüller & Goldenberg, 2010). As the use of signs progresses and as his or her communication needs grow, other concepts can be added to the learner's sign vocabulary (Dark et al., 2019; Grove & Walker, 1990; Hockema & Smith, 2009; Walker,

Mitha, & Riddington, 2019). In addition, it is critically important that assessments of the communication skills and needs of adults and older persons be tailored to their vocabulary needs by including more mature topics of conversation and age-appropriate concerns (Grove & Woll, 2017).

Other signs that teachers and caregivers should consider including in their teaching plans are signs that may help the main user understand what events are going to occur in his or her environment and what people want him or her to do (von Tetzchner & Martinsen, 2000). Often, individuals with severe language impairments, such as many persons with autism spectrum disorder, become anxious and upset when they are unable to understand what is happening in their environment and what others expect of them (Frith, 1989).

In addition to teaching signs that meet a communication need, teach signs for objects, actions, or persons that are highly important or interesting to the main user. These signs are likely to generate strong motivation and an underlying basis for learning signs; for example, a person who enjoys sports may want to know how to ask for the basketball he or she cannot find. In fact, the communication partner may have deliberately hidden the ball to create the need for asking. Try to avoid teaching signs that are of little interest or value to the user. Overburdening a person with signs that seem irrelevant could possibly diminish the user's ability to remember more helpful and necessary signs.

Although the particular objects or actions that are especially motivating, interesting, or reinforcing will vary from person to person, certain guidelines should be followed when picking an initial sign lexicon (Sundberg & Partington, 1998). One recommendation is to avoid more complex concepts such as *please, like,* and *help* in favor of more distinct or clear-cut concepts such as *food, cat,* and *book.* The latter concepts can be identified or demonstrated relatively easily, whereas the former are more difficult to demonstrate and involve some degree of social understanding. This is not to say that the former concepts should not be taught, but rather that they should not be the focus of the very first sign-teaching efforts.

A second recommendation when selecting the initial signs to teach is to avoid signs that resemble each other formationally (Sundberg &

Partington, 1998). For example, the signs EAT and DRINK both involve the signer's hand arcing up to the lips. To avoid confusion and the potential blending of sign formations by the learner, it would be unwise for the initial vocabulary to include signs that are produced in the same location or that too closely resemble each other. Once the individual has acquired one of the signs and is paying attention to the different sign formational parameters (i.e., handshape, location, and movement), then introduce the other, formationally similar, sign.[2] Also, because many teachers and caregivers utter the word equivalent of a sign while making the sign, it would be better for the learner if words that rhyme or sound similar were avoided in the initial lexicon.

A third guideline is to avoid signs that are conceptually similar (Doherty, 1985; Stremel-Campbell, Cantrell, & Halle, 1977). Confusion may arise for the learner when the meaning of one sign is subsumed by that of another sign, as in the signs BERRIES and FOOD (listed as EAT in our lexicon). Misunderstandings also may occur if two signs are related in meaning and are taught at the same time, as would be the case for SHIRT and COAT. Again, once the learner has acquired one of the signs and understands its meaning, then the related sign may be introduced.

Finally, select signs that vary in their motivating or reinforcing aspects (Sundberg & Partington, 1998). For example, if the signs being taught or introduced in a specific session are all foods or all forms of physical play, then the user's motivation to learn likely will decrease when he or she is no longer hungry or if he or she becomes physically tired. To avoid such potential satiation, consider varying the types or categories of signs being taught in a particular set or session and spread signing throughout the day's naturally occurring activities.

---

2   We should note that there is also a potential advantage to teaching formationally similar signs. That is, if a sign learner acquires the ability to form a certain sign, then he or she probably has the capacity to acquire formationally similar signs. But to avoid possible confusion in the learning process, we would not recommend that two or more formationally similar signs be taught in the same early teaching session.

What If the Simplified Sign System Does Not Provide a Sign for a Needed Concept?

The lexicon of the Simplified Sign System is designed to be used in the majority of daily interactions between caregivers and target users; it is not, however, meant to convey every single concept or represent every possible object with which a user may come into contact. For an item for which there is no specific sign in the Simplified Sign System, caregivers or users may wish to simply point to the object (if it is visible). If the object is of considerable importance to a user or is a common topic of conversation, however, a caregiver may feel the need to add that concept to the person's sign vocabulary. If this is the case, we recommend the following steps:

1. Make sure that none of the signs in the current system can be used. Remember that signs are not direct translations of words, but rather represent the underlying concepts. For example, suppose the user really enjoys playing with dolls. Instead of creating a separate sign for the concept *dollhouse*, try just using the sign HOUSE. The more widely individual signs are used, the more powerful the system is.

2. If a single existing sign is not specific enough (for example, if one is often confused about which meaning is being indicated), consider combining two signs from the lexicon. For example, *dollhouse* could be conveyed by combining the signs DOLL and HOUSE or possibly SMALL and HOUSE. It should be noted, however, that combining signs in this way requires greater amounts of cognitive and motor skills and may not be helpful for non-speaking individuals whose sign communications are usually limited to single signs. Only those individuals who have learned how to combine signs to convey more complex utterances will be able to benefit from this option.

3. If the above strategies do not work, create a new sign. One may find that outlining the general shape of an object is an effective approach to creating a sign for a needed object. Also, observe the user in the context for which the sign is needed. One's observations may uncover movements or actions that are typical to that concept and which in turn can be used to

create the needed sign for an action or activity. For example, one may use an imitation of a machine's turning wheels or another visually obvious section of it to represent a specific machine. Regardless, make the sign as iconic or representative as possible — its meaning should be readily apparent. Use easily formed handshapes (see Appendix B for options) and reduce multiple movements to a single movement. Also, try to have the sign make contact with the torso, head, arms, or hands, especially if it is a one-handed sign (Grove, 1990; Lloyd & Doherty, 1983). Once the sign is as iconic and as easy to form as possible, test the sign with other caregivers. This will help determine whether another person can accurately guess a sign's meaning and remember how to make it. If the sign is not sufficiently memorable or is too confusing, try again. It may take multiple attempts to come up with a sign that is easily understood, remembered, and produced. Finally, once a sign has been created and tested, make sure that both the main user and all communication partners know the sign.

What If a Potential User Already Knows Some Signs, such as ASL Signs?

There is nothing magical about Simplified Signs. Their power is in the fact that they are easy to learn, remember, recognize, and produce. If a potential user already knows some signs from a different source and is able to produce them accurately, then there is no need for him or her to learn the corresponding signs in our system. The other signs can co-exist with any new signs taught from the Simplified Sign System. If, however, the person has difficulty forming a particular sign from another sign language or system, it may be worthwhile teaching and using the corresponding Simplified Sign instead.

When Are Name Signs Necessary and How Should They Be Developed?

Individuals already using a sign language or a sign system to communicate may already have signs to represent themselves, their close friends or family members, and others in the environment with whom they come into frequent contact. For those individuals who are just now starting to use a sign language or sign system such as the Simplified Sign System, some time will need to be spent creating signs to represent the important persons in a user's life. Who ranks as important is a judgment call, but fundamentally, these are the persons with whom the user has frequent, meaningful interactions. Not all of these individuals, however, will need to have a name sign.

An individual's mother and father do not need name signs because the user can refer to them with the signs MOTHER and FATHER; stepparents may, on the other hand, require name signs. The signs GRANDMOTHER and GRANDFATHER can be used for grandparents, although one may wish to distinguish between one's maternal and paternal grandparents or among various great-grandparents. Brothers or sisters may need name signs if an individual has more than one or a person can refer to them as *brother* or *sister*. Any other family members who interact frequently with the main user may need name signs, as do the individual's friends. Other people in the environment can usually be referred to by their occupation, such as TEACHER (listed under TEACH in our lexicon), DOCTOR, etc.

One source of information about the creation of name signs is the way that they emerge in the Deaf community. When Deaf parents in the United States select a name sign for their children, they typically use handshapes from the manual alphabet for the initial letter of the children's first or, less frequently, last names. These handshapes are made in the area in front of the signer's torso where fingerspelling usually occurs or on certain areas of the signer's arms, hands, head, or torso (Supalla, 1990). Because the handshapes of the manual alphabet do not resemble particular characteristics of the persons being named, these name signs often are considered arbitrary name signs. Most children who grow up deaf, however, have hearing parents. These children often do not receive their name signs from their parents, who usually have limited or no signing skills and who are not part of the Deaf community. Rather, these children typically receive name signs from their peers at educational institutions for deaf students (Meadow, 1977). These name signs often are based on particularly striking or identifying aspects of an individual's physical appearance, behavior, personality, or interests. For example, a name sign might reflect a person's prominent scar or extra-thick glasses. Because these signs are directly tied to characteristics of those persons being named, these name signs are often called descriptive (Supalla, 1990).

In recent years, a number of hearing persons with some background in signing often have chosen to create name signs for themselves by combining the arbitrary and descriptive approaches. In this combined approach, a sign that refers to a prominent physical, emotional, or other characteristic of an individual typically is modified by incorporating the manual alphabet handshape for the initial letter of that person's first name.[3] For example, Alan may be a cheerful and happy fellow; his name sign may modify the sign for HAPPY by changing the handshape to an "A" for Alan. Catherine may be such a hard worker that her friends refer to her with the sign for WORK, but modify the handshape to a "C" for Catherine. Other name signs may focus on a person's favorite activities or on physical characteristics such as long or short hair, height, weight, or facial features. If one opts to use this approach to create a name sign, focus first on that person's most salient characteristic and then modify the sign for that characteristic to represent the first letter of the individual's name or nickname.[4] If the letter's handshape is too difficult for the user to form, consider modifying it or simply leaving it out. Also, this strategy of modifying a sign to refer to a person may be too confusing and complicated for certain non-speaking individuals to understand. In this case, one may need to create name signs from that person's existing gestural repertoire, taking care not to overlap with existing sign vocabulary.

If a decision is made to develop a name sign for an individual, several types of sign forms should be avoided (Mindess, 1990). First, a name sign for a specific person should not be the same as that of another person in the group or immediate environment. Second, a name sign should not be identical to a commonly used sign in the sign language or system being employed. These two recommendations to avoid duplication of

---

3   The reaction of members of the American Deaf community to this hearing persons'
     approach — modifying an ASL sign with the handshape for the initial letter of a
     person's first name — has been mixed at best (Mindess, 1990).

4   See Appendix B for the list of handshapes used in our lexicon; see a sign language
     dictionary for the full manual alphabet of the sign language of your country.

sign forms should greatly lessen the chance of confusion over to whom or what one is referring. A third suggestion is that a name sign should not look like a gesture that is used in swearing or that has strong sexual connotations in that culture. Finally, name signs should not be difficult to form or located in places that are hard to see.

Why Is the Use of Manual Communication with Non-Speaking Hearing Individuals Relatively Recent?

Although this is a frequently asked question, it is based on an inaccurate impression. Signs were successfully taught to a limited number of hearing individuals with an intellectual disability at least as early as the 1840s (Bonvillian & Miller, 1995). Furthermore, there are reports of the use of the manual alphabet by hearing individuals who had lost their ability to speak because of medical illnesses, such as throat cancer, that go back hundreds of years (Lane, 1984). What has changed relatively recently is that efforts to use signs with non-speaking persons are more widespread.

Unfortunately, for many years most educators and linguists believed that language could only be expressed in speech or writing. Signs were considered inferior and unfit to carry linguistic structure in the same way as speech. In short, sign languages were not considered languages at all, but just a collection of readily understood gestures. Although these opinions were not based on scientific findings, the use of ASL and other sign languages in educational settings frequently was discouraged. These views had wide-ranging negative effects, especially for Deaf people, as instruction in sign language often was prohibited and all sign communication discouraged (see Chapter 3 for more information). Many hearing, but non-speaking, people who might have benefited from the use of signs also suffered as a consequence.

Once the sign languages of Deaf persons gained value and recognition within linguistic and educational circles, their use with other populations gained more widespread acceptance. However, many non-speaking individuals with an intellectual disability, autism spectrum disorder, cerebral palsy, or aphasia still had limited success with the acquisition of signs from full and genuine sign languages. This is probably attributable to these individuals' specific motor and cognitive impairments, as well as the formational complexity and abstract (or arbitrary) nature of many signs in those sign languages.

In response to these difficulties, several sign systems, among them the Simplified Sign System, have used the sign languages of Deaf persons as starting points in developing tailored communication systems for hearing, but non-speaking, persons. These systems adapt signs for use with various populations whose members are unable to successfully learn and use a full and genuine sign language. These creative efforts rely on the findings of a number of studies of individuals with specific disabilities that have only recently become available. In the past two decades, much has been learned about the acquisition of sign language formational parameters, as well as the motor difficulties of non-speaking persons. These advances have in turn had a positive effect on the use of sign languages or sign-communication systems.

Why Do Simplified Signs Work?

There are a number of reasons why the use of Simplified Signs may help individuals with communication limitations. Some of these reasons are particular to signs in the Simplified Sign System and others to sign languages more generally. First, many Simplified Signs are highly iconic: they visually resemble what they represent. For example, SMILE is conveyed by tracing a smile on one's face. Few words in spoken languages are onomatopoeic and thus sound like what they stand for. Because they often visually resemble their referents, Simplified Signs often are easier to understand and remember than spoken words (and many signs from full sign languages). Second, the handshapes and movements of Simplified Signs make them easier to produce than many of the manual signs from the full and genuine sign languages of Deaf people. Simplified Signs may therefore require less motor ability and fine motor coordination to produce accurately than signs in other languages or systems.

Third, signing depends on the use of one's arms, hands, fingers, body, and facial expression. Unlike the parts of the body involved in speech production (tongue, vocal cords, etc.), which are primarily internal, the body parts used in signing are located on the periphery of the anatomical system. This makes it easier for signs to be imitated as an individual can see himself or herself make the signs. A caregiver or teacher also can physically mold a user's hands into the correct handshape, place the hand in the proper location, and then trace the movement of the sign. A similar degree of control and guidance is not possible in the formation of spoken words. A fourth possible reason is that teachers may considerably slow down their rates of sign production, or even come to full stops, to help learners grasp correct sign formation. It is probably much easier to manipulate production rates in the visual and gestural modalities than in the auditory mode. Fifth, many individuals may simply be better at processing visual information than auditory information. Indeed, human memory retention for auditory events often is inferior to that for visual and tactile material (Bigelow & Poremba, 2014). A sixth reason is that because the specific neural mechanisms for signs in memory processes are not identical to those for speech (Rönnberg, Rudner, & Ingvar, 2004), then it is possible that the neural architecture involved in memory for signs might be more intact than that for spoken language, making signs a preferred modality in some instances. Finally, signs, when used with speech, may accentuate the message and make it easier to understand than speech alone.

The use of manual signs likely will be helpful to different persons for different reasons. A person who is not able to coordinate the mouth, lip, and tongue movements necessary for speaking may still have the motor abilities needed to form signs. In this case, signs may be easier because they do not require the same movements or types of fine motor coordination as speech. Even if the signs are imperfectly formed, they may still be more understandable to the user's communication partners than his or her speech. On the other hand, a child with a severe developmental speech delay may benefit from the use of signs because he or she cannot process sounds as well as he or she can process visual information.

What If One Arm or Hand of a Potential User Is Fully or Partially Paralyzed (or Unable to Be Used)?

Many Simplified Signs require the use of only one hand and arm. It does not matter whether this is the left hand or the right hand. Two-handed symmetrical signs (those signs whose handshapes and movements are mirror images of each other) can be made either with both hands or with the single hand that is available — the result is still understandable. For two-handed asymmetrical signs (those signs where one hand serves as a stationary base and the other hand performs the action of the sign), the signer uses the available hand to perform the main action of the sign. The stationary hand is either deleted or the sign is performed on top of an existing surface; for example, a table, a desk, one's chest, or the paralyzed arm itself. For those individuals with substantial bilateral impairment of their arms, it will likely be necessary to utilize an augmentative and/or alternative communication system other than manual signs until rehabilitation efforts have resulted in sufficient motor control of at least one arm.

Will Signing Keep My Child or Loved One from Learning to Speak or Regaining Speech Skills?

This is probably the most persistent myth or misconception about signs and sign learning (see the "Dispelling Myths" section in Chapter 5). It is based on the belief that signs and speech are incompatible — that our mind can either process one or the other, but not both — and that once a person chooses one of these modalities, the other will deteriorate or decline. For a long time, many clinicians and professional educators were convinced that manual signing would hinder the development of speech and speech skills. They assumed that the mind had limitations in processing language in more than one mode and that if a person learned signs then she would not be able to learn or understand spoken language.

There is no evidence to support this belief; on the contrary, many clinical reports show that signs and speech positively reinforce each other (Barrera et al., 1980; Blischak et al., 2003; Branson & Demchak, 2009; Carr et al., 1984; DeThorne et al., 2009; Dunst et al., 2011; Fouts, 1997; Fulwiler & Fouts, 1976; Goodwyn & Acredolo, 1998; Grove & Walker, 1990; Kouri, 1989; Launonen, 1996, 1998; Launonen & Grove, 2003; Layton & Savino, 1990; Millar et al., 2006; Pattison & Robertson, 2016; Remington & Clarke, 1983; Schaeffer et al., 1977, 1980; Sheehy & Duffy, 2009; Silverman, 1995; Singh et al., 2017; Vandereet et al., 2011). Furthermore, hearing children of Deaf parents are often reared by parents who use a sign language as their principal means of communication, yet these children are still able to acquire fluency in the spoken language of the larger hearing society in which they live. These children who acquire fluency in both a signed language and a spoken language are known as bimodal bilinguals.

In addition, using a manual sign requires understanding a mental symbol, much as using a spoken word does. Through signing, a person can acquire and develop symbolic skills that may then be used to learn and acquire a spoken language. Typically developing infants who are not yet able to speak can still understand symbols; using signs thus gives the child practice in communication and symbol use (Acredolo & Goodwyn, 1990). Not only does signing give children a chance to practice using language, but it even appears to enhance acquisition of spoken vocabulary items (Daniels, 2001). Sign-communication training with hearing, but non-speaking, persons also may help facilitate the processing of speech in the brains of these individuals and subsequently help them gain speech skills (Fouts, 1997). For all of these reasons, teachers, caregivers, and family members should not fear that learning signs will prevent a user from acquiring speech. One should keep in mind, however, that some users may never gain the ability to produce intelligible speech.

How Long Will It Take Me to Become Skilled at Using the Simplified Sign System?

A frequently expressed concern of teachers, staff, and caregivers is that learning to sign will require a substantial time commitment. While acquiring proficiency in a full or genuine sign language would probably require at least several years of study and practice (Kemp, 1998), this is unlikely to occur in the learning of Simplified Signs. First, the signs in the Simplified Sign System were selected or developed for their ease of production, learning, and recall. Overall, the handshapes and movements used in the formation of signs in the Simplified Sign System are easier to produce than the ones used in the formation of signs in a full sign language. This means that our system is not as formationally complex or as difficult as full sign languages. This should make Simplified Signs relatively easier to learn and produce. Also, many of the signs in our system are iconic or resemble the concepts for which they stand; this should make them easier to learn and remember than less iconic signs. Third, the Simplified Sign System is not a language and thus does not have its own grammatical or syntactical rules that need to be mastered. Instead, we recommend that teachers and caregivers combine Simplified Signs with their speech in an approach called key word signing. In this technique, teachers and caregivers continue to speak full sentences as they always have (in the grammatically correct sentence order of their spoken language) but they also sign the important words of the sentence as those words are uttered.

Another reason why teachers and caregivers should not be particularly worried about the time commitment involved in acquiring proficiency in Simplified Signs is that initially they will not need to know all of the signs or be particularly adept at signing them. Instead, only a small group of signs needs to be learned at any particular time. At the beginning of a sign-communication intervention program, teachers and caregivers will need to agree on which signs will be the first ones taught to the main user. The teachers and caregivers then learn how those particular signs are formed; once they are comfortable using this first group of signs, they teach those signs to the main user. Once the main user has achieved some command of these signs (which may take a while), teachers and caregivers can meet to decide which signs will be taught in the next group. This process is then repeated periodically as the main user's sign vocabulary continues to expand. Although the time commitment on the part of the teachers and caregivers to learning a relatively small number of Simplified Signs each week or month is unlikely to be a very substantial one, it should be recognized that some time will need to be set aside on a regular basis for deciding which signs will be taught and for learning how they are formed. Finally, it should be noted that this investment in time and effort to learning Simplified Signs probably will be small in comparison with the improved communication efficacy that is achieved.

Will It Be Difficult to Learn to Combine Gestures or Signs with Spoken Words?

Nearly all individuals who speak accompany their speech with gestures (McNeill, 1992). For example, a speaker might accompany the sentence

"She went up the hill, looked around, and then ran back down" with three gestures: an upward moving gesture, a pantomimic look-around gesture, and a downward rushing gesture. Most speakers are perfectly comfortable combining speech and gestures in this way. In fact, when speakers want to make sure that they get their point across, they will often make much greater use of hand, body, and facial gestures (Kendon, 2014). When giving directions, for instance, a person will often point in the proper direction and use other gestures to convey additional information about the trip. By using gestures and pantomimic signs, people can express their need to use a telephone, drive a car, find a restroom, or convey feelings of illness. Such non-spoken communication takes place in many forms and in very different arenas of interaction (Remland, 2004). Gestures can even help two people communicate who do not speak the same language. Furthermore, there is a growing recognition among researchers and educators that when speech is accompanied by gestures, communication is significantly enhanced (Hostetter, 2011; Launonen & Grove, 2019). In fact, the opposite is also true — when forbidden from using gestures along with their speech, people find it much harder to access or convey complicated information (Pine, Bird, & Kirk, 2007). Given the highly iconic nature of many Simplified Signs, caregivers and teachers should not find it too difficult to incorporate them into their spoken language interactions with potential users of the system.

How Does One Know If a Person Is Making Reasonable Progress in the Use of the Simplified Sign System? What Can Be Expected?

As discussed previously in the "Guidelines for Using the Simplified Sign System" section, it takes time for an individual to become accustomed to using signs or to learning specific signs. This is especially true for persons with motor impairments and other disabilities (Dennis et al., 1982; Dunn, 1982; Grove et al., 2019). Progress during this period will most likely be slow and gradual and may be contingent upon the sign learner's degree of fine motor control. To better assess a person's progress, it is helpful to prepare a communication plan, maintain a record of signs learned and progress made in communicating with signs, and document any secondary effects that may result from the introduction of signs.

Preparing a communication plan. Decide which signs should be taught, when they should be taught, how they will be taught, who will teach them, and where the signs will be used outside of the teaching/learning situations (this should be in as many places as conveniently possible). Also, set goals for sign recognition and spontaneous production by the user, as well as appropriate goals for all communication partners. Allow enough time for everyone to become accustomed to the Simplified Sign System. Remember that the communication plan must be part of a general intervention strategy. Communication is not a separate component in the development of a person; it is integral to that person's identity and development. The fact that communication is part of the general intervention plan invites all of the individual's communication partners (e.g., parents, counselors, educators, workshop supervisors, occupational therapists, speech-language pathologists, friends) to assume responsibility. Make sure that these people know and use signs with the main learner and have acquired a style and technique of encouraging the production of signs. When assessing progress, verify that the use of Simplified Signs will not be just a separate component of the intervention plan by ensuring the commitment and involvement of all communication partners to using signs.

Maintaining a record. Keep records of which signs are taught, when they are understood by the main user, when they are produced or made by him or her for the first time, how often they are employed, and the errors made when forming them. When evaluating progress, keep a record of all the signs taught and note which ones are understood and which ones are produced. Typically, individuals with disabilities will understand more signs than they are able to correctly produce themselves.

It is also important to determine whether the main user employs the signs he or she has learned in new settings he or she encounters and with additional persons with whom he or she interacts. If generalization of sign learning has not occurred, then specific procedures designed to facilitate such generalization will need to be added to the sign intervention program. These procedures include varying the settings where sign learning takes place, varying the learner's communication partners, and changing the conditions of instruction and materials used.[5] In general, a user will understand a sign before he or she begins to produce it spontaneously. In some instances, a user will never produce a certain sign, even though he or she understands it. Such a person may rely heavily on producing a few "favorite" signs to convey a wide range of information in diverse situations. If this person shows any interest in or need for another sign, then make an effort to teach him or her a new one. Regardless, it is important to compare your records periodically with the goals set in the communication plan and determine whether previous expectations were realistic or whether they were instead underestimating the main user's potential. Make adjustments as necessary.

Documenting secondary effects. Keep an eye out for changes in the main user's behavior that may be an indirect result of learning Simplified Signs. Often the learning and use of a sign-communication system reduces problem or challenging behaviors (tantrums, soiling incidents, etc.) because the person is more successful in conveying his or her needs or desires and consequently feels less frustration. The main user may also show more interest in the surrounding environment, initiate more interactions, or ask more questions. When assessing progress, see if there have been any non-linguistic or collateral effects in the user's behavior and interactions with others.

Concluding Remarks

In writing the present chapter, we were thinking primarily of how to teach Simplified Signs to children with cognitive and motor disabilities. Indeed, we most sincerely hope that if the above guidelines and recommendations are followed, then many of these youngsters will show greatly increased communication skills. While we believe that many of our suggested procedures will work well with quite diverse populations, we recognize that they are not for everyone. Older individuals who have lost their hearing, for example, are quite different

---

5   For additional information on facilitating sign generalization, see the "Teaching Generalization and Spontaneous Communication Skills" section in Chapter 5 and the "Recommendations for Enhancing the Sign-Learning Environment" section in Chapter 4.

in their learning abilities from young children with autism spectrum disorder. It would therefore be a mistake to insist on a single training or teaching approach for all non-speaking or minimally verbal individuals. In addition, the characteristics of individual sign learners may change over time, necessitating modifications in the teaching strategies or techniques that are employed. This may be the case because as children grow older, their interests and skill levels often change. Furthermore, some individuals may gain or regain speech skills or show improved motor control of their arms and hands. As a consequence, teachers, caregivers, and family members may need to modify our recommended procedures for teaching and using the Simplified Sign System to meet these individuals' particular needs. Regardless, we wish everyone who uses Simplified Signs the best possible outcome in their lives and communicative interactions, and we look forward to your helpful feedback.

Appendix A

Sign Language Dictionaries
and Other Sources

The following is a listing of the sign language dictionaries and other sources we consulted when selecting the initial 1000 signs to use in the Simplified Sign System:

Acredolo, L. P., & Goodwyn, S. W. (1996). *Baby signs: How to talk with your baby before your baby can talk*. Chicago, IL: Contemporary Books.

Bakken, A., & Holm, S. G. (1985). *Barnas tegn-ordbok, vol. 1*. Bergen, Norway: Døves Forlag.

Barakat, R. A. (1975). *The Cistercian Sign Language: A study in non-verbal communication*. Kalamazoo, MI: Cistercian Publications.

Bergmann, R., Hansen, B., Nielsen, K., & Engberg-Pedersen, E. (eds.). (1992). *Tegn til børn: Tegnordbog for forældre og pædagoger*. København, Denmark: Døves Center for Total Kommunikation.

Chao, C., Chu, H., & Liu, C. (eds.). (1988). *Taiwan natural sign language*. Republic of China: Deaf Sign Language Research Association.

Costello, E. (2000). *Random House Webster's American Sign Language medical dictionary*. New York, NY: Random House.

Duffy, L. (1977). *An innovative approach to the development of communication skills for severely speech handicapped cerebral palsied children*. Unpublished master's thesis, University of Nevada, Las Vegas, NV.

Eastman, G. C., with M. Noretsky & S. Censoplano. (1989). *From mime to sign*. Silver Spring, MD: T. J. Publishers.

Edinburgh and East of Scotland Society for the Deaf (ed.). (1985). *Seeing the signs! in Scotland*. Edinburgh, Scotland: Edinburgh & East of Scotland Society for the Deaf.

Grove, N., & Walker, M. (1990). The Makaton Vocabulary: Using manual signs and graphic symbols to develop interpersonal communication. *Augmentative and Alternative Communication*, 6, 15–28, https://doi.org/10.1080/074346190 12331275284

Gustason, G., & Zawolkow, E. (eds.). (1982). *Signos para el inglés exacto* (M. S. Cargill, Trans.). Los Alamitos, CA: Modern Signs Press.

Hadley, L. F. (1893). *Indian sign talk*. Chicago, IL: Baker.

Henson, R. (1983). *Las señas de los sordomudos de México*. Mexico: Ronald Henson.

Hofsinde, R. (1956). *Indian Sign Language*. New York, NY: William Morrow.

Hussain, M. T., & Dossani, A. (eds.). (1987). *A dictionary of Pakistan Sign Language: Focus on Karachi*. Karachi, Pakistan: ABSA School for the Deaf.

Japanese Federation of the Deaf, Institute for Sign Language Studies (ed.). (1991). *An English dictionary of basic Japanese signs*. Tokyo, Japan: Japanese Federation of the Deaf.

Jeanes, R. C., & Reynolds, B. E. (eds.). (1982). *Dictionary of Australasian signs for communication with the deaf*. Melbourne, Victoria, Australia: Victorian School for Deaf Children.

Johnston, T. (1989). *Auslan dictionary: A dictionary of the sign language of the Australian deaf community*. Petersham, New South Wales, Australia: Deafness Resources, Australia.

Kennedy, G., with R. Arnold & P. Dugdale. (eds.). (1997). *A dictionary of New Zealand Sign Language*. Auckland, New Zealand: Auckland University Press and Bridget Williams Books.

Lancz, E. (1999). *Dictionary of Hungarian Sign Language* (S. Berbeco, Ed.). Budapest, Hungary: National Association for the Deaf and Hard-of-Hearing, and SHL Hungary Kft., Budapest.

Loncke, F., Nijs, M., & Smet, L. (1998). *Spreken met ondersteuning van gebaren: Het handboek* [Manual signing supporting speech: The handbook]. Leuven, Belgium: Garant.

National Association for the Deaf & Sign Language Tutors Association of Ireland. (eds.). (1992). *Sign on: Basic signs used by Irish deaf people*. Dublin, Ireland: National Association for the Deaf and the Sign Language Tutors Association of Ireland.

Nieder-Heitmann, N. (1980). *Talking to the deaf: A visual manual of standardized signs for the deaf in South Africa*. Staatsdrukker, Pretoria, Republic of South Africa: Department of Education and Training & S.A. National Council for the Deaf.

O'Rourke, T. J., & Parsons, F. M. (1973). *Curso básico en comunicación manual: Programa de adiestramiento en comunicación*. Silver Spring, MD: National Association of the Deaf.

Paget, R., Gorman, P., & Paget, G. (1976). *The Paget Gorman sign system* (6th ed.). London, U.K.: Association for Experiment in Deaf Education, London.

Peydro, F. J. P. (1981). *Diccionario mímico español*. Valladolid, Spain: Sever-Cuesta.

Riekehof, L. L. (1978). *The joy of signing: The new illustrated guide for mastering sign language and the manual alphabet*. Springfield, MO: Gospel Publishing House.

Romeo, O. (1991). *Dizionario dei segni: La lingua dei segni in 1400 immagini*. Bologna, Italy: Zanichelli.

Ross, P., Devkota, N. K., & Maskey, D. M. (1989). *Nepali Sign Language dictionary*. Naxal, Kathmandu, Nepal: The Welfare Society for the Hearing Impaired, School for the Deaf.

Sandager, O. (1986). *Sign languages around the world*. North Hollywood, CA: OK Publishing.

Seton, E. T. (1918). *Sign talk: A universal signal code, without apparatus, for use in the army, the navy, camping, hunting, and daily life*. Garden City, NY: Doubleday, Page.

Skelly, M. (1979). *Amer-Ind gestural code based on universal American Indian Hand Talk*. New York, NY: Elsevier North Holland.

Sternberg, M. L. A. (1981). *American Sign Language: A comprehensive dictionary*. New York, NY: Harper & Row.

Stokoe, W. C., Jr., Casterline, D. C., & Croneberg, C. G. (1965). *A dictionary of American Sign Language on linguistic principles*. Washington, DC: Gallaudet College Press.

Suwanarat, M., & Reilly, C. (1986). *The Thai Sign Language dictionary: Book one* (Owen Wrigley, Ed.). Bangkok, Thailand: National Association of the Deaf in Thailand and International Human Assistance Programs/Thailand.

Tanzania Association of the Deaf (ed.). (1993). *The Tanzania Sign Language dictionary*. Dar es Salaam, Tanzania: Tanzania Association of the Deaf.

Tomkins, W. (1931/1969). *Indian Sign Language*. New York, NY: Dover Publications. [Corrected republication of the 1931 fifth edition originally published in San Diego, CA under the title *Universal Indian Sign Language of the Plains Indians of North America*.]

Tytgat, M.-G., Peltier, E., Wechseler, R., & Masquelier, M. (1995). *Coghamo: Lexique adulte*. Brussels, Belgium: Centre La Famille.

Walker, M. (1977). *Line drawing illustrations for the revised Makaton vocabulary*. Action, London, U.K.: Royal Association of the Deaf and Dumb.

World Federation of the Deaf, Unification of Signs Commission (ed.). (1975). *Gestuno: International Sign Language of the deaf*. Carlisle, England: The British Deaf Association on behalf of The World Federation of the Deaf.

Appendix B
Handshapes

Handshape refers to the configuration or physical form/shape of the hand(s) during the production of a sign. Below you will find the written descriptions, as well as drawings (from the viewer's perspective), of the primary handshapes used in the Simplified Sign System. The signer's right hand is depicted. (See also "Tips for Using the Sign Lexicon and Sign Index" in Chapter 10, Volume 2, for a more detailed discussion of each handshape, along with any acceptable variations that may exist.)

Baby O-hand: the index finger and thumb are curved and touch at their tips from an otherwise closed hand.

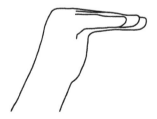

Bent-hand: the fingers are together and extended at a right angle with respect to the palm.

 https://doi.org/10.11647/OBP.0205.11

C-hand: the fingers are together and curved, with the thumb opposite the fingers.

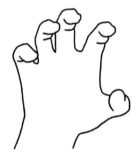

Claw-hand: the fingers are spread apart and bent.

Curved-hand: the fingers and thumb are together and curved.

Fist: the hand forms a fist.

Flat-hand: the hand is flat with fingers together and extended.

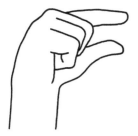

G-hand: the index finger and thumb are extended from an otherwise closed hand and are parallel.

H-hand: the index and middle fingers are together and extended from an otherwise closed hand.

Horns-hand: the little finger and thumb are extended from an otherwise closed hand.

L-hand: the index finger and thumb are extended from an otherwise closed hand and form a right angle.

Okay-hand: the index finger and thumb are curved and touch at their tips from an otherwise open hand.

Pointing-hand: the index finger is extended from an otherwise closed hand.

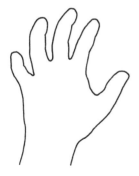

Spread curved-hand: the fingers are spread apart and curved.

Spread- or 5-hand: the hand is flat with fingers spread apart and extended.

Tapered- or O-hand: the fingers are together and curved, with the finger tips touching the thumb tip.

V-hand: the index and middle fingers are spread apart and extended from an otherwise closed hand in the shape of a "V."

Appendix C
Palm, Finger, and Knuckle Orientation

Palm Orientation

Palm orientation describes the positioning of the palm(s) of the hand(s) during the production of a sign; in other words, the direction each palm faces as a sign is being formed. Below you will find the written descriptions, as well as drawings, of the common orientations of the palm(s) during signing. (See also "Tips for Using the Sign Lexicon and Sign Index" in Chapter 10, Volume 2.) A flat-hand (the hand is flat with fingers together and extended) is used in the illustrations, which are drawn from the viewer's perspective. In most instances, the signer's right hand is depicted.

Palm facing down: the position of the hand when the palm faces down toward the floor.

Palm facing in: the position of the hand when the palm faces in toward the signer.

 https://doi.org/10.11647/OBP.0205.12

Palm facing out: the position of the hand when the palm faces out or away from the signer.

Palm facing to the side: the position of the hand when the palm faces to one side or the other. (For a signer who uses the right hand as the dominant hand, the natural position is with the palm of that hand facing to his or her left. For a signer who uses the left hand as the dominant hand, the natural position is with the palm of that hand facing to his or her right.)

Palm facing to the side (rare): the position of the right hand when the palm faces to the right, with the little finger above the thumb (i.e., the little finger is closer to the ceiling). Or, the position of the left hand when the palm faces to the left, with the little finger above the thumb (i.e., the little finger is closer to the ceiling).

Palm facing up: the position of the hand when the palm faces up toward the ceiling.

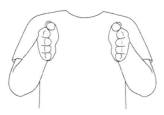

Palms facing each other (and to opposite sides): for two-handed signs, the position of the hands when they are side by side with the palms facing each other and toward opposite sides. (In this example, the fingers point forward, but it is also possible for the fingers to point up or down.)

Palms facing each other (up and down): for two-handed signs, the position of the hands when one is above the other, with the palms facing toward each other. The palm of the upper hand faces down, and the palm of the lower hand faces up. (In this example, the fingers point forward, but it is also possible for the fingers to point to the right or to the left.)

Finger/Knuckle Orientation

Finger/knuckle orientation describes the positioning of the finger(s) or knuckles of the hand during the production of a sign; in other words, the direction the finger(s) or knuckles point as a sign is being formed. (See also "Tips for Using the Sign Lexicon and Sign Index" in Chapter 10, Volume 2.) In the written descriptions of how the signs are formed, we often include the orientation of the finger(s) or knuckles because palm orientation alone may not be specific enough. For example, consider the following (a flat-hand is used for the illustrations, which are drawn from the viewer's perspective):

Palm facing down, fingers pointing forward: the position of the hand when the palm faces down toward the floor and the fingers point out or away from the signer.

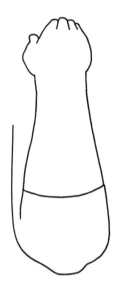

Palm facing down, fingers pointing in: the position of the hand when the palm faces down toward the floor and the fingers point in toward the signer.

Palm facing down, fingers pointing to the (left) side: the position of the hand when the palm faces down toward the floor and the fingers point to the signer's left side.

Palm facing down, fingers pointing to the (right) side: the position of the hand when the palm faces down toward the floor and the fingers point to the signer's right side.

Palm facing down, fingers pointing diagonally forward and to the opposite (left) side: the position of the right hand when the palm faces down toward the floor and the fingers point diagonally forward to the opposite (left) side.

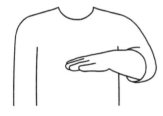

Palm facing down, fingers pointing diagonally forward and to the opposite (right) side: the position of the left hand when the palm faces down toward the floor and the fingers point diagonally forward to the opposite (right) side.

Generally, the most natural hand orientation when a sign is made in front of the body is with the fingers pointing diagonally forward and to the opposite side.

All of the above examples use a palm down orientation, yet the orientation of the fingers varies. Since the fingers are not always extended during the production of a sign, we have also included drawings of the various orientations of the knuckles. The convention used for describing finger/knuckle orientation mirrors the convention used for describing palm orientation. A pointing-hand (the index finger is extended from an otherwise closed hand) is used in the finger orientation illustrations and a fist (the hand forms a fist) is used in the knuckle orientation illustrations. Both are drawn from the viewer's perspective, with the signer's right hand depicted in most instances.

Finger/knuckles pointing down, palm facing in: the finger/knuckles point down toward the floor and the palm faces in toward the signer.

Finger/knuckles pointing down, palm facing out: the finger/knuckles point down toward the floor and the palm faces out or away from the signer.

Finger/knuckles pointing forward: the finger/knuckles point out or away from the signer.

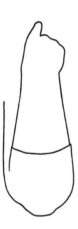

Finger/knuckles pointing in: the finger/ knuckles point in toward the signer.

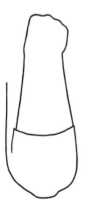

Finger/knuckles pointing to the (left) side: the finger/knuckles point to the signer's left side.

Finger/knuckles pointing to the (right) side: the finger/knuckles point to the signer's right side.

Finger/knuckles pointing up: the finger/knuckles point up toward the ceiling.

Palm facing down, finger/knuckles pointing diagonally forward and to the opposite (left) side: the position of the right hand when the palm faces down toward the floor and the finger/knuckles point diagonally forward to the opposite (left) side.

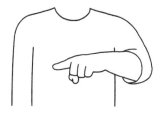

Palm facing down, finger/knuckles pointing diagonally forward and to the opposite (right) side: the position of the left hand when the palm faces down toward the floor and the finger/knuckles point diagonally forward to the opposite (right) side.

Again, the most natural hand orientation when a sign is made in front of the body is with the finger or knuckles pointing diagonally forward and to the opposite side.

Glossary

AAC — abbreviation for augmentative and alternative communication.

Abstract concepts — mental representations that cannot be directly experienced through the senses (sight, hearing, touch, smell, taste); for example, honor, loyalty, and imagination. Abstract concepts typically are more difficult to express iconically in a sign-communication system than physical objects or overt actions.

Accelerative Integrated Methodology (AIM) — a relatively recent approach to foreign language teaching and learning. This approach incorporates pantomimic or iconic gestures together with listening and speaking in the learning process.

Acquired childhood aphasia — a loss or disturbance of language function that occurs in childhood after the onset of language acquisition; it is often the result of a head injury, stroke, infection, tumor, seizure activity, or progressive disorder.

Acquired epileptic aphasia — also known as Landau-Kleffner syndrome.

Acquired neurological disorder — an abnormal or disturbed function of the nervous system whose onset begins after birth and is not genetic in origin. These disorders can result from traumatic brain injuries (TBIs), infectious diseases of the central nervous system (e.g., encephalitis), electrical shock, near drowning, drug overdoses, and exposure to toxic chemicals.

Active hand — the hand that moves or performs the principal action during the production of a manual sign. See dominant hand and hand preference.

 https://doi.org/10.11647/OBP.0205.13

Adaptive behaviors — positive actions or behaviors such as increased attention span, bowel/bladder control, self-help skills, social interaction, and emotional control. The ability to adjust to or apply familiar skills to new situations (generalization).

Adult-acquired apraxia of speech — a neuromotor speech disorder acquired in adulthood (rather than during the developmental stages of childhood) consisting of loss of or impairment in the ability to coordinate the movements involved in speech and that results in impaired speaking or an inability to speak. Adult-acquired apraxia of speech is typically the product of a stroke or brain injury. See apraxia of speech.

Agent — in linguistics, the actor or being that performs the action of the verb within a sentence.

Agglutination of signs — the combination of two or more signs to convey one concept; for example, using the signs HOUSE plus BOOK to represent the concept *library*. See compound signs.

Aided communication — communication systems that rely on pictures, real objects, electronic devices, voice synthesizers, speech-generating devices, and/or other equipment. Compare with unaided communication.

Akbar — sixteenth-century emperor of Hindustan who conducted an experiment to determine humankind's most fundamental language. By rearing children in silence, he hoped to resolve the question of whether speech arises spontaneously in children and, if so, which language they would speak.

Alphabetic language — a language that uses characters or symbols to represent speech sounds in their written form. The letters of the modern English alphabet are derived from the Roman alphabet.

Alternative communication system — a communication system meant to serve as an alternative or replacement for speech or signs; for example, the use of a speech-generating device in place of a person's use of natural speech.

American Indian Hand Talk — also known as Plains Indian Sign Language (PISL) or North American Indian Sign Language.

American School for the Deaf — the first public school for deaf students in the United States; it was founded in 1817 by Laurent Clerc and Thomas H. Gallaudet.

American Sign Language (ASL) — the primary language of the Deaf community in the United States; it has its own linguistic structure (grammar and phonology) that is quite different from English and other spoken languages.

Amer-Ind — a sign-communication system based on signs from Plains Indian Sign Language (PISL); many of its signs are clearly iconic. Originally devised by Madge Skelly for use with people whose tongues had been surgically removed, Amer-Ind was later adapted for use with individuals with aphasia or other language impairments.

Amodal symbol processing — the view that symbols or concepts are processed in the brain without regard to the modality or form in which they were learned or used. In this approach, symbols are abstract notions that are devoid of specific forms or modality.

Angelman syndrome — a form of severe or profound intellectual disability that typically involves an absence of speech and a loss of coordination of muscle movement; it is a relatively rare genetic disorder.

Aphasia — a disorder that affects the production and/or understanding of language; often the result of a stroke, brain infection, tumor, head injury, or lack of oxygen. The type of aphasia varies depending on the site and extent of the damage. Milder forms are often known as dysphasia.

Applied behavior analysis (ABA) — an approach often used in the behavioral training or treatment of non-speaking or minimally verbal individuals with autism spectrum disorder (or other disabilities). This approach typically first involves systematic observation to determine what behaviors are beneficial to the individual and should be increased as well as what behaviors are harmful and should be eliminated. Therapists and parents then reward behaviors deemed beneficial, and may use mild punishment or extinction to reduce the frequency of or eliminate harmful behaviors. Positive behaviors are developed in the individual through rewards for behaviors that are closer and closer to the desired new behaviors in a process called shaping.

Apraxia — a neuromotor disorder in which a person has lost the ability to accurately and purposefully control movements and motor configurations in the absence of muscle weakness or paralysis. Apraxia is often the result of a stroke, brain infection, tumor, or head injury. This disorder may involve the limbs and/or oral-motor movements. Also known as dyspraxia.

Apraxia of speech — a neuromotor speech disorder that results in impaired speaking or an inability to speak. In this disorder, one has a loss of or impairment in the ability to plan, coordinate, or execute the actions or movements involved in speech production; there are often disruptions in the timing and rhythm of speech. Also known as verbal apraxia (or dyspraxia).

Apraxia test battery — a series of tests designed to evaluate an individual's purposeful gross and fine motor skills.

Arbitrary name signs — name signs that are not based on any personally identifiable characteristics of an individual. These name signs often use the handshape for the initial letter of the person's first name and are made in the neutral signing space or on the arms, hands, head, or torso. Compare with descriptive name signs.

Arbitrary signs — signs with no clearly discernible ties to the concepts they represent.

Arcuate fasciculus — the white matter tract (or bundle of nerve fibers) of the brain that connects the principal language comprehension region of the brain (Wernicke's area) with the principal speech-generating region of the brain (Broca's area). The lack of development of the arcuate fasciculus may explain the absence of spoken language in many children with Angelman syndrome. Persons who have certain forms of aphasia and children with autism also have abnormalities of the arcuate fasciculus.

Articulation — the motor act of producing or forming speech sounds (in auditory-vocal languages) or, less frequently, signs (in visual-motor languages).

Articulatory disorder — an impairment or disturbance in speech production, commonly caused by structural anomalies (e.g., cleft palate or lip), hearing impairment, weakness of the oral musculature, or delayed onset of language.

Articulatory gestures — the locations, shapes/formations, and movements of the mouth, lips, tongue, jaw, and vocal tract during the production of speech sounds.

ASD — abbreviation for autism spectrum disorder.

ASL — abbreviation for American Sign Language.

Asperger, Hans — clinician who conducted important early investigations of children with autism. He described children with difficulties in social interaction and repetitive behaviors, but otherwise the children varied across a wide range of abilities.

Asperger syndrome — an autism spectrum disorder (ASD). Persons identified with Asperger syndrome historically were depicted as experiencing social interaction difficulties, but having average or above-average intelligence and intact formal language abilities. In the past, many researchers and clinicians considered the diagnosis of Asperger syndrome to be largely the same as that of high-functioning autism.

Asymmetrical signs — signs made with two hands and whose handshapes, movements, and/or locations are asymmetrical or different on each hand. Also known as two-handed asymmetrical signs.

Ataxia — a loss of or inability to coordinate muscular movement. Ataxia is often present in individuals with Angelman syndrome or cerebral palsy.

Attention-deficit hyperactivity disorder (ADHD) — a disorder that is typically diagnosed in childhood and that often persists into adolescence and/or adulthood. ADHD may negatively impact an individual's attention span or ability to sustain attention (he or she often is easily distracted, forgetful, or experiences difficulty focusing or finishing tasks), impulse control (is impatient or prone to emotional outbursts), and behavioral regulation (is hyperactive, overly talkative, or unable to sit still).

Attrition rate — in this book, the rate at which research participants withdraw from or fail to complete a scientific study before that study ends.

Auditory memory — the ability to store and remember information obtained through hearing; the capacity to perceive, encode, rehearse, and recall acoustic- or sound-based material. Auditory memory is related to phonological memory and verbal memory.

Auditory processing — the ability of a person to successfully distinguish, recognize, understand, and remember environmental or speech sounds. Auditory processing is related to phonological processing and verbal processing.

Auditory sequencing — the ability of a person to process and correctly order a succession or connected series of environmental or speech sounds. Auditory sequencing is related to phonological sequencing and verbal sequencing.

Auditory-temporal processing deficit — an inability or a decreased ability to understand speech or recognize and process sounds that are present for only a short duration.

Auditory training — instruction that aims to improve the ability to perceive, distinguish, identify, and interpret sounds important to spoken language processing.

Auditory-vocal languages — also known as spoken languages.

Auditory-vocal modality — the use of one's hearing and mind to perceive and process sounds or speech and the use of one's voice to transmit information. See speech modality.

Augmentative and alternative communication (AAC) — systems and approaches that support and enhance typical communication forms such as signs or speech (augmentative) or that provide a substitute for them (alternative).

Augmentative communication system — a communication system meant to serve as a support to the main system of communication, which is often either speech or signs. Augmentative communication may include the use of pictures, gestures, manual signs, eye blinking, and digitized or pre-recorded speech output.

Australian Sign Language — the primary language of some members of the Deaf communities in Australia. Also known as Auslan or Australasian Sign Language.

Autism — a developmental disorder first evident in infancy or early childhood that results in social, behavioral, cognitive, motor, and communication impairments or atypicalities. The identifying characteristics often include limited social affect, bizarre mannerisms or gestures, a preoccupation with maintaining sameness in the environment, and difficulty in using language. Classic autism was first identified by Leo Kanner. Autism is believed to have a strong genetic component and to be the result of an organic or neurochemical dysfunction of the brain. Also known as childhood autism.

Autism spectrum disorder (ASD) — the relatively recent view that the characteristics or behaviors that constitute autism occur across a wide range. These characteristics include difficulties in reciprocal social-interaction skills, communication atypicalities, and the frequent presence of repetitive and stereotyped behaviors. In previous years, clinicians and investigators often identified individuals as having more delimited disorders, such as Asperger syndrome and childhood autism.

Autonomous speech — spoken language production that is essentially independent of external control or influence. These vocal utterances are not reflexive cries and do not need to rely on gestures for communicative support.

Aversives — in behavior modification approaches, aversives are noxious or punishing stimuli that make responses less likely to occur in the future.

Axon — the part of a neuron (nerve cell) that conducts impulses away from the cell body to other neurons, glands, or muscles.

Babbling — an important stage in the typical language development of an infant (whether deaf or hearing). Babbling consists of the speech-like sounds or sign-like movements produced by infants primarily between four and twelve months of age. Babbling may include the vocalization of syllables, in which a consonant and a vowel sound are combined (in auditory-vocal language development).

Baby O-hand — a sign handshape used in the Simplified Sign System (SSS) and by babies learning to sign. The index finger and thumb are curved and touch at their tips from an otherwise closed hand; similar to a pincer grip.

Baby-signing — a relatively recent trend in which hearing parents teach their hearing infants to sign as a way to enhance communicative exchanges with their babies before they can communicate effectively through speech.

Basal ganglia — a system of subcortical structures located in each cerebral hemisphere that are important in the production of planned actions or movements. The basal ganglia receive input from the cerebral cortex and send output to motor centers of the brain.

Base — in signing, the hand or arm (and at times an object) that is part of a sign's production, but which does not move. This stationary hand or arm is acted upon by the other hand or arm.

Behavior modification (speech) training — the process of changing a person's behavior by offering rewards for desired behaviors, and, at times, punishment for undesired ones. Often used to teach speech skills. Also known as operant (speech) training.

Belgian Sign Language — the primary language of some members of the Deaf communities in Belgium. In recent years, some researchers have asserted that there are two separate sign languages in Belgium: Flemish Sign Language (also known as Vlaamse Gebarentaal or VGT) in the northern, Dutch-speaking part of the country and French Belgian Sign Language (also known as Langue des Signes Belge Francophone or LSFB) in the southern, French-speaking region.

Benhaven — an educational institution for children and youth with autism located in New Haven, Connecticut. Benhaven instructors and staff members conducted pioneering programs using manual signs with deaf and hearing individuals with autism.

Bent-hand — a sign handshape used in the Simplified Sign System (SSS); the fingers are together and extended at a right angle with respect to the palm.

Bilateral — on or of two sides; on both sides of the body.

Bimodal bilinguals — persons who acquire fluency in two languages that have distinct modalities. In this book, refers to those persons who become fluent in both a signed language such as American Sign Language (ASL) (visual-motor modality) and a spoken language such as English (speech modality). Such individuals typically learn to sign and to speak during their childhoods.

Bimodal input — information that is provided in two different modalities; for example, signing and speaking at the same time (a process known as simultaneous communication) provides information in the gestural (or visual-motor) modality and in the speech (or auditory-vocal) modality. Providing information in more than one modality may increase the likelihood that the information is retained in memory.

Birth language — the language to which an infant is exposed from birth onward.

Blissymbols — a graphic symbol communication system initially widely used with non-speaking children with cerebral palsy. It is based on a "universal" pictographic system designed by Charles Bliss. See pictographic line drawings.

Brain stem — the part of the brain that is between the cerebrum and spinal cord. The brain stem is composed of the thalamus, midbrain, pons, and medulla oblongata. The brain stem is involved in regulating many of the body's basic life processes (e.g., breathing, blood pressure, heartbeat).

British Sign Language (BSL) — the primary language of the Deaf community in Great Britain.

Broca's aphasia — a form of expressive language loss or nonfluent aphasia in which persons experience great difficulty with the production of speech, although their understanding of speech may not be impaired. Persons with Broca's aphasia typically have lesions in their left frontal lobes.

Cabeza de Vaca, Álvar Núñez —sixteenth-century Spaniard who utilized the sign-communication system of the Native Americans of the Great Plains in his travels throughout North America. See Plains Indian Sign Language (PISL).

Case study — research that focuses on one individual or a small number of individuals.

Central nervous system — the brain and spinal cord, which receive sensory information and relay nerve impulses to control motor actions.

Central symbolic deficit — a type of aphasia in which a person has difficulty understanding and using various symbol forms in addition to words; examples of these other symbol forms are musical notes and military insignia.

Cerebellum — a part of the hindbrain situated between the back of the cerebrum and the brain stem. The cerebellum is involved in muscular coordination (including the timing and sequencing of complex motor movements), the maintenance of equilibrium, and the modulation of various cognitive processes (including language).

Cerebral cortex — the outermost layer of the cerebral hemispheres and the part of the brain responsible for most mental processes.

Cerebral hemorrhage — extensive bleeding from the rupture of a blood vessel in the brain. See stroke.

Cerebral palsy — a disability characterized by a loss of or decrease in voluntary muscular control and coordination as a result of brain damage. Some persons with cerebral palsy may have other disabling conditions, such as an impairment in hearing or intellectual disability. Common types of cerebral palsy include spastic unilateral or spastic bilateral CP, which is characterized by increased muscle tone and stiff muscles (subtypes include diplegia and quadriplegia). Dyskinetic CP is characterized by uncontrollable movements and muscle tone that can alternate between too tight and too loose (subtypes include athetoid, dystonic, and choreoathetoid). Ataxic CP is characterized by problems with balance and coordination. A person may also have a mixed form of cerebral palsy in which symptoms of two or more types are present.

Cerebrovascular accident (CVA) — also known as a stroke.

Cerebrum — the largest, upper portion of the brain; it consists of two hemispheres. The cerebrum is primarily responsible for mental processes in humans. See forebrain.

Challenging behaviors — also known as maladaptive behaviors.

C-hand — a sign handshape used in the Simplified Sign System (SSS); the fingers are together and curved, with the thumb opposite the fingers.

Chereme — also known as a sign phoneme.

Childhood apraxia of speech — a disorder in which children experience great difficulty in the production and sequencing of speech sounds. It is evidently based in deficits in the planning and programming of the movements underlying speech. Also known as childhood dyspraxia (of speech), childhood verbal apraxia (or dyspraxia), developmental apraxia of speech, and developmental articulatory apraxia.

Childhood autism — also known as autism or autism spectrum disorder.

Chromosomes — rod-shaped structures containing DNA located in the nucleus of an organism's cells. Chromosomes contain an organism's genes, the units of hereditary transmission.

Chronic aphasia — a loss of language ability that persists over a long period and does not noticeably or substantially improve with time.

Classifiers — in sign language research, particular handshapes in a sign language that symbolically represent a general class of items (such as vehicles, animals, objects, or people). Classifiers are typically used to convey an object's location and/or movement in space.

Claw-hand — a sign handshape used in the Simplified Sign System (SSS); the fingers are spread apart and bent.

Cleft lip or palate — an opening in the upper lip or palate (the hard and soft portions of the roof of the mouth); it occurs during early fetal development when the tissue of the lip or palate fails to fuse. A cleft lip or palate often interferes with one's ability to produce recognizable speech.

Clerc, Laurent — a prominent teacher of deaf students, he taught initially at the school for deaf students in Paris. Clerc was persuaded by Thomas H. Gallaudet to move to the United States, where together they founded the first American public school for deaf students (the American School for the Deaf) in 1817. Clerc's knowledge and use of French signs greatly influenced the development of American Sign Language (ASL).

Cochlea — a coiled structure in the inner ear that plays an essential role in the reception and transmission of sound to the brain. The cochlea transforms sound vibrations into electrical signals that then travel to the brain.

Cognitive impairment — a disruption of one's cognitive functions or thought processes, such as receiving, processing, analyzing, and understanding information.

Collateral effects — in this book, the secondary or indirect effects of a treatment program; for example, teaching a non-speaking person to use signs has the primary effect of teaching communicative skills but may also have the secondary effect of improving that person's emotional well-being.

Columbus, Christopher — famous voyager who first sailed to North America in 1492; in his log of this journey, he documented the use of signs and gestures by the Native Americans he encountered.

Communication assessment — a comprehensive assessment or evaluation of a person's expressive and receptive language abilities. The evaluation may examine the person's use of speech, signs, gestures, object manipulation, and/or other forms of communication in a variety of settings. It may include measures of phonological mastery, vocabulary size, knowledge of grammatical rules, and social or pragmatic language usage.

Communication (or picture) board or book — an augmentative and alternative communication aid or device in which persons may use pictures, symbols, printed words, or letters on a board, screen, or book to communicate. A communication (or picture) board is a piece of material, such as wood, plastic, or cardboard, on which pictures or drawings of desired objects, persons, or actions typically are attached. A communication (or picture) book is a book, notebook, or scrapbook that contains pictures or drawings of objects, persons, or actions that are important to non-speaking individuals. The minimally verbal user often indicates desired objects or activities by pointing to, touching, or gazing at the appropriate picture or drawing.

Communication disorder — an inability or impaired ability to transmit or receive information, typically because of difficulties understanding or producing language.

Communication intervention system — a system of strategies and techniques used to enhance the communication skills of an individual or group.

Communication plan — a relatively detailed strategy for teaching or developing a person's communication skills. For sign communication, this plan may include which signs to teach, when to teach them, how to teach them, who will teach them, and where the signs will be taught.

Communicative competence — the ability to use signs, speech, or other forms of communication to effectively convey one's needs, interests, or desires. Such competence involves linguistic ability together with knowledge of the social rules involved in language use.

Communicative spontaneity — the ability to communicate in various settings, without prior prompting, through the use of words, signs, or other symbols. This communication often is used to express needs and to make requests.

Comorbidity — the simultaneous existence of two or more chronic medical disorders, diseases, or conditions in a single patient. Comorbidity increases the complexity of diagnosis and treatment of a patient.

Complex communication needs — a term applied to the situation of persons who are unable to successfully communicate their daily needs through a spoken, written, or signed language. Persons with complex communication needs typically have more than one disabling condition or impairment.

Compound signs — two or more different signs that are used together or combined in order to represent a single concept. See agglutination of signs.

Computed tomography (CT) scan — a diagnostic procedure that uses x-rays to take pictures of cross sections of a part of the body; these images are then compiled or put together for viewing by a computer program.

Concentration — a game or task in which the player turns over two cards from a number of cards that have been placed face down on a flat surface. If the two cards are the same, then they are removed from the playing surface. If the cards do not match, then they are returned to their original positions. The game continues until all the cards are removed. This game has been used to investigate visual memory.

Concept — an idea derived from specific instances; an abstract representation of an object, action, person, or idea. Words and signs stand for concepts.

Concordance rate — the likelihood or probability that a pair of individuals will have the same characteristic if one of them has that characteristic. In this book, the rate at which twins inherit or have the same condition, disorder, or disease.

Concrete nouns — people, places, or things that can be directly experienced through the senses (sight, hearing, touch, smell, taste). Concrete nouns are real things or a class of such things. Concrete nouns typically are relatively easy to express iconically in a sign-communication system.

Condillac, Etienne Bonnot de — eighteenth-century French philosopher and essayist who developed the view that all knowledge comes from the senses as opposed to innate ideas. He also wrote about the early gestural communication of two imaginary young children.

Congenital — present at birth, although not necessarily genetic.

Congenitally aphasic — someone whose language skills are impaired from birth.

Congruent gesture — in this book, a gesture that matches (or is in accord with) the meaning of a spoken word that is being learned; an iconic or representative gesture. Production of congruent gestures typically helps or enhances a person's acquisition of paired foreign spoken language vocabulary items.

Consecutive movements — in this book, movements made during a sign's production that occur one after the other. Also known as sequential movements.

Contralateral — on the other side. Each hemisphere of a typically developed brain controls the motor actions of the contralateral arm and hand; for example, the right hemisphere of the brain controls the left side of the body, and the left hemisphere of the brain controls the right side of the body.

Convention — a custom or way of thinking; often, an unstated agreement or principle that is accepted as true or correct.

Copula verb — in grammar, a linking verb that joins or connects the subject of a sentence with an adjective or noun in the predicate of that sentence without indicating that a distinct action is performed. In English, the different forms of the verb *be* (is, am, are, was, were) are frequently used in this capacity; for example, "The dogs *are* friendly." "The woman *is* a teacher." "The birds *were* hungry." Signed languages typically omit or do not have equivalents of the copular verb *be*. That is, there is not a distinct sign for the *be* verb used to express a predicate's state or quality.

Core sign vocabulary — a collection of signs that have been learned and that represent important and necessary objects or aspects of one's environment.

Corsi block-tapping test — a visuospatial (nonverbal) short-term memory test that assesses a person's ability to remember and repeat sequences in which up to nine identical blocks are tapped or indicated. Both the number of correct sequences and the longest sequence remembered (visuospatial memory span) are recorded. Compare with Digit Span Task.

Cortex/cortices — the outermost layer(s) of an organ. Often refers to the cerebral cortex.

Cri du chat syndrome — a rare genetic disorder characterized by a high-pitched, cat-like cry. Persons with this syndrome often have poor muscle tone and motor skills, intellectual disability, a small head and/or jaw, an abnormal larynx, and delayed or nonexistent speech.

Criterion/criteria — standards or minimal requirements; in this book, primarily the minimum level of recall accuracy necessary to include a sign in the Simplified Sign System (SSS).

Cross-modal activation — the use of one modality, such as signs (manual modality), that may result in the use of or improvement of skills in another area, such as spoken language (speech modality).

Cross-modal transfer — information from one sensory modality moves to or is integrated with information from another; for example, information conveyed in a sign may be stored in a speech code.

Cued-recall memory task — a memory research method in which an experimenter presents information (the cue) to a participant along with an item to be remembered and then subsequently presents the cue again to the participant, who is instructed to remember the paired item shown or heard earlier. In this book, the experimenter demonstrated a sign and provided its English translation, then later cued the participant to produce that sign by providing its English translation (or cued the participant to provide the English translation by producing the sign).

Cueing — an aphasia treatment technique in which prompts or prestimulation, such as pictures, gestures, written words, or manual signs, are used to facilitate an individual's lexical retrieval or comprehension. Effective gestural cueing for names of objects and actions often involves the use of iconic gestures or signs.

Curved-hand — a sign handshape used in the Simplified Sign System (SSS); the fingers and thumb are together and curved.

Deaf/deaf — in this book, *deaf* is used to refer to any person with a substantial hearing loss, as well as to indicate the medical condition of deafness or the physical aspects of hearing loss. The word *Deaf* is used to indicate those persons, typically with hearing impairments, who communicate primarily through a sign language (such as American Sign Language), who interact frequently with other signers, and who self-identify with Deaf culture.

Deblocking — an aphasia treatment technique in which a disturbed language function is paired with an intact or less impaired language function. See sign-communication deblocking therapy.

Declarative memory — a memory system that consists of knowledge, such as that of facts and events, that can be expressed by a person in words.

Deictic gestures — showing or indicating gestures; also known as indexical (or pointing) signs.

Delayed recall — a task that tests the participant's ability to produce some item from memory after an intervening period or delay has been introduced following the earlier presentation of that item.

de l'Épée, Abbé Charles-Michel — founder of the first school for the education of deaf students, irrespective of social condition, in Paris, France in 1760.

De novo mutation — an alteration in a gene that is present for the first time in a family member often as a result of a mutation in a parent's germ cell (egg or sperm) or in the fertilized egg itself; a new or spontaneous mutation in genetic material. A substantial number of all cases of childhood autism are believed to be a result of de novo mutations.

Deoxyribonucleic acid (DNA) — the building blocks of life that contain an organism's genetic code.

Depth of processing — a theory in which a person's ability to remember or recall information is dependent upon the level at which that information is encoded or mentally processed; a greater depth of processing would lead to a stronger, longer-lasting memory. The formation of a visual image, the hearing and saying of a word, thinking about an item's meaning, and the production of a representative (iconic) gesture may increase depth of processing of an item.

Descriptive name signs — name signs that are based on individuals' identifiable characteristics, such as physical appearance, behavior, personality, or interests. Compare with arbitrary name signs.

Designator — also known as handshape or sign handshape; one of the three principal formational parameters of manual signs.

Developmental delay — a lag in the appearance or emergence of one or more abilities during childhood, such as the ability to mentally or physically perceive, understand, or interact with aspects of the environment.

Developmental dysphasia — also known as specific language impairment or developmental language disorder (DLD).

Developmental dyspraxia — a neuromotor disorder present from infancy or early childhood in which a person has an impaired ability to accurately and purposefully control or coordinate movements and motor configurations in the absence of muscle weakness or paralysis. See apraxia.

Developmental language disorder (DLD) — a recent consensus term for the various language difficulties or impairments experienced by some children and that are not attributable to brain injury, hearing loss, intellectual disability, autism spectrum disorder, or genetic syndromes. Children with such speech or communicative impairments may have previously been diagnosed with developmental dysphasia or specific language impairment.

Diagnostic substitution — a phenomenon by which one term for a condition or disorder is replaced by another term. This shift in terminology often results in a decrease of the incidence of the first condition or disorder and an increase of the incidence of the second condition or disorder.

Digit Span Task — a short-term memory test that typically assesses a person's ability to remember and repeat a series of numbers that have been read out loud or presented on a computer screen. Both the number of correct sequences and the longest sequence remembered (digit memory span) are recorded. Compare with Corsi block-tapping test.

Discrete trial training — in this book, a method of teaching words or signs to a learner through highly structured training sessions that typically involve the use of reinforcement (reward, punishment) contingencies. Compare with general exposure and incidental teaching program.

Dizygotic twins — twins that develop from two separate fertilized eggs; fraternal twins. Compare with monozygotic twins.

Dominant hand — the hand that a person uses to perform most manual tasks or to produce the movement parameter or aspect of the majority of his or her signs; usually the right hand. See active hand and hand preference.

Down syndrome — a congenital condition typically characterized by a mild or moderate intellectual disability, short stature, a recessed mandible (lower jaw bone), and epicanthic eye folds (small folds of skin from the upper eyelids in the inner corners of the eyes). Down syndrome occurs because of trisomy (three copies of chromosomes instead of the normal two) in chromosome 21.

Dysgraphia — a disorder that affects writing or the production of written language.

Dyslexia — a disorder that affects reading or the understanding of written language.

Early intervention — in this book, therapeutic services that are provided to a person early in development or as close to the onset of a disabling condition as possible. Although certain intervention approaches may be applied at any point in such a person's rehabilitation, beginning as soon as possible after the onset of a condition (as well as providing more frequent therapy) may produce better, longer-lasting results.

Echolalia — the phenomenon of echoing or repeating another person's speech or signs; also designates the largely involuntary verbal repetition present in some individuals with autism or an intellectual disability. See verbal imitation program.

Electroencephalogram (EEG) — typically a noninvasive test that records brain waves that trace electrical activity in a person's brain. EEGs are commonly used to detect seizures, to diagnose epilepsy, coma, and sleep disorders, or to confirm brain death.

Embodied actions — movements that involve the body (e.g., arms, hands, trunk, legs, feet). Often, the view that reasoning or cognition (perception, awareness) arises primarily from the body and bodily experiences. See embodied cognition.

Embodied cognition — the view that cognition is primarily the product of the brain's systems of perception, action, and introspection. This view contrasts markedly with the approach emphasizing amodal symbol processing. See embodied actions.

Empirical — based on experimental evidence, direct observation, or verifiable experience instead of theory.

Enactment effect — the positive or facilitative effect on one's memory for verbal material (particularly phrases that describe actions) that is achieved by physically performing the action associated with that verbal material. Foreign language acquisition research over the last few decades has shown that accompanying a to-be-learned foreign language word or phrase with an iconic or representative gesture helps in the learning and longer-term retention or recall of such words or phrases.

Encephalitis — an inflammation of the brain, usually the result of an infection, that can result in brain damage, paralysis, or death. See acquired neurological disorder.

English translation/word equivalent — the English translation of a sign or of a word from another language. See gloss.

Enhanced milieu teaching (EMT) program — an incidental teaching program. This method typically involves the use of parents in addition to teachers to foster learning through natural interaction processes.

Environmental cues — information gathered from context or from the surrounding environment that may help support the meaning of a signed or spoken communication; for example, pictures, posters, drawings, toys, or other objects.

Epilepsy — a disorder of the nervous system that involves seizures caused by abnormal electrical activity in the brain.

Essentially correct (sign) recall — in this book, the production by a study participant of a Simplified Sign System (SSS) sign or an American Sign Language (ASL) sign that is formationally close to the sign demonstrated by the experimenter, but which contains a small error in handshape, location, or movement.

Etiology — the cause of a condition, disorder, disease, disability, or injury.

Executive functioning skills — the cognitive abilities involved in problem solving and goal-directed tasks. These skills may include planning, inhibition of actions, and error correction.

Exemplar — a particular instance or typical example of a concept. For example, *tree* is a broad conceptual category that includes such specific exemplars as oak trees, maple trees, palm trees, and pine trees.

Expressive aphasia — a type of aphasia in which a person has difficulty producing language (speech or signs) even though he or she may retain the ability to understand language. Also known as productive aphasia. See Broca's aphasia.

Expressive language skills — the extent to which a person can produce speech, signs, gestures, or written language. Also known as productive language skills.

Expressive speech aphasia — a type of aphasia in which an individual can produce very little or no speech. Also known as productive speech aphasia.

Expressive vocabulary — the extent to which a person can produce different signs or spoken words; the signs or words that a person produces. Also known as productive vocabulary.

Eye-hand coordination — the synchronization of the movement of the hand(s) in accord with movements of the eye(s); visual-motor coordination. The ability to successfully reach for and touch (or grab) objects that are seen by one's eyes.

Facial discrimination — in psychological testing, the ability to match or identify a target face (or faces) from among various options. Studies have shown that deaf and hearing signers are often better at this task than non-signers.

Facial expression — in this book, the expression on a signer's face that is often helpful in clarifying or supporting the meaning of a signed communication. In American Sign Language (ASL) and other sign languages, facial expression is a component of many signs and contributes to the understanding of their meanings and syntactical relationships. A form of nonverbal communication.

Facial Recognition test — a neuropsychological test of a person's ability to match or locate a target face from among six options. The faces are presented under different viewing conditions (e.g., identical front view, partial side view, front view under different lighting conditions). This test may be administered to persons with suspected neurological damage or impairments, autism, or aphasia.

Field testing — in this book, the testing of the Simplified Sign System (SSS) in natural settings with members of the populations for whom it was primarily developed.

Fine motor movements — relatively small motor movements or actions, often of the hands or face. These movements require a high degree of control or accuracy.

Finger orientation — the direction that the finger(s) of the hand(s) point during a sign's production.

Fingerspelling — spelling a word from an alphabetical language by manually producing the handshapes that represent each letter in that word. See manual alphabet.

Fist — a sign handshape used in the Simplified Sign System (SSS); the hand forms a fist. The hand is clenched with the fingers bent into the palm.

Flat-hand — a sign handshape used in the Simplified Sign System (SSS); the hand is flat with fingers together and extended.

Flemish Sign Language — also known as Vlaamse Gebarentaal or VGT. See Belgian Sign Language.

Fluent aphasia — a type of language loss in which a person may produce effortless speech that is lacking in content or meaning. See Wernicke's aphasia.

Forebrain — in humans, the largest portion of the brain; it includes the cerebral hemispheres. Among the forebrain's many functions are the storing of new information, sequencing voluntary actions, abstract thinking, processing of sensory information, language production and comprehension, and the learning and remembering of emotional events. See cerebrum.

Fragile X syndrome — a genetic disorder, more often present in males than females, that usually results in intellectual disability. Expressive language skills typically are more adversely affected than receptive language skills.

French Belgian Sign Language — also known as Langue des Signes Belge Francophone or LSFB. See Belgian Sign Language.

French Sign Language — the primary language of the Deaf community in France. Many American Sign Language (ASL) signs are related to or derived from signs in French Sign Language. Also known as Langue des Signes Française or LSF.

Frontal lobe — the anterior (frontmost), upper lobe of each cerebral hemisphere primarily responsible for thought and consciousness, as well as certain aspects of speech.

Gallaudet, Thomas H. — American educator of deaf students. After studying methods of education for deaf students in Europe, he helped found the first public school for deaf students (the American School for the Deaf) in the United States in 1817.

Gallaudet University — the first institution of higher education or learning for Deaf students in the world, located in Washington, DC. Gallaudet College was established in 1864 and became Gallaudet University in 1986.

General exposure — in this book, a method of teaching signs to the main user or learner by incorporating sign usage throughout the surrounding environment or while in the presence of the main user (even if not communicating directly with him or her). The main user may spontaneously or indirectly acquire signs by seeing how those signs are used by other people in conversation. Compare with discrete trial training and incidental teaching program.

Generalization — what is learned in one context is extended to others. The ability to apply a concept, word, or sign to multiple examples (exemplars) or situations; this is often a problem for children with autism spectrum disorder. See adaptive behaviors.

Genetic — inherited or passed on through one's genes. See chromosomes and Deoxyribonucleic acid (DNA).

Genitive — the grammatical case that indicates possession.

German measles — a viral infection that when contracted by a pregnant woman may cause brain damage, an intellectual disability, and/or deafness in the developing child. Also known as rubella.

Gestation — the length of time that a child develops within the womb; the time between the first day of the mother's last menstrual period and the birth of a child, which is approximately 284 days for babies born full-term.

Gestuno — a system of signs created by the World Federation of the Deaf for use in international settings or interactions between deaf people who do not use the same sign language. Most signs in Gestuno were borrowed from a small number of European sign languages and American Sign Language (ASL). See International Sign.

Gestural imitation — the ability to copy or reproduce a person's gestural movements.

Gestural modality — the use of one's hands, arms, and/or upper body to transmit information. See manual modality, tactile modality, and visual-gestural modality.

Gestural processing — the ability of a person to successfully distinguish, recognize, understand, and remember gestures.

Gestural sequencing — the ability of a person to process and correctly order a succession or connected series of movements of the hands, arms, and/or upper body.

Gestures/gestural communication — the movement of the body or limbs to convey information; for example, pantomime, pointing, and facial expressions.

G-hand — a sign handshape used in the Simplified Sign System (SSS); the index finger and thumb are extended from an otherwise closed hand and are parallel to each other.

Global aphasia — extensive loss or considerable damage to most or all aspects involved in the understanding and production of language. Global aphasia is often the result of major brain damage caused by a stroke, brain infection, tumor, or head injury.

Gloss — a brief explanation of a foreign or unknown word. In this book, the spoken language translation of a sign. See English translation/word equivalent.

Glossectomy — the surgical removal of the tongue.

Grammar — the rules that describe the structure and principles of a language's operation; often used to refer to the system of inflections and syntax of a language.

Gross motor movements — bodily movements or actions that involve large muscle groups and not the smaller, typically more precise, movements of fine motor actions. Examples include crawling, walking, running, or throwing an object.

Hand-internal movements — movements made within a signer's hand, such as the opening and closing of the hand.

Hand preference — the hand that a person prefers to use when performing most manual tasks or producing the movement parameter of signs; usually the right hand. See active hand and dominant hand.

Handshape — one of the three major sign formational parameters or aspects identified by linguist and sign language researcher William C. Stokoe that distinguish meaning in sign languages. The configuration of the hand(s) during the production of a sign; for example, C-hand, L-hand, and spread- or 5-hand. Also known as designator or sign handshape. See sign phoneme.

Haptic — of or pertaining to the sense of touch; relating to the perception, grasping, and manipulation of objects through touch, typically by use of one's hands.

Hemiparesis — muscular weakness or partial paralysis of one side of the body. See hemiplegia.

Hemiplegia — severe weakness in or paralysis of the muscles on one side of the body resulting from damage to motor centers in the brain (areas of the brain that control muscular activity or movement).

Herpes encephalitis — a potentially fatal viral infection of the nervous system that may infect the temporal lobes of the brain and cause severe brain damage and seizures.

H-hand — a sign handshape used in the Simplified Sign System (SSS); the index and middle fingers are together and extended from an otherwise closed hand.

Hindbrain — the rearmost portion of the brain consisting of the cerebellum, pons, and medulla oblongata. The hindbrain is responsible for equilibrium and the regulation of essential biological functions (e.g., blood circulation, breathing).

Hippocampus — a region in the temporal lobe of the brain involved in forming and storing memories.

Homesigns — a basic gestural communication system that is created by a non-speaking (often deaf) child and his or her relatives in the absence of exposure to a full sign language. See personal signs.

Horns-hand — a sign handshape used in the Simplified Sign System (SSS); the little finger and thumb are extended from an otherwise closed hand.

Iconicity — a property of a sign in which the sign bears a resemblance to or close association with the action, object, or characteristic it represents. There is a correspondence between the form of a sign and its meaning. See onomatopoeia.

Identifiable (sign) recall — in this book, the production by a study participant of a sign that, despite being imperfectly formed, is sufficiently close formationally to the sign demonstrated by the experimenter as to be recognized or identified as an attempt to produce that sign.

Idiom or idiomatic expression — a phrase or an expression that has a figurative (not literal) meaning; a figure of speech. Idioms are difficult to translate into other languages, as a literal interpretation of each word in the phrase renders a different meaning of the expression (the figurative meaning of the entire phrase or expression is different from the literal meaning of each word in the phrase). For example, "It costs an arm and a leg" means that something is very expensive (not that one literally has to use an arm and a leg as the form of payment). Idiomatic expressions are often difficult for foreign language students to learn.

Imitation skills — the ability to observe the actions of another and to reproduce or copy those same actions. Children with autism often need to be specifically and painstakingly taught to attend to and copy the actions of another person.

Immediate recall — a task that tests the participant's ability to produce some item from memory very shortly after it has been presented. In this book, the ability to manually produce a sign after no significant time delay.

Incidence/incidence rate — the number of or rate at which new cases of a condition, disorder, or disease occurs in a population in a given time frame. Compare with prevalence.

Incidental teaching program — an educational approach that utilizes the natural interactions (or naturally occurring situations) between teachers or caregivers and their students or clients throughout the day for instructional purposes. When parents also are involved in the teaching, the approach is known as an enhanced milieu teaching program. Compare with discrete trial training and general exposure.

Incongruent gesture — in this book, a gesture that does not match the meaning of a spoken word that is being learned. Production of incongruent gestures does not help, and may have a negative effect on, a person's acquisition of foreign language vocabulary items when paired with those items.

Indexical signs — gestures that are linguistic pointers or direct indicators of something; for example, pointing directly at an object. Also known as deictic gestures.

Initial sign lexicon — the sign vocabulary that is taught to or acquired by a new sign language learner. The vocabulary items that are taught should in most cases focus primarily on discrete objects and actions useful and important to enhancing the quality of the sign learner's environment and communication skills.

Inner ear — the portion of the ear that includes the vestibule, the semicircular canals, and the cochlea. This essential organ of hearing is responsible for the transduction or conversion of sound vibrations into auditory signals, which are then sent to the brain where they are interpreted.

Instrument — in linguistics, the means by which the action of the verb is performed within a sentence; the thing employed by the agent to accomplish the action.

Intellectual disability — a condition characterized by significantly below average cognitive functioning, impaired adaptive behavior, and often limited motor development and communication skills. Formerly known as mental retardation.

Intelligible/intelligibility — in this book, how well a person's speech, manual signs, or gestures are understood by that person's communication partners.

Internal models or representations — the mental pictures or frameworks for comparison that a person has for understanding and learning information; a mental portrayal or description of something. See object visualization and visual image.

International Sign — a system of signs that incorporates signs from different sign languages from around the world, and that has been allowed to evolve relatively naturally. Signs that are considered useful, easily learned and remembered, as well as readily formed, are often included.

International Society for Augmentative and Alternative Communication (ISAAC) — an organization that promotes the use and study of augmentative and alternative communication strategies with various non-speaking or minimally verbal persons.

Intervention program — a course of treatment meant to improve functioning in an area such as communication or social behavior. In this book, we often recommend the use of the Simplified Sign System (SSS) in a sign-communication intervention program to help improve an individual's communicative interactions.

IQ test — a measure of one's intelligence quotient; a standardized test used to assess or determine one's level of intelligence relative to the performance of others of the same age.

Joint attention — a state or situation in which two individuals are attending to or paying attention to the same thing or action at the same time.

Kanner, Leo — psychiatrist who is credited as being the first to identify and describe the major characteristics of childhood autism.

Key words — content words; words that contain the principal or content information of an utterance.

Key word signing — an approach to communication that involves signing only the principal or content words in a sentence while speaking the entire sentence. Key word signing is related to simultaneous communication.

Kinesthetic system — the system that senses movement and orientation of the body through information transmitted from receptors in the muscles, tendons, and joints.

Knuckle orientation — the direction that the knuckles of the hand(s) point during a sign's production.

Landau-Kleffner syndrome — a relatively rare form of childhood epilepsy that results in a severe loss of receptive language skills (comprehension, understanding) even though the ability to hear is not impaired. Expressive language skills (speech) are often seriously impaired as well. This condition is associated with the onset of seizure activity; persons with Landau-Kleffner syndrome have abnormal electrical activity in the brain. Recovery varies widely. Also known as acquired epileptic aphasia or verbal auditory agnosia.

Language — the use of auditory-vocal or written symbols (words) or visual-gestural symbols (signs) in an organized pattern to communicate ideas or feelings. Usually refers to human communication, which can take place in a variety of settings and be expressed and perceived in many different forms (vocal, auditory, visual, tactile, manual, written, etc.). Although most people consider speech or spoken language to be the predominant means of human communication, sign languages and sign-communication systems are also common.

Language milestones — important developmental steps or tasks that are used to evaluate an individual's level of language achievement or linguistic skills; for example, the onset of vocal or manual babbling, the production of one's first word or sign, and the combination of words or signs.

Language modality — the medium that a language uses to produce and transmit information; the mode of production and reception of a language. Examples include auditory-vocal, gestural, manual, speech, tactile, or visual-gestural.

Laryngectomy — the surgical removal of the larynx, which holds the vocal cords.

Larynx — a part of the respiratory tract that contains the vocal cords; the voice box.

Late talkers — toddlers or young children who do not achieve productive (expressive) language milestones within the typical time frame; young children whose speech skills and vocabulary lag well behind those of other children of the same age.

Left hemisphere of the brain — one of the two lateral halves of the cerebrum (the topmost portion of the brain). The cerebral hemispheres consist of the left and right hemispheres, each of which is further divided into four lobes. The left hemisphere of the brain controls the right side of the body. In most humans, areas in the left hemisphere are specialized for language.

L-hand — a sign handshape used in the Simplified Sign System (SSS); the index finger and thumb are extended from an otherwise closed hand and form a right angle.

Limb apraxia — a type of apraxia in which a person experiences a loss of or disturbance in the ability to purposefully control the movements of the arms, hands, legs, or feet.

Lingua franca — a common or hybrid language (or communication system) employed among users of different languages when they need to communicate with each other.

Linguistic deprivation — a situation in which a child is raised without access to full linguistic input (either spoken language or signed language) and is therefore severely limited in his or her ability to communicate with others.

Linguistic family — a grouping of distinct languages whose characteristics nevertheless indicate that they are related to each other; for example, Spanish, French, Italian, Romanian, and

Portuguese are all descended from vulgar Latin and thus belong to the same linguistic family.

Linguistics — the scientific study of language (whether signed or spoken), including its origins, history, evolution, structure, social variation and application, biological bases, and psychological underpinnings.

Lip reading — a skill in which a person depends on his or her ability to visually observe (or, less often, physically touch and feel) the speech movements of another person's mouth, lips, and face to understand what that person is saying (often without actually hearing what is being said). Also known as speech reading.

List intrusion — in this book, the production of an item during a recall study that was presented in a different list (other than the one currently being tested).

Literacy — the ability to read and write.

Location — one of the three major sign formational parameters or aspects identified by linguist and sign language researcher William C. Stokoe that distinguish meaning in sign languages. The area(s) on or near the body where a sign is made; the place or location of the hand or hands during the production of a sign. Examples include the chin, chest, forehead, or arm. Also known as the sign location or tabula. See sign phoneme.

Locative — the grammatical case that indicates location or place.

Longer-term recall study — in this book, a task that tests the participant's ability to manually produce or recognize a sign after a delay often consisting of more than a few days.

Longitudinal study — a study that is conducted over an extended period of time on the same participants. Observations are made at various time intervals to provide information on the course of development and to measure long-term effects.

Magnetic resonance imaging (MRI) — a diagnostic or research procedure that uses radio waves and magnets to create images of cross sections of the body; these images are compiled or put together for viewing by a computer program.

Main user — in this book, the person who will use the Simplified Sign System (SSS) as a primary language or communication system. See target population or users.

Makaton Vocabulary — initially, a vocabulary or lexicon of several hundred basic signs from British Sign Language (BSL) for use with non-speaking persons with an intellectual disability in Great Britain. It has been expanded and used with other non-speaking populations as well. When used in other countries, signs are taken from the principal sign language(s) of the Deaf persons of those countries.

Maladaptive behaviors — negative, challenging, or problem behaviors that interfere with a person's daily life activities; may include self-injury, tantrums, aggression, stereotypies, and destruction of property.

Mandible — the lower jaw bone.

Manual alphabet — handshapes used in manual communication to represent the individual letters of words from a spoken language. See fingerspelling.

Manual apraxia — a type of apraxia in which a person experiences a loss of or disturbance in the ability to purposefully control the movements of the hands and arms.

Manual dexterity — the muscular abilities of one's hands and arms; the extent to which a person can control the movements of the hands and arms. Manual dexterity often refers to a person's skill and ease in performing manual acts.

Manual modality — the use of one's hands, arms, and facial expression to transmit information. See gestural modality, tactile modality, and visual-gestural modality.

Manual numeration — handshapes, locations, and movements used in manual communication to represent individual numbers.

Manual skills — abilities or skills that involve the use of or movement of the hands or limbs; for example, object manipulation and forming correct handshapes.

Maternal chromosomal deletion — a loss or deletion of genetic material from a maternal chromosome. In about 70% of all cases of Angelman syndrome, genetic material on chromosome 15 (q11-13) is not passed from the mother to the child.

Mean — arithmetic average, obtained by adding the scores and then dividing by the number of scores.

Medulla oblongata — the lowest part of the hindbrain and brain stem, located at the top of the spinal cord. The medulla oblongata is involved in the control of breathing, circulation, balance, and certain protective reflexes.

Melodic Intonation Therapy — a language therapy technique that uses musical melodies, rhythms, and intonations to stimulate areas of the brain related to language; it is used mostly with persons with expressive speech aphasia to help them regain the ability to speak. A therapist typically first demonstrates and then teaches a client to rhythmically hum or sing words or phrases. This language therapy technique may also be combined with the production of manual signs.

Memory aid or cue — in this book, a sentence or phrase provided with each sign in the Simplified Sign System (SSS) lexicon to illuminate the link between that sign and the concept for which it stands. See mnemonic explanation.

Mendelian inheritance pattern — a set of rules or principles that describe the way in which biological traits are passed from one generation to another. This pattern of genetic transmission was initially discovered by Austrian monk and botanist Gregor Mendel in the 1800s. These principles state that the inheritance of a trait is determined by genes that are passed from the parent generation to the next (child) generation unchanged. For each trait described, the child receives one gene from each parent. Traits that are suppressed in the parent (or current) generation can still be passed on and expressed in the child (or next) generation.

Mental rotation skills — a set of visuospatial skills that allow a person to compare one object or shape with another. These skills include the ability to form a mental image of a two- or three-dimensional object, to mentally rotate or move that object around, to compare the mentally-rotated object with the original object, and then to make a determination as to whether the two objects match or are the same. Mental rotation skills are important to a wide range of cognitive tasks.

Metaphor — a non-literal linguistic formulation of a concept that cannot be represented directly. A word, sign, or phrase that often designates one thing is instead used to describe or designate another, thus suggesting likeness (e.g., drowning in money).

Metonymic signs — signs that represent or imitate relatively minor or obscure features of their referents. The relationships between these signs and their referents would not be immediately apparent to most observers.

Midbrain — the portion of the brain located vertically between the forebrain and the hindbrain and horizontally between the cerebellum and pons. The midbrain is involved in arousal, body temperature regulation, eye movement control, the sleep-waking cycle, and other actions.

Middle ear — the portion of the ear that extends from the eardrum to the inner ear. The middle ear amplifies and transmits sound-produced vibrations to the inner ear. The middle ear contains a chain of tiny bones (the malleus, incus, and stapes) that is involved in this sound wave transmission.

Midface — the region of the face near the eyes and nose; a common sign location.

Mild intellectual disability — a category of below average mental functioning (IQ range: 55–69); about 85–89% of persons with an intellectual disability are in this category. These individuals typically develop communication, language, and social skills and may achieve academically up to the sixth-grade level. As adults, they may be able to be employed and live independently, although some support and supervision often are needed.

Mirror image signs — also known as symmetrical signs.

Mirror neurons — neurons in the brain that are activated or fire when a monkey or a person views certain actions performed by others; these same neurons also activate or fire when the observer performs those actions. Recent studies into mirror neurons may provide insight into the origins of language. See observation matching system.

Mnemonic explanation — a memory aid or cue. In this book, an explanation of how a sign and its meaning are related that may help a person to remember that sign.

Moderate intellectual disability — a category of below average mental functioning (IQ range: 40–54); about 6–10% of persons with an intellectual disability are in this category. These individuals develop some communication, language, and social skills and often achieve academic skills at the intermediate elementary school level, typically through special education. As adults, with some support, they may be able to be employed in unskilled or semiskilled jobs.

Monozygotic twins — twins that develop from a single fertilized egg; identical twins. Compare with dizygotic twins.

Motor ability — a person's ability to purposefully control the movements of her arms, hands, legs, and body.

Motor complexity — the level of difficulty involved in purposefully controlling or producing a specific movement. When used in reference to signs, it is based on the type and number of movements contained in a sign, the spatial orientation of the sign, and the sign's particular handshape(s) and location(s).

Motor coordination — the ability to control and combine muscular activity or movement.

Motor cortex — the region of the brain that controls movement and motor activity. The motor cortex is a part of the cerebral cortex.

Motor embodiment — in this book, a person's ability to imagine himself or herself in another person's body and to view things from that other person's perspective or vantage point. Signers typically produce sign utterances from their own viewpoints, while perceivers of these sign utterances learn to adopt the perspectives of the sign producers.

Motor imagery — in this book, the creation of visual or mental images of oneself performing motor actions or movements without overtly or physically producing such movements; a recent technique or approach to rehabilitating motor abilities and control in stroke patients with physical impairments.

Motor milestones — important developmental steps or tasks that are used to evaluate an individual's level of motor achievement or motor skills; for example, sitting, crawling, and walking.

Motor planning — the mental formulation for muscular activity or movement of part of the body; the ability to organize sensory information in order to plan and carry out motor activity.

Motor processing skills — the ability of a person to successfully distinguish, recognize, understand, and/or remember movements or motor-based information.

Motor programming process — the planning or organizing of a motor action or actions. Because both signing and speaking involve sequential motor actions, these actions need to be planned or organized so that the resulting actions are appropriately coordinated and sequenced.

Motor sequencing — the ability of a person to process and correctly order a succession or connected series of movements of part of the body.

Motor speech disorder — a dysfunction of motor abilities involved in producing speech.

Movement — one of the three major sign formational parameters or aspects identified by linguist and sign language researcher William C. Stokoe that distinguish meaning in sign languages. The action or movement of the hands or arms in making a sign; for example, nodding or bending of the wrists, up and down movements of the arms or hands, and wiggling of the fingers. Also known as signation or sign movement. See sign phoneme.

Multi-channel system — in this book, the use of facial expression (involving the eyes, eyebrows, nose, and mouth), head and eye movements, body posture, and hand movement to convey meaning in sign languages.

Multimodal — having or occurring in several forms or modalities. The gestural, manual, auditory-vocal, tactile, and visual modalities may be involved in communication.

Multimodal communication system — a communication system that provides information in multiple different modalities; for example, the use of manual signs, speech, printed material, pictures, photos, and/or real objects in communication.

Multi-movement signs or gestures — signs or gestures that involve more than one manual movement.

Multi-term sign utterance — a signed sentence/phrase composed of two or more signs.

Mute — unable or unwilling to produce intelligible speech.

Name sign — a sign that represents a specific person. In American Deaf communities, it is common practice to create a name sign by using the handshape from the manual alphabet for the initial letter of the person's first name or by modifying an existing sign that refers to a prominent physical, emotional, or other characteristic of that person. See arbitrary name signs and descriptive name signs.

Native user — a person who has grown up learning a specific language and is fluent in that language. See principal language.

Natural language — in contemporary usage, a language that has its own vocabulary and grammar and that is learned by native signers or speakers; examples include American Sign Language (ASL), English, French, Russian, and Mandarin Chinese.

Neural plasticity — the ability of the brain to adapt to new stimuli, incorporate new information, or successfully adjust to a brain injury. Younger children's brains typically have greater neural plasticity (and thus adaptive ability) than the brains of adults.

Neuro-imaging techniques — procedures that record and map brain activity, including computed tomography (CT) scans, magnetic resonance imaging (MRI), and positron emission tomography (PET) scans.

Neuromotor impairment — damage to the nerves or muscles that results in a decreased ability or loss of control of motor activity.

Neuropathology — the study of the characteristics, causes, and effects of diseases of the nervous system; a disease or dysfunction of the nervous system.

Neurophysiology — the study of the structure, function, and processes of the body's nervous system and neural circuitry.

Neutral place or space — the area in front of the signer's torso; a common sign location.

Nondeclarative memory — also known as procedural memory.

Nonfluent aphasia — a type of expressive or productive language loss that is characterized by labored and effortful speech. See Broca's aphasia.

Non-oral communication system — a communication system that does not use speech; for example, the use of sign communication, symbols, pictures, or objects. See augmentative and alternative communication.

Nonverbal communication — communication that does not involve vocalized speech; it includes gestures, pantomime, facial expression, and the positioning and movements of various parts of the body.

Nonverbal intelligence — a measure of mental ability (or abilities) that does not involve the production or understanding of speech (or language). See Raven Progressive Matrices.

Non-vocal sounds — environmental sounds; sounds not produced by the human voice.

North American Indian Sign Language — also known as Plains Indian Sign Language (PISL).

Object visualization — the formation in one's mind of a picture-like mental image of an object. Visualizing an object or the use of that object may help some people with language impairments to remember the name of that object. See internal models or representations and visual image.

Observation matching system — the ability of a person to match sensory stimuli (e.g., auditory or visual input) with the correct mental understanding of the stimuli; the ability to observe an action and then execute or perform that same action. See mirror neurons.

Occipital lobe — the posterior (rearmost) lobe of each cerebral hemisphere; it contains the primary visual projection area or visual cortex.

Okay-hand — a sign handshape used in the Simplified Sign System (SSS); the index finger and thumb are curved and touch at their tips from an otherwise open hand.

Onomatopoeia — spoken words that imitate the sounds associated with the designated concept or object; for example, quack, cuckoo, moo, or buzz. See iconicity.

Operant (speech) training — also known as behavior modification (speech) training.

Oral cavity — the area of the mouth; the opening in the head that is bounded externally by the lips and internally by the pharynx.

Oral educational programs — educational programs for deaf students that focus on speech and lip reading; sign language and fingerspelling are not included. Oral-only educational programs prohibit the use of sign language and fingerspelling.

Oral-motor/oromotor apraxia — an inability or significantly decreased ability to control the movement of the muscles of the jaw, tongue, mouth, lips, larynx, pharynx, and velum. Such a disruption in movement may interfere with speech and swallowing.

Oral-motor/oromotor coordination — the ability to control and combine the muscular activity or movement of the jaw, tongue, mouth, lips, larynx, pharynx, and velum.

Oral-motor/oromotor planning — the mental formulation for muscular activity or movement of the jaw, tongue, mouth, lips, larynx, pharynx, and velum.

Oral-motor/oromotor sequencing — the ability of a person to process and correctly order a succession or connected series of movements of the muscles of the jaw, tongue, mouth, lips, larynx, pharynx, and velum.

Oral-motor/oromotor skills — skills that involve movement of the muscles of the jaw, tongue, mouth, lips, larynx, pharynx, and velum. These skills are important in speech, chewing, and swallowing.

Otitis media — inflammation of the middle ear that may cause pain, fever, and hearing impairment. Children with Down syndrome are especially vulnerable to otitis media.

Paget-Gorman sign system — a sign-communication system devised in England to render English manually (on the hands).

Palate — the roof of the mouth; there is both a hard palate and a soft palate (velum).

Palm down — the position of the hand when the palm faces down toward the floor.

Palm in — the position of the hand when the palm faces in toward the signer.

Palm orientation — the direction that the palm of the hand(s) faces during a sign's production.

Palm out — the position of the hand when the palm faces out or away from the signer.

Palm to the side — the position of the hand when the palm faces to one side or the other.

Palm up — the position of the hand when the palm faces up toward the ceiling.

Panacea — a remedy or solution (often mythical) to all of one's problems or ills.

Pantomime — the conveying of information by body movement and realistic gestures; frequently it involves the use of the entire body in a continuous sequence of image-evoking movements or actions. Also known as mime. In signing, a type of highly iconic sign or gesture that clearly resembles and acts out in some significant way the action, object, or characteristic it represents (its referent). Pantomimic signs are formed by using the hands, arms, shoulders, and the face.

Parameters — in this book, a more recent term for the aspects that make up a manual sign's formation: handshape, location, and movement. See sign phoneme.

Parietal lobe — one of the four lobes of each cerebral hemisphere, the parietal lobe is located between the frontal and occipital (rearmost) lobes. The parietal lobe is the region of the brain involved with the sense of touch and the experience of one's body in space and movement.

Peabody Picture Vocabulary Test-Revised (PPVT-R) — a standardized test of receptive English vocabulary typically given to children. The test involves the test administrator saying a word and then the person being tested selecting the picture from a collection of four pictures that best represents that word. The test measures verbal ability and scholastic aptitude.

PECS — abbreviation for Picture Exchange Communication System.

Pedagogical/pedagogy — pertaining to the science or art of teaching and instruction; the educational principles, techniques, and methods a teacher or professor employs.

Perfect (sign) recall — in this book, the production by a study participant of a Simplified Sign System (SSS) sign or an American Sign Language (ASL) sign that is formationally identical to the sign demonstrated by the experimenter.

Peripheral vision — vision at the edges or boundaries of one's field of sight.

Personal signs — a communication system often based on the various gestures that a particular non-speaking individual produces naturally (without training). Individuals with Angelman syndrome may use personal signs to communicate. See homesigns.

Pharynx — in humans, the anatomical channel, together with its enclosing muscles and mucous membrane, that is located behind the nasal cavity and mouth and extends to the esophagus; the throat. The pharynx serves as a passage for air and food.

Phoneme — the smallest unit of speech or sound that may signal a difference in meaning; a class of speech sounds that is perceived as having a single distinct sound in a language.

Phonemic sequencing errors — errors in speech production in which a succession or connected series of sounds are produced in the incorrect order or out of sequence.

Phonological memory — the ability to process, store, and remember information based on speech sounds. This includes the capacities to perceive, encode, rehearse, and recall verbal material. Phonological memory is related to auditory memory and verbal memory.

Phonological processing — the ability of a person to successfully distinguish, recognize, understand, and remember speech sounds. Young children often systematically alter the sounds of the adult language to fit their limited production repertoires. Phonological processing is related to auditory processing and verbal processing.

Phonological sequencing — the ability of a person to process and correctly order a succession or connected series of speech sounds. Phonological sequencing is related to auditory sequencing and verbal sequencing.

Phonology — the linguistic study of the basic units of sound in a spoken language or the basic units of sign in a signed language, as well as their rules for combination.

Physical prompter — a person who guides an individual's (typically a child's) hand in grasping and then releasing a picture of a desired item in the Picture Exchange Communication System.

Pictographic line drawings — simple drawings that are used to represent concepts and are often pictorial in nature; they are frequently used with individuals who have trouble communicating through either speech or signs. See Blissymbols.

Picture board or book — see communication (or picture) board or book.

Picture Exchange Communication System (PECS) — an alternative communication system in which a physical prompter teaches an individual (typically a child) to associate a particular item with its picture by presenting both to that individual and then guiding him or her to grasp and then give the picture to the caregiver in exchange for the item.

Pincer grip — a handshape similar to the baby O-hand. The tips of the index finger and thumb close together. The pincer grip typically emerges early in an infant's development.

Pivotal response treatment — an intervention approach for children with autism spectrum disorder that uses behavioral learning techniques within the context of ongoing interactions between the child and those persons around him or her.

Plains Indians — Native Americans who lived on the Great Plains and who often used a sign-communication system known as Plains Indians Sign Language (PISL) to communicate with members of other tribes or nations who did not speak the same language.

Plains Indian Sign Language (PISL) — a manual sign-communication system used in North America among members of different tribes or nations of Plains Indians who did not speak the same language. Also known as American Indian Hand Talk or North American Indian Sign Language.

Play therapy — a psychotherapeutic approach in which children are encouraged to reveal their feelings and conflicts through their play.

Pointing-hand — a sign handshape used in the Simplified Sign System (SSS); the index finger is extended from an otherwise closed hand.

Ponce de León, Pedro — sixteenth-century Benedictine monk who undertook the first systematic instruction of deaf students in Spain.

Pons — the thickened area of the hindbrain located below the midbrain and at the top end of the medulla oblongata. The pons is involved in the integration and coordination of facial sensations and movements, as well as regulating attentiveness, sleep, and arousal. See brain stem.

Poor (reading) comprehenders — a term applied to persons who have reading comprehension impairment. Poor comprehenders typically can read aloud at an age-appropriate level, but have difficulty understanding the meaning of what they have just read. See reading comprehension impairment.

Portable prompt system — an item or a collection of items that can be easily carried from place to place and that may serve as a memory aid for its user. For example, a reference card with a picture or drawing of a sign, the sign's meaning, and a brief description of how the sign is made.

Positron emission tomography (PET) scan — a diagnostic procedure that produces images of chemical activity in the body using the injection of a radioactive substance. It helps determine how well organs and tissues are functioning by measuring blood flow, oxygen use, and sugar metabolism.

Postlingually deaf — a person who becomes deaf or loses his or her hearing after gaining some considerable amount of speech or spoken language skills.

Praxis — the ability to purposefully control one's movements or to use (or to understand the uses of) objects.

Preactivation — in this book, the activation of parts of the brain through motor activity (such as standing) in the hopes of improving or enhancing another activity (such as remembering words or vocabulary). This recall strategy may be helpful for persons who have language or memory impairments.

Prehominid — refers to the extinct primates that resemble or are related by ancestry to humans; the time period before the appearance of humans.

Prelingually deaf — a person who is born deaf or loses his or her hearing before gaining any significant speech or spoken language skills.

Prelinguistic gestures — gestures produced by an infant or young child prior to his or her production of referential words (words used to name or label new instances of a concept). Such gestures might include the acts of showing or giving something to another. These early emerging communicative gestures typically are absent or occur very infrequently in infants who are subsequently diagnosed with autism or on the autism spectrum.

Prestimulation — the act of giving a participant some form of advance knowledge of or information about a forthcoming stimulus that may increase the likelihood (or ease) that the stimulus will be recalled or recognized. See cueing and prompts.

Preterm infant — a premature infant; an infant born before thirty-seven weeks of gestation.

Prevalence — the number of cases of a condition, disorder, or disease in a population at any given time. Compare with incidence/incidence rate.

Primary progressive aphasia — a clinical syndrome in which there is a gradual deterioration of language functioning over a period of at least two years while other cognitive abilities are largely preserved. In later stages, some individuals may also show marked disturbances in cognition (perception, memory) and behavior.

Primate — a member of the biological order or grouping Primates. Examples of living primates include apes, chimpanzees, gorillas, monkeys, lemurs, and humans.

Principal language — the language one uses as a primary means of communication or for the majority of one's communicative interactions. See native user.

Problem behaviors — also known as maladaptive behaviors.

Procedural memory — a memory system that consists of knowledge of how to do something, such as how to ride a bike or do a certain dance. A person may demonstrate this knowledge through performance of actions or behaviors, but not be able to express this knowledge through words. Also known as nondeclarative memory.

Productive aphasia — also known as expressive aphasia.

Productive language skills — also known as expressive language skills.

Productive speech aphasia — also known as expressive speech aphasia.

Productive vocabulary — also known as expressive vocabulary.

Profound intellectual disability — a category of below average mental functioning (IQ below 25); about 1–2% of persons with an intellectual disability are in this category. These individuals have extremely limited language and communication skills, which are often achieved through augmentative and alternative communication. Many persons with a profound intellectual disability also have serious physical difficulties and neurological damage. Some may learn basic self-help skills but typically require close supervision in a sheltered setting.

Prognosis — outlook or prospect of recovery; often used in medical settings to forecast or predict the outcome of a particular health condition, disease, disorder, or treatment program.

Progressive disorder — a condition that worsens or deteriorates over time.

Project Head Start — an intervention program started in the United States in the 1960s in an attempt to combat the effects of poverty on young children's development. Mainstays of the program include the provision of nutritious meals, access to regular medical and dental care, and educational instruction for pre-school children (mostly three- and four-year-olds) from low-income families.

Proloquo2Go — an augmentative and alternative communication (AAC) software application for certain electronic devices geared toward helping minimally verbal persons to communicate effectively with others. The system is based on the selection of graphic symbols or pictures on a screen to communicate; it also offers a voice-output (or speech-generating) feature.

Prompts — verbal, gestural, physical, or visual encouragement to perform an activity. See cueing, physical prompter, and prestimulation.

Proprioception — the ability to perceive the spatial position or movement of one's body.

Proximalization error — an error in the production of a manual sign in which the movement is displaced from one joint (e.g., the knuckles of the hand) to a joint closer to the trunk of the body (e.g., the wrist, elbow, or shoulder).

Pseudo-words — word-like constructions; made-up or invented words. Combinations of sounds that resemble the way words are constructed in a particular language, but which are not actual words from that language.

Psychodynamic therapy — a treatment or therapeutic approach that is based on the view that symptoms are largely the product of unresolved unconscious conflicts from childhood.

Raven Progressive Matrices — a standardized, nonverbal test of mental ability that involves the detection of patterns and analysis of figures. The test measures abstract reasoning, problem solving, and learning ability.

Reading comprehension impairment — a difficulty or limitation in the ability to understand text passages that one has adequately read aloud. Persons with reading comprehension impairment have intact phonological skills, but tend to have weak vocabulary knowledge, problems with listening comprehension, difficulty understanding figurative language (metaphors, idioms), and problems with processing grammatical information. One of the main strategies for addressing reading comprehension impairment is to focus on teaching vocabulary. See poor (reading) comprehenders.

Rebus — a representation of syllables, words, or phrases by pictures of objects, arrangements of letters, or symbols whose names in sound resemble the intended syllables, words, or phrases.

Receptive aphasia — a form of language loss or aphasia in which an individual has difficulty understanding or processing language.

Receptive language skills — the extent to which a person can understand other persons' speech or signs; a person's ability to understand language.

Receptive vocabulary — the words or signs that a person understands; the extent to which a person can understand other persons' spoken words or signs.

Recognizable (sign) recall — in this book, the production by a study participant of a sign from memory that is either produced correctly or includes only a small formational error in comparison with the sign demonstrated by the experimenter. Used in the Simplified Sign System (SSS)/American Sign Language (ASL) comparison study to encompass perfect (sign) recalls and essentially correct (sign) recalls.

Referent — the object, action, property, or concept that a word or sign represents.

Register — in linguistics, the level of formality of a person's language; register usually varies according to the setting and audience. For example, a researcher giving a presentation at a professional conference would be expected to use formal, highly grammatical, and more complex speech when describing the results of a scientific study. That same person, however, would likely use less formal speech and grammar when interacting with a family member or friend.

Rehabilitation program — a treatment program or plan of activity by which an individual may improve or regain the use of damaged functions of the body.

Representative gesture — a gesture that visually resembles the concept for which it stands; a highly iconic gesture.

Residential program — a treatment program that typically provides housing, shelter, care, social development, and rehabilitation to clients who cannot function independently.

Right hemisphere of the brain — one of the two lateral halves of the cerebrum (the topmost portion of the brain). The cerebral hemispheres consist of the left and right hemispheres, each of which is further divided into four lobes. The right hemisphere of the brain controls the left side of the body.

Ritalin — a neural stimulant medication often given to treat persons with attention-deficit hyperactivity disorder (ADHD); trademark for methylphenidate preparation.

Rubella — also known as German measles.

Sapir-Whorf hypothesis — the view advanced by anthropologist and linguist Benjamin Lee Whorf and his academic mentor Edward Sapir that one's language affects one's thoughts. Sapir and Whorf claimed that one's language might limit the scope of one's thinking and that language might influence thought.

Scott, W. R. — the principal of an English institution for deaf students in the mid-1800s who embraced signing as a form of instruction. Teachers from his school often were successful in teaching signs to individuals with a significant intellectual disability.

Second-first language acquisition — the process by which an internationally adopted child (who has to that point been exposed to the language of his or her native country) learns the new (and different) language of his or her adoptive parents. The language skills of internationally adopted children in their new language tend to lag behind those of non-adopted children of the same age and family socioeconomic background.

Seizure — loss of control of one's movements, behavior, or consciousness brought on by abnormal electrical activity in the brain; a seizure may occur as a result of a brain infection, tumor, injury, or stroke. See epilepsy and Landau-Kleffner syndrome.

Semantic — having to do with the meaning component of language.

Semantic category — an overarching notion or concept, such as *chair*, that is exemplified by many different physical forms, such as a wing chair, a wooden chair, a high-backed chair, a folding chair, etc.

Semantic encoding — the storage in memory of the meaning that is conveyed by language.

Semantic relations — the roles of the principal words or signs in an utterance; the limited set of meanings often present in children's early spoken or signed utterances.

Semicircular canals — a part of the inner ear involved in sensing motion and balance.

Sensorimotor actions — acts produced by an individual that may involve the use of his or her limbs (e.g., arms, legs), bodily motor activities, and senses (e.g., vision, touch). Much early development may depend on sensorimotor (also spelled sensorymotor) actions.

Sequential movements — also known as consecutive movements.

Severe intellectual disability — a category of below average mental functioning (IQ range: 25–39); about 3–4% of persons with an intellectual disability are in this category. These individuals often have quite limited language abilities, poor motor skills, and limited self-help skills. With special education, they can improve their communication skills, but rarely demonstrate academic achievement. They require a supportive environment with supervision.

Signation — also known as movement or sign movement; one of the three principal formational parameters of manual signs.

Sign-communication deblocking therapy — an aphasia treatment method in which a manual sign typically is produced at the same time as the corresponding spoken word (or appropriate oral movements); the goal is for the impaired speech skills to improve as a result of being paired with the more intact signing skills. See deblocking.

Sign-communication system — a form of manual communication often based on signs from sign languages used by Deaf persons and/or Native Americans. See Amer-Ind, Paget-Gorman sign system, and Simplified Sign System (SSS).

Sign-communication training or teaching — the instruction of persons in the use of signs from a sign language or sign-communication system.

Sign dialect — an often regional variation within a sign language, akin to dialects in spoken languages, which may involve differences in sign vocabulary or sign formation. For example, the formation of the sign CHICKEN in American Sign Language (ASL) may vary according to where one lives.

Signed English — a manual and visual form of English that puts American Sign Language (ASL) signs in English word order and makes greater use of fingerspelling; the signs may be further modified to indicate specific English words, plurality, or verb tense. Signing Exact English is a form of Signed English.

Signed languages — also known as sign languages.

Sign handshape — also known as designator or handshape.

Sign language psycholinguistics — the study of how sign languages are acquired (as a native language and as a second or additional language), how sign languages are processed in the brain or understood, and how sign languages are produced. Sign language psycholinguistics may cover such topics as the neurobiological bases for the origins of sign language, similarities and differences between sign language acquisition and spoken language acquisition, how brain damage affects the production and comprehension of sign language (aphasia), and the use of sign languages with special populations.

Sign languages — languages that rely on the transmission of meaning through manually produced and seen signs. Deaf persons in most countries have their own distinct sign languages. Also known as signed languages, visual-gestural languages, or visual-motor languages.

Sign location — also known as location or tabula.

Sign movement — also known as movement or signation.

Sign notation(al) system — a system of symbols used to describe a sign's handshape, movement, and location in written form; for example, Stokoe notation. See sign phoneme.

Sign phoneme — a sign's basic unit of formation that can signal a difference in meaning; a sign's particular handshape, location, or movement. Also known as a chereme (sign language linguist William C. Stokoe's term). See parameters.

Signs — in this book, concepts that are produced manually (primarily by the hands and arms) and are composed of the formational parameters or aspects known as handshape, location, and movement.

Simplified Sign System (SSS) — the sign-communication system originally designed for use with hearing, but non-speaking, populations by the present authors. Most SSS signs resemble their concepts.

Simultaneous communication — an approach to communication in which the user speaks and signs at the same time. Often the user produces signs according to the word order of the spoken language. Simultaneous communication is related to key word signing.

Simultaneous movements — movements made during a sign's production that occur at the same time.

Skelly, Madge — person who developed the sign-communication system Amer-Ind by selecting and adapting signs from Plains Indian Sign Language (PISL). These signs initially were used to meet the communication needs of patients who had undergone a glossectomy or laryngectomy because of cancer.

Social interaction skills — the ability to successfully communicate and interact with other people and to understand the communication of others. Social interaction skills encompass the use and understanding of nonverbal cues (e.g., facial expressions, body posturing), conversational rules (e.g., appropriate topics, turn taking, reciprocity), and other social customs. Social interaction skills are important for establishing self-esteem, building friendships, and gaining acceptance into one's community.

Social touch aversion — the dislike of or strong preference to avoid common means of interacting or contact with others through touch (e.g., hugging, touching of the hands or arms). Often present in children with autism.

Socioeconomic status (SES) — the position one has in society largely as a result of one's material wealth. Other factors include one's level of education and occupation.

Sound symbolism — the view that sounds of a word often are linked or related to the meaning of the word to some extent.

Spatial memory — the ability to perceive and remember the relations and locations of objects or actions in space. This ability may include that of remembering the sequencing of actions produced in space. See Corsi block-tapping test.

Spatial orientation — in signing, the positioning of the arms and/or hands in space.

Spatial relations/relationships — the ability to perceive and understand the positioning of objects in space relative to each other (including their size, volume, distance apart, order, and direction).

Spatial skills/spatial cognition skills — the ability to perceive and comprehend relations in the spatial domain. Tests of spatial ability might involve finding embedded figures and mentally rotating shapes.

Specific language impairment (SLI) — delayed or atypical language development with no apparent cognitive or sensory dysfunction. Also known as developmental dysphasia or developmental language disorder (DLD).

Speech-generating device — an electronic device that allows the user to produce digitized or pre-recorded speech. See voice output communication aid (VOCA).

Speech-language center of the brain — the portion of the brain responsible for the processing of language input and output; in most persons, language processing occurs primarily in the left hemisphere of the cerebrum. See speech signals.

Speech-language pathologist (SLP) — a professional trained to assist in the development or recovery of speech and language skills in persons with communication disorders. See speech therapy.

Speech modality — the use of the voice to transmit information. See auditory-vocal modality.

Speech reading — also known as lip reading.

Speech signals — the sound waves of speech that have been converted into electrical impulses on the way to the brain's language center. Speech signals may be disrupted along these neural pathways, resulting in an impaired ability to understand spoken language.

Speech therapy — a system of spoken language training in which an individual is trained in perceiving speech sounds and assisted in learning how to form speech sounds, words, and sentences; speech exercises. See speech-language pathologist.

Spinal cord — the cord or column of nervous tissue that extends from the brain along the length of the back. The spinal cord, a part of the central nervous system, carries nerve impulses to and from the brain.

Spoken languages — languages that rely on the transmission of meaning through spoken and heard words; also known as auditory-vocal languages.

Spontaneous communication — a person's ability to initiate communication, typically through signs or speech, without immediate prior prompting or usage by others.

Spread curved-hand — a sign handshape used in the Simplified Sign System (SSS); the fingers are spread apart and curved.

Spread- or 5-hand — a sign handshape used in the Simplified Sign System (SSS); the hand is flat with fingers spread apart and extended. Known as the 5-hand in Stokoe's sign notational system.

SSS — abbreviation for the Simplified Sign System.

Standard deviation — a measurement of the variation or distribution of values within a data set with respect to the mean (the arithmetic average of the values). A higher standard deviation reflects a greater distance from the average (expected) result. This statistic is obtained by calculating the difference between each value and the mean, squaring each result, adding the squared values together and dividing by the number of values to obtain the variance, and then taking the square root of the variance.

Standardization — in reference to the Simplified Sign System (SSS), the selection and use of one consistent sign or gesture to convey a particular concept, even if many acceptable gestural variations exist.

Stanford-Binet IQ test — a well-respected and individually administered test of intelligence. The test has its roots in the intelligence test developed by Alfred Binet (1857–1911) in France; it then was revised and adapted for use in America by Lewis Terman of Stanford University. The test measures a person's performance on a broad range of tasks that vary in content and difficulty.

Stationary hand — a hand that is part of the production of some two-handed manual signs. A stationary hand often serves as a non-moving base in the formation of a two-handed asymmetrical sign.

Stereotyped motor movements — frequently repeated, routinized, or stereotypical behaviors such as finger flicking, hand flapping, or rocking back and forth; these behaviors are common among children with autism. Also known as stereotypies.

Stereotypies — also known as stereotyped motor movements.

Stokoe notation — a system of symbols developed by linguist and sign language researcher William C. Stokoe to describe in a written or printed form a sign's formational parameters or aspects of handshape, location, and movement. See sign notation(al) system and sign phoneme.

Stokoe, William C., Jr. — pioneering linguist who showed that American Sign Language (ASL) is a genuine language with its own distinct structure that is quite different from that of English and other spoken languages. See sign phoneme.

Stroke — a rupture (cerebral hemorrhage) of or obstruction (clot) in a blood vessel in the brain that may result in a sudden loss or reduction of sensation, consciousness, and voluntary movement. A loss or disturbance of language abilities and/or paralysis of one side of the body (hemiplegia) may occur as well. Also known as a cerebrovascular accident (CVA).

Subject performed task effect — for a maximum facilitative effect of gestures on memory (or enactment effect), the gestures need to be produced by each individual participant. Also known as self-performed task effect.

Sublexical — referring to or pertaining to the constituent parts of a word or sign (such as the phonemes within a word or sign).

Swiss-French Sign Language — the primary language of some members of the Deaf communities in Switzerland. Also known as SSR.

Symbol — a word, sign, or other token that stands for a concept, but which typically does not bear any clearly apparent vocal, manual, or visual connection to that concept.

Symbolic coding system — a communication system composed of symbols that are used to represent concepts. Examples include speech and manual signs.

Symbolic gestures/gesturing — manual gestures that are used to represent objects, actions, and properties in one's environment. These gestures frequently bear a resemblance to the concepts they represent. Infants make use of symbolic gestures as part of the typical course of both signed and spoken language development.

Symbol-processing skills — the capacity to recognize that something can stand for or represent something else. In most instances, the ability to perceive and understand visual or auditory signs, marks, or characters.

Symbol system — a system in which certain things stand for or represent something else, typically concepts. Language is an important symbol system.

Symmetrical signs — signs made with two hands and whose handshapes, movements, and locations are the same or mirror images of each other. Also known as mirror image signs or two-handed symmetrical signs.

Synesthesia — a condition in which one sense affects or spills over into another sense. One of the most common forms is the association of specific letters and/or numbers with specific colors; other forms include seeing shapes or colors when one hears sounds, and hearing sounds in response to visual input. Perhaps the result of cross-activation of neighboring regions of the brain or of enhanced white matter connectivity in certain areas of the brain. Also known as sensory blending.

Syntax — the study or description of how words or signs are arranged or combined into phrases, clauses, and sentences.

Tabula — also known as location or sign location; one of the three principal formational parameters of manual signs.

Tactile modality — the use of one's hands (or other body parts) to transmit and receive information through the sense of touch. See gestural modality and manual modality.

Tangible symbols — symbols that may be perceived, especially through the sense of touch. See haptic.

Tapered- or O-hand — a sign handshape used in the Simplified Sign System (SSS); the fingers are together and curved, with the finger tips touching the thumb tip.

Target population or users — in this book, persons who are to be the main users or beneficiaries of a communication intervention program.

Temporal lobe — the region of the brain lying below the temple in each cerebral hemisphere. It includes the primary auditory projection area of the brain and is important in hearing and language processing.

Temporal relations — the ability to perceive and understand the positioning or arrangement of objects or events in time relative to each other (including their chronology or order of appearance, their synchronicity or simultaneous occurrence, or their asynchrony or unrelated occurrence).

Text-to-speech alternative communication device — an electronic device that stores text for later retrieval and conversion into speech; a speech-generating device. See augmentative and alternative communication and voice output communication aid (VOCA).

Thalamus — a portion of the brain stem above the midbrain that is responsible for relaying sensory information (e.g., temperature, pain) to the cerebral cortex; it plays a major role in motor control. The thalamus also is involved in functions such as arousal, sleep, memory, emotion, attention, and consciousness.

Topicalization — in sign language linguistics, the practice of an accomplished signer first establishing the topic or focus of a conversation at the beginning of a signed sentence before continuing with new information about that topic in the rest of the signed utterance (known as the comment). For example, signing CAT before describing what the cat did.

Total Physical Response — a method for teaching foreign languages developed by James Asher. Total Physical Response coordinates the production of spoken language by the teacher with physical movement or bodily action from the student as the student acts out what has been said. Initial stages of this method focus on a student's ability to understand what the teacher is saying (listening comprehension) and to respond to the teacher's commands. The student's ability to speak the language is allowed to develop naturally and spontaneously.

Toxic chemicals — poisons or substances that may have a harmful, and potentially fatal, effect on an organism's health.

Translucency — in this book, the extent to which the relationship between a sign and its meaning can be discerned or understood after the meaning of the sign is provided.

Transparency — in this book, the extent to which one can accurately perceive or guess the meaning of an unfamiliar sign.

Traumatic brain injury (TBI) — damage to the brain that results from a blow to the head, a fall, an accident, physical abuse, a concussive force (such as an explosive device), or another type of head injury.

Trunk — the area of a signer's body from approximately the shoulders to the waist, not including the head or limbs; a common sign location.

Tuberculous meningitis — a potentially fatal bacterial infection of the membranes surrounding the brain and spinal cord; it may cause motor impairments, paralysis, or seizures.

Tumor — an abnormal overgrowth of cells in an organism; a tumor can be benign (non-life threatening) or malignant (life-threatening).

Two-handed asymmetrical signs — also known as asymmetrical signs.

Two-handed symmetrical signs — also known as symmetrical signs.

Unaided communication — communication systems (such as speech, manual signs, or gestures) that do not rely on elements outside the communicator's own body (such as pictures, real objects, electronic devices, voice synthesizers or speech-generating devices, and other equipment). Compare with aided communication.

Universal design — the design of an environment, product, or service so that it can be accessed, understood, and utilized to the greatest extent possible by all people regardless of their age, size, ability, or disability. Universal design for learning is an inclusive educational model in which the needs of persons with disabilities are considered and enacted on a broad scale to the benefit of all students (not just those persons with disabilities).

Unmarked handshapes — basic handshapes or hand configurations that are the most easily formed handshapes present in sign languages. Unmarked handshapes typically are acquired early by children learning to sign and occur in sign languages worldwide. Such handshapes often are substituted for handshapes that are more difficult to form or articulate by young signing children. Unmarked handshapes include the flat-hand, the spread- or 5-hand, the pointing-hand, and the fist.

Upper respiratory tract — the upper portion (mouth, nose, and throat) of an organ system through which air passes in the breathing process.

Velum — soft palate; the mucous membrane that partially separates the mouth from the pharynx and is important in closing the nasal passages during swallowing.

Verbal apraxia (or dyspraxia) — also known as apraxia of speech.

Verbal auditory agnosia — also known as Landau-Kleffner syndrome.

Verbal imitation program — a speech therapy approach or program in which individuals are encouraged to repeat or imitate the speech of others. See echolalia.

Verbal memory — the ability to store and remember spoken or written material; memory for words. Verbal memory is related to auditory memory and phonological memory.

Verbal processing — the ability of a person to successfully distinguish, recognize, understand, and remember spoken or written material. Verbal processing is related to auditory processing and phonological processing.

Verbal sequencing — the ability of a person to process and correctly order a succession or connected series of spoken or written material. Verbal sequencing is related to auditory sequencing and phonological sequencing.

Vestibule — a part of the inner ear important in sensing the spatial position of one's body.

V-hand — a sign handshape used in the Simplified Sign System (SSS); the index and middle fingers are spread apart and extended from an otherwise closed hand in the shape of a "V."

Visual cortex — the region of the occipital lobes (rearmost lobes of the cerebral hemispheres) in which visual (obtained by sight) information is processed.

Visual field — the area that is visible to a person when not moving one's eyes or head.

Visual-gestural languages — also known as sign languages.

Visual-gestural modality — the use of one's eyes to perceive manual signs and gestures and the use of movements of one's hands, limbs, and body, together with facial expressions, to communicate. Also known as visual-motor modality. See gestural modality and manual modality.

Visual image — a mental picture or representation of something that typically is based on visual information. See internal models or representations and object visualization.

Visual-motor languages — also known as sign languages.

Visual-motor modality — also known as visual-gestural modality.

Visual Patterns Test — this test measures a participant's short-term visual memory. A participant is shown a matrix, for three seconds, with some of its cells (squares) filled. The participant then tries to reproduce the recently seen pattern of filled squares in a blank grid.

Visual perspective-taking — the ability of a person to successfully process and understand the spatial relationships among objects in the visual environment. In this book, the ability to understand the movements or gestures produced by another person, mentally flip and rotate them, and then produce those same movements or gestures. For example, watching a person move her right hand from the right side of her body to the left side of her face and then moving one's own right hand from the right side of one's body to the left side of one's face. One possible error in visual perspective-taking (in this example) would be to move one's left hand from the left side of one's body to the right side of one's face (producing a mirror image of the original movement).

Visual-processing skills — the ability of a person to successfully distinguish, recognize, understand, and remember visual information.

Visual sequencing — the ability of a person to process and correctly order a succession or connected series of visual information.

Visuospatial immediate memory skills — the ability to remember or recall information presented visually with no significant time delay.

Vocal cords — muscular flaps located in one's voice box or larynx that vibrate during the production of certain sounds.

Vocal inflection — the intonation, pitch, and/or volume with which speech is produced that may provide information on how to interpret an oral communication.

Vocal stimuli — spoken or speech-based cues or prompts; for example, saying the initial /b/ sound to help another person access or remember the word *book*.

Voice output communication aid (VOCA) — an electronic device often used by non-speaking or minimally verbal persons to generate spoken (or written) text; a speech-generating device.

Washoe — a chimpanzee taught by researchers R. Allen Gardner and Beatrix Gardner to communicate using American Sign Language (ASL) signs.

Wechsler scales of intelligence — standardized tests of intelligence for children and adults that measure verbal and performance skills. In this book, many research studies refer to the WISC-R (Wechsler Intelligence Scale for Children — Revised) or the WISC-III (Wechsler Intelligence Scale for Children — III) editions of the test.

Wernicke's aphasia — a loss or disturbance of language ability as a result of damage to a particular part of the brain (Wernicke's area). A type of fluent aphasia in which the speech of a person usually retains its grammatical structure, but it is without much meaning because of the omission of content words (nouns, verbs, adjectives, and adverbs). Language comprehension often is very poor.

White matter (tract) of the brain — neural fibers in the brain that are beneath the cerebral cortex and that run to and from cortical cells. These fibers (or tracts) are insulated with a fatty material that is whitish in appearance.

Williams syndrome — a rare disorder that results in an intellectual disability and poor visuospatial abilities; speech and expressive language abilities are less impaired.

Word retrieval — the ability of a person to successfully remember and produce a specific word on demand; persons with certain types of aphasia often have difficulty accessing or retrieving words from memory.

Word-sign pairs — a collection of signs together with their spoken language translations. See English translation/word equivalent and gloss.

Working memory — the maintenance of incoming information in short-term storage as it is being processed in a preliminary way.

References

AAIDD Ad Hoc Committee on Terminology and Classification. (2010). *Intellectual disability: Definition, classification, and systems of supports* (11th ed.). Washington, DC: American Association on Intellectual and Developmental Disabilities.

Abernathy, E. R. (1959). An historical sketch of the manual alphabets. *American Annals of the Deaf*, 104, 232–240.

Abrahamsen, A., Lamb, M., Brown-Williams, J., & McCarthy, S. (1991). Boundary conditions on language emergence: Contributions from atypical learners and input. In P. Siple & S. D. Fischer (eds.), *Theoretical issues in sign language research, vol. 2. Psychology* (pp. 231–254). Chicago, IL: University of Chicago Press.

Achmadi, D., Sigafoos, J., van der Meer, L., Sutherland, D., Lancioni, G. E., O'Reilly, M. F., Hodis, F., Green, V. A., McLay, L., & Marschik, P. B. (2014). Acquisition, preference, and follow-up data on the use of three AAC options by four boys with developmental disability/delay. *Journal of Developmental and Physical Disabilities*, 26, 565–583, https://doi.org/10.1007/s10882-014-9379-z

Acosta, M. T., & Pearl, P. L. (2006). Genetic aspects of autism. In R. Tuchman & I. Rapin (eds.), *Autism: A neurological disorder of early brain development* (pp. 93–114). London, U.K.: Mac Keith Press.

Acredolo, L., & Goodwyn, S. (2000, July). *The longterm impact of symbolic gesturing during infancy on IQ at age 8*. Paper presented at the International Conference on Infant Studies, Brighton, U.K., https://pursuitofresearch.org/wp-content/uploads/2014/03/Longterm-Impact-of-Symbolic-Gesturing.pdf

Acredolo, L., Goodwyn, S., & Abrams, D. (2002). *Baby signs: How to talk with your baby before your baby can talk*. New York, NY: McGraw-Hill.

Acredolo, L. P., & Goodwyn, S. W. (1990). Sign language in babies: The significance of symbolic gesturing for understanding language development. In R. Vasta (ed.), *Annals of child development, vol. 7* (pp. 1–42). London, U.K.: Jessica Kingsley Publishers.

Acredolo, L. P., & Goodwyn, S. W. (1996). *Baby signs: How to talk with your baby before your baby can talk*. Chicago, IL: Contemporary Books.

Adams, D. J., Susi, A., Erdie-Lalena, C. R., Gorman, G., Hisle-Gorman, E., Rajnik, M., Elrod, M., & Nylund, C. M. (2016). Otitis media and related complications among children with autism spectrum disorders. *Journal of Autism and Developmental Disorders*, 46, 1636–1642, https://doi.org/10.1007/s10803-015-2689-x

Adams, J. (2016). *The effects of Simplified Sign on language acquisition for typically developing adults.* Unpublished master's thesis, The Chicago School of Professional Psychology, Chicago, IL.

Adams, L. (1998). Oral-motor and motor-speech characteristics of children with autism. *Focus on Autism and Other Developmental Disabilities*, 13, 108–112, https://doi.org/10.1177/108835769801300207

Adams, M. J. (1990). *Beginning to read: Thinking and learning about print.* Cambridge, MA: MIT Press.

Adorno, R., & Pautz, P. C. (1999). *Álvar Núñez Cabeza de Vaca, vol. 1. His account, his life, and the expedition of Pánfilo de Narváez.* Lincoln, NE: University of Nebraska Press. [This volume includes the translation by Adorno and Pautz of Cabeza de Vaca's *Relación*, first published in 1542 in Zamora, Spain.]

Ahlsén, E. (1991). Body communication as compensation for speech in a Wernicke's aphasic — A longitudinal study. *Journal of Communication Disorders*, 24, 1–12, https://doi.org/10.1016/0021-9924(91)90029-I

Akita, K. (2009). *A grammar of sound-symbolic words in Japanese: Theoretical approaches to iconic and lexical properties of mimetics.* Unpublished doctoral dissertation, Kobe University, Kobe, Japan, http://www.lib.kobe-u.ac.jp/repository/thesis/d1/D1004724.pdf

Akita, K. (2013). The lexical iconicity hierarchy and its grammatical correlates. In L. Elleström, O. Fischer, & C. Ljungberg (eds.), *Iconic investigations* (pp. 331–350). Amsterdam, The Netherlands: John Benjamins Publishing, https://doi.org/10.1075/ill.12.24aki

Albert, M. L., Goodglass, H., Helm, N. A., Rubens, A. B., & Alexander, M. P. (1981). *Clinical aspects of dysphasia.* New York, NY: Springer-Verlag, https://doi.org/10.1007/978-3-7091-8605-3

Alexander, K., Entwisle, D., & Olson, L. (2014). *The long shadow: Family background, disadvantaged urban youth, and the transition to adulthood.* New York, NY: Russell Sage Foundation.

Alibali, M. W., & Nathan, M. J. (2012). Embodiment in mathematics teaching and learning: Evidence from learners' and teachers' gestures. *The Journal of the Learning Sciences*, 21, 247–286, https://doi.org/10.1080/10508406.2011.611446

Allen, G. (2005). The cerebellum in autism. *Clinical Neuropsychiatry*, 2, 321–337.

Allen, G. (2006). Cerebellar contributions to autism spectrum disorders. *Clinical Neuroscience Research*, 6, 195–207, https://doi.org/10.1016/j.cnr.2006.06.002

Allen, L. Q. (1995). The effects of emblematic gestures on the development and access of mental representations of French expressions. *The Modern Language Journal*, 79, 521–529, https://doi.org/10.1111/j.1540-4781.1995.tb05454.x

Allen, L. Q. (2000). Nonverbal accommodations in foreign language teacher talk. *Applied Language Learning*, 11, 155–176.

Allsop, L., Woll, B., & Brauti, J. M. (1995). International Sign: The creation of an international deaf community and sign language. In H. Bos & T. Schermer (eds.), *Sign language research 1994: Proceedings of the Fourth European Congress on Sign Language Research, Munich, September 1–3, 1994* (pp. 171–188). Hamburg, Germany: Signum.

Alpert, C. L. (1980). Procedures for determining the optimal nonspeech mode with autistic children. In R. L. Schiefelbusch (ed.), *Nonspeech language and communication: Analysis and intervention* (pp. 389–420). Baltimore, MD: University Park Press.

Alvares, R. L., & Downing, S. F. (1998). A survey of expressive communication skills in children with Angelman syndrome. *American Journal of Speech-Language Pathology*, 7, 14–24, https://doi.org/10.1044/1058-0360.0702.14

Alvarez, W., Fuente, A., Coloma, C. J., & Quezada, C. (2015). Association between temporal resolution and specific language impairment: The role of nonsensory processing. *International Journal of Pediatric Otorhinolaryngology*, 79, 1702–1707, https://doi.org/10.1016/j.ijporl.2015.07.029

Alzrayer, N. M., Banda, D. R., & Koul, R. (2017). Teaching children with autism spectrum disorder and other developmental disabilities to perform multistep requesting using an iPad. *Augmentative and Alternative Communication*, 33, 65–76, https://doi.org/10.1080/07434618.2017.1306881

American Association on Mental Retardation. (1992). *Mental retardation: Definition, classification, and systems of support* (9th ed.). Washington, DC: Author.

American Psychiatric Association. (1994). *Diagnostic and statistical manual of mental disorders* (4th ed.). Washington, DC: Author.

American Psychiatric Association. (2013). *Diagnostic and statistical manual of mental disorders* (5th ed.). Arlington, VA: Author, https://doi.org/10.1176/appi.books.9780890425596

Amraei, K., Amirsalari, S., & Ajalloueyan, M. (2017). Comparison of intelligence quotients of first- and second-generation deaf children with cochlear implants. *International Journal of Pediatric Otorhinolaryngology*, 92, 167–170, https://doi.org/10.1016/j.ijporl.2016.10.005

Andersen, G. L., Irgens, L. M., Haagaas, I., Skranes, J. S., Meberg, A. E., & Vik, T. (2008). Cerebral palsy in Norway: Prevalence, subtypes and severity. *European Journal of Paediatric Neurology*, 12, 4–13, https://doi.org/10.1016/j.ejpn.2007.05.001

Anderson, A. E. (2001). *Augmentative communication and autism: A comparison of sign language and the Picture Exchange Communication System.* Unpublished doctoral dissertation, University of California, San Diego, CA. (UMI Microform No.: 3027052).

Anderson, D. (2006). Lexical development of deaf children acquiring signed languages. In B. Schick, M. Marschark, & P. E. Spencer (eds.), *Advances in the sign language development of deaf children* (pp. 135–160). New York, NY: Oxford University Press, https://doi.org/10.1093/acprof:oso/9780195180947.003.0006

Anderson, D., & Reilly, J. (2002). The MacArthur Communicative Development Inventory: Normative data for American Sign Language. *Journal of Deaf Studies and Deaf Education, 7,* 83–106, https://doi.org/10.1093/deafed/7.2.83

Anderson, D. E., & Reilly, J. S. (1997). The puzzle of negation: How children move from communicative to grammatical negation in ASL. *Applied Psycholinguistics, 18,* 411–429, https://doi.org/10.1017/s0142716400010912

Anderson, S. W., Damasio, H., Damasio, A. R., Klima, E. S., Bellugi, U., & Brandt, J. P. (1992). Acquisition of signs from American Sign Language in hearing individuals following left hemisphere damage and aphasia. *Neuropsychologia, 30,* 329–340, https://doi.org/10.1016/0028-3932(92)90106-v

Angeleri, R., Gabbatore, I., Bosco, F. M., Sacco, K., & Colle, L. (2016). Pragmatic abilities in children and adolescents with autism spectrum disorder: A study with the ABaCo battery. *Minerva Psichiatrica, 57,* 93–103.

Arbib, M. (2005). The mirror system hypothesis: How did protolanguage evolve? In M. Tallerman (ed.), *Language origins: Perspectives on evolution* (pp. 21–47). New York, NY: Oxford University Press.

Arbib, M. A. (2013). Précis of how the brain got language: The mirror system hypothesis. *Language and Cognition, 5,* 107–131, https://doi.org/10.1515/langcog-2013-0007

Archibald, L. M. D., & Gathercole, S. E. (2006). Visuospatial immediate memory in specific language impairment. *Journal of Speech, Language, and Hearing Research, 49,* 265–277, https://doi.org/10.1044/1092-4388(2006/022)

Archibald, L. M. D., & Griebeling, K. H. (2016). Rethinking the connection between working memory and language impairment. *International Journal of Language & Communication Disorders, 51,* 252–264, https://doi.org/10.1111/1460-6984.12202

Armstrong, D. F. (1983). Iconicity, arbitrariness, and duality of patterning in signed and spoken languages: Perspectives on language evolution. *Sign Language Studies, 38,* 51–83, https://doi.org/10.1353/sls.1983.0013

Armstrong, D. F. (1988). Review article: The world turned inside out. *Sign Language Studies, 61,* 419–428, https://doi.org/10.1353/sls.1988.0030

Armstrong, D. F. (2008). The gestural theory of language origins. *Sign Language Studies*, 8, 289–314, https://doi.org/10.1353/sls.2008.0005

Armstrong, D. F. (2011). *Show of hands: A natural history of sign language.* Washington, DC: Gallaudet University Press.

Armstrong, D. F., Stokoe, W. C., & Wilcox, S. E. (1995). *Gesture and the nature of language.* Cambridge, U.K.: Cambridge University Press, https://doi.org/10.1017/CBO9780511620911

Armstrong, D. F., & Wilcox, S. E. (2007). *The gestural origin of language.* New York, NY: Oxford University Press, https://doi.org/10.1093/acprof:oso/9780195163483.001.0001

Arnold, P., & Murray, C. (1998). Memory for faces and objects by deaf and hearing signers and hearing nonsigners. *Journal of Psycholinguistic Research*, 27, 481–497, https://doi.org/10.1023/A:1023277220438

Arnott, S. (2011). Exploring the dynamic relationship between the Accelerative Integrated Method (AIM) and the core French teachers who use it: Why agency and experience matter. *The Canadian Journal of Applied Linguistics*, 14, 156–176.

Asher, J. J. (1969). The Total Physical Response approach to second language learning. *The Modern Language Journal*, 53, 3–17, https://doi.org/10.1111/j.1540-4781.1969.tb04552.x

Assaneo, M. F., Nichols, J. I., & Trevisan, M. A. (2011). The anatomy of onomatopoeia. *PLoS One*, 6, e28317, https://doi.org/10.1371/journal.pone.0028317

Atkinson, J. R., Woll, B., & Gathercole, S. (2002). The impact of developmental visuospatial learning difficulties on British Sign Language. *Neurocase*, 8, 424–441, https://doi.org/10.1076/neur.8.5.424.16176

Autism Genome Project Consortium. (2007). Mapping autism risk loci using genetic linkage and chromosomal rearrangements. *Nature Genetics*, 39, 319–328, https://doi.org/10.1038/ng1985

Autism Speaks. (2017). *Autism and health: Advances in understanding and treating the health conditions that frequently accompany autism*, https://www.autismspeaks.org/sites/default/files/2018-09/autism-and-health-report.pdf

Avramidis, E., & Norwich, B. (2002). Teacher's attitudes towards integration/inclusion: A review of the literature. *European Journal of Special Needs Education*, 17, 129–147, https://doi.org/10.1080/08856250210129056

Axtell, J. (2000). Babel of tongues: Communicating with the Indians in eastern North America. In E. G. Gray & N. Fiering (eds.), *The language encounter in the Americas, 1492–1800* (pp. 15–60). New York, NY: Berghahn Books.

Axtell, R. E. (1991). *Gestures: The do's and taboos of body language around the world.* New York, NY: John Wiley & Sons.

Aziz, A. A., Shohdi, S., Osman, D. M., & Habib, E. I. (2010). Childhood apraxia of speech and multiple phonological disorders in Cairo-Egyptian Arabic speaking children: Language, speech, and oro-motor differences. *International Journal of Pediatric Otorhinolaryngology*, 74, 578–585, https://doi.org/10.1016/j.ijporl.2010.02.003

Bailey, A., Le Couteur, A., Gottesman, I., Bolton, P., Simonoff, E., Yuzda, E., & Rutter, M. (1995). Autism as a strongly genetic disorder: Evidence from a British twin study. *Psychological Medicine*, 25, 63–77, https://doi.org/10.1017/s0033291700028099

Baird, G., Charman, T., Baron-Cohen, S., Cox, A., Swettenham, J., Wheelwright, S., & Drew, A. (2000). A screening instrument for autism at 18 months of age: A 6-year follow-up study. *Journal of the American Academy of Child and Adolescent Psychiatry*, 39, 694–702, https://doi.org/10.1097/00004583-200006000-00007

Baker, A., van den Bogaerde, B., Pfau, R., & Schermer, T. (eds.). (2016). *The linguistics of sign languages: An introduction.* Amsterdam, The Netherlands: John Benjamins Publishing, https://doi.org/10.1075/z.199

Baker, A. E., & van den Bogaerde, B. (1996). Language input and attentional behavior. In C. E. Johnson & J. H. V. Gilbert (eds.), *Children's Language, vol. 9* (pp. 209–217). Mahwah, NJ: Lawrence Erlbaum Associates.

Bakheit, A. M. O., Shaw, S., Carrington, S., & Griffiths, S. (2007). The rate and extent of improvement with therapy from the different types of aphasia in the first year after stroke. *Clinical Rehabilitation*, 21, 941–949, https://doi.org/10.1177/0269215507078452

Banajee, M., Dicarlo, C., & Stricklin, S. B. (2003). Core vocabulary determination for toddlers. *Augmentative and Alternative Communication*, 19, 67–73, https://doi.org/10.1080/0743461031000112034

Bangerter, A. (2004). Using pointing and describing to achieve joint focus of attention in dialogue. *Psychological Science*, 15, 415–419, https://doi.org/10.1111/j.0956-7976.2004.00694.x

Barakat, R. A. (1975). *The Cistercian Sign Language: A study in non-verbal communication.* Kalamazoo, MI: Cistercian Publications.

Baranek, G. T. (1999). Autism during infancy: A retrospective video analysis of sensory-motor and social behaviors at 9–12 months of age. *Journal of Autism and Developmental Disorders*, 29, 213–224, https://doi.org/10.1023/A:1023080005650

Baranek, G. T. (2002). Efficacy of sensory and motor interventions for children with autism. *Journal of Autism and Developmental Disorders*, 32, 397–422, https://doi.org/10.1023/A:1020541906063

Baratz, R. (1985). A case study: Manual communication training for a global aphasic patient. *Aphasia-Apraxia-Agnosia*, 3, 19–44.

Barkley, R. A. (2003). Issues in the diagnosis of attention-deficit/hyperactivity disorder in children. *Brain and Development*, 25, 77–83, https://doi.org/10.1016/s0387-7604(02)00152-3

Barnes, E. F., Roberts, J., Long, S. H., Martin, G. E., Berni, M. C., Mandulak, K. C., & Sideris, J. (2009). Phonological accuracy and intelligibility in connected speech of boys with fragile X syndrome or Down syndrome. *Journal of Speech, Language, and Hearing Research*, 52, 1048–1061, https://doi.org/10.1044/1092-4388(2009/08-0001)

Barnes, E. F., Roberts, J., Mirrett, P., Sideris, J., & Misenheimer, J. (2006). A comparison of oral structure and oral-motor function in young males with fragile X syndrome and Down syndrome. *Journal of Speech, Language, and Hearing Research*, 49, 903–917, https://doi.org/10.1044/1092-4388(2006/065)

Barnes, S. K. (2010). Sign language with babies: What difference does it make? *Dimensions of Early Childhood*, 38, 21–29.

Barnett, D. (1990). The art of gesture. In V. Kapp (ed.), *Die sprache der zeichen und bilder: Rhetorik und nonverbale kommunikation in der frühen neuzeit* (pp. 65–76). Marburg, Germany: Hitzeroth.

Barrera, R. D., Lobato-Barrera, D., & Sulzer-Azaroff, B. (1980). A simultaneous treatment comparison of three expressive language training programs with a mute autistic child. *Journal of Autism and Developmental Disorders*, 10, 21–37, https://doi.org/10.1007/bf02408430

Barrera, R. D., & Sulzer-Azaroff, B. (1983). An alternating treatment comparison of oral and total communication training programs with echolalic autistic children. *Journal of Applied Behavior Analysis*, 16, 379–394, https://doi.org/10.1901/jaba.1983.16-379

Barsalou, L. W. (2008). Grounded cognition. *Annual Review of Psychology*, 59, 617–645, https://doi.org/10.1146/annurev.psych.59.103006.093639

Bartlett, D. E. (1853). Family education for young deaf-mute children. *American Annals of the Deaf and Dumb*, 5, 32–35.

Bates, E., Benigni, L., Bretherton, I., Camaioni, L., & Volterra, V. (1979). *The emergence of symbols: Cognition and communication in infancy*. New York, NY: Academic Press.

Batorowicz, B., Campbell, F., von Tetzchner, S., King, G., & Missiuna, C. (2014). Social participation of school-aged children who use communication aids: The views of children and parents. *Augmentative and Alternative Communication*, 30, 237–251, https://doi.org/10.3109/07434618.2014.940464

Battison, R. (1978). *Lexical borrowing in American Sign Language*. Silver Spring, MD: Linstok Press.

Bauman, M. L., & Kemper, T. L. (2005). Neuroanatomic observations of the brain in autism: A review and future directions. *International Journal of Developmental Neuroscience*, 23, 183–187, https://doi.org/10.1016/j.ijdevneu.2004.09.006

Baus, C., Carreiras, M., & Emmorey, K. (2013). When does iconicity in sign language matter? *Language and Cognitive Processes*, 28, 261–271, https://doi.org/10.1080/01690965.2011.620374

Beattie, G., & Shovelton, H. (2011). An exploration of the other side of semantic communication: How the spontaneous movements of the human hand add crucial meaning to narrative. *Semiotica*, 184, 33–51, https://doi.org/10.1515/semi.2011.021

Bébian, R.-A. (1817/1984). Essay on the deaf and natural language or introduction to a natural classification of ideas with their proper signs (F. Philip, Trans., 1984). In H. Lane (ed.), *The deaf experience: Classics in language and education* (pp. 127–160). Cambridge, MA: Harvard University Press. [Originally published in 1817 as *Essai sur les sourds-muets et sur le langage naturel*. Paris, France: Dentu.]

Becker, E. B. E., & Stoodley, C. J. (2013). Autism spectrum disorder and the cerebellum. *International Review of Neurobiology*, 113, 1–34, https://doi.org/10.1016/b978-0-12-418700-9.00001-0

Béland, R., & Ska, B. (1992). Interaction between verbal and gestural language in progressive aphasia: A longitudinal case study. *Brain and Language*, 43, 355–385, https://doi.org/10.1016/0093-934X(92)90107-P

Bellugi, U., & Klima, E. S. (1976). Two faces of sign: Iconic and abstract. In S. R. Harnad, H. D. Steklis, & J. Lancaster (eds.), *The origins and evolution of language and speech* (pp. 514–538). New York, NY: New York Academy of Sciences, https://doi.org/10.1111/j.1749-6632.1976.tb25514.x

Bellugi, U., O'Grady, L., Lillo-Martin, D., O'Grady Hynes, M., van Hoek, K., & Corina, D. (1990). Enhancement of spatial cognition in deaf children. In V. Volterra & C. J. Erting (eds.), *From gesture to language in hearing and deaf children* (pp. 278–298). Berlin, Germany: Springer-Verlag, https://doi.org/10.1007/978-3-642-74859-2_22

Benson, D. F., & Ardila, A. (1996). *Aphasia: A clinical perspective*. New York, NY: Oxford University Press.

Benton, A. L., Hamsher, K., Varney, N. R., & Spreen, O. (1983). *Facial recognition: Stimuli and multiple choice pictures*. New York, NY: Oxford University Press.

Berglund, E., Eriksson, M., & Johansson, I. (2001). Parental reports of spoken language skills in children with Down syndrome. *Journal of Speech, Language, and Hearing Research*, 44, 179–191, https://doi.org/10.1044/1092-4388(2001/016)

Bernier, R., Dawson, G., Webb, S., & Murias, M. (2007). EEG mu rhythm and imitation impairments in individuals with autism spectrum disorder. *Brain and Cognition*, 64, 228–237, https://doi.org/10.1016/j.bandc.2007.03.004

Bernstein Ratner, N. (2017). Atypical language development. In J. Berko Gleason & N. Bernstein Ratner (eds.), *The development of language* (9th ed., pp. 215–256). Boston, MA: Pearson.

Berry, J. O. (1987). Strategies for involving parents in programs for young children using augmentative and alternative communication. *Augmentative and Alternative Communication*, 3, 90–93, https://doi.org/10.1080/074346187 12331274319

Bettger, J. G., Emmorey, K., McCullough, S. H., & Bellugi, U. (1997). Enhanced facial discrimination: Effects of experience with American Sign Language. *Journal of Deaf Studies and Deaf Education*, 2, 223–233, https://doi.org/10.1093/oxfordjournals.deafed.a014328

Beukelman, D. R., Fager, S., Ball, L., & Dietz, A. (2007). AAC for adults with acquired neurological conditions: A review. *Augmentative and Alternative Communication*, 23, 230–242, https://doi.org/10.1080/07434610701553668

Beukelman, D. R., Jones, R., & Rowan, M. (1989). Frequency of word usage by nondisabled peers in integrated preschool classrooms. *Augmentative and Alternative Communication*, 5, 243–248, https://doi.org/10.1080/0743461891 2331275296

Beukelman, D. R., & Mirenda, P. (2005). *Augmentative and alternative communication: Supporting children and adults with complex communication needs* (3rd ed.). Baltimore, MD: Paul H. Brookes Publishing.

Beukelman, D. R., & Mirenda, P. (2013). *Augmentative and alternative communication: Supporting children and adults with complex communication needs* (4th ed.). Baltimore, MD: Paul H. Brookes Publishing.

Beverly, B. L., McGuinness, T. M., & Blanton, D. J. (2008). Communication and academic challenges in early adolescence for children who have been adopted from the former Soviet Union. *Language, Speech, and Hearing Services in Schools*, 39, 303–313, https://doi.org/10.1044/0161-1461(2008/029)

Bezuidenhout, A., & Sroda, M. S. (1998). Children's use of contextual cues to resolve referential ambiguity: An application of relevance theory. *Pragmatics & Cognition*, 6, 265–299, https://doi.org/10.1075/pc.6.1-2.14bez

Bhat, A. N., Srinivasan, S. M., Woxholdt, C., & Shield, A. (2016). Differences in praxis performance and receptive language during fingerspelling between deaf children with and without autism spectrum disorder. *Autism*, 22, 271–282, https://doi.org/10.1177/1362361316672179

Bhogal, S. K., Teasell, R., & Speechley, M. (2003). Intensity of aphasia therapy, impact on recovery. *Stroke*, 34, 987–993, https://doi.org/10.1161/01.STR.0000062343.64383.D0

Biederman, J., & Faraone, S. V. (2005). Attention-deficit hyperactivity disorder. *The Lancet*, 366, 237–248, https://doi.org/10.1016/S0140-6736(05)66915-2

Bigelow, J., & Poremba, A. (2014). Achilles' ear? Inferior human short-term and recognition memory in the auditory modality. *PLoS ONE*, 9, e89914, https://doi.org/10.1371/journal.pone.0089914

Binkofski, F., & Buccino, G. (2004). Motor functions of the Broca's region. *Brain and Language*, 89, 362–369, https://doi.org/10.1016/s0093-934x(03)00358-4

Biscaldi, M., Rauh, R., Irion, L., Jung, N. H., Mall, V., Fleischhaker, C., & Klein, C. (2014). Deficits in motor abilities and developmental fractionation of imitation performance in high-functioning autism spectrum disorders. *European Child and Adolescent Psychiatry*, 23, 599–610, https://doi.org/10.1007/s00787-013-0475-x

Biscaldi, M., Rauh, R., Müller, C., Irion, L., Saville, C. W. N., Schulz, E., & Klein, C. (2015). Identification of neuromotor deficits common to autism spectrum disorder and attention deficit/hyperactivity disorder, and imitation deficits specific to autism spectrum disorder. *European Child and Adolescent Psychiatry*, 24, 1497–1507, https://doi.org/10.1007/s00787-015-0753-x

Bishop, D. V. M. (1985). Age of onset and outcome in "acquired aphasia with convulsive disorder" (Landau-Kleffner syndrome). *Developmental Medicine & Child Neurology*, 27, 705–712, https://doi.org/10.1111/j.1469-8749.1985.tb03793.x

Bishop, D. V. M. (2006). What causes specific language impairment in children? *Current Directions in Psychological Science*, 15, 217–221, https://doi.org/10.1111/j.1467-8721.2006.00439.x

Bishop, D. V. M. (2017). Why is it so hard to reach agreement on terminology? The case of developmental language disorder (DLD). *International Journal of Language & Communication Disorders*, 52, 671–680, https://doi.org/10.1111/1460-6984.12335

Bishop, D. V. M., North, T., & Donlan, C. (1996). Nonword repetition as a behavioural marker for inherited language impairment: Evidence from a twin study. *Journal of Child Psychology and Psychiatry*, 37, 391–403, https://doi.org/10.1111/j.1469-7610.1996.tb01420.x

Blake, J., Myszczyszyn, D., Jokel, A., & Bebiroglu, N. (2008). Gestures accompanying speech in specifically language-impaired children and their timing with speech. *First Language*, 28, 237–253, https://doi.org/10.1177/0142723707087583

Blischak, D. M., Lombardino, L. J., & Dyson, A. T. (2003). Use of speech-generating devices: In support of natural speech. *Augmentative and Alternative Communication*, 19, 29–35, https://doi.org/10.1080/0743461032000056478

Blischak, D. M., Loncke, F., & Waller, A. (1997). Intervention for persons with developmental disabilities. In L. L. Lloyd, D. R. Fuller, & H. H. Arvidson (eds.), *Alternative and augmentative communication: A handbook of principles and practices* (pp. 299–339). Boston, MA: Allyn and Bacon.

Bloomberg, K., Karlan, G. R., & Lloyd, L. L. (1990). The comparative translucency of initial lexical items represented in five graphic symbol systems and sets. *Journal of Speech and Hearing Research*, 33, 717–725, https://doi.org/10.1044/jshr.3304.717

Bluestone, C. D. (1998). Epidemiology and pathogenesis of chronic suppurative otitis media: Implications for prevention and treatment. *International Journal of Pediatric Otorhinolaryngology,* 42, 207–223, https://doi.org/10.1016/s0165-5876(97)00147-x

Bluestone, C. D., & Klein, J. O. (2007). *Otitis media in infants and children* (4th ed.). Hamilton, Ontario, Canada: B C Decker.

Bo, J., Lee, C.-M., Colbert, A., & Shen, B. (2016). Do children with autism spectrum disorders have motor learning difficulties? *Research in Autism Spectrum Disorders,* 23, 50–62, https://doi.org/10.1016/j.rasd.2015.12.001

Bodison, S., & Mostofsky, S. (2014). Motor control and motor learning processes in autism spectrum disorders. In F. R. Volkmar, R. Paul, S. J. Rogers, & K. A. Pelphrey (eds.), *Handbook of autism and pervasive developmental disorders, vol. 1. Diagnosis, development, and brain mechanisms* (4th ed., pp. 354–377). Hoboken, NJ: John Wiley & Sons, https://doi.org/10.1002/9781118911389

Bohn, M., Call, J., & Tomasello, M. (2016). Comprehension of iconic gestures by chimpanzees and human children. *Journal of Experimental Child Psychology,* 142, 1–17, https://doi.org/10.1016/j.jecp.2015.09.001

Bondy, A., & Frost, L. (1994). The Picture-Exchange Communication System. *Focus on Autistic Behavior,* 9, 1–19, https://doi.org/10.1177/108835769400900301

Bondy, A., & Frost, L. (2002). *A picture's worth: PECS and other visual communication strategies in autism.* Bethesda, MD: Woodbine House.

Bondy, A., & Frost, L. (2009a). Generalization issues pertaining to the Picture Exchange Communication System (PECS). In C. Whalen (ed.), *Real life, real progress for children with autism spectrum disorders: Strategies for successful generalization in natural environments* (pp. 57–81). Baltimore, MD: Paul H. Brookes Publishing.

Bondy, A., & Frost, L. (2009b). The Picture Exchange Communication System: Clinical and research applications. In P. Mirenda & T. Iacono (eds.), *Autism spectrum disorders and AAC* (pp. 279–302). Baltimore, MD: Paul H. Brookes Publishing.

Bonet, J. P. (1620). *Reducción de las letras y arte para enseñar a hablar los mudos.* Madrid, Spain: Francisco Abarca de Angulo.

Bonnet-Brilhault, F. (2017). L'autisme: Un trouble neuro-développemental précoce. *Archives de Pédiatrie,* 24, 384–390, https://doi.org/10.1016/j.arcped.2017.01.014

Bonvillian, J. D. (1999). Sign language development. In M. Barrett (ed.), *The development of language* (pp. 277–310). Hove, U.K.: Psychology Press.

Bonvillian, J. D. (2002). Sign communication training and motor functioning in children with autistic disorder and in other populations. In D. F. Armstrong, M. A. Karchmer, & J. V. Van Cleve (eds.), *The study of signed languages: Essays in honor of William C. Stokoe* (pp. 190–212). Washington, DC: Gallaudet University Press.

Bonvillian, J. D. (2019). Sign acquisition and development by hearing children with autism spectrum disorders. In N. Grove & K. Launonen (eds.), *Manual sign acquisition in children with developmental disabilities* (pp. 115–131). New York, NY: Nova Science Publishers, Inc.

Bonvillian, J. D., & Blackburn, D. W. (1991). Manual communication and autism: Factors relating to sign language acquisition. In P. Siple & S. D. Fischer (eds.), *Theoretical issues in sign language research, vol. 2. Psychology* (pp. 255–277). Chicago, IL: University of Chicago Press.

Bonvillian, J. D., & Friedman, R. J. (1978). Language development in another mode: The acquisition of signs by a brain-damaged adult. *Sign Language Studies*, 19, 111–120, https://doi.org/10.1353/sls.1978.0013

Bonvillian, J. D., Garber, A. M., & Dell, S. B. (1997). Language origin accounts: Was the gesture in the beginning? *First Language*, 17, 219–239, https://doi.org/10.1177/014272379701705110

Bonvillian, J. D., Ingram, V. L., & McCleary, B. M. (2009). Observations on the use of manual signs and gestures in the communicative interactions between Native Americans and Spanish explorers of North America: The accounts of Bernal Díaz del Castillo and Álvar Núñez Cabeza de Vaca. *Sign Language Studies*, 9, 132–165, https://doi.org/10.1353/sls.0.0013

Bonvillian, J. D., & Miller, A. J. (1995). Everything old is new again: Observations from the nineteenth century about sign communication training with mentally retarded children. *Sign Language Studies*, 88, 245–254, https://doi.org/10.1353/sls.1995.0019

Bonvillian, J. D., & Nelson, K. E. (1976). Sign language acquisition in a mute autistic boy. *Journal of Speech and Hearing Disorders*, 41, 339–347, https://doi.org/10.1044/jshd.4103.339

Bonvillian, J. D., & Nelson, K. E. (1978). Development of sign language in autistic children and other language-handicapped individuals. In P. Siple (ed.), *Understanding language through sign language research* (pp. 187–212). New York, NY: Academic Press.

Bonvillian, J. D., Nelson, K. E., & Rhyne, J. M. (1981). Sign language and autism. *Journal of Autism and Developmental Disorders*, 11, 125–137, https://doi.org/10.1007/bf01531345

Bonvillian, J. D., Orlansky, M. D., & Novack, L. L. (1983). Developmental milestones: Sign language acquisition and motor development. *Child Development*, 54, 1435–1445, https://doi.org/10.2307/1129806

Bonvillian, J. D., Richards, H. C., & Dooley, T. T. (1997). Early sign language acquisition and the development of hand preference in young children. *Brain and Language*, 58, 1–22, https://doi.org/10.1006/brln.1997.1754

Bonvillian, J. D., & Siedlecki, T., Jr. (1996). Young children's acquisition of the location aspect of American Sign Language signs: Parental report findings. *Journal of Communication Disorders*, 29, 13–35, https://doi.org/10.1016/0021-9924(94)00015-8

Bonvillian, J. D., & Siedlecki, T., Jr. (1998). Young children's acquisition of the movement aspect in American Sign Language: Parental report findings. *Journal of Speech, Language, and Hearing Research*, 41, 588–602, https://doi.org/10.1044/jslhr.4103.588

Bonvillian, J. D., & Siedlecki, T., Jr. (2000). Young children's acquisition of the formational aspects of American Sign Language: Parental report findings. *Sign Language Studies*, 1, 45–64, https://doi.org/10.1353/sls.2000.0002

Borghi, A. M., Capirci, O., Gianfreda, G., & Volterra, V. (2014). The body and the fading away of abstract concepts and words: A sign language analysis. *Frontiers in Psychology (Hypothesis and Theory)*, 5, AR 811, https://doi.org/10.3389/fpsyg.2014.00811

Borgia, M. E. (2014). Using gesture to teach Seneca in a language nest school. *Language Documentation & Conservation*, 8, 92–99.

Bornman, J., & Alant, E. (1999). Training teachers to facilitate interaction with autistic children using digital voice output devices. *South African Journal of Education*, 19, 364–373.

Bornstein, H. (1974). Signed English: A manual approach to English language development. *Journal of Speech and Hearing Disorders*, 39, 330–343, https://doi.org/10.1044/jshd.3903.330

Bornstein, H., & Jordan, I. K. (1984). *Functional signs: A new approach from simple to complex*. Baltimore, MD: University Park Press.

Bornstein, H., Saulnier, K. L., & Miller, R. (1984). *The Signed English starter*. Washington, DC: Gallaudet College Press.

Botha, R. (2007). On homesign systems as a potential window on language evolution. *Language and Communication*, 27, 41–53, https://doi.org/10.1016/j.langcom.2005.10.001

Botting, N. (2002). Narrative as a tool for the assessment of linguistic and pragmatic impairments. *Child Language Teaching and Therapy*, 18, 1–21, https://doi.org/10.1191/0265659002ct224oa

Botting, N. (2014). Specific language impairment (overview). In P. J. Brooks & V. Kempe (eds.), *Encyclopedia of language development* (pp. 567–573). Los Angeles, CA: SAGE, https://doi.org/10.4135/9781483346441.n181

Botting, N., Riches, N., Gaynor, M., & Morgan, G. (2010). Gesture production and comprehension in children with specific language impairment. *British Journal of Developmental Psychology*, 28, 51–69, https://doi.org/10.1348/026151009x482642

Bottos, M., Granato, T., Allibrio, G., Gioachin, C., & Puato, M. L. (1999). Prevalence of cerebral palsy in north-east Italy from 1965 to 1989. *Developmental Medicine & Child Neurology*, 41, 26–39, https://doi.org/10.1111/j.1469-8749.1999.tb00006.x

Boukhris, T., Sheehy, O., Mottron, L., & Bérard. A. (2016). Antidepressant use during pregnancy and the risk of autism spectrum disorder in children. *JAMA Pediatrics*, 170, 117–124, https://doi.org/10.1001/jamapediatrics.2015.3356

Bourdages, J. S., & Vignola, M.-J. (2009). Évaluation des habiletés de communication orale chez des élèves de l'élémentaire utilisant AIM. *The Canadian Modern Language Review*, 65, 731–755, https://doi.org/10.3138/cmlr.65.5.731

Bowles, C., & Frizelle, P. (2016). Investigating peer attitudes towards the use of key word signing by children with Down syndrome in mainstream schools. *British Journal of Learning Disabilities*, 44, 284–291, https://doi.org/10.1111/bld.12162

Boyes Braem, P. (1973/1990). Acquisition of the handshape in American Sign Language: A preliminary analysis. In V. Volterra & C. Erting (eds.), *From gesture to language in hearing and deaf children* (pp. 107–127). Heidelberg, Germany: Springer-Verlag, https://doi.org/10.1007/978-3-642-74859-2_10

Boyes Braem, P. (1986). Two aspects of psycholinguistic research: Iconicity and temporal structure. In B. T. Tervoort (ed.), *Signs of life: Proceedings of the Second European Congress on Sign Language Research* (pp. 65–74). Amsterdam, The Netherlands: Publication of the Institute for General Linguistics, University of Amsterdam.

Braden, J. P. (1994). *Deafness, deprivation, and IQ*. New York, NY: Plenum Press, https://doi.org/10.1007/978-1-4757-4917-5

Brady, N. C., Skinner, D., Roberts, J., & Hennon, E. (2006). Communication in young children with fragile X syndrome: A qualitative study of mothers' perspectives. *American Journal of Speech-Language Pathology*, 15, 353–364, https://doi.org/10.1044/1058-0360(2006/033)

Brady, N. C. (2008). Augmentative and alternative communication for children with Down syndrome or fragile X syndrome. In J. E. Roberts, R. S. Chapman, & S. F. Warren (eds.), *Speech & language development & intervention in Down syndrome & fragile X syndrome* (pp. 255–274). Baltimore, MD: Paul H. Brookes Publishing.

Brady, N. C., Thiemann-Bourque, K., Fleming, K., & Matthews, K. (2013). Predicting language outcomes for children learning augmentative and alternative communication: Child and environmental factors. *Journal of Speech, Language, and Hearing Research*, 56, 1595–1612, https://doi.org/10.1044/1092-4388(2013/12-0102)

Bragg, L. (1997). Visual-kinetic communication in Europe before 1600: A survey of sign lexicons and finger alphabets prior to the rise of deaf education.

Journal of Deaf Studies and Deaf Education, 2, 1–25, https://doi.org/10.1093/oxfordjournals.deafed.a014306

Bram, S., Meier, M., & Sutherland, P. J. (1977). A relationship between motor control and language development in an autistic child. *Journal of Autism and Childhood Schizophrenia*, 7, 57–67, https://doi.org/10.1007/bf01531115

Branson, D., & Demchak, M. (2009). The use of augmentative and alternative communication methods with infants and toddlers with disabilities: A research review. *Augmentative and Alternative Communication*, 25, 274–286, https://doi.org/10.3109/07434610903384529

Brennan, M. (1998). *The hidden Maya*. Santa Fe, NM: Bear & Company.

Brennan, M. (2005). Conjoining word and image in British Sign Language (BSL): An exploration of metaphorical signs in BSL. *Sign Language Studies*, 5, 360–382, https://doi.org/10.1353/sls.2005.0007

Brentari, D. (1998). *A prosodic model of sign language phonology*. Cambridge, MA: MIT Press, https://doi.org/10.7551/mitpress/5644.001.0001

Brereton, A. (2008). Sign language use and the appreciation of diversity in hearing classrooms. *Early Years*, 28, 311–324, https://doi.org/10.1080/09575140802393702

Brereton, A. (2009). Alana: How one hearing child used sign language to move from "disruptive" student to a classroom expert. *Early Childhood Education Journal*, 36, 461–465, https://doi.org/10.1007/s10643-008-0297-5

Brian, J., Bryson, S. E., Smith, I. M., Roberts, W., Roncadin, C., Szatmari, P., & Zwaigenbaum, L. (2016). Stability and change in autism spectrum disorder diagnosis from age 3 to middle childhood in a high-risk sibling cohort. *Autism*, 20, 888–892, https://doi.org/10.1177/1362361315614979

Bristol, M. M., Cohen, D. J., Costello, E. J., Denckla, M., Eckberg, T. J., Kallen, R., Kraemer, H. C., Lord, C., Maurer, R., McIlvane, W. J., Minshew, N., Sigman, M., & Spence, M. A. (1996). State of the science in autism: Report to the National Institutes of Health. *Journal of Autism and Developmental Disorders*, 26, 121–154, https://doi.org/10.1007/bf02172002

Broberg, M., Ferm, U., & Thunberg, G. (2012). Measuring responsive style in parents who use AAC with their children: Development and evaluation of a new instrument. *Augmentative and Alternative Communication*, 28, 243–253, https://doi.org/10.3109/07434618.2012.740686

Brock, J. (2007). Language abilities in Williams syndrome: A critical review. *Development and Psychopathology*, 19, 97–127, https://doi.org/10.1017/s095457940707006x

Brookner, S. P., & Murphy, N. O. (1975). The use of a total communication approach with a nondeaf child: A case study. *Language, Speech, and Hearing Services in Schools*, 6, 131–139, https://doi.org/10.1044/0161-1461.0603.131

Brown, R. (1979). Why are signed languages easier to learn than spoken languages? In W. C. Stokoe (ed.), *Proceedings of the national symposium on sign language research and teaching* (pp. 9–24). Silver Spring, MD: National Association of the Deaf.

Brown, T. E. (2005). *Attention deficit disorder: The unfocused mind in children and adults.* New Haven, CT: Yale University Press.

Bruce, S., DiNatale, P., & Ford, J. (2008). Meeting the needs of deaf and hard of hearing students with additional disabilities through professional teacher development. *American Annals of the Deaf, 153,* 368–375, https://doi.org/10.1353/aad.0.0058

Bruce, S. G. (2007). *Silence and sign language in medieval monasticism: The Cluniac tradition c. 900–1200.* Cambridge, U.K.: Cambridge University Press, https://doi.org/10.1017/CBO9780511496417

Bryen, D. N., Goldman, A. S., & Quinlisk-Gill, S. (1988). Sign language with students with severe/profound mental retardation: How effective is it? *Education and Training in Mental Retardation, 23,* 129–137.

Bryen, D. N., & Joyce, D. G. (1985). Language intervention with the severely handicapped: A decade of research. *The Journal of Special Education, 19,* 7–39, https://doi.org/10.1177/002246698501900103

Bryen, D. N., & Joyce, D. G. (1986). Sign language and the severely handicapped. *The Journal of Special Education, 20,* 183–194, https://doi.org/10.1177/002246698602000205

Bryen, D. N., & McGinley, V. (1991). Sign language input to community residents with mental retardation. *Education and Training in Mental Retardation, 26,* 207–213.

Buccino, G., Solodkin, A., & Small, S. L. (2006). Functions of the mirror neuron system: Implications for neurorehabilitation. *Cognitive and Behavioral Neurology, 19,* 55–63, https://doi.org/10.1097/00146965-200603000-00007

Buckingham, J., Beaman, R., & Wheldall, K. (2014). Why poor children are more likely to become poor readers: The early years. *Educational Review, 66,* 428–446, https://doi.org/10.1080/00131911.2013.795129

Budiyanto, Sheehy, K., Kaye, H., & Rofiah, K. (2018). Developing Signalong Indonesia: Issues of happiness and pedagogy, training and stigmatisation. *International Journal of Inclusive Education, 22,* 543–559, https://doi.org/10.1080/13603116.2017.1390000

Bulwer, J. (1644/1974). *Chirologia: Or the natural language of the hand and Chironomia: Or the art of manual rhetoric* (J. W. Cleary, Ed., 1974). Carbondale, IL: Southern Illinois University Press. [This updated, expanded, and annotated edition is based on the text of the first edition, originally published in 1644 by Thomas Harper and sold by R. Whitaker, and on the illustrations from the edition sold by Henry Twyford.]

Burroughs, G. E. R. (1957). *A study of the vocabulary of young children.* Edinburgh, Scotland: Oliver & Boyd.

Calculator, S., & Diaz-Caneja Sela, P. (2015). Overview of the enhanced natural gestures instructional approach and illustration of its use with three students with Angelman syndrome. *Journal of Applied Research in Intellectual Disabilities*, 28, 145–158, https://doi.org/10.1111/jar.12110

Calculator, S. N. (2013a). Parents' reports of patterns of use and exposure to practices associated with AAC acceptance by individuals with Angelman syndrome. *Augmentative and Alternative Communication*, 29, 146–158, https://doi.org/10.3109/07434618.2013.784804

Calculator, S. N. (2013b). Use and acceptance of AAC systems by children with Angelman syndrome. *Journal of Applied Research in Intellectual Disabilities*, 26, 557–567, https://doi.org/10.1111/jar.12048

Calculator, S. N. (2016). Description and evaluation of a home-based, parent-administered program for teaching Enhanced Natural Gestures to individuals with Angelman syndrome. *American Journal of Speech-Language Pathology*, 25, 1–13, https://doi.org/10.1044/2015_ajslp-15-0017

Camarata, S. M. (2014). *Late-talking children: A symptom or a stage?* Cambridge, MA: MIT Press, https://doi.org/10.7551/mitpress/10035.001.0001

Campbell, C. R., & Jackson, S. T. (1995). Transparency of one-handed Amer-Ind hand signals to nonfamiliar viewers. *Journal of Speech and Hearing Research*, 38, 1284–1289, https://doi.org/10.1044/jshr.3806.1284

Campbell, L. (1997). *American Indian languages: The historical linguistics of Native America.* New York, NY: Oxford University Press.

Campbell, R., & Woll, B. (2003). Space is special in sign. *Trends in Cognitive Sciences*, 7, 5–7, https://doi.org/10.1016/s1364-6613(02)00012-8

Campos, J. G., & Guevara, L. G. de. (2007). Landau-Kleffner syndrome. *Journal of Pediatric Neurology*, 5, 93–99, https://doi.org/10.1055/s-0035-1557366

Caparulo, B. K., & Cohen, D. J. (1977). Cognitive structures, language, and emerging social competence in autistic and aphasic children. *Journal of the American Academy of Child Psychiatry*, 16, 620–645, https://doi.org/10.1016/s0002-7138(09)61183-3

Capirci, O., Cattani, A., Rossini, P., & Volterra, V. (1998). Teaching sign language to hearing children as a possible factor in cognitive enhancement. *Journal of Deaf Studies and Deaf Education*, 3, 135–142, https://doi.org/10.1093/oxfordjournals.deafed.a014343

Caplan, D. (1995). *Neurolinguistics and linguistic aphasiology: An introduction.* Cambridge, U.K.: Cambridge University Press. [Reprint; first published in 1987.]

Caraballo, R. H., Cejas, N., Chamorro, N., Kaltenmeier, M. C., Fortini, S., & Soprano, A. M. (2014). Landau-Kleffner syndrome: A study of 29 patients. *Seizure, 23,* 98–104, https://doi.org/10.1016/j.seizure.2013.09.016

Carbone, V. J., Sweeney-Kerwin, E. J., Attanasio, V., & Kasper, T. (2010). Increasing the vocal responses of children with autism and developmental disabilities using manual sign mand training and prompt delay. *Journal of Applied Behavior Analysis, 43,* 705–709, https://doi.org/10.1901/jaba. 2010.43-705

Carey, B. (2015). *How we learn: The surprising truth about when, where, and why it happens.* New York, NY: Random House.

Carmo, P. do, Mineiro, A., Castelo Branco, J., Quadros, R. M. de, & Castro-Caldas, A. (2013). Handshape is the hardest path in Portuguese Sign Language acquisition: Towards a universal modality constraint. *Sign Language & Linguistics, 16,* 75–90, https://doi.org/10.1075/sll.16.1.03car

Carr, D., & Felce, J. (2007). The effects of PECS teaching to phase III on the communicative interactions between children with autism and their teachers. *Journal of Autism and Developmental Disorders, 37,* 724–737, https://doi.org/10.1007/s10803-006-0203-1

Carr, E. G. (1982). Sign language. In R. L. Koegel, A. Rincover, & A. L. Egel (eds.), *Educating and understanding autistic children* (pp. 142–157). San Diego, CA: College-Hill Press.

Carr, E. G., & Durand, V. M. (1985). Reducing behavior problems through functional communication training. *Journal of Applied Behavior Analysis, 18,* 111–126, https://doi.org/10.1901/jaba.1985.18-111

Carr, E. G., & Kologinsky, E. (1983). Acquisition of sign language by autistic children: II. Spontaneity and generalization effects. *Journal of Applied Behavior Analysis, 16,* 297–314, https://doi.org/10.1901/jaba.1983.16-297

Carr, E. G., Pridal, C., & Dores, P. A. (1984). Speech versus sign comprehension in autistic children: Analysis and prediction. *Journal of Experimental Child Psychology, 37,* 587–597, https://doi.org/10.1016/0022-0965(84)90078-x

Carretti, B., Lanfranchi, S., & Mammarella, I. C. (2013). Spatial-simultaneous and spatial-sequential working memory in individuals with Down syndrome: The effect of configuration. *Research in Developmental Disabilities, 34,* 669–675, https://doi.org/10.1016/j.ridd.2012.09.011

Cartmill, E. A., Beilock, S., & Goldin-Meadow, S. (2012). A word in the hand: Action, gesture and mental representation in humans and non-human primates. *Philosophical Transactions of the Royal Society B, 367,* 129–143, https://doi.org/10.1098/rstb.2011.0162

Caselli, N. K., & Pyers, J. E. (2017). The road to language learning is not entirely iconic: Iconicity, neighborhood density, and frequency facilitate acquisition of sign language. *Psychological Science, 28,* 979–987, https://doi. org/10.1177/0956797617700498

Caselli, N. K., Sevcikova Sehyr, Z., Cohen-Goldberg, A. M., & Emmorey, K. (2017). ASL-LEX: A lexical database of American Sign Language. *Behavior Research Methods*, 49, 784–801, https://doi.org/10.3758/s13428-016-0742-0

Casey, B., Erkut, S., Ceder, I., & Young, J. M. (2008). Use of a storytelling context to improve girls' and boys' geometry skills in kindergarten. *Journal of Applied Developmental Psychology*, 29, 29–48, https://doi.org/10.1016/j.appdev.2007.10.005

Casey, B. M. (2013). Individual and group differences in spatial ability. In D. Waller & L. Nadel (eds.), *Handbook of spatial cognition* (pp. 117–134). Washington, DC: American Psychological Association, https://doi.org/10.1037/13936-007

Cassidy, S., Hannant, P., Tavassoli, T., Allison, C., Smith, P., & Baron-Cohen, S. (2016). Dyspraxia and autistic traits in adults with and without autism spectrum conditions. *Molecular Autism*, 7, 48, https://doi.org/10.1186/s13229-016-0112-x

Castañeda, P. de. *The journey of Francisco Vazquez de Coronado, 1540–1542 (as told by Pedro de Castañeda, Francisco Vazquez de Coronado, and others)* (G. P. Winship, Trans., Ed., 1933). San Francisco, CA: The Grabhorn Press.

Castillo, E. M., Butler, I. J., Baumgartner, J. E., Passaro, A., & Papanicolaou, A. C. (2008). When epilepsy interferes with word comprehension: Findings in Landau-Kleffner syndrome. *Journal of Child Neurology*, 23, 97–101, https://doi.org/10.1177/0883073807308701

Cates, D., Gutiérrez, E., Hafer, S., Barrett, R., & Corina, D. (2013). Location, location, location. *Sign Language Studies*, 13, 433–461, https://doi.org/10.1353/sls.2013.0014

Cattaneo, L., Fabbri-Destro, M., Boria, S., Pieraccini, C., Monti, A., Cossu, G., & Rizzolatti, G. (2007). Impairment of actions chains in autism and its possible role in intention understanding. *Proceedings of the National Academy of Sciences*, 104, 17825–17830, https://doi.org/10.1073/pnas.0706273104

Centre for Excellence in Universal Design. (2020). *What is universal design.* Dublin, Ireland: Centre for Excellence in Universal Design, National Disability Authority, http://universaldesign.ie/What-is-Universal-Design/

Centers for Disease Control and Prevention. (2018). Prevalence of autism spectrum disorder among children aged 8 years — Autism and Developmental Disabilities Monitoring Network, 11 sites, United States, 2014. *MMWR Surveillance Summaries Publication 67 (No. SS-6)*, https://doi.org/10.15585/mmwr.ss6706a1

Chadwick, D. D., & Jolliffe, J. (2008). A pilot investigation into the efficacy of a signing training strategy for staff working with adults with intellectual disabilities. *British Journal of Learning Disabilities*, 37, 34–42, https://doi.org/10.1111/j.1468-3156.2008.00503.x

Chamberlain, C., Morford, J. P., & Mayberry, R. I. (2000). *Language acquisition by eye*. Mahwah, NJ: Lawrence Erlbaum Associates.

Chan, H. S. S., Lau, P. H. B., Fong, K. H., Poon, D., & Lam, C. C. C. (2005). Neuroimpairment, activity limitation, and participation restriction among children with cerebral palsy in Hong Kong. *Hong Kong Medical Journal*, 11, 342–350, https://www.hkmj.org/abstracts/v11n5/342.htm

Chapman, R. S., & Hesketh, L. J. (2000). Behavioral phenotype of individuals with Down syndrome. *Mental Retardation and Developmental Disabilities Research Reviews*, 6, 84–95, https://doi. org/10.1002/1098-2779(2000)6:2<84::aid-mrdd2>3.0.co;2-p

Chapman, T., Stormont, M., & McCathren, R. (1998). What every educator should know about Landau-Kleffner syndrome. *Focus on Autism and Other Developmental Disabilities*, 13, 39–44, https://doi. org/10.1177/108835769801300105

Chatley, N. (2013). *Development of the enactment effect: Examining individual differences in executive function to predict increased memory for action*. Unpublished master's thesis, University of North Carolina at Greensboro, Greensboro, NC.

Chaves, T. L. de, & Soler, J. L. (1974). Pedro Ponce de León, first teacher of the deaf. *Sign Language Studies*, 5, 48–63, https://doi.org/10.1353/sls.1974.0001

Chawarska, K., Klin, A., Paul, R., Macari, S., & Volkmar, F. (2009). A prospective study of toddlers with ASD: Short-term diagnostic and cognitive outcomes. *Journal of Child Psychology and Psychiatry*, 50, 1235–1245, https://doi. org/10.1111/j.1469-7610.2009.02101.x

Chawarska, K., Shic, F., Macari, S., Campbell, D. J., Brian, J., Landa, R., Hutman, T., Nelson, C. A., Ozonoff, S., Tager-Flusberg, H., Young, G. S., Zwaigenbaum, L., Cohen, I. L., Charman, T., Messinger, D. S., Klin, A., Johnson, S., & Bryson, S. (2014). 18-month predictors of later outcomes in younger siblings of children with autism spectrum disorder: A baby siblings research consortium study. *Journal of the American Academy of Child & Adolescent Psychiatry*, 53, 1317–1327, https://doi.org/10.1016/j.jaac.2014.09.015

Cheek, A., Cormier, K., Repp, A., & Meier, R. P. (2001). Prelinguistic gesture predicts mastery and error in the production of early signs. *Language*, 77, 292–323, https://doi.org/10.1353/lan.2001.0072

Chen, H.-L. (1994). Hearing in the elderly: Relation of hearing loss, loneliness, and self-esteem. *Journal of Gerontological Nursing*, 20, 22–28, https://doi. org/10.3928/0098-9134-19940601-07

Chen Pichler, D., & Koulidobrova, E. (2015). Acquisition of sign language as a second language. In M. Marschark & P. E. Spencer (eds.), *The Oxford handbook of Deaf studies in language* (pp. 218–230). Oxford, U.K.: Oxford University Press, https://doi.org/10.1093/oxfordhb/9780190241414.013.14

Cheron, G., Márquez-Ruiz, J., & Dan, B. (2016). Oscillations, timing, plasticity, and learning in the cerebellum. *Cerebellum*, 15, 122–138, https://doi.org/10.1007/s12311-015-0665-9

Chiang, M.-C., Reiss, A. L., Lee, A. D., Bellugi, U., Galaburda, A. M., Korenberg, J. R., Mills, D. L., Toga, A. W., & Thompson, P. M. (2007). 3D pattern of brain abnormalities in Williams syndrome visualized using tensor-based morphometry. *NeuroImage*, 36, 1096–1109, https://doi.org/10.1016/j.neuroimage.2007.04.024

Chiat, S., Armon-Lotem, S., Marinis, T., Polišenská, K., Roy, P., & Seeff-Gabriel, B. (2013). Assessment of language abilities in sequential bilingual children: The potential of sentence imitation tasks. In V. C. Mueller Gathercole (ed.), *Issues in the assessment of bilinguals* (pp. 56–89). Bristol, U.K.: Multilingual Matters, https://doi.org/10.21832/9781783090105-005

Chiat, S., & Roy, P. (2008). Early phonological and sociocognitive skills as predictors of later language and social communication outcomes. *Journal of Child Psychology and Psychiatry*, 49, 635–645, https://doi.org/10.1111/j.1469-7610.2008.01881.x

Christopoulou, C., & Bonvillian, J. D. (1985). Sign language, pantomime, and gestural processing in aphasic persons: A review. *Journal of Communication Disorders*, 18, 1–20, https://doi.org/10.1016/0021-9924(85)90010-3

Chu, M., & Kita, S. (2011). The nature of gestures' beneficial role in spatial problem solving. *Journal of Experimental Psychology: General*, 140, 102–116, https://doi.org/10.1037/a0021790

Chukoskie, L., Townsend, J., & Westerfield, M. (2013). Motor skill in autism spectrum disorders: A subcortical view. *International Review of Neurobiology*, 113, 207–249, https://doi.org/10.1016/b978-0-12-418700-9.00007-1

Clark, W. P. (1885). *The Indian Sign Language, with brief explanatory notes of the gestures taught deaf-mutes in our institutions for their instruction and a description of some of the peculiar laws, customs, myths, superstitions, ways of living, code of peace and war signals of our aborigines.* Philadelphia, PA: L. R. Hamersly.

Clarke, P. J., Snowling, M. J., Truelove, E., & Hulme, C. (2010). Ameliorating children's reading-comprehension difficulties: A randomized controlled trial. *Association for Psychological Science*, 21, 1106–1116, https://doi.org/10.1177/0956797610375449

Clay, R. A. (2017). In search of hope and home. *Monitor on Psychology*, 48, 34–40.

Clayton-Smith, J. (1993). Clinical research on Angelman syndrome in the United Kingdom: Observations on 82 affected individuals. *American Journal of Medical Genetics*, 46, 12–15, https://doi.org/10.1002/ajmg.1320460105

Clibbens, J. (1998). Research on the acquisition of British Sign Language: Current issues. *Deafness and Education*, 22, 10–15.

Clibbens, J. (2001). Signing and lexical development in children with Down syndrome. *Down Syndrome Research and Practice, 7,* 101–105, https://doi.org/10.3104/reviews.119

Clibbens, J., & Harris, M. (1993). Phonological processes and sign language development. In D. J. Messer & G. J. Turner (eds.), *Critical influences on child language acquisition and development* (pp. 197–208). New York, NY: Macmillan, https://doi.org/10.1007/978-1-349-22608-5_10

Clibbens, J., Powell, G. G., & Atkinson, E. (2002). Strategies for achieving joint attention when signing to children with Down's syndrome. *International Journal of Language & Communication Disorders, 37,* 309–323, https://doi.org/10.1080/13682820210136287

Cockerell, I., Bølling, G., & Nakken, K. O. (2011). Landau-Kleffner syndrome in Norway: Long-term prognosis and experiences with the health services and educational systems. *Epilepsy & Behavior, 21,* 153–159, https://doi.org/10.1016/j.yebeh.2011.03.019

Cocks, N., Dipper, L., Middleton, R., & Morgan, G. (2011). What can iconic gestures tell us about the language system? A case of conduction aphasia. *International Journal of Language & Communication Disorders, 46,* 423–436, https://doi.org/10.3109/13682822.2010.520813

Cocks, N., Dipper, L., Pritchard, M., & Morgan, G. (2013). The impact of impaired semantic knowledge on spontaneous iconic gesture production. *Aphasiology, 27,* 1050–1069, https://doi.org/10.1080/02687038.2013.770816

Cocks, N., Sautin, L., Kita, S., Morgan, G., & Zlotowitz, S. (2009). Gesture and speech integration: An exploratory study of a man with aphasia. *International Journal of Language & Communication Disorders, 44,* 795–804, https://doi.org/10.1080/13682820802256965

Code, C., & Gaunt, C. (1986). Treating severe speech and limb apraxia in a case of aphasia. *British Journal of Disorders of Communication, 21,* 11–20, https://doi.org/10.3109/13682828609018540

Coelho, C. A. (1990). Acquisition and generalization of simple manual sign grammars by aphasic subjects. *Journal of Communication Disorders, 23,* 383–400, https://doi.org/10.1016/0021-9924(90)90026-u

Coelho, C. A., & Duffy, R. J. (1986). Effects of iconicity, motoric complexity, and linguistic function on sign acquisition in severe aphasia. *Perceptual and Motor Skills, 63,* 519–530, https://doi.org/10.2466/pms.1986.63.2.519

Coelho, C. A., & Duffy, R. J. (1987). The relationship of the acquisition of manual signs to severity of aphasia: A training study. *Brain and Language, 31,* 328–345, https://doi.org/10.1016/0093-934x(87)90078-2

Coelho, C. A., & Duffy, R. J. (1990). Sign acquisition in two aphasic subjects with limb apraxia. *Aphasiology, 4,* 1–8, https://doi.org/10.1080/02687039008249050

Cohen, J. (1969). *Operant behavior and operant conditioning*. Chicago, IL: Rand McNally & Company.

Cohen, R. L. (1981). On the generality of some memory laws. *Scandinavian Journal of Psychology*, 22, 267–281, https://doi.org/10.1111/j.1467-9450.1981.tb00402.x

Coleman, A., Weir, K. A., Ware, R. S., & Boyd, R. N. (2013). Relationship between communication skills and gross motor function in preschool-aged children with cerebral palsy. *Archives of Physical Medicine and Rehabilitation*, 94, 2210–2217, https://doi.org/10.1016/j.apmr.2013.03.025

Collier, B. (2000). *See what we say: Situational vocabulary for adults who use augmentative and alternative communication*. Baltimore, MD: Paul H. Brookes Publishing.

Collier, B., McGhie-Richmond, D., & Self, H. (2010). Exploring communication assistants as an option for increasing communication access to communities for people who use augmentative communication. *Augmentative and Alternative Communication*, 26, 48–59, https://doi.org/10.3109/07434610903561498

Cologon, K., & Mevawalla, Z. (2018). Increasing inclusion in early childhood: Key word sign as a communication partner intervention. *International Journal of Inclusive Education*, 22, 902–920, https://doi.org/10.1080/13603116.2017.1412515

Columbus, C. (1492/1987). *The log of Christopher Columbus* (R. H. Fuson, Trans., 1987). Camden, ME: International Marine Publishing Company.

Conant, K. D., Thibert, R. L., & Thiele, E. A. (2009). Epilepsy and the sleep-wake patterns found in Angelman syndrome. *Epilepsia*, 50, 2497–2500, https://doi.org/10.1111/j.1528-1167.2009.02109.x

Condillac, E. B. de (1746/2001). *Essay on the origin of human knowledge* (H. Aarsleff, Trans., Ed., 2001). Cambridge, U.K.: Cambridge University Press, https://doi.org/10.1017/CBO9781139164160

Condon, W. S. (1975). Multiple response to sound in dysfunctional children. *Journal of Autism and Childhood Schizophrenia*, 5, 37–56, https://doi.org/10.1007/bf01537971

Conlin, K. E., Mirus, G. R., Mauk, C., & Meier, R. P. (2000). The acquisition of first signs: Place, handshape and movement. In C. Chamberlain, J. P. Morford, & R. I. Mayberry (eds.), *Language acquisition by eye* (pp. 51–69). Mahwah, NJ: Lawrence Erlbaum Associates.

Contemori, C., & Garraffa, M. (2010). Comparison of modalities in SLI syntax: A study on the comprehension and production of non-canonical sentences. *Lingua*, 120, 1940–1955, https://doi.org/10.1016/j.lingua.2010.02.011

Conti-Ramsden, G. (2003). Processing and linguistic markers in young children with specific language impairment (SLI). *Journal of Speech, Language, and Hearing Research,*46,1029–1037,https://doi.org/10.1044/1092-4388(2003/082)

Conti-Ramsden, G., & Botting, N. (2000). Educational placements for children with specific language impairments. In D. V. M. Bishop & L. B. Leonard (eds.), *Speech and language impairments in children: Causes, characteristics, intervention and outcome* (pp. 211–225). Hove, East Sussex, U.K.: Psychology Press.

Conti-Ramsden, G., Botting, N., & Faragher, B. (2001). Pyscholinguistic markers for specific language impairment (SLI). *Journal of Child Psychology and Psychiatry,* 42, 741–748, https://doi.org/10.1111/1469-7610.00770

Conti-Ramsden, G., & Hesketh, A. (2003). Risk markers for SLI: A study of young language-learning children. *International Journal of Language & Communication Disorders,* 38, 251–263, https://doi.org/10.1080/1368282031000092339

Cook, S. W., Friedman, H. S., Duggan, K. A., Cui, J., & Popescu, V. (2017). Hand gesture and mathematics learning: Lessons from an avatar. *Cognitive Science,* 41, 518–535, https://doi.org/10.1111/cogs.12344

Cook, S. W., Yip, T. K., & Goldin-Meadow, S. (2010). Gesturing makes memories that last. *Journal of Memory and Language,* 63, 465–475, https://doi.org/10.1016/j.jml.2010.07.002

Cooney, A., & Knox, G. (1981). An evaluation of a sign language programme taught to a group of severely/profound retarded children. In G. McIntyre & T. R. Parmenter (eds.), *Preparation for life: Programmes for mentally handicapped people in Australia in the 1980s* (pp. 350–364). Sydney, Australia: Prentice-Hall.

Cooper, B. R., & Lanza, S. T. (2014). Who benefits most from Head Start? Using latent class moderation to examine differential treatment effects. *Child Development,* 85, 2317–2338, https://doi.org/10.1111/cdev.12278

Corballis, M. C. (2002). *From hand to mouth: The origins of language.* Princeton, NJ: Princeton University Press.

Corballis, M. C. (2009). Language as gesture. *Human Movement Science,* 28, 556–565, https://doi.org/10.1016/j.humov.2009.07.003

Corballis, M. C. (2010). Mirror neurons and the evolution of language. *Brain and Language,* 112, 25–35, https://doi.org/10.1016/j.bandl.2009.02.002

Corballis, M. C. (2013). Toward a Darwinian perspective on language evolution. In Y. Coello & A. Bartolo (eds.), *Language and action in cognitive neuroscience* (pp. 33–58). Hove, East Sussex, U.K.: Psychology Press.

Corballis, M. C. (2017a). Language evolution: A changing perspective. *Trends in Cognitive Sciences,* 21, 229–236, https://doi.org/10.1016/j.tics.2017.01.013

Corballis, M. C. (2017b). The evolution of language: Sharing our mental lives. *Journal of Neurolinguistics,* 43, 120–132, https://doi.org/10.1016/j.jneuroling.2016.06.003

Corby, D., Taggart, L., & Cousins, W. (2018). The lived experience of people with intellectual disabilities in post-secondary or higher education. *Journal of Intellectual Disabilities*, October 9, https://doi.org/10.1177/1744629518805603

Corina, D. P., Poizner, H., Bellugi, U., Feinberg, T., Dowd, D., & O'Grady-Batch, L. (1992). Dissociation between linguistic and nonlinguistic gestural systems: A case for compositionality. *Brain and Language*, 43, 414–447, https://doi.org/10.1016/0093-934X(92)90110-Z

Corkin, S. (2013). *Permanent present tense: The unforgettable life of the amnesic patient, H. M.* New York, NY: Basic Books.

Cornforth, A. R. T., Johnston, K., & Walker, M. (1974). Teaching sign language to the deaf mentally handicapped adults. *Apex*, 2, 23–25, https://doi.org/10.1111/j.1468-3156.1974.tb00075.x

Corriveau, K., Pasquini, E., & Goswami, U. (2007). Basic auditory processing skills and specific language impairment: A new look at an old hypothesis. *Journal of Speech, Language, and Hearing Research*, 50, 647–666, https://doi.org/10.1044/1092-4388(2007/046)

Costello, E. (2000). *Random House Webster's American Sign Language medical dictionary*. New York, NY: Random House.

Coulter, G. R. (1990). Emphatic stress in ASL. In S. D. Fischer & P. Siple (eds.), *Theoretical issues in sign language research, vol. 1. Linguistics* (pp. 109–125). Chicago, IL: University of Chicago Press.

Couper, L., van der Meer, L., Schäfer, M. C. M., McKenzie, E., McLay, L., O'Reilly, M. F., Lancioni, G. E., Marschik, P. B., Sigafoos, J., & Sutherland, D. (2014). Comparing acquisition of and preference for manual signs, picture exchange, and speech-generating devices in nine children with autism spectrum disorder. *Developmental Neurorehabilitation*, 17, 99–109, https://doi.org/10.3109/17518423.2013.870244

Courchesne, E., Carper, R., & Akshoomoff, N. (2003). Evidence of brain overgrowth in the first year of life in autism. *Journal of the American Medical Association*, 290, 337–344, https://doi.org/10.1001/jama.290.3.337

Craik, F. I. M., & Lockhart, R. S. (1972). Levels of processing: A framework for memory research. *Journal of Verbal Learning and Verbal Behavior*, 11, 671–684, https://doi.org/10.1016/s0022-5371(72)80001-x

Craik, F. I. M., & Tulving, E. (1975). Depth of processing and the retention of words in episodic memory. *Journal of Experimental Psychology: General*, 104, 268–294, https://doi.org/10.1037/0096-3445.104.3.268

Crawford, D. C., Acuña, J. M., & Sherman, S. L. (2001). FMR1 and the fragile X syndrome: Human genome epidemiology review. *Genetics in Medicine*, 3, 359–371, https://doi.org/10.1097/00125817-200109000-00006

Creedon, M. P. (1973). *Language development in nonverbal autistic children using a simultaneous communication system.* Paper presented at the biennial meeting of the Society for Research in Child Development, Philadelphia, PA.

Cress, C. J., & Marvin, C. A. (2003). Common questions about AAC services in early intervention. *Augmentative and Alternative Communication, 19,* 254–272, https://doi.org/10.1080/07434610310001598242

Crippa, A., Del Vecchio, G., Busti Ceccarelli, S., Nobile, M., Arrigoni, F., & Brambilla, P. (2016). Cortico-cerebellar connectivity in autism spectrum disorder: What do we know so far? *Frontiers in Psychiatry, 7,* AR 20, https://doi.org/10.3389/fpsyt.2016.00020

Croen, L. A., Grether, J. K., Hoogstrate, J., & Selvin, S. (2002). The changing prevalence of autism in California. *Journal of Autism and Developmental Disorders, 32,* 207–215, https://doi.org/10.1023/a:1015453830880

Culp, D. M. (1989). Developmental apraxia and augmentative or alternative communication — A case example. *Augmentative and Alternative Communication, 5,* 27–34, https://doi.org/10.1080/07434618912331274936

Cumley, G. D., & Swanson, S. (1999). Augmentative and alternative communication options for children with developmental apraxia of speech: Three case studies. *Augmentative and Alternative Communication, 15,* 110–125, https://doi.org/10.1080/07434619912331278615

Dachkovsky, S., & Sandler, W. (2009). Visual intonation in the prosody of a sign language. *Language and Speech, 52,* 287–314, https://doi.org/10.1177/0023830909103175

Dada, S., Horn, T., Samuels, A., & Schlosser, R. W. (2016). Children's attitudes toward interaction with an unfamiliar peer with complex communication needs: Comparing high- and low-technology devices. *Augmentative and Alternative Communication, 32,* 305–311, https://doi.org/10.1080/07434618.2016.1216597

Dahle, A. J., & McCollister, F. P. (1986). Hearing and otologic disorders in children with Down syndrome. *American Journal of Mental Deficiency, 90,* 636–642.

Damasio, H. (2008). Neural basis of language disorders. In R. Chapey (ed.), *Language intervention strategies in aphasia and related neurogenic communication disorders* (5th ed., pp. 20–41). Philadelphia, PA: Lippincott Williams & Wilkins.

Dammeyer, J., & Ask Larsen, F. (2016). Communication and language profiles of children with congenital deafblindness. *British Journal of Visual Impairment, 34,* 214–224, https://doi.org/10.1177/0264619616651301

Daniels, M. (2001). *Dancing with words: Signing for hearing children's literacy.* Westport, CT: Bergin and Garvey.

Daniels, M. (2004). Happy hands: The effect of ASL on hearing children's literacy. *Reading Research and Instruction*, 44, 86–100, https://doi.org/10.1080/19388070409558422

Daniloff, J. K., Fritelli, G., Buckingham, H. W., Hoffman, P. R., & Daniloff, R. G. (1986). Amer-Ind versus ASL: Recognition and imitation in aphasic subjects. *Brain and Language*, 28, 95–113, https://doi.org/10.1016/0093-934x(86)90094-5

Daniloff, J. K., Lloyd, L. L., & Fristoe, M. (1983). Amer-Ind transparency. *Journal of Speech and Hearing Disorders*, 48, 103–110, https://doi.org/10.1044/jshd.4801.103

Daniloff, J. K., & Vergara, D. (1984). Comparison between the motoric constraints for Amer-Ind and ASL sign formation. *Journal of Speech and Hearing Research*, 27, 76–88, https://doi.org/10.1044/jshr.2701.76

Dapretto, M., Davies, M. S., Pfeifer, J. H., Scott, A. A., Sigman, M., Bookheimer, S. Y., & Iacoboni, M. (2006). Understanding emotions in others: Mirror neuron dysfunction in children with autism spectrum disorders. *Nature Neuroscience*, 9, 28–30, https://doi.org/10.1038/nn1611

Dark, L., Brownlie, E., & Bloomberg, K. (2019). Selecting, developing and supporting key word sign vocabularies for children with developmental disabilities. In N. Grove & K. Launonen (eds.), *Manual sign acquisition in children with developmental disabilities* (pp. 215–245). New York, NY: Nova Science Publishers, Inc.

Daumüller, M., & Goldenberg, G. (2010). Therapy to improve gestural expression in aphasia: A controlled clinical trial. *Clinical Rehabilitation*, 24, 55–65, https://doi.org/10.1177/0269215509343327

Davis, G. A. (2007). *Aphasiology: Disorders and clinical practice* (2nd ed.). Boston, MA: Allyn and Bacon, Pearson.

Davis, J. (2005). Evidence of a historical signed lingua franca among North American Indians. *Deaf Worlds*, 21, 47–72.

Davis, J. (2017, May 10). Native American signed languages. *Oxford Handbooks Online*, https://doi.org/10.1093/oxfordhb/9780199935345.013.42

Davis, J. E. (2006). A historical linguistic account of sign language among North American Indians. In C. Lucas (ed.), *Multilingualism and sign languages: From the Great Plains to Australia, vol. 12* (pp. 3–35). Washington, DC: Gallaudet University Press.

Davis, J. E. (2010). *Hand talk: Sign language among American Indian nations*. Cambridge, U.K.: Cambridge University Press.

Davis, J. E. (2014). American Indian Sign Language: Documentary linguistic methodologies and technologies. In M. C. Jones (ed.), *Endangered languages and new technologies* (pp. 161–178). Cambridge, U.K.: Cambridge University Press, https://doi.org/10.1017/CBO9781107279063.015

Davis, J. E. (2016). The linguistic vitality of American Indian Sign Language: Endangered, yet not vanished. *Sign Language Studies*, 16, 535–562, https://doi.org/10.1353/sls.2016.0011

Dawson, G., Jones, E. J. H., Merkle, K., Venema, K., Lowy, R., Faja, S., Kamara, D., Murias, M., Greenson, J., Winter, J., Smith, M., Rogers, S. J., & Webb, S. J. (2012). Early behavioral intervention is associated with normalized brain activity in young children with autism. *Journal of the American Academy of Child & Adolescent Psychiatry*, 51, 1150–1159, https://doi.org/10.1016/j.jaac.2012.08.018

Dawson, G., Munson, J., Webb, S. J., Nalty, T., Abbott, R., & Toth, K. (2007). Rate of head growth decelerates and symptoms worsen in the second year of life in autism. *Biological Psychiatry*, 61, 458–464, https://doi.org/10.1016/j.biopsych.2006.07.016

Dawson, M., Soulières, I., Gernsbacher, M. A., & Mottron, L. (2007). The level and nature of autistic intelligence. *Psychological Science*, 18, 657–662, https://doi.org/10.1111/j.1467-9280.2007.01954.x

Dayanim, S., & Namy, L. L. (2015). Infants learn baby signs from video. *Child Development*, 86, 800–811, https://doi.org/10.1111/cdev.12340

de Beer, C., Carragher, M., van Nispen, K., Hogrefe, K., de Ruiter, J. P., & Rose, M. L. (2017). How much information do people with aphasia convey via gesture? *American Journal of Speech-Language Pathology*, 26, 483–497, https://doi.org/10.1044/2016_AJSLP-15-0027

Deckers, S. R. J. M., Van Zaalen, Y., Mens, E. J. M., van Balkom, H., & Verhoeven, L. (2016). The concurrent and predictive validity of the Dutch version of the Communicative Development Inventory in children with Down syndrome for the assessment of expressive vocabulary in verbal and signed modalities. *Research in Developmental Disabilities*, 56, 99–107, https://doi.org/10.1016/j.ridd.2016.05.017

Deckers, S. R. J. M., Van Zaalen, Y., van Balkom, H., & Verhoeven, L. (2017). Core vocabulary of young children with Down syndrome. *Augmentative and Alternative Communication*, 33, 77–86, https://doi.org/10.1080/07434618.2017.1293730

Degener, T. (2016). Disability in a human rights context. *Laws*, 5, 35–59, https://doi.org/10.3390/laws5030035

Della Sala, S., Gray, C., Baddeley, A., Allamano, N., & Wilson, L. (1999). Pattern span: A tool for unwelding visuo-spatial memory. *Neuropsychologia*, 37, 1189–1199, https://doi.org/10.1016/s0028-3932(98)00159-6

DeLoache, J. S., Chiong, C., Sherman, K., Islam, N., Vanderborght, M., Troseth, G. L., Strouse, G. A., & O'Doherty, K. (2010). Do babies learn from baby media? *Psychological Science*, 21, 1570–1574, https://doi.org/10.1177/0956797610384145

DeLoache, J. S., Miller, K. F., & Rosengren, K. S. (1997). The credible shrinking room: Very young children's performance with symbolic and nonsymbolic relations. *Psychological Science*, 8, 308–313, https://doi.org/10.1111/j.1467-9280.1997.tb00443.x

DeLoache, J. S., Pierroutsakos, S. L., & Uttal, D. H. (2003). The origins of pictorial competence. *Current Directions in Psychological Science*, 12, 114–118, https://doi.org/10.1111/1467-8721.01244

Delprato, D. J. (2001). Comparisons of discrete-trial and normalized behavioral language intervention for young children with autism. *Journal of Autism and Developmental Disorders*, 31, 315–325, https://doi.org/10.1023/a:1010747303957

De Meulder, M. (2015). The legal recognition of sign languages. *Sign Language Studies*, 15, 498–506, https://doi.org/10.1353/sls.2015.0018

Demopoulos, C., & Lewine, J. D. (2016). Audiometric profiles in autism spectrum disorders: Does subclinical hearing loss impact communication? *Autism Research*, 9, 107–120, https://doi.org/10.1002/aur.1495

Denes, G. (2016). *Neural plasticity across the lifespan: How the brain can change.* London, U.K.: Routledge, https://doi.org/10.4324/9781315849461

Denmark, T., Atkinson, J., Campbell, R., & Swettenham, J. (2014). How do typically developing deaf children and deaf children with autism spectrum disorder use the face when comprehending emotional facial expressions in British Sign Language? *Journal of Autism and Developmental Disorders*, 44, 2584–2592, https://doi.org/10.1007/s10803-014-2130-x

Dennis, R., Reichle, J., Williams, W., & Vogelsberg. R. T. (1982). Motoric factors influencing the selection of vocabulary for sign production programs. *Journal of the Association for the Severely Handicapped*, 7, 20–32, https://doi.org/10.1177/154079698200700103

Deonna, T. (1991). Acquired epileptiform aphasia in children (Landau-Kleffner syndrome). *Journal of Clinical Neurophysiology*, 8, 288–298, https://doi.org/10.1097/00004691-199107010-00005

Deonna, T. (2000). Acquired epileptic aphasia (AEA) or Landau-Kleffner syndrome: From childhood to adulthood. In D. V. M. Bishop & L. B. Leonard (eds.), *Speech and language impairments in children: Causes, characteristics, intervention and outcome* (pp. 261–272). Hove, East Sussex, U.K.: Psychology Press.

Deonna, T., Peter, C., & Ziegler, A.-L. (1989). Adult follow-up of the acquired aphasia-epilepsy syndrome in childhood. Report of 7 cases. *Neuropediatrics*, 20, 132–138, https://doi.org/10.1055/s-2008-1071278

Deonna, T., Prelaz-Girod, A.-C., Mayor-Dubois, C., & Roulet-Perez, E. (2009). Sign language in Landau-Kleffner syndrome. *Epilepsia*, 50 (Suppl. 7), 77–82, https://doi.org/10.1111/j.1528-1167.2009.02226.x

de Radonvilliers, C.-F. L. (1768). *De la manière d'apprendre les langues*. Paris, France: Saillant.

de Ruiter, J. P. (2006). Can gesticulation help aphasic people speak, or rather, communicate? *International Journal of Speech-Language Pathology*, 8, 124–127, https://doi.org/10.1080/14417040600667285

de Ruiter, J. P., & de Beer, C. (2013). A critical evaluation of models of gesture and speech production for understanding gesture in aphasia. *Aphasiology*, 27, 1015–1030, https://doi.org/10.1080/02687038.2013.797067

De Smet, H. J., Baillieux, H., De Deyn, P. P., Mariën, P., & Paquier, P. (2007). The cerebellum and language: The story so far. *Folio Phoniatrica et Logopaedica*, 59, 165–170, https://doi.org/10.1159/000102927

DeThorne, L. S., Johnson, C. J., Walder, L., & Mahurin-Smith, J. (2009). When "Simon says" doesn't work: Alternatives to imitation for facilitating early speech development. *American Journal of Speech-Language Pathology*, 18, 133–145, https://doi.org/10.1044/1058-0360(2008/07-0090)

Deuce, G., & Rose, S. (2019). Sign acquisition in children who are deafblind. In N. Grove & K. Launonen (eds.), *Manual sign acquisition in children with developmental disabilities* (pp. 175–193). New York, NY: Nova Science Publishers, Inc.

Deuchar, M. (1990). Are the signs of language arbitrary? In H. Barlow, C. Blakemore, & M. Weston-Smith (eds.), *Images and understanding* (pp. 168–179). Cambridge, U.K.: Cambridge University Press.

Díaz del Castillo, B. *The true history of the conquest of New Spain, vol. 1* (A. P. Maudslay, Trans., 1908; G. García, Ed.). London, U.K.: Hakluyt Society, https://doi.org/10.1017/CBO9780511686979.006

Didden, R., Sigafoos, J., Korzilius, H., Baas, A., Lancioni, G. E., O'Reilly, M. F., & Curfs, L. M. G. (2009). Form and function of communicative behaviours in individuals with Angelman syndrome. *Journal of Applied Research in Intellectual Disabilities*, 22, 526–537, https://doi.org/10.1111/j.1468-3148.2009.00520.x

Dierssen, M., Herault, Y., & Estivill, X. (2009). Aneuploidy: From a physiological mechanism of variance to Down syndrome. *Physiological Reviews*, 89, 887–920, https://doi.org/10.1152/physrev.00032.2007

Dimitrova, N., Özçalişkan, Ş., & Adamson, L. B. (2016). Parents' translations of child gesture facilitate word learning in children with autism, Down syndrome and typical development. *Journal of Autism and Developmental Disorders*, 46, 221–231, https://doi.org/10.1007/s10803-015-2566-7

Dingemanse, M. (2012). Advances in the cross-linguistic study of ideophones. *Language and Linguistics Compass*, 6, 654–672, https://doi.org/10.1002/lnc3.361

Dingemanse, M., Blasi, D. E., Lupyan, G., Christiansen, M. H., & Monaghan, P. (2015). Arbitrariness, iconicity, and systematicity in language. *Trends in Cognitive Sciences*, 19, 603–615, https://doi.org/10.1016/j.tics.2015.07.013

Divale, W. T., & Zipin, C. (1977). Hunting and the development of sign language: A cross-cultural test. *Journal of Anthropological Research*, 33, 185–201, https://doi.org/10.1086/jar.33.2.3629738

Dodd, J. L., & Gorey, M. (2014). AAC intervention as an immersion model. *Communication Disorders Quarterly*, 35, 103–107, https://doi.org/10.1177/1525740113504242

Dodge, R. I. (1882/1978). The sign language — Wonderful expertness of Indian sign-talkers. In D. J. Umiker-Sebeok & T. A. Sebeok (eds.), *Aboriginal sign languages of the Americas and Australia, vol. 2* (pp. 3–18). New York, NY: Plenum Press. [Originally published 1882 in *Our wild Indians: Thirty-three years personal experience among the red men of the great west* (pp. 379–394). Hartford, CT: Hartford Publishing.]

Doherty, C. P., Fitzsimons, M., Asenbauer, B., McMackin, D., Bradley, R., King, M., & Staunton, H. (1999). Prosodic preservation in Landau-Kleffner syndrome: A case report. *European Journal of Neurology*, 6, 227–234, https://doi.org/10.1111/j.1468-1331.1999.tb00017.x

Doherty, J. E. (1985). The effects of sign characteristics on sign acquisition and retention: An integrative review of the literature. *Augmentative and Alternative Communication*, 1, 108–121, https://doi.org/10.1080/07434618512331273601

Dollaghan, C., & Campbell, T. F. (1998). Nonword repetition and child language impairment. *Journal of Speech, Language, and Hearing Research*, 41, 1136–1146, https://doi.org/10.1044/jslhr.4105.1136

Donkin, A., Roberts, J., Tedstone, A., & Marmot, M. (2014). Family socio-economic status and young children's outcomes. *Journal of Children's Services*, 9, 83–95, https://doi.org/10.1108/jcs-01-2014-0004

Donvan, J., & Zucker, C. (2016). *In a different key: The story of autism*. New York, NY: Crown Publishers.

Dolly, A., & Noble, E. (2018). "Lámh signs combined" — Investigating a whole school approach to augmentative and alternative communication (AAC) intervention through research in practice. *REACH Journal of Special Needs Education in Ireland*, 31, 53–68.

Dowell, L. R., Mahone, E. M., & Mostofsky, S. H. (2009). Associations of postural knowledge and basic motor skill with dyspraxia in autism: Implication for abnormalities in distributed connectivity and motor learning. *Neuropsychology*, 23, 563–570, https://doi.org/10.1037/a0015640

Duffy, C., & Healy, O. (2011). Spontaneous communication in autism spectrum disorder: A review of topographies and intervention. *Research in Autism Spectrum Disorders*, 5, 977–983, https://doi.org/10.1016/j.rasd.2010.12.005

Duffy, R. J., & Duffy, J. R. (1981). Three studies of deficits in pantomimic expression and pantomimic recognition in aphasia. *Journal of Speech and Hearing Research,* 24, 70–84, https://doi.org/10.1044/jshr.2401.70

Duffy, R. J., & Duffy, J. R. (1990). The relationship between pantomime expression and recognition in aphasia: The search for causes. In G. R. Hammond (ed.), *Cerebral control of speech and limb movements* (pp. 417–449). Amsterdam, The Netherlands: Elsevier Science Publishers, https://doi.org/10.1016/S0166-4115(08)60657-3

Duffy, R. J., Duffy, J. R., & Pearson, K. L. (1975). Pantomime recognition in aphasics. *Journal of Speech and Hearing Research,* 18, 115–132, https://doi.org/10.1044/jshr.1801.115

Dunn, L. M., & Dunn, L. M. (1981). *Peabody Picture Vocabulary Test-Revised.* Circle Pines, MN: American Guidance Service.

Dunn, M. L. (1982). *Pre-sign language motor skills: Skill starters for motor development.* Tucson, AZ: Communication Skill Builders.

Dunst, C. J., Meter, D., & Hamby, D. W. (2011). Influences of sign and oral language interventions on the speech and oral language production of young children with disabilities. *CELLreviews,* 4, 1–20.

Duran, M. H. C., Guimarães, C. A., Medeiros, L. L., & Guerreiro, M. M. (2009). Landau-Kleffner syndrome: Long-term follow-up. *Brain and Development,* 31, 58–63, https://doi.org/10.1016/j.braindev.2008.09.007

Dykens, E. M., Hodapp, R. M., & Finucane, B. M. (2000). *Genetics and mental retardation syndromes: A new look at behavior and interventions.* Baltimore, MD: Paul H. Brookes Publishing.

Dziuk, M. A., Gidley Larson, J. C., Apostu, A., Mahone, E. M., Denckla, M. B., & Mostofsky, S. H. (2007). Dyspraxia in autism: Association with motor, social, and communicative deficits. *Developmental Medicine & Child Neurology,* 49, 734–739, https://doi.org/10.1111/j.1469-8749.2007.00734.x

Eagleson, H. M., Jr., Vaughn, G. R., & Knudson, A. B. C. (1970). Hand signals for dysphasia. *Archives of Physical Medicine and Rehabilitation,* 51, 111–113.

Ebbels, S. H., Dockrell, J. E., & van der Lely, H. K. J. (2012). Non-word repetition in adolescents with specific language impairment (SLI). *International Journal of Language & Communication Disorders,* 47, 257–273, https://doi.org/10.1111/j.1460-6984.2011.00099.x

Eberhard, D. M., Simons, G. F., & Fennig, C. D. (eds.). (2020). *Ethnologue: Languages of the world* (23rd ed.). Dallas, TX: SIL International, https://www.ethnologue.com

Eccarius, P. N. (2008). *A constraint-based account of handshape contrast in sign languages.* Unpublished doctoral dissertation, Purdue University, West Lafayette, IN, https://docs.lib.purdue.edu/dissertations/AAI3330229/

Eco, U. (1995). *The search for the perfect language* (J. Fentress, Trans.). Oxford, U.K.: Blackwell.

Edelson, M. G. (2006). Are the majority of children with autism mentally retarded? A systematic evaluation of the data. *Focus on Autism and Other Developmental Disabilities*, 21, 66–83, https://doi.org/10.1177/10883576060210020301

Edwards, L. A. (2014). A meta-analysis of imitation abilities in individuals with autism spectrum disorders. *Autism Research*, 7, 363–380, https://doi.org/10.1002/aur.1379

Ege, B., & Mouridsen, S. E. (1998). Linguistic development in a boy with the Landau-Kleffner syndrome: A five year follow-up study. *Journal of Neurolinguistics*, 11, 321–328, https://doi.org/10.1016/s0911-6044(97)00013-4

Eggenberger, N., Preisig, B. C., Schumacher, R., Hopfner, S., Vanbellingen, T., Nyffeler, T., Gutbrod, K., Annoni, J.-M., Bohlhalter, S., Cazzoli, D., & Müri, R. M. (2016). Comprehension of co-speech gestures in aphasic patients: An eye movement study. *PLoS ONE*, 11, e0146583, https://doi.org/10.1371/journal.pone.0146583

Eigsti, I.-M., Stevens, M. C., Schultz, R. T., Barton, M., Kelley, E., Naigles, L., Orinstein, A., Troyb, E., & Fein, D. A. (2016). Language comprehension and brain function in individuals with an optimal outcome from autism. *NeuroImage: Clinical*, 10, 182–191, https://doi.org/10.1016/j.nicl.2015.11.014

Eisenberg, L. (1956). The autistic child in adolescence. *American Journal of Psychiatry*, 112, 607–612, https://doi.org/10.1176/ajp.112.8.607

Eldevik, S., Hastings, R. P., Hughes, J. C., Jahr, E., Eikeseth, S., & Cross, S. (2009). Meta-analysis of early intensive behavioral intervention for children with autism. *Journal of Clinical Child & Adolescent Psychology*, 38, 439–450, https://doi.org/10.1080/15374410902851739

El Hachioui, H., Lingsma, H. F., van de Sandt-Koenderman, M. E., Dippel, D. W. J., Koudstaal, P. J., & Visch-Brink, E. G. (2013). Recovery of aphasia after stroke: A 1-year follow-up study. *Journal of Neurology*, 260, 166–171, https://doi.org/10.1007/s00415-012-6607-2

Elwér, Å., Gustafson, S., Byrne, B., Olson, R. K., Keenan, J. M., & Samuelsson, S. (2015). A retrospective longitudinal study of cognitive and language skills in poor reading comprehension. *Scandinavian Journal of Psychology*, 56, 157–166, https://doi.org/10.1111/sjop.12188

Emmons, H. M. (2004). *Evaluating the efficacy of a Simplified Sign System compared with American Sign Language signs: Immediate and delayed recall studies*. Unpublished master's thesis, University of Virginia, Charlottesville, VA.

Emmorey, K. (2002). *Language, cognition, and the brain: Insights from sign language research*. Mahwah, NJ: Lawrence Erlbaum Associates, https://doi.org/10.4324/9781410603982

Emmorey, K. (ed.). (2003a). *Perspectives on classifier constructions in sign languages*. Mahwah, NJ: Lawrence Erlbaum Associates, https://doi.org/10.4324/9781410607447

Emmorey, K. (2003b). The neural systems underlying sign languages. In M. Marschark & P. E. Spencer (eds.), *Oxford handbook of deaf studies, language, and education* (pp. 361–376). New York, NY: Oxford University Press.

Emmorey, K. (2014). Iconicity as structure mapping. *Philosophical Transactions of the Royal Society B*, 369, 20130301, https://doi.org/10.1098/rstb.2013.0301

Emmorey, K., Klima, E., & Hickok, G. (1998). Mental rotation within linguistic and non-linguistic domains in users of American Sign Language. *Cognition*, 68, 221–246, https://doi.org/10.1016/s0010-0277(98)00054-7

Emmorey, K., Kosslyn, S. M., & Bellugi, U. (1993). Visual imagery and visual-spatial language: Enhanced imagery abilities in deaf and hearing ASL signers. *Cognition*, 46, 139–181, https://doi.org/10.1016/0010-0277(93)90017-p

Emmorey, K., & Sevcikova Sehyr, Z. (2018). *Measuring iconicity in sign language: Effects of linguistic knowledge and transparency on perceived iconicity*. Paper presented at the International Society for Gesture Studies Conference, July 8, Cape Town, South Africa.

Enders, J. (2001). Of miming and signing: The dramatic rhetoric of gesture. In C. Davidson (ed.), *Gesture in medieval drama and art* (pp. 1–25). Early Drama, Art, and Music Monograph Series 28. Western Michigan University, Kalamazoo, MI: Medieval Institute Publications.

Engberg-Pedersen, E. (1993). *Space in Danish Sign Language: The semantics and morphosyntax of the use of space in a visual language*. Hamburg, Germany: Signum.

Engelkamp, J., & Krumnacker, H. (1980). Imaginale und motorische prozesse beim behalten verbalen materials [Imagery and motor processes in memory of verbal material]. *Zeitschrift für experimentelle und angewandte Psychologie*, 27, 511–533.

Engelkamp, J., & Zimmer, H. D. (1984). Motor programme information as a separable memory unit. *Psychological Research*, 46, 283–299, https://doi.org/10.1007/bf00308889

Engelkamp, J., & Zimmer, H. D. (1994). *Human memory: A multimodal approach*. Seattle, WA: Hogrefe & Huber Publishers.

Engineer, C. T., Centanni, T. M., Im, K. W., Rahebi, K. C., Buell, E. P., & Kilgard, M. P. (2014). Degraded speech sound processing in a rat model of fragile X syndrome. *Brain Research*, 1564, 72–84, https://doi.org/10.1016/j.brainres.2014.03.049

Erlenkamp, S., & Kristoffersen, K. E. (2010). Sign communication in Cri du chat syndrome. *Journal of Communication Disorders*, 43, 225–251, https://doi.org/10.1016/j.jcomdis.2010.03.002

European Sign Language Centre. (2018). *Spread the sign*, https://www. spreadthesign.com/en.gb/search/

Evans, J. L., Alibali, M. W., & McNeil, N. M. (2001). Divergence of verbal expression and embodied knowledge: Evidence from speech and gesture in children with specific language impairment. *Language and Cognitive Processes*, 16, 309–331, https://doi.org/10.1080/01690960042000049

Falchook, A. D., Burtis, D. B., Acosta, L. M., Salazar, L., Hedna, V. S., Khanna, A. Y., & Heilman, K. M. (2014). Praxis and writing in a right-hander with crossed aphasia. *Neurocase*, 20, 317–327, https://doi.org/10.1080/13554794. 2013.770883

Fallon, K. A., Light, J. C., & Paige, T. K. (2001). Enhancing vocabulary selection for preschoolers who require augmentative and alternative communication (AAC). *American Journal of Speech-Language Pathology*, 10, 81–94, https://doi. org/10.1044/1058-0360(2001/010)

Farb, P. (1968). *Man's rise to civilization as shown by the Indians of North America from primeval times to the coming of the industrial state*. New York, NY: Dutton.

Farnell, B. (1995). *Do you see what I mean? Plains Indian Sign Talk and the embodiment of action*. Austin, TX: University of Texas Press.

Fay, N., Lister, C. J., Ellison, T. M., & Goldin-Meadow, S. (2014). Creating a communication system from scratch: Gesture beats vocalization hands down. *Frontiers in Psychology*, 5, AR 354, https://doi.org/10.3389/fpsyg.2014.00354

Fein, D., Barton, M., Eigsti, I.-M., Kelley, E., Naigles, L., Schultz, R. T., Stevens, M., Helt, M., Orinstein, A., Rosenthal, M., Troyb, E., & Tyson, K. (2013). Optimal outcome in individuals with a history of autism. *Journal of Child Psychology and Psychiatry*, 54, 195–205, https://doi.org/10.1111/jcpp.12037

Fenn, G., & Rowe, J. A. (1975). An experiment in manual communication. *British Journal of Disorders of Communication*, 10, 3–16, https://doi. org/10.3109/13682827509011270

Fenson, L., Dale, P. S., Reznick, J. S., Bates, E., Thal, D. J., & Pethick, S. J. (1994). Variability in early communicative development. *Monographs of the Society for Research in Child Development*, 59, 1–185, https://doi.org/10.2307/1166093

Fenson, L., Dale, P. S., Reznick, J. S., Thal, D. J., Bates, E., Hartung, J., Pethick, S., & Reilly, J. S. (1993). *Guide and technical manual for the MacArthur Communicative Development Inventories*. San Diego, CA: Singular Press.

Fernald, A., Marchman, V. A., & Weisleder, A. (2013). SES differences in language processing skill and vocabulary are evident at 18 months. *Developmental Science*, 16, 234–248, https://doi.org/10.1111/desc.12019

Ferrari, P. F., Gallese, V., Rizzolatti, G., & Fogassi, L. (2003). Mirror neurons responding to the observation of ingestive and communicative mouth actions in the monkey ventral premotor cortex. *European Journal of Neuroscience*, 17, 1703–1714, https://doi.org/10.1046/j.1460-9568.2003.02601.x

Fey, M. E., Finestack, L. H., Gajewski, B. J., Popescu, M., & Lewine, J. D. (2010). A preliminary evaluation of Fast ForWord-Language as an adjuvant treatment in language intervention. *Journal of Speech, Language, and Hearing Research*, 53, 430–449, https://doi.org/10.1044/1092-4388(2009/08-0225)

Fey, M. E., Long, S. H., & Finestack, L. H. (2003). Ten principles of grammar facilitation for children with specific language impairments. *American Journal of Speech-Language Pathology*, 12, 3–15, https://doi.org/10.1044/1058-0360(2003/048)

Fey, M. E., Warren, S. F., Brady, N., Finestack, L. H., Bredin-Oja, S. L., Fairchild, M., Sokol, S., & Yoder, P. J. (2006). Early effects of responsivity education/prelinguistic milieu teaching for children with developmental delays and their parents. *Journal of Speech, Language, and Hearing Research*, 49, 526–547, https://doi.org/10.1044/1092-4388(2006/039)

Finestack, L. H., & Abbeduto, L. (2010). Expressive language profiles of verbally expressive adolescents and young adults with Down syndrome or fragile X syndrome. *Journal of Speech, Language, and Hearing Research*, 53, 1334–1348, https://doi.org/10.1044/1092-4388(2010/09-0125)

Finestack, L. H., Sterling, A. M., & Abbeduto, L. (2013). Discriminating Down syndrome and fragile X syndrome based on language ability. *Journal of Child Language*, 40, 244–265, https://doi.org/10.1017/s0305000912000207

Fischer, R. (2002). The study of natural sign language in eighteenth-century France. *Sign Language Studies*, 2, 391–406, https://doi.org/10.1353/sls.2002.0017

Fischer, S. (1973). *Verbs in American Sign Language*. Unpublished paper, Salk Institute, San Diego, CA.

Fischer, S., & Gong, Q. (2010). Variation in East Asian sign language structures. In D. Brentari (ed.), *Sign languages* (pp. 499–518). Cambridge, U.K.: Cambridge University Press, Cambridge Language Surveys Series, https://doi.org/10.1017/CBO9780511712203.023

Fischer, S., & Gong, Q. (2011). Marked hand configurations in Asian sign languages. In R. Channon & H. van der Hulst (eds.), *Formational units in sign languages* (pp. 19–42). Berlin, Germany: Mouton de Gruyter, Sign Language Typology Series 3, https://doi.org/10.1515/9781614510680.19

Fischer, S., & Gough, B. (1978). Verbs in American Sign Language. *Sign Language Studies*, 18, 17–48, https://doi.org/10.1353/sls.1978.0014

Fitzgerald, A. (2001). *Gesture imitation and memory in children with autistic disorder*. Unpublished distinguished major thesis, University of Virginia, Charlottesville, VA.

Fitzpatrick, E. M., Thibert, J., Grandpierre, V., & Johnston, J. C. (2014). How HANDy are baby signs? A systematic review of the impact of gestural communication on typically developing, hearing infants under the age of 36 months. *First Language*, 34, 486–509, https://doi.org/10.1177/0142723714562864

Flippin, M., Reszka, S., & Watson, L. R. (2010). Effectiveness of the Picture Exchange Communication System (PECS) on communication and speech for children with autism spectrum disorders: A meta-analysis. *American Journal of Speech-Language Pathology*, 19, 178–195, https://doi.org/10.1044/1058-0360(2010/09-0022)

Floris, D. L., Barber, A. D., Nebel, M. B., Martinelli, M., Lai, M.-C., Crocetti, D., Baron-Cohen, S., Suckling, J., Pekar, J. J., & Mostofsky, S. H. (2016). Atypical lateralization of motor circuit functional connectivity in children with autism is associated with motor deficits. *Molecular Autism*, 7, AR 35, https://doi.org/10.1186/s13229-016-0096-6

Focaroli, V., Taffoni, F., Parsons, S. M., Keller, F., & Iverson, J. M. (2016). Performance of motor sequences in children at heightened vs. low risk for ASD: A longitudinal study from 18 to 36 months of age. *Frontiers in Psychology*, 7, AR 724, https://doi.org/10.3389/fpsyg.2016.00724

Foley, M. A., & Ratner, H. H. (2001). The role of action-based structures in activity memory. In H. D. Zimmer, R. L. Cohen, M. J. Guynn, J. Engelkamp, R. Kormi-Nouri, & M. A. Foley (eds.), *Memory for action: A distinct form of episodic memory?* (pp. 112–135). New York, NY: Oxford University Press.

Folven, R. J., & Bonvillian, J. D. (1991). The transition from nonreferential to referential language in children acquiring American Sign Language. *Developmental Psychology*, 27, 806–816, https://doi.org/10.1037/0012-1649.27.5.806

Fombonne, E. (2005). Epidemiological studies of pervasive developmental disorders. In F. R. Volkmar, R. Paul, A. Klin, & D. Cohen (eds.), *Handbook of autism and pervasive developmental disorders, vol. 1. Diagnosis, development, neurobiology, and behavior* (3rd ed., pp. 42–69). Hoboken, NJ: John Wiley & Sons, https://doi.org/10.1002/9780470939345.ch2

Fombonne, E. (1999). The epidemiology of autism: A review. *Psychological Medicine*, 29, 769–786, https://doi.org/10.1017/s0033291799008508

Fontanella, C. A., Hiance, D. L., Phillips, G. S., Bridge, J. A., & Campo, J. V. (2014). Trends in psychotropic medication use for Medicaid-enrolled preschool children. *Journal of Child and Family Studies*, 23, 617–631, https://doi.org/10.1007/s10826-013-9761-y

Foreman, C. T. (1949). Lewis Francis Hadley: The long-haired sign talker. *Chronicles of Oklahoma*, 27, 41–55.

Fouts, R., with S. T. Mills. (1997). *Next of kin: What chimpanzees have taught me about who we are*. New York, NY: William Morrow.

Fowler, A. E. (1990). Language abilities in children with Down syndrome: Evidence for a specific syntactic delay. In D. Cicchetti & M. Beeghly (eds.), *Children with Down syndrome: A developmental perspective* (pp. 302–328). Cambridge, U.K.: Cambridge University Press, https://doi.org/10.1017/CBO9780511581786.010

Fowler, A. E. (1998). Language in mental retardation: Associations with and dissociations from general cognition. In T. A. Burack, R. M. Hodapp, & E. Zigler (eds.), *Handbook of mental retardation and development* (pp. 290–333). Cambridge, U.K.: Cambridge University Press.

Fox Tree, E. (2009). Meemul Tziij: An indigenous sign language complex of Mesoamerica. *Sign Language Studies*, 9, 324–366, https://doi.org/10.1353/sls.0.0016

Frankel, R., Leary, M., & Kilman, B. (1987). Building social skills through pragmatic analysis: Assessment and treatment implications for children with autism. In D. Cohen, A. Donnellan, & R. Paul (eds.), *Handbook of autism and pervasive developmental disorders* (pp. 333–359). New York, NY: John Wiley & Sons.

Frick-Horbury, D., & Guttentag, R. E. (1998). The effects of restricting hand gesture production on lexical retrieval and free recall. *The American Journal of Psychology*, 111, 43–62, https://doi.org/10.2307/1423536

Fried-Oken, M., & More, L. (1992). An initial vocabulary for nonspeaking preschool children based on developmental and environmental language sources. *Augmentative and Alternative Communication*, 8, 41–56, https://doi.org/10.1080/07434619212331276033

Frishberg, N. (1975). Arbitrariness and iconicity: Historical change in American Sign Language. *Language*, 51, 696–719, https://doi.org/10.2307/412894

Fritelli, G., & Daniloff, J. K. (1982). *Amer-Ind versus ASL: Recognition and imitation in aphasic subjects*. Paper presented at the annual meeting of the American Speech-Language-Hearing Association, Toronto, Ontario, Canada.

Frith, U. (1989). *Autism: Explaining the enigma*. Oxford, U.K.: Blackwell.

Frith, U. (2008). *Autism: A very short introduction*. Oxford, U.K.: Oxford University Press, https://doi.org/10.1093/actrade/9780199207565.001.0001

Fulwiler, R. L., & Fouts, R. S. (1976). Acquisition of American Sign Language by a noncommunicating autistic child. *Journal of Autism and Childhood Schizophrenia*, 6, 43–51, https://doi.org/10.1007/bf01537941

Fusellier-Souza, I. (2006). Emergence and development of signed languages: From a semiogenetic point of view. *Sign Language Studies*, 7, 30–56, https://doi.org/10.1353/sls.2006.0030

Gaines, R., Leaper, C., Monahan, C., & Weickgenant, A. (1988). Language learning and retention in young language-disordered children. *Journal of Autism and Developmental Disorders*, 18, 281–296, https://doi.org/10.1007/bf02211953

Gainotti, G. (1988). Nonverbal cognitive disturbances in aphasia. In H. A. Whitaker (ed.), *Contemporary reviews in neuropsychology* (pp. 127–158). New York, NY: Springer-Verlag, https://doi.org/10.1007/978-1-4612-3780-8_5

Gainotti, G., & Lemmo, M. A. (1976). Comprehension of symbolic gestures in aphasia. *Brain and Language*, 3, 451–460, https://doi.org/10.1016/0093-934x(76)90039-0

Galeote, M., Sebastián, E., Checa, E., Rey, R., & Soto, P. (2011). The development of vocabulary in Spanish children with Down syndrome: Comprehension, production, and gestures. *Journal of Intellectual and Developmental Disability*, 36, 184–196, https://doi.org/10.3109/13668250.2011.599317

Gamsiz, E. D., Sciarra, L. N., Maguire, A. M., Pescosolido, M. F., van Dyck, L. I., & Morrow, E. M. (2015). Discovery of rare mutations in autism: Elucidating neurodevelopmental mechanisms. *Neurotherapeutics*, 12, 553–571, https://doi.org/10.1007/s13311-015-0363-9

Ganz, J. B., Davis, J. L., Lund, E. M., Goodwyn, F. D., & Simpson, R. L. (2012). Meta-analysis of PECS with individuals with ASD: Investigation of targeted versus non-targeted outcomes, participant characteristics, and implementation phase. *Research in Developmental Disabilities*, 33, 406–418, https://doi.org/10.1016/j.ridd.2011.09.023

Ganz, J. B., & Simpson, R. L. (2004). Effects on communicative requesting and speech development of the Picture Exchange Communication System in children with characteristics of autism. *Journal of Autism and Developmental Disorders*, 34, 395–409, https://doi.org/10.1023/b:jadd.0000037416.59095.d7

Garces, E., Thomas, D., & Currie, J. (2002). Longer-term effects of Head Start. *The American Economic Review*, 92, 999–1012, https://doi.org/10.1257/00028280260344560

Gardner, B. T., & Gardner, R. A. (1971). Two-way communication with an infant chimpanzee. In A. M. Schrier & F. Stollnitz (eds.), *Behavior of nonhuman primates: Modern research trends, vol. 4* (pp. 117–184). New York, NY: Academic Press.

Gardner, R. A., & Gardner, B. T. (1969). Teaching sign language to a chimpanzee. *Science*, 165, 664–672, https://doi.org/10.1126/science.165.3894.664

Gates, G. E., & Edwards, R. P. (1989). Acquisition of American Sign Language versus Amerind signs in a mentally handicapped sample. *Journal of Communication Disorders*, 22, 423–435, https://doi.org/10.1016/0021-9924(89)90035-x

Gauthier, K., & Genesee, F. (2011). Language development in internationally adopted children: A special case of early second language learning. *Child Development*, 82, 887–901, https://doi.org/10.1111/j.1467-8624.2011.01578.x

Gauthier, L. V., Taub, E., Perkins, C., Ortmann, M., Mark, V. W., & Uswatte, G. (2008). Remodeling the brain: Plastic structural brain changes produced by different motor therapies after stroke. *Stroke*, 39, 1520–1525, https://doi.org/10.1161/strokeaha.107.502229

Gellevij, M., Van der Meij, H., Jong, T. de, & Pieters, J. (2002). Multimodal versus unimodal instruction in a complex learning context. *The Journal of Experimental Education*, 70, 215–239, https://doi.org/10.1080/00220970209599507

Gentilucci, M., & Campione, G. C. (2013). From action to speech. In Y. Coello & A. Bartolo (eds.), *Language and action in cognitive neuroscience* (pp. 59–79). Hove, East Sussex, U.K.: Psychology Press.

Gentilucci, M., & Corballis, M. C. (2006). From manual gesture to speech: A gradual transition. *Neuroscience and Biobehavioral Reviews*, 30, 949–960, https://doi.org/10.1016/j.neubiorev.2006.02.004

Geraci, C., Gozzi, M., Papagno, C., & Cecchetto, C. (2008). How grammar can cope with limited short-term memory: Simultaneity and seriality in sign languages. *Cognition*, 106, 780–804, https://doi.org/10.1016/j.cognition.2007.04.014

Gernsbacher, M. A., Dawson, M., & Goldsmith, H. H. (2005). Three reasons not to believe in an autism epidemic. *Current Directions in Psychological Science*, 14, 55–58, https://doi.org/10.1111/j.0963-7214.2005.00334.x

Gernsbacher, M. A., Sauer, E. A., Geye, H. M., Schweigert, E. K., & Goldsmith, H. H. (2008). Infant and toddler oral- and manual-motor skills predict later speech fluency in autism. *Journal of Child Psychology and Psychiatry*, 49, 43–50, https://doi.org/10.1111/j.1469-7610.2007.01820.x

Gernsbacher, M. A., Stevenson, J. L., Khandakar, S., & Goldsmith, H. H. (2008). Why does joint attention look atypical in autism? *Child Development Perspectives*, 2, 38–45, https://doi.org/10.1111/j.1750-8606.2008.00039.x

Gervais, H., Belin, P., Boddaert, N., Leboyer, M., Coez, A., Sfaello, I., Barthélémy, C., Brunelle, F., Samson, Y., & Zilbovicius, M. (2004). Abnormal cortical voice processing in autism. *Nature Neuroscience*, 7, 801–802, https://doi.org/10.1038/nn1291

Geschwind, N. (1979). Foreword. In A. Kertesz, *Aphasia and associated disorders: Taxonomy, localization, and recovery* (pp. xiii–xiv). New York, NY: Grune & Stratton.

Gevarter, C., O'Reilly, M. F., Rojeski, L., Sammarco, N., Lang, R., Lancioni, G. E., & Sigafoos, J. (2013). Comparing communication systems for individuals with developmental disabilities: A review of single-case research studies. *Research in Developmental Disabilities*, 34, 4415–4432, https://doi.org/10.1016/j.ridd.2013.09.017

Gidley Larson, J. C., & Mostofsky, S. H. (2006). Motor deficits in autism. In R. Tuchman & I. Rapin (eds.), *Autism: A neurological disorder of early brain development* (pp. 231–247). London, U.K.: Mac Keith Press.

Girolametto, L., Sussman, F., & Weitzman, E. (2007). Using case study methods to investigate the effects of interactive intervention for children with autism spectrum disorders. *Journal of Communication Disorders*, 40, 470–492, https://doi.org/10.1016/j.jcomdis.2006.11.001

Glacken, M., Healy, D., Gilrane, U., Healy-McGowan, S., Dolan, S., Walsh-Gallagher, D., & Jennings, C. (2019). Key word signing: Parents' experiences of an unaided form of augmentative and alternative communication (Lámh). *Journal of Intellectual Disabilities*, 23, 327–343, https://doi.org/10.1177/1744629518790825

Glennen, S. (2002). Language development and delay in internationally adopted infants and toddlers: A review. *American Journal of Speech-Language Pathology*, 11, 333–339, https://doi.org/10.1044/1058-0360(2002/038)

Glennen, S. (2009). Speech and language guidelines for children adopted from abroad at older ages. *Topics in Language Disorders*, 29, 50–64, https://doi.org/10.1097/tld.0b013e3181976df4

Glennen, S., & Bright, B. J. (2005). Five years later: Language in school-age internationally adopted children. *Seminars in Speech and Language*, 26, 86–101, https://doi.org/10.1055/s-2005-864219

Glennen, S., & Masters, M. G. (2002). Typical and atypical language development in infants and toddlers adopted from eastern Europe. *American Journal of Speech-Language Pathology*, 11, 417–433, https://doi.org/10.1044/1058-0360(2002/045)

Glück, S., & Pfau, R. (1999). A distributed morphology account of verbal inflection in German Sign Language. In T. Cambier-Langeveld, A. Lipták, M. Redford, & E. J. van der Torre (eds.), *Proceedings of the seventh annual conference of the student organization of linguistics in Europe* (pp. 65–80). Leiden, South Holland: SOLE.

Goddard, I. (1996). Introduction. In I. Goddard (ed.), *Handbook of North American Indians, vol. 17. Languages* (pp. 1–16). Washington, DC: Smithsonian Institution.

Goldbart, J., & Marshall, J. (2004). "Pushes and pulls" on the parents of children who use AAC. *Augmentative and Alternative Communication*, 20, 194–208, https://doi.org/10.1080/07434610400010960

Goldenberg, G., & Randerath, J. (2015). Shared neural substrates of apraxia and aphasia. *Neuropsychologia*, 75, 40–49, https://doi.org/10.1016/j.neuropsychologia.2015.05.017

Golder, H. (1996). Making a scene: Gesture, tableau, and the tragic chorus. *Arion: A Journal of Humanities and the Classics*, 4, 1–19.

Goldin-Meadow, S. (1998). The development of gesture and speech as an integrated system. *New Directions for Child Development*, 79, 29–42, https://doi.org/10.1002/cd.23219987903

Goldin-Meadow, S. (2003). *The resilience of language: What gesture creation in deaf children can tell us about how all children learn language*. New York, NY: Psychology Press.

Goldin-Meadow, S., & Beilock, S. L. (2010). Action's influence on thought: The case of gesture. *Perspectives on Psychological Science*, 5, 664–674, https://doi.org/10.1177/1745691610388764

Goldin-Meadow, S., & Brentari, D. (2017). Gesture, sign, and language: The coming of age of sign language and gesture studies. *Behavioral and Brain Sciences*, 40, e46, https://doi.org/10.1017/S0140525X15001247

Goldin-Meadow, S., Butcher, C., Mylander, C., & Dodge, M. (1994). Nouns and verbs in a self-styled gesture system: What's in a name? *Cognitive Psychology*, 27, 259–319, https://doi.org/10.1006/cogp.1994.1018

Goldin-Meadow, S., Levine, S. C., Hedges, L. V., Huttenlocher, J., Raudenbush, S. W., & Small, S. L. (2014). New evidence about language and cognitive development based on a longitudinal study: Hypotheses for intervention. *American Psychologist*, 69, 588–599, https://doi.org/10.1037/a0036886

Goldstein, H. (2002). Communication intervention for children with autism: A review of treatment efficacy. *Journal of Autism and Developmental Disorders*, 32, 373–396, https://doi.org/10.1023/a:1020589821992

Goldstein, S. (2011). Attention-deficit/hyperactivity disorder. In S. Goldstein & C. R. Reynolds (eds.), *Handbook of neurodevelopmental and genetic disorders in children* (2nd ed., pp. 131–150). New York, NY: The Guilford Press.

Gonsiorowski, A., Williamson, R. A., & Robins, D. L. (2016). Brief report: Imitation of object-directed acts in young children with autism spectrum disorders. *Journal of Autism and Developmental Disorders*, 46, 691–697, https://doi.org/10.1007/s10803-015-2596-1

Goodman, L., Wilson, P. S., & Bornstein, H. (1978). Results of a national survey of sign language programs in special education. *Mental Retardation*, 16, 104–106.

Goodwin, C. (2000). Gesture, aphasia, and interaction. In D. McNeill (ed.), *Language and gesture* (pp. 84–98). Cambridge, U.K.: Cambridge University Press, https://doi.org/10.1017/CBO9780511620850.006

Goodwin, C. (2006). Human sociality as mutual orientation in a rich interactive environment: Multimodal utterances and pointing in aphasia. In N. J. Enfield & S. C. Levinson (eds.), *Roots of human sociality: Culture, cognition, and interaction* (pp. 97–125). Oxford, U.K.: Berg.

Goodwyn, S. W., & Acredolo, L. P. (1993). Symbolic gesture versus word: Is there a modality advantage for onset of symbol use? *Child Development*, 64, 688–701, https://doi.org/10.2307/1131211

Goodwyn, S. W., & Acredolo, L. P. (1998). Encouraging symbolic gestures: A new perspective on the relationship between gesture and speech. In J. M. Iverson & S. Goldin-Meadow (eds.), *The nature and functions of gesture in children's communication* (pp. 61–73). San Francisco, CA: Jossey-Bass, https://doi.org/10.1002/cd.23219987905

Goodwyn, S. W., Acredolo, L. P., & Brown, C. A. (2000). Impact of symbolic gesturing on early language development. *Journal of Nonverbal Behavior*, 24, 81–103, https://doi.org/10.1023/a:1006653828895

Gordon, K., Pasco, G., McElduff, F., Wade, A., Howlin, P., & Charman, T. (2011). A communication-based intervention for nonverbal children with autism: What changes? Who benefits? *Journal of Consulting and Clinical Psychology*, 79, 447–457, https://doi.org/10.1037/a0024379

Gordon, N. (2004). The neurology of sign language. *Brain and Development*, 26, 146–150, https://doi.org/10.1016/s0387-7604(03)00128-1

Grandin, T. (1995). *Thinking in pictures and other reports from my life with autism.* New York, NY: Doubleday.

Grandin, T., & Panek, R. (2013). *The autistic brain: Thinking across the spectrum.* New York, NY: Houghton Mifflin Harcourt.

Granlund, M., Björck-Åkesson, E., Wilder, J., & Ylvén, R. (2008). AAC interventions for children in a family environment: Implementing evidence in practice. *Augmentative and Alternative Communication*, 24, 207–219, https://doi.org/10.1080/08990220802387935

Gray, S. (2003). Word-learning by preschoolers with specific language impairment: What predicts success? *Journal of Speech, Language, and Hearing Research*, 46, 56–67, https://doi.org/10.1044/1092-4388(2003/005)

Green, E. M. (2014). Building the tower of Babel: International Sign, linguistic commensuration, and moral orientation. *Language in Society*, 43, 445–465, https://doi.org/10.1017/s0047404514000396

Greenblatt, S. (1991). *Marvelous possessions: The wonder of the New World.* Chicago, IL: University of Chicago Press, https://doi.org/10.7208/chicago/9780226306575.001.0001

Greenspan, S. I., & Weider, S. (1997). Developmental patterns and outcomes in infants and children with disorders in relating and communicating. A chart review of 200 cases of children with autistic spectrum diagnoses. *Journal of Developmental and Learning Disorders*, 1, 87–141.

Grieco, J., Pulsifer, M., Seligsohn, K., Skotko, B., & Schwartz, A. (2015). Down syndrome: Cognitive and behavioral functioning across the lifespan. *American Journal of Medical Genetics Part C (Seminars in Medical Genetics)*, 169c, 135–149, https://doi.org/10.1002/ajmg.c.31439

Griffith, P. L., & Robinson, J. H. (1980). Influence of iconicity and phonological similarity on sign learning by mentally retarded children. *American Journal of Mental Deficiency*, 85, 291–298.

Griffith, P. L., Robinson, J. H., & Panagos, J. M. (1981). Perception of iconicity in American Sign Language by hearing and deaf subjects. *Journal of Speech and Hearing Disorders*, 46, 388–397, https://doi.org/10.1044/jshd.4604.388

Grinnell, M. F., Detamore, K. L., & Lipke, B. A. (1976). Sign it successful — Manual English encourages expressive communication. *Teaching Exceptional Children, 8,* 123–124, https://doi.org/10.1177/004005997600800308

Grosse, J., & Reker, J. (2010). *Don't get me wrong! The global gestures guide.* Munich, Germany: Bierke Publishing.

Grosso, B. (1993). *Iconicity and arbitrariness in Italian Sign Language: An experimental study.* Padua, Italy: University of Padua.

Grove, N. (1980). Nonspeech systems of communication: An introduction. *Makaton Vocabulary Development Project Research Information Service, 1,* 1–20.

Grove, N. (1990). Developing intelligible signs with learning-disabled students: A review of the literature and an assessment procedure. *British Journal of Disorders of Communication, 25,* 265–293, https://doi.org/10.3109/13682829009011978

Grove, N. (1994). The acquisition of sign and word combinations in the bimodal communication of children with learning difficulties. In M. Brennan & G. H. Turner (eds.), *Word-order issues in sign language: Working papers* (pp. 159–169). Durham, U.K.: The International Sign Linguistics Association and the University of Durham.

Grove, N. (2019a). Multi-sign utterances by children with intellectual disabilities: Patterns of use, assessment and intervention. In N. Grove & K. Launonen (eds.), *Manual sign acquisition in children with developmental disabilities* (pp. 271–292). New York, NY: Nova Science Publishers, Inc.

Grove, N. (2019b). Pragmatic skills of key word signers. In N. Grove & K. Launonen (eds.), *Manual sign acquisition in children with developmental disabilities* (pp. 293–314). New York, NY: Nova Science Publishers, Inc.

Grove, N., & Colville, D. (1990). *An approach to the remediation of sign production errors.* Paper presented at the 2nd national conference of the International Society of Augmentative and Alternative Communication, September 24–25, Lancaster, U.K.

Grove, N., Dark, L., Brownlie, E., & Bloomberg, K. (2019). Assessment and intervention for problems in sign production. In N. Grove & K. Launonen (eds.), *Manual sign acquisition in children with developmental disabilities* (pp. 247–270). New York, NY: Nova Science Publishers, Inc.

Grove, N., & Dockrell, J. (2000). Multisign combinations by children with intellectual impairments: An analysis of language skills. *Journal of Speech, Language, and Hearing Research, 43,* 309–323, https://doi.org/10.1044/jslhr.4302.309

Grove, N., & McDougall, S. (1991). Exploring sign use in two settings. *British Journal of Special Education, 18,* 149–156, https://doi.org/10.1111/j.1467-8578.1991.tb00862.x

Grove, N., & Walker, M. (1990). The Makaton Vocabulary: Using manual signs and graphic symbols to develop interpersonal communication. *Augmentative and Alternative Communication*, 6, 15–28, https://doi.org/10.1080/074346190 12331275284

Grove, N., & Woll, B. (2017). Assessing language skills in adult key word signers with intellectual disabilities: Insights from sign linguistics. *Research in Developmental Disabilities*, 62, 174–183, https://doi.org/10.1016/j. ridd.2017.01.017

Grush, R. (2004). The emulation theory of representation: Motor control, imagery, and perception. *Behavioral and Brain Sciences*, 27, 377–396, https:// doi.org/10.1017/s0140525x04000093

Gruson-Wood, J. F. (2016). Autism, expert discourses, and subjectification: A critical examination of applied behavioural therapies. *Studies in Social Justice*, 10, 38–58, https://doi.org/10.26522/ssj.v10i1.1331

Guardino, C. A. (2008). Identification and placement for deaf students with multiple disabilities: Choosing the path less followed. *American Annals of the Deaf*, 153, 55–64, https://doi.org/10.1353/aad.0.0004

Guidi, S., Ciani, E., Bonasoni, P., Santini, D., & Bartesaghi, R. (2011). Widespread proliferation impairment and hypocellularity in the cerebellum of fetuses with Down syndrome. *Brain Pathology*, 21, 361–373, https://doi. org/10.1111/j.1750-3639.2010.00459.x

Gullberg, M. (2006). Some reasons for studying gesture and second language acquisition (hommage à Adam Kendon). *International Review of Applied Linguistics*, 44, 103–124, https://doi.org/10.1515/iral.2006.004

Guralnick, M. J. (2017). Early intervention for children with intellectual disabilities: An update. *Journal of Applied Research in Intellectual Disabilities*, 30, 211–229, https://doi.org/10.1111/jar.12233

Haar, S., Berman, S., Behrmann, M., & Dinstein, I. (2016). Anatomical abnormalities in autism? *Cerebral Cortex*, 26, 1440–1452, https://doi. org/10.1093/cercor/bhu242

Hadley, L. F. (1893). *Indian sign talk*. Chicago, IL: Baker.

Hahn, L. J., Zimmer, B. J., Brady, N. C., Swinburne Romine, R. E., & Fleming, K. K. (2014). Role of maternal gesture use in speech use by children with fragile X syndrome. *American Journal of Speech-Language Pathology*, 23, 146–159, https://doi.org/10.1044/2013_ajslp-13-0046

Haiman, J. (1980). The iconicity of grammar: Isomorphism and motivation. *Language*, 56, 515–540, https://doi.org/10.2307/414448

Haiman, J. (ed.). (1985). *Iconicity in syntax: Proceedings of a symposium on iconicity in syntax, Stanford, June 24–26, 1983*. Amsterdam, The Netherlands: John Benjamins Publishing, https://doi.org/10.1075/tsl.6

Hall, S. M., & Talkington, L. W. (1970). Evaluation of a manual approach to programming for deaf retarded. *American Journal of Mental Deficiency, 75,* 378–380.

Hall, S. S. (2015). Solving the autism puzzle. *MIT Technology Review, 118,* 36–43.

Hallmayer, J., Cleveland, S., Torres, A., Phillips, J., Cohen, B., Torigoe, T., Miller, J., Fedele, A., Collins, J., Smith, K., Lotspeich, L., Croen, L. A., Ozonoff, S., Lajonchere, C., Grether, J. K., & Risch, N. (2011). Genetic heritability and shared environmental factors among twin pairs with autism. *Archives of General Psychiatry,* 68, 1095–1102, https://doi.org/10.1001/archgenpsychiatry.2011.76

Halpern, D. F., Benbow, C. P., Geary, D. C., Gur, R. C., Hyde, J. S., & Gernsbacher, M. A. (2007). The science of sex differences in science and mathematics. *Psychological Science in the Public Interest,* 8, 1–51, https://doi.org/10.1111/j.1529-1006.2007.00032.x

Hamilton, A. F. de C., Brindley, R., & Frith, U. (2009). Visual perspective taking impairment in children with autistic spectrum disorder. *Cognition,* 113, 37–44, https://doi.org/10.1016/j.cognition.2009.07.007

Hamilton, B. L., & Snell, M. E. (1993). Using the milieu approach to increase spontaneous communication book use across environments by an adolescent with autism. *Augmentative and Alternative Communication,* 9, 259–272, https://doi.org/10.1080/07434619312331276681

Hamilton, C. (1993). Investigation of the articulatory patterns of young adults with Down's syndrome using electropalatography. *Down Syndrome Research and Practice,* 1, 15–28, https://doi.org/10.3104/reports.7

Hammond, S. A., & Meiners, L. H. (1993). American Indian deaf children and youth. In K. M. Christensen & G. L. Delgado (eds.), *Multicultural issues in deafness* (pp. 143–166). White Plains, NY: Longman Publishing Group.

Hanlon, R. E., Brown, J. W., & Gerstman, L. J. (1990). Enhancement of naming in nonfluent aphasia through gesture. *Brain and Language,* 38, 298–314, https://doi.org/10.1016/0093-934x(90)90116-x

Harrington, T. R. (2006, August). *Sign languages of the world by name.* Washington, DC: Gallaudet University Library, http://libguides.gallaudet.edu/content.php?pid=114804&sid=991940

Harrington, T. R., & Hamrick, S. (2010, May). *Sign languages of the world by country.* Washington, DC: Gallaudet University Library, http://libguides.gallaudet.edu/content.php?pid=114804&sid=991920

Harris, M., Clibbens, J., Chasin, J., & Tibbitts, R. (1989). The social context of early sign language development. *First Language,* 9, 81–97, https://doi.org/10.1177/014272378900902507

Hart, B., & Risley, T. R. (1995). *Meaningful differences in the everyday experience of young American children.* Baltimore, MD: Paul H. Brookes Publishing.

Hart, B., & Risley, T. R. (2003). The early catastrophe: The 30 million word gap by age 3. *American Educator*, 27, 4–9.

Haskill, A. M., & Tyler, A. A. (2007). A comparison of linguistic profiles in subgroups of children with specific language impairment. *American Journal of Speech-Language Pathology*, 16, 209–221, https://doi.org/10.1044/1058-0360(2007/026)

Haswell, C. C., Izawa, J., Dowell, L. R., Mostofsky, S. H., & Shadmehr, R. (2009). Representation of internal models of action in the autistic brain. *Nature Neuroscience*, 12, 970–972, https://doi.org/10.1038/nn.2356

Haug, T. (2005). Review of sign language assessment instruments. *Sign Language & Linguistics*, 8, 61–98, https://doi.org/10.1075/sll.8.1.04hau

Haug, T., & Mann, W. (2008). Adapting tests of sign language assessment for other sign languages — A review of linguistic, cultural, and psychometric problems. *Journal of Deaf Studies and Deaf Education*, 13, 138–147, https://doi.org/10.1093/deafed/enm027

Hauser, P. C., & Kartheiser, G. (2014). Advantages of learning a signed language. In H-D. L. Bauman & J. J. Murray (eds.), *Deaf gain: Raising the stakes for human diversity* (pp. 133–145). Minneapolis, MN: University of Minnesota Press.

Hazlett, H. C., Gu, H., Munsell, B. C., Kim, S. H. Styner, M., Wolff, J. J., Elison, J. T., Swanson, M. R., Zhu, H., Botteron, K. N., Collins, D. L., Constantino, J. N., Dager, S. R., Estes, A. M., Evans, A. C., Fonov, V. S., Gerig, G., Kostopoulos, P., McKinstry, R. C., Pandey, J., Paterson, S., Pruett, J. R., Jr., Schultz, R. T., Shaw, D. W., Zwaigenbaum, L., Piven, J., & the IBIS Network. (2017). Early brain development in infants at high risk for autism spectrum disorder. *Nature*, 542, 348–351, https://doi.org/10.1038/nature21369

Heilman, K., Rothi, L., Campanella, D., & Wolfson, S. (1979). Wernicke's and global aphasia without alexia. *Archives of Neurology*, 36, 129–133, https://doi.org/10.1001/archneur.1979.00500390047003

Heimann, M., Nordqvist, E., Strid, K., Connant Almrot, J., & Tjus, T. (2016). Children with autism respond differently to spontaneous, elicited and deferred imitation. *Journal of Intellectual Disability Research*, 60, 491–501, https://doi.org/10.1111/jir.12272

Helfrich-Miller, K. R. (1984). Melodic intonation therapy with developmentally apraxic children. *Seminars in Speech and Language*, 5, 119–126, https://doi.org/10.1055/s-0028-1082518

Helfrich-Miller, K. R. (1994). A clinical perspective: Melodic intonation therapy for developmental apraxia. *Clinics in Communication Disorders*, 4, 175–182.

Hellendoorn, A., Wijnroks, L., & Leseman, P. P. M. (2015). Unraveling the nature of autism: Finding order amid change. *Frontiers in Psychology*, 6, AR 359, https://doi.org/10.3389/fpsyg.2015.00359

Heller, I., Manning, D., Pavur, D., & Wagner, K. (1998). Let's all sign! Enhancing language development in an inclusive preschool. *Teaching Exceptional Children*, 30, 50–53, https://doi.org/10.1177/004005999803000309

Hepburn, S., Philofsky, A., Fidler, D. J., & Rogers, S. (2008). Autism symptoms in toddlers with Down syndrome: A descriptive study. *Journal of Applied Research in Intellectual Disabilities*, 21, 48–57, https://doi.org/10.1111/j.1468-3148.2007.00368.x

Hepburn, S. L., & Stone, W. L. (2006). Longitudinal research on motor imitation in autism. In S. J. Rogers & J. H. G. Williams (eds.), *Imitation and the social mind: Autism and typical development* (pp. 310–328). New York, NY: The Guilford Press.

Herman, R., Grove, N., Holmes, S., Morgan, G., Sutherland, H., & Woll, B. (2004). *Assessing British Sign Language development: Production test (Narrative skills)*. London, U.K.: City University Publication.

Herman, R., Holmes, S., & Woll, B. (1999). *Assessing British Sign Language development: Receptive skills test*. Gloucester, U.K.: The Forest Bookshop.

Herman, R., Rowley, K., Mason, K., & Morgan, G. (2014). Deficits in narrative abilities in child British Sign Language users with specific language impairment. *International Journal of Language & Communication Disorders*, 49, 343–353, https://doi.org/10.1111/1460-6984.12078

Herman, R., Shield, A., & Morgan, G. (2019). Sign language development in deaf children with language impairments and autism spectrum disorders. In N. Grove & K. Launonen (eds.), *Manual sign acquisition in children with developmental disabilities* (pp. 133–149). New York, NY: Nova Science Publishers, Inc.

Herrmann, M., Reichle, T., Lucius-Hoene, G., Wallesch, C.-W., & Johannsen-Horbach, H. (1988). Nonverbal communication as a compensatory strategy for severely nonfluent aphasics? A quantitative approach. *Brain and Language*, 33, 41–54, https://doi.org/10.1016/0093-934X(88)90053-3

Herrmann, A., & Steinbach, M. (eds.). (2013). *Nonmanuals in sign language*. Amsterdam, The Netherlands: John Benjamins Publishing, https://doi.org/10.1075/bct.53

Hertz-Picciotto, I., & Delwiche, L. (2009). The rise in autism and the role of age at diagnosis. *Epidemiology*, 20, 84–90, https://doi.org/10.1097/ede.0b013e3181902d15

Hetzroni, O. E., & Roth, T. (2003). Effects of a positive support approach to enhance communicative behaviors of children with mental retardation who have challenging behaviors. *Education and Training in Developmental Disabilities*, 38, 95–105.

Hewes, G. W. (1974). Gesture language in culture contact. *Sign Language Studies*, 4, 1–34, https://doi.org/10.1353/sls.1974.0010

Hewes, G. W. (1976). The current status of the gestural theory of language origins. *Annals of the New York Academy of Sciences*, 280, 482–504, https://doi.org/10.1111/j.1749-6632.1976.tb25512.x

Heyns, B. (1978). *Summer learning and the effects of schooling.* New York, NY: Academic Press.

Hickok, G., Love-Geffen, T., & Klima, E. S. (2002). Role of the left hemisphere in sign language comprehension. *Brain and Language*, 82, 167–178, https://doi.org/10.1016/S0093-934X(02)00013-5

Hiddinga, A., & Crasborn, O. (2011). Signed languages and globalization. *Language in Society*, 40, 483–505, https://doi.org/10.1017/s0047404511000480

Hildebrandt, U., & Corina, D. (2002). Phonological similarity in American Sign Language. *Language and Cognitive Processes*, 17, 593–612, https://doi.org/10.1080/01690960143000371

Hill, E. L. (2001). Non-specific nature of specific language impairment: A review of the literature with regard to concomitant motor impairments. *International Journal of Language and Communication Disorders*, 36, 149–171, https://doi.org/10.1080/13682820010019874

Hill, F., Reichart, R., & Korhonen, A. (2014). Multi-modal models for concrete and abstract concept meaning. *Transactions of the Association for Computational Linguistics*, 2, 285–296, https://doi.org/10.1162/tacl_a_00183

Hillis, A. E. (2007). Aphasia: Progress in the last quarter of a century. *Neurology*, 69, 200–213, https://doi.org/10.1212/01.wnl.0000265600.69385.6f

Himmelmann, K., Beckung, E., Hagberg, G., & Uvebrant, P. (2006). Gross and fine motor function and accompanying impairments in cerebral palsy. *Developmental Medicine & Child Neurology*, 48, 417–423, https://doi.org/10.1111/j.1469-8749.2006.tb01289.x

Hirsh-Pasek, K., Adamson, L. B., Bakeman, R., Owen, M. T., Golinkoff, R. M., Pace, A., Yust, P. K. S., & Suma, K. (2015). The contribution of early communication quality to low-income children's language success. *Psychological Science*, 26, 1071–1083, https://doi.org/10.1177/0956797615581493

Hobson, P. A., & Duncan, P. (1979). Sign learning and profoundly retarded people. *Mental Retardation*, 17, 33–37.

Hockema, S. A., & Smith, L. B. (2009). Learning your language, outside-in and inside-out. *Linguistics*, 47, 453–479, https://doi.org/10.1515/LING.2009.016

Hockett, C. F. (1978). In search of Jove's brow. *American Speech*, 53, 243–313, https://doi.org/10.2307/455140

Hoemann, H. W. (1975). The transparency of meaning of sign language gestures. *Sign Language Studies*, 7, 151–161, https://doi.org/10.1353/sls.1975.0019

Hoff, E. (2003). The specificity of environmental influence: Socioeconomic status affects early vocabulary development via maternal speech. *Child Development*, 74, 1368–1378, https://doi.org/10.1111/1467-8624.00612

Hoff, E. (2009). *Language development* (4th ed.). Belmont, CA: Wadsworth.

Hoff, E. (2013). Interpreting the early language trajectories of children from low-SES and language minority homes: Implications for closing achievement gaps. *Developmental Psychology*, 49, 4–14, https://doi.org/10.1037/a0027238

Hoffmeister, R. J., & Farmer, A. (1972). The development of manual sign language in mentally retarded and deaf individuals. *Journal of Rehabilitation of the Deaf*, 6, 19–26.

Hogrefe, K., Ziegler, W., Weidinger, N., & Goldenberg, G. (2012). Non-verbal communication in severe aphasia: Influence of aphasia, apraxia, or semantic processing? *Cortex*, 48, 952–962, https://doi.org/10.1016/j.cortex.2011.02.022

Hogrefe, K., Ziegler, W., Wiesmayer, S., Weidinger, N., & Goldenberg, G. (2013). The actual and potential use of gestures for communication in aphasia. *Aphasiology*, 27, 1070–1089, https://doi.org/10.1080/02687038.2013.803515

Holcomb, T. K. (2013). *Introduction to American Deaf culture*. New York, NY: Oxford University Press.

Holmes, J. M. (1975). *Manual signing with an aphasic patient*. Paper presented at the 13th Academy of Aphasia meeting, Victoria, British Columbia, Canada.

Holmes, K. M., & Holmes, D. W. (1980). Signed and spoken language development in a hearing child of hearing parents. *Sign Language Studies*, 28, 239–254, https://doi.org/10.1353/sls.1980.0012

Holzrichter, A. S., & Meier, R. P. (2000). Child-directed signing in American Sign Language. In C. Chamberlain, J. P. Morford, & R. I. Mayberry (eds.), *Language acquisition by eye* (pp. 25–40). Mahwah, NJ: Lawrence Erlbaum Associates.

Hoodin, R. B., & Thompson, C. K. (1983). Facilitation of verbal labeling in adult aphasia by gestural, verbal or verbal plus gestural training. In R. H. Brookshire (ed.), *Clinical aphasiology: Proceedings of the conference, 1983* (pp. 62–64). Minneapolis, MN: BRK Publishers.

Hooper, J., Connell, T. M., & Flett, P. J. (1987). Blissymbols and manual signs: A multimodal approach to intervention in a case of multiple disability. *Augmentative and Alternative Communication*, 3, 68–76, https://doi.org/10.1080/07434618712331274299

Hornberger, N. H. (1998). Language policy, language education, language rights: Indigenous, immigrant, and international perspectives. *Language in Society*, 27, 439–458, https://doi.org/10.1017/s0047404500020182

Horner, R. H., & Budd, C. M. (1985). Acquisition of manual sign use: Collateral reduction of maladaptive behavior and factors limiting generalization. *Education and Training of the Mentally Retarded*, 20, 39–47.

Hornig, M., Bresnahan, M. A., Che, X., Schultz, A. F., Ukaigwe, J. E., Eddy, M. L., Hirtz, D., Gunnes, N., Lie, K. K., Magnus, P., Mjaaland, S., Reichborn-Kjennerud, T., Schjølberg, S., Øyen, A.-S., Levin, B., Susser, E. S., Stoltenberg, C., & Lipkin, W. I. (2017). Prenatal fever and autism risk. *Molecular Psychiatry*, 23, 759–766, http://dx.doi.org/10.1038/mp.2017.119

Hostetter, A. B. (2011). When do gestures communicate? A meta-analysis. *Psychological Bulletin*, 137, 297–315, https://doi.org/10.1037/a0022128

Hou, L., & Meier, R. P. (2018). The morphology of first-person object forms of directional verbs in ASL. *Glossa: A Journal of General Linguistics*, 3, 114, https://doi.org/10.5334/gjgl.469

Hough, R. (1994). *Captain James Cook*. New York, NY: W. W. Norton.

Howard, D., & Hatfield, F. M. (1987). *Aphasia therapy: Historical and contemporary issues*. Hove and London, U.K.: Lawrence Erlbaum Associates.

Howard, D. A. (1997). *Conquistador in chains: Cabeza de Vaca and the Indians of the Americas*. Tuscaloosa, AL: The University of Alabama Press.

Howard, J., Soo, B., Graham, H. K., Boyd, R. N., Reid, S., Lanigan, A., Wolfe, R., & Reddihough, D. S. (2005). Cerebral palsy in Victoria: Motor types, topography and gross motor function. *Journal of Paediatrics and Child Health*, 41, 479–483, https://doi.org/10.1111/j.1440-1754.2005.00687.x

Howlin, P., Goode, S., Hutton, J., & Rutter, M. (2004). Adult outcome for children with autism. *Journal of Child Psychology and Psychiatry*, 45, 212–229, https://doi.org/10.1111/j.1469-7610.2004.00215.x

Hughes, C. (1996). Brief report: Planning problems in autism at the level of motor control. *Journal of Autism and Developmental Disorders*, 26, 99–107, https://doi.org/10.1007/bf02276237

Hulme, C., Nash, H. M., Gooch, D., Lervåg, A., & Snowling, M. J. (2015). The foundations of literacy development in children at familial risk of dyslexia. *Psychological Science*, 26, 1877–1886, https://doi.org/10.1177/0956797615603702

Hulme, C., & Snowling, M. J. (2011). Children's reading comprehension difficulties: Nature, causes, and treatments. *Current Directions in Psychological Science*, 20, 139–142, https://doi.org/10.1177/0963721411408673

Humes, L. E., Dubno, J. R., Gordon-Salant, S., Lister, J. J., Cacace, A. T., Cruickshanks, K. J., Gates, G. A., Wilson, R. H., & Wingfield, A. (2012). Central presbycusis: A review and evaluation of the evidence. *Journal of the American Academy of Audiology*, 23, 635–666, https://doi.org/10.3766/jaaa.23.8.5

Hundert, J. (1981). Stimulus generalization after training an autistic deaf boy in manual signs. *Education and Treatment of Children*, 4, 329–337.

Hustad, K. C., & Garcia, J. M. (2005). Aided and unaided speech supplementation strategies: Effect of alphabet cues and iconic hand gestures on dysarthric speech. *Journal of Speech, Language, and Hearing Research*, 48, 996–1012, https://doi.org/10.1044/1092-4388(2005/068)

Hux, K., Weissling, K., & Wallace, S. (2008). Communication-based interventions: Augmentative and alternative communication for people with aphasia. In R. Chapey (ed.), *Language intervention strategies in aphasia and related neurogenic communication disorders* (5th ed., pp. 814–836). Philadelphia, PA: Lippincott Williams & Wilkins.

Hwa-Froelich, D. A. (2009). Communication development in infants and toddlers adopted from abroad. *Topics in Language Disorders*, 29, 32–49, https://doi.org/10.1097/01.tld.0000346060.63964.c2

Hwang, S., Jeon, H.-S., Yi, C.-h., Kwon, O.-y., Cho, S.-h., & You, S.-h. (2010). Locomotor imagery training improves gait performance in people with chronic hemiparetic stroke: A controlled clinical trial. *Clinical Rehabilitation*, 24, 514–522, https://doi.org/10.1177/0269215509360640

Hyde, M. B., & Power, D. J. (1991). Teachers' use of simultaneous communication: Effects on the signed and spoken components. *American Annals of the Deaf*, 136, 381–387, https://doi.org/10.1353/aad.2012.0434

Iacono, T., & Cameron, M. (2009). Australian speech-language pathologists' perceptions and experiences of augmentative and alternative communication in early childhood intervention. *Augmentative and Alternative Communication*, 25, 236–249, https://doi.org/10.3109/07434610903322151

Iacono, T., Lyon, K., Johnson, H., & West, D. (2013). Experiences of adults with complex communication needs receiving and using low tech AAC: An Australian context. *Disability and Rehabilitation: Assistive Technology*, 8, 392–401, https://doi.org/10.3109/17483107.2013.769122

Ingersoll, B., & Lalonde, K. (2010). The impact of object and gesture imitation training on language use in children with autism spectrum disorder. *Journal of Speech, Language, and Hearing Research*, 53, 1040–1051, https://doi.org/10.1044/1092-4388(2009/09-0043)

Ingersoll, B., & Meyer, K. (2011). Examination of correlates of different imitative functions in young children with autism spectrum disorders. *Research in Autism Spectrum Disorders*, 5, 1078–1085, https://doi.org/10.1016/j.rasd.2010.12.001

Ingersoll, B., & Schreibman, L. (2006). Teaching reciprocal imitation skills to young children with autism using a naturalistic behavioral approach: Effects on language, pretend play, and joint attention. *Journal of Autism and Developmental Disorders*, 36, 487–505, https://doi.org/10.1007/s10803-006-0089-y

Iossifov, I., O'Roak, B. J., Sanders, S. J., Ronemus, M., Krumm, N., Levy, D., Stessman, H. A., Witherspoon, K. T., Vives, L., Patterson, K. E., Smith, J. D., Paeper, B., Nickerson, D. A., Dea, J., Dong, S., Gonzalez, L. E., Mandell, J. D., Mane, S. M., Murtha, M. T., Sullivan, C. A., Walker, M. F., Waqar, Z., Wei,

L., Willsey, A. J., Yamrom, B., Lee, Y.-H., Grabowska, E., Dalkic, E., Wang, Z., Marks, S., Andrews, P., Leotta, A., Kendall, J., Hakker, I., Rosenbaum, J., Ma, B., Rodgers, L., Troge, J., Narzisi, G., Yoon, S., Schatz, M. C., Ye, K., McCombie, W. R., Shendure, J., Eichler, E. E., State, M. W., & Wigler, M. (2014). The contribution of *de novo* coding mutations to autism spectrum disorder. *Nature*, 515, 216–221, https://doi.org/10.1038/nature13908

Iverson, J. M., Capirci, O., & Caselli, M. C. (1994). From communication to language in two modalities. *Cognitive Development*, 9, 23–43, https://doi.org/10.1016/0885-2014(94)90018-3

Iverson, J. M., & Braddock, B. A. (2011). Gesture and motor skill in relation to language in children with language impairment. *Journal of Speech, Language, and Hearing Research*, 54, 72–86, https://doi.org/10.1044/1092-4388(2010/08-0197)

Iverson, J. M., & Goldin-Meadow, S. (1997). What's communication got to do with it? Gesture in children blind from birth. *Developmental Psychology*, 33, 453–467, https://doi.org/10.1037/0012-1649.33.3.453

Iverson, J. M., & Goldin-Meadow, S. (2005). Gesture paves the way for language development. *Psychological Science*, 16, 367–371, https://doi.org/10.1111/j.0956-7976.2005.01542.x

Iverson, J. M., & Thelen, E. (1999). Hand, mouth and brain: The dynamic emergence of speech and gesture. *Journal of Consciousness Studies*, 6, 19–40.

Jackson, E., Leitao, S., & Claessen, M. (2016). The relationship between phonological short-term memory, receptive vocabulary, and fast mapping in children with specific language impairment. *International Journal of Language & Communication Disorders*, 51, 61–73, https://doi.org/10.1111/1460-6984.12185

Jacobs, B., Drew, R., Ogletree, B. T., & Pierce, K. (2004). Augmentative and alternative communication (AAC) for adults with severe aphasia: Where we stand and how we can go further. *Disability and Rehabilitation*, 26, 1231–1240, https://doi.org/10.1080/09638280412331280244

Jenkins, J. M., Farkas, G., Duncan, G. J., Burchinal, M., & Vandell, D. L. (2016). Head Start at ages 3 and 4 versus Head Start followed by state pre-K: Which is more effective? *Educational Evaluation and Policy Analysis*, 38, 88–112, https://doi.org/10.3102/0162373715587965

Jernigan, T. L., & Bellugi, U. (1990). Anomalous brain morphology on magnetic resonance images in Williams syndrome and Down syndrome. *Archives of Neurology*, 47, 529–533, https://doi.org/10.1001/archneur.1990.00530050049011

Jiménez, L., Ortiz-Tudela, J., Méndez, C., & Lorda, M. J. (2015). Mimicry deficits in autism are not just *storm* effects. *Research in Autism Spectrum Disorders*, 17, 64–69, https://doi.org/10.1016/j.rasd.2015.06.003

Johnson, R. E., & Liddell, S. K. (2010). Toward a phonetic representation of signs: Sequentiality and contrast. *Sign Language Studies*, 11, 241–274, https://doi.org/10.1353/sls.2010.0008

Johnston, J. C., Durieux-Smith, A., & Bloom, K. (2005). Teaching gestural signs to infants to advance child development: A review of the evidence. *First Language*, 25, 235–251, https://doi.org/10.1177/0142723705050340

Jolleff, N., Emmerson, F., Ryan, M., & McConachie, H. (2006). Communication skills in Angelman syndrome: Matching phenotype to genotype. *Advances in Speech-Language Pathology*, 8, 28–33, https://doi.org/10.1080/14417040500459684

Jordan, M. (2016, March 30). Foreign adoptions sharply lower. *The Wall Street Journal*, A2.

Judge, S. L. (1999). Eastern European adoptions: Current status and implications for intervention. *Topics in Early Childhood Special Education*, 19, 244–252, https://doi.org/10.1177/027112149901900405

Juncos, O., Caamaño, A., Justo, M. J., López, E., Rivas, M. R., López, M. T., & Sola, F. (1997). Primeras palabras en la Lengua de Signos Española (LSE): Estructura formal, semántica, y contextual. *Revista de Logopedia, Foniatría, y Audiología*, 17, 170–180, https://doi.org/10.1016/S0214-4603(97)75662-6

Jure, R., Rapin, I., & Tuchman, R. F. (1991). Hearing-impaired autistic children. *Developmental Medicine and Child Neurology*, 33, 1062–1072, https://doi.org/10.1111/j.1469-8749.1991.tb14828.x

Justice, L. M., Petscher, Y., Schatschneider, C., & Mashburn, A. (2011). Peer effects in preschool classrooms: Is children's language growth associated with their classmates' skills? *Child Development*, 82, 1768–1777, https://doi.org/10.1111/j.1467-8624.2011.01665.x

Kaga, M. (1999). Language disorders in Landau-Kleffner syndrome. *Journal of Child Neurology*, 14, 118–122, https://doi.org/10.1177/088307389901400210

Kagohara, D. M., van der Meer, L., Ramdoss, S., O'Reilly, M. F., Lancioni, G. E., Davis, T. N., Rispoli, M., Lang, R., Marschik, P. B., Sutherland, D., Green, V. A., & Sigafoos, J. (2013). Using iPods® and iPads® in teaching programs for individuals with developmental disabilities: A systematic review. *Research in Developmental Disabilities*, 34, 147–156, https://doi.org/10.1016/j.ridd.2012.07.027

Kahn, J. V. (1996). Cognitive skills and sign language knowledge of children with severe and profound mental retardation. *Education and Training in Mental Retardation and Developmental Disabilities*, 31, 162–168.

Kaiser, A. P., & Roberts, M. Y. (2013). Parent-implemented enhanced milieu teaching with preschool children who have intellectual disabilities. *Journal of Speech, Language, and Hearing Research*, 56, 295–309, https://doi.org/10.1044/1092-4388(2012/11-0231)

Kanner, L. (1943). Autistic disturbances of affective contact. *The Nervous Child*, 2, 217–250.

Karaaslan, O., & Mahoney, G. (2013). Effectiveness of responsive teaching with children with Down syndrome. *Intellectual and Developmental Disabilities*, 51, 458–469, https://doi.org/10.1352/1934-9556-51.6.458

Karnopp, L. B. (2002). Phonology acquisition in Brazilian Sign Language. In G. Morgan & B. Woll (eds.), *Directions in sign language acquisition* (pp. 29–53). Amsterdam, The Netherlands: John Benjamins Publishing, https://doi.org/10.1075/tilar.2.05kar

Kates-McElrath, K., & Axelrod, S. (2006). Behavioral intervention for autism: A distinction between two behavior analytic approaches. *The Behavior Analyst Today*, 242–252, https://doi.org/10.1037/h0100085

Kaufman, C. M. (2003). *Parental attitudes towards using total communication intervention with children who are non-verbal.* Unpublished doctoral dissertation, Teachers College, Columbia University, New York, NY. (UMI Microform No.: 3091261).

Kay-Raining Bird, E., & Chapman, R. S. (1994). Sequential recall in individuals with Down syndrome. *Journal of Speech and Hearing Research*, 37, 1369–1380, https://doi.org/10.1044/jshr.3706.1369

Kay-Raining Bird, E., Gaskell, A., Babineau, M. D., & MacDonald, S. (2000). Novel word acquisition in children with Down syndrome: Does modality make a difference? *Journal of Communication Disorders*, 33, 241–266, https://doi.org/10.1016/S0021-9924(00)00022-8

Kearns, K. P., Simmons, N. N., & Sisterhen, C. (1982). Gestural sign (Amer-Ind) as a facilitator of verbalization in patients with aphasia. In R. H. Brookshire (ed.), *Clinical aphasiology: Proceedings of the conference, 1982* (pp. 183–191). Minneapolis, MN: BRK Publishers.

Keehner, M., & Gathercole, S. E. (2007). Cognitive adaptations arising from nonnative experience of sign language in hearing adults. *Memory & Cognition*, 35, 752–761, https://doi.org/10.3758/bf03193312

Kellett, K. A., Stevenson, J. L., & Gernsbacher, M. A. (2012). What role does the cerebellum play in language processing? In M. Faust (ed.), *The handbook of the neuropsychology of language, vol. 1. Language processing in the brain: Basic science* (pp. 294–316). Chichester, West Sussex, U.K.: Wiley-Blackwell, https://doi.org/10.1002/9781118432501.ch15

Kelley, B. (2017). The statistic in the room. *Hearing Loss Magazine*, 38, 8–9.

Kelly, S. D., McDevitt, T., & Esch, M. (2009). Brief training with co-speech gesture lends a hand to word learning in a foreign language. *Language and Cognitive Processes*, 24, 313–334, https://doi.org/10.1080/01690960802365567

Kelly, S. D., Özyürek, A., & Maris, E. (2010). Two sides of the same coin: Speech and gesture mutually interact to enhance comprehension. *Psychological Science, 21*, 260–267, https://doi.org/10.1177/0956797609357327

Kemp, M. (1998). Why is learning American Sign Language a challenge? *American Annals of the Deaf, 143*, 255–259, https://doi.org/10.1353/aad.2012.0157

Kemper, T. L., & Bauman, M. (1998). Neuropathology of infantile autism. *Journal of Neuropathology and Experimental Neurology, 57*, 645–652, https://doi.org/10.1097/00005072-199807000-00001

Kendon, A. (1990). Signs in the cloister and elsewhere. *Semiotica, 79*, 307–329.

Kendon, A. (2011). Gesture first or speech first in language origins? In G. Mathur & D. J. Napoli (eds.), *Deaf around the world: The impact of language* (pp. 251–267). New York, NY: Oxford University Press, https://doi.org/10.1093/acprof:oso/9780199732548.003.0014

Kendon, A. (2014). Semiotic diversity in utterance production and the concept of "language." *Philosophical Transactions of the Royal Society B, 369*, 20130293, https://doi.org/10.1098/rstb.2013.0293

Kenin, M., & Swisher, L. P. (1972). A study of pattern of recovery in aphasia. *Cortex, 8*, 56–68, https://doi.org/10.1016/s0010-9452(72)80027-3

Kent-Walsh, J., Murza, K. A., Malani, M. D., & Binger, C. (2015). Effects of communication partner instruction on the communication of individuals using AAC: A meta-analysis. *Augmentative and Alternative Communication, 31*, 271–284, https://doi.org/10.3109/07434618.2015.1052153

Kern, J. K., Geier, D. A., Sykes, L. K., Geier, M. R., & Deth, R. C. (2015). Are ASD and ADHD a continuum? A comparison of pathophysiological similarities between the disorders. *Journal of Attention Disorders, 19*, 805–827, https://doi.org/10.1177/1087054712459886

Kertesz, A. (1979). *Aphasia and associated disorders: Taxonomy, localization, and recovery.* New York, NY: Grune & Stratton.

Kertesz, A. (2000). Behavioral and cognitive disorders. In R. W. Evans, D. S. Baskin, & F. M. Yatsu (eds.), *Prognosis of neurological disorders* (2nd ed., pp. 610–622). New York, NY: Oxford University Press.

Kielinen, M., Linna, S.-L., & Moilanen, I. (2000). Autism in northern Finland. *European Child and Adolescent Psychiatry, 9*, 162–167, https://doi.org/10.1007/s007870070039

Kiernan, C., & Reid, B. (1984). The use of augmentative communication systems in schools and units for autistic and aphasic children in the United Kingdom. *British Journal of Disorders of Communication, 19*, 47–61, https://doi.org/10.3109/13682828409019835

Kiernan, C., Reid, B., & Jones, L. (1982). *Signs and symbols: A review of literature and survey of the use of non-vocal communication systems.* London, U.K.: Heinemann Educational Books.

Kilincaslan, A., & Mukaddes, N. M. (2009). Pervasive developmental disorders in individuals with cerebral palsy. *Developmental Medicine & Child Neurology*, 51, 289–294, https://doi.org/10.1111/j.1469-8749.2008.03171.x

Kim, M. J., Stierwalt, J. A. G., LaPointe, L. L., & Bourgeois, M. S. (2015). The use of gesture following traumatic brain injury: A preliminary analysis. *Aphasiology*, 29, 665–684, https://doi.org/10.1080/02687038.2014.976536

Kim, S. H., & Lord, C. (2014). Autism and language development. In P. J. Brooks & V. Kempe (eds.), *Encyclopedia of language development* (pp. 36–39). Los Angeles, CA: SAGE Publications.

Kim, Y. S., Leventhal, B. L., Koh, Y.-J., Fombonne, E., Laska, E., Lim, E.-C., Cheon, K.-A., Kim, S.-J., Kim, Y.-K., Lee, H., Song, D.-H., & Grinker, R. R. (2011). Prevalence of autism spectrum disorders in a total population sample. *American Journal of Psychiatry*, 168, 904–912, https://doi.org/10.1176/appi.ajp.2011.10101532

Kimura, D. (1976). The neural basis of language qua gesture. In H. Whitaker & H. A. Whitaker (eds.), *Studies in neurolinguistics, vol. 2* (pp. 145–156). New York, NY: Academic Press, https://doi.org/10.1016/B978-0-12-746302-5.50011-6

Kimura, D. (1993). *Neuromotor mechanisms in human communication*. New York, NY: Oxford University Press, https://doi.org/10.1093/acprof:oso/9780195054927.001.0001

Kipp, D. R. (2007). Observations on a tribal language revitalization program. In G. P. Horse Capture, D. Champagne, & C. C. Jackson (eds.), *American Indian nations: Yesterday, today, and tomorrow* (pp. 105–111). Lanham, MD: AltaMira Press.

Kirk, E. (2009). *The impact of encouraging infants to gesture on their language development*. Unpublished doctoral dissertation, University of Hertfordshire, Hertfordshire, U.K.

Kirk, E., Howlett, N., Pine, K. J., & Fletcher, B. C. (2013). To sign or not to sign? The impact of encouraging infants to gesture on infant language and maternal mind-mindedness. *Child Development*, 84, 574–590, https://doi.org/10.1111/j.1467-8624.2012.01874.x

Kirk, E., Pine, K. J., & Ryder, N. (2011). I hear what you say but I see what you mean: The role of gestures in children's pragmatic comprehension. *Language and Cognitive Processes*, 26, 149–170, https://doi.org/10.1080/01690961003752348

Kirschner, A., Algozzine, B., & Abbott, T. B. (1979). Manual communication systems: A comparison and its implications. *Education and Training of the Mentally Retarded*, 14, 5–10.

Kirshner, H. S., & Webb, W. G. (1981). Selective involvement of the auditory-verbal modality in an acquired communication disorder: Benefit from sign language therapy. *Brain and Language*, 13, 161–170, https://doi.org/10.1016/0093-934x(81)90136-x

Kissane, N. (2001). *Memory and recall of signs: The development of a simplified sign system*. Unpublished distinguished major thesis, University of Virginia, Charlottesville, VA.

Klein, S., Fries, L., & Emmons, M. M. (2017). Early care and education arrangements and young children's risk of foster placement: Findings from a national child welfare sample. *Children and Youth Services Review*, 83, 168–178, https://doi.org/10.1016/j.childyouth.2017.09.006

Klima, E. S., & Bellugi, U. (1979). *The signs of language*. Cambridge, MA: Harvard University Press.

Klimesch, W. (1987). A connectivity model for semantic processing. *Psychological Research*, 49, 53–61, https://doi.org/10.1007/bf00309203

Kljajevic, V. (2012). *Comprehension of wh-dependencies in Broca's aphasia*. Newcastle upon Tyne, U.K.: Cambridge Scholars Publishing.

Knowlson, J. R. (1965). The idea of gesture as a universal language in the XVIIth and XVIIIth centuries. *Journal of the History of Ideas*, 26, 495–508, https://doi.org/10.2307/2708496

Knox, D. (1990). Late medieval and renaissance ideas on gesture. In V. Kapp (ed.), *Die sprache der zeichen und bilder: Rhetorik und nonverbale kommunikation in der frühen neuzeit* (pp. 11–39). Marburg, Germany: Hitzeroth.

Knudsen, E. I. (2004). Sensitive periods in the development of the brain and behavior. *Journal of Cognitive Neuroscience*, 16, 1412–1425, https://doi.org/10.1162/0898929042304796

Knudsen, E. I., Heckman, J. J., Cameron, J. L., & Shonkoff, J. P. (2006). Economic, neurobiological, and behavioral perspectives on building America's future workforce. *Proceedings of the National Academy of Sciences of the United States of America*, 103, 10155–10162, https://doi.org/10.1073/pnas.0600888103

Koegel, R. L., Bimbela, A., & Schreibman, L. (1996). Collateral effects of parent training on family interactions. *Journal of Autism and Developmental Disorders*, 26, 347–359, https://doi.org/10.1007/bf02172479

Kogan, M. D., Blumberg, S. J., Schieve, L. A., Boyle, C. A., Perrin, J. M., Ghandour, R. M., Singh, G. K., Strickland, B. B., Trevathan, E., & van Dyck, P. C. (2009). Prevalence of parent-reported diagnosis of autism spectrum disorder among children in the U.S., 2007. *Pediatrics*, 124, 1395–1403, https://doi.org/10.1542/peds.2009-1522

Kohl, F. L. (1981). Effects of motoric requirements on the acquisition of manual sign responses by severely handicapped students. *American Journal of Mental Deficiency*, 85, 396–403.

Kong, A. P.-H., Law, S.-P., Wat, W. K.-C., & Lai, C. (2015). Co-verbal gestures among speakers with aphasia: Influence of aphasia severity, linguistic and semantic skills, and hemiplegia on gesture employment in oral discourse. *Journal of Communication Disorders*, 56, 88–102, https://doi.org/10.1016/j.jcomdis.2015.06.007

Konstantareas, M. M. (1985). Review of evidence on the relevance of sign language in the early communication training of autistic children. *Australian Journal of Human Communication Disorders*, 13, 77–97, https://doi.org/10.3109/asl2.1985.13.issue-2.05

Konstantareas, M. M., Oxman, J., & Webster, C. D. (1978). Iconicity: Effects on the acquisition of sign language by autistic and other severely dysfunctional children. In P. Siple (ed.), *Understanding language through sign language research* (pp. 213–237). New York, NY: Academic Press.

Kopchick, G. A., & Lloyd, L. L. (1976). Total communication for the severely language impaired: A 24-hour approach. In L. L. Lloyd (ed.), *Communication assessment and intervention strategies* (pp. 501–523). Baltimore, MD: University Park Press.

Kopchick, G. A., Jr., Rombach, D. W., & Smilovitz, R. (1975). A total communication environment in an institution. *Mental Retardation*, 13, 22–23.

Korkman, M., Granström, M.-L., Appelqvist, K., & Liukkonen, E. (1998). Neuropsychological characteristics of five children with the Landau-Kleffner syndrome: Dissociation of auditory and phonological discrimination. *Journal of the International Neuropsychological Society*, 4, 566–575, https://doi.org/10.1017/S1355617798466050

Koulidobrova, H., Luchkina, T., & Palmer, J. L. (2019). *Testing the two models of sign language phonology in ASL: Deaf L2 learns vs. naïve.* Paper presented at the 42nd annual GLOW (Generative Linguistics in the Old World) conference, May 7, University of Oslo, Oslo, Norway.

Kouri, T. (1989). How manual sign acquisition relates to the development of spoken language: A case study. *Language, Speech, and Hearing Services in Schools*, 20, 50–62, https://doi.org/10.1044/0161-1461.2001.50

Kraat, A. W. (1990). Augmentative and alternative communication: Does it have a future in aphasia rehabilitation? *Aphasiology*, 4, 321–338, https://doi.org/10.1080/02687039008249086

Krägeloh-Mann, I., & Cans, C. (2009). Cerebral palsy update. *Brain & Development*, 31, 537–544, https://doi.org/10.1016/j.braindev.2009.03.009

Krakow, R. A., Tao, S., & Roberts, J. (2005). Adoption age effects on English language acquisition: Infants and toddlers from China. *Seminars in Speech and Language*, 26, 33–43, https://doi.org/10.1055/s-2005-864214

Krauss, R. M., Chen, Y., & Gottesman, R. F. (2000). Lexical gestures and lexical access: A process model. In D. McNeill (ed.), *Language and gesture* (pp. 261–283). Cambridge, U.K.: Cambridge University Press, https://doi.org/10.1017/CBO9780511620850.017

Kuhl, P. K., Coffey-Corina, S., Padden, D., & Dawson, G. (2005). Links between social and linguistic processing of speech in preschool children with autism: Behavioral and electrophysiological measures. *Developmental Science*, 8, F1-F12, https://doi.org/10.1111/j.1467-7687.2004.00384.x

Kumin, L. (1996). Speech and language skills in children with Down syndrome. *Mental Retardation and Developmental Disabilities Research Reviews*, 2, 109–115, https://doi.org/10.1002/(sici)1098-2779(1996)2:2<109::aid-mrdd9>3.0.co;2-o

Kumin, L. (2003). *Early communication skills for children with Down syndrome: A guide for parents and professionals* (2nd ed.). Bethesda, MD: Woodbine House.

Kumin, L. (2006). Speech intelligibility and childhood verbal apraxia in children with Down syndrome. *Down Syndrome Research and Practice*, 10, 10–22, https://doi.org/10.3104/reports.301

Kuriakose, S., Lang, R., Boyer, K., Lee, A., & Lancioni, G. (2012). Rehabilitation issues in Landau-Kleffner syndrome. *Developmental Neurorehabilitation*, 15, 317–321, https://doi.org/10.3109/17518423.2012.701241

Kusters, A., Spotti, M., Swanwick, R., & Tapio, E. (2017). Beyond languages, beyond modalities: Transforming the study of semiotic repertoires. *International Journal of Multilingualism*, 14, 219–232, https://doi.org/10.1080/14790718.2017.1321651

Lajonchere, C. M., & the AGRE Consortium. (2010). Changing the landscape of autism research: The Autism Genetic Resource Exchange. *Neuron*, 68, 187–191, https://doi.org/10.1016/j.neuron.2010.10.009

Lal, R. (2010). Effect of alternative and augmentative communication on language and social behavior of children with autism. *Educational Research and Reviews*, 5, 119–125.

Landa, R. (2007). Early communication development and intervention for children with autism. *Mental Retardation and Developmental Disabilities Research Reviews*, 13, 16–25, https://doi.org/10.1002/mrdd.20134

Landau, W. M., & Kleffner, F. R. (1957). Syndrome of acquired aphasia with convulsive disorder in children. *Neurology*, 7, 523–530, https://doi.org/10.1212/wnl.7.8.523

Landrigan, P. J. (2010). What causes autism? Exploring the environmental contribution. *Current Opinion in Pediatrics*, 22, 219–225, https://doi.org/10.1097/mop.0b013e328336eb9a

Lane, H. (1984). *When the mind hears: A history of the deaf.* New York, NY: Random House.

Lang, H. G. (2003). Perspectives on the history of deaf education. In M. Marschark & P. E. Spencer (eds.), *Oxford handbook of deaf studies, language, and education* (pp. 9–20). New York, NY: Oxford University Press.

Lanyon, L., & Rose, M. L. (2009). Do the hands have it? The facilitation effects of arm and hand gesture on word retrieval in aphasia. *Aphasiology*, 23, 809–822, https://doi.org/10.1080/02687030802642044

Laska, A. C., Hellblom, A., Murray, V., Kahan, T., & von Arbin, M. (2001). Aphasia in acute stroke and relation to outcome. *Journal of Internal Medicine*, 249, 413–422, https://doi.org/10.1046/j.1365-2796.2001.00812.x

Launonen, K. (1996). Enhancing communication skills of children with Down syndrome: Early use of manual signs. In S. von Tetzchner & M. H. Jensen (eds.), *Augmentative and alternative communication: European perspectives* (pp. 213–231). San Diego, CA: Singular Publishing Group.

Launonen, K. (1998). Early manual sign intervention: Eight-year follow-up of children with Down syndrome. In *1998 ISAAC Conference Proceedings (Dublin/ Ireland)* (pp. 370–371). Dublin, Ireland: ISAAC/Ashfield Publications.

Launonen, K. (2003). Manual signing as a tool of communicative interaction and language: The development of children with Down syndrome and their parents. In S. von Tetzchner & N. Grove (eds.), *Augmentative and alternative communication: Developmental issues* (pp. 83–122). London, U.K.: Whurr Publishers.

Launonen, K. (2019a). Sign acquisition in Down syndrome: Longitudinal perspectives. In N. Grove & K. Launonen (eds.), *Manual sign acquisition in children with developmental disabilities* (pp. 89–113). New York, NY: Nova Science Publishers, Inc.

Launonen, K. (2019b). Signing at home. In N. Grove & K. Launonen (eds.), *Manual sign acquisition in children with developmental disabilities* (pp. 337–358). New York, NY: Nova Science Publishers, Inc.

Launonen, K., & Grove, N. (2003). A longitudinal study of sign and speech development in a boy with Down syndrome. In S. von Tetzchner & N. Grove (eds.), *Augmentative and alternative communication: Developmental issues* (pp. 123–154). London, U.K.: Whurr Publishers.

Launonen, K., & Grove, N. (2019). Looking back, looking forward: Conclusions. In N. Grove & K. Launonen (eds.), *Manual sign acquisition in children with developmental disabilities* (pp. 427–437). New York, NY: Nova Science Publishers, Inc.

Lavelli, M., Barachetti, C., & Florit, E. (2015). Gesture and speech during shared book reading with preschoolers with specific language impairment. *Journal of Child Language*, 42, 1191–1218, https://doi.org/10.1017/s0305000914000762

LaVigna, G. W. (1977). Communication training in mute autistic adolescents using the written word. *Journal of Autism and Childhood Schizophrenia*, 7, 135–149, https://doi.org/10.1007/bf01537725

Lavoie, C., & Villeneuve, S. (2000). Acquisition du lieu d'articulation en Langue des Signes Québécoise chez trois enfants sourds: Étude de cas. *Revue Québécoise de Linguistique*, 28, 99–125, https://doi.org/10.7202/603200ar

Lawler, L. B. (1964). *The dance of the ancient Greek theatre.* Iowa City, IA: University of Iowa Press.

Laws, G., & Gunn, D. (2004). Phonological memory as a predictor of language comprehension in Down syndrome: A five-year follow-up study. *Journal of Child Psychology and Psychiatry*, 45, 326–337, https://doi.org/10.1111/j.1469-7610.2004.00224.x

Laws, G., & Hall, A. (2014). Early hearing loss and language abilities in children with Down syndrome. *International Journal of Language & Communication Disorders*, 49, 333–342, https://doi.org/10.1111/1460-6984.12077

Layton, T. L. (1987). Manual communication. In T. L. Layton (ed.), *Language and treatment of autistic and developmentally disordered children* (pp. 189–213). Springfield, IL: Charles C Thomas.

Layton, T. L., & Savino, M. A. (1990). Acquiring a communication system by sign and speech in a child with Down syndrome: A longitudinal investigation. *Child Language Teaching and Therapy*, 6, 59–76, https://doi.org/10.1177/026565909000600107

Layton, T. L., & Watson, L. R. (1995). Enhancing communication in nonverbal children with autism. In K. A. Quill (ed.), *Teaching children with autism: Strategies to enhance communication and socialization* (pp. 73–101). New York, NY: Delmar Publishers.

Lazaraton, A. (2004). Gesture and speech in the vocabulary explanations of one ESL teacher: A microanalytic inquiry. *Language Learning*, 54, 79–117, https://doi.org/10.1111/j.1467-9922.2004.00249.x

Lazenby, D. C., Sideridis, G. D., Huntington, N., Prante, M., Dale, P. S., Curtin, S., Henkel, L., Iverson, J. M., Carver, L., Dobkins, K., Akshoomoff, N., Tagavi, D., Nelson, C. A., III, & Tager-Flusberg, H. (2016). Language differences at 12 months in infants who develop autism spectrum disorder. *Journal of Autism and Developmental Disorders*, 46, 899–909, https://doi.org/10.1007/s10803-015-2632-1

LeBarton, E. S., & Iverson, J. M. (2016a). Associations between gross motor and communicative development in at-risk infants. *Infant Behavior and Development*, 44, 59–67, https://doi.org/10.1016/j.infbeh.2016.05.003

LeBarton, E. S., & Iverson, J. M. (2016b). Gesture development in toddlers with an older sibling with autism. *International Journal of Language & Communication Disorders*, 51, 18–30, https://doi.org/10.1111/1460-6984.12180

Lee, J. (2011). Size matters: Early vocabulary as a predictor of language and literacy competence. *Applied Psycholinguistics*, 32, 69–92, https://doi.org/10.1017/s0142716410000299

Leiner, H. C., Leiner, A. L., & Dow, R. S. (1989). Reappraising the cerebellum: What does the hindbrain contribute to the forebrain? *Behavioral Neuroscience*, 103, 998–1008, https://doi.org/10.1037/0735-7044.103.5.998

Leiner, H. C., Leiner, A. L., & Dow, R. S. (1993). Cognitive and language functions of the human cerebellum. *Trends in Neuroscience*, 16, 444–447, https://doi.org/10.1016/0166-2236(93)90072-t

Lervåg, A., & Aukrust, V. G. (2010). Vocabulary knowledge is a critical determinant of the difference in reading comprehension growth between first and second language learners. *The Journal of Child Psychology and Psychiatry*, 51, 612–620, https://doi.org/10.1111/j.1469-7610.2009.02185.x

Lettick, A. L. (1972, June). *Pre-vocational training program at Benhaven*. Paper presented at the 4th annual meeting of the National Society for Autistic Children, Flint, MI.

Lettick, A. L. (1979). *Benhaven then and now*. New Haven, CT: The Benhaven Press.

Leung, A. K. C., & Hon, K. L. (2016). Attention-deficit/hyperactivity disorder. *Advances in Pediatrics*, 63, 255–280, https://doi.org/10.1016/j.yapd.2016.04.017

Levett, L. M. (1969). A method of communication for non-speaking severely subnormal children. *British Journal of Disorders of Communication*, 4, 64–66, https://doi.org/10.3109/13682826909011471

Levett, L. M. (1971). A method of communication for non-speaking severely subnormal children — Trial results. *British Journal of Disorders of Communication*, 6, 125–128, https://doi.org/10.3109/13682827109011537

Levin, K. (1999). Babbling in infants with cerebral palsy. *Clinical Linguistics & Phonetics*, 13, 249–267, https://doi.org/10.1080/026992099299077

Levinson, S. C., & Holler, J. (2014). The origin of human multi-modal communication. *Philosophical Transactions of the Royal Society B*, 369, 20130302, https://doi.org/10.1098/rstb.2013.0302

Lewis, B. A., Freebairn, L. A., Hansen, A., Taylor, H. G., Iyengar, S., & Shriberg, L. D. (2004). Family pedigrees of children with suspected childhood apraxia of speech. *Journal of Communication Disorders*, 37, 157–175, https://doi.org/10.1016/j.jcomdis.2003.08.003

Li, M., & Kirby, J. R. (2014). Unexpected poor comprehenders among adolescent ESL students. *Scientific Studies of Reading*, 18, 75–93, https://doi.org/10.1080/10888438.2013.775130

Liberman, A. M., Cooper, F. S., Shankweiler, D. P., & Studdert-Kennedy, M. (1967). Perception of the speech code. *Psychological Review*, 74, 431–461, https://doi.org/10.1037/h0020279

Liddell, S. K. (2003). *Grammar, gesture, and meaning in American Sign Language*. Cambridge, U.K.: Cambridge University Press, https://doi.org/10.1017/CBO9780511615054

Liddell, S. K., & Johnson, R. E. (1989). American Sign Language: The phonological base. *Sign Language Studies*, 64, 195–277, https://doi.org/10.1353/sls.1989.0027

Lieberman, P. (1998). *Eve spoke: Human language and human evolution.* New York, NY: W. W. Norton.

Lieberman, P. (2000). *Human language and our reptilian brain: The subcortical bases of speech, syntax, and thought.* Cambridge, MA: Harvard University Press.

Lieberth, A. K., & Gamble, M. E. B. (1991). The role of iconicity in sign language learning by hearing adults. *Journal of Communication Disorders, 24,* 89–99, https://doi.org/10.1016/0021-9924(91)90013-9

Light, J., & McNaughton, D. (2015). Designing AAC research and intervention to improve outcomes for individuals with complex communication needs. *Augmentative and Alternative Communication, 31,* 85–96, https://doi.org/10.31 09/07434618.2015.1036458

Light, J. C., Roberts, B., Dimarco, R., & Greiner, N. (1998). Augmentative and alternative communication to support receptive and expressive communication for people with autism. *Journal of Communication Disorders, 31,* 153–180, https://doi.org/10.1016/s0021-9924(97)00087-7

Lillo-Martin, D., & Meier, R. P. (2011). On the linguistic status of "agreement" in sign languages. *Theoretical Linguistics, 37,* 95–141, https://doi.org/10.1515/ thli.2011.009

Lin, F. R. (2017). Where we are and where we're headed — The importance of over-the-counter hearing aids to the future of hearing health care. *Hearing Loss Magazine, 38,* 18–23.

Lindstromberg, S., & Boers, F. (2005). From movement to metaphor with manner-of-movement verbs. *Applied Linguistics, 26,* 241–261, https://doi. org/10.1093/applin/ami002

Lloyd, L., Loeding, B., & Doherty, J. (1985). Role of iconicity in sign acquisition: A response to Orlansky and Bonvillian (1984). *Journal of Speech and Hearing Disorders, 50,* 299–301, https://doi.org/10.1044/jshd.5003.299

Lloyd, L. L., & Doherty, J. E. (1983). The influence of production mode on the recall of signs in normal adult subjects. *Journal of Speech, Language, and Hearing Research, 26,* 595–600, https://doi.org/10.1044/jshr.2604.595

Lloyd, L. L., & Fuller, D. R. (1990). The role of iconicity in augmentative and alternative communication — Symbol learning. In W. I. Fraser (ed.), *Key issues in mental retardation research* (pp. 295–306). London, U.K.: Routledge.

Lloyd, M., MacDonald, M., & Lord, C. (2011). Motor skills of toddlers with autism spectrum disorders. *Autism, 17,* 133–146, https://doi. org/10.1177/1362361311402230

Loeding, B. L., Zangari, C., & Lloyd, L. L. (1990). A "working party" approach to planning in-service training in manual signs for an entire public school staff. *Augmentative and Alternative Communication, 6,* 38–49, https://doi.org/1 0.1080/07434619012331275304

Loncke, F. (2019). Manual signing and psycholinguistics. In N. Grove & K. Launonen (eds.), *Manual sign acquisition in children with developmental disabilities* (pp. 23–35). New York, NY: Nova Science Publishers, Inc.

Loncke, F., & Bos, H. (1997). Unaided AAC symbols. In L. L. Lloyd, D. R. Fuller, & H. H. Arvidson (eds.), *Augmentative and alternative communication: A handbook of principles and practices* (pp. 80–106). Boston, MA: Allyn and Bacon.

Loncke, F., Weng, P.-L., Hilton, J., & Corthals, P. (2009, October). *Testing the multimodality hypothesis: Learning printed words with and without auditory and gesture feedback.* Paper presented at the 3rd annual Clinical Augmentative and Alternative Research Conference, Pittsburgh, PA.

Loncke, F. T., Campbell, J., England, A. M., & Haley, T. (2006). Multimodality: A basis for augmentative and alternative communication — Psycholinguistic, cognitive, and clinical/educational aspects. *Disability and Rehabilitation, 28,* 169–174, https://doi.org/10.1080/09638280500384168

Loncke, F. T., Nijs, M., & Smet, L. (2012). *SMOG: Spreken met ondersteuning van gebaren: Het handbook* [*Speaking with support of signs: The manual*]. Leuven, Belgium: Garant.

Loonen, M. C. B., & Van Dongen, H. R. (1990). Acquired childhood aphasia: Outcome one year after onset. *Archives of Neurology, 47,* 1324–1328, https://doi.org/10.1001/archneur.1990.00530120068012

Lorah, E. R., & Parnell, A. (2017). Acquisition of tacting using a speech-generating device in group learning environments for preschoolers with autism. *Journal of Developmental and Physical Disabilities, 29,* 597–609, https://doi.org/10.1007/s10882-017-9543-3

Lord, C., & Bailey, A. (2002). Autism spectrum disorders. In M. Rutter & E. Taylor (eds.), *Child and adolescent psychiatry* (4th ed., pp. 636–663). Oxford, U.K.: Blackwell Science.

Lord, C., & Paul, R. (1997). Language and communication in autism. In D. J. Cohen & F. R. Volkmar (eds.), *Handbook of autism and pervasive developmental disorders* (2nd ed., pp. 195–225). New York, NY: John Wiley & Sons.

Lord, C., Risi, S., & Pickles, A. (2004). Trajectory of language development in autistic spectrum disorders. In M. L. Rice & S. F. Warren (eds.), *Developmental language disorders: From phenotypes to etiologies* (pp. 7–29). Mahwah, NJ: Lawrence Erlbaum Associates.

Lotter, V. (1974). Factors related to outcome in autistic children. *Journal of Autism and Childhood Schizophrenia, 4,* 263–277, https://doi.org/10.1007/bf02115232

Loukusa, S., Mäkinen, L., Gabbatore, I., Laukkanen-Nevala, P., & Leinonen, E. (2017). Understanding contextual and social meaning in typically developing Finnish-speaking four- to eight-year-old children. *Psychology of Language and Communication, 21,* 408–428, https://doi.org/10.1515/plc-2017-0020

Lovaas, O. I. (1977). *The autistic child: Language development through behavior modification.* New York, NY: Irvington Publishers, John Wiley & Sons.

Lovaas, O. I. (1987). Behavioral treatment and normal educational and intellectual functioning in young autistic children. *Journal of Consulting and Clinical Psychology, 55,* 3–9, https://doi.org/10.1037/0022-006x.55.1.3

Lovaas, O. I., Koegel, R., Simmons, J. Q., & Long, J. S. (1973). Some generalization and follow-up measures on autistic children in behavior therapy. *Journal of Applied Behavior Analysis, 6,* 131–165, https://doi.org/10.1901/jaba.1973.6-131

Lovaas, O. I., Schaeffer, B., & Simmons, J. Q. (1965). Experimental studies in childhood schizophrenia: Building social behavior in autistic children by use of electric shock. *Journal of Experimental Research in Personality, 1,* 99–109.

Love, J. M., Chazan-Cohen, R., & Raikes, H. (2007). Forty years of research knowledge and use: From Head Start to Early Head Start and beyond. In J. L. Aber, S. J. Bishop-Josef, S. M. Jones, K. T. McLearn, & D. A. Phillips (eds.), *Child development and social policy: Knowledge for action* (pp. 79–95). Washington, DC: American Psychological Association, https://doi.org/10.1037/11486-005

Lu, J., Jones, A., & Morgan, G. (2016). The impact of input quality on early sign development in native and non-native language learners. *Journal of Child Language, 43,* 537–552, https://doi.org/10.1017/S0305000915000835

Luftig, R. L. (1983). Translucency of sign and concreteness of gloss in the manual sign learning of moderately/severely mentally retarded students. *American Journal of Mental Deficiency, 88,* 279–286.

Lukowski, A. F., Wiebe, S. A., Haight, J. C., DeBoer, T., Nelson, C. A., & Bauer, P. J. (2005). Forming a stable memory representation in the first year of life: Why imitation is more than child's play. *Developmental Science, 8,* 279–298, https://doi.org/10.1111/j.1467-7687.2005.00415.x

Luyster, R. J., Kadlec, M. B., Carter, A., & Tager-Flusberg, H. (2008). Language assessment and development in toddlers with autism spectrum disorders. *Journal of Autism and Developmental Disorders, 38,* 1426–1438, https://doi.org/10.1007/s10803-007-0510-1

Lyn, H. (2017). The question of capacity: Why enculturated and trained animals have much to tell us about the evolution of language. *Psychonomic Bulletin & Review, 24,* 85–90, https://doi.org/10.3758/s13423-016-1129-z

Macedonia, M. (2014). Bringing back the body into the mind: Gestures enhance word learning in foreign language. *Frontiers in Psychology, 5,* AR 1467, https://doi.org/10.3389/fpsyg.2014.01467

Macedonia, M., & Klimesch, W. (2014). Long-term effects of gestures on memory for foreign language words trained in the classroom. *Mind, Brain, and Education, 8,* 74–88, https://doi.org/10.1111/mbe.12047

Macedonia, M., & Knösche, T. R. (2011). Body in mind: How gestures empower foreign language learning. *Mind, Brain, and Education*, 5, 196–211, https://doi.org/10.1111/j.1751-228x.2011.01129.x

Macedonia, M., & Mueller, K. (2016). Exploring the neural representation of novel words learned through enactment in a word recognition task. *Frontiers in Psychology*, 7, AR 953, https://doi.org/10.3389/fpsyg.2016.00953

Macedonia, M., Müller, K., & Friederici, A. D. (2011). The impact of iconic gestures on foreign language word learning and its neural substrate. *Human Brain Mapping*, 32, 982–998, https://doi.org/10.1002/hbm.21084

Macedonia, M., & Repetto, C. (2017). Why your body can jog your mind. *Frontiers in Psychology*, 8, AR 362, https://doi.org/10.3389/fpsyg.2017.00362

Mackenzie, M., Cologon, K., & Fenech, M. (2016). "Embracing everybody": Approaching the inclusive early childhood education of a child labeled with autism from a social relational understanding of disability. *Australasian Journal of Early Childhood*, 41, 4–12, https://doi.org/10.1177/183693911604100202

MacSweeney, M., Capek, C. M., Campbell, R., & Woll, B. (2009). The signing brain: The neurobiology of sign language. *Trends in Cognitive Sciences*, 12, 432–440, https://doi.org/10.1016/j.tics.2008.07.010

Mady, C., Arnott, S., & Lapkin, S. (2009). Assessing AIM: A study of grade 8 students in an Ontario school board. *The Canadian Modern Language Review*, 65, 703–729, https://doi.org/10.3138/cmlr.65.5.703

Magiati, I., & Howlin, P. (2003). A pilot evaluation study of the Picture Exchange Communication System (PECS) for children with autistic spectrum disorders. *Autism: International Journal of Research and Practice*, 7, 297–320.

Magid, R. W., & Pyers, J. E. (2017). "I use it when I see it": The role of development and experience in Deaf and hearing children's understanding of iconic gesture. *Cognition*, 162, 73–86, https://doi.org/10.1016/j.cognition.2017.01.015

Magnuson, M. (2000). Infants with congenital deafness: On the importance of early sign language acquisition. *American Annals of the Deaf*, 145, 6–14, https://doi.org/10.1353/aad.2012.0256

Mahoney, G., Perales, F., Wiggers, B., & Herman, B. (2006). Responsive teaching: Early intervention for children with Down syndrome and other disabilities. *Down Syndrome Research and Practice*, 11, 18–28, https://doi.org/10.3104/perspectives.311

Malaia, E., & Wilbur, R. B. (2010). Early acquisition of sign language: What neuroimaging data tell us. *Sign Language & Linguistics*, 13, 183–199, https://doi.org/10.1075/sll.13.2.03mal

Mallery, G. (1880). *Introduction to the study of sign language among the North American Indians as illustrating the gesture speech of mankind*. Washington, DC: Bureau of Ethnology, Government Printing Office.

Mallery, G. (1881/2001). *Sign language among North American Indians compared with that among other peoples and deaf-mutes.* Mineola, NY: Dover Publications. [Originally published, 1881. Washington, DC: Bureau of Ethnology.]

Mancil, G. R. (2009). Milieu therapy as a communication intervention: A review of the literature related to children with autism spectrum disorder. *Education and Training in Developmental Disabilities*, 44, 105–117.

Mancini, L. S. (2005). A positive sign: An overview of the benefits of signing in the classroom. In K. Denham & A. Lobeck (eds.), *Language in the schools: Integrating linguistic knowledge into K-12 teaching* (pp. 87–96). Mahwah, NJ: Lawrence Erlbaum Associates.

Mandak, K., O'Neill, T., Light, J., & Fosco, G. M. (2017). Bridging the gap from values to actions: A family systems framework for family-centered AAC services. *Augmentative and Alternative Communication*, 33, 32–41, https://doi.org/10.1080/07434618.2016.1271453

Mann, W., Marshall, C. R., Mason, K., & Morgan, G. (2010). The acquisition of sign language: The impact of phonetic complexity on phonology. *Language Learning and Development*, 6, 60–86, https://doi.org/10.1080/15475440903245951

Manwaring, S. S., Mead, D. L., Swineford, L., & Thurm, A. (2017). Modelling gesture use and early language development in autism spectrum disorder. *International Journal of Language & Communication Disorders*, 52, 637–651, https://doi.org/10.1111/1460-6984.12308

Marangolo, P., Bonifazi, S., Tomaiuolo, F., Craighero, L., Coccia, M., Altoè, G., Provinciali, L., & Cantagallo, A. (2010). Improving language without words: First evidence from aphasia. *Neuropsychologia*, 48, 3824–3833, https://doi.org/10.1016/j.neuropsychologia.2010.09.025

Marcell, M. M. (1995). Relationships between hearing and auditory cognition in Down syndrome youth. *Down Syndrome Research and Practice*, 3, 75–91, https://doi.org/10.3104/reports.54

Marcell, M. M., & Cohen, S. (1992). Hearing abilities of Down syndrome and other mentally handicapped adolescents. *Research in Developmental Disabilities*, 13, 533–551, https://doi.org/10.1016/0891-4222(92)90048-b

Marentette, P., Pettenati, P., Bello, A., & Volterra, V. (2016). Gesture and symbolic representation in Italian and English-speaking Canadian 2-year-olds. *Child Development*, 87, 944–961, https://doi.org/10.1111/cdev.12523

Marentette, P. F., & Mayberry, R. I. (2000). Principles for an emerging phonological system: A case study of early ASL acquisition. In C. Chamberlain, J. P. Morford, & R. I. Mayberry (eds.), *Language acquisition by eye* (pp. 71–90). Mahwah, NJ: Lawrence Erlbaum Associates.

Marquardt, T. P., Sanchez, S., & Munoz, M. L. (1999). Gestural communication learning in mentally retarded adults with Down's syndrome. *Journal of Developmental and Physical Disabilities*, 11, 221–236, https://doi.org/10.1023/a:1021896515483

Marschark, M. (1997). *Raising and educating a deaf child*. New York, NY: Oxford University Press.

Marschark, M., Lang, H. G., & Albertini, J. A. (2002). *Educating deaf students: From research to practice*. New York, NY: Oxford University Press.

Marschark, M., Spencer, L. J., Durkin, A., Borgna, G., Convertino, C., Machmer, E., Kronenberger, W. G., & Trani, A. (2015). Understanding language, hearing status, and visual-spatial skills. *Journal of Deaf Studies and Deaf Education*, 20, 310–330, https://doi.org/10.1093/deafed/env025

Marshall, C., Mason, K., Rowley, K., Herman, R., Atkinson, J., Woll, B., & Morgan, G. (2015). Sentence repetition in deaf children with specific language impairment in British Sign Language. *Language Learning and Development*, 11, 237–251, https://doi.org/10.1080/15475441.2014.917557

Marshall, C., & Morgan, G. (2016). Investigating sign language development, delay, and disorder in deaf children. In M. Marschark & P. E. Spencer (eds.), *The Oxford handbook of deaf studies in language: Research, policy, and practice* (pp. 311–344). Oxford, U.K.: Oxford University Press, https://doi.org/10.1093/oxfordhb/9780190241414.013.21

Marshall, C. R., Denmark, T., & Morgan, G. (2006). Investigating the underlying causes of SLI: A non-sign repetition test in British Sign Language. *Advances in Speech-Language Pathology*, 8, 347–355, https://doi.org/10.1080/14417040600970630

Marshall, C. R., Mann, W., & Morgan, G. (2011). Short-term memory in signed languages: Not just a disadvantage for serial recall. *Frontiers in Psychology*, 2, AR 102, https://doi.org/10.3389/fpsyg.2011.00102

Marshall, C. R., Rowley, K., Mason, K., Herman, R., & Morgan, G. (2013). Lexical organization in deaf children who use British Sign Language: Evidence from a semantic fluency task. *Journal of Child Language*, 40, 193–220, https://doi.org/10.1017/S0305000912000116

Marshall, J. (2006). The roles of gesture in aphasia therapy. *Advances in Speech-Language Pathology*, 8, 110–114, https://doi.org/10.1080/14417040600672384

Marshall, J., Atkinson, J., Smulovitch, E., Thacker, A., & Woll, B. (2004). Aphasia in a user of British Sign Language: Dissociation between sign and gesture. *Cognitive Neuropyschology*, 21, 537–554, https://doi.org/10.1080/02643290342000249

Marshall, J., Atkinson, J., Woll, B., & Thacker, A. (2005). Aphasia in a bilingual user of British Sign Language and English: Effects of cross-linguistic cues. *Cognitive Neuropsychology*, 22, 719–736, https://doi.org/10.1080/02643290442000266

Marshall, J., Best, W., Cocks, N., Cruice, M., Pring, T., Bulcock, G., Creek, G., Eales, N., Mummery, A. L., Matthews, N., & Caute, A. (2012). Gesture and naming therapy for people with severe aphasia: A group study. *Journal of Speech, Language, and Hearing Research*, 55, 726–738, https://doi. org/10.1044/1092-4388(2011/11-0219)

Marshall, J., & Goldbart, J. (2008). "Communication is everything I think." Parenting a child who needs augmentative and and alternative communication (AAC). *International Journal of Language & Communication Disorders*, 43, 77–98, https://doi.org/10.1080/13682820701267444

Marshall, N. R., & Hegrenes, J. (1972). The use of written language as a communication system for an autistic child. *Journal of Speech and Hearing Disorders*, 37, 258–261, https://doi.org/10.1044/jshd.3702.258

Martin, G. E., Klusek, J., Estigarribia, B., & Roberts, J. E. (2009). Language characteristics of individuals with Down syndrome. *Topics in Language Disorders*, 29, 112–132, https://doi.org/10.1097/tld.0b013e3181a71fe1

Martin, G. E., Losh, M., Estigarribia, B., Sideris, J., & Roberts, J. (2013). Longitudinal profiles of expressive vocabulary, syntax, and pragmatic language in boys with fragile X syndrome or Down syndrome. *International Journal of Language & Communication Disorders*, 48, 432–443, https://doi. org/10.1111/1460-6984.12019

Martins, I. P. (2004). Persistent acquired childhood aphasia. In F. Fabbro (ed.), *Neurogenic language disorders in children* (pp. 231–251). Amsterdam, The Netherlands: Elsevier.

Marton, K. (2009). Imitation of body postures and hand movements in children with specific language impairment. *Journal of Experimental Child Psychology*, 102, 1–13, https://doi.org/10.1016/j.jecp.2008.07.007

Masataka, N. (2000). The role of modality and input in the earliest stage of language acquisition: Studies of Japanese Sign Language. In C. Chamberlain, J. P. Morford, & R. I. Mayberry (eds.), *Language acquisition by eye* (pp. 3–24). Mahwah, NJ: Lawrence Erlbaum Associates.

Mason, K., Rowley, K., Marshall, C. R., Atkinson, J. R., Herman, R., Woll, B., & Morgan, G. (2010). Identifying specific language impairment in deaf children acquiring British Sign Language: Implications for theory and practice. *British Journal of Developmental Psychology*, 28, 33–49, https://doi. org/10.1348/026151009X484190

Mastrogiuseppe, M., Capirci, O., Cuva, S., & Venuti, P. (2015). Gestural communication in children with autism spectrum disorders during mother-child interaction. *Autism*, 19, 469–481, https://doi. org/10.1177/1362361314528390

Matas, J., Mathy-Laikko, P., Beukelman, D. R., & Legresley, K. (1985). Identifying the nonspeaking population: A demographic study. *Augmentative and Alternative Communication*, 1, 17–31, https://doi.org/10.1080/074346185123 31273491

Maurer, R., & Damasio, A. (1982). Childhood autism from the point of view of behavioral neurology. *Journal of Autism and Developmental Disorders*, 12, 195–205, https://doi.org/10.1007/bf01531309

May, T., McGinley, J., Murphy, A., Hinkley, T., Papadopoulos, N., Williams, K. J., McGillivray, J., Enticott, P. G., Leventer, R. J., & Rinehart, N. J. (2016). A multidisciplinary perspective on motor impairment as an early behavioural marker in children with autism spectrum disorder. *Australian Psychologist*, 51, 296–303, https://doi.org/10.1111/ap.12225

Mayberry, R. I. (1994). The importance of childhood to language acquisition: Evidence from American Sign Language. In J. C. Goodman & H. C. Nusbaum (eds.), *The development of speech perception* (pp. 57–90). Cambridge, MA: MIT Press.

Mayer, K. M., Yildiz, I. B., Macedonia, M., & von Kriegstein, K. (2015). Visual and motor cortices differentially support the translation of foreign language words. *Current Biology*, 25, 530–535, https://doi.org/10.1016/j.cub.2014.11.068

Mayer, R. E., & Sims, V. K. (1994). For whom is a picture worth a thousand words? Extensions of a dual-coding theory of multimedia learning. *Journal of Educational Psychology*, 86, 389–401, https://doi.org/10.1037/0022-0663.86.3.389

Maynard, A., Slavoff, G., & Bonvillian, J. (1994). Learning and recall of word-sign pairs: The impact of sign etymology. *Sign Language Studies*, 82, 55–78, https://doi.org/10.1353/sls.1994.0013

McCarty, T. L. (2008). Native American languages as heritage mother tongues. *Language, Culture and Curriculum*, 21, 201–225, https://doi.org/10.1080/07908310802385881

McDonnell, A. P., Hawken, L. S., Johnston, S. S., Kidder, J. E., Lynes, M. J., & McDonnell, J. J. (2014). Emergent literacy practices and support for children with disabilities: A national survey. *Education and Treatment of Children*, 37, 495–529, https://doi.org/10.1353/etc.2014.0024

McEwen, I. R., & Lloyd, L. L. (1990). Some considerations about the motor requirements of manual signs. *Augmentative and Alternative Communication*, 6, 207–216, https://doi.org/10.1080/07434619012331275474

McGee, G. G., Krantz, P. J., Mason, D., & McClannahan, L. E. (1983). A modified incidental-teaching procedure for autistic youth: Acquisition and generalization of receptive object labels. *Journal of Applied Behavior Analysis*, 16, 329–338, https://doi.org/10.1901/jaba.1983.16-329

McIntire, M. L. (1977). The acquisition of American Sign Language hand configurations. *Sign Language Studies*, 16, 247–266, https://doi.org/10.1353/sls.1977.0019

McKay-Cody, M. R. (1998). Plains Indian Sign Language: A comparative study of alternative and primary signers. In C. Carroll (ed.), *Deaf studies V: Toward*

2000: Unity and diversity: Conference proceedings, April 17–20, 1997 (pp. 17–77). Washington, DC: College for Continuing Education, Gallaudet University.

McLay, L., van der Meer, L., Schäfer, M. C. M., Couper, L., McKenzie, E., O'Reilly, M. F., Lancioni, G. E., Marschik, P. B., Green, V. A., Sigafoos, J., & Sutherland, D. (2015). Comparing acquisition, generalization, maintenance, and preference across three AAC options in four children with autism spectrum disorder. *Journal of Developmental and Physical Disabilities, 27*, 323–339, https://doi.org/10.1007/s10882-014-9417-x

McLean, L. P., & McLean, J. E. (1974). A language training program for nonverbal autistic children. *Journal of Speech and Hearing Disorders, 39*, 186–193, https://doi.org/10.1044/jshd.3902.186

McNeill, D. (1992). *Hand and mind: What gestures reveal about thought.* Chicago, IL: University of Chicago Press.

McNeill, D., & Duncan, S. D. (2005). Review of: *Grammar, gesture, and meaning in American Sign Language* by Scott K. Liddell. *Sign Language Studies, 5*, 506–523, https://doi.org/10.1353/sls.2005.0016

McShane, D. A., & Plas, J. M. (1982). Otitis media, psychoeducational difficulties, and Native Americans: A review and a suggestion. *Journal of Preventive Psychiatry, 1*, 277–292.

McWhorter, J. H. (2014). *The language hoax: Why the world looks the same in any language.* New York, NY: Oxford University Press.

Meadow, K. P. (1977). Name signs as identity symbols in the Deaf community. *Sign Language Studies, 16*, 237–246, https://doi.org/10.1353/sls.1977.0015

Meadow, K. P. (1980). *Deafness and child development.* Berkeley, CA: University of California Press.

Meadow-Orlans, K. P. (1990). Research on developmental aspects of deafness. In D. F. Moores & K. P. Meadow-Orlans (eds.), *Educational and developmental aspects of deafness* (pp. 283–298). Washington, DC: Gallaudet University Press.

Meier, R. P. (1981). Icons and morphemes: Models of the acquisition of verb agreement in ASL. *Papers and Reports on Child Language Development, 20*, 92–99.

Meier, R. P. (1987). Elicited imitation of verb agreement in American Sign Language: Iconically or morphologically determined? *Journal of Memory and Language, 26*, 362–376, https://doi.org/10.1016/0749-596x(87)90119-7

Meier, R. P. (1991). Language acquisition by deaf children. *American Scientist, 79*, 60–70.

Meier, R. P. (2002). Why different, why the same? Explaining effects and non-effects of modality upon linguistic structure in sign and speech. In R. P. Meier, K. Cormier, & D. Quinto-Pozos (eds.), *Modality and structure in signed and spoken languages* (pp. 1–25). Cambridge, U.K.: Cambridge University Press, https://doi.org/10.1017/CBO9780511486777.001

Meier, R. P. (2019). Acquiring signed languages as first languages: The milestones of acquisition and the form of early signs. In N. Grove & K. Launonen (eds.), *Manual sign acquisition in children with developmental disabilities* (pp. 59–86). New York, NY: Nova Science Publishers, Inc.

Meier, R. P., Cormier, K., & Quinto-Pozos, D. (2002). Gesture and iconicity in sign and speech. In R. P. Meier, K. Cormier, & D. Quinto-Pozos (eds.), *Modality and structure in signed and spoken languages* (pp. 167–174). Cambridge, U.K.: Cambridge University Press, https://doi.org/10.1017/CBO9780511486777.008

Meier, R. P., Mauk, C. E., Cheek, A., & Moreland, C. J. (2008). The form of children's early signs: Iconic or motor determinants? *Language Learning and Development*, 4, 63–98, https://doi.org/10.1080/15475440701377618

Meier, R. P., & Willerman, R. (1995). Prelinguistic gesture in deaf and hearing infants. In K. Emmorey & J. S. Reilly (eds.), *Language, gesture, and space* (pp. 391–409). Hillsdale, NJ: Lawrence Erlbaum Associates.

Meinzer, M., Breitenstein, C., Westerhoff, U., Sommer, J., Rösser, N., Rodriguez, A. D., Harnish, S., Knecht, S., & Flöel, A. (2011). Motor cortex preactivation by standing facilitates word retrieval in aphasia. *Neurorehabilitation and Neural Repair*, 25, 178–187, https://doi.org/10.1177/1545968310376577

Meir, I. (2010). Iconicity and metaphor: Constraints on metaphorical extension of iconic forms. *Language*, 86, 865–896, https://doi.org/10.1353/lan.2010.0044

Meir, I., Padden, C., Aronoff, M., & Sandler, W. (2013). Competing iconicities in the structure of languages. *Cognitive Linguistics*, 24, 309–343, https://doi.org/10.1515/cog-2013-0010

Meister, I. G., Boroojerdi, B., Foltys, H., Sparing, R., Huber, W., & Töpper, R. (2003). Motor cortex hand area and speech: Implications for the development of language. *Neuropsychologia*, 41, 401–406, https://doi.org/10.1016/s0028-3932(02)00179-3

Melinger, A., & Levelt, W. J. M. (2004). Gesture and the communicative intention of the speaker. *Gesture*, 4, 119–141, https://doi.org/10.1075/gest.4.2.02mel

Mellon, J. (2001). *An analysis of the quantity and quality of speech and sign use in children with severe learning difficulties in response to frequency of sign use by adults*. Unpublished master's thesis, City University, London, U.K.

Mesch, J. (2013). Tactile signing with one-handed perception. *Sign Language Studies*, 13, 238–263, https://doi.org/10.1353/sls.2013.0005

Mesibov, G. B., Adams, L. W., & Klinger, L. G. (1997). *Autism: Understanding the disorder*. New York, NY: Plenum Press, https://doi.org/10.1007/978-1-4757-9343-7

Methé, S., Huber, W., & Paradis, M. (1993). Inventory and classification of rehabilitation methods. In M. Paradis (ed.), *Foundations of aphasia rehabilitation* (pp. 3–60). Oxford, U.K.: Pergamon Press.

Metz-Lutz, M. N., de Saint Martin, A., Monpiou, S., Massa, R., Hirsch, E., & Marescaux, C. (1999). Early dissociation of verbal and nonverbal gestural ability in an epileptic deaf child. *Annals of Neurology*, 46, 929–932, https://doi.org/10.1002/1531-8249(199912)46:6<929::aid-ana19>3.0.co;2-c

Meuris, K., Maes, B., De Meyer, A.-M., & Zink, I. (2014). Manual signing in adults with intellectual disability: Influence of sign characteristics on functional sign vocabulary. *Journal of Speech, Language, and Hearing Research*, 57, 990–1010, https://doi.org/10.1044/2014_jslhr-l-12-0402

Meuris, K., Maes, B., & Zink, I. (2015). Teaching adults with intellectual disability manual signs through their support staff: A key word signing program. *American Journal of Speech-Language Pathology*, 24, 545–560, https://doi.org/10.1044/2015_ajslp-14-0062

Meyer, A., & Rose, D. H. (2000). Universal design for individual differences. *Educational Leadership*, 58, 39–43, http://www.ascd.org/publications/educational-leadership/nov00/vol58/num03/Universal-Design-for-Individual-Differences.aspx

Micheletti, S., Palestra, F., Martelli, P., Accorsi, P., Galli, J., Giordano, L., Trebeschi, V., & Fazzi, E. (2016). Neurodevelopmental profile in Angelman syndrome: More than low intelligence quotient. *Italian Journal of Pediatrics*, 42, AR 91, https://doi.org/10.1186/s13052-016-0301-4

Miles, H. L. W. (1994). ME CHANTEK: The development of self-awareness in a signing orangutan. In S. T. Parker, R. W. Mitchell, & M. L. Boccia (eds.), *Self-awareness in animals and humans: Developmental perspectives* (pp. 254–272). Cambridge, U.K.: Cambridge University Press, https://doi.org/10.1017/CBO9780511565526.018

Millar, D. C. (2009). Effects of AAC on the natural speech development of individuals with autism spectrum disorders. In P. Mirenda & T. Iacono (eds.), *Autism spectrum disorders and AAC* (pp. 171–192). Baltimore, MD: Paul H. Brookes Publishing.

Millar, D. C., Light, J. C., & Schlosser, R. W. (2006). The impact of augmentative and alternative communication intervention on the speech production of individuals with developmental disabilities: A research review. *Journal of Speech, Language, and Hearing Research*, 49, 248–264, https://doi.org/10.1044/1092-4388(2006/021)

Miller, J. F. (1992). Development of speech and language in children with Down syndrome. In I. T. Lott & E. E. McCoy (eds.), *Down syndrome: Advances in medical care* (pp. 39–50). New York, NY: Wiley-Liss.

Miller, J. F., Leddy, M., & Leavitt, L. A. (1999). A view toward the future: Improving the communication of people with Down syndrome. In J. F. Miller,

M. Leddy, & L. A. Leavitt (eds.), *Improving the communication of people with Down syndrome* (pp. 241–262). Baltimore, MD: Paul H. Brookes Publishing.

Miller, N. (1969). Language therapy with an autistic nonverbal boy. *Exceptional Children*, 35, 555–557, https://doi.org/10.1177/001440296903500707

Milner, B. (1971). Interhemispheric differences in the localization of psychological processes in man. *British Medical Bulletin*, 27, 272–277, https://doi.org/10.1093/oxfordjournals.bmb.a070866

Mindel, E. D., & Vernon, M. (1971). *They grow in silence*. Silver Spring, MD: National Association of the Deaf.

Mindess, A. (1990). What name signs can tell us about Deaf culture. *Sign Language Studies*, 66, 1–23, https://doi.org/10.1353/sls.1990.0009

Mindess, A. (2014). *Reading between the signs: Intercultural communication for sign language interpreters*. Boston, MA: Intercultural Press.

Ming, X., Brimacombe, M., & Wagner, G. C. (2007). Prevalence of motor impairment in autism spectrum disorders. *Brain & Development*, 29, 565–570, https://doi.org/10.1016/j.braindev.2007.03.002

Mira Pastor, R., & Grau, C. (2017). Los sistemas alternativos y aumentativos de comunicación (SAAC) como instrumento para disminuir conductas desafiantes en el alumnado con TEA: Estudio de un caso. *Revista Española de Discapacidad*, 5, 113–132, https://doi.org/10.5569/2340-5104.05.01.07

Mirenda, P. (2003). Toward functional augmentative and alternative communication for students with autism: Manual signs, graphic symbols, and voice output communication aids. *Language, Speech, and Hearing Services in Schools*, 34, 203–216, https://doi.org/10.1044/0161-1461(2003/017)

Mirenda, P. (2008). A back door approach to autism and AAC. *Augmentative and Alternative Communication*, 24, 220–234, https://doi.org/10.1080/08990220802388263

Mirenda, P. (2014). Augmentative and alternative communication. In F. R. Volkmar, R. Paul, S. J. Rogers, & K. A. Pelphrey (eds.), *Handbook of autism and pervasive developmental disorders, vol. 2. Assessment, interventions, and policy* (4th ed., pp. 813–825). Hoboken, NJ: John Wiley & Sons, https://doi.org/10.1002/9781118911389

Mirenda, P., & Locke, P. A. (1989). A comparison of symbol transparency in nonspeaking persons with intellectual disabilities. *Journal of Speech and Hearing Disorders*, 54, 131–140, https://doi.org/10.1044/jshd.5402.131

Mirenda, P., & Santogrossi, J. (1985). A prompt-free strategy to teach pictorial communication system use. *Augmentative and Alternative Communication*, 1, 143–150, https://doi.org/10.1080/07434618512331273641

Mirenda, P., & Schuler, A. L. (1988). Augmenting communication for persons with autism: Issues and strategies. *Topics in Language Disorders*, 9, 24–43, https://doi.org/10.1097/00011363-198812000-00004

Mirus, G. R., Rathmann, C., & Meier, R. P. (2001). Proximalization and distalization of sign movement in adult learners. In V. Dively, M. Metzger, S. Taub, & A. M. Baer (eds.), *Signed languages: Discoveries from international research* (pp. 103–119). Washington, DC: Gallaudet University Press.

Mistry, M., & Barnes, D. (2013). The use of Makaton for supporting talk, through play, for pupils who have English as an Additional Language (EAL) in the Foundation Stage. *Education 3–13*, 41, 603–616, https://doi.org/10.1080/030 04279.2011.631560

Mitchell, P., & Ropar, D. (2004). Visuo-spatial abilities in autism: A review. *Infant and Child Development*, 13, 185–198, https://doi.org/10.1002/icd.348

Mitchell, R. E., & Karchmer, M. A. (2004). Chasing the mythical ten percent: Parental hearing status of deaf and hard of hearing students in the United States. *Sign Language Studies*, 4, 138–163, https://doi.org/10.1353/ sls.2004.0005

Mohammadzaheri, F., Koegel, L. K., Rezaee, M., & Rafiee, S. M. (2014). A randomized clinical trial comparison between pivotal response treatment (PRT) and structured applied behavior analysis (ABA) intervention for children with autism. *Journal of Autism and Developmental Disorders*, 44, 2769–2777, https://doi.org/10.1007/s10803-014-2137-3

Mol, L., Krahmer, E., & van de Sandt-Koenderman, M. (2013). Gesturing by speakers with aphasia: How does it compare? *Journal of Speech, Language, and Hearing Research*, 56, 1224–1236, https://doi. org/10.1044/1092-4388(2012/11-0159)

Molteni, B., Sarti, D., Airaghi, G., Falcone, C., Mantegazza, G., Baranello, G., Riva, F., Saletti, V., Paruta, N., & Riva, D. (2010). Language abilities and gestural communication in a girl with bilateral perisylvian syndrome: A clinical and rehabilitative follow-up. *Neurological Science*, 31, 471–481, https://doi. org/10.1007/s10072-010-0309-2

Montgomery, J. W., Magimairaj, B. M., & Finney, M. C. (2010). Working memory and specific language impairment: An update on the relation and perspectives on assessment and treatment. *American Journal of Speech-Language Pathology*, 19, 78–94, https://doi.org/10.1044/1058-0360(2009/09-0028)

Moodie-Ramdeen, T. (2008). *Sign language versus Picture Exchange Communication System in language acquisition in young children with autism.* Unpublished doctoral dissertation, Capella University, Minneapolis, MN. (UMI Microform No.: 3339029).

Moody, B. (2002). International Sign: A practitioner's perspective. *Journal of Interpretation*, 1–47.

Moody, E. J. (1982). Sign language acquisition by a global aphasic. *The Journal of Nervous and Mental Disease*, 170, 113–116, https://doi. org/10.1097/00005053-198202000-00009

Moore, D. G. (2001). Reassessing emotion recognition performance in people with mental retardation: A review. *American Journal on Mental Retardation*, 106, 481–502, https://doi.org/10.1352/0895-8017(2001)106<0481:rerpip>2.0.co;2

Moores, D. F. (1996). *Educating the deaf: Psychology, principles, and practices* (4th ed.). Boston, MA: Houghton Mifflin.

Moores, D. F. (2010). The history of language and communication issues in deaf education. In M. Marschark & P. E. Spencer (eds.), *The Oxford handbook of deaf studies, language, and education, vol. 2* (pp. 17–30). New York, NY: Oxford University Press, https://doi.org/10.1093/oxfordhb/9780195390032.013.0002

Moores, D. F., & Miller, M. S. (eds.). (2009). *Deaf people around the world: Educational and social perspectives*. Washington, DC: Gallaudet University Press.

Morgan, G. (2014). On language acquisition in speech and sign: Development of combinatorial structure in both modalities. *Frontiers in Psychology*, 5, AR 1217, https://doi.org/10.3389/fpsyg.2014.01217

Morgan, G., Barrett-Jones, S., & Stoneham, H. (2007). The first signs of language: Phonological development in British Sign Language. *Applied Psycholinguistics*, 28, 3–22, https://doi.org/10.1017/S0142716407070014

Morgan, G., Barrière, I., & Woll, B. (2006). The influence of typology and modality on the acquisition of verb agreement morphology in British Sign Language. *First Language*, 26, 19–43, https://doi.org/10.1177/0142723706060739

Morgan, G., Herman, R., Barrière, I., & Woll, B. (2008). The onset and mastery of spatial language in children acquiring British Sign Language. *Cognitive Development*, 23, 1–9, https://doi.org/10.1016/j.cogdev.2007.09.003

Morgan, G., Herman, R., & Woll, B. (2007). Language impairments in sign language: Breakthroughs and puzzles. *International Journal of Language & Communication Disorders*, 42, 97–105, https://doi.org/10.1080/13682820600783178

Morgan, G., & Woll, B. (eds.). (2002). *Directions in sign language acquisition*. Amsterdam, The Netherlands: John Benjamins Publishing, https://doi.org/10.1075/tilar.2

Moseley, R. L., Correia, M. M., Baron-Cohen, S., Shtyrov, Y., Pulvermüller, F., & Mohr, B. (2016). Reduced volume of the arcuate fasciculus in adults with high-functioning autism spectrum conditions. *Frontiers in Human Neuroscience*, 10, AR 214, https://doi.org/10.3389/fnhum.2016.00214

Mostofsky, S. H., Dubey, P., Jerath, V. K., Jansiewicz, E. M., Goldberg, M. C., & Denckla, M. B. (2006). Developmental dyspraxia is not limited to imitation in children with autism spectrum disorders. *Journal of the International Neuropsychological Society*, 12, 314–326, https://doi.org/10.1017/s1355617706060437

Moulton, E., Barton, M., Robins, D. L., Abrams, D. N., & Fein, D. (2016). Early characteristics of children with ASD who demonstrate optimal progress between age two and four. *Journal of Autism and Developmental Disorders, 46,* 2160–2173, https://doi.org/10.1007/s10803-016-2745-1

Mueller, V., & Acosta, A. (2015). Infants' use of baby sign to extract unfamiliar words from the speech stream. *Early Child Development and Care, 185,* 943–951, https://doi.org/10.1080/03004430.2014.970184

Mueller, V., Sepulveda, A., & Rodriguez, S. (2014). The effects of baby sign training on child development. *Early Child Development and Care, 184,* 1178–1191, https://doi.org/10.1080/03004430.2013.854780

Muhle, R., Trentacoste, S. V., & Rapin, I. (2004). The genetics of autism. *Pediatrics,* 113, e472-e486, https://doi.org/10.1542/peds.113.5.e472

Nadel, L. (2003). Down's syndrome: A genetic disorder in biobehavioral perspective. *Genes, Brain and Behavior, 2,* 156–166, https://doi.org/10.1034/j.1601-183x.2003.00026.x

Næss, K.-A. B., Lervåg, A., Lyster, S.-A. H., & Hulme, C. (2015). Longitudinal relationships between language and verbal short-term memory skills in children with Down syndrome. *Journal of Experimental Child Psychology, 135,* 43–55, https://doi.org/10.1016/j.jecp.2015.02.004

Nafstad, A. V., & Rødbroe, I. B. (2015). *Communicative relations: Interventions that create communication with persons with congenital deafblindness* (English edition). Aalborg, Denmark: Materialcentret.

Namy, L. L., & Waxman, S. R. (1998). Words and gestures: Infants' interpretations of different forms of symbolic reference. *Child Development, 69,* 295–308, https://doi.org/10.1111/j.1467-8624.1998.tb06189.x

Napoli, D. J., & Sutton-Spence, R. (2011). Sign language humor, human singularities, and the origins of language. In G. Mathur & D. J. Napoli (eds.), *Deaf around the world: The impact of language* (pp. 231–250). New York, NY: Oxford University Press, https://doi.org/10.1093/acprof:oso/9780199732548.003.0013

Napoli, D. J., & Sutton-Spence, R. (2010). Limitations on simultaneity in sign language. *Language, 86,* 647–662, https://doi.org/10.1353/lan.2010.0018

National Center on Birth Defects and Developmental Disabilities. (2019). *What is cerebral palsy?* Bethesda, MD: NCBDDD, Centers for Disease Control, National Institutes of Health, https://www.cdc.gov/ncbddd/cp/facts.html

National Institute of Neurological Disorders and Stroke. (2019). *NINDS aphasia information page.* Bethesda, MD: NINDS, National Institutes of Health, https://www.ninds.nih.gov/Disorders/All-Disorders/Aphasia-Information-Page

Needlman, R., & Silverstein, M. (2004). Pediatric interventions to support reading aloud: How good is the evidence? *Journal of Developmental and Behavioral Pediatrics, 25,* 352–363, https://doi.org/10.1097/00004703-200410000-00007

Nelson, C. A. (2000). The neurobiological bases of early intervention. In J. P. Shonkoff & S. J. Meisels (eds.), *Handbook of early childhood intervention* (pp. 204–228). New York, NY: Cambridge University Press, https://doi.org/10.1017/CBO9780511529320.012

Nespor, M., & Sandler, W. (1999). Prosody in Israeli Sign Language. *Language and Speech*, 42, 143–176, https://doi.org/10.1177/00238309990420020201

Neuman, S. B., Kaefer, T., & Pinkham, A. M. (2018). A double dose of disadvantage: Language experiences for low-income children in home and school. *Journal of Educational Psychology*, 110, 102–118, https://doi.org/10.1037/edu0000201

Newport, E. L., & Ashbrook, E. (1977). The emergence of semantic relations in American Sign Language. *Papers and Reports on Child Language Development*, 13, 16–21.

Newport, E. L., & Meier, R. P. (1985). The acquisition of American Sign Language. In D. I. Slobin (ed.), *The crosslinguistic study of language acquisition, vol. 1. The data* (pp. 881–938). Hillsdale, NJ: Lawrence Erlbaum Associates, https://doi.org/10.4324/9781315802541-12

Nicola, K., & Watter, P. (2016). Visual-motor integration performance in children with severe specific language impairment. *Child: care, health and development*, 42, 742–749, https://doi.org/10.1111/cch.12365

Nightengale, E., Yoon, P., Wolter-Warmerdam, K., Daniels, D., & Hickey, F. (2017). Understanding hearing and hearing loss in children with Down syndrome. *American Journal of Audiology*, 26, 301–308, https://doi.org/10.1044/2017_AJA-17-0010

Nitschke, A. (1997). Sign language and gestures in medieval Europe: Monasteries, courts of justice, and society. In U. Segerstråle & P. Molnár (eds.), *Nonverbal communication: Where nature meets culture* (pp. 263–274). Mahwah, NJ: Lawrence Erlbaum Associates.

Nollet, M. D. (2008). *A systematic investigation of picture exchange and sign language for the acquisition of mands in young children with autism.* Unpublished master's thesis, University of Nevada, Reno, NV. (UMI Microform No.: 1455653).

Noterdaeme, M., Amorosa, H., Mildenberger, K., Sitter, S., & Minow, F. (2001). Evaluation of attention problems in children with autism and children with a specific language disorder. *European Child and Adolescent Psychiatry*, 10, 58–66, https://doi.org/10.1007/s007870170048

Notoya, M., Suzuki, S., & Furukawa, M. (1994). Effects of early manual instruction on the oral-language development of two deaf children. *American Annals of the Deaf*, 139, 348–351, https://doi.org/10.1353/aad.2012.0334

Occhino, C., Anible, B., Wilkinson, E., & Morford, J. P. (2017). Iconicity is in the eye of the beholder. *Gesture*, 16, 100–126, https://doi.org/10.1075/gest.16.1.04occ

Offir, C. W. (1976, June). Visual speech: Their fingers do the talking. *Psychology Today*, 10, 72–78.

Ohler, N. (1986/1989). *The medieval traveler* (C. Hillier, Trans., 1989). Suffolk, U.K.: Boydell Press.

Olfson, M., Crystal, S., Huang, C., & Gerhard, T. (2010). Trends in antipsychotic drug use by very young, privately insured children. *Journal of the American Academy of Child & Adolescent Psychiatry*, 49, 13–23, https://doi.org/10.1016/j.jaac.2009.09.003

Olsson, M. B., Westerlund, J., Lundström, S., Giacobini, M., Fernell, E., & Gillberg, C. (2015). "Recovery" from the diagnosis of autism — And then? *Neuropsychiatric Disease and Treatment*, 11, 999–1005, https://doi.org/10.2147/ndt.s78707

O'Neill, H., & Chiat, S. (2015). What our hands say: Exploring gesture use in subgroups of children with language delay. *Journal of Speech, Language, and Hearing Research*, 58, 1319–1325, https://doi.org/10.1044/2015_jslhr-l-14-0187

Openden, D., Whalen, C., Cernich, S., & Vaupel, M. (2009). Generalization and autism spectrum disorders. In C. Whalen (ed.), *Real life, real progress for children with autism spectrum disorders: Strategies for successful generalization in natural environments* (pp. 1–18). Baltimore, MD: Paul H. Brookes Publishing.

Orlansky, M. D., & Bonvillian, J. D. (1984). The role of iconicity in early sign language acquisition. *Journal of Speech and Hearing Disorders*, 49, 287–292, https://doi.org/10.1044/jshd.4903.287

Orlansky, M. D., & Bonvillian, J. D. (1988). Early sign language acquisition. In M. D. Smith & J. L. Locke (eds.), *The emergent lexicon: The child's development of a linguistic vocabulary* (pp. 263–292). New York, NY: Academic Press.

Orsini, A., Grossi, D., Capitani, E., Laiacona, M., Papagno, C., & Vallar, G. (1987). Verbal and spatial immediate memory span: Normative data from 1355 adults and 1112 children. *Italian Journal of Neurological Sciences*, 8, 537–548, https://doi.org/10.1007/bf02333660

Ortega, G. (2017). Iconicity and sign lexical acquisition: A review. *Frontiers in Psychology*, 8, AR 1280, https://doi.org/10.3389/fpsyg.2017.01280

Ortega, G., Sümer, B., & Özyürek, A. (2017). Type of iconicity matters in the vocabulary development of signing children. *Developmental Psychology*, 53, 89–99, https://doi.org/10.1037/dev0000161

Ospina, M. B., Krebs Seida, J., Clark, B., Karkhaneh, M., Hartling, L., Tjosvold, L., Vandermeer, B., & Smith, V. (2008). Behavioural and developmental interventions for autism spectrum disorder: A clinical systematic review. *PLoS ONE*, 3, e3755, https://doi.org/10.1371/journal.pone.0003755

Osterling, J., & Dawson, G. (1994). Early recognition of children with autism: A study of first birthday home videotapes. *Journal of Autism and Developmental Disorders*, 24, 247–257, https://doi.org/10.1007/bf02172225

Östling, R., Börstell, C., & Courtaux, S. (2018). Visual iconicity across sign languages: Large-scaled automated video analysis of iconic articulators and locations. *Frontiers in Psychology*, 9, AR 725, https://doi.org/10.3389/fpsyg.2018.00725

Özçalişkan, Ş., Adamson, L. B., Dimitrova, N., Bailey, J., & Schmuck, L. (2016). Baby sign but NOT spontaneous gesture predicts later vocabulary in children with Down syndrome. *Journal of Child Language*, 43, 948–963, https://doi.org/10.1017/s030500091500029x

Özçalişkan, Ş., Adamson, L. B., Dimitrova, N., & Baumann, S. (2017). Early gesture provides a helping hand to spoken vocabulary development for children with autism, Down syndrome, and typical development. *Journal of Cognition and Development*, 18, 325–337, https://doi.org/10.1080/15248372.2017.1329735

Padden, C., Hwang, S.-O., Lepic, R., & Seegers, S. (2015). Tools for language: Patterned iconicity in sign language nouns and verbs. *Topics in Cognitive Science*, 7, 81–94, https://doi.org/10.1111/tops.12121

Padden, C. A., Meir, I., Hwang, S.-O., Lepic, R., Seegers, S., & Sampson, T. (2013). Patterned iconicity in sign language lexicons. *Gesture*, 13, 287–308, https://doi.org/10.1075/gest.13.3.03pad

Page, J., & Boucher, J. (1998). Motor impairments in children with autistic disorder. *Child Language Teaching and Therapy*, 14, 233–259, https://doi.org/10.1177/026565909801400301

Paivio, A. (1971). *Imagery and verbal processes*. New York, NY: Holt, Rinehart and Winston.

Paivio, A. (1990). *Mental representation: A dual coding approach*. New York, NY: Oxford University Press, https://doi.org/10.1093/acprof:oso/9780195066661.001.0001

Pakula, A. T., Van Naarden Braun, K., & Yeargin-Allsopp, M. (2009). Cerebral palsy: Classification and epidemiology. *Physical Medicine and Rehabilitation Clinics of North America*, 20, 425–452, https://doi.org/10.1016/j.pmr.2009.06.001

Palmen, S. J. M. C., van Engeland, H., Hof, P. R., & Schmitz, C. (2004). Neuropathological findings in autism. *Brain*, 127, 2572–2583, https://doi.org/10.1093/brain/awh287

Pan, B. A., Rowe, M. L., Singer, J. D., & Snow, C. E. (2005). Maternal correlates of growth in toddler vocabulary production in low-income families. *Child Development*, 76, 763–782, https://doi.org/10.1111/1467-8624.00498-i1

Papagno, C., Della Sala, S., & Basso, A. (1993). Ideomotor apraxia without aphasia and aphasia without apraxia: The anatomical support for a double dissociation. *Journal of Neurology, Neurosurgery, and Psychiatry*, 56, 286–289, https://doi.org/10.1136/jnnp.56.3.286

Paquet, A., Olliac, B., Bouvard, M.-P., Golse, B., & Vaivre-Douret, L. (2016). The semiology of motor disorders in autism spectrum disorders as highlighted from a standardized neuro-psychomotor assessment. *Frontiers in Psychology*, 7, AR 1292, https://doi.org/10.3389/fpsyg.2016.01292

Paquet, A., Olliac, B., Golse, B., & Vaivre-Douret, L. (2016). Current knowledge on motor disorders in children with autism spectrum disorder (ASD). *Child Neuropsychology*, 22, 763–794, https://doi.org/10.1080/09297049.2015.108550 1

Paquier, P. F., & Mariën, P. (2005). A synthesis of the role of the cerebellum in cognition. *Aphasiology*, 19, 3–19, https://doi.org/10.1080/02687030444000615

Paquier, P. F., Van Dongen, H. R., & Loonen, M. C. B. (1992). The Landau-Kleffner syndrome or "acquired aphasia with convulsive disorder": Long-term follow-up of six children and a review of the recent literature. *Archives of Neurology*, 49, 354–359, https://doi.org/10.1001/archneur.1992.00530280034019

Parasnis, I., Samar, V. J., Bettger, J. G., & Sathe, K. (1996). Does deafness lead to enhancement of visual spatial cognition in children? Negative evidence from deaf nonsigners. *Journal of Deaf Studies and Deaf Education*, 1, 145–152, https://doi.org/10.1093/oxfordjournals.deafed.a014288

Parkhouse, C., & Smith, G. (2019). "Yes, no, maybe": A call for a paradigm shift in attitudes towards key word signing. In N. Grove & K. Launonen (eds.), *Manual sign acquisition in children with developmental disabilities* (pp. 315–333). New York, NY: Nova Science Publishers, Inc.

Pashek, G. V. (1997). A case study of gesturally cued naming in aphasia: Dominant versus nondominant hand training. *Journal of Communication Disorders*, 30, 349–366, https://doi.org/10.1016/s0021-9924(96)00079-2

Pattee, C., Von Berg, S., & Ghezzi, P. (2006). Effects of alternative communication on the communicative effectiveness of an individual with a progressive language disorder. *International Journal of Rehabilitation Research*, 29, 151–153, https://doi.org/10.1097/01.mrr.0000210046.02044.4d

Patterson, F. (1978). Conversations with a gorilla. *National Geographic*, 134, 438–465, https://www.nationalgeographic.co.uk/animals/2018/06/conversations-gorilla

Patterson, J. P., & Chapey, R. (2008). Assessment of language disorders in adults. In R. Chapey (ed.), *Language intervention strategies in aphasia and related neurogenic communication disorders* (5th ed., pp. 64–160). Philadelphia, PA: Lippincott Williams & Wilkins.

Pattison, A. E., & Robertson, R. E. (2016). Simultaneous presentation of speech and sign prompts to increase MLU in children with intellectual disability. *Communication Disorders Quarterly*, 37, 141–147, https://doi.org/10.1177/1525740115583633

Paul, R., & Roth, F. P. (2011). Characterizing and predicting outcomes of communication delays in infants and toddlers: Implications for clinical practice. *Language, Speech, and Hearing Services in Schools*, 42, 331–340, https://doi.org/10.1044/0161-1461(2010/09-0067)

Pearce, W. M., James, D. G. H., & McCormack, P. F. (2010). A comparison of oral narratives in children with specific language and non-specific language impairment. *Clinical Linguistics & Phonetics*, 24, 622–645, https://doi.org/10.3109/02699201003736403

Pearl, P. L., Carrazana, E. J., & Holmes, G. L. (2001). The Landau-Kleffner syndrome. *Epilepsy Currents*, 1, 39–45, https://doi.org/10.1111/j.1469-5812.2005.00134.x-i1

Pearson, E., Wilde, L., Heald, M., Royston, R., & Oliver, C. (2019). Communication in Angelman syndrome: A scoping review. *Developmental Medicine & Child Neurology*, 61, 1266–1274, https://doi.org/10.1111/dmcn.14257

Pease, L. (2000). Creating a communicating environment. In S. Aitken, M. Buultjens, C. Clark, J. T. Eyre, & L. Pease (eds.), *Teaching children who are deafblind: Contact, communication and learning* (pp. 35–82). London, U.K.: David Fulton Publishers.

Pedersen, P. M., Jørgensen, H. S., Nakayama, H., Raaschou, H. O., & Olsen, T. S. (1995). Aphasia in acute stroke: Incidence, determinants, and recovery. *Annals of Neurology*, 38, 659–666, https://doi.org/10.1002/ana.410380416

Peeters, T., & Gillberg, C. (1999). *Autism: Medical and educational aspects*. London, U.K.: Whurr Publishers.

Pellegrino, L. (2007). Cerebral palsy. In M. L. Batshaw, L. Pellegrino, & N. J. Roizen (eds.), *Children with disabilities* (6th ed., pp. 387–408). Baltimore, MD: Paul H. Brookes Publishing.

Penner, K. A., Johnston, J., Faircloth, B. H., Irish, P., & Williams, C. A. (1993). Communication, cognition, and social interaction in the Angelman syndrome. *American Journal of Medical Genetics*, 46, 34–39, https://doi.org/10.1002/ajmg.1320460108

Pepperberg, I. M. (2017). Animal language studies: What happened? *Psychonomic Bulletin & Review*, 24, 181–185, https://doi.org/10.3758/s13423-016-1101-y

Perlman, M., Little, H., Thompson, B., & Thompson, R. L. (2018). Iconicity in signed and spoken vocabulary: A comparison between American Sign Language, British Sign Language, English, and Spanish. *Frontiers in Psychology*, 9, AR 1433, https://doi.org/10.3389/fpsyg.2018.01433

Perniss, P., Lu, J. C., Morgan, G., & Vigliocco, G. (2017). Mapping language to the world: The role of iconicity in the sign language input. *Developmental Science*, 21, e12551, https://doi.org/10.1111/desc.12551

Perniss, P., Thompson, R. L., & Vigliocco, G. (2010). Iconicity as a general property of language: Evidence from spoken and signed languages. *Frontiers in Psychology*, 1, AR 227, https://doi.org/10.3389/fpsyg.2010.00227

Perniss, P., & Vigliocco, G. (2014). The bridge of iconicity: From a world of experience to the experience of language. *Philosophical Transactions of the Royal Society B*, 369, 20130300, https://doi.org/10.1098/rstb.2013.0300

Peter, B., Wijsman, E. M., Nato, Jr., A. Q., University of Washington Center for Mendelian Genomics, Matsushita, M. M., Chapman, K. L., Stanaway, I. B., Wolff, J., Oda, K., Gabo, V. B., & Raskind, W. H. (2016). Genetic candidate variants in two multigenerational families with childhood apraxia of speech. *PLoS ONE*, 11, e0153864, https://doi.org/10.1371/journal.pone.0153864

Peterson, L. N., & Kirshner, H. S. (1981). Gestural impairment and gestural ability in aphasia: A review. *Brain and Language*, 14, 333–348, https://doi.org/10.1016/0093-934x(81)90084-5

Petitto, L. A. (1988). "Language" in the pre-linguistic child. In F. Kessel (ed.), *The development of language and language researchers* (pp. 187–221). Hillsdale, NJ: Lawrence Erlbaum Associates.

Petitto, L. A., & Marentette, P. F. (1991). Babbling in the manual mode: Evidence for the ontogeny of language. *Science*, 251, 1493–1496, https://doi.org/10.1126/science.2006424

Pfau, R., & Bos, H. (2016). Syntax: Simple sentences. In A. Baker, B. van den Bogaerde, R. Pfau, & T. Schermer (eds.), *The linguistics of sign languages: An introduction* (pp. 117–147). Amsterdam, The Netherlands: John Benjamins Publishing, https://doi.org/10.1075/z.199.06pfa

Phillips, G. M. (1973). *An analysis of the results of a sign language training program on selected aphasic children: As a function of degree of aphasia, chronological age, and intelligence.* Unpublished doctoral dissertation, The American University, Washington, DC. (UMI Microform No.: 75–17,483).

Pickell, H., Klima, E., Love, T., Kritchevsky, M., Bellugi, U., & Hickok, G. (2005). Sign language aphasia following *right* hemisphere damage in a left-hander: A case of reversed cerebral dominance in a deaf signer? *Neurocase*, 11, 194–203, https://doi.org/10.1080/13554790590944717

Pickett, E., Pullara, O., O'Grady, J., & Gordon, B. (2009). Speech acquisition in older nonverbal individuals with autism: A review of features, methods, and prognosis. *Cognitive and Behavioral Neurology*, 22, 1–21, https://doi.org/10.1097/wnn.0b013e318190d185

Pierpont, E. I., Richmond, E. K., Abbeduto, L., Kover, S. T., & Brown, W. T. (2011). Contributions of phonological and verbal working memory to language development in adolescents with fragile X syndrome. *Journal of Neurodevelopmental Disorders*, 3, 335–347, https://doi.org/10.1007/s11689-011-9095-2

Pietrandrea, P. (2002). Iconicity and arbitrariness in Italian Sign Language. *Sign Language Studies*, 2, 296–321, https://doi.org/10.1353/sls.2002.0012

Pimperton, H., & Nation, K. (2014). Poor comprehenders in the classroom: Teacher ratings of behavior in children with poor reading comprehension and its relationship with individual differences in working memory. *Journal of Learning Disabilities*, 47, 199–207, https://doi.org/10.1177/0022219412454172

Pine, K. J., Bird, H., & Kirk, E. (2007). The effects of prohibiting gestures on children's lexical retrieval ability. *Developmental Science*, 10, 747–754, https://doi.org/10.1111/j.1467-7687.2007.00610.x

Pirila, S., van der Meere, J., Pentikainen, T., Ruusu-Niemi, P., Korpela, R., Kilpinen, J., & Nieminen, P. (2007). Language and motor speech skills in children with cerebral palsy. *Journal of Communication Disorders*, 40, 116–128, https://doi.org/10.1016/j.jcomdis.2006.06.002

Pizer, G., Meier, R. P., & Shaw Points, K. (2011). Child-directed signing as a linguistic register. In R. Channon & H. van der Hulst (eds.), *Formational units in sign languages* (pp. 65–84). Berlin, Germany: Mouton de Gruyter, https://doi.org/10.1515/9781614510680.65

Pizer, G., Walters, K., & Meier, R. P. (2007). Bringing up baby with baby signs: Language ideologies and socialization in hearing families. *Sign Language Studies*, 7, 387–430, https://doi.org/10.1353/sls.2007.0026

Pizzuto, E., & Volterra, V. (2000). Iconicity and transparency in sign languages: A cross-linguistic cross-cultural view. In K. Emmorey & H. L. Lane (eds.), *The signs of language revisited: An anthology to honor Ursula Bellugi and Edward Klima* (pp. 229–250). Mahwah, NJ: Lawrence Erlbaum Associates.

Plann, S. (1997). *A silent minority: Deaf education in Spain, 1550–1835*. Berkeley, CA: University of California Press.

Plato. Cratylus (B. Jowett, Trans., 1961). In E. Hamilton & H. Cairns (eds.), *The collected dialogues of Plato* (pp. 421–474). Princeton, NJ: Princeton University Press, https://doi.org/10.1515/9781400835867-017

Poizner, H., Klima, E. S., & Bellugi, U. (1987). *What the hands reveal about the brain*. Cambridge, MA: MIT Press.

Pollick, A. S., & de Waal, F. B. M. (2007). Ape gestures and language evolution. *Proceedings of the National Academy of Sciences*, 104, 8184–8189, https://doi.org/10.1073/pnas.0702624104

Porch, B. E. (1970). Personal communication; cited in M. Kenin & L. P. Swisher (1972). A study of pattern of recovery in aphasia. *Cortex*, 8, 56–68, https://doi.org/10.1016/s0010-9452(72)80027-3

Porter, A. (2016). A helping hand with language learning: Teaching French vocabulary with gesture. *The Language Learning Journal*, 44, 236–256, https://doi.org/10.1080/09571736.2012.750681

Powell, G. G., & Clibbens, J. (1994). Actions speak louder than words: Signing and speech intelligibility in adults with Down syndrome. *Down Syndrome Research and Practice*, 2, 127–129, https://doi.org/10.3104/reports.43

Premack, D. (1971). Language in chimpanzee? *Science*, 172, 808–822, https://doi.org/10.1126/science.172.3985.808

Premack, D., & Premack, A. J. (1974). Teaching visual language to apes and language-deficient persons. In R. L. Schiefelbusch & L. L. Lloyd (eds.), *Language perspectives: Acquisition, retardation, and intervention* (pp. 347–376). Baltimore, MD: University Park Press.

Preston, D., & Carter, M. (2009). A review of the efficacy of the Picture Exchange Communication System intervention. *Journal of Autism and Developmental Disorders*, 39, 1471–1486, https://doi.org/10.1007/s10803-009-0763-y

Prinz, P. M., & Prinz, E. A. (1979). Simultaneous acquisition of ASL and spoken English (in a hearing child of a deaf mother and hearing father): Phase I, early lexical development. *Sign Language Studies*, 25, 283–296, https://doi.org/10.1353/sls.1979.0005

Prior, M. R. (1977). Psycholinguistic disabilities of autistic and retarded children. *Journal of Mental Deficiency Research*, 21, 37–45, https://doi.org/10.1111/j.1365-2788.1977.tb00023.x

Pritchard, M., Dipper, L., Morgan, G., & Cocks, N. (2015). Language and iconic gesture use in procedural discourse by speakers with aphasia. *Aphasiology*, 29, 826–844, https://doi.org/10.1080/02687038.2014.993912

Prizant, B. M., with Fields-Meyer, T. (2015). *Uniquely human: A different way of seeing autism.* New York, NY: Simon & Schuster.

Proctor, A. (2014). Apraxia of speech, childhood. In P. J. Brooks & V. Kempe (eds.), *Encyclopedia of language development* (pp. 16–18). Los Angeles, CA: SAGE.

Proulx, T., & Inzlicht, M. (2012). The five "A"s of meaning maintenance: Finding meaning in the theories of sense-making. *Psychological Inquiry*, 23, 317–335, https://doi.org/10.1080/1047840x.2012.702372

Pullens, P., Pullens, W., Blau, V., Sorger, B., Jansma, B. M., & Goebel, R. (2015). Evidence for normal letter-sound integration, but altered language pathways in a case of recovered Landau-Kleffner syndrome. *Brain and Cognition*, 99, 32–45, https://doi.org/10.1016/j.bandc.2015.07.003

Pulvermüller, F. (2005). Brain mechanisms linking language and action. *Nature Reviews: Neuroscience*, 6, 576–582, https://doi.org/10.1038/nrn1706

Pulvermüller, F., & Berthier, M. L. (2008). Aphasia therapy on a neuroscience basis. *Aphasiology*, 22, 563–599, https://doi.org/10.1080/02687030701612213

Purser, H. R. M., & Jarrold, C. (2005). Impaired verbal short-term memory in Down syndrome reflects a capacity limitation rather than atypically rapid forgetting. *Journal of Experimental Child Psychology*, 91, 1–23, https://doi.org/10.1016/j.jecp.2005.01.002

Pyers, J. E., Perniss, P., & Emmorey, K. (2015). Viewpoint in the visual-spatial modality: The coordination of spatial perspective. *Spatial Cognition & Computation*, 15, 143–169, https://doi.org/10.1080/13875868.2014.1003933

Quadros, R., & Lillo-Martin, D. (2007). Gesture and the acquisition of verb agreement in sign languages. In H. Caunt-Nulton, S. Kulatilake, & I. Woo (eds.), *Proceedings of the 31ˢᵗ annual Boston University conference on language development* (pp. 520–531). Somerville, MA: Cascadilla Press.

Quinn, D. B. (ed.). (1979). *New American world: A documentary history of North America to 1612, vol. 1.* New York, NY: Arno Press and Hector Bye.

Quinn, E. D., & Rowland, C. (2017). Exploring expressive communication skills in a cross-sectional sample of children and young adults with Angelman syndrome. *American Journal of Speech-Language Pathology*, 26, 369–382, https://doi.org/10.1044/2016_AJSLP-15-0075

Quinto-Pozos, D., Forber-Pratt, A. J., & Singleton, J. L. (2011). Do developmental communication disorders exist in the signed modality? Perspectives from professionals. *Language, Speech, and Hearing Services in Schools*, 42, 423–443, https://doi.org/10.1044/0161-1461(2011/10-0071)

Radford, L. (2009). Why do gestures matter? Sensuous cognition and the palpability of mathematical meanings. *Educational Studies in Mathematics*, 70, 111–126, https://doi.org/10.1007/s10649-008-9127-3

Raikes, H., Pan, B. A., Luze, G., Tamis-LeMonda, C. S., Brooks-Gunn, J., Constantine, J., Tarullo, L. B., Raikes, H. A., & Rodriguez, E. T. (2006). Mother-child bookreading in low-income families: Correlates and outcomes during the first three years of life. *Child Development*, 77, 924–953, https://doi.org/10.1111/j.1467-8624.2006.00911.x

Ramachandran, V. S., & Hubbard, E. M. (2003). Hearing colors, tasting shapes: Mingled signals. *Scientific American*, 288, 52–59, https://doi.org/10.1038/scientificamerican0503-52

Rao, P. R. (2001). Use of Amer-Ind code by persons with severe aphasia. In R. Chapey (ed.), *Language intervention strategies in aphasia and related neurogenic communication disorders* (4ᵗʰ ed., pp. 688–701). Baltimore, MD: Lippincott Williams & Wilkins.

Rao, P. R., & Horner, J. (1978). Gesture as a deblocking modality in a severe aphasic patient. In R. Brookshire (ed.), *Clinical aphasiology: Proceedings of the conference, 1978* (pp. 239–247). Minneapolis, MN: BRK Publishers.

Rapin, I., Mattis, S., Rowan, A. J., & Golden, G. G. (1977). Verbal auditory agnosia in children. *Developmental Medicine and Child Neurology*, 19, 192–207, https://doi.org/10.1111/j.1469-8749.1977.tb07969.x

Ratusnik, C. M., & Ratusnik, D. L. (1974). A comprehensive communication approach for a ten-year-old nonverbal autistic child. *American Journal of Orthopsychiatry*, 44, 396–403, https://doi.org/10.1111/j.1939-0025.1974.tb00892.x

Rautakoski, P. (2011). Training total communication. *Aphasiology*, 25, 344–365, https://doi.org/10.1080/02687038.2010.530671

Raven, J., Raven, J. C., & Court, J. H. (1998). *Raven manual: Section 3. Standard progressive matrices*. Oxford, U.K.: Oxford Psychologists Press.

Raven, J. C. (1949). *Progressive matrices (1947). Sets A, Ab, B. Board and book forms*. London, U.K.: Lewis.

Rée, J. (1999). *I see a voice: Deafness, language and the senses — A philosophical history*. New York, NY: Henry Holt.

Reed, P. (2016). *Interventions for autism: Evidence for educational and clinical practice*. Chichester, U.K.: John Wiley & Sons, https://doi.org/10.1002/9781118897553

Reed, V. A., Patchell, F. C., Coggins, T. E., & Hand, L. S. (2007). Informativeness of the spoken narratives of younger and older adolescents with specific language impairment and their counterparts with normal language. *Clinical Linguistics & Phonetics*, 21, 953–960, https://doi.org/10.1080/02699200701587246

Reichle, J., & Sigafoos, J. (1991). Establishing spontaneity and generalization. In J. Reichle, J. York, & J. Sigafoos (eds.), *Implementing augmentative and alternative communication: Strategies for learners with severe disabilities* (pp. 157–171). Baltimore, MD: Paul H. Brookes Publishing.

Reichle, J., York, J., & Sigafoos, J. (eds.). (1991). *Implementing augmentative and alternative communication: Strategies for learners with severe disabilities*. Baltimore, MD: Paul H. Brookes Publishing.

Reid, S. M., Modak, M. B., Berkowitz, R. G., & Reddihough, D. S. (2011). A population-based study and systematic review of hearing loss in children with cerebral palsy. *Developmental Medicine & Child Neurology*, 53, 1038–1045, https://doi.org/10.1111/j.1469-8749.2011.04069.x

Reilly, J. S., McIntire, M., & Bellugi, U. (1990). The acquisition of conditionals in American Sign Language: Grammaticalized facial expressions. *Applied Psycholinguistics*, 11, 369–392, https://doi.org/10.1017/S0142716400009632

Remington, B., & Clarke, S. (1983). Acquisition of expressive signing by autistic children: An evaluation of the relative effects of simultaneous communication and sign-alone training. *Journal of Applied Behavior Analysis*, 16, 315–327, https://doi.org/10.1901/jaba.1983.16-315

Remington, B., & Clarke. S. (1996). Alternative and augmentative systems of communication for children with Down's syndrome. In J. Rondal, J. Perera, L. Nadel, & A. Comblain (eds.), *Down's syndrome: Psychological, psychobiological and socio-educational perspectives* (pp. 129–143). San Diego, CA: Singular Publishing Group.

Remland, M. S. (2004). *Nonverbal communication in everyday life* (2ⁿᵈ ed.). Boston, MA: Houghton Mifflin.

Rescorla, L. (2009). Age 17 language and reading outcomes in late-talking toddlers: Support for a dimensional perspective on language delay. *Journal of Speech, Language, and Hearing Research*, 52, 16–30, https://doi.org/10.1044/1092-4388(2008/07-0171)

Reséndez, A. (2007). *A land so strange: The epic journey of Cabeza de Vaca*. New York, NY: Basic Books.

Reuterskiöld-Wagner, C., Sahlén, B., & Nyman, A. (2005). Non-word repetition and non-word discrimination in Swedish preschool children. *Clinical Linguistics & Phonetics*, 19, 681–699, https://doi.org/10.1080/02699200400000343

Rice, M. L., & Hoffman, L. (2015). Predicting vocabulary growth in children with and without specific language impairment: A longitudinal study from 2;6 to 21 years of age. *Journal of Speech, Language, and Hearing Research*, 58, 345–359, https://doi.org/10.1044/2015_jslhr-l-14-0150

Richardson, T. (1975). Sign language for the SMR and PMR. *Mental Retardation*, 13, 17.

Riches, N. G., Loucas, T., Baird, G., Charman, T., & Simonoff, E. (2010). Sentence repetition in adolescents with specific language impairments and autism: An investigation of complex syntax. *International Journal of Language & Communication Disorders*, 45, 47–60, https://doi.org/10.3109/13682820802647676

Riseborough, M. G. (1981). Physiographic gestures as decoding facilitators: Three experiments exploring a neglected facet of communication. *Journal of Nonverbal Behavior*, 5, 172–183, https://doi.org/10.1007/bf00986134

Rispoli, M. J., Machalicek, W., & Lang, R. (2010). Communication interventions for individuals with acquired brain injury. *Developmental Neurorehabilitation*, 13, 141–151, https://doi.org/10.3109/17518420903468464

Rivers, W. M. (1991). Psychological validation of methodological approaches and foreign language classroom practices. In B. F. Freed (ed.), *Foreign language acquisition research and the classroom* (pp. 283–294). Lexington, MA: D. C. Heath.

Rizzolatti, G., & Arbib, M. A. (1998). Language within our grasp. *Trends in Neurosciences*, 21, 188–194, https://doi.org/10.1016/s0166-2236(98)01260-0

Rizzolatti, G., & Sinigaglia, C. (2008). *Mirrors in the brain — How our minds share actions and emotions* (F. Anderson, Trans.). Oxford, U.K.: Oxford University Press.

Roberts, J. E., & Medley, L. P. (1995). Otitis media and speech-language sequelae in young children: Current issues in management. *American Journal of Speech-Language Pathology*, 4, 15–24, https://doi.org/10.1044/1058-0360.0401.15

Roberts, J. E., Price, J., & Malkin, C. (2007). Language and communication development in Down syndrome. *Mental Retardation and Developmental Disabilities Research Reviews*, 13, 26–35, https://doi.org/10.1002/mrdd.20136

Roberts, J. M. A. (2014). Echolalia and language development in children with autism. In J. Arciuli & J. Brock (eds.), *Communication in autism* (pp. 55–73). Amsterdam, The Netherlands: John Benjamins Publishing.

Robinson, K. (1997). *Sign in education: The teaching of hearing children British Sign Language in school*. Birmingham, U.K.: Teesside Tec.

Robinson, R. O., Baird, G., Robinson, G., & Simonoff, E. (2001). Landau-Kleffner syndrome: Course and correlates with outcome. *Developmental Medicine & Child Neurology*, 43, 243–247, https://doi.org/10.1111/j.1469-8749.2001. tb00197.x

Rodriguez, E. T., Tamis-LeMonda, C. S., Spellmann, M. E., Pan, B. A., Raikes, H., Lugo-Gil, J., & Luze, G. (2009). The formative role of home literacy experiences across the first three years of life in children from low-income families. *Journal of Applied Developmental Psychology*, 30, 677–694, https://doi. org/10.1016/j.appdev.2009.01.003

Rogers, S. J. (2006). Evidence-based interventions for language development in young children with autism. In T. Charman & W. Stone (eds.), *Social and communication development in autism spectrum disorders: Early identification, diagnosis, and intervention* (pp. 143–179). New York, NY: The Guilford Press.

Rogers, S. J., & Bennetto, L. (2000). Intersubjectivity in autism: The roles of imitation and executive function. In A. M. Wetherby & B. M. Prizant (eds.), *Autism spectrum disorders: A transactional developmental perspective, vol. 9* (pp. 79–107). Baltimore, MD: Paul H. Brookes Publishing.

Rogers, S. J., Bennetto, L., McEvoy, R., & Pennington, B. F. (1996). Imitation and pantomime in high-functioning adolescents with autism spectrum disorders. *Child Development*, 67, 2060–2073, https://doi.org/10.2307/1131609

Rogers, S. J., & Williams, J. H. G. (2006). Imitation in autism: Findings and controversies. In S. J. Rogers & J. H. G. Williams (eds.), *Imitation and the social mind: Autism and typical development* (pp. 277–309). New York, NY: The Guilford Press.

Rogers, T. T., & Patterson, K. (2007). Object categorization: Reversals and explanations of the basic-level advantage. *Journal of Experimental Psychology: General*, 136, 451–469, https://doi.org/10.1037/0096-3445.136.3.451

Roizen, N. (1997). Hearing loss in children with Down syndrome: A review. *Down Syndrome Quarterly*, 2, 1–4.

Roizen, N. J. (2007). Down syndrome. In M. L. Batshaw, L. Pellegrino, & N. J. Roizen (eds.), *Children with disabilities* (6th ed., pp. 263–273). Baltimore, MD: Paul H. Brookes Publishing.

Rombouts, E., Maes, B., & Zink, I. (2017a). Beliefs and habits: Staff experiences with key word signing in special schools and group residential homes. *Augmentative and Alternative Communication*, 33, 87–96, https://doi.org/10.10 80/07434618.2017.1301550

Rombouts, E., Maes, B., & Zink, I. (2017b). Maintenance of key word signing in adults with intellectual disabilities: Novel signed turns facilitated by partners' consistent input and sign imitation. *Augmentative and Alternative Communication*, 33, 121–130, https://doi.org/10.1080/07434618.2017.1326066

Rombouts, E., Maes, B., & Zink, I. (2017c). Key word signing usage of adults with intellectual disabilities: Influence of communication partners' sign usage and responsivity. *American Journal of Speech-Language Pathology*, 26, 853–864, https://doi.org/10.1044/2017_AJSLP-16-0051

Rombouts, E., Maes, B., & Zink, I. (2018a). Use of key word signing by staff in special schools and in day centers for adults with intellectual disabilities. *Journal of Intellectual Disability Research*, 62, 21–29, https://doi.org/10.1111/jir.12444

Rombouts, E., Maes, B., & Zink, I. (2018b). Manual signing throughout the day: Influence from staff's sign use and type of activity. *Journal of Intellectual Disability Research*, 62, 737–745, https://doi.org/10.1111/jir.12509

Rombouts, E., Sheehy, K., Buchanan-Mellon, J., & Grove, N. (2019). Signing in school. In N. Grove & K. Launonen (eds.), *Manual sign acquisition in children with developmental disabilities* (pp. 359–378). New York, NY: Nova Science Publishers, Inc.

Romero Lauro, L. J., Crespi, M., Papagno, C., & Cecchetto, C. (2014). Making sense of an unexpected detrimental effect of sign language use in a visual task. *Journal of Deaf Studies and Deaf Education*, 19, 358–365, https://doi.org/10.1093/deafed/enu001

Romski, M., Sevcik, R. A., Barton-Hulsey, A., & Whitmore, A. S. (2015). Early intervention and AAC: What a difference 30 years makes. *Augmentative and Alternative Communication*, 31, 181–202, https://doi.org/10.3109/07434618.2 015.1064163

Romski, M. A., & Sevcik, R. A. (1996). *Breaking the speech barrier: Language development through augmented means*. Baltimore, MD: Paul H. Brookes Publishing.

Romski, M. A., & Sevcik, R. A. (1997). Augmentative and alternative communication for children with developmental disabilities. *Mental Retardation and Developmental Disabilities Research Reviews*, 3, 363–368, https://doi.org/10.1002/(sici)1098-2779(1997)3:4<363::aid-mrdd12>3.0.co;2-t

Rönnberg, J., Rudner, M., & Ingvar, M. (2004). Neural correlates of working memory for sign language. *Cognitive Brain Research*, 20, 165–182, https://doi.org/10.1016/j.cogbrainres.2004.03.002

Rose, M. (2010). Expressing one's self in the context of aphasia: The utility of arm and hand gestures in aphasia treatments. In E. Morsella (ed.), *Expressing oneself/expressing one's self: Communication, cognition, language, and identity* (pp. 23–48). New York, NY: Psychology Press.

Rose, M., & Douglas, J. (2001). The differential facilitatory effects of gesture and visualisation processes on object naming in aphasia. *Aphasiology, 15*, 977–990, https://doi.org/10.1080/02687040143000339

Rose, M., & Douglas, J. (2003). Limb apraxia, pantomime, and lexical gesture in aphasic speakers: Preliminary findings. *Aphasiology, 17*, 453–464, https://doi.org/10.1080/02687030344000157

Rose, M. L. (2006). The utility of arm and hand gestures in the treatment of aphasia. *Advances in Speech-Language Pathology, 8*, 92–109, https://doi.org/10.1080/14417040600657948

Rose, M. L. (2013). Releasing the constraints on aphasia therapy: The positive impact of gesture and multimodality treatments. *American Journal of Speech-Language Pathology, 22*, S227-S239, https://doi.org/10.1044/1058-0360(2012/12-0091)

Rose, M. L., Mok, Z., & Sekine, K. (2017). Communicative effectiveness of pantomime gesture in people with aphasia. *International Journal of Language & Communication Disorders, 52*, 227–237, https://doi.org/10.1111/1460-6984.12268

Rosen, R. S. (2004). Beginning L2 production errors in ASL lexical phonology: A cognitive phonology model. *Sign Language & Linguistics, 7*, 31–61, https://doi.org/10.1075/sll.7.1.04beg

Rosenbek, J. C., LaPointe, L. L., & Wertz, R. T. (1989). *Aphasia: A clinical approach.* Austin, TX: PRO-ED.

Rosenberg, R. E., Law, J. K., Yenokyan, G., McGready, J., Kaufmann, W. E., & Law, P. A. (2009). Characteristics and concordance of autism spectrum disorders among 277 twin pairs. *Archives of Pediatrics and Adolescent Medicine, 163*, 907–914, https://doi.org/10.1001/archpediatrics.2009.98

Rosenfeld, S. (2001). *A revolution in language: The problem of signs in late eighteenth-century France.* Stanford, CA: Stanford University Press.

Rosenstock, R. (2004). *An investigation of International Sign: Analyzing structure and comprehension.* Unpublished doctoral dissertation, Gallaudet University, Washington, DC. (UMI Microform No.: 3181450).

Rosenstock, R. (2008). The role of iconicity in International Sign. *Sign Language Studies, 8*, 131–159, https://doi.org/10.1353/sls.2008.0003

Rosenstock, R., & Napier, J. (eds.). (2016). *International Sign: Linguistic, usage, & status issues.* Washington, DC: Gallaudet University Press.

Roth, W.-M. (2001). Gestures: Their role in teaching and learning. *Review of Educational Research, 71*, 365–392, https://doi.org/10.3102/00346543071003365

Rothi, L. J. G., Mack, L., & Heilman, K. M. (1986). Pantomime agnosia. *Journal of Neurology, Neurosurgery, and Psychiatry*, 49, 451–454, https://doi.org/10.1136/jnnp.49.4.451

Roulet Perez, E., Davidoff, V., Prélaz, A.-C., Morel, B., Rickli, F., Metz-Lutz, M.-N., Boyes Braem, P., & Deonna, T. (2001). Sign language in childhood epileptic aphasia (Landau-Kleffner syndrome). *Developmental Medicine and Child Neurology*, 43, 739–744, https://doi.org/10.1111/j.1469-8749.2001.tb00154.x

Rowe, M. L., & Goldin-Meadow, S. (2009a). Differences in early gesture explain SES disparities in child vocabulary size at school entry. *Science*, 323, 951–953, https://doi.org/10.1126/science.1167025

Rowe, M. L., & Goldin-Meadow, S. (2009b). Early gesture *selectively* predicts later language learning. *Developmental Science*, 12, 182–187, https://doi.org/10.1111/j.1467-7687.2008.00764.x

Rowe, M. L., Özçalişkan, Ş., & Goldin-Meadow, S. (2008). Learning words by hand: Gesture's role in predicting vocabulary development. *First Language*, 28, 182–199, https://doi.org/10.1177/0142723707088310

Rowland, C., & Schweigert, P. (1990). *Tangible symbol systems: Symbolic communication for individuals with multisensory impairments*. Tucson, AZ: Communication Skill Builders.

Rowland, C., & Schweigert, P. (2000). Tangible symbols, tangible outcomes. *Augmentative and Alternative Communication*, 16, 61–78, https://doi.org/10.1080/07434610012331278914

Ruble, L., McDuffie, A., King, A. S., & Lorenz, D. (2008). Caregiver responsiveness and social interaction behaviors of young children with autism. *Topics in Early Childhood Special Education*, 28, 158–170, https://doi.org/10.1177/0271121408323009

Rudd, H., Grove, N., & Pring, T. (2007). Teaching productive sign modifications to children with intellectual disabilities. *Augmentative and Alternative Communication*, 23, 154–163, https://doi.org/10.1080/07434610601124867

Rudolph, J. M., & Leonard, L. B. (2016). Early language milestones and specific language impairment. *Journal of Early Intervention*, 38, 41–58, https://doi.org/10.1177/1053815116633861

Rutter, M., & Thapar, A. (2014). Genetics of autism spectrum disorders. In F. R. Volkmar, R. Paul, S. J. Rogers, & K. A. Pelphrey (eds.), *Handbook of autism and pervasive developmental disorders, vol. 1. Diagnosis, development, and brain mechanisms* (4th ed., pp. 411–423). Hoboken, NJ: John Wiley & Sons, https://doi.org/10.1002/9781118911389

Rygvold, A.-L., & Theie, S. (2016). Internationally adopted children's reading comprehension in second grade. *Adoption Quarterly*, 19, 166–187, https://doi.org/10.1080/10926755.2016.1182954

Samarin, W. J. (1987). Demythologizing Plains Indian Sign Language history. *International Journal of American Linguistics*, 53, 65–73, https://doi.org/10.1086/466044

Sandberg, A. D., & Dahlgren, SO. (2012). Theory of mind in children with cerebral palsy: The impact of limited expressive linguistic abilities. In M. Siegal & L. Surian (eds.), *Access to language and cognitive development* (pp. 62–79). New York, NY: Oxford University Press, https://doi.org/10.1093/acprof:oso/9780199592722.003.0004

Sandberg, C. W. (2017). Hypoconnectivity of resting-state networks in persons with aphasia compared with healthy age-matched adults. *Frontiers in Human Neuroscience*, 11, AR 91, https://doi.org/10.3389/fnhum.2017.00091

Sandler, W. (2012). The phonological organization of sign languages. *Language and Linguistics Compass*, 6, 162–182, https://doi.org/10.1002/lnc3.326

Sandler, W., & Lillo-Martin, D. (2006). *Sign language and linguistic universals*. Cambridge, U.K.: Cambridge University Press, https://doi.org/10.1017/CBO9781139163910

Sanz Aparicio, M. T., & Balaña, J. M. (2002). Early language stimulation of Down's syndrome babies: A study on the optimum age to begin. *Early Child Development and Care*, 172, 651–656, https://doi.org/10.1080/03004430215098

Sarno, J. E., Swisher, L. P., & Sarno, M. T. (1969). Aphasia in a congenitally deaf man. *Cortex*, 5, 398–414, https://doi.org/10.1016/S0010-9452(69)80016-X

Sarno, M. T. (1998). Recovery and rehabilitation in aphasia. In M. T. Sarno (ed.), *Acquired aphasia* (3rd ed., pp. 595–631). San Diego, CA: Academic Press, https://doi.org/10.1016/B978-012619322-0/50021-X

Savage-Rumbaugh, S., McDonald, K., Sevcik, R. A., Hopkins, W. D., & Rubert, E. (1986). Spontaneous symbol acquisition and communicative use by pygmy chimpanzees *(Pan paniscus)*. *Journal of Experimental Psychology: General*, 115, 211–235, https://doi.org/10.1037/0096-3445.115.3.211

Scarbro-McLaury, J. (2004). *The effects of sign language on the vocal responses of a child with autism*. Unpublished master's thesis, Department of Behavior Analysis, University of North Texas, Denton, TX. (UMI Microform No.: 1419751).

Schaaf, C. P., & Zoghbi, H. Y. (2011). Solving the autism puzzle a few pieces at a time. *Neuron*, 70, 806–808, https://doi.org/10.1016/j.neuron.2011.05.025

Schaeffer, B. (1978). Teaching spontaneous sign language to nonverbal children: Theory & method. *Sign Language Studies*, 21, 317–352, https://doi.org/10.1353/sls.1978.0002

Schaeffer, B., Kollinzas, G., Musil, A., & McDowell, P. (1977). Spontaneous verbal language for autistic children through signed speech. *Sign Language Studies*, 17, 287–328, https://doi.org/10.1353/sls.1977.0009

Schaeffer, B., Musil, A., & Kollinzas, G. (1980). *Total communication: A signed speech program for nonverbal children.* Champaign, IL: Research Press.

Schalock, R. L., Luckasson, R. A., & Shogren, K. A., with S. Borthwick-Duffy, V. Bradley, W. H. E. Buntinx, D. L. Coulter, E. M. Craig, S. C. Gomez, Y. Lachapelle, A. Reeve, M. E. Snell, S. Spreat, M. J. Tassé, J. R. Thompson, M. A. Verdugo, M. L. Wehmeyer, & M. H. Yeager. (2007). The renaming of *mental retardation*: Understanding the change to the term *intellectual disability. Intellectual and Developmental Disabilities*, 45, 116–124, https://doi.org/10.1352/1934-9556(2007)45[116:TROMRU]2.0.CO;2

Schein, J. D., & Delk, M. T., Jr. (1974). *The deaf population of the United States.* Silver Spring, MD: National Association of the Deaf.

Schein, J. D., & Stewart, D. A. (1995). *Language in motion: Exploring the nature of sign.* Washington, DC: Gallaudet University Press.

Schembri, A., Cormier, K., & Fenlon, J. (2018). Indicating verbs as typologically unique constructions: Reconsidering verb "agreement" in sign languages. *Glossa: A Journal of General Linguistics*, 3, 89, https://doi.org/10.5334/gjgl.468

Schembri, A., Jones, C., & Burnham, D. (2005). Comparing action gestures and classifier verbs of motion: Evidence from Australian Sign Language, Taiwan Sign Language, and nonsigners' gestures without speech. *Journal of Deaf Studies and Deaf Education*, 10, 272–290, https://doi.org/10.1093/deafed/eni029

Schepis, M. M., Reid, D. H., Fitzgerald, J. R., Faw, G. D., Van Den Pol, R. A., & Welty, P. A. (1982). A program for increasing manual signing by autistic and profoundly retarded youth within the daily environment. *Journal of Applied Behavior Analysis*, 15, 363–379, https://doi.org/10.1901/jaba.1982.15-363

Schick, B. (2003). The development of American Sign Language and manually coded English systems. In M. Marschark & P. E. Spencer (eds.), *Oxford handbook of deaf studies, language, and education* (pp. 219–231). New York, NY: Oxford University Press.

Schick, B., Marschark, M., & Spencer, P. E. (eds.). (2005). *Advances in the sign language development of deaf children.* New York, NY: Oxford University Press, https://doi.org/10.1093/acprof:oso/9780195180947.001.0001

Schlesinger, H. S., & Meadow, K. P. (1972). *Sound and sign: Childhood deafness and mental health.* Berkeley, CA: University of California Press.

Schlosser, R. W., & Sigafoos, J. (2006). Augmentative and alternative communication interventions for persons with developmental disabilities: Narrative review of comparative single-subject experimental studies. *Research in Developmental Disabilities*, 27, 1–29, https://doi.org/10.1016/j.ridd.2004.04.004

Schlosser, R. W., Sigafoos, J., & Koul, R. K. (2009). Speech output and speech-generating devices in autism spectrum disorders. In P. Mirenda & T. Iacono (eds.), *Autism spectrum disorders and AAC* (pp. 141–169). Baltimore, MD: Paul H. Brookes Publishing.

Schlosser, R. W., & Wendt, O. (2008). Effects of augmentative and alternative communication intervention on speech production in children with autism: A systematic review. *American Journal of Speech-Language Pathology, 17,* 212–230, https://doi.org/10.1044/1058-0360(2008/021)

Schmitt, S. A., Simpson, A. M., & Friend, M. (2011). A longitudinal assessment of the home literacy environment and early language. *Infant and Child Development, 20,* 409–431, https://doi.org/10.1002/icd.733

Schreibman, L., Stahmer, A. C., & Suhrheinrich, J. (2009). Enhancing generalization of treatment effects via pivotal response training and the individualization of treatment protocols. In C. Whalen (ed.), *Real life, real progress for children with autism spectrum disorders: Strategies for successful generalization in natural environments* (pp. 21–39). Baltimore, MD: Paul H. Brookes Publishing.

Schuchardt, K., Maehler, C., & Hasselhorn, M. (2011). Functional deficits in phonological working memory in children with intellectual disabilities. *Research in Developmental Disabilities, 32,* 1934–1940, https://doi.org/10.1016/j.ridd.2011.03.022

Schunk, H. A. (1999). The effect of singing paired with signing on receptive vocabulary skills of elementary ESL students. *The Journal of Music Therapy, 36,* 110–124, https://doi.org/10.1093/jmt/36.2.110

Schwartz, I. S., Davis, C., McLaughlin, A., & Rosenberg, N. E. (2009). Generalization in school settings: Strategies for planning and teaching. In C. Whalen (ed.), *Real life, real progress for children with autism spectrum disorders: Strategies for successful generalization in natural environments* (pp. 195–212). Baltimore, MD: Paul H. Brookes Publishing.

Schwartz, I. S., Garfinkle, A. N., & Bauer, J. (1998). The Picture Exchange Communication System: Communicative outcomes for young children with disabilities. *Topics in Early Childhood Special Education, 18,* 144–159, https://doi.org/10.1177/027112149801800305

Schwartz, J. B., & Nye, C. (2006). Improving communication for children with autism: Does sign language work? *EBP Briefs, 1,* 1–17.

Scott, H. L. (1898/1978). The sign language of the Plains Indian. In D. J. Umiker-Sebeok & T. A. Sebeok (eds.), *Aboriginal sign languages of the Americas and Australia, vol. 2* (pp. 53–67). New York, NY: Plenum Press. [Originally published 1898 in *Archives of the International Folk-Lore Association, 1,* 206–220.]

Scott, K. A., Roberts, J. A., & Glennen, S. (2011). How well do children who are internationally adopted acquire language? A meta-analysis. *Journal of Speech, Language, and Hearing Research, 54,* 1153–1169, https://doi.org/10.1044/1092-4388(2010/10-0075)

Scott, K. A., Pollock, K., Roberts, J. A., & Krakow, R. (2013). Phonological processing skills of children adopted internationally. *American Journal of Speech-Language Pathology*, 22, 673–683, https://doi.org/10.1044/1058-0360(2013/12-0133)

Scott, W. R. (1847). *Remarks, theoretical and practical, on the education of idiots, and children of weak intellect*. Exeter, U.K.: Spreat & Wallis.

Seal, B. C., & Bonvillian, J. D. (1997). Sign language and motor functioning in students with autistic disorder. *Journal of Autism and Developmental Disorders*, 27, 437–466, https://doi.org/10.1023/a:1025809506097

Seal, B. C., & DePaolis, R. A. (2014). Manual activity and onset of first words in babies exposed and not exposed to baby signing. *Sign Language Studies*, 14, 444–465, https://doi.org/10.1353/sls.2014.0015

Sebat, J., Lakshmi, B., Malhotra, D., Troge, J., Lese-Martin, C., Walsh, T., Yamrom, B., Yoon, S., Krasnitz, A., Kendall, J., Leotta, A., Pai, D., Zhang, R., Lee, Y.-H., Hicks, J., Spence, S. J., Lee, A. T., Puura, K., Lehtimäki, T., Ledbetter, D., Gregersen, P. K., Bregman, J., Sutcliffe, J. S., Jobanputra, V., Chung, W., Warburton, D., King, M.-C., Skuse, D., Geschwind, D. H., Gilliam, T. C., Ye, K., & Wigler, M. (2007). Strong association of de novo copy number mutations with autism. *Science*, 316, 445–449, https://doi.org/10.1126/science.1138659

Seigel, J. P. (1969). The Enlightenment and the evolution of a language of signs in France and England. *Journal of the History of Ideas*, 30, 96–115, https://doi.org/10.2307/2708248

Sekine, K., & Rose, M. L. (2013). The relationship of aphasia type and gesture production in people with aphasia. *American Journal of Speech-Language Pathology*, 22, 662–672, https://doi.org/10.1044/1058-0360(2013/12-0030)

Sekine, K., Rose, M. L., Foster, A. M., Attard, M. C., & Lanyon, L. E. (2013). Gesture production patterns in aphasic discourse: In-depth description and preliminary predictions. *Aphasiology*, 27, 1031–1049, https://doi.org/10.1080/02687038.2013.803017

Sennott, S., & Bowker, A. (2009). Autism, AAC, and Proloquo2Go. *Perspectives on Augmentative and Alternative Communication*, 18, 137–145, https://doi.org/10.1044/aac18.4.137

Sennott, S. C., Light, J. C., & McNaughton, D. (2016). AAC modeling intervention research review. *Research and Practice for Persons with Severe Disabilities*, 41, 101–115, https://doi.org/10.1177/1540796916638822

Seton, E. T. (1918). *Sign talk: A universal signal code, without apparatus, for use in the army, the navy, camping, hunting, and daily life*. Garden City, NY: Doubleday, Page.

Sharma, N., Pomeroy, V. M., & Baron, J.-C. (2006). Motor imagery: A backdoor to the motor system after stroke? *Stroke*, 37, 1941–1952, https://doi.org/10.1161/01.str.0000226902.43357.fc

Sharma, S. R., Sharma, N., & Yeolekar, M. E. (2011). An adolescent boy with acquired epileptic aphasia — Landau Kleffner syndrome: A rare case report. *Journal of Nepal Paediatric Society*, 31, 57–60, https://doi.org/10.3126/jnps. v31i1.3543

Shaw, E., & Delaporte, Y. (2010). New perspectives on the history of American Sign Language. *Sign Language Studies*, 11, 158–204, https://doi.org/10.1353/ sls.2010.0006

Sheehan, J., Martyn, M. M., & Kilburn, K. L. (1968). Speech disorders in retardation. *American Journal of Mental Deficiency*, 73, 251–256.

Sheehy, K., & Duffy, H. (2009). Attitudes to Makaton in the ages of integration and inclusion. *International Journal of Special Education*, 24, 91–102, http://oro. open.ac.uk/id/eprint/19897

Shelton, I. S., & Garves, M. M. (1985). Use of visual techniques in therapy for developmental apraxia of speech. *Language, Speech, and Hearing Services in Schools*, 16, 129–131, https://doi.org/10.1044/0161-1461.1602.129

Sherley-Appel, C., & Bonvillian, J. D. (2014). Manual signs and gestures of the Inuit of Baffin Island: Observations during the three voyages led by Martin Frobisher. In H-D. L. Bauman & J. J. Murray (eds.), *Deaf gain: Raising the stakes for human diversity* (pp. 159–181). Minneapolis, MN: University of Minnesota Press.

Shic, F., Macari, S., & Chawarska, K. (2014). Speech disturbs face scanning in 6-month-old infants who develop autism spectrum disorder. *Biological Psychiatry*, 75, 231–237, https://doi.org/10.1016/j.biopsych.2013.07.009

Shield, A. (2014). Preliminary findings of similarities and differences in the signed and spoken language of children with autism. *Seminars in Speech and Language*, 35, 309–320, https://doi.org/10.1055/s-0034-1389103

Shield, A., Cooley, F., & Meier, R. P. (2017). Sign language echolalia in deaf children with autism spectrum disorder. *Journal of Speech, Language, and Hearing Research*, 60, 1622–1634, https://doi.org/10.1044/2016_jslhr-l-16-0292

Shield, A., Knapke, K., Henry, M., Srinivasan, S., & Bhat, A. (2017). Impaired praxis in gesture imitation by deaf children with autism spectrum disorder. *Autism & Developmental Language Impairments*, 2, 1–14, https://doi. org/10.1177/2396941517745674

Shield, A., & Meier, R. P. (2012). Palm reversal errors in native-signing children with autism. *Journal of Communication Disorders*, 45, 439–454, https://doi. org/10.1016/j.jcomdis.2012.08.004

Shield, A., & Meier, R. P. (2018). Learning an embodied visual language: Four imitation strategies available to sign learners, *Frontiers in Psychology*, 9, AR 811, https://doi.org/10.3389/fpsyg.2018.00811

Shield, A., Meier, R. P., & Tager-Flusberg, H. (2015). The use of sign language pronouns by native-signing children with autism. *Journal of Autism and Developmental Disorders*, 45, 2128–2145, https://doi.org/10.1007/s10803-015-2377-x

Shield, A., Pyers, J., Martin, A., & Tager-Flusberg, H. (2016). Relations between language and cognition in native-signing children with autism spectrum disorder. *Autism Research*, 9, 1304–1315, https://doi.org/10.1002/aur.1621

Shield, A. M. (2010). *The signing of deaf children with autism: Lexical phonology and perspective-taking in the visual-spatial modality*. Unpublished doctoral dissertation, University of Texas at Austin, Austin, TX, http://www.academia.edu/383379/The_Signing_of_Deaf_Children_With_Autism_Lexical_Phonology_and_Perspective-Taking_In_the_Visual-Spatial_Modality

Shneidman, L. A., Arroyo, M. E., Levine, S. C., & Goldin-Meadow, S. (2013). What counts as effective input for word learning? *Journal of Child Language*, 40, 672–686, https://doi.org/10.1017/s0305000912000141

Shott, S. R., Joseph, A., & Heithaus, D. (2001). Hearing loss in children with Down syndrome. *International Journal of Pediatric Otorhinolaryngology*, 61, 199–205, https://doi.org/10.1016/s0165-5876(01)00572-9

Sibscota, G. (1670/1967). *The deaf and dumb man's discourse 1670*. Menston, U.K.: The Scolar Press.

Siedlecki, T., Jr., & Bonvillian, J. D. (1993). Location, handshape and movement: Young children's acquisition of the formational aspects of American Sign Language. *Sign Language Studies*, 78, 31–52, https://doi.org/10.1353/sls.1993.0016

Siedlecki, T., Jr., & Bonvillian, J. D. (1997). Young children's acquisition of the handshape aspect of American Sign Language signs: Parental report findings. *Applied Psycholinguistics*, 18, 17–39, https://doi.org/10.1017/s0142716400009851

Sieratzki, J. S., Calvert, G. A., Brammer, M., David, A., & Woll, B. (2001). Accessibility of spoken, written, and sign language in Landau-Kleffner syndrome: A linguistic and functional MRI study. *Epileptic Disorders*, 3, 79–89.

Sigafoos, J., & Drasgow, E. (2001). Conditional use of aided and unaided AAC: A review and clinical case demonstration. *Focus on Autism and Other Developmental Disabilities*, 16, 152–161, https://doi.org/10.1177/108835760101600303

Silberman, S. (2015). *NeuroTribes: The legacy of autism and the future of neurodiversity*. New York, NY: Avery.

Silver, S., & Miller, W. R. (1997). *American Indian languages: Cultural and social contexts*. Tucson, AZ: The University of Arizona Press.

Silverman, F. H. (1995). *Communication for the speechless* (3rd ed.). Boston, MA: Allyn and Bacon.

Singh, S. J., Hussein, N. H., Kamal, R. M., & Hassan, F. H. (2017). Reflections of Malaysian parents of children with developmental disabilities on their experiences with AAC. *Augmentative and Alternative Communication*, 33, 110–120, https://doi.org/10.1080/07434618.2017.1309457

Skelly, M. (1979). *Amer-Ind gestural code based on universal American Indian Hand Talk*. New York, NY: Elsevier North Holland.

Skelly, M., Schinsky, L., Smith, R. W., Donaldson, R. C., & Griffin, J. M. (1975). American Indian sign: A gestural communication system for the speechless. *Archives of Physical Medicine and Rehabilitation*, 56, 156–160.

Skelly, M., Schinsky, L., Smith, R. W., & Fust, R. S. (1974). American Indian sign (Amerind) as a facilitator of verbalization for the oral verbal apraxic. *Journal of Speech and Hearing Disorders*, 39, 445–456, https://doi.org/10.1044/jshd.3904.445

Slavoff, G. (1998). *Motor development in children with autism*. Unpublished doctoral dissertation, University of Virginia, Charlottesville, VA. (UMI Microform No.: 9824251).

Slobin, D. I. (2008). Breaking the molds: Signed languages and the nature of human language. *Sign Language Studies*, 8, 114–130, https://doi.org/10.1353/sls.2008.0004

Smith, A., Marks, R., Haan, E., Dixon, J., & Trent, R. J. (1997). Clinical features in four patients with Angelman syndrome resulting from paternal uniparental disomy. *Journal of Medical Genetics*, 34, 426–429, https://doi.org/10.1136/jmg.34.5.426

Smith, A. L., Romski, M. A., & Sevcik, R. A. (2013). Examining the role of communication on sibling relationship quality and interaction for sibling pairs with and without a developmental disability. *American Journal on Intellectual and Developmental Disabilities*, 118, 394–409, https://doi.org/10.1352/1944-7558-118.5.394

Smith, I. M., & Bryson, S. E. (1994). Imitation and action in autism: A critical review. *Psychological Bulletin*, 116, 259–273, https://doi.org/10.1037/0033-2909.116.2.259

Smith, I. M., & Bryson, S. E. (1998). Gesture imitation in autism I: Nonsymbolic postures and sequences. *Cognitive Neuroscience*, 15, 747–770, https://doi.org/10.1080/026432998381087

Smith, I. M., & Bryson, S. E. (2007). Gesture imitation in autism: II. Symbolic gestures and pantomimed object use. *Cognitive Neuropsychology*, 24, 679–700, https://doi.org/10.1080/02643290701669703

Snoddon, K. (2014). Baby sign as deaf gain. In H-D. L. Bauman & J. J. Murray (eds.), *Deaf gain: Raising the stakes for human diversity* (pp. 146–158). Minneapolis, MN: University of Minnesota Press.

Snow, C. E. (2014). Language, literacy, and the needs of the multilingual child. *Perspectives in Education*, 32, 7–16.

Snyder-McLean, L. (1978). *Functional stimulus and response variables in sign training with retarded subjects*. Paper presented at the Annual Convention of the American Speech and Hearing Association, San Francisco, CA.

So, W.-C., Wong, M. K.-Y., Lui, M., & Yip, V. (2015). The development of co-speech gesture and its semantic integration with speech in 6- to 12-year-old children with autism spectrum disorders. *Autism*, 19, 956–968, https://doi.org/10.1177/1362361314556783

Soorya, L. V. (2003). *Evaluation of motor proficiency and apraxia in autism: Effects on sign language acquisition*. Unpublished doctoral dissertation, Binghamton University, State University of New York, Binghamton, NY. (UMI Microform No.: 3102088).

Soprano, A. M., Garcia, E. F., Caraballo, R., & Fejerman, N. (1994). Acquired epileptic aphasia: Neuropsychologic follow-up of 12 patients. *Journal of Pediatric Neurology*, 11, 230–235, https://doi.org/10.1016/0887-8994(94)90108-2

Sorby, S. A. (2009). Educational research in developing 3-D spatial skills for engineering students. *International Journal of Science Education*, 31, 459–480, https://doi.org/10.1080/09500690802595839

Souriau, J., Vege, G., Estenberger, M., & Nyling, P. (2008). Emergence of gestures based on shared experiences. In J. Souriau, I. Rødbroe, & M. Janssen (eds.), *Communication and congenital deafblindness. III: Meaning making*. Aalborg: The Danish Resource Centre on Congenital Deafblindness/Viataal.

Sparaci, L., Lasorsa, F. R., & Capirci, O. (2019). More than words: Gestures in typically developing children and in children with autism. In N. Grove & K. Launonen (eds.), *Manual sign acquisition in children with developmental disabilities* (pp. 37–58). New York, NY: Nova Science Publishers, Inc.

Spencer, L. J., & Tomblin, J. B. (2006). Speech production and spoken language development of children using "total communication." In P. E. Spencer & M. Marschark (eds.), *Advances in the spoken language development of deaf and hard-of-hearing children* (pp. 166–192). New York, NY: Oxford University Press, https://doi.org/10.1093/acprof:oso/9780195179873.003.0008

Spencer, P. E., & Harris, M. (2006). Patterns and effects of language input to deaf infants and toddlers from deaf and hearing mothers. In B. Schick, M. Marschark, & P. E. Spencer (eds.), *Advances in the sign language development of deaf children* (pp. 71–101). New York, NY: Oxford University Press, https://doi.org/10.1093/acprof:oso/9780195180947.003.0004

Sperdin, H. F., & Schaer, M. (2016). Aberrant development of speech processing in young children with autism: New insights from neuroimaging biomarkers. *Frontiers in Neuroscience*, 10, AR 393, https://doi.org/10.3389/fnins.2016.00393

Spiker, D. (2011). The history of early intervention for infants and young children with Down syndrome and their families: Where have we been and where are we going? In J.-A. Rondal, J. Perera, & D. Spiker (eds.),

Neurocognitive rehabilitation of Down syndrome: The early years (pp. 15–35). Cambridge, U.K.: Cambridge University Press, https://doi.org/10.1017/CBO9780511919299.003

Spragale, D. M., & Micucci, D. (1990). Signs of the week: A functional approach to manual sign training. *Augmentative and Alternative Communication, 6,* 29–37, https://doi.org/10.1080/07434619012331275294

Spratt, J., & Florian, L. (2015). Inclusive pedagogy: From learning to action. Supporting each individual in the context of "everybody." *Teaching and Teacher Education, 49,* 89–96, https://doi.org/10.1016/j.tate.2015.03.006

Stadskleiv, K., Jahnsen, R., Andersen, G. L., & von Tetzchner, S. (2018). Neuropyschological profiles of children with cerebral palsy. *Developmental Neurorehabilitation, 21,* 108–120, https://doi.org/10.1080/17518423.2017.1282054

Stamenova, V., Roy, E. A., & Black, S. E. (2010). Associations and dissociations of transitive and intransitive gestures in left and right hemisphere stroke patients. *Brain and Cognition, 72,* 483–490, https://doi.org/10.1016/j.bandc.2010.01.004

Stedt, J. D. (1984). *The effects of translucency, mnemonic explanations, and age on the recall of American Sign Language signs in normal hearing subjects.* Unpublished doctoral dissertation, The Pennsylvania State University, State College, PA. (AAT No.: 8506687).

Steenbergen, B., & Gordon, A. M. (2006). Activity limitation in hemiplegic cerebral palsy: Evidence for disorders in motor planning. *Developmental Medicine & Child Neurology, 48,* 780–783, https://doi.org/10.1111/j.1469-8749.2006.tb01367.x

Stefanatos, G. (2011). Changing perspectives on Landau-Kleffner syndrome. *The Clinical Neuropsychologist, 25,* 963–988, https://doi.org/10.1080/13854046.2011.614779

Stefanini, S., Recchia, M., & Caselli, M. C. (2008). The relationship between spontaneous gesture production and spoken lexical ability in children with Down syndrome in a naming task. *Gesture, 8,* 197–218, https://doi.org/10.1075/gest.8.2.05ste

Steinhausen, H.-C., Mohr Jensen, C., & Lauritsen, M. B. (2016). A systematic review and meta-analysis of the long-term overall outcome of autism spectrum disorders in adolescence and adulthood. *Acta Psychiatrica Scandinavica, 133,* 445–452, https://doi.org/10.1111/acps.12559

Stevenson, R. A., Segers, M., Ferber, S., Barense, M. D., Camarata, S., & Wallace, M. T. (2016). Keeping time in the brain: Autism spectrum disorder and audiovisual temporal processing. *Autism Research, 9,* 720–738, https://doi.org/10.1002/aur.1566

Stillman, R., & Battle, C. W. (1984). Developing prelanguage communication in the severely handicapped: An interpretation of the van Dijk method. *Seminars in Speech and Language, 5,* 159–170, https://doi.org/10.1055/s-0028-1085175

St. John, T., Estes, A. M., Dager, S. R., Kostopoulos, P., Wolff, J. J., Pandey, J., Elison, J. T., Paterson, S. J., Schultz, R. T., Botteron, K., Hazlett, H., & Piven, J. (2016). Emerging executive functioning and motor development in infants at high and low risk for autism spectrum disorder. *Frontiers in Psychology*, 7, AR 1016, https://doi.org/10.3389/fpsyg.2016.01016

Stokes, S. F., Wong, A. M.-Y., Fletcher, P., & Leonard, L. B. (2006). Nonword repetition and sentence repetition as clinical markers of specific language impairment: The case of Cantonese. *Journal of Speech, Language, and Hearing Research*, 49, 219–236, https://doi.org/10.1044/1092-4388(2006/019)

Stokes, T., & Baer, D. (1977). An implicit technology of generalization. *Journal of Applied Behavior Analysis*, 10, 349–367, https://doi.org/10.1901/jaba.1977.10-349

Stokoe, W. C. (1978/1987). Sign language and the monastic use of lexical gestures. In J. Umiker-Sebeok & T. A. Sebeok (eds.), *Monastic sign languages* (pp. 325–338). Berlin, Germany: Mouton de Gruyter. [Originally published 1978 in *Semiotica*, 24, 181–194.]

Stokoe, W. C. (1991). Semantic phonology. *Sign Language Studies*, 71, 107–114, https://doi.org/10.1353/sls.1991.0032

Stokoe, W. C. (2001). *Language in hand: Why sign came before speech*. Washington, DC: Gallaudet University Press.

Stokoe, W. C., Jr. (1960). Sign language structure: An outline of the visual communication systems of the American deaf. *Studies in Linguistics*, Occasional Papers: 8. Buffalo, NY: University of Buffalo.

Stokoe, W. C., Jr., Casterline, D. C., & Croneberg, C. G. (1965). *A dictionary of American Sign Language on linguistic principles*. Washington, DC: Gallaudet College Press.

Stone, C., & Russell, D. (2016). Comparative analysis of depicting signs in International Sign and natural sign language interpreting. In R. Rosenstock & J. Napier (eds.), *International Sign: Linguistic, usage, and status issues* (pp. 65–83). Washington, DC: Gallaudet University Press.

Stone, W. L., Ousley, O. Y., Yoder, P. J., Hogan, K. L., & Hepburn, S. L. (1997). Nonverbal communication in two- and three-year-old children with autism. *Journal of Autism and Developmental Disorders*, 27, 677–696, https://doi.org/10.1023/a:1025854816091

Stone, W. L., & Yoder, P. J. (2001). Predicting spoken language level in children with autism spectrum disorders. *Autism*, 5, 341–361, https://doi.org/10.1177/1362361301005004002

Stoner, R., Chow, M. L., Boyle, M. P., Sunkin, S. M., Mouton, P. R., Roy, S., Wynshaw-Boris, A., Colamarino, S. A., Lein, E. S., & Courchesne, E. (2014). Patches of disorganization in the neocortex of children with autism. *The New England Journal of Medicine*, 370, 1209–1219, https://doi.org/10.1056/nejmoa1307491

Storch, S. A., & Whitehurst, G. J. (2002). Oral language and code-related precursors to reading: Evidence from a longitudinal structural model. *Developmental Psychology*, 38, 934–947, https://doi.org/10.1037/0012-1649.38.6.934

Strawbridge, W. J., Wallhagen, M. I., Shema, S. J., & Kaplan, G. A. (2000). Negative consequences of hearing impairment in old age: A longitudinal analysis. *The Gerontologist*, 40, 320–326, https://doi.org/10.1093/geront/40.3.320

Stremel-Campbell, K., Cantrell, D., & Halle, J. (1977). Manual signing as a language system and as a speech initiator for the non-verbal severely handicapped student. In E. Sontag, J. Smith, & N. Certo (eds.), *Educational programming for the severely and profoundly handicapped* (pp. 335–347). Reston, VA: Division on Mental Retardation, The Council for Exceptional Children.

Strome, S. E., & Strome, M. (1992). Down syndrome: An otolaryngologic perspective. *The Journal of Otolaryngology*, 21, 394–397.

Strong, G. K., Torgerson, C. J., Torgerson, D., & Hulme, C. (2011). A systematic meta-analytic review of evidence for the effectiveness of the "Fast ForWord" language intervention program. *Journal of Child Psychology and Psychiatry*, 52, 224–235, https://doi.org/10.1111/j.1469-7610.2010.02329.x

Stuart, S., Beukelman, D. R., & King, J. (1997). Vocabulary use during extended conversations by two cohorts of older adults. *Augmentative and Alternative Communication*, 13, 40–47, https://doi.org/10.1080/07434619712331277828

Summers, J., & Szatmari, P. (2009). Using discrete trial instruction to teach children with Angelman syndrome. *Focus on Autism and Other Developmental Disabilities*, 24, 216–226, https://doi.org/10.1177/1088357609334057

Sundberg, C. T., & Sundberg, M. L. (1990). Comparing topography-based verbal behavior with stimulus selection-based verbal behavior. *The Analysis of Verbal Behavior*, 8, 31–41, https://doi.org/10.1007/bf03392845

Sundberg, M. L., & Partington, J. W. (1998). *Teaching language to children with autism or other developmental disabilities*. Pleasant Hill, CA: Behavior Analysts.

Sundqvist, A., & Rönnberg, J. (2010). Advanced theory of mind in children using augmentative and alternative communication. *Communication Disorders Quarterly*, 31, 86–97, https://doi.org/10.1177/1525740109333967

Supalla, S. J. (1990). The arbitrary name sign system in American Sign Language. *Sign Language Studies*, 67, 99–126, https://doi.org/10.1353/sls.1990.0006

Sutcliffe, J. S. (2008). Insights into the pathogenesis of autism. *Science*, 321, 208–209, https://doi.org/10.1126/science.1160555

Sutherland, D. E., Gillon, G. G., & Yoder, D. E. (2005). AAC use and service provision: A survey of New Zealand speech-language therapists. *Augmentative and Alternative Communication*, 21, 295–307, https://doi.org/10.1080/07434610500103483

Sutherland, G. F., & Beckett, J. W. (1969). Teaching the mentally retarded sign language. *Journal of Rehabilitation of the Deaf*, 2, 56–60.

Sutton-Spence, R. L., & Kaneko, M. (2016). *Introducing sign language literature: Folklore and creativity*. London, U.K.: Palgrave Macmillan.

Sutton-Spence, R. L., & Woll, B. (1999). *The linguistics of British Sign Language: An introduction*. Cambridge, U.K.: Cambridge University Press, https://doi.org/10.1017/CBO9781139167048

Szaflarski, J. P., Ball, A. L., Grether, S., Al-fwaress, F., Griffith, N. M., Neils-Strunjas, J., Newmeyer, A., & Reichhardt, R. (2008). Constraint-induced aphasia therapy stimulates language recovery in patients with chronic aphasia after ischemic stroke. *Medical Science Monitor: International Medical Journal of Experimental and Clinical Research*, 14, CR243-CR250.

Szatmari, P., Bryson, S. E., Boyle, M. H., Streiner, D. L., & Duku, E. (2003). Predictors of outcome among high functioning children with autism and Asperger syndrome. *Journal of Child Psychology and Psychiatry*, 44, 520–528, https://doi.org/10.1111/1469-7610.00141

Szymanski, C., & Brice, P. J. (2008). When autism and deafness coexist in children: What we know now. *Odyssey: New Directions in Deaf Education*, 9, 10–15, https://eric.ed.gov/?id=EJ903163

Szymanski, C. A., Brice, P. J., Lam, K. H., & Hotto, S. A. (2012). Deaf children with autism spectrum disorders. *Journal of Autism and Developmental Disorders*, 42, 2027–2037, https://doi.org/10.1007/s10803-012-1452-9

Tager-Flusberg, H. (1999). Language development in atypical children. In M. Barrett (ed.), *The development of language* (pp. 311–348). Hove, U.K.: Psychology Press.

Tager-Flusberg, H., & Kasari, C. (2013). Minimally verbal school-aged children with autism spectrum disorder: The neglected end of the spectrum. *Autism Research*, 6, 468–478, https://doi.org/10.1002/aur.1329

Takkinen, R. (2003). Variations of handshape features in the acquisition process. In A. Baker, B. van den Bogaerde, & O. Crasborn (eds.), *Cross-linguistic perspectives in sign language research: Selected papers from TISLR 2000* (pp. 81–91). Hamburg, Germany: Signum.

Talbot, K. F., & Haude, R. H. (1993). The relationship between sign language skill and spatial visualization ability: Mental rotation of three-dimensional objects. *Perceptual and Motor Skills*, 77, 1387–1391, https://doi.org/10.2466/pms.1993.77.3f.1387

Tallal, P. (2003). Language learning disabilities: Integrating research approaches. *Current Directions in Psychological Science*, 12, 206–211, https://doi.org/10.1046/j.0963-7214.2003.01263.x

Tallal, P., Miller, S., & Fitch, R. H. (1993). Neurobiological basis of speech: A case for the preeminence of temporal processing. In P. Tallal, A. M.

Galaburda, R. R. Llinás, & C. von Euler (eds.), *Temporal information processing in the central nervous system: Special reference to dyslexia and dysphasia* (pp. 27–47). New York, NY: The New York Academy of Sciences, https://doi.org/10.1111/j.1749-6632.1993.tb22957.x

Tallal, P., & Stark, R. (1981). Speech acoustic-cue discrimination abilities of normally developing and language-impaired children. *Journal of the Acoustical Society of America*, 69, 568–574, https://doi.org/10.1121/1.385431

Tamis-LeMonda, C. S., Song, L., Leavell, A. S., Kahana-Kalman, R., & Yoshikawa, H. (2012). Ethnic differences in mother-infant language and gestural communications are associated with specific skills in infants. *Developmental Science*, 15, 384–397, https://doi.org/10.1111/j.1467-7687.2012.01136.x

Tan, T. X., Loker, T., Dedrick, R. F., & Marfo, K. (2012). Second-first language acquisition: Analysis of expressive language skills in a sample of girls adopted from China. *Journal of Child Language*, 39, 365–382, https://doi.org/10.1017/s0305000911000109

Tan, T. X., & Yang, Y. (2005). Language development of Chinese adoptees 18–35 months old. *Early Childhood Research Quarterly*, 20, 57–68, https://doi.org/10.1016/j.ecresq.2005.01.004

Tan, X. Y., Trembath, D., Bloomberg, K., Iacono, T., & Caithness, T. (2014). Acquisition and generalization of key word signing by three children with autism. *Developmental Neurorehabilitation*, 17, 125–136, https://doi.org/10.3109/17518423.2013.863236

Tang, G. (2007). *Hong Kong Sign Language: A trilingual dictionary with linguistic descriptions*. Hong Kong: The Chinese University Press.

Tartter, V. C. (1998). *Language processing in atypical populations*. Thousand Oaks, CA: Sage Publications.

Taub, S. F. (2001). *Language from the body: Iconicity and metaphor in American Sign Language*. Cambridge, U.K.: Cambridge University Press, https://doi.org/10.1017/CBO9780511509629

Tavares, L., & Peixoto, A. (2003). Late development of independent conversation skills with manual and graphic signs through joint activities. In S. von Tetzchner & N. Grove (eds.), *Augmentative and alternative communication: Developmental issues* (pp. 272–286). London, U.K.: Whurr Publishers.

Teitelbaum, P., Teitelbaum, O., Nye, J., Fryman, J., & Maurer, R. G. (1998). Movement analysis in infancy may be useful for early diagnosis of autism. *Proceedings of the National Academy of Sciences*, 95, 13982–13987, https://doi.org/10.1073/pnas.95.23.13982

te Kaat-van den Os, D. J. A., Jongmans, M. J., Volman, M. J. M., & Lauteslager, P. E. M. (2015). Do gestures pave the way?: A systematic review of the transitional role of gesture during the acquisition of early lexical and syntactic milestones in young children with Down syndrome. *Child Language Teaching and Therapy*, 31, 71–84, https://doi.org/10.1177/0265659014537842

Tellier, M. (2010). The effect of gestures on second language memorisation by young children. In M. Gullberg & K. de Bot (eds.), *Gestures in language development* (pp. 75–91). Amsterdam, The Netherlands: John Benjamins Publishing, https://doi.org/10.1075/bct.28.06tel

ten Holt, G. A., van Doorn, A. J., de Ridder, H., Reinders, M. J. T., & Hendriks, E. A. (2009). Which fragments of a sign enable its recognition? *Sign Language Studies*, 9, 211–239, https://doi.org/10.1353/sls.0.0012

Tessler, R., Gamache, G., & Liu, L. (1999). *West meets east: Americans adopt Chinese children*. Westport, CT: Bergin & Garvey.

Tharpe, A. M., & Olson, B. J. (1994). Landau-Kleffner syndrome: Acquired epileptic aphasia in children. *Journal of the American Academy of Audiology*, 5, 146–150, https://www.audiology.org/sites/default/files/journal/JAAA_05_02_10.pdf

Thompson, R. H., Cotnoir-Bichelman, N. M., McKerchar, P. M., Tate, T. L., & Dancho, K. A. (2007). Enhancing early communication through infant sign training. *Journal of Applied Behavior Analysis*, 40, 15–23, https://doi.org/10.1901/jaba.2007.23-06

Thompson, R. L., Vinson, D. P., Woll, B., & Vigliocco, G. (2012). The road to language learning is iconic: Evidence from British Sign Language. *Psychological Science*, 23, 1443–1448, https://doi.org/10.1177/0956797612459763

Tierney, C., Mayes, S., Lohs, S. R., Black, A., Gisin, E., & Veglia, M. (2015). How valid is the checklist for autism spectrum disorder when a child has apraxia of speech? *Journal of Developmental and Behavioral Pediatrics*, 36, 569–574, https://doi.org/10.1097/dbp.0000000000000189

Tincani, M. (2004). Comparing the Picture Exchange Communication System and sign language training for children with autism. *Focus on Autism and Other Developmental Disabilities*, 19, 152–163, https://doi.org/10.1177/10883576040190030301

Tolar, T. D., Lederberg, A. R., Gokhale, S., & Tomasello, M. (2008). The development of the ability to recognize the meaning of iconic signs. *Journal of Deaf Studies and Deaf Education*, 13, 225–240, https://doi.org/10.1093/deafed/enm045

Tomasello, M., Striano, T., & Rochat, P. (1999). Do young children use objects as symbols? *British Journal of Developmental Psychology*, 17, 563–584, https://doi.org/10.1348/026151099165483

Tomblin, J. B., Records, N. L., Buckwalter, P., Zhang, X., Smith, E., & O'Brien, M. (1997). Prevalence of specific language impairment in kindergarten children. *Journal of Speech, Language, and Hearing Research*, 40, 1245–1260, https://doi.org/10.1044/jslhr.4006.1245

Tomblin, J. B., Zhang, X., Buckwalter, P., & O'Brien, M. (2003). The stability of primary language disorder: Four years after kindergarten diagnosis.

Journal of Speech, Language, and Hearing Research, 46, 1283–1296, https://doi.org/10.1044/1092-4388(2003/100)

Tomkins, W. (1931/1969). *Indian Sign Language*. New York, NY: Dover Publications. [Corrected republication of the 1931 fifth edition originally published in San Diego, CA under the title *Universal Indian Sign Language of the Plains Indians of North America*.]

Topping, K., Dekhinet, R., & Zeedyk, S. (2013). Parent-infant interaction and children's language development. *Educational Psychology*, 33, 391–426, https://doi.org/10.1080/01443410.2012.744159

Toth, A. (2009). Bridge of signs: Can sign language empower non-deaf children to triumph over their communication disabilities? *American Annals of the Deaf*, 154, 85–95, https://doi.org/10.1353/aad.0.0084

Toth, K., Munson, J., Meltzoff, A. N., & Dawson, G. (2006). Early predictors of communication development in young children with autism spectrum disorder: Joint attention, imitation, and toy play. *Journal of Autism and Developmental Disorders*, 36, 993–1005, https://doi.org/10.1007/s10803-006-0137-7

Trembath, D., Balandin, S., & Togher, L. (2007). Vocabulary selection for Australian children who use augmentative and alternative communication. *Journal of Intellectual & Developmental Disability*, 32, 291–301, https://doi.org/10.1080/13668250701689298

Trevarthen, C., & Delafield-Butt, J. T. (2013). Autism as a developmental disorder in intentional movement and affective engagement. *Frontiers in Integrative Neuroscience*, 7, AR 49, https://doi.org/10.3389/fnint.2013.00049

Trillingsgaard, A., & Ostergaard, J. R. (2004). Autism in Angelman syndrome: An exploration of comorbidity. *Autism*, 8, 163–174, https://doi.org/10.1177/1362361304042720

Trivette, C. M. (2007). Influence of caregiver responsiveness on the development of young children with or at risk for developmental disabilities. *Winterberry Research Syntheses*, 1, 1–15.

Trosman, S., Matusik, D. K., Ferro, L., Gao, W., & Saadia-Redleaf, M. (2012). Presbycusis occurs after cochlear implantation also: A retrospective study of pure tone thresholds over time. *Otology & Neurotology*, 33, 1543–1548, https://doi.org/10.1097/mao.0b013e318271c1ef

Turner, G., Webb, T., Wake, S., & Robinson, H. (1996). Prevalence of fragile X syndrome. *American Journal of Medical Genetics*, 64, 196–197, https://doi.org/10.1002/(sici)1096-8628(19960712)64:1<196::aid-ajmg35>3.0.co;2-g

Turner, S., Alborz, A., & Gayle, V. (2008). Predictors of academic attainments of young people with Down's syndrome. *Journal of Intellectual Disability Research*, 52, 380–392, https://doi.org/10.1111/j.1365-2788.2007.01038.x

Tylor, E. B. (1878). *Researches into the early history of mankind and the development of civilization* (3rd ed., rev.). London, U.K.: John Murray.

Tzeng, C. Y., Nygaard, L. C., & Namy, L. L. (2017). Developmental change in children's sensitivity to sound symbolism. *Journal of Experimental Child Psychology*, 160, 107–118, https://doi.org/10.1016/j.jecp.2017.03.004

Udwin, O., & Yule, W. (1990). Augmentative communication systems taught to cerebral palsied children — A longitudinal study. I. The acquisition of signs and symbols, and syntactic aspects of their use over time. *British Journal of Disorders of Communication*, 25, 295–309, https://doi.org/10.3109/13682829009011979

Udwin, O., & Yule, W. (1991). Augmentative communication systems taught to cerebral-palsied children — A longitudinal study. III. Teaching practices and exposure to sign and symbol use in schools and homes. *British Journal of Disorders of Communication*, 26, 149–162, https://doi.org/10.3109/13682829109012000

Uecker, A., Mangan, P. A., Obrzut, J. E., & Nadel, L. (1993). Down syndrome in neurobiological perspective: An emphasis on spatial cognition. *Journal of Clinical Child Psychology*, 22, 266–276, https://doi.org/10.1207/s15374424jccp2202_12

U.S. Department of Health and Human Services. (2010). *Head Start impact study: Final report*. Washington, DC: U.S. Government Printing Office.

Uttal, D. H., Miller, D. I., & Newcombe, N. S. (2013). Exploring and enhancing spatial thinking: Links to achievement in science, technology, engineering, and mathematics? *Current Directions in Psychological Science*, 22, 367–373, https://doi.org/10.1177/0963721413484756

Valentino, A. L., & Shillingsburg, M. A. (2011). Acquisition of mands, tacts, and intraverbals through sign exposure in an individual with autism. *The Analysis of Verbal Behavior*, 27, 95–101, https://doi.org/10.1007/bf03393094

Valentino, A. L., Shillingsburg, M. A., Call, N. A., Burton, B., & Bowen, C. N. (2011). An investigation of extinction-induced vocalizations. *Behavior Modification*, 35, 284–298, https://doi.org/10.1177/0145445511398412

Vallar, G., & Papagno, C. (1993). Preserved vocabulary acquisition in Down's syndrome: The role of phonological short-term memory. *Cortex*, 29, 467–483, https://doi.org/10.1016/S0010-9452(13)80254-7

Valli, C., Lucas, C., & Mulrooney, K. J. (2005). *Linguistics of American Sign Language: An introduction* (4th ed.). Washington, DC: Gallaudet University Press.

Vance, M. (1991). Educational and therapeutic approaches used with a child presenting with acquired aphasia with convulsive disorder (Landau-Kleffner syndrome). *Child: Language Teaching and Therapy*, 7, 41–60, https://doi.org/10.1177/026565909100700103

Van Cleve, J. V. (ed.). (1987). *Gallaudet encyclopedia of deaf people and deafness.* New York, NY: McGraw-Hill.

Vandereet, J., Maes, B., Lembrechts, D., & Zink, I. (2010). Predicting expressive vocabulary acquisition in children with intellectual disabilities: A 2-year longitudinal study. *Journal of Speech, Language, and Hearing Research,* 53, 1673–1686, https://doi.org/10.1044/1092-4388(2010/09-0187)

Vandereet, J., Maes, B., Lembrechts, D., & Zink, I. (2011). The role of gestures in the transition from one- to two-word speech in a variety of children with intellectual disabilities. *International Journal of Language & Communication Disorders,* 46, 714–727, https://doi.org/10.1111/j.1460-6984.2011.00050.x

Vanderheiden, G. C., & Lloyd, L. L. (1986). Communication systems and their components. In S. W. Blackstone (ed.), *Augmentative communication: An introduction* (pp. 49–161). Rockville, MD: American Speech-Language-Hearing Association.

van der Hulst, H. (1993). Units in the analysis of signs. *Phonology,* 10, 209–241, https://doi.org/10.1017/S095267570000004X

van der Kooij, E. (2002). *Phonological categories in Sign Language of the Netherlands: The role of phonetic implementation and iconicity.* Amsterdam, The Netherlands: Netherlands Graduate School of Linguistics, Landelijke Onderzoekschool Taalwetenschap (LOT), https://www.lotpublications.nl/phonological-categories-in-sign-language-of-the-netherlands-phonological-categories-in-sign-language-of-the-netherlands-the-role-of-phonetic-implementation-and-iconicity

van der Meer, L., Sigafoos, J., O'Reilly, M. F., & Lancioni, G. E. (2011). Assessing preferences for AAC options in communication interventions for individuals with developmental disabilities: A review of the literature. *Research in Developmental Disabilities,* 32, 1422–1431, https://doi.org/10.1016/j.ridd.2011.02.003

van der Schuit, M., Segers, E., van Balkom, H., & Verhoeven, L. (2011a). Early language intervention for children with intellectual disabilities: A neurocognitive perspective. *Research in Developmental Disabilities,* 32, 705–712, https://doi.org/10.1016/j.ridd.2010.11.010

van der Schuit, M., Segers, E., van Balkom, H., & Verhoeven, L. (2011b). How cognitive factors affect language development in children with intellectual disabilities. *Research in Developmental Disabilities,* 32, 1884–1894, https://doi.org/10.1016/j.ridd.2011.03.015

van Dijk, J. (1966). The first steps of the deaf-blind child towards language. *International Journal for the Education of the Blind,* 15, 112–114.

van Dijk, J. (2004). Educating deaf students with multiple disabilities. In D. Power & G. Leigh (eds.), *Educating deaf students: Global perspectives* (pp. 27–39). Washington, DC: Gallaudet University Press.

van Dijk, R., Kappers, A. M. L., & Postma, A. (2013). Haptic spatial configuration learning in deaf and hearing individuals. *PLoS ONE*, 8, e61336, https://doi.org/10.1371/journal.pone.0061336

van Dijk, R., Nelson, C., Postma, A., & van Dijk, J. (2010). Deaf children with severe multiple disabilities: Etiologies, intervention, and assessment. In M. Marschark & P. E. Spencer (eds.), *The Oxford handbook of deaf studies, language, and education, vol. 2* (pp. 172–191). New York, NY: Oxford University Press.

Van Dongen, H. R., & Loonen, M. C. B. (1977). Factors related to prognosis of acquired aphasia in children. *Cortex*, 13, 131–136, https://doi.org/10.1016/s0010-9452(77)80004-x

Van keer, I., Colla, S., Van Leeuwen, K., Vlaskamp, C., Ceulemans, E., Hoppenbrouwers, K., Desoete, A., & Maes, B. (2017). Exploring parental behavior and child interactive engagement: A study on children with a significant cognitive and motor developmental delay. *Research in Developmental Disabilities*, 64, 131–142, https://doi.org/10.1016/j.ridd.2017.04.002

van Nispen, K., van de Sandt-Koenderman, M., Mol, L., & Krahmer, E. (2014). Should pantomime and gesticulation be assessed separately for their comprehensibility in aphasia? A case study. *International Journal of Language & Communication Disorders*, 49, 265–271, https://doi.org/10.1111/1460-6984.12064

Van Slyke, P. A. (2002). Classroom instruction for children with Landau-Kleffner syndrome. *Child Language Teaching and Therapy*, 18, 23–42, https://doi.org/10.1191/0265659002ct225oa

Vanvuchelen, M., Roeyers, H., & De Weerdt, W. (2007). Nature of motor imitation problems in school-aged boys with autism: A motor or a cognitive problem? *Autism*, 11, 225–240, https://doi.org/10.1177/1362361307076846

Vanvuchelen, M., Roeyers, H., & De Weerdt, W. (2011). Do imitation problems reflect a core characteristic in autism?: Evidence from a literature review. *Research in Autism Spectrum Disorders*, 5, 89–95, https://doi.org/10.1016/j.rasd.2010.07.010

Veness, C., Prior, M., Eadie, P., Bavin, E., & Reilly, S. (2014). Predicting autism diagnosis by 7 years of age using parent report of infant social communication skills. *Journal of Paediatrics and Child Health*, 50, 693–700, https://doi.org/10.1111/jpc.12614

Vermeerbergen, M., Leeson, L., & Crasborn, O. (eds.) (2007). *Simultaneity in signed languages: Form and function*. Amsterdam, The Netherlands: John Benjamins Publishing, https://doi.org/10.1075/cilt.281

Vernon, M., & Koh, S. D. (1970). Early manual communication and deaf children's achievement. *American Annals of the Deaf*, 115, 527–536.

Vernon, M., & Koh, S. D. (1971). Effects of oral preschool compared to early manual communication on education and communication in deaf children. *American Annals of the Deaf*, 116, 569–574.

Verrazzano, G. da (1524/[1896]). Verrazzano's voyage. In *Old South Leaflets, General Series, No. 17* [1896]. Boston, MA: D. C. Heath. [Letter translated by J. G. Cogswell and first published by the New York Historical Society, 1841.]

Vicari, S. (2006). Motor development and neuropsychological patterns in persons with Down syndrome. *Behavior Genetics*, 36, 355–364, https://doi.org/10.1007/s10519-006-9057-8

Vicari, S., Bates, E., Caselli, M. C., Pasqualetti, P., Gagliardi, C., Tonucci, F., & Volterra, V. (2004). Neuropsychological profile of Italians with Williams syndrome: An example of a dissociation between language and cognition? *Journal of the International Neuropsychological Society*, 10, 862–876, https://doi.org/10.1017/s1355617704106073

Vigliocco, G., Perniss, P., & Vinson, D. (2014). Language as a multimodal phenomenon: Implications for language learning, processing and evolution. *Philosophical Transactions of the Royal Society B*, 369, 20130292, https://doi.org/10.1098/rstb.2013.0292

Vinson, D. P., Cormier, K., Denmark, T., Schembri, A., & Vigliocco, G. (2008). The British Sign Language (BSL) norms for age of acquisition, familiarity, and iconicity. *Behavior Research Methods*, 40, 1079–1087, https://doi.org/10.3758/BRM.40.4.1079

Vivanti, G., & Hamilton, A. (2014). Imitation in autism spectrum disorders. In F. R. Volkmar, R. Paul, S. J. Rogers, & K. A. Pelphrey (eds.), *Handbook of autism and pervasive developmental disorders, vol. 1. Diagnosis, development, and brain mechanisms* (4th ed., pp. 278–301). Hoboken, NJ: John Wiley & Sons, https://doi.org/10.1002/9781118911389

Volkmar, F. R., Reichow, B., Westphal, A., & Mandell, D. S. (2014). Autism and the autism spectrum: Diagnostic concepts. In F. R. Volkmar, R. Paul, S. J. Rogers, & K. A. Pelphrey (eds.), *Handbook of autism and pervasive developmental disorders, vol. 1. Diagnosis, development, and brain mechanisms* (4th ed., pp. 3–27). Hoboken, NJ: John Wiley & Sons, https://doi.org/10.1002/9781118911389

Volterra, V., & Caselli, M. C. C. (1985). From gestures and vocalizations to signs and words. In W. C. Stokoe & V. Volterra (eds.), *S L R '83: Proceedings of the third international symposium on sign language research* (pp. 1–9). Silver Spring, MD: Linstok Press.

von Humboldt, W. (1836/1988). *On language: The diversity of human language-structure and its influence on the mental development of mankind* (P. Heath, Trans., H. Aarsleff, Intro., 1988). Cambridge, U.K.: Cambridge University Press.

von Tetzchner, S. (1984a). Facilitation of early speech development in a dysphatic child by use of signed Norwegian. *Scandinavian Journal of Psychology*, 25, 265–275, https://doi.org/10.1111/j.1467-9450.1984.tb01018.x

von Tetzchner, S. (1984b). First signs acquired by a Norwegian deaf child with hearing parents. *Sign Language Studies*, 44, 225–257, https://doi.org/10.1353/sls.1984.0007

von Tetzchner, S., & Martinsen, H. (2000). *Introduction to augmentative and alternative communication: Sign teaching and the use of communication aids for children, adolescents and adults with developmental disorders* (2nd ed.). London, U.K.: Whurr Publishers.

Wacker, D. P., Steege, M. W., Northup, J., Sasso, G., Berg, W., Reimers, T., Cooper, L., Cigrand, K., & Donn, L. (1990). A component analysis of functional communication training across three topographies of severe behavior problems. *Journal of Applied Behavior Analysis*, 23, 417–429, https://doi.org/10.1901/jaba.1990.23-417

Wai, J., Lubinski, D., & Benbow, C. P. (2009). Spatial ability for STEM domains: Aligning over 50 years of cumulative psychological knowledge solidifies its importance. *Journal of Educational Psychology*, 101, 817–835, https://doi.org/10.1037/a0016127

Walker, M., Mitha, S., & Riddington, C. (2019). Cultural issues in developing and using signs within the Makaton language programme in different countries. In N. Grove & K. Launonen (eds.), *Manual sign acquisition in children with developmental disabilities* (pp. 391–408). New York, NY: Nova Science Publishers, Inc.

Wang, X.-l., Bernas, R., & Eberhard, P. (2004). Engaging ADHD students in tasks with hand gestures: A pedagogical possibility for teachers. *Educational Studies*, 30, 217–229, https://doi.org/10.1080/0305569042000224189

Ward, N. S., & Cohen, L. G. (2004). Mechanisms underlying recovery of motor function after stroke. *Archives of Neurology*, 61, 1844–1848, https://doi.org/10.1001/archneur.61.12.1844

Watson, L. R., Crais, E. R., Baranek, G. T., Dykstra, J. R., & Wilson, K. P. (2013). Communicative gesture use in infants with and without autism: A retrospective home video study. *American Journal of Speech-Language Pathology*, 22, 25–39, https://doi.org/10.1044/1058-0360(2012/11-0145)

Watson, R. M., & Pennington, L. (2015). Assessment and management of the communication difficulties of children with cerebral palsy: A UK survey of SLT practice. *International Journal of Language & Communication Disorders*, 50, 241–259, https://doi.org/10.1111/1460-6984.12138

Waxman, R. P., & Spencer, P. E. (1997). What mothers do to support infant visual attention: Sensitivities to age and hearing status. *Journal of Deaf Studies and Deaf Education*, 2, 104–114, https://doi.org/10.1093/oxfordjournals.deafed.a014311

Webster, C. D., Fruchter, D., Dean, J., Konstantareas, M. M., & Sloman, L. (2016). Lessons that linger: A 40-year follow-along note about a boy with autism taught to communicate by gestures when aged six. *Journal of Autism and Developmental Disorders, 46*, 2561–2564, https://doi.org/10.1007/s10803-016-2773-x

Wechsler, D. (1974). *Wechsler Intelligence Scale for Children — Revised.* New York, NY: The Psychological Corporation.

Wechsler, D. (1991). *Wechsler Intelligence Scale for Children — Third Edition.* San Antonio, TX: The Psychological Corporation.

Weiss, P. H., Rahbari, N. N., Hesse, M. D., & Fink, G. R. (2008). Deficient sequencing of pantomimes in apraxia. *Neurology, 70*, 834–840, https://doi.org/10.1212/01.wnl.0000297513.78593.dc

Weiss, P. H., Ubben, S. D., Kaesberg, S., Kalbe, E., Kessler, J., Liebig, T., & Fink, G. R. (2016). Where language meets meaningful action: A combined behavior and lesion analysis of aphasia and apraxia. *Brain Structure & Function, 221*, 563–576, https://doi.org/10.1007/s00429-014-0925-3

Wendt, O. (2009). Research on the use of manual signs and graphic symbols in autism spectrum disorders: A systematic review. In P. Mirenda & T. Iacono (eds.), *Autism spectrum disorders and AAC* (pp. 83–139). Baltimore, MD: Paul H. Brookes Publishing.

Werner, E., Dawson, G., Osterling, J., & Dinno, N. (2000). Brief report: Recognition of autism spectrum disorder before one year of age: A retrospective study based on home videotapes. *Journal of Autism and Developmental Disorders, 30*, 157–162, https://doi.org/10.1023/a:1005463707029

Wertz, R. T., LaPointe, L. L., & Rosenbek, J. (1984). *Apraxia of speech in adults: The disorder and its management.* Orlando, FL: Grune & Stratton.

Wetherby, A. M. (1986). Ontogeny of communicative functions in autism. *Journal of Autism and Developmental Disorders, 16*, 295–316, https://doi.org/10.1007/bf01531661

Wetherby, A. M. (2006). Understanding and measuring social communication in children with autism spectrum disorders. In T. Charman & W. Stone (eds.), *Social and communication development in autism spectrum disorders: Early identification, diagnosis, and intervention* (pp. 3–34). New York, NY: The Guilford Press.

Wetherell, D., Botting, N., & Conti-Ramsden, G. (2007). Narrative in adolescent specific language impairment (SLI): A comparison with peers across two different narrative genres. *International Journal of Language & Communication Disorders, 42*, 583–605, https://doi.org/10.1080/13682820601056228

Whitehouse, A. J. O., & Bishop, D. V. M. (2008). Cerebral dominance for language function in adults with specific language impairment or autism. *Brain, 131*, 3193–3200, https://doi.org/10.1093/brain/awn266

Whitehurst, G. J. (1997). Language processes in context: Language learning in children reared in poverty. In L. B. Adamson & M. A. Romski (eds.), *Communication and language acquisition: Discoveries from atypical development* (pp. 233–265). Baltimore, MD: Paul H. Brookes Publishing.

Whynot, L. (2016). Telling, showing, and representing: Conventions of the lexicon in International Sign expository text. In R. Rosenstock & J. Napier (eds.), *International Sign: Linguistic, usage, and status issues* (pp. 35–64). Washington, DC: Gallaudet University Press.

Wikipedia. (2020). *Word order*, https://en.wikipedia.org/wiki/Word_order

Wilbur, R. B. (1993). Syllables and segments: Hold the movement and move the holds! In G. R. Coulter (ed.), *Phonetics and phonology, vol. 3. Current issues in ASL phonology* (pp. 135–168). San Diego, CA: Academic Press, https://doi.org/10.1016/B978-0-12-193270-1.50012-1

Wilbur, R. B. (2011). Sign syllables. In M. van Oostendorp, C. J. Ewen, E. V. Hume, & K. Rice (eds.), *The Blackwell companion to phonology, vol. 2. Suprasegmental and prosodic phonology* (pp. 1309–1334). Chichester, West Sussex, U.K.: Wiley-Blackwell, https://doi.org/10.1002/9781444335262.wbctp0056

Wilbur, R. B., & Petersen, L. (1998). Modality interactions of speech and signing in simultaneous communication. *Journal of Speech, Language, and Hearing Research*, 41, 200–212, https://doi.org/10.1044/jslhr.4101.200

Wilcox, S. E. (2009). William C. Stokoe and the gestural theory of language origins. *Sign Language Studies*, 9, 398–409, https://doi.org/10.1353/sls.0.0028

Wiley, T. G., Moore, S. C. K., & Fee, M. S. (2012). A "language for jobs" initiative. *Renewing America: Policy Innovation Memorandum No. 24*, Council on Foreign Relations, https://www.cfr.org/report/languages-jobs-initiative

Willems, R. M., Labruna, L., D'Esposito, M., Ivry, R., & Casasanto, D. (2011). A functional role for the motor system in language understanding: Evidence from theta-burst transcranial magnetic stimulation. *Psychological Science*, 22, 849–854, https://doi.org/10.1177/0956797611412387

Williams, J. H., Whiten, A., & Singh, H. (2004). A systematic review of action imitation in autistic spectrum disorder. *Journal of Autism and Developmental Disorders*, 34, 285–299, https://doi.org/10.1023/b:jadd.0000029551.56735.3a

Wilson, F. R. (1998). *The hand: How its use shapes the brain, language, and human culture*. New York, NY: Pantheon Books.

Wilson, M., Bettger, J. G., Niculae, I., & Klima, E. S. (1997). Modality of language shapes working memory: Evidence from digit span and spatial span in ASL signers. *Journal of Deaf Studies and Deaf Education*, 2, 150–160, https://doi.org/10.1093/oxfordjournals.deafed.a014321

Wilson, B. J., Sundaram, S. K., Huq, A. H. M., Jeong, J.-W., Halverson, S. R., Behen, M. E., Bui, D. Q., & Chugani, H. T. (2011). Abnormal language pathway in children with Angelman syndrome. *Pediatric Neurology*, 44, 350–356, https://doi.org/10.1016/j.pediatrneurol.2010.12.002

Windsor, J., & Fristoe, M. (1991). Key word signing: Perceived and acoustic differences between signed and spoken narratives. *Journal of Speech and Hearing Research*, 34, 260–268, https://doi.org/10.1044/jshr.3402.260

Winkielman, P., McIntosh, D. N., & Oberman, L. (2009). Embodied and disembodied emotion processing: Learning from and about typical and autistic individuals. *Emotion Review*, 1, 178–190, https://doi.org/10.1177/1754073908100442

Winter, S., Autry, A., Boyle, C., & Yeargin-Allsopp, M. (2002). Trends in the prevalence of cerebral palsy in a population-based study. *Pediatrics*, 110, 1220–1225, https://doi.org/10.1542/peds.110.6.1220

Wodka, E. L., Mathy, P., & Kalb, L. (2013). Predictors of phrase and fluent speech in children with autism and severe language delay. *Pediatrics*, 131, e1128-e1134, https://doi.org/10.1542/peds.2012-2221

Woll, B., & Barnett, S. (1998). Toward a sociolinguistic perspective on augmentative and alternative communication. *Augmentative and Alternative Communication*, 14, 200–211, https://doi.org/10.1080/07434619812331278376

Woll, B., & Grove, N. (1996). On language deficits and modality in children with Down syndrome: A case study of twins bilingual in BSL and English. *Journal of Deaf Studies and Deaf Education*, 1, 271–278, https://doi.org/10.1093/oxfordjournals.deafed.a014302

Woll, B., & Grove, N. (2019). Bilingual, bimodal development of signed and spoken language in twins with Down syndrome. In N. Grove & K. Launonen (eds.), *Manual sign acquisition in children with developmental disabilities* (pp. 151–164). New York, NY: Nova Science Publishers, Inc.

Woll, B., Kyle, J. G., & Ackerman, J. (1988). Providing sign language models: Strategies used by deaf mothers. In G. Collis, A. Lewis, & V. Lewis (eds.), *Proceedings of the child language seminar* (pp. 217–228). Coventry, U.K.: University of Warwick.

Woll, B., & Morgan, G. (2012). Language impairments in the development of sign: Do they reside in a specific modality or are they modality-independent deficits? *Bilingualism: Language and Cognition*, 15, 75–87, https://doi.org/10.1017/s1366728911000459

Woll, B., & Sieratski, J. (2019). The role of sign language in Landau-Kleffner syndrome. In N. Grove & K. Launonen (eds.), *Manual sign acquisition in children with developmental disabilities* (pp. 165–174). New York, NY: Nova Science Publishers, Inc.

Woll, B., & Sieratski, J. S. (1996). Sign language for children with acquired aphasia. *Journal of Child Neurology*, 11, 347–348, https://doi.org/10.1177/088307389601100419

Wooderson, J. R., Cuskelly, M., & Meyer, K. A. (2014). A systematic review of interventions for improving the work performance of direct support staff. *Research and Practice in Intellectual and Developmental Disabilities*, 1, 160–173, https://doi.org/10.1080/23297018.2014.941967

Woodward, J. (1978). Historical bases of American Sign Language. In P. Siple (ed.), *Understanding language through sign language research* (pp. 333–348). New York, NY: Academic Press.

Woodward, J. (1982). *How you gonna get to heaven if you can't talk with Jesus: On depathologizing deafness*. Silver Spring, MD: T. J. Publishers, Inc.

Woodward, J. C., Jr. (1975, March). *How you gonna get to heaven if you can't talk with Jesus: The educational establishment vs. the deaf community*. Paper presented at the annual meeting of the Society for Applied Anthropology, Amsterdam, The Netherlands.

Woolfe, T., Herman, R., Roy, P., & Woll, B. (2010). Early vocabulary development in deaf native signers: A British Sign Language adaptation of the communicative development inventories. *Journal of Child Psychology and Psychiatry*, 51, 322–331, https://doi.org/10.1111/j.1469-7610.2009.02151.x

World Federation of the Deaf, Unification of Signs Commission. (ed.). (1975). *Gestuno: International Sign Language of the deaf*. Carlisle, England: The British Deaf Association on behalf of The World Federation of the Deaf.

Wozniak, R. H., Leezenbaum, N. B., Northrup, J. B., West, K. L., & Iverson, J. M. (2017). The development of autism spectrum disorders: Variability and causal complexity. *WIREs Cognitive Science*, 8, e1426, https://doi.org/10.1002/wcs.1426

Wraikat, R., Sundberg, C. T., & Michael, J. (1991). Topography-based and selection-based verbal behavior: A further comparison. *The Analysis of Verbal Behavior*, 9, 1–17, https://doi.org/10.1007/bf03392856

Wray, C., Norbury, C. F., & Alcock, K. (2016). Gestural abilities of children with specific language impairment. *International Journal of Language & Communication Disorders*, 51, 174–182, https://doi.org/10.1111/1460-6984.12196

Wright, C., Bonvillian, J. D., & Schulman, A. (in press). Memory for gestures: Recall of American Sign Language signs by nonsigning hearing students. *Sign Language Studies*.

Wright, C. A., & Kaiser, A. P. (2017). Teaching parents enhanced milieu teaching with words and signs using the teach-model-coach-review model. *Topics in Early Childhood Special Education*, 36, 192–204, https://doi.org/10.1177/0271121415621027

Wright, C. A., Kaiser, A. P., Reikowsky, D. I., & Roberts, M. Y. (2013). Effects of a naturalistic sign intervention on expressive language of toddlers with Down syndrome. *Journal of Speech, Language, and Hearing Research*, 56, 994–1008, https://doi.org/10.1044/1092-4388(2012/12-0060)

Wurtzburg, S., & Campbell, L. (1995). North American Indian Sign Language: Evidence of its existence before European contact. *International Journal of American Linguistics*, 61, 153–167, https://doi.org/10.1086/466249

Yang, Y., Conners, F. A., & Merrill, E. C. (2014). Visuo-spatial ability in individuals with Down syndrome: Is it really a strength? *Research in Developmental Disabilities*, 35, 1473–1500, https://doi.org/10.1016/j.ridd.2014.04.002

Yoder, P., Woynaroski, T., Fey, M., & Warren, S. (2014). Effects of dose frequency of early communication intervention in young children with and without Down syndrome. *American Journal on Intellectual and Developmental Disabilities*, 119, 17–32, https://doi.org/10.1352/1944-7558-119.1.17

Yoder, P. J., & Warren, S. F. (2002). Effects of prelinguistic milieu teaching and parent responsivity education on dyads involving children with intellectual disabilities. *Journal of Speech, Language, and Hearing Research*, 45, 1158–1174, https://doi.org/10.1044/1092-4388(2002/094)

Yoder, P. J., Woynaroski, T., & Camarata, S. (2016). Measuring speech comprehensibility in students with Down syndrome. *Journal of Speech, Language, and Hearing Research*, 59, 460–467, https://doi.org/10.1044/2015_jslhr-s-15-0149

Yorkston, K. M., Beukelman, D. R., Strand, E. A., & Bell, K. R. (1999). *Management of motor speech disorders in children and adults* (2nd ed.). Austin, TX: PRO-ED.

Yoshinaga-Itano, C. (2006). Early identification, communication modality, and the development of speech and spoken language skills: Patterns and considerations. In P. E. Spencer & M. Marschark (eds.), *Advances in the spoken language development of deaf and hard-of-hearing children* (pp. 298–327). New York, NY: Oxford University Press, https://doi.org/10.1093/acprof:oso/9780195179873.003.0013

Yuen, R. K. C., Merico, D., Bookman, M., Howe, J. L., Thiruvahindrapuram, B., Patel, R. V., Whitney, J., Deflaux, N., Bingham, J., Wang, Z., Pellecchia, G., Buchanan, J. A., Walker, S., Marshall, C. R., Uddin, M., Zarrei, M., Deneault, E., D'Abate, L., Chan, A. J. S., Koyanagi, S., Paton, T., Pereira, S. L., Hoang, N., Engchuan, W., Higginbotham, E. J., Ho, K., Lamoureux, S., Li, W., MacDonald, J. R., Nalpathamkalam, T., Sung, W. W. L., Tsoi, F. J., Wei, J., Xu, L., Tasse, A.-M., Kirby, E., Van Etten, W., Twigger, S., Roberts, W., Drmic, I., Jilderda, S., Modi, B. M., Kellam, B., Szego, M., Cytrynbaum, C., Weksberg, R., Zwaigenenbaum, L., Woodbury-Smith, M., Brian, J., Senman, L., Iaboni, A., Doyle-Thomas, K., Thompson, A., Chrysler, C., Leef, J., Savion-Lemieux, T., Smith, I. M., Liu, X., Nicolson, R., Seifer, V., Fedele, A., Cook, E. H., Dager, S., Estes, A., Gallagher, L., Malow, B. A., Parr, J. R., Spence, S. J., Vorstman, J., Frey, B. J., Robinson, J. T., Strug, L. J., Fernandez, B. A., Elsabbagh, M., Carter, M. T., Hallmayer, J., Knoppers, B. M., Anagnostou, E., Szatmari, P., Ring, R. H., Glazer, D., Pletcher, M. T., & Scherer, S. W. (2017). Whole genome sequencing resource identifies 18 new candidate genes for autism spectrum disorder. *Nature Neuroscience*, 20, 602–611, https://doi.org/10.1038/nn.4524

Zampini, L., & D'Odorico, L. (2009). Communicative gestures and vocabulary development in 36-month-old children with Down's syndrome. *International Journal of Language & Communication Disorders*, 44, 1063–1073, https://doi.org/10.1080/13682820802398288

Zampini, L., & D'Odorico, L. (2013). Vocabulary development in children with Down syndrome: Longitudinal and cross-sectional data. *Journal of Intellectual & Developmental Disability*, 38, 310–317, https://doi.org/10.3109/13668250.2013.828833

Zauche, L. H., Thul, T. A., Mahoney, A. E. D., & Stapel-Wax, J. L. (2016). Influence of language nutrition on children's language and cognitive development: An integrated review. *Early Childhood Research Quarterly*, 36, 318–333, https://doi.org/10.1016/j.ecresq.2016.01.015

Zhang, J. Y., Oskoui, M., & Shevell, M. (2015). A population-based study of communication impairment in cerebral palsy. *Journal of Child Neurology*, 30, 277–284, https://doi.org/10.1177/0883073814538497

Zimmer, H. D., & Cohen, R. L. (2001). Remembering actions: A specific type of memory? In H. D. Zimmer, R. L. Cohen, M. J. Guynn, J. Engelkamp, R. Kormi-Nouri, & M. A. Foley, *Memory for action: A distinct form of episodic memory?* (pp. 3–24). Oxford, U.K.: Oxford University Press.

Zimmer, H. D., Cohen, R. L., Guynn, M. J., Engelkamp, J., Kormi-Nouri, R., & Foley, M. A. (2001). *Memory for action: A distinct form of episodic memory?* Oxford, U.K.: Oxford University Press.

Zwaigenbaum, L., Bryson, S., Lord, C., Rogers, S., Carter, A., Carver, L., Chawarska, K., Constantino, J., Dawson, G., Dobkins, K., Fein, D., Iverson, J., Klin, A., Landa, R., Messinger, D., Ozonoff, S., Sigman, M., Stone, W., Tager-Flusberg, H., & Yirmiya, N. (2009). Clinical assessment and management of toddlers with suspected autism spectrum disorder: Insights from studies of high-risk infants. *Pediatrics*, 123, 1383–1391, https://doi.org/10.1542/peds.2008-1606

Zwaigenbaum, L., Bryson, S. E., Brian, J., Smith, I. M., Roberts, W., Szatmari, P., Roncadin, C., Garon, N., & Vaillancourt, T. (2016). Stability of diagnostic assessment for autism spectrum disorder between 18 and 36 months in a high-risk cohort. *Autism Research*, 9, 790–800, https://doi.org/10.1002/aur.1585

Author Biographies

John D. Bonvillian was a faculty member in the Psychology Department at the University of Virginia for thirty-seven years. He also chaired the University's Interdepartmental Program in Linguistics. He was known for his contributions to the study of sign language, child development, psycholinguistics, and language acquisition. His research focused on typically developing children, deaf children, and children with disabilities. For the last seventeen years of his career he worked on a simplified, manual sign-communication system. The initial focus of this work was to create an easily-adopted signing system for minimally verbal populations, such as individuals with autism spectrum disorder (ASD), Down syndrome, or cerebral palsy. Later, he studied applications of the Simplified Sign System for foreign language acquisition and for children in limited language environments. He and his research colleagues developed and tested a lexicon of approximately 1850 easily-formed, highly iconic signs or gestures, some of which are presented in these volumes.

Bonvillian received his Ph.D. in Psychology from Stanford University, where he held a National Science Foundation doctoral fellowship. His B.A. was from Johns Hopkins University in Psychology. He authored over 100 journal articles and was an editor of the journal *Sign Language Studies*. Before taking his position at the University of Virginia, Bonvillian taught at Vassar College. He also served as a visiting faculty member at Gallaudet University in Washington, DC and the University of Canterbury in New Zealand. He died in 2018.

Tracy T. Dooley was an undergraduate honors student at the University of Virginia and a member of Dr. Bonvillian's research group in the early 1990s, where she studied handedness in the young sign-learning children of Deaf parents. After earning B.A. degrees in Linguistics and Spanish with a minor in Psychology, she obtained her Master of Divinity degree from Emory University's Candler School of Theology in Atlanta, GA. While studying theology, she also pursued training in sign language interpretation at DeKalb College (now Georgia State University Perimeter College). After moving back to Virginia in 2003, Ms. Dooley rejoined Dr. Bonvillian's research group, where she focused on the expansion of the Simplified Sign System to include more concepts, the writing and editing of Volumes 1 and 2, and overseeing the development of the sign illustrations. After Dr. Bonvillian's death, Ms. Dooley updated both volumes of the system in preparation for publication.

Nicole Kissane Lee, M.D., Ed.M., had the privilege of formally starting the "Simplified Sign System" project with Dr. John Bonvillian in 1997 when she was a first-year pre-medical student at the University of Virginia. After many hours meticulously studying and testing the memory and recall of simplified signs, Dr. Lee and Dr. Bonvillian published the "Simplified Sign System" on the internet in the spring of 2001 which exponentially launched its soon-to-be international notoriety. Dr. Lee graduated from the University of Virginia in 2001 with High Distinction in Psychology under the mentorship of Dr. Bonvillian, with her thesis work on the "Simplified Sign System" gaining recognition for its unique innovation from *The Today Show*, CNN, *The Washington Post*, and *CosmoGirl*, to name a few. Dr. Lee went on to obtain her medical degree from the Medical College of Virginia, in Richmond, VA, her surgical residency training at the University of Florida, in Gainesville, FL, and fellowship training in advanced laparoscopic surgery at Massachusetts General Hospital in Boston, MA. Dr. Lee continued her education while in Boston, obtaining additional fellowship training in Medical Simulation from Brigham and Women's Hospital. She also obtained an Ed.M. with a focus in Technology and Innovation from Harvard University in 2013.

Dr. Lee is currently a minimally invasive and bariatric surgeon at Indiana University. She is an Assistant Professor of Surgery and the Director of the Indiana University Surgical Skills Center. She is also Co-Director of the Indiana University Surgical Education Research Fellowship. Dr. Lee is an active member of the American College of Surgeons Accredited Education Institute (ACS/AEI) as a member of the

Accreditation Review Committee, national site reviewer, and Co-Editor of the ACS/AEI Online Communities. Dr. Lee remains proud and grateful to be associated with the legendary works of her former mentor, Dr. Bonvillian. It was his enthusiasm in education and research which launched her career in medical education and related research.

Filip T. Loncke is a psycholinguist from Belgium who came to the United States in 1997 as a professor at the Curry School of Education and Human Development at the University of Virginia. Prior to his arrival in the U.S., he worked for twenty years as an educational psychologist and as a school superintendent for services for children with disabilities. He obtained his B.A. and M.A. degrees in Special Education from the University of Ghent, and an M.A. and Ph.D. degree in neurolinguistics from the University of Brussels. While in Belgium, he was a co-developer of a manual sign system that is currently still in use in parts of Europe. Since his arrival in the U.S. in the late 1990s until Dr. Bonvillian's passing, he collaborated with Dr. Bonvillian on several research projects related to the Simplified Sign System.

Val Nelson-Metlay was born hard-of-hearing in Chicago, IL and is now Deaf. It wasn't until she was about twenty-five years old that she started to pick up ASL. She graduated from the University of Kansas with a B.F.A. and went on to work at several jobs: cartoonist for a small advertising agency, color separation for two greeting cards, pre-press keyliner, layout artist, and typesetter, book designer, newspaper editor and layout, and finally freelance artist. She is grateful for the opportunity to illustrate these volumes, and for the full support she has received from her family, her dear hearing friends, and many Deaf and hard-of-hearing friends.

Name Index

Subject Index

About the publishing team

Alessandra Tosi was the managing editor for this book.

Adèle Kreager performed the copy-editing, proofreading and indexing.

Anna Gatti designed the cover using InDesign. The cover was produced in InDesign using Fontin (titles) and Calibri (text body) fonts.

Luca Baffa typeset the book in InDesign. The text font is Tex Gyre Pagella; the heading font is Californian FB. Luca created all of the editions — paperback, hardback, EPUB, MOBI, PDF, HTML, and XML — the conversion is performed with open source software freely available on our GitHub page (https://github.com/OpenBookPublishers).

This book need not end here...

Share

All our books — including the one you have just read — are free to access online so that students, researchers and members of the public who can't afford a printed edition will have access to the same ideas. This title will be accessed online by hundreds of readers each month across the globe: why not share the link so that someone you know is one of them?

This book and additional content is available at:

https://doi.org/10.11647/OBP.0205

Customise

Personalise your copy of this book or design new books using OBP and third-party material. Take chapters or whole books from our published list and make a special edition, a new anthology or an illuminating coursepack. Each customised edition will be produced as a paperback and a downloadable PDF.

Find out more at:

https://www.openbookpublishers.com/section/59/1

9 781783 749232